WORLD ERAS

VOLUME 6

CLASSICAL GREEK CIVILIZATION

800-323 B.C.E.

WORLD ERAS

VOLUME 6

CLASSICAL GREEK CIVILIZATION
800-323 B.C.E.

JOHN T. KIRBY

A MANLY, INC. BOOK

GALE GROUP

Detroit
New York
San Francisco
London
Boston
Woodbridge, CT

WORLD ERAS VOL. 6 CLASSICAL GREEK CIVILIZATION
800-323 BCE

Matthew J. Bruccoli and Richard Layman, *Editorial Directors*

Anthony J. Scotti Jr., *Series Editor*

Library Of Congress Cataloging-in-Publication Data
World Eras vol. 6: Classical Greek Civilization, 800-323 B.C.E. /
    edited by John T. Kirby.
        p. cm.
    "A Manly, Inc. book."
    Includes bibliographical references and index.
    ISBN 0-7876-1707-5 (alk. paper)
    1. Greece—Civilization—To 146 B.C.   I. Kirby, John T.
DF77.W67 2001
938—dc21   00-047648

Printed in the United States of America
10 9 8 7 6 5 4 3 2 1

ADVISORY BOARD

FOR MY FATHER

CONTENTS

ABOUT THE SERIES xv

TIMELINE xvii

INTRODUCTION xxv

ACKNOWLEDGEMENTS xxxi

CHAPTER 1: WORLD EVENTS

Chronology 3

CHAPTER 2: GEOGRAPHY

Chronology 26
Overview 29

Topics in Geography

Ethnographers and Geographers 29
Greece: the Land and People 33
Herodotus and His Travels 33
The Military Campaigns of Alexander The Great 34
The Physical World of Homer 36
Trade, Colonization, Travel 37
Documentary Sources 39

CHAPTER 3: THE ARTS

Chronology 42
Overview 49

Topics in the Arts

Architecture 53
Comedy 57
Didactic Poetry 59
Elegy and Iambics 60
History 63
Lyric 64
Oratory 64
Philosophy 65
Pottery, Painting, and Mosaics 66
Rhetoric 73
Satyr Plays 75
Sculpture 76
Tragedy 82

Significant People

Aeschylus 85
Apelles Of Colophon 85

Aristophanes 86
Euripides 86
Herodotus 87
Hesiod 87
Lysippus and Lysistratus 88
Parrhasius 88
Pheidias 89
Pindar 89
Polyclitus 90
Praxiteles 90
Sappho 91
Scopas 91
Sophocles 92
Thucydides 92
Zeuxis 93

Documentary Sources 93

CHAPTER 4: COMMUNICATION, TRANSPORTATION, AND EXPLORATION

Chronology 96
Overview 98

Topics in Communication, Transportation, and Exploration

Language 99
Means of Communication 102
Patterns and Practices of Transportation 107
Roads and Land Traffic 113
Sea Transport 118

Significant People

Sostratus of Aegina 124
Documentary Sources 125

CHAPTER 5: SOCIAL CLASS SYSTEM AND THE ECONOMY

Chronology 128
Overview 131

Topics in Social Class System and the Economy

Archaic Period: Social and Agricultural Crisis 133
Athens 134
Boeotia 138
Classical Period: Economic Crisis 138
Colonization 140
Corinth 142
Economic Activities 143
Ionia And The Aegean Islands 145
Sicily and Southern Italy 143
Social Organization 147
Sparta 148
Technological Advances and Innovations 151
Thessaly 153

Trading Posts... 153
Transportation and Exchange of Goods and Services.............. 155
The Tyrants.. 156

Significant People

Hippias.. 158
Periander.. 158
Polycrates... 158

Documentary Sources.. 159

CHAPTER 6: POLITICS, LAW, AND THE MILITARY

Chronology... 162
Overview... 172

Topics in Politics, Law, and the Military

The Archaic Greek World.. 174
Athens and Sparta.. 176
The Battle of Marathon... 181
The Macedonian Art of Warfare.................................. 182
Oratory and Rhetoric... 183
The Persian Menace... 184
The Polis in Decline... 187
Political Assemblies of Athens................................. 190
Punishment... 191
The Second Peloponnesian War................................... 192
War Engines: Land and Sea...................................... 195
Weaponry... 196

Significant People

Alcibiades... 198
Alexander The Great.. 198
Demosthenes.. 201
Pericles... 201
Philip II.. 202
Solon.. 203
Themistocles... 204

Documentary Sources.. 204

CHAPTER 7: LEISURE, RECREATION, AND DAILY LIFE

Chronology... 208
Overview... 211

Topics in Leisure, Recreation, and Daily Life

Climate and Landscape.. 212
Clothing and Adornment... 213
Food... 219
Games.. 224
Housing.. 229
Leisure and Festivals.. 233
Symposia... 235

Documentary Sources. 238

CHAPTER 8: THE FAMILY AND SOCIAL TRENDS

Chronology. 240
Overview 244

Topics in the Family and Social Trends

Children and Education 248
Conception and Childbirth. 251
Marriage 254
Sexual Misconduct 257
Sexuality 259
Social Roles in the Household. 264

Significant People

Aspsia 269
Cleisthenes 269
Draco. 269
Lycurgus 270
Pisistratus 270

Documentary Sources

Chapter 9: RELIGION AND PHILOSOPHY

Chronology. 273
Overview 277

Topics in Religion and Philosophy

Gods and Goddesses 278
Heroes. 282
Minor Deities and Monsters 283
Older Sophists. 289
Philosophy: Parameters 290
Philosophy: Terms, Concepts, and Places 291
Presocratics 293
Religion: Parameters 297
Religion: Terms, Concepts, and Places 300
Seven Sages 306
Socratics, Later Sophists, ad Cynics 307

Documentary Sources. 311

Chapter 10: SCIENCE, TECHNOLOGY AND HEALTH

Chronology. 313
Overview 318

Topics in Science, Technology and Health

Ancient Myths and Legends. 319
Ancient Technology 321
The Early Philosophers 323
Early Speculation. 325
Early Speculation: The Cult of Pythagoras 327

Early Speculation: Cycles of Change. 328

Early Speculation: Pluralism 330

Leucippus and Atomism 332

Medicine Social Content. 333

Medicine: The Theory of Healing 334

Medicine Therapy. 338

The Science of Plato 340

The Science of Plato: Astronomy 341

The Scientific Research of Aristotle 344

Teleology of Aristotle 346

The Unmoved Mover and Aristotle: Cosmology 348

Significant People 351

Anaxagoras 351

Anaximander. 351

Anaximenes 352

Aristotle. 352

Empedocles 352

Heraclitus 353

Plato 353

Pythagoras 354

Thales 354

Documentary Sources. 355

GLOSSARY. 357

GENERAL REFERENCES 365

CONTRIBUTORS 373

INDEX OF PHOTOGRAPHS 375

INDEX 381

ABOUT THE SERIES

PROJECT DESCRIPTION

Patterned after the well-received *American Decades* and *American Eras* series, *World Eras* is a cross-disciplinary reference series. It comprises volumes examining major civilizations that have flourished from antiquity to modern times, with a global perspective and a strong emphasis on daily life and social history. Each volume provides in-depth coverage of one era, focusing on a specific cultural group and its interaction with other peoples of the world. The *World Eras* series is geared toward the needs of high-school students studying subjects in the humanities. Its purpose is to provide students—and general reference users as well—a reliable, engaging reference resource that stimulates their interest, encourages research, and prompts comparison of the lives people led in different parts of the world, in different cultures, and at different times.

The goal of *World Eras* volumes is to enrich the traditional historical study of "kings and battles" with a resource that promotes understanding of daily life and the cultural institutions that affect people's beliefs and behavior.

What kind of work did people in a certain culture perform?

What did they eat?

How did they fight their battles?

What laws did they have and how did they punish criminals?

What were their religious practices?

What did they know of science and medicine?

What kind of art, music, and literature did they enjoy?

These are the types of questions *World Eras* volumes seek to answer.

VOLUME DESIGN

World Eras is designed to facilitate comparative study. Thus volumes employ a consistent ten-chapter structure so that teachers and students can readily access standard topics in various volumes. The chapters in each *World Eras* volume are

1. World Events
2. Geography
3. The Arts
4. Communication, Transportation, and Exploration
5. Social Class System and the Economy
6. Politics, Law, and the Military
7. Leisure, Recreation, and Daily Life
8. The Family and Social Trends
9. Religion and Philosophy
10. Science, Technology, and Health

World Eras volumes begin with two chapters designed to provide a broad view of the world against which a specific culture can be measured. Chapter 1 provides students today with a means to understand where a certain people stood within our concept of world history. Chapter 2 describes the world from the perspective of the people being studied—what did they know of geography and how did geography and climate affect their lives? The following eight chapters address major aspects of people's lives to provide a sense of what defined their culture. The ten chapters in *World Eras* will remain constant in each volume. Teachers and students seeking to compare religious beliefs in Roman and Greek cultures, for example, can easily locate the information they require by consulting chapter 9 in the appropriate volumes, tapping a rich source for class assignments and research topics. Volume-specific glossaries and a checklist of general references provide students assistance in studying unfamiliar cultures.

CHAPTER CONTENTS

Each chapter in *World Eras* volumes also follows a uniform structure designed to provide users quick access to the information they need. Chapters are arranged into five types of material:

- **Chronology** provides an historical outline of significant events in the subject of the chapter in time-line form.

- **Overview** provides a narrative overview of the chapter topic during the period and discusses the material of the chapter in a global context.

- **Topical Entries** provide focused information in easy-to-read articles about people, places, events, institutions, and matters of general concern to the people of the time. A references rubric includes sources for further study.

• **Biographical Entries** profiles people of enduring significance regarding the subject of the chapter.

• **Documentary Sources** is an annotated checklist of documentary sources from the historical period that are the basis for the information presented in the chapter.

Chapters are supplemented throughout with primary-text sidebars that include interesting short documentary excerpts or anecdotes chosen to illuminate the subject of the chapter: recipes, letters, daily-life accounts, excerpts from important documents. Each *World Eras* volume includes about 150 illustrations, maps, diagrams, and line drawings linked directly to material discussed in the text. Illustrations are chosen with particular emphasis on daily life.

INDEXING

A general two-level subject index for each volume includes significant terms, subjects, theories, practices, people, organizations, publications, and so forth, mentioned in the text. Index citations with many page references are broken down by subtopic. Illustrations are indicated both in the general index, by use of italicized page numbers, and in a separate illustrations index, which provides a description of each item.

EDITORS AND CONTRIBUTORS

An advisory board of history teachers and librarians has provided valuable advice about the rationale for this series. They have reviewed both series plans and individual volume plans. Each *World Eras* volume is edited by a distinguished specialist in the subject of his or her volume. The editor is responsible for enlisting other scholar-specialists to write each of the chapters in the volume and of assuring the quality of their work. The editorial staff at Manly, Inc., rigorously checks factual information, line edits the manuscript, works with the editor to select illustrations, and produces the books in the series, in cooperation with Gale Group editors.

The *World Eras* series is for students of all ages who seek to enrich their study of world history by examining the many aspects of people's lives in different places during different eras. This series continues Gale's tradition of publishing comprehensive, accurate, and stimulating historical reference works that promote the study of history and culture.

The following timeline, included in every volume of *World Eras,* is provided as a convenience to users seeking a ready chronological context.

TIMELINE

This timeline, compiled by editors at Manly, Inc., is provided as a convenience for students seeking a broad global and historical context for the materials in this volume of World Eras. *It is not intended as a self-contained resource. Students who require a comprehensive chronology of world history should consult sources such as William L. Langer, comp. and ed.,* The New Illustrated Encyclopedia of World History, *2 volumes (New York: Harry N. Abrams, 1975).*

CIRCA 4 MILLION TO 1 MILLION B.C.E.
Era of *Australopithecus,* the first hominid

CIRCA 1.5 MILLION TO 200,000 B.C.E.
Era of *Homo erectus,* "upright-walking human"

CIRCA 1,000,000-10,000 B.C.E.
Paleothic Age: hunters and gathers make use of stone tools in Eurasia

CIRCA 250,000 B.C.E.
Early evolution of *Homo sapiens,* "consciously thinking humans"

CIRCA 40,000 B.C.E.
Migrations from Siberia to Alaska lead to the first human inhabitation of North and South America

CIRCA 8000 B.C.E.
Neolithic Age: settled agrarian culture begins to develop in Eurasia

5000 B.C.E.
The world population is between 5 million and 20 million

CIRCA 4000-3500 B.C.E.
Earliest Sumerian cities: artificial irrigation leads to increased food supplies and populations in Mesopotamia

CIRCA 3000 B.C.E.
Bronze Age begins in Mesopotamia and Egypt, where bronze is primarily used for making weapons; invention of writing

CIRCA 2900-1150 B.C.E.
Minoan society on Crete: lavish palaces and commercial activity

CIRCA 2700-2200 B.C.E.
Egypt: Old Kingdom and the building of the pyramids

CIRCA 2080-1640 B.C.E.
Egypt: Middle Kingdom plagued by internal strife and invasion by the Hyksos

CIRCA 2000-1200 B.C.E.
Hittites build a powerful empire based in Anatolia (present-day Turkey) by using horse-drawn war chariots

CIRCA 1792-1760 B.C.E.
Old Babylonian Kingdom; one of the oldest extant legal codes is compiled

CIRCA 1766-1122 B.C.E.
Shang Dynasty in China: military expansion, large cities, written language, and introduction of bronze metallurgy

CIRCA 1570-1075 B.C.E.
Egypt: New Kingdom and territorial expansion into Palestine, Lebanon, and Syria

CIRCA 1500 B.C.E.
The Aryans, an Indo-European people from the steppes of present-day Ukraine and southern Russia, expand into northern India

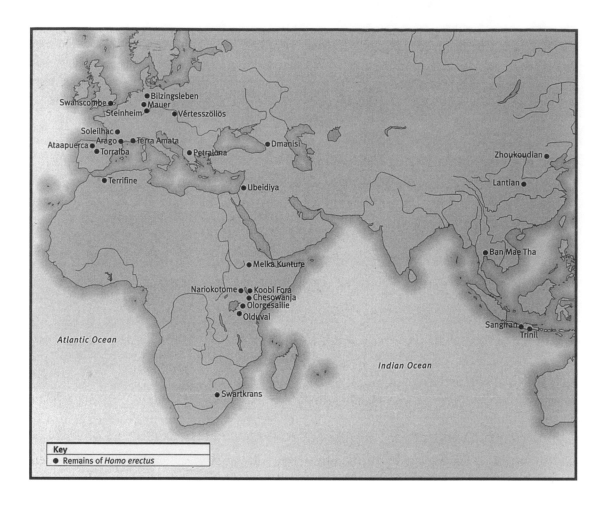

Key
● Remains of *Homo erectus*

CIRCA 1500 B.C.E.
Phoenicians create the first alphabet

CIRCA 1400-1200 B.C.E.
Hittites develop the technology of iron-smelting, improving weaponry and agricultural implements, as well as stimulating trade

CIRCA 1200-800 B.C.E.
Phoenicians establish colonies throughout the Mediterranean

CIRCA 1122- 221 B.C.E.
Zhou Dynasty in China: military conquests, nomadic invasions, and introduction of iron metallurgy

CIRCA 1100-750 B.C.E.
Greek Dark Ages: foreign invasions, civil disturbances, decrease in agricultural production, and population decline

1020-587 B.C.E.
Israelite monarchies consolidate their power in Palestine

CIRCA 1000-612 B.C.E.
Assyrians create an empire encompassing Mesopotamia, Syria, Palestine, and most of Anatolia and Egypt; they deport populations to various regions of the realm

1000 B.C.E.
The world population is approximately 50 million

CIRCA 814-146 B.C.E.
The city-state of Carthage is a powerful commercial and military power in the western Mediterranean

753 B.C.E.
Traditional date of the founding of Rome

CIRCA 750-700 B.C.E.
Rise of the polis, or city-state, in Greece

558-330 B.C.E.
Achaemenid Dynasty establishes the Persian Empire (present-day Iran, Turkey, Afghanistan, and Iraq); satraps rule the various provinces

509 B.C.E.
Roman Republic is established

500 B.C.E.
The world population is approximately 100 million

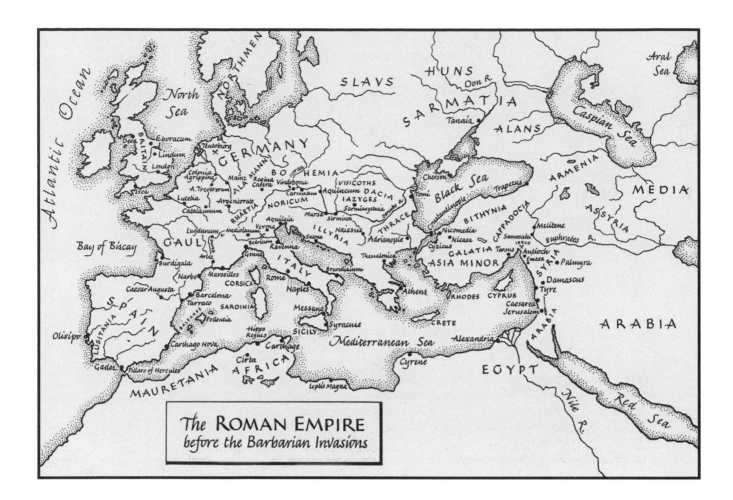

The ROMAN EMPIRE
before the Barbarian Invasions

CIRCA 400 B.C.E.
Spread of Buddhism in India

338-323 B.C.E.
Macedon, a kingdom in the central Balkan peninsula, conquers the Persian Empire

323-301 B.C.E.
Ptolemaic Kingdom (Egypt), Seleucid Kingdom (Syria), and Antigonid Dynasty (Macedon) are founded

247 B.C.E.-224 C.E.
Parthian Empire (Parthia, Persia, and Babylonia): clan leaders build independent power bases in their satrapies, or provinces

215-168 B.C.E.
Rome establishes hegemony over the Hellenistic world

206 B.C.E. TO 220 C.E.
Han Dynasty in China: imperial expansion into central Asia, centralized government, economic prosperity, and population growth

CIRCA 100 B.C.E.
Tribesmen on the Asian steppes develop the stirrup, which eventually revolutionizes warfare

1 C.E.
The world population is approximately 200 million

CIRCA 100 C.E.
Invention of paper in China

224-651 C.E.
Sasanid Empire (Parthia, Persia, and Babylonia): improved government system, founding of new cities, increased trade, and the introduction of rice and cotton cultivation

340 C.E.
Constantinople becomes the capital of the Eastern Roman, or Byzantine, Empire

CIRCA 320-550 C.E.
Gupta Dynasty in India: Golden Age of Hindu civilization marked by stability and prosperity throughout the subcontinent

395 C.E.
Christianity becomes the official religion of the Roman Empire

CIRCA 400 C.E.
The first unified Japanese state arises and is centered at Yamato on the island of Honshu; Buddhism arrives in Japan by way of Korea

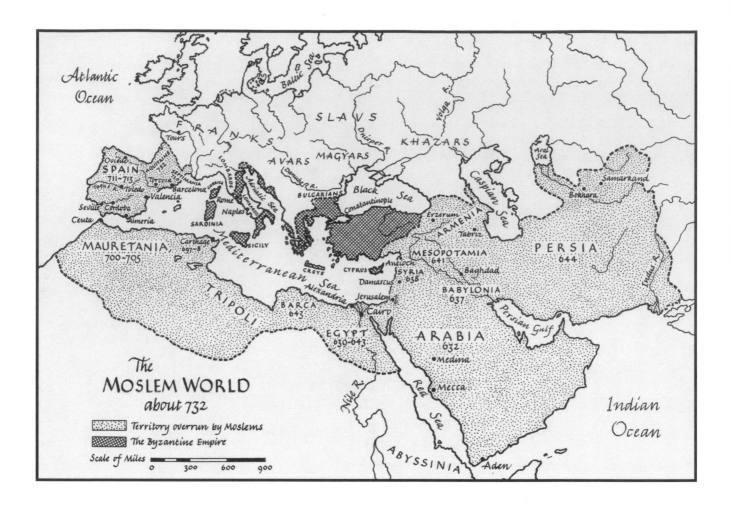

The Moslem World about 732

Territory overrun by Moslems
The Byzantine Empire

Scale of Miles
0   300   600   900

CIRCA 400 C.E.
The nomadic Huns begin a westward migration from central Asia, causing disruption in the Roman Empire

CIRCA 400 C.E.
The Mayan Empire in Mesoamerica evolves into city-states

476 C.E.
Rome falls to barbarian hordes and the Western Roman Empire collapses

CIRCA 500-1500 C.E.
Middle Ages, or medieval period, in Europe: gradual recovery from political disruption and increase in agricultural productivity and population

618-907 C.E.
Tang Dynasty in China: territorial expansion, government bureaucracy, agricultural improvements, and transportation and communication networks

632-733 C.E.
Muslim expansion and conquests in Arabia, Syria, Palestine, Mesopotamia, Egypt, North Africa, Persia, northwestern India, and Iberia

CIRCA 700 C.E.
Origins of feudalism, a political and social organization that dominates Europe until the fifteenth century; based on the relationship between lords and vassals

CIRCA 900 C.E.
Introduction of the horseshoe in Europe and black powder in China

960-1279 C.E.
Song Dynasty in China: civil administration, industry, education, and the arts

962-1806 C.E.
Holy Roman Empire of western and central Europe, created in an attempt to revive the old Roman Empire

1000 C.E.
The world population is approximately 300 million

1096-1291 C.E.
Western Christians undertake the Crusades, a series of religiously inspired military campaigns, to recapture the Holy Land from the Muslims

1200 TO 1400 C.E.
The Mali empire in Africa dominates the trans-Saharan trade network of camel caravans

1220-1335 C.E.
The Mongols, nomadic horsemen from the high steppes of eastern central Asia, build an empire that includes China, Persia, and Russia

CIRCA 1250 C.E.
Inca Empire develops in Peru: Civil administration, road networks, and sun worshipping

1299-1919 C.E.
Ottoman Empire, created by nomadic Turks and Christian converts to Islam, encompasses Asia Minor, the Balkans, Greece, Egypt, North Africa, and the Middle East

1300 C.E.
The world population is approximately 396 million

1337-1453 C.E.
Hundred Years' War, a series of intermittent military campaigns between England and France over control of Continental lands claimed by both countries

1347-1350 C.E.
Black Death, or the bubonic plague, kills one-quarter of the European population

1368-1644 C.E.
Ming Dynasty in China: political, economic, and cultural revival; the Great Wall is built

1375-1527 C.E.
The Renaissance in Western Europe, a revival in the arts and learning

1428-1519 C.E.
The Aztecs expand in central Mexico, developing trade routes and a system of tribute payments

1450 C.E.
Invention of the printing press

1453 C.E.
Constantinople falls to the Ottoman Turks, ending the Byzantine Empire

1464-1591 C.E.
Songhay Empire in Africa: military expansion, prosperous cities, control of the trans-Saharan trade

1492 C.E.
Discovery of America; European exploration and colonization of the Western Hemisphere begins

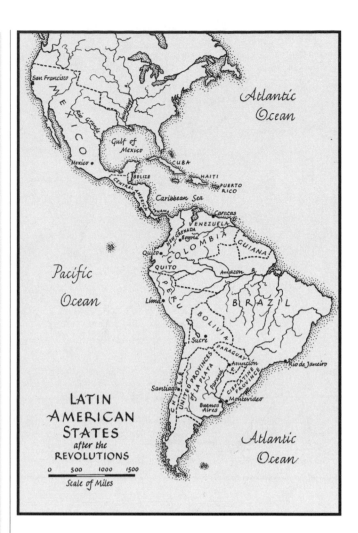

LATIN AMERICAN STATES after the REVOLUTIONS
0   500   1000   1500
Scale of Miles

CIRCA 1500-1867 C.E.
Transatlantic slave trade results in the forced migration of between 12 million and 16 million Africans to the Western Hemisphere

1500 C.E.
The world population is approximately 480 million

1517 C.E.
Beginning of the Protestant Reformation, a religious movement that ends the spiritual unity of western Christendom

1523-1763 C.E.
Mughal Empire in India: military conquests, productive agricultural economy, and population growth

1600-1867 C.E.
Tokugawa Shogunate in Japan: shoguns (military governors) turn Edo, or Tokyo, into the political, economic, and cultural center of the nation

1618-1648 C.E.
Thirty Years' War in Europe between Catholic and Protestant states

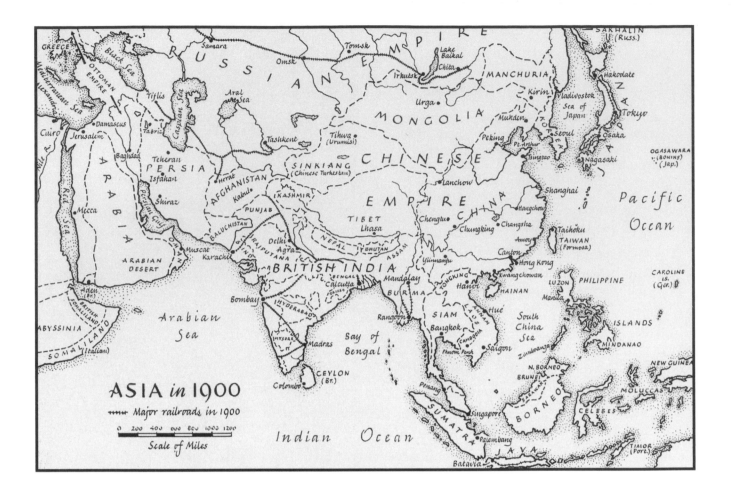

ASIA in 1900

Major railroads in 1900

Scale of Miles
0 200 400 600 800 1000 1200

1644-1911 C.E.
Qing Dynasty in China: military expansion and scholar-bureaucrats

1700 C.E.
The world population is approximately 640 million

CIRCA 1750 C.E.
Beginning of the Enlightenment, a philosophical movement marked by an emphasis on rationalism and scientific inquiry

1756-1763 C.E.
Seven Years' War: England and Prussia versus Austria, France, Russia, Saxony, Spain, and Sweden

CIRCA 1760-1850 C.E.
Industrial Revolution in Britain is marked by mass production through the division of labor, mechanization, a great increase in the supply of iron, and the use of the steam engine

1775-1783 C.E.
American War of Independence; the United States becomes an independent republic

1789 C.E.
French Revolution topples the monarchy and leads to a period of political unrest followed by a dictatorship

1793-1815 C.E.
Napoleonic wars: Austria, England, Prussia, and Russia versus France and its satellite states

1794-1824 C.E.
Latin American states conduct wars of independence against Spain

1900 C.E.
The world population is approximately 1.65 billion

1914-1918 C.E.
World War I, or the Great War: the Allies (England, France, Russia, and the United States) versus Central Powers (Austria-Hungary, Germany, and the Ottoman Empire)

1917-1921 C.E.
Russian Revolution: a group of Communists known as the Bolsheviks seize control of the country following a civil war

1939-1945 C.E.
World War II: the Allies (China, England, France, the Soviet Union, and the United States) versus the Axis (Germany, Italy, and Japan)

1945 C.E.
Successful test of the first atomic weapon; beginning of the Cold War, a period of rivalry, mistrust, and, occasionally, open hostility between the capitalist West and communist East

1947-1975 C.E.
Decolonization occurs in Africa and Asia as European powers relinquish control of colonies in those regions

1948
Israel becomes the first independent Jewish state in nearly two thousand years

1949
Communists seize control of China

1950-1951
Korean War: the United States attempts to stop Communist expansion in the Korean peninsula

1957 C.E.
The Soviet Union launches *Sputnik* ("fellow traveler of earth"), the first man-made satellite; the Space Age begins

1965-1973
Vietnam War: the United States attempts to thwart the spread of Communism in Vietnam

1989 C.E.
East European Communist regimes begin to falter and multi-party elections are held

1991 C.E.
Soviet Union is dissolved and replaced by the Commonwealth of Independent States

2000 C.E.
The world population is 6 billion

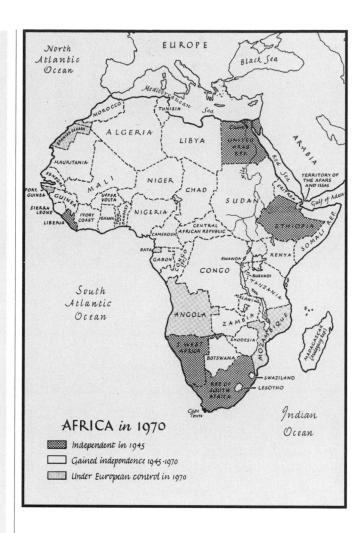

AFRICA in 1970
- Independent in 1945
- Gained independence 1945-1970
- Under European control in 1970

Editor's Introduction

The Glory That Was Greece. Nobody who encountered that phrase a hundred years ago would have needed much explanation for it: a vivid sense of the debt owed by western civilization to the ancient Greeks was part of the educational systems, not only of most of the Mediterranean world, but also of the Anglo/American tradition. Indeed it was common to attribute all that was good in our culture to the legacy of the ancient Greeks, from philosophy to technology.

Incalculable Debt. Things have changed rather dramatically. No longer can the average student be expected to be familiar with this vanished civilization; on the contrary, to most people in the English-speaking world today, their customs, their way of life, their language and literature, and many of their interests will doubtless seem alien and remote. And yet we do indeed owe them a great, an incalculable debt: it is safe to say, in fact, that our own culture would not be what it is if it were not for the ancient Greeks. So it behooves us to inquire as closely as possible into the details of their world.

Vanished Civilization. The Greeks of today are (to a certain extent) descended from the ancient Hellenes, just as their language is (partially) descended from ancient Greek; they inhabit the same land as their forebears, living literally among the ancient monuments (some of which you will find depicted on these pages), and proudly (if not always with great specificity) conscious of their august heritage. But getting a nuanced sense of ancient Greek civilization is not a simple matter of going to Greece, or even of being Greek. This is part of what makes Classics a difficult and, in some ways, obscure discipline. The classicist must learn a difficult language, a "dead" one (which means that it is no longer spoken in any living culture), and then attempt to piece together the elements of a civilization that has vanished from the planet, leaving only tantalizing traces of what its life and achievements were like. In looking at the artefacts that have survived the wrack of time, the classicist must sometimes do the work of a sleuth, imagining, inferring, puzzling, or detecting what a broken piece of pottery or a chunk of stone might once have been. The very best classical scholars learn everything they can about this vanished world, bringing to their work as broad a knowledge and exposure as possible, so that new connections can more easily occur to them. In this slow, laborious way, bit by bit, our understanding of antiquity is advanced.

Many Subdisciplines. Training in Classics, in the twentieth century at least, was principally distributed under two headings: *philology* and *archaeology*. (Other related disciplines, such as history and philosophy, have made use of the combined results of philology and archaeology.) By "philology" I intend not its narrow focus on linguistic scrutiny—although that is surely an important aspect of philology—but its older meaning of textual studies in the broadest sense: the philologist was expected to have competence to work with ancient texts, in every conceivable way. Most widely construed, this includes the actual ability to decode ancient documents. Such work requires expertise in the fields of *papyrology* and *palaeography*. Johannes Gutenberg did not invent his movable-type printing press until the fifteenth century, so prior to that time, virtually all books in the western world were laboriously copied one at a time, by hand, whether onto papyrus, parchment, or (in the case of some mediaeval manuscripts) an early form of paper. It is from such hand-written documents that our modern printed editions of all ancient authors are made. This process demands skill in *textual criticism*, in which palaeography and/or papyrology may play an important part. More durable (but generally much briefer) textual remains are those preserved on stone or metal; the field that studies such inscriptions is called *epigraphy*. Aside from the actual matters they discuss, epigraphic inscriptions can also preserve precious information about such things as alphabetic styles and norms of spelling current at the time in which they were produced. A hybrid field, poised midway amongst those of philology, epigraphy, and archaeology (on which see below), is that of *numismatics*, the study of coins, which may have not only pictorial images but also verbal inscriptions on them.

Studying the Text. Once palaeographers, papyrologists, epigraphers, and other textual critics have done their work, and a critical text is established and published, the wider community of philologists can set to work studying the text. For Hellenists, this of course demands not only expertise in the language—the grammar and linguistic phenomena—but also, ideally, a broad base of knowledge about other texts that were produced in the same time and place.

If one is working on a Greek tragedy, for example—let us say, the *Antigone* of Sophocles—it is very helpful to have the greatest possible familiarity with all the other extant tragedies of Sophocles. More than this, one will want to know as much as possible about all the tragedies that have survived—those of Aeschylus and Euripides, as well as those of Sophocles—and one will try to scout out information about other tragedies that have not survived, or of which only fragments now remain. One will want to discover as much as one can about the history of Athens, of the region (called "Attica") in which Athens was situated, and of Greece as a whole, both in the time of Sophocles and before. For that matter, one may want to know what happened in Athens (or Attica, or Greece) *after* the time of Sophocles, so that one can trace what happened to the *Antigone* (or to tragedy generally) in the ensuing years. (In the case of most ancient Greek texts, actually, one will want to know, not only about Greece, but the rest of the Mediterranean world, including Egypt and Asia Minor, because the history of these texts is partly bound up with the book-trade in those regions, and with the way in which books were stored there in libraries after the classical period.)

Other Skills. To continue with our imagined study of *Antigone:* Attic tragedy is a very particular type of textual production, and in order to understand it deeply, the classicist will need some special skills. Since it is written in verse, and since ancient Greek verse is very different from our own, one needs to know something about *metrics*, the study of different metrical patterns in classical verse (indeed the textual critic will already have needed to consider metrical issues in establishing a critical text of the play, so there is some circularity here). The actual diction used in tragedy was more formal than that in ordinary Athenian conversational Greek (although to a certain extent we have to infer the nature of the latter from documents like Plato's dialogues and Aristophanes' comedies), so the classicist may want to make a lexical study of the text as well (again, *lexicology* may already have played an important part of the process of editing the text for publication). In order to enrich our knowledge of the text, one will want next to inquire into a number of different realms of knowledge: What were the ancient myths and legends from which Sophocles drew his tale? Has he innovated on those in any significant way, and if so, how? What was an ancient play-performance like? How, when, where, and why were these plays performed? Who performed them, and who watched the performances? What were the theater, the costumes, the sets, the music, the special effects like? It emerges that these tragedies, which were performed at an annual festival in central Athens, had not only a religious, but also a political significance. So the classicists who are interested in this text may find themselves hunting down information in these areas of study.

Other Texts. There are, of course, many different kinds of text besides an Attic tragedy; one might want to know, for example, about a work of philosophy, or of oratory, or of medical science, or of epic poetry. Each of these genres is

a different kind of cultural production; the questions the classicist is going to ask will vary, and differ, not only according to the genre of the text under study, but also by virtue of the kind of use he wants to make of it.

Material Culture. The archaeologist is especially interested in the remains of what we call "material culture" — that is, in the physical objects that the ancient Greeks left behind, and that have survived to this day. These include such things as buildings (public and private, sacred and secular); works of art, such as paintings and sculpture; pottery, which was often painted with extraordinary skill and beauty; coins; tools and weapons, and machinery of both war and peace; jewelry and other forms of adornment; devices for personal grooming; and so on. The more durable the material, of course, the longer-lasting the artefact (stone lasts longer than wood; metal lasts longer than ceramic; and so forth). One has only to walk around an archaeological site in Greece to get a strong sense of the palpability of the past. Potsherds, which might be three thousand years old, are sometimes just lying on the ground. (Indeed, ironically, while innumerable ancient bronze statues were at some point melted down for the use of their metal, the humbler clay pot has often survived to the present day.) Much careful work of recuperation and restoration has been done, especially in the past couple hundred years, and some ancient sites that were literally buried underground have been painstakingly dug out and, as much as possible, meticulously put back together as they once were. The great museums of the world, even those outside Greece itself, contain many painted pots and other artefacts that can shed precious light on the darkness of the past, giving us a glimpse into the humanity of these long-dead peoples.

Art History. That aspect of Classics now known as *art history* is an extension of classical archaeology, studying as it does in stylistic and formal terms the images bequeathed to us by antiquity. The classical art-historian will be particularly interested in assessing the development of artistic techniques in the various media, and also in relating these to our larger sociocultural picture of the civilizations that produced them.

Reciprocal Influences. Again the influences are circular: the work of the archaeologist is much illuminated by the information we can glean from ancient texts (Pausanias' *Guide to Greece*, written in the second century C.E., is still one of the richest sources of information on the region and its ancient monuments). Conversely, the philologists who do not avail themselves of the visual enrichment that archaeological scholarship can provide are impoverished readers. So each of these sub-disciplines nourishes the other in a vital way.

Historical Inquiry. The *historian*, whose job it is to ask questions about the events of the past and their significance, advances the work both of philologists and of archaeologists in order to piece together a coherent narrative about the culture in question. Traditionally such narratives have focused on matters of government, of warfare, of the grand-scale evolution and devolution of societies. As we move into the twenty-first century, however, we find that ancient historians are inquiring more and more into the life of the ordinary person of antiquity. To a certain extent, this parallels recent trends in cultural studies programs that focus on current cultures: as the canons of literature and the other arts have been called into question, we are seeing a shift away from "high culture" and toward the everyday. To an extent as well, this reflects the sense (shared by many) that the world is, after all, largely composed of ordinary people leading everyday lives.

Traditional Patterns. Such, then, was traditional Classics as it was practiced into the twentieth century. Some of these patterns of scholarship were in place before the Enlightenment; indeed some of them have roots as far back as the Renaissance, or even earlier. And except for some of the very youngest generation, most classicists now alive were trained in this approach. With the extraordinary changes and developments we have seen in the humanities generally over the past few decades, it should not be surprising that Classics too has changed.

Different Approaches and Values. The differences have evinced themselves not only in terms of the *topics* that scholars tend to find interesting and important—such as the shift, just mentioned, toward the everyday—but also (and perhaps especially) in terms of *methodology*. More simply put, there have been massive changes, not only in *what* classical scholars tend to study, but also in *how*. As the academic world has become more and more internationalized, there is a good deal of cross-pollination from one culture to another. In the nineteenth century, Classics in America was largely shaped according to German styles of scholarship; in the twentieth century, the greatest impact came from French theorists, in literary theory and anthropology especially. These new influences have substantially changed the kinds of questions classicists are likely to ask about ancient peoples (and thus, necessarily, the kinds of answers they are likely to find). As Marxist thought and psychoanalytic theory have entered the critical vocabulary of scholars, for example, recent research has inevitably come to reflect these schools of thought. Issues of class and gender, too, have been much foregrounded in recent work on antiquity; to return again to our sample case: Attic tragedy, and the *Antigone* especially, raise many important questions under the rubric of gender studies. What was it like to be a woman in ancient Greece? What can a play about a woman in a difficult situation, set in the mythical past, and written by a man in an overwhelmingly androcentric society, tell us about the way women might have been perceived, represented, or treated (by men and by other women) in Sophocles' own day? Other literary schools and approaches, too, will have new light to shed on classical texts. Semiotics, narratology, reader-response criticism—all these, and others as well, promise to open up new vistas for the student of antiquity.

Different Conclusions. In view of all this, it is important to realize that, no matter what approach one takes, the data themselves do not change: that is, the traditionalist will, at the end of the day, have read the same texts, have examined the same vase-paintings, as the most avant-garde scholar. Rather what determines one's findings is (on the one hand) one's worldview, and (on the other) the kinds of questions that one asks of the data.

Why This Volume? There are many books available on the ancient Greeks, including a number of truly admirable reference works. So why, at the brink of a new millennium, have we undertaken to compile a new one? The *World Eras* series was conceived with the rationale of providing, in such a way as to reflect changing curricular needs, a cross-disciplinary overview of world history, with a strong emphasis on daily life and social history. Such a project is both difficult and profoundly needed in the study of Greek culture; until recently, because of the way the discipline of Classics was established, the Greeks were uniformly put on a pedestal, with the predictable double result that they were not only lionized, but also became quite unreachable. In the past few decades we have seen a marked reversal of this trend, but much work still remains to be done, and there are still many things about life in ancient Greece that remain shrouded in mystery for us. It is our hope that *Classical Greek Civilization: 800–323 B.C.E.* will help in this exciting work of discovery.

Triple Goal. I have asked my contributors to keep ever before them the triple goal of *accuracy*, *clarity*, and *accessibility*: we have made every effort to present the materials in such a way as to avoid factual error, obscurity, or abstruseness. Hopefully, the reader will also find that they have also managed to be interesting.

How To Use This Book. It is, of course, impossible to freeze any culture in time. How, for example, could we accurately say what "American culture" is? Is it possible to say what American culture is like, even if we restrict our inquiry to "American culture in the year 2001"? Upon reflection it quickly becomes clear that any culture is going to be multifaceted, and to look radically different depending on one's vantage point. I would like, just as a point of departure, to suggest three different factors that will radically affect one's perception of any culture, ancient or modern: *place*, *time*, and *class*. *Place*, of course, was even more a factor in ancient cultures than it is in modern. Because of the physical and logistical difficulties attendant upon any attempt to travel (see chapter 4), and because the ancients lacked the mass-media—television, radio, film, and the internet—that help to homogenize our culture and make it more instantaneous, Greek-speaking peoples on the west coast of what is now Turkey (for example) would inevitably have a different way of life—many different ways of life—than, say, those living on islands in the Ionian Sea. *Time*, too, plays a crucial role: if Aristotle was right in defining time as the measure of *change*, then it should not be surprising that Greek life in Homer's day was dramatically different from Greek life in Aristotle's own time. By *class* I mean the socioeconomic factors that divide and distinguish groups of people even when they coexist in the same place and time: the poor living in downtown Los Angeles have a life unimaginably different from that of the captains of industry whose mansions are only a few miles away in Beverly Hills. A similar class-spectrum was in place, for example, in fifth-century Athens, and can probably be found in all times and places.

Classical Greek Civilization. With these facts in mind, the reader should consider that a label like "Classical Greek Civilization" is, inevitably, an over-simplification. There was no such thing as a monolithic classical Greek civilization. Even the word "classical" is potentially misleading, because it is used by experts in more than one way. In the strictest sense, it has regularly been applied to the culture of Athens in the fifth and fourth centuries B.C.E. (on the grounds that Athens in this period, as "the Greece of Greece," represents the finest flower of Hellenic civilization). In other contexts, however, "classical" is taken as a convenient way of distinguishing ancient Greek culture from Byzantine and modern Greek cultures (again, as though any of them were or could be monolithic). It is in the latter sense that this volume has been assigned its title of *Classical Greek Civilization*. But the reader should keep in mind that this umbrella-term covers a sizeable period of time, which could more carefully be broken down into a number of different periods: the Archaic, the early Classical, the High Classical, and the Hellenistic (the latter term referring to the breathtaking dissemination, by Alexander the Great, of Hellenic culture among non-Hellenic peoples). Even this list of terms does not account for earlier periods of civilization in what came to be seen as the Greek world, such as the Helladic, Cycladic, Minoan, and Mycenaean. But we must begin somewhere; and we must find a way of sorting the data into categories of which we can somehow make sense. That is the spirit in which this book has been put together. But the reader should always keep in mind that formulae like "The Greeks were X" or "The Greeks did Y" are, and can only be, in some sense reductive.

Topics. Each volume in the *World Eras* series is scheduled to have the same basic table of contents. This will ensure that the student who wishes to compare details of (say) marriage in a variety of cultures, can do so quickly and easily. It has also meant that the contributors to this volume have, to a certain extent, had their projects arranged for them in advance, and in ways that otherwise might not have occurred to them. But the overall result, I think, has led to a volume that is perspicuously structured and easy to consult.

Wealth of Material. Readers who want to know details of what life and culture were like in the Greek-speaking world of the first millennium B.C.E. will find a wealth of material here to reward them. Are you curious about what a typical Greek breakfast was like? Turn to chapter 7. Would you like to know how a Greek doctor would set broken bones? You will find information about this in chapter 10. Have you ever wondered about how taxes were levied in the ancient world? They are discussed in chapter 5. Do you

know what an ancient Greek funeral was like? If not, you can find out in chapter 8. If you would like details on the way law-courts were run, look in chapter 6. Chapter 3 describes the arts — verbal, visual, and performing — that have made ancient Greece the wellspring of high culture for all subsequent western culture. And there is a great deal of information about the myths and legends of ancient Greece, as well as about their religious practices and philosophy, in chapter 9. Chapter 1 provides a summary overview, in chronological format, of major events occurring outside the Greek-speaking world during the period covered by the book, while chapter 2 offers a geographical overview of the entire region during this period. We have also added, at the end, a glossary of technical terms and of the Greek words used in the text, as well as a chapter-by-chapter bibliography full of suggestions for further reading.

Pronunciation. We do not know with absolute certainty how the ancient Greeks pronounced their language. What we do know is that [1] there were several different dialects of Greek scattered throughout what we think of as the Greek-speaking world, and [2] patterns of pronunciation appear to have changed, in some cases dramatically, over time. The best that can be done is to offer some recommendations about how Greek words should be pronounced. With those caveats, the following tentative conjectures can be made regarding what might have been the pronunciation of Attic Greek (the dialect spoken in and around Athens) in the fifth and fourth centuries B.C.E.

Vowels. Greek vowels follow a more consistent logic, at least in their pronunciation, than do modern English vowels. In ancient Greek, a long vowel, for example, was not really a different sound than a short one, but rather one that took (precisely) more time to pronounce than its short counterpart.

• Thus a long A, "alpha," takes longer to pronounce than a short one, but both appear to have had the value of *a* in *ah*.

• Short E, "epsilon," had the value of *e* in *get*. Long E, known as "eta," was apparently pronounced as a longer, more open version of epsilon; its nature is not entirely certain, but by way of convenient distinction most scholars today pronounce it either like the *a* in *way*, or the *a* in our *cat*.

• Long and short I, "iota," are somewhere between the *i* in *prestige* and the *i* in *hit*.

• Modern American English probably does not have any sounds that are exactly like the long and short O of ancient Greek, the "omega" and "omicron" respectively, but omicron was probably somewhere in the spectrum between the *o* in *soft* and that in *drove*, while omega might have been like the *aw* in *caw*, or the *au* in *caught* (as that word is pronounced in the northeast United States, not the Midwest, where *caught* and *cot* are difficult to distinguish audially).

• The U sound, represented by long and short "upsilon," appears to have been something like the *u* in French *tu* or German *Grüß*.

• Our own half-vowels, Y and W, are problematic in different ways. Our letter Y is drawn like the ancient capital upsilon (hence its French name, "igrec"), but is essentially used in English either to represent a semivowel (as in *your*) or as another way of representing a long *i* sound (as in *Kirby*). Our W may be used as part of what is essentially a diphthong (as in *how*), or as part of a semivowel (as in *wool*); the Greeks, apparently, had a letter for this sound, which we call "digamma"; it looked like our capital F, and fell out of written use after the sound itself disappeared from spoken Attic Greek.

Diphthongs. A "diphthong" is, essentially, a single syllable composed of two vowel-sounds; in pronouncing a diphthong, one glides from the sound of the first vowel to the sound of the second. Ancient Greek had quite a number of such composite vowels, although some are far less common than others. Here are some of those most frequently encountered (and, again, one should bear in mind that some of these are dramatically different in modern Greek):

• AI was probably pronounced like the *ai* in our *aisle*.

• AU was something like the vowel-sound in our *how*.

• EI was apparently like the vowel-sound in our *vein*.

• EU as the Greeks appear to have pronounced it is not a sound current in American English; it seems to have been a glide from the *e* of *get* to the *u* of *truth* (imagine Henry Higgins saying "Oh!").

• OI was comparable to the *oi* in *oil*.

• OU (traditionally pronounced in Britain like the *ou* in *mouse*) was probably like the *ou* in *soup*.

• UI again has no American English counterpart; it seems to have been a glide from the *u* (of French *tu*) to the *i* of *prestige*.

Consonants. The Greek B, D, G, K, L, M, N, P, S, and T were probably pronounced more or less as we would pronounce them (G being always hard, as in *get*, and S being usually or always unvoiced).

• They also had letters to represent the aspirated forms of the consonants K, P, and T; these are known as "chi," "phi," and "theta," respectively, and, in the classical period, represented not the *ch*, *ph*, and *th* in *loch*, *phlox*, and *thin*, but the stop-sound followed by the expulsion of breath, as in *cat*, *pot*, and *top* (rather than the "drier" sounds of *c*, *p*, and *t* in *bloc*, *tip*, and *pat*. (Even modern Greek is different in this respect; modern phi, for example, is pronounced like our F.)

• There were two convenience-letters for combinations with S: "xi" for *k* + *s*, and "psi" for *p* + *s*. These seem to have been pronounced like the X in *axe* and the PS in *lapse*.

• R appears to have been pronounced toward the front of the mouth, and typically trilled as in Spanish or Italian;

Z was pronounced like the *sd* in *wisdom* or the *dz* in *adze* (again modern Greek is different in this respect).

• Our letter Q is derived from the ancient "qoppa," which looked like a stick-drawing of a lollipop, and which appears to have been pronounced rather like kappa; it is found, however, more frequently in inscriptions on stone than in manuscripts on papyrus or animal skin.

• Most ancient Greeks did aspirate some initial vowels; that is, they sometimes began words with an *h* sound. This is also the case for words that began with R; consequently such words are transliterated with RH- at the beginning (as in the name for the Greek letter R itself, "rho").

Spelling. In this volume we have tried to maintain orthographic consistency throughout, although that has not always been possible—partly because there is no single universally-adopted system of transliteration, and because certain Greek words already have a familiar "look" in English. Eta and omega have been rendered, usually, as *ê* and *ô* respectively; sometimes a final *ê* will be marked *ë* (to show that it is indeed pronounced, and not a silent E as in such English words as *time* or *bake*). As a rule we have used *k* and *kh* rather than *c* and *ch* to represent the Greek letters kappa and chi. The Greek double consonants GG and GK have usually been transliterated as such, although the reader should know that they were probably pronounced like the *ng* in *angle* and the *nk* in *ankle*, respectively; many scholars will actually transliterate them according to the latter convention. So too the combination gamma-chi, which was probably pronounced like the central cluster in *anchor*, will be represented by *gkh* rather than *nkh*. Some scholars will use *y* to represent upsilon, but wherever possible we have transliterated the latter as *u*.

Acknowledgments. I have been extremely fortunate to have the collaboration of a skilled and distinguished team of contributors, for whose excellent work I am most grateful. In addition, I would like to express my gratitude for the advice and assistance of Ward Briggs, Ralph Gallucci, Neil and Patrick O'Sullivan, Kirk Ormand, and Rex Wallace. Richard Layman and Anthony Scotti, of Manly, Inc., have lent their unfailing expertise and assistance; without them this book literally could not have come into existence. Dr. Scotti, moreover, chose and placed the many beautiful images for the volume. Robert Wright has, as always, been an inexhaustible fund of sapience and encouragement. I am especially grateful to my students over the past two decades—at Choate, at Chapel Hill, at Smith, and at Purdue—who, by their unfailing hunger and thirst for knowledge, have enabled me to keep my reading audience clearly in mind as this book came into focus. That audience, esteemed reader, now includes you: and whoever you may be, wherever you are, whenever this book shall come into your hands, I salute you, and invite you in to the captivating world of the ancient Greeks.

John T. Kirby
Purdue University

ACKNOWLEDGMENTS

This book was produced by Manly, Inc. Karen L. Rood is senior editor and Anthony J. Scotti Jr. is series editor.

Production manager is Philip B. Dematteis.

Administrative support was provided by Ann M. Cheschi, Dawnca T. Williams, and Mary A. Womble.

Accountant is Kathy Weston. Accounting assistant is Amber L. Coker.

Copyediting supervisor is Phyllis A. Avant. The copyediting staff includes Brenda Carol Blanton, Allen E. Friend Jr., Melissa D. Hinton, William Tobias Mathes, Jennifer S. Reid, Nancy E. Smith, and Elizabeth Jo Ann Sumner. Freelance copyeditor is Rebecca Mayo.

Editorial associates are Michael S. Allen and Michael S. Martin.

Layout and graphics supervisor is Janet E. Hill. The graphics staff includes Karla Corley Brown and Zoe R. Cook.

Office manager is Kathy Lawler Merlette.

Permissions editor is Jeff Miller.

Photography editors are Charles Mims, Scott Nemzek, and Paul Talbot.

Digital photographic copy work was performed by Joseph M. Bruccoli.

SGML supervisor is Cory McNair. The SGML staff includes Frank Graham, Linda Dalton Mullinax, Jason Paddock, and Alex Snead.

Systems manager is Marie L. Parker.

Typesetting supervisor is Kathleen M. Flanagan. The typesetting staff includes Mark J. McEwan, Patricia Flanagan Salisbury, and Alison Smith. Freelance typesetters are Wanda Adams and Vicki Grivetti.

Walter W. Ross did library research. He was assisted by Steven Gross and the following librarians at the Thomas Cooper Library of the University of South Carolina: circulation department head Tucker Taylor; reference department head Virginia W. Weathers; Brette Barclay, Marilee Birchfield, Paul Cammarata, Gary Geer, Michael Macan, Tom Marcil, Rose Marshall, and Sharon Verba; interlibrary loan department head John Brunswick; and Robert Arndt, Hayden Battle, Barry Bull, Jo Cottingham, Marna Hostetler, Marieum McClary, Erika Peake, and Nelson Rivera, interlibrary loan staff.

WORLD ERAS

VOLUME 6

CLASSICAL GREEK CIVILIZATION

800-323 B.C.E.

WORLD EVENTS:
SELECTED OCCURRENCES OUTSIDE GREECE

by MICHAEL S. ALLEN

800-550*
B.C.E.

- The Indian Aryans continue their expansion on the Asian subcontinent, settling westward along the Gangetic plain. During this period the first of the *Upanishads,* the chief mystical and philosophical scriptures of Hinduism, are composed.

800

- Menua becomes king of Urartu, or Van. Under his fifteen-year reign the strength of this kingdom north of Assyria is consolidated and its borders expanded.

798-782

- The kingdom of Israel, led by Joash, wars with the Aramaean armies of Ben Hadad II, recovering territories formerly lost to Hazael of Damascus; Judah, including its capital at Jerusalem, subsequently falls to Joash as well, losing its independence.

790

- Babylon makes a treaty with Assyria, submitting to its protection.

783-748

- Under the reign of Jeroboam II, Damascus and Hamath become tributaries of Israel.

776

- A poem later anthologized in the Chinese work *Shi-Ching* (Classic of Poetry) notes a solar eclipse occurring in this year, the earliest recorded observation of such a phenomenon.

* Denotes circa date

771 • Hao, the capital of the Chou Dynasty in China, is sacked by Western invaders.

770 • The Chou relocate their capital to Loyang, marking the beginning of the Eastern Chou Dynasty.

765-735 • The Hebrew prophets Amos and Hosea, the first to record their prophecies in writing, warn Israel of its corruption during the reign of Jeroboam II.

760* • The Greeks began colonizing Italy and Sicily.

755-735 • Following in the victories of his predecessor Argishti I, Sarduri II continues to expand the borders of Urartu, conquering Commagene, Melitene, and Carchemish.

755 • Matiel of Aramea submits to vassalage under Assurnirari V, king of Assyria, only to rebel later; he will bring the Aramaean states into a treaty with Ketek, an ally of Urartu, the greatest threat to Assyria's power.

753 • According to traditional sources, the city of Rome is founded by Romulus, the son of a princess of Alba Longa and the god Mars.

748 • Jeroboam II of Israel dies, and Uzziah of Judah takes charge of a western coalition opposed to Assyria. Zechariah, Jeroboam's successor, is assassinated by Shallum, marking the end of the Jehu dynasty in Israel. In the midst of the political unrest Shallum is killed by Menahem, who in turn ascends to the throne in Israel.

743 • Tiglath-pileser III of Assyria launches his first major campaign against neighboring states to the west, besieging the Urartean allies at Arpad.

739	• Tiglath-pileser III begins a successful war against the coalition headed by Uzziah of Judah.
738	• Tiglath-pileser III receives tribute from Israel, Damascus, Phoenicia, and other members of the failing anti-Assyrian coalition.
736	• Pekahiah, the successor to Menahem in Israel, is killed by Pekah, the leader of a rising anti-Assyrian faction.
735	• Tiglath-pileser III invades Urartu.
734	• Ahaz becomes king of Judah and is entreated by the Syro-Ephraimite coalition, composed of Pekah of Israel and Rezin of Aram, son of Ben Hadad II, to join their alliance; Ahaz turns to Assyria for support, ignoring the counsel of the prophet Isaiah.
733-732	• In a second wave of attacks against his western opposition, Tiglath-pileser III defeats Israel and Damascus. Gilead, Galilee, and Damascus are made into Assyrian provinces, while Israel is placed under the kingship of Hoshea.
733-701	• The prophets Isaiah and Micah minister in Judah, attacking corruption and warning of God's wrath and impending destruction.
731	• Revolution breaks out in Babylon; Tiglath-pileser III returns from his western campaign in order to put it down.
728	• Tiglath-pileser III regains full control over Babylon, appointing himself king.

725

- Against the protests of the prophet Isaiah, Hoshea of Israel rebels against Assyria, looking to Egypt for support; meanwhile, Shalmaneser V of Assyria besieges Samaria, the capital of Israel.

722

- Samaria falls to Assyria; Shalmaneser V is succeeded by his son, Sargon II, at whose orders thousands of Israelites are taken away captive into Mesopotamia.

722-706

- Sargon recaptures Hamath, Ekron, and Gaza; he conquers Tyre after a five-year siege.

721

- The Elamites, led by Humbanigash and allied with Merodach-baladan of Babylon, engage in battle at Der with the forces of Sargon of Assyria, but the outcome is indecisive.

720

- Judah capitulates to Sargon II and pays tribute to the Assyrian king.

720*

- In China the Hung Kou (Great Ditch) is constructed, connecting a tributary of the Huai to the Yellow River.

717-716

- The Neo-Hittite city of Carchemish is conquered and annexed by Sargon II; the Egyptian Pharaoh Osorkon likewise meets Assyrian defeat at Raphia.

715*

- Pi'ankhi, advancing north from his capital at Napata, invades Egypt; with little effort he is able to overthrow the Twenty-fourth Dynasty and found a new Ethiopian Dynasty.

- Hezekiah is anointed king of Judah.

- Numa Pompilius, tradition holds, becomes the first king of Rome, after Romulus and Remus; he is also considered to be the founder of Roman religion.

714
- Sargon II of Assyria defeats the Urartean armies and raids their royal treasury, effectively bringing an end to Urarta's role in world affairs.

712
- The Assyrian armies of Sargon II attack the city of Ashdod, dissolving an alliance between Egypt and the southern states of Palestine.

710
- Babylon revolts against Assyrian rule; Merodach-baladan becomes king.

709
- Sargon II of Assyria sends Merodach-baladan into exile, declaring himself king in his place.

705
- After the death of Sargon II, Sennacherib becomes king of Assyria.

703
- Merodach-baladan reclaims his throne in Babylon, intending to bring an end to Assyrian domination; Assyria, under the rule of Sennacherib, once again puts down the Babylonian insurgents, but only with great difficulty.

701
- Judah, Phoenicia, Egypt, and Philistia ally themselves against Assyria. Sennacherib marches westward against the new conspiracy and, after easily overcoming the Phoenicians and Philistines, defeats the Egyptian troops of the Pharaoh Shabaka at Elteqeh; he then attacks the armies of Hezekiah, razing almost all of Judah.

700*
- After a lengthy and indecisive siege on Jerusalem, Hezekiah agrees to pay tribute to Sennacherib; Sidon and Tyre likewise submit to vassalage under Assyria.
- Celtic peoples begin to settle in Spain.

692
- Allied with the Elamites, the Chaldean faction in Babylon wrests control of the city away from the Assyrians.

690	• Cimmeria invades Phrygia, devastating the Anatolian kingdom.
689	• In response to thirteen years of continual insurrection, Sennacherib sacks the city of Babylon.
681*	• Esarhaddon, Sennacherib's son and heir, puts down a rebellion instigated by one of his brothers, who had murdered their father; Esarhaddon becomes king of Assyria.
677	• Esarhaddon puts down a Phoenician rebellion at Sidon, razing the city, dissolving its alliance with Egypt, and annexing the province.
675-674	• Esarhaddon begins his first raids into Egypt, but without a decisive outcome.
671	• Esarhaddon captures Memphis, and the Pharaoh Tirhaqah is forced to flee south to Ethiopia.
669	• Esarhaddon dies at Harran, and Tirhaqah returns to Memphis.
668	• Assurbanipal succeeds Esarhaddon as king of Assyria; a patron of Assyrian and Babylonian culture, he compiles a vast library of tablets chronicling literature, history, science, and religion.
667	• The Assyrians again expel the Pharaoh Tirhaqah from Memphis.
664	• Tirhaqah's successor, the Pharaoh Tanuatamun, reclaims Egyptian power at Memphis.

663

- Assyria captures Thebes, defeating Tanuatamun and putting an end to Ethiopian power in Egypt. Psammetichus I becomes Pharaoh of the new dynasty; looking back to Old Kingdom Egypt for his model, he initiates what is known as the Saite Revival, a renaissance in religion, art, and literature.

660*

- Zoroaster, the Persian prophet and founder of Zoroastrianism, is born.
- The Cimmerians invade Lydia, but its king, Gyges, allied with Assurbanipal of Assyria, is able to repel their attacks.
- The Ainus in Japan are pushed out by a Mongolian people, most likely coming from Korea; according to tradition, Jimmu becomes the first emperor of Japan.

658

- Gyges of Lydia, breaking his alliance with Assyria, sends Ionian and Carian mercenary support to Psammetichus I of Egypt, who begins a successful campaign to drive the Assyrians out of the country.

652

- The Cimmerians return to Lydia, sacking its capital at Sardis and killing King Gyges.
- Civil war breaks out in Assyria at the instigation of Assurbanipal's brother Shamashshumukin, king of Babylon, who forms an alliance with the Chaldeans, the Armenians, the Egyptians, and the Elamites.

650

- The anti-Assyrian allies are defeated at the battle of Babsame on the Tigris River.

648

- Shamashshumkin surrenders Babylon to Assyria.

642

- According to tradition, Ancus Martius becomes king of Rome; during his reign he constructs a bridge over the Tiber River.

639

- The Elamite city of Susa is sacked by Assurbanipal of Assyria.

631
- Assurbanipal dies, and rebellion quickly begins to spread through the territories of the overextended Assyrian empire.

627
- Josiah claims the formerly Assyrian provinces of Samaria, Gilead, and Galilee for Judah.

626
- Nabopolassar consolidates Chaldean power in Babylon, declaring himself king.
- Scythian invaders from the north spill into Syria and Palestine; they destroy the Philistines and reach as far as Egypt.

623-616
- Babylon and Assyria wage a long but indecisive war.

622
- In Judah, Josiah inaugurates comprehensive religious and political reforms on the basis of a rediscovered version of the book of Deuteronomy.

616*
- Tarquinius Priscus, the first in a line of Etruscan rulers, becomes king in Rome; the Cloaca Maxima (a canal through Rome), the Temple of Jupiter Capitolinus, and the Circus Maximus (an arena for chariot racing) are all built under his reign.

614
- Cyaxares of Media allies his kingdom with Babylon.

612
- The Scythians join the alliance already existing between Cyaxares and Nabopolassar; the city of Nineveh falls to the combined Median, Babylonian, and Scythian forces. The Medes and Scythians conquer Urarta, bringing a final end to the kingdom of Van.

611
- Nabopolassar leads his armies against Harran, where Assuruballit II had been trying to muster his Assyrian forces; however, with his Median allies absent, Nabopolassar is unable to capture the Assyrian fortress.

610
- The Medes rejoin the Babylonians, and the Assyrians flee Harran.

609
- The remaining Assyrian armies, allied with Egypt, attempt to recapture Harran, but without success. Neko II succeeds Psammetichus I in Egypt and leads his armies north to aid Assyria.

608
- On his march north, Neko II meets Josiah of Judah at Megiddo. Josiah is killed and Judah conquered, but the Egyptian army is prevented from reaching their Assyrian allies in time to save them from defeat.

605
- The crown prince Nebuchadrezzer of Babylon overwhelmingly defeats the Egyptian armies of Neko II at the battle of Carchemish, forcing them out of Syria-Palestine. He then becomes king of Babylon and ruler of the newly conquered Assyrian provinces.

601
- Nebuchadrezzar attacks Egypt, but without decisive outcome.

600-500*
- The Olmec, founders of the earliest of Mesoamerican civilizations, abandon their center at La Venta; Tres Zapotes emerges as the new chief city in the region.

600*
- An expedition of Phoenician ships successfully circumnavigates Africa.
- In Lydia the use of coined money is introduced.
- *The Book of Odes,* an anthology of poetry dating back to the time of the Shang, appears in China.

598
- Nebuchadrezzar launches another western campaign, this time against Judah.

597
- The Babylonian armies besiege Jerusalem. When it falls, after nearly three months, thousands of Israelites are taken captive to Babylon.

592
- Ezekiel begins to prophesize in Israel, maintaining that Jerusalem will be destroyed and eventually rebuilt.

590*
- Cyaxares of Media attacks Lydia.
- The arch is first used in Roman architecture.

588
- Against the counsel of the prophet Jeremiah, Zedekiah allies with Egypt and revolts against Babylon; Nebuchadrezzar once again invests Jerusalem.

587
- The Pharaoh Apries meets the Babylonian armies briefly but then retreats to Egypt, leaving the besieged Israelites without an ally.

586
- Jerusalem falls to Nebuchadrezzar, who razes the city and takes away captive to Babylon a second wave of Jews. This defeat marks the end of Judah as a nation.

586-561
- Nebuchadrezzar lavishes wealth upon the city of Babylon, making it a wonder of the ancient world.

585
- After five years of indecisive war, Media and Lydia make peace.

582
- Following the murder of Gedaliah, the governor of Judah, a third wave of Jews are exiled to Babylon.

578-534
- Rome, under the reign of Servius Tullius, enters the Latin League.

573
- Tyre surrenders to Nebuchadrezzar, after thirteen years of siege.

570

- In an attempt to aid Libyan allies attacking the Greek city of Cyrene in North Africa, the Pharaoh Apries is defeated and dethroned.

561

- Nebuchadrezzar dies.

560*

- Croesus becomes king of Lydia and begins a successful campaign to gain control throughout Asia Minor.
- Siddhartha Gautama, The Buddha, is born.

559

- Cyrus the Great ascends to power in Anshan, in what will later be known as Persia.

556

- Following the death of Neriglissar, Nebuchadrezzar's successor, the Medes capture Harran. The new Babylonian king, Nabonidus, allies with Cyrus of Anshan against the Medes.

555

- Nabonidus of Babylon lays siege to Harran.

553

- Nabonidus marches south to Teima, a city approximately one hundred miles east of Akaba in Arabia, in an attempt to establish a safer capital; he leaves Belshazzar as his regent in Babylon.

551*

- Confucius is born.

550*

- Cyrus usurps the throne of Media.
- Celtic tribes begin to settle throughout Ireland, Scotland, and England.
- Lao-tzu, traditionally the author of the *Tao Te Ching* and founder of Taoism, flourishes in China.

547 • Cyrus the Great, having united the Medes and the Persians, conquers Lydia, which had become a sizable power in Asia Minor by this time.

545 • Persia exacts tribute from the Greek cities along the coast of Asia Minor.

540 • Vardhamana Mahavira, the founder of Jainism, is born.

• Cyrus the Great, after first conquering the local Bedouins surrounding Teima, forces Nabonidus to flee from his new capital.

539 • Cyrus the Great takes the city of Babylon, and the Jews in exile are released from their captivity.

534 • The Temple of Juno is constructed on the Roman Capitol, under the rule of Tarquinius Superbus (the Proud).

533 • Cyrus the Great enters India, exacting tribute from cities in the Indus River Valley. He establishes, according to Herodotus, what will become the twentieth of the Persian satrapies, or provinces, in Gandhara.

530 • Cyrus is killed in a battle against the Massagetae, an Asiatic people from a region near the Sea of Aral.

525 • Cambyses of Persia, the son of Cyrus the Great, attacks the Egyptian armies of Psammetichus III, who surrenders at the battle of Pelusium.

521-519 • Darius I of Persia quells revolts in the extensive empire, which is divided into twenty satrapies. Zoroastrianism is made the official religion.

520-515
- The Jewish Temple at Jerusalem is rebuilt at the insistence of the prophet Haggai.

515*
- Under the reign of Darius I, a canal is built joining the Nile River to the Red Sea, an effort begun by Neko II but left incomplete. A sea route from India to Persia is also established.

512
- With the aid of Greek soldiers drafted from Asia Minor, Darius I invades Thrace; both Thrace and Macedonia are forced to acknowledge Persian rule.

510
- Tarquinius Superbus is expelled from power during a Roman revolt. Tradition holds that the revolt was begun by Lucius Junius Brutus, outraged at the rape of Lucretia by the king's son, Sextus Tarquinius.

509
- The Roman republic is founded, according to traditional histories; Lucius Junius Brutus and Lucius Tarquinius Collatinus (Lucretia's husband) are made consuls. The Temple of Jupiter Optimus Maximus is constructed on the Capitoline Hill.

506
- According to traditional sources, Rome and Carthage sign a treaty of mutual noninterference, granting each other sole rights to activity in Latium and Africa, respectively.

500*
- Darius I is forced to respond to a widespread revolt of Ionian Greek cities in Asia. Around this time the Persians undertake to build the vast 1,677-mile Royal Road. Darius I also begins construction of a new capital city known as Parsae (Persepolis).
- The Bantu peoples of Africa begin their migrations.
- Iron is introduced in China.
- The Nok culture of West Africa begins to flourish.

496

- The Roman dictator Postumius defeats the Latins at the battle of Lake Regillus. The Latin armies had been led by Lars Porsenna, allied with Tarquinius Superbus, the exiled king of Rome.

494

- Darius I sacks Miletus, effectively ending the Ionian revolt.
- The plebeians of Rome leave the city for the Sacred Mount, threatening permanent secession; they demand political reform from the patricians before their return.

493

- Spurius Cassius makes a treaty with the Latin League, agreeing to colonize new lands together and to share the spoils of war equally; marriage and trade are also officially sanctioned between the participating states.

492

- Persia reasserts its control over Thrace and Macedonia but loses some of its ships off the coast of Mount Athos.

491

- According to tradition, Gnaeus Marcius Coriolanus of Rome offers the plebeians free grain, hoping they will turn over the tribunate. He is charged with bribery but escapes to Volsci, where he gathers an army of plebeians. The women of Rome, led by Coriolanus's mother and wife, convince him to lay aside his plans to attack the city.

490

- Darius I loses the battle of Marathon to the mainland Greeks.
- Hanno of Carthage sets out on an extensive voyage of exploration and colonization around the continent of Africa.
- The philosopher Mo Ti flourishes in China.

487

- Under the supervision of the Chinese state of Wu, a canal is built joining the Huai and Yangtze rivers.

486

- The Roman consul Spurius Cassius is executed after a failed attempt at tyranny.

485*
- Siddhartha Gautama (The Buddha) dies; his followers convene a council to codify his teachings and to organize the monastic community he had established.

483
- Rome goes to war with the Etruscan city of Veii, which is allied with Fidenae, a town situated on the upper Tiber and therefore essential to Roman power in the region.

480
- Xerxes I of Persia is defeated by the Greek navy at Salamis.
- The Celtic tribes that had earlier spread through the British Isles in small numbers now begin to arrive en masse.

479
- The army of Xerxes I meets defeat at Plataea and Mycale. Following these losses the Persians abandon their attempts to conquer Greece.

477
- The Romans lose the battle of Cremera to the Veientines.

474
- Rome and Veii make peace.

470*
- Confucius's disciples compile the collection of his sayings and teachings known as the *Analects*.

458-424
- Chin, a chief state in imperial China, is divided among the three houses of Han, Chao, and Wei.

458
- The Romans entreat Lucius Quinctius Cincinnatus to become dictator; he helps defeat the Aequi at the valley of Algidus.

456-454
- Egypt, supported by Greek troops sent from Athens, revolts against Artaxerxes I of Persia; the Greek fleet is destroyed, its armies forced to retreat, and the rebellion put down.

451
- The plebeians of Rome demand the codification of Roman law; the resulting Twelve Tables will serve as the basis of Roman law for approximately the next three hundred years.

450
- The Persian armies put down another rebellion aided by the Greeks, this time in Cyprus.

446
- Persia and Greece make peace.

445
- Nehemiah becomes governor of Jerusalem.

444
- Chinese mathematicians accurately calculate the length of the year at 365¼ days.

439
- The walls of Jerusalem are rebuilt under the supervision of Nehemiah, despite opposition from the neighboring governors of Samaria and Ammon.
- According to Roman tradition, Spurius Maelius, suspected of attempting tyranny by freely distributing grain to the people, is condemned to death by Servius Ahala, the dictator Cincinnatus's master of the horse.

438*
- Ezra institutes Jewish legal and religious reforms.
- Fidenae and Veii declare war against Rome.

431
- The Roman dictator Postumius Tubertus expels the Aequi and the Volsci from the Algidus Valley.

426
- The Roman dictator Mamercus Aemilius, together with Aulus Cornelius Cossus, the master of the horse, razes the town of Fidenae, the ally of Veii.

425
- Following the Roman victory at Fidenae, Veii makes peace.
- The biblical book of *Esther* is composed.

410*
- Celtic tribes later known to the Romans as Gauls begin their southward migration across the Alps.

409
- Carthaginian forces invade Sicily, conquering its Greek inhabitants at the second battle of Himera.

406
- Carthage launches a second Sicilian invasion but is forced to return after an outbreak of plague.

405
- Carthage and Sicily make peace.
- War resumes between Rome and Veii.

404
- Persian rule relaxes in Egypt, leaving the country relatively independent. Artaxerxes II, son of Darius II, succeeds his father in Persia.

403
- The official recognition by the royalty of Chin of the state's threefold division initiates the almost two-hundred-year Era of Warring States.

401
- At Cunaxa, a city near Babylon, Artaxerxes II of Persia brings an end to a rebellion started by his brother Cyrus, the satrap of Anatolia, who had received Greek mercenary support.

400*

- The Indian scholar Panini composes the earliest and still authoritative work on Sanskrit grammar.

396

- After nine years of siege, the Romans sack the city of Veii, without the help of their Latin allies; accordingly, the newly conquered territory is not shared with the Latins, and Rome is thenceforth stronger than its allies.

393

- Achoris becomes pharaoh of Egypt. Allied with Evagoras of Salamis, he prevents Artaxerxes II from reasserting Persian control in his country.

390

- The Romans are defeated by Gallic invaders, led by Brennus, at the battle of Allia. The city of Rome is subsequently besieged, and only the Capitol does not fall. Following the conquest of the Gauls, the Latins and the Hernici end their alliance with Rome.
- Cyprus, under the rule of King Evagoras, again receives Athenian aid in a rebellion against Persia.

385*

- Approximately one hundred years after the death of The Buddha, a second Buddhist council convenes to address the monastic code of discipline.

384

- According to tradition, the Roman patrician Marcus Manlius Capitolinus is sentenced to death after having forgiven plebeians their debts, an act seen as an attempt at tyranny.

381

- King Evagoras makes peace with the Persians, and Cyprus submits to the empire.

373*

- Artaxerxes II launches a major attack on Egypt but without any lasting success.
- The Chinese philosopher Mencius is born.

367-349 • Rome, in response to Celtic invasions in central Italy, fights four wars with the Gauls.

366-360 • Datames, the governor of Persian-controlled Cappadocia in Asia Minor, revolts; other satraps of the Western Empire follow in rebellion.

362-345 • Rome subjugates the local tribes in Italy. The Hernici are conquered, and the Latin cities that had revolted are pacified; they are forced to reenter the Latin League, but at great disadvantage to themselves. Rome further puts down the Volsci and the Aurunci and takes control of southern Etruria.

361 • Egypt, receiving the aid of Athenian mercenaries and one thousand Spartan hoplites, plans to launch an attack on Persia but is forced to abandon its expediton in order to suppress a domestic rebellion.

360 • The Egyptian Pharaoh Teos, faced with a revolt supported by Agesilaus of Sparta, his former ally, makes peace with Persia.

• Gallic invaders again attack Rome but this time are successfully repelled.

358-338 • Artaxerxes III Ochus becomes king of Persia and manages to quell the widespread rebellion seething throughout his empire.

356 • To defend against the Huns, China constructs its first wall along its borders; along with others to be built later, it will serve as part of the Great Wall.

354 • The Romans and the Samnites become allies.

350* • Artaxerxes III sends Persian armies to Egypt, and their defeats lead to further rebellion in the Persian empire.

- Rome decisively repels another Gallic invasion.

- Tennes of Sidon revolts against the Persians, but Artaxerxes III destroys his Phoenician armies.

- China begins to use coined money.

348

- Carthage signs a second treaty with Rome, agreeing not to attack the Latin states that remain loyal to Rome.

343

- The Romans send military aid to a faction of Samnites facing attack from the neighboring hill tribes, launching the First Samnite War.

- Artaxerxes III personally leads a march against Egypt, bringing to an end the last of the Egyptian dynasties.

341

- After several minor Roman victories, Rome and the Samnites make peace, renewing their alliance.

340-338

- The Latin cities, unsatisfied with their inferior status in the Latin League, withdraw and revolt against their former Roman allies. The so-called Latin War that ensues comes to a close with the Roman victory at Trifanum, under the consul Titus Manlius. The Romans disband the Latin League and force its one-time allies to become its dependents.

339-329

- Chuang-tzu, a major interpreter of Taoism and celebrated literary stylist, flourishes in China.

336

- Philip of Macedon is assassinated, and his son, Alexander the Great, becomes king.

- In the wake of several years of intrigue and murder, Darius III becomes king of Persia.

334

- The Persian army is defeated by Alexander at the river Granicus in Asia Minor.

- The Chinese state of Ch'u annexes the state of Yueh to the east.
- Rome and the Gauls make peace after a series of wars spanning more than thirty years.

333

- Darius III of Persia is defeated at the battle of Issus; following this battle, all of Phoenicia except the city of Tyre capitulates to Alexander.
- Su Ch'in organizes an alliance of six Chinese states in an attempt to stop the expansion of the state of Ch'in.

332

- Egypt is freed from Persian rule by Alexander the Great, who meets no opposition while there. Meanwhile, Azemilkos of Tyre defies Alexander, and his city is besieged; after seven months it falls to the Macedonians.

331

- Alexander the Great founds the city of Alexandria in Egypt. Within the same year he defeats the Persians at Gaugamela, and the Macedonians capture Babylon, Susa, and Persepolis.

330

- In the spring Darius flees from Alexander through Media, but he is betrayed and murdered by the satrap Bessus. The Caspian region also falls to Alexander, who continues south.

328

- Spitamenes leads the Iranians against the Macedonian armies; he is able to delay Alexander's conquest with some success but is eventually overcome.

327-325

- Alexander the Great invades India.

327

- The Romans once again intervene in Samnite affairs, besieging the city of Naples and entering what is known as the Second Samnite War.

326

- The Indian king Porus is defeated by Alexander the Great at the battle of the Hydaspes, a tributary of the Indus River.

- After penetrating as far as the river Hydaspes in India, Alexander's armies refuse to proceed further, and they begin the two-year march back to Babylon.

323

- While in Babylon, Alexander the Great succumbs to a fever and dies.

Sources:

Stuart J. Fiedel, *Prehistory of the Americas* (Cambridge, U.K.: Cambridge University Press, 1987).

Harry A. Gailey, *History of Africa from Earliest Times to 1800* (Hinsdale, Ill.: Holt, Rinehart & Winston, 1970).

Charles O. Hucker, *China's Imperial Past* (Stanford, Cal.: Stanford University Press, 1975).

William L. Langer, comp. and ed., *The New Illustrated Encyclopedia of World History,* 2 volumes (New York: Harry N. Abrams, 1975).

H. E. L. Mellersh, *Chronology of the Ancient World* (London: Barries & Jenkins, 1976).

Chester G. Starr, *History of the Ancient World* (New York: Oxford University Press, 1974).

The Athenian treasury on Delphi, built with the booty taken from the Persians after the Battle of Marathon in 490 B.C.E.
(Courtesy of Ecole Française d'Archéologie, Athens)

CHAPTER TWO

GEOGRAPHY

by KELLY OLSON

CONTENTS

CHRONOLOGY
25

OVERVIEW
29

TOPICS IN GEOGRAPHY

Ethnographers and
Geographers. 29

*Did the Ancient Greeks Believe the Earth
was Round?* 31

Greece: The Land
and People. 33

Herodotus and His
Travels 33

The Military Campaigns of
Alexander The Great 34

The History of Herodotus 34

*Alexander Finds the Source of
the Nile* 35

The Physical World
of Homer 36

Trade, Colonization, and
Travel 37

The Persian Pony Express 37

DOCUMENTARY SOURCES
39

Sidebars and tables are listed in italics.

800* B.C.E.

- Oral composition (attributed to Homer) of the epic poems *Iliad* and *Odyssey*, which contain the earliest accounts in ancient Greece of foreign people and faraway lands.

750*

- The age of colonization begins, and among the first city-states that send out expeditions are Chalcis, Eretria, Corinth, Megara, Miletus, and Phocaea. Settlements are made throughout the Mediterranean world, especially in Italy, Sicily, Egypt, and Ionia.

610

- The philosopher and astronomer Anaximander of Miletus is born. He is the first Greek to draw a map of the inhabited world, which he describes as a flat disk.

600*

- Euthymenes leads a Phoenician expedition around Africa; the journey takes two years.

525*

- The Carthaginian Himilco journeys beyond the Pillars of Hercules (Straits of Gibraltar) and to the north, where he encounters dense fog and an area of water filled with dense seaweed (the Sargasso Sea).

510*

- Under the orders of Darius I of Persia, Scylax of Caryanda explores the Indus Valley and the Arabian, or Persian, Gulf. His expedition takes two and one-half years to complete.

500*

- Hecataeus of Miletus writes his *Periodos Gês,* or Journey Round the World. It provides information about places and peoples encountered on a clockwise coastal voyage around the Mediterranean and the Black Sea. It starts at the Pillars of Hercules and ends in North Africa, and among the regions described are various Mediterranean islands, Scythia, Persia, India, Egypt, and Nubia.
- The Carthaginian Hanno journeys to Africa. An account of his travels is inscribed on a stone tablet and describes many frightening scenes.

450*

- The Persian Sataspes leads an abortive expedition around Africa. He reports many fanciful sightings to King Xerxes I, who does not believe him and orders his execution.

* Denotes circa date

420*

- Herodotus writes his *History of the Persian Wars*, a narrative of the struggle between the Greek city-states and Persia. The account also provides detailed observations made by Herodotus on his travels to the Italian peninsula, Tyre, the island of Thasos, the Black Sea settlements, Babylon, and Egypt.

410*

- Ctesias of Cnidus compiles a geographical treatise on India called *Ta Indika* (Writings on India). A Greek doctor at the court of Persian king Artaxerxes II, Ctesias is considered unreliable, even by ancient standards.

400*

- The philosopher Plato maintains that the earth is a globe that hangs unsupported in the middle of the universe.

350*

- The philosopher and scientist Aristotle advances the theories that the earth is either spherical or flat and shaped like a drum.

334

- Alexander the Great crosses into Asia Minor and defeats the Persians in battle at the Granicus River. He wins another victory the following year at Issus and in 332 takes the seaports of Tyre and Gaza in present-day Lebanon and Israel, respectively.

331

- After a winter in Egypt (during which time he establishes the city of Alexandria), Alexander the Great invades Mesopotamia and defeats the Persians at Gaugamela. Babylon and Susa fall without resistance, while at Persepolis, Alexander seizes the treasury and burns the royal palace.

329

- Alexander the Great embarks on another series of military campaigns, marching his army eastward through Areia, Drangiana, and Arachosia (present-day eastern Iran and western Afghanistan). He then crosses the Hindu Kush and invades Bactria. A revolt in Sogdiana (Uzbekistan) is crushed in the spring of 327.

326

- At the invitation of local rulers in the Kabul valley and Punjab, Alexander the Great marches into India. By the spring he is at Taxila, east of the Indus River. He crosses the Hydaspes River and drives all opposition before him, but his troops refuse to move beyond the Ganges River.

325

- Alexander the Great leads his troops westward through the Gedrosian Desert; they reach Susa early the next year.

323

- Alexander the Great dies in Babylon, and his principal generals dismember his vast kingdom (which stretches from Egypt to the Indus River).

The temple of Poseidon on Cape Sunium in Attica (M. Nicholson/*Ancient Civilizations*)

OVERVIEW

Imperfect Knowledge. The state of Greek knowledge concerning world geography was poor in comparison with geographical knowledge today. Maps in ancient Greece, along with most geographical lore, were possessed only by the upper classes and, even then, were fragmentary and imperfect, filled with incredible tales of distant flora and fauna, outlandish human customs, and misinformed pronouncements about the size and extent of different regions. Exploration for its own sake was rarely undertaken, and such discoveries as existed about the inhabited world came about through expeditions launched for purposes of trade or colonization. Still, the Greeks showed a laudable curiosity about the inhabited regions around them, even if the information they gathered was not always correct.

Mountainous Terrain. The geography of Greece had a profound impact on the political, economic, cultural, and social development of Greece. Mountainous terrain limited the areas for settlements and influenced the rise of the city-state. Although frequently rivals, the Greeks in the various *poleis* did have enough sense of common ancestry that they designated all non-Greek peoples as *barbaroi*.

Expansion and Early Explorers. Because most of their inhabitable land was within twenty-five miles of the ocean, the Greeks became mariners early on in their history. They developed trade routes and established colonies throughout the Mediterranean world. At times expeditions were sent out into the Atlantic Ocean to probe the outer limits of the known world, and in circa 600 B.C.E. one explorer rounded the Cape of Good Hope in Africa.

Cartography. Mapmaking in ancient Greece was, at best, a crude science. The first map of the inhabitable world was made around 550 B.C.E. by Anaximander of Miletus, but his assertion of the world's being a flat disk met with skepticism from Aristotle, Plato, and others. Many Greeks relied on the travel accounts of individuals such as Herodotus or Ctesias of Cnidus to get a vague understanding of what was outside the immediate Greek world.

Hellenization. The military conquests of Alexander the Great between 336 and 323 B.C.E. helped spread Greek language and culture across the Near East and surrounding areas. After his death, the Greek world joined the wider culture of the Mediterranean. In the centuries that followed, the ancient world knew much more of the Greeks than it had in any previous time period, thanks to the veneration of Greek literature, culture, and political forms across the Mediterranean.

TOPICS IN GEOGRAPHY

ETHNOGRAPHERS AND GEOGRAPHERS

Select Audience. In the centuries following Homer, most geographers were educated and wealthy men with leisure time to devote to writing and research. They composed descriptions of inhabited lands and drew maps for a tiny and highly specialized audience (educated and wealthy like themselves), and their works were not in wide circulation. The knowledge of the ancient geographer was limited: he relied mainly on earlier authors and the accounts of colonists, traders, and

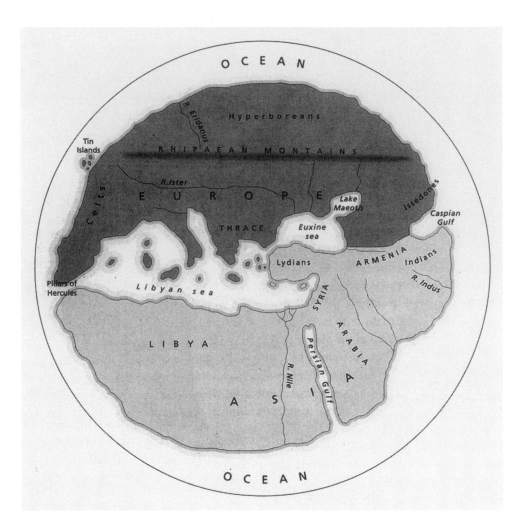

A map of the world by Hecataeus of Miletus, circa 500 B.C.E.

early explorers. There were many traveler's tales that circulated in antiquity; most geographers merely selected those they thought credible (and a few they found merely plausible) for insertion into their own work. The position of most of the places which the geographers wrote about and indicated on maps would have been unknown to the average Greek of the period. Because advances made by early explorers and geographers were confined to a small number of people, the typical Greek farmer or tradesman probably clung to Homer's idea of the earth as a flat disk on which an island-like landmass was surrounded by the vast and terrifying river, Ocean.

Ethnography. Closely connected to the study of geography was ethnography (the study of the customs and way of life of foreign peoples). The Greeks had a natural curiosity about distant lands and peoples (both real and imaginary), and mythical and fantastic ethnographical material was often woven into geographical studies. The Greeks perceived themselves and the Mediterranean basin to be at the center of the earth (in fact the sanctuary of Delphi was known as the *Omphalos,* or navel, of the inhabited world), and Greek ethnography often explores the grotesque and bizarre aspects of peo-

ples far removed from the "center." That geographers inserted bizarre ethnographical elements into their work was not due to ignorance or naiveté: the type of writing demanded such insertions for reasons of pleasure and novelty.

Hecataeus of Miletus. The earliest geographical writings are attributed to Hecataeus of Miletus, who wrote a work in the late sixth century B.C.E. called the *Periodos Gês* (The Circuit of the Earth), divided into two parts: *Europe* and *Asia.* This work, which unfortunately exists only in fragments quoted by later writers, assembled information about the ends of the earth known at that time (from the author's travels, the reports of others, and pure fantasy) and had a map attached as well. The author described a clockwise coastal voyage around both the Mediterranean Sea and Black Sea, starting at the Pillars of Hercules and finishing on the Atlantic coast of Morocco (he included Scythia, Persia, India, Egypt, and Nubia), giving interesting facts about each place. Because Hecataeus's work, like all ancient geography, was in fact a blend of geography and ethnography, he also listed the names of the different peoples around the Mediterranean basin and provided a description of their customs, which was a mixture of fact and fantasy.

Early Explorers. Geographers like Hecataeus obtained their information not only from their own travels but also from the tales of early explorers and traders. Explorations were probably launched in the Greek world not for the sake of finding new lands or adding to existing geographical knowledge, but to open up new trade routes or for purposes of colonization. A few accounts of these journeys (preserved by later authors) survive.

Euthymenes. The earliest of these stories seems to have been around 600 B.C.E., when, at the behest of an Egyptian king, an expedition of Phoenicians (led by a man called Euthymenes) managed to sail around Africa, a journey that took two years. An account of this expedition is preserved by the historian Herodotus and is full of "things which others can believe if they want to but I cannot, namely that in sailing around Africa they had the sun on their right side." This item, which Herodotus singles out for disbelief, is actually the most convincing item in the whole account, and indicates that the Phoenicians' ship must have pushed beyond the Tropic of Capricorn.

Himilco. Another early explorer named Himilco (from Carthage in North Africa) made a northern expedition out of the Pillars around 525 B.C.E., probably again for purposes of colonization or trade. His descrip-

---

---

tion of what the ship encountered is preserved by a later writer: "No breeze pushes the craft onward, and a torpid flow of heavy water dulls the ship's progress. [Himilco] adds this as well, that there is a mass of seaweed among the waves and like a hedge it impedes the prow. . . . Wild sea-creatures stand in the way on all sides, and sea-monsters swim among the sluggish and lazily crawling ships . . . a dark fog enshrouds the air as if in a kind of cloak. . . ." Himilco's description of the fantastic sailing conditions may be, some scholars feel, an early encounter with the Sargasso Sea (which is full of seaweed and subject to dense fog). Yet, there are mythic elements in his account as well, in the form of the grotesque monsters that live in the seas north of the Pillars, which again confirmed ancient conviction that danger lay past this point.

Scylax of Caryanda. Scylax of Caryanda was sent around 510 B.C.E. by the Persian king Darius I into the Indus Valley and as far as the Arabian Gulf (a journey that took thirty months). Scylax had many wonders to report on his return about the natives he had seen: men with parasol-shaped feet, one-eyed men, and men whose ears were so huge they could shelter their owners from the sun. These outlandish characteristics conformed to the expectations of Greek audiences, who had firm ideas about the strange inhabitants of distant worlds.

Hanno. Another early Carthaginian explorer was a man named Hanno. He was captain of a colonizing expedition that sailed out of the Pillars of Hercules and south along the coast of Africa around 500 B.C.E. Hanno reported strange phenomena along his journey, which surely satisfied ancient tastes for the bizarre and the fantastic. He heard eerie music coming out of the darkness, for instance, and saw rivers of flame and a mountain that caught fire after nightfall. As the journey went on, Hanno reported his crew was becoming frightened. Finally the ship encountered "hairy wild men" that his native guides called "gorillas" (which were not the great apes that are known today, as none existed in the regions Hanno visited; what exactly the crew encountered is debated among scholars). Hanno was unable to capture any of the creatures alive and had to kill them instead; at this point, running low on provisions, he had to turn the ship around and head for home. Hanno had an account of his journey put up on a tablet when he returned to Carthage, and it stands as a vivid confirmation of the frightening world that existed outside the Pillars.

Sataspes and Pytheas. A Persian named Sataspes, ordered to make a journey around Africa by the Persian king Xerxes (circa 450 B.C.E.), reported seeing dwarflike people wearing clothes of palm leaves, who fled from his ship whenever he landed. Sataspes' ship eventually got stuck trying to make the circumnavigation, and he was forced to return home (where his stories were disbelieved and he was executed). In 310 B.C.E. Pytheas, a captain from Massilia, made an expedition northward (perhaps hunting for a source of tin), circumnavigated Britain, and pushed on up into the North Sea. He glimpsed a landmass six days' sail

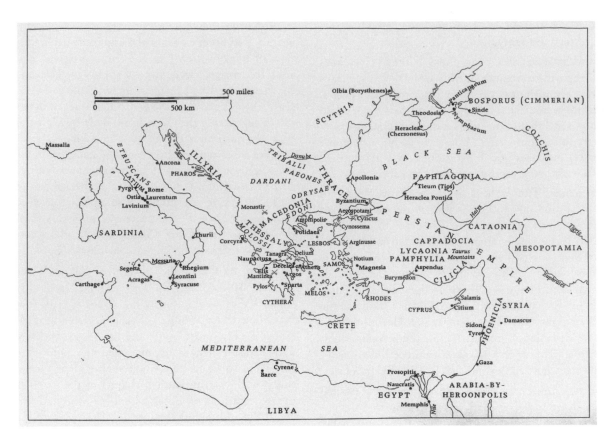

A map of Greece and the Mediterranean during the time period 800–323 B.C.E.

north of Britain, which he could not approach because of the dense fog and thick waters. It could have been Iceland, but perhaps it was part of Norway, which Pytheas mistook for an island. Above it was a water mass he called the Frozen Sea. The northern landmass glimpsed by Pytheas became known as the island of Thule and came to represent the furthest reaches of the earth in ancient thought.

Written Accounts. Stories from explorers such as these were among the sources from which Greek ethnographers drew in their writing. Ethnographers and geographers were especially interested in exotic lands such as India and Africa, which were characterized by strange phenomena and bizarre human races (as in the account of Hanno). Ctesias of Cnidus was one such writer, a doctor at the Persian court in the late fifth and early fourth centuries B.C.E. Merchants passed through his city with fabulous tales of the East, which Ctesias collected into a work called *Ta Indika* (*Writings on India*, a work that survives only in a summary by a later author. The Greek title is a form of adjective naming the people and their locale). The purpose of the work was entertainment, not necessarily accurate information, and the stories Ctesias relates seem to be based on Indian fable and folklore. Ctesias describes a land fabulously rich, brimming with gold, silver, amber, and gemstones, and full of purple dyes and perfumes. There were natural wonders too, such as rivers flowing with honey and fine oil that could be skimmed off the surface of certain lakes, exotic races of strange dog-headed men, and fearsome beasts, one of which excretes a poison so fearsome that coming into contact with even the tiniest amount causes one's brain to instantly dissolve and run out the nostrils.

Again, the unbelievable curiosities that form the bulk of Ctesias's work were not inserted due to ignorance on the part of the author; the genre of ethnography demanded the unconfirmed report of the improbable and even the impossible. Greek audiences thus expected authors of geography and ethnography to record "memorable" or "amazing" things.

Maps. Ethnographers and geographers did not have accurate maps at their disposal. Although earlier maps certainly existed, Anaximander of Miletus was credited as being the first to draw a map of the inhabited world (around 550 B.C.E.), which was included as an illustration to his *Periodos Gês*. This map represented the earth as a flat disk. Later, the geographer Hecataeus illustrated his own *Periodos Gês* with a map, an improved version of Anaximander's. The historian Herodotus, writing in the fifth century, criticized existing cartography: "I laugh when I see the many men who draw maps of the world and don't bother to use their heads. They make the earth a perfect circle, better even than one drawn with a compass, with Ocean running around it, and Europe and Asia of equal size." He also complains that there were many variations of shape and distance on maps depicting the same region.

Sources:

Lionel Casson, *Travel in the Ancient World* (Baltimore & London: Johns Hopkins University Press, 1974).

Charles W. Fornara, *The Nature of History in Ancient Greece and Rome* (Berkeley: University of California Press, 1983).

James S. Romm, *The Edges of the Earth in Ancient Thought* (Princeton: Princeton University Press, 1992).

J. O. Thomson, *Everyman's Classical Atlas* (New York: E. P. Dutton, 1961).

GREECE: THE LAND AND PEOPLE

Geographic and Political Divisions. Greece itself is a terrain divided by the Pindos mountain chain into small sections of land (the mountain chain extends out into the Aegean Sea as well, forming small islands). These mountains create natural pocketlike regions, often large enough to contain just one settlement. The geography of Greece, therefore, had important ramifications for the development of political structure: Greece did not develop as a "nation" with a unified purpose and common outlook, but as a collection of small and dissimilar settlements, each with its own customs, ways of life, and dialect. The Greeks, in fact, did not speak of their country as "Greece," but merely in terms of individual city-states (*poleis*) such as Athens, Thebes, Sparta, and so on. Poleis would sometimes band together for a limited period to unite against a common enemy, as when Greece fought its wars with Persia in the early fifth century B.C.E.; for purposes of retaining what had been won in such wars, as in the Delian League of 478 (so called because the treasury of the league was located on the island of Delos); or for purposes of foreign policy, such as the collection of Greek states organized by the Macedonian king Philip II in 338 B.C.E. However, rarely did individual poleis unify in pursuit of a common goal, and for much of Greece's history the city-states were rivals, competing among themselves for land and power. The natural divisions of the Greek region also made for political divisions.

Barbarians. Nevertheless, the Greeks did possess a sense of common ancestry and myth (the Greeks' word for themselves was *Hellênes,* after Hellen, a mythical figure whom the Greeks took as their common ancestor), and Greeks in Classical times (the fifth century B.C.E. and beyond) collectively felt that they were somehow different from the inhabitants of other countries. They called all non-Greeks (regardless of where they were from) *barbaroi,* from the way these foreign languages sounded to the Greek ear: an incomprehensible ba-ba-ba. The modern English word *barbarian* comes from *barbaroi,* and the ancient word had all the derogatory connotations of its modern counterpart: most Greeks seem to have looked at foreigners with a definite recognition of their own superiority and sense of national pride. Some Greek intellectuals stretched this polarity between Greeks and barbarians to its limits: the philosopher Aristotle, for instance, claimed that certain (mainly Eastern) races of people were "natural slaves" simply by virtue of the fact that they were barbarians.

Greek World. Greece was found, therefore, wherever Greek was spoken: in mainland Greece; on the small islands that dotted the Aegean Sea; even, through colonization, in such diverse and faraway places as the west coast of Asia Minor or southern Italy. The physical range of the Greek world in antiquity was extensive and fragmented.

Sources:

Peter D. Arnott, *An Introduction to the Greek World* (London: Macmillan; New York: St. Martin's Press, 1967).

Nancy Demand, *A History of Ancient Greece* (Boston: McGraw-Hill, 1996).

The World of Athens: An Introduction to Classical Athenian Culture. Joint Association of Classical Teachers (Cambridge: Cambridge University Press, 1984).

HERODOTUS AND HIS TRAVELS

Significance. By the fifth century B.C.E., geographical and ethnographical writings were taking a newer, more scientific turn, in which real information about distant lands was prized, not just bizarre traveler's tales. Herodotus of Halicarnassus was an early ethnographer and travel writer, a wealthy and well-educated man. He had much curiosity and interest in the affairs of countries outside Greece, especially in matters concerning religion. His *History of the Persian Wars* includes a description of the physical geography of different lands, as well as plentiful ethnography which, while not always accurate, serves in the tradition of such writing to refresh the reader and add intriguing information about the region in question.

New Approach. Besides providing new information about the customs of different peoples of the inhabited world, Herodotus subjected known geography to a detailed reexamination. He rejected, for instance, the old ideas about Ocean ("I know of no river called Ocean and I think that Homer or some other of the early poets invented the name and inserted it into his poetry"), which represented a dramatic shift from earlier authors, who assumed as a matter of course the existence of this vast river.

Observations. Herodotus made several small voyages: to southern Italy and Sicily, Tyre in Phoenicia, Thasos, the Black Sea, and as far East as Babylon. However, the largest ethnographical portion of his book is devoted to his travels in Egypt, where he went not to view Egyptian art and architecture but to continue his research into deities and temples (he does mention the pyramids, a destination for tourists in Egypt today, but only to speculate on the time, the work gangs, and the cash outlay needed to build such monuments). Herodotus inquires, for instance, the way bulls were sacrificed to the Egyptian goddess Isis; the ritual attitude toward pigs; which foods were considered unclean for priests; available types of embalming; and whether Greek divinities were derived from Egyptian or vice versa. He claims the Ethiopians worship Dionysus; examines past oracles; and describes the ritual practices of tribes in northern Russia. Yet, Herodotus does not merely give scholars information on religious matters: he reported on everything that he found interesting or significant in the inhabited world, from a type of cloth woven from hemp made in southern Russia, to the candy made in a certain town in Asia Minor, to the marriage practices of the Babylonians (they auction off the beautiful girls to the highest bidders and use the money as dowries for the less attractive women). Nor is Herodotus resistant to the wonders of the East: in Arabia he reports that flying snakes guard incense trees and that certain types of birds build their nests with cinnamon sticks. In his description of India, he lists such wonders as giant snakes, dog-headed men, headless men with eyes in their breasts, and other wild men and women. He also recounts a story of ants bigger than

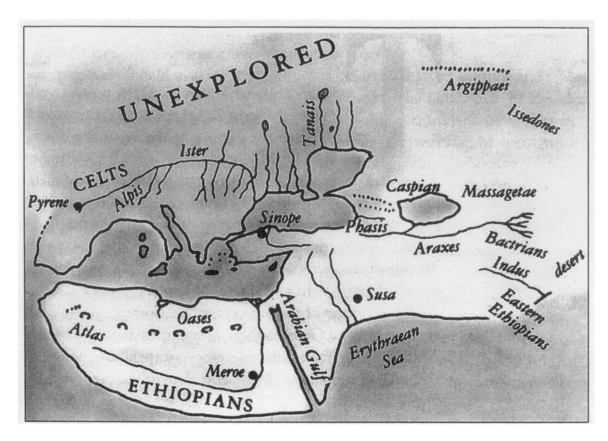

Herodotus's map of the world, originally made circa 430 B.C.E. (Thames & Hudson Ltd, London, from O. A. W. Dilke: "Greek and Roman Maps," (1985); used by permission of the publisher and Cornell University Press)

foxes, who dig for gold in the Indian desert (although Herodotus is doubtful as to the truth of this and tells his audience he got the story from the Persians). As for northern Russia, Herodotus repeats information about the existence of griffins, goat-footed people, and men who sleep six months out of the year; even further north, he says, lives a race of cannibals. Although Herodotus claims he does not believe such accounts himself, it is significant that he repeats them: the reader expected such bizarre and diverting anecdotes in the genre of ethnographical writing.

Doubtful Knowledge. By the fifth century B.C.E. the well-educated or well-traveled Greek (and there were not many of these), then, was knowledgeable about the whole of the Mediterranean and Black Sea areas and had some idea of size and outlines. Nonetheless, the geographical knowledge of the Greeks was never extensive: they were vague, for example, about regions remote from urban areas and where exactly the people they called the Celts lived. They knew something of southern Russia (a people called the Scythians lived there), but nothing north of the Black Sea except some fantastic tales that Herodotus repeats (further north was a terrain they called "the snowy desert"). Africa remained largely mysterious, although the Greeks did know it was surrounded by water. Their knowledge of Asia included Arabia and as far east as the Indus valley: east of India was all burning desert (a hypothesis repeated by Herodotus); the Greeks did not know of the existence of China.

Sources:

Lionel Casson, *Travel in the Ancient World* (Baltimore & London: Johns Hopkins University Press, 1974).

James S. Romm, *The Edges of the Earth in Ancient Thought* (Princeton: Princeton University Press, 1992).

THE HISTORY OF HERODOTUS

The Massagetae wear the same kinds of clothes as the Scythians and live much the same. . . . These are their customs: each of them marries a wife, but the wives they have in common. . . . There are no definite limits to life other than this: when a man grows very old, all his relatives come together and kill him, and sheep and goats along with him, and stew all the meat together and have a banquet of it. This is regarded as the happiest lot; any man who dies of disease they do not eat, but bury him in the ground, lamenting that he did not come to being eaten. They do not sow land but live off cattle and also fish, which they have in abundance from the river Araxes. They are drinkers of milk. Of the gods, they worship the sun only, to whom they sacrifice horses, and their argument for the sacrifice is this: to the swiftest of all gods they assign the swiftest of all mortal things.

Source: Herodotus, *The History*, translated by David Greene (Chicago: University of Chicago Press, 1987).

THE MILITARY CAMPAIGNS OF ALEXANDER THE GREAT

Alexander III. In 336 B.C.E., at the age of twenty, the Macedonian king Alexander III, or Alexander the Great, inherited the resources and wealth of the Macedonian state left to him by his father, Philip II. The problems began almost immediately. Alexander was forced to execute several pretenders to his throne, subdue the Thracians and Illyrians (old enemies of the Macedonians), and quell a Greek revolt before he could travel with his army into Asia Minor to begin his conquest of Persia (in 334). By 331 he had defeated the Persian king Darius in two important battles and crossed into Egypt. The priests there crowned him Pharaoh, and he founded the city of Alexandria (later a center of learning and Greek culture). He invaded Mesopotamia next, where he defeated Darius yet again, pushed across the mountains into Persia proper, and seized the mound of royal treasure that had been accumulating for over two centuries at Persepolis. He journeyed on into Ecbatana and to another battle with Darius, but as Alexander approached, the Persian king was assassinated by his own guards, who then fled. Alexander now had full control of Persian lands. Many commanders would have then moved to more civilized regions to consolidate their conquests, but not Alexander. He knew that to retain Mesopotamia he would have to retain control of the Iranian plateau, subject in the north and east to marauding nomads from central Asia. Moreover, Alexander wanted to push his conquests to the edge of the known world (which he thought could not be much further east than the Indus).

Adventure into the Unknown. Alexander's last major campaign was the conquest of India, an expedition that was not only a military venture but also a fantastic journey to the outer limits of the world. Marching with his men to what Alexander thought was the edge of his new territory, he discovered more land to the east and another great river, the Ganges. His army refused to press further east (although Alexander was eager to travel further), and he was forced to lead his men back (through southern Iran, losing many of his men in the unforgiving heat of the Gedrosian Desert), reaching Susa by 324 B.C.E.

Audience Expectation. When he marched east in 326 B.C.E., Alexander's expedition included a geographer and other scientific staff: he was thus armed to record information as well as make conquests. Unfortunately, although there were reports of a more scientific nature that were handed down, most of the literary works that came out of Alexander's march did little more than earlier writings about the east, which were catalogues of Eastern monsters and marvels. This approach was not a sign of naiveté on the part of the geographers but a recognition of audience expectation (and reader ignorance: the later geographer Strabo states that these writers were not able to resist exploiting the innocence of their audience, "because the expedition took place at the ends of Asia, far from us, and the distant is difficult to dis-

---

ALEXANDER FINDS THE SOURCE OF THE NILE

There was much curiosity among educated Greeks about the Nile River in Egypt. What was its source and its upper course? Why did it flood yearly? Geographers had tried for centuries to answer these questions, with varying degrees of success; the mysterious Nile had come to represent a mythic geographical riddle. While in India in 324 B.C.E. Alexander the Great thought he had the answer. The historian Arrian tells the story:

> Alexander fancied at this time that he had discovered the source of the Nile, his reasons being that he had, on a previous occasion, seen crocodiles in the Indus, and in no other river except the Nile, and had also observed a kind of bean like the Egyptian bean growing on the banks of the Aescines, which, he was told, flowed into the Indus. His notion was that the Nile (under the name of Indus) rose somewhere in that part of India and then flowed through a vast desert tract, where it lost its original name and received that of the Nile from the Ethiopians and Egyptians at that point where it began to flow through inhabited country again, ultimately flowing into the Mediterranean.

Source: Arrian, *The Campaigns of Alexander,* translated by Aubrey de Sélincourt (New York: Penguin, 1958).

---

prove.") Also, because Alexander did not journey east of the Hyphasis, that land remained a source of mystery and exotica for centuries. Geographers who wrote in the period following Alexander's death about this mysterious area, unpenetrated by any traveler, are summarized by Strabo:

> Everything about [the trans-Hyphasis frontier] is reported as bigger and more freakish, such as the gold-mining ants, and other beasts and men who have singular forms, or in some way have totally different qualities; like the Seres, whom they say are long-lived, prolonging their lives beyond two hundred years. They also tell of a certain aristocratic system of government, made up of 5000 counselors, each of whom furnishes an elephant for public use. And Megasthenes says the tigers among the Prasians are the biggest of all . . . and that the long-tailed apes are bigger than the biggest dogs . . . and that stones are dug up have the color of frankincense and are sweeter in flavor than figs or honey; elsewhere there are snakes two cubits long with webbed wings, like bats, which fly by night, and let fall drops of urine (some say of sweat) which cause the skin of the unwary to rot away; and that there are winged scorpions, exceeding all others in size; and that ebony grows there; and that there are powerful dogs, which do not let go of whatever they bite until water is poured into their nostrils.

Quest. Although Alexander had been frustrated in his quest for the eastern edge of Ocean (a goal he still hoped for even at his death), some later works claimed he had penetrated East further than he actually had and had

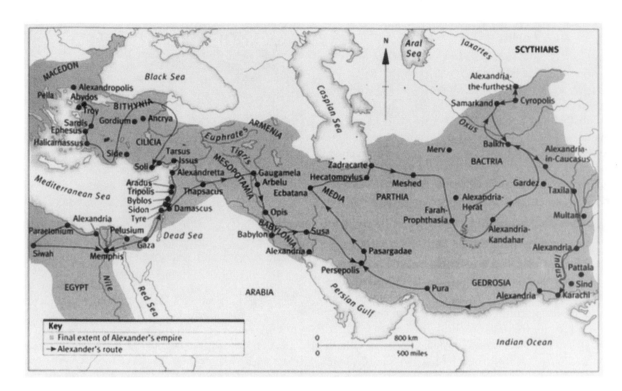

A map of Alexander the Great's military campaigns

made a mythical journey beyond the Ganges and into confrontation with freaks and monsters. There exist several "miracle-letters" which are purported to be written by Alexander himself (which they certainly were not), describing journeys to the edge of the earth and encounters with strange creatures. In these letters, "Alexander" reports seeing wild races of hairy subhuman creatures, nine feet tall; talking trees; emeralds collected from the carcasses of snakes who wear them as necklaces; and bats with teeth the size of a man's. He is at last directed by divine voices to return to the inhabited world (and at the same time receives a prophecy of his own death). Tales like these were probably circulated in order to increase the young king's heroism; amplification of Alexander into a mythic explorer could be easily accomplished with fantastic tales of his feats east of the Ganges, since no expedition had actually traveled that far.

Sources:
D. Brendan Nagle, *The Ancient World: A Social and Cultural History* (Upper Saddle River, N.J.: Prentice Hall, 1999).

James S. Romm, *The Edges of the Earth in Ancient Thought* (Princeton: Princeton University Press, 1992).

THE PHYSICAL WORLD OF HOMER

Pillars of Herakles. Greeks in the eighth century (and perhaps even earlier) conceived the earth to be a flat disk, on which the landmass of Europe, Asia, and Africa was surrounded by a vast river called Ocean. Thus, the inhabited earth was thought to be an "island" encircled by water. In the eighth century B.C.E. Homer and Hesiod used this image to good effect in their poetry; early Greek maps also showed this characterization. Although the water encircling the inhabited world was described as

a "river," the ancient poets do not say what the boundary of Ocean was: early Ocean just stretches away into the measureless distance. The Greeks knew that the Strait of Gibraltar (the ancients called this spot the Pillars of Herakles) was to the west, and for them it marked the boundary between the known and the unknown; between ease and fear: the later poet Pindar terms what lay beyond the Pillars as "the untrodden sea."

Geographical Reality. Homer's *Iliad* and *Odyssey* appear to be a mixture of memories from the twelfth century (the time period in which the events of the stories are thought to take place), the eighth century (in which Homer himself lived), and some picturesque fantasy. The "Catalogue of Ships" in Book Two of the *Iliad*, in which all the Greek participants in the Trojan War are designated, names 152 towns or districts in Greece and 19 in Thrace and Asia Minor; most of the action of the *Iliad* and the *Odyssey* takes place bounded by the island of Ithaca (Odysseus's homeland) in the west, Troy in the east, and the island of Crete to the south. Homer, however, does describe some peoples and places further distant (possibly preserving some early travelers' tales). Unknown lands and peoples held a fascination for the Greeks, and in Homer scholars find mention of Egypt and Libya, pygmies and Ethiopians in the south, Sidon and the Phoenicians to the east, and the Cimmerians to the north. As for Odysseus's decade of extravagant wanderings after the end of the Trojan War, the Greeks themselves located these travels mainly in the western Mediterranean (perhaps reflecting the fact that pockets of Greek civilization were being established there at this time). However, most of the places mentioned in the *Odyssey*, (the island of the beautiful witch Circe, the land of the

Lotus-Eaters, or the Underworld) have their basis in myth or folk tales and do not represent geographical reality.

Sources:

James S. Romm, *The Edges of the Earth in Ancient Thought* (Princeton: Princeton University Press, 1992).

Richard J. A. Talbert, ed., *Atlas of Classical History* (London & New York: Routledge, 1985).

TRADE, COLONIZATION, AND TRAVEL

Seafarers. The Greeks seem to have been a natural seafaring people whose lives were closely linked with the sea and ships. There are many metaphors and expressions in Greek literature that stem from the sea and sailing, and artistic motifs such as octopi, shells, and dolphins are found on coins, painted pottery, and colorful wall frescoes.

Mediterranean World. Seventy-two percent of the land that makes up Greece is within twenty-five miles of the sea, and there is evidence for travel and trade by sea in Greece as early as 7000 B.C.E. The Mediterranean has many islands, and the sailing seasons and winds are largely predictable (fierce storms are frequent during the winter months, however, so ships were usually laid up from early November to late March). Expertise in seafaring had political ramifications for the Greeks as well, both overseas and closer to home: their aptitude for sailing meant distant colonies could be established, and naval supremacy in the area of well-designed ships allowed Athens to dominate Greece for much of the fifth century B.C.E. In addition, many parts of Greece are poor in natural resources, which forced dependence on trade with more fortunate areas (timber and silver, for instance, were never abundant in southern Greece); and since import and export was done by water transport, city-states that achieved wealth and importance were usually seaports.

Sailing. Ship design under the Greeks reached a high level of competence and success. The earliest seagoing vessels in the ancient world were probably very small rafts or boats, but larger vessels were soon developed because of a need for greater capacity and security. By the end of the second millennium B.C.E. ships equipped with oars and a square sail were found all over the Mediterranean.

Trade. Much of Greek trading both within Greece and to distant ports was meant to secure food, timber, and metals, but there was also a smaller trade in luxuries: fine wine, pottery and art, olive oil (which was valuable because of its varied uses as food, fuel, cleansing agent, and a base for perfume). Some trade was conducted over land, but this was slow and expensive, and sea travel was the preferred method. Traders mainly went from port to port, connecting different parts of Greece, Italy and Sicily, Ionia, the Hellespont, and Egypt: procuring grain from southern Russia, olive oil from Athens, timber from Palestine, and fine woolen fabrics from Miletus. Long voyages over the open sea were avoided whenever possible, and ships hugged the coastline or islands. Greek trading ships were deep, rounded vessels, with a short square sail and damp sand in the hold for ballast. Merchant ships were constructed for capacity and safety, not speed.

THE PERSIAN PONY EXPRESS

A system of Persian dispatch riders was established by the Persian king Cyrus (ruled from 550 to 530 B.C.E.) who posted stations every fifteen miles or so along the road from Susa to Sardis. This system provided the fastest means of long-distance communication in antiquity, greatly admired by the Greeks. Herodotus wrote:

There is no mortal man who can accomplish a journey faster than these Persian messengers. The idea was invented by the Persians. For it is reported that as many days as there are for the entire trip, so many are the horses and men posted, a horse and a man for each day's journey. Not snow, not rain, not heat, not night hinder these men from covering the stage assigned to them as quickly as possible. The first rider passes the dispatch to the second, the second to the third, and so on. . . .

Source: John Humphrey, John P. Oleson, and Andrew Sherwood, eds., *Greek and Roman Technology: A Sourcebook* (London & New York: Routledge, 1998).

Evidence. When did long-distance seaborne commerce between Greece and other countries begin? The earliest literary mention of trade is in the poetry of Homer (when Odysseus is accused of looking like a scruffy merchant skipper), but contact with foreign countries and peoples may also be identified through archeological evidence such as pottery finds. Greek artifacts turn up in foreign countries for a variety of reasons: for the use of the Greeks in overseas colonies; indicating perhaps an export market in Greek pottery; or representing pieces that merely traveled down from trading posts or colonies. Contact with foreign countries influenced Greece as well: art historians have detected Near Eastern patterns and motifs influences in Greek painted pottery after 750 B.C.E. or so, which implies early interaction with countries such as Persia.

Colonies. The period 750–550 B.C.E. marked a great burst of intensive foreign settlement on the part of the Greeks. A decision by a polis to establish a colony overseas (at a site chosen on the advice of traders or travelers) usually stemmed from practical reasons such as famine or land shortage, and such a decision was formed by the ruling body of the city-state, not by any one individual. The polis selected a wealthy *oikistês* (aristocratic founder) who would lead the expedition and draw up plans for the new city, and for his efforts receive heroic honors after his death. Once established, the colony was bound to the mother-state only by ties of kinship, religion, and sentiment. It could call on its mother-state (or vice versa) in times of trouble, but a colony was just as self-sufficient a city-state as the founding polis, and was under no obligation to serve the economic interests of its mother city. During this period, Greek city-states established colonies in Italy and Sicily, at Naucratis in Egypt, in southern France and Spain, to the east along the coast of

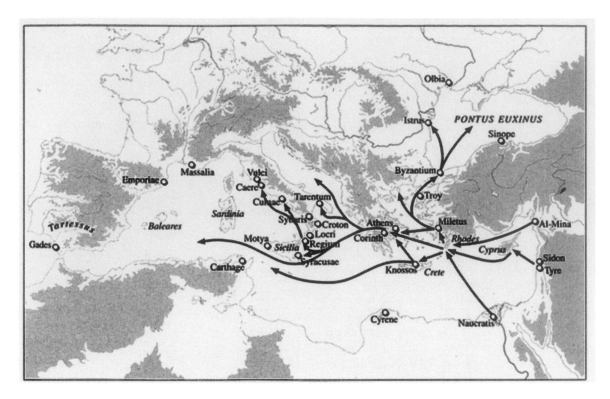

A map of the principal sea routes used by Greek mariners during the period 800 to 323 B.C.E.

modern Turkey, in Libya, and in the northeast along the Black Sea, which spread Greek culture throughout the regions of the Mediterranean and into Asia Minor.

Travelers. Apart from traders and colonists, there were other ancient Greek travelers. Many people traveled to the great religious and athletic festivals held in different parts of Greece: the Olympic games (held every four years); the Pythian games (held every eight years); and the Nemean and Isthmian games (held every other year). Another reason for travel was illness: the sick or infirm journeyed to sanctuaries of Aesclepius (the Greek god of healing) for cures and relief. Some travelers were seekers of the Greek oracles (prophetic deities) at Dodona or Delphi. There were some Greeks who traveled simply as tourists (who would, for example, journey to Egypt to see the sights), but travel for its own sake required leisure and money, and there were few people with both in Greek society.

Highwaymen and Pirates. In addition, taking a trip in the ancient world was not easy, another obstacle to travel for its own sake. Journeys by land were slow and strenuous. Most roads were not well built or well maintained and tended to be narrow, rocky, shadeless, and peopled by highwaymen and other robbers. Inns and taverns did dot the roads, but the upper-class Greek would stay at the homes of his friends along the way, since roadside inns tended to be dirty, bug ridden, and rife with crime. To go on foot was the easiest (although most tiring), since not all roads were built for wheeled traffic, and some were nearly impassable by a cart or wagon. Travelers would carry their clothing, provisions for the journey, even their bedding with them, as well as a hefty supply of ready money. There were no banks or savings accounts in antiquity, and robbers could be fairly certain that travelers had well-filled purses. On the seas, although travel by water was quicker and less exhausting, one ran the risk of pirates or shipwreck.

Limited Worldview. For the typical Greek, then, life was mostly lived out in his home terrain, on his farm, or in the town. Few were traders or tourists, and because travel was difficult and expensive, the average Greek did not journey extensively. Maps and detailed geography were the province of the wealthy and educated class.

Sources:

John Boardman, *The Greeks Overseas* (London: Penguin, 1964).

Lionel Casson, *Ships and Seafaring in Ancient Times* (London: British Museum Press, 1994).

Casson, *Travel in the Ancient World* (Baltimore & London: Johns Hopkins University Press, 1974).

John Humphrey, John P. Oleson, and Andrew Sherwood, eds., *Greek and Roman Technology: A Sourcebook* (London & New York: Routledge, 1998).

DOCUMENTARY SOURCES

Note: Unfortunately, many of the sources used for this chapter are extremely fragmentary and exist only as quotations by later writers such as Arrian and Strabo. Listed below are the more important works that survive whole or in large pieces, embedded in the works of other Greek authors.

Hecataeus, *Periodos Gês* or *Periêgêsis* (sixth–fifth centuries B.C.E.)—summarized by Herodotus in his *History of the Persian Wars*. A literary tour of the inhabited world in the early fifth century, with interesting characteristics of lands and peoples.

Herodotus, *History of the Persian Wars* (fifth century B.C.E.)—often called the first travel writer, Herodotus's work, although purportedly a history, contains much information about world geography as it was known at the time, including fantastic tales of just about every country.

Homer, *Iliad* and *Odyssey* (circa eighth–seventh centuries B.C.E.)—these epic poems contain both the earliest mention in Greek literature of faraway peoples and places and travelers' tales of the mythic and the bizarre.

Plato, *Phaedo* (fourth century B.C.E.)—a philosophical work that includes a section on ancient ideas of the shape of the earth and the geography of the inhabited world.

A surviving fragment of the decree for the Athenian expedition to Sicily in 415 B.C.E. (Epigraphical Museum, Athens)

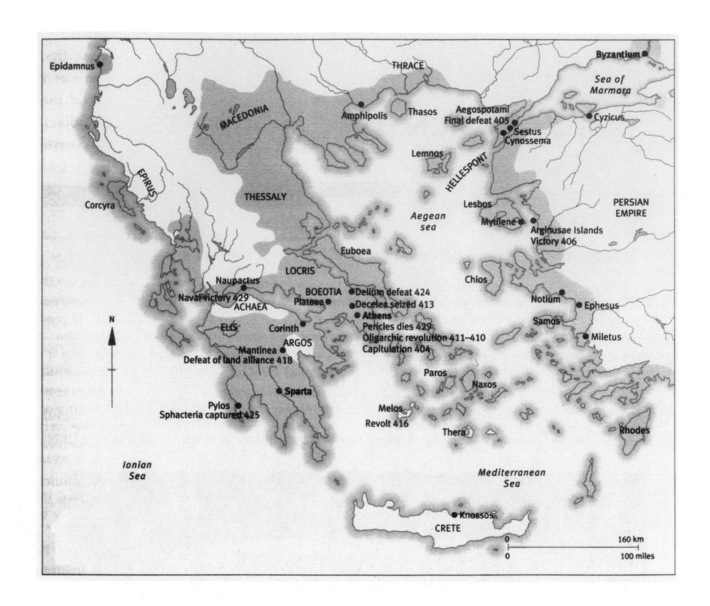

A map of Greece

CHAPTER THREE

THE ARTS

by NEIL O'SULLIVAN and PATRICK O'SULLIVAN

CONTENTS

CHRONOLOGY

42

OVERVIEW

49

TOPICS IN THE ARTS

Architecture 53
Inspiration 53
Praise for Pheidias's Zeus 56
Comedy 57
Tragedy's Only Joke? 58
Didactic Poetry 59
The Root Of All Evil 59
Elegy and Iambics 60
Epics 60
Odysseus Strings The Bow 62
The Meaning of Life 62
History 63

Lyric 64
Oratory 64
Philosophy 65
Pottery, Painting, And
    Mosaics 66
Zeuxis V. Parrhasius 68
A Platonic Criticism of Painting . . 68
Rhetoric 73
Satyr Plays 75
The Fruits of Victory 75
Sculpture 76
A Homeric Simile for an Artisan . . 76
The Seduction 81
Tragedy 82
Oedipus Blinds Himself. 84

**SIGNIFICANT
PEOPLE**

Aeschylus 85
Apelles Of Colophon 85

Aristophanes 86
Euripides 86
Herodotus 87
Hesiod. 87
Lysippus and Lysistratus 88
Parrhasius. 88
Pheidias 89
Pindar 89
Polyclitus 90
Polygnotus 90
Praxiteles 90
Sappho 91
Scopas 91
Sophocles 92
Thucydides 92
Zeuxis 93

**DOCUMENTARY
SOURCES**

93

Sidebars and tables are listed in italics.

800*

- The Homeric poems are composed. The two epics, the *Iliad* and the *Odyssey*, are considered by many to be the greatest works of Greek literature. The *Iliad* tells the story of Achilles and the Trojan War, and the *Odyssey* is about the trials and travails of Odysseus.

800-750* **B.C.E.**

- The Greeks develop an alphabetic form of writing that is based on the system of the Phoenicians, but differs in that it records vowels as well as consonants. (Linear B, the earliest Greek method of writing developed by the Mycenaeans, was syllabic in nature and seems to have been used only for the keeping of records, not for the communication of literature.)

800-700*

- Among the most significant innovations in Greek visual arts is the widespread return of the human figure after being mostly absent during the Dark Ages (a period of relative cultural obscurity from circa 1200 to circa 800 B.C.E.). Contacts with the East and Eastern images provides some stimulus to Greek artisans depicting human and supernatural bodies, as do the rediscovery of Mycenaean Greek palace sites and artifacts dating from 1600–1200 B.C.E.

700*

- The Hesiodic poems are composed. *Theogony* is the earliest surviving systematic account of the Greek gods while *Works and Days* is the only surviving Archaic Greek poem on farming.

700-650*

- Fuller contact with the East leads to a new style in pottery in Athens known as "Proto-Attic." Some vases are painted with scenes from myths.

650*

- The Daedalic style of sculpture (statues with frontal poses painted in bright colors) is prevalent in Corinth and later Corcyra.

- Corinth pottery exhibits a new style that departs from the prevailing geometric approach of straight lines, circles, triangles, and other symbols. The new pottery has floral patterns and animal imagery painted in a precise manner with a variety of colors.

620*

- Aristocratic commemorative marble and stone statues known as *kouros* (youth) and *korê* (maiden) begin to appear in Attica.

* Denotes circa date

600*

- On the island of Lesbos, Sappho and Alcaeus compose lyric poems. Sappho focuses on themes of love and personal relationships, often with other women. Of her nine books of lyrical verse and one of elegiac, only one poem and a few fragments are extant. In addition to drinking and love songs, Alcaeus writes hymns and political odes against tyrants.

- As a leading center of pottery, Attica makes great advances in black-figure vase painting. Female figures are represented in white while male figures are painted in black.

534*

- Thespis, considered the father of the tragic drama, wins first prize for tragedy at the City Dionysia, an early spring festival in Athens. (The word *thespian* is used today to designate an actor.) Thespis introduces monologues and perhaps dialogues in the choruses of hymns to Dionysus and other deities.

520*

- Attica pioneers the technique of red-figure vase painting with the result that more vivid images are used. (The background is painted black while the figures are left the color of the unpainted vase.)

510–480*

- Bronze becomes a favored medium for sculpture. Some of the prominent sculptors in bronze include Polyclitus and the brothers Lysippus and Lysistratus.

498*

- Pindar writes the first of his *Epinikia*, four collections of athletic victory odes celebrating the Panhellenic festivals (the Olympian, Pythian, Nemean, and Isthmian).

486*

- Comedy competitions begin in Athens.

484

- Aeschylus wins his first victory for tragedy at the Great Dionysia.

480*

- The first free-standing statues appear in the *contrapposto* pose, which implies movement by shifting weight onto one leg.

470-430

- Civic monuments commemorating mythic and recent actual victories over the Persians appear in Athens and Delphi and in paintings by Polygnotus and Micon, and in sculptures by Pheidias.

472

- *Persians,* the oldest surviving play of Aeschylus, is produced. It describes the great Athenian naval victory of Salamis (480), in which Aeschylus supposedly participated.

468

- Sophocles wins his first victory for tragedy at the City Dionysia; he wins altogether as many as twenty-four times.

467

- Aeschylus writes *Seven Against Thebes*, a play about two brothers who murder each other and fulfill their father's curse.

463

- Aeschylus writes *Suppliant Women,* a play about marriage and fertility.

460*

- The sculptor Pheidias is active. His grand and majestic statues include Athena Parthenos (447–438) and Zeus at Olympia (circa 430).

458

- Aeschylus produces the *Oresteia*, which is the only surviving Greek trilogy and probably the playwright's last work. It includes the tragic plays *Agamemnon, Libation Bearers,* and *Eumenides,* and the lost satyr play *Proteus. Oresteia* addresses the issues of justice, freedom, and destiny.

450*

- Herodotus, often called the "Father of History," writes his *History of the Persian Wars* detailing the resistance of the Greek city-states against the Persian Empire.

- Polygnotus paints several works, including *The Rape of the Daughters of Leucippus* and *Odysseus After Slaying the Suitors.* His *Sack of Troy* supposedly gains him Athenian citizenship.

Parrhasius specializes in painting heroes at times of great distress; for example, his *Feigned Madness of Odysseus* depicts strong emotion. Parrhasius supposedly tortures an old slave to death in order to capture the anguish for his painting of Prometheus in chains.

447

Laborers under the supervision of the architects Ictinus and Callicrates begin construction on the Parthenon, the temple of Athena on the Athenian Acropolis. Upon completion in 432, the Parthenon is a prime example of the Doric order of architecture. The thick columns have twenty-two grooves each, vertical incisions, and metopes (spaces on the area above the columns with sculptures). Other examples of the Doric style include the treasury of the Sicyonians at Delphi (built circa 540 B.C.E.) and the temple to Zeus at Olympia (built circa 470–456).

441*

Sophocles writes what is sometimes considered his greatest play, *Antigone,* a tragedy about a young woman's love for and dedication to her dead brother.

441

The tragic poet Euripides wins his first award at the City Dionysia.

438

Euripides composes *Alcestis,* his earliest extant play. It is the story of Admetus, king of Pherae in Thessaly, who receives a special privilege not accorded to other mortals.

431

Euripides produces *Medea,* the tragic story of spurned love, revenge, and infanticide.

428

Hippolytus, by Euripides, is the tale of revenge taken by Aphrodite against Hippolytus, illegitimate son of Theseus by an Amazon woman.

427

The sophist Gorgias of Leontini journeys to Athens as the leader of a delegation that requests military aid against Syracuse. The Athenians are so impressed with his rhythmic style of speaking that they agree to make an alliance with Leontini.

425

- Aristophanes writes the comedy *Acharnians*, his earliest extant work, which tells the story of an ordinary farmer who becomes the savior of his polis.

424

- Aristophanes composes the comedy *Knights*, in which Athenian democracy is compared to a troubled private household.

422

- *Wasps*, a play by Aristophanes, satirizes the jury system and the conflict between generations.

421

- Work begins on the Erekhtheion, a temple on the Athenian Acropolis. Construction continues until 407, and when it is finished the Erekhtheion is an example of Ionic order architecture with its tall, slender columns (each with twenty-four grooves and surmounted by two heavy spirals) and a continuous sculpted frieze above the colonnade. Other examples of the Ionic order include the Siphnian treasury at Delphi (built circa 530 B.C.E.) and the Athena Nikê at Athens (built in the late fifth century B.C.E.).
- Aristophanes's *Peace I* is a play that lampoons the peace proceedings between Athens and Sparta during the Second Peloponnesian War (431–404).

418*

- *Clouds II* by Aristophanes is a comic play on education.

415

- Euripides composes *Trojan Women*, a protest of the excesses of war.

414

- In the lyric poetry of *Birds*, Aristophanes satirizes the imperial ambitions of the Athenians.

413

- The painter Zeuxis begins to decorate the palace of the Macedonian tyrant Archelaus. Known for his realism, Zeuxis could deceive birds with his paintings of natural scenes.

IMPORTANT EVENTS OF 800-323 B.C.E.

412	• Euripides produces *Helen,* a play about the devotion between a husband and wife.
411	• Aristophanes writes two comic plays, *Lysistrata* and *Thesmophoriazousai I.* Both plays are apolitical in nature and deal with gender relations.
410*	• *Phoenician Women,* by Euripides, is a retelling of the story of the Seven against Thebes.
409	• Sophocles composes *Philoctetes,* the story of a hero of the Trojan War marooned on an island.
408	• Euripides produces *Orestes,* a tragic play about murder and revenge.
405	• Aristophanes composes *Frogs,* a comedy about literary criticism in the underworld.
401	• Sophocles' play *Oedipus at Colonus* is performed posthumously; its theme is the bitterness of a character betrayed by those close to him.
400*	• Thucydides writes *History of the Peloponnesian War,* a narrative of the great struggle between Athens and Sparta and their respective allies between 431 and 404 B.C.E.
388	• Aristophanes' satire *Wealth II,* the last surviving play of Classical Greece, is produced. *Wealth II* examines inequality by posing the question of what would happen if the god Wealth were cured of his blindness and only the deserving in life received rewards.

370*

- The marble sculptor Scopas is active and becomes famous for his statues of divinities such as Aphrodite, Poseidon, and Achilles.

360*

- Praxiteles finishes the nude *Aphrodite of Cnidus* or *Cnidia*. The marble sculptor reportedly uses his mistress as a model; the King of Bithynia is so taken with the finished product that he offers to buy it by paying the national debt of Cnidus.

350*

- Leading Greek architects and sculptors build grand monuments and tombs dedicated to individual rulers, such as the royal burial vault at Vergina (believed by some to be that of Philip II) and the Mausoleum (or the tomb to the ruler Mausolus) at Halicarnassus.

332*

- The painter Apelles is active. He paints the royal portraits of Philip II and his son Alexander the Great. His most famous work is *Aphroditê Anaduomenê* (Aphrodite Rising from the Sea). Horses reportedly neigh at his painted horses.

"Leonidas at Thermopylae," painted by Jacques Louis David in 1814 (Louvre, Cliché des Musées Nationaux, Paris)

OVERVIEW

Literature. No aspect of the legacy of Greece to later Western culture has been as influential as its literature. The words by which we describe so many literary forms—*epic, hymn, didactic, drama (tragedy* and *comedy), lyric, history, rhetoric, philosophy*—are Greek in origin and thus betray the fact that they are in effect Greek inventions. In some cases we can now glimpse at developed literary forms from earlier cultures predating our earliest known Greek examples, but these were unknown to Greeks in historical times and certainly to their European heirs; in effect, Western literary culture begins with the Greeks and, it is widely thought, also reaches its highest development in the pioneering yet sophisticated work of the Archaic (700–480 B.C.E.) and Classical (480–323 B.C.E.) periods of Greece.

Homeric Poems. Many aspects of this overall picture can be illustrated already in what is probably the earliest literature to survive from the Greek world, the Homeric poems. They appear to leap onto the world stage, with no surviving precedents, and yet the *Iliad* and the *Odyssey* (both composed circa eighth–seventh centuries B.C.E.) are arguably the two finest poems ever composed, and are certainly the two most influential. Yet, the poems should be seen as an ending as well as a beginning, for they represent the culmination of what must have been centuries of illiterate poetic composition. It is unlikely to be coincidence that the Greeks rediscovered the art of writing (adapting the script of the Phoenicians) early in the eighth century B.C.E., shortly before the Homeric poems were given the fixed form in which they became known to later Greeks and then to the rest of the world.

Poetry. The Latin-derived word *literature* goes with the essentially Roman idea that literature is what gets written down. However, Greek poetry reached great sophistication without this medium, and their culture never accepted the equation of great works of language as things of their nature written down. To translate what modern society means by literature into Greek of the Archaic and Classical ages, it would have to be called by the suggestive name of *mousikê* (the origin of our word *music*, but clearly of a broader scope). Poetry was closer to the performed song than to the written word.

Lyric Poetry. The Homeric poems probably were sung in their earliest performances—certainly they describe poets singing to the lyre—and it is no surprise that some of the earliest nonepic poetry to survive was composed to be always sung: hence its name *lyric*. Again, the first surviving lyric poets, who include the best-known woman from ancient Greece, Sappho, must represent a long tradition, one phase of which has been preserved (albeit imperfectly) because of the introduction of writing. The songs these poets composed, whether performed by large choirs or by solo artists, again indicate that there was nothing bookish about Greek mousikê in this period.

Didactic Poetry. The close connection between music and Greek poetry should not lead one to think that entertainment was the sole, or even most important goal its producers set themselves. A rich tradition of didactic (that is, instructional) poetry runs from the beginnings of surviving literature, and the Greeks themselves debated whether the first such extant poetry, that of Hesiod in the eighth century, should not be placed earlier than Homer himself. Hesiod's surviving poetry deals with mythology as a catalogue (*Theogony* or *Origin of the Gods*) and with the rudiments of farming (*Works and Days*); but the latter especially draws on folk wisdom (much of it evidently of an Eastern origin) and can be said to be a work more concerned with morality than the real techniques of agriculture. Didactic poetry was not actually a genre much fostered by the Greeks of the Archaic and Classical periods, but the strongly moralizing tendency of Hesiod's work was to find itself reworked in the essentially political poetry of the Athenian statesman Solon and in the conservative collection of poetry which goes under the name of *Theognis*.

Drama. The great works of Athenian drama were also the product of a profoundly political process. Although its beginnings lie in the predemocratic period of Athens' history, Greek tragedy is associated above all with the democratic (within the ancient definitions of that word) city-state of Athens in the fifth century B.C.E., when all our surviving Greek tragedies were written. Athens so dominates the modern view of ancient Greece that it must be remembered that it only rose to real prominence in the Greek world as late as that century; and Greek tragedy in fact shows how late it was on the scene. For although they were written by Athenians, and performed by and for Athenians at large and popular festivals, the plays make only limited reference to the city-state itself. With the exception of a couple of famous and early examples, the plays are based on earlier Greek mythology, the product of a time when Athens was of little account in comparison with the great centers of Mycenae and Thebes (also reflected in the embarrassingly few references to Athens in the Homeric poems). The three great Athenian tragedians—Aeschylus, Sophocles, and Euripides—did their best by inventing events in the lives of the heroes of mythology which somehow tied them to Athens, but it was a bit of an effort. Greek tragedy, like the epic, was really more at home with the far away and the long ago, dealing with characters who are, as Aristotle put it in his *Poetics,* better than us.

Comedy. Yet, this same city in the same century also produced a radically different type of drama, the comedy of Aristophanes and his rivals. While tragedy dealt with traditional stories and larger-than-life characters, Aristophanes' comedy was concerned with the immediate political and domestic issues of contemporary Athens and was peopled with characters Aristotle was happy to describe as "worse than us." Boisterous and blasphemous, yet lyrical and in many ways reactionary, Aristophanes' plays were the product of a deeply irreverent conservative, living with and making use of the intellectual world against which his plays direct such scorn.

Prose. Aristophanes died early in the fourth century B.C.E., by which stage the intellectual culture about which he was so ambivalent had truly taken hold of Greek literature. Perhaps the clearest indication of this change is the new preference for prose over poetry. That preference was beginning to emerge in the fifth century and goes hand in hand with the emergence of new literary genres in Greece, especially in Athens. The formal study of rhetoric, instigated according to Aristotle by the birth of democracy in Greek cities in Sicily, spread to Athens where the democracy also made it welcome: the citizen who had need to address the sovereign assembly, or to defend himself in front of a large jury, was able to make use of the new techniques of composing prose speeches, or at least to pay others to compose them for him. The influence of this development on other literary genres (especially drama) was considerable, but it also led to the emergence of a new genre in its own right: in the last quarter of the fifth century B.C.E., speechwriters began publishing the speeches they had written for clients or on their own behalf. The following century was to see the emergence of Athenian orators regarded by many later Greeks as the greatest of all prose writers, especially Demosthenes.

Philosophy. The flourishing of philosophy as a literary form in its own right occurred in the fourth century B.C.E. Philosophers were writing prose of sorts (now surviving only in fragments) in the fifth and even sixth centuries B.C.E.; and again, the Greek colonies led the way rather than the homeland. Yet, once again (to judge on the incomplete historical records), Athens produced the standard by which later Greeks were to measure excellence in prose. A description of Plato's philosophy has no place in this chapter, but his merits as a writer of Greek prose must be mentioned; those of his pupil Aristotle must be taken on trust, as his surviving works are not those he wrote as polished works of art for a general audience.

History. The final new prose form to mention is that of history. The title "the Father of History" is traditionally assigned to Herodotus from the Carian city of Halicarnassus; his sprawling account of the Persian invasions of Greece in the early fifth century was clearly pioneering, and contains an enormous amount of geographical and ethnographical information along with history as the word is presently used. More bracing, and much more scientific, is Thucydides, another Athenian taking a colonial invention to a new literary height. His history of the Second Peloponnesian War (fought between Athens and Sparta from 431 to 404 B.C.E.) was written at the end of the fifth century and, although preoccupied with military matters, has been called the greatest work on politics ever written. Of great interest in it is the influence of the new art of rhetoric, especially in the many set speeches that feature in it.

Turning Point. The death of Alexander the Great in 323 B.C.E. has been regarded as a turning point in Greek literature from at least the first century B.C.E. The Hellenistic Period (323–31 B.C.E.) which it inaugurated lies beyond the scope of this chapter, but must be mentioned briefly in the context of the posthumous life of Archaic and Classical literature. For although Hellenistic literature was in some ways more influential on later European literature than the strictly Classical canon, it was essentially built on and developed the literary genres of earlier Greece. During the Hellenistic Age Rome developed its own literature, but it did so in conscious and often awkward imitation of Greek models; as the Roman poet Horace stated, "conquered Greece conquered her savage captor, and brought her arts into rustic Latium." The Romans often chose more contemporary Greek literature, rather than older models for imitation, but those contemporary works were usually deeply indebted to Greek ancestors. Thus, New Comedy, a domesticated development of Old Comedy, was what the Romans took over and gave to Europe: a timeless and essentially unpolitical genre, but one firmly based on features of earlier comedy. Also, although the Hellenistic Period did originate some genres (notably pastoral, much imitated by the Romans and their heirs), most of its literature reworked (often in highly original ways) the forms of literature established before the fourth century B.C.E.

Established Norms. Deeply conscious of their artistic inferiority to the Greeks, the Romans nevertheless produced a culture through which Greek literary and artistic forms became the established ones of the European tradition. The education of the *Pax Romana* was, above all, Greek in inspiration, and the stability and breadth of the Roman Empire gave Greek culture a place that it would not have enjoyed in a more-turbulent world. When the Roman Empire came to an end in Western Europe and direct contact with ancient Greek literature was lost, Latin kept knowledge of it alive: even today, the figures of Greek literature are still more familiar to us in their Latin spellings than in their Greek (thus Aeschylus and Thucydides rather than Aiskhulos and Thoukudides). The return of the knowledge of Greek to Western Europe in the Renaissance was probably not of great consequence for the subsequent literature of that region: the difficulties of the language, and the fact that so much of its mythology and literature were available already through Latin, occasioned this predominance of Latin.

Sculpture and Painted Pottery. It has often been said that the central subject of Greek art is the human, usually male, figure. Developments in rendering human figures are most noticeable in different styles of sculpture that emerged over the period 800–323 B.C.E., as well as on painted pottery, which brought the rise of black-figure and red-figure styles. One of the main reasons for the importance of the human figure in Greek art is that so much painting and sculpture refers to a well-known myth or narrative involving, for instance, scenes from the Trojan War (twelfth or thirteenth centuries B.C.E.), or episodes in the life of the Olympian gods or heroes such as Heracles. At the same time, of course, much surviving Greek art is not obviously narrative. Many artifacts served as either private dedications celebrating athletic victories, or as memorials to the the dead; and painted pottery could be used in a domestic context such as a drinking party (symposium), depicting anonymous men and women dancing, at work, play, love, and war.

Architecture. Also important are architectural changes during the period under consideration. Large-scale architecture made from durable materials such as stone was, like the human figure in Greek art, mostly absent after the Mycenaean Era (1600–1200 B.C.E.) until the 700s B.C.E. By the 600s B.C.E. large stone temples began to appear in different regions of Greece, and as separate city-states began to develop into commercial and cultural centers, there was increased demand for civic buildings such as treasuries, law courts, town halls, and marketplaces, as well as temples and shrines. Such civic architecture became prominent especially from the sixth century B.C.E. onward and is most famously exemplified by Pericles' building of the Athenian Acropolis, crowned by the Parthenon. The rise in importance of sanctuaries at Delphi and Olympia provided a further impetus for city-states to display their wealth and power by building their own treasuries and clubhouses; there they could also make public dedications to celebrate military victories and to secure the favor of the oracle who acted as the mouthpiece of the gods. Many public buildings included architectural sculptures, sculpted friezes that reveal Eastern influences, and various types of columns such as the Doric, Ionic, and Corinthian orders.

Artists. Except for a couple of fragments, the writings about art by practicing artists and others in the Classical Period are all lost. In addition to the ancient artifacts themselves and public inscriptions, there are literary sources on ancient art. While some are from a much later period and do not primarily deal with visual art, they often draw on earlier sources and have been crucial in shaping subsequent ideas on the nature of Greek art and artists. As for the lives of Greek artists, little is known. Although their works were admired in antiquity, interest in the personal history of visual artists or artisans is an alien concept to the ancient world. Many artisans, then, are anonymous, or are simply names that have come down to us because they signed their works. Yet, for some artists of the fifth and fourth centuries B.C.E. there is a little more biographical information, often from later sources of the Roman Period. While these texts tend to concentrate on aspects of the artists' works and perceived qualities of style, they include some anecdotes; although not always to be taken as fact, these usually reflect interesting features of the ancient reception of these artists and their works and again draw on earlier sources.

Legacy. The works produced by Greek sculptors, painters, and architects have been the most enduring achievements of the ancient world. Just as Greek drama continues to be performed and reinterpreted in various forms all over the world, so too Classical Greek art and architecture remain a source for practicing artists worldwide, and continue to attract visitors to ancient sites and museums who wish to catch a closer look at statues, vases, and remains of buildings. Already in antiquity its impact was widespread and has endured periodically for over two millennia, profoundly affecting developments in Western art.

Roman Influence. In the mid fourth century B.C.E., a Persian ruler in the eastern Aegean called Mausolus set up a huge funerary memorial to himself that broadly used Greek artistic elements; this memorial was literally his Mausoleum. He employed eminent Greek architects and sculptors to depict several Greek mythic scenes, such as the legendary wars with the Amazons. In Pergamon in Asia Minor, a dynasty known as the Attalids who rose to power in the third century B.C.E., looked to Athens as its cultural model, and, to commemorate victories over the Celts or Gauls, produced monuments that followed Greek sculptural forms. About 167 B.C.E. a huge altar in Pergamon was dedicated to Zeus that similarly echoed Greek styles of sculpture and architecture and depicted the Greek myth of the battle of gods and giants. Greek works were emulated by the Romans, their conquerors by 146 B.C.E., and readers have come to know many Greek works through Roman copies. This appropriation has been crucial for the long-term impact of Greek art, since many Greek original statues have been lost but have become known through Roman copies.

Sources. The legacy of Classical Greek art in the Roman Period is also evident in the ancient sources for the history of Greek art. These writings by Pliny, Pausanias, and others constantly focus on the artists and architecture of the fifth and fourth centuries B.C.E. Modern scholars also know that in antiquity there were revivals of earlier Greek styles in certain sculptures; for instance, a statue of the first century B.C.E. imitates the early Classical style of the early fifth century B.C.E. Beyond the Greco-Roman world Greek art made an impact that can be detected in, for instance, an ancient sculpture from Gandhara, dated to the first century C.E., which depicts one of Buddha's guardians as Herakles with lionskin and club.

Italian Renaissance. After antiquity the next great era of the dominance of the Greek legacy in art began with the Italian Renaissance of the 1400s–1500s. When Greek statues (or at least Roman copies of them) were being rediscovered at this time, they exercised profound effects on artists of all kinds, notably Michelangelo, whose famous statue of David owes a great deal to such Classical sculptors as Polyclitus and Lysippus. Throughout the Renaissance and Baroque periods other artists such as Raphael, Titian, and Bernini not only worked with themes from Greek history and mythology but added a monumental grandeur to their figures, reminiscent of Classical statues.

Winckelmann. By the eighteenth century Greek art had attained an idealized status in the minds of connoisseurs and critics such as the renowned German scholar J. J. Winckelmann, who claimed that the greatness of Greek art was linked to the liberty enjoyed by Greeks, such as Periclean democracy of the fifth century B.C.E. Winckelmann never visited Greece, and the pieces of art he most admired long postdate the fifth century B.C.E; but his own account added a political dimension to appreciation of Greek art and architecture, even if many would now see his notion of Greek liberty as certainly exaggerated. Yet, such notions were widespread and were further fueled by the desire to fight against the empire of the Turks in the Greek War of Independence (1820s), whose most famous casualty was the thirty-six-year old George Gordon, Lord Byron.

English Treasure. In England the fashion for Greek art received a major boost with the arrival of the sculptures from the Athenian Acropolis, and especially from the Parthenon, under the supervision of Lord Elgin in the early nineteenth century. The circumstances of the appropriation were, and still are, controversial; after Elgin sold the marbles to the British government some dissenting voices could still be heard, but they petered out amidst widespread enthusiasm for the sculptures. Until this time, Greek art was mostly known in Western Europe through Roman copies, but now here were prime examples of the real thing, which added to romantic notions of the Classical past. The revival of Grecian and Roman style architecture in the late 1700s into the 1800s thus often carried political overtones and was frequently used to convey connotations of liberty and/or power, or cultural enlightenment. As such, it has been used for parliamentary and legal buildings and memorials, notably Hyde Park Gate, which celebrates the defeat of Napoleon, and the Lincoln Memorial in Washington, D.C. It is some measure of the vast appeal of this style of architecture and sculpture that it continued variously to be used for two centuries or more to express republican ideals, regal and totalitarian power, as well as housing art treasures, banks, and churches.

French Neoclassical Style. The Classical heritage has also had a huge stylistic and political impact on the painting and sculpture of recent centuries. The works of French painter Jacques-Louis David embodied republican sentiment in France around the time of the revolution of 1789 by depicting figures in neoclassical style from Greek and Roman history as paradigms of heroic virtue. Napoleon, David's chief patron, had an infatuation with ancient art that resulted not only in the pillaging of Greco-Roman artworks, but in depictions of himself in the pose of a Greek hero. David's pupil and successor, Jean-Auguste-Dominique Ingres, continued the neoclassical style in his paintings, many of which depicted scenes from Greek mythology, such as *Oedipus and the Sphinx* (1808), among others.

Vases. The trade in tourism and antiquities over the past two hundred years broadened familiarity with Greek art, especially vase painting, which was long overlooked, but is now at the forefront of any study of Greek art. As John Keats's *Ode on a Grecian Urn* (1819) testifies, Greek vases soon caught the attention of lovers of the ancient world, who came upon them in Italy, especially Etruria, where they had been exported in antiquity. The impact of Greek art on artists continued into the nineteenth century, evident in Auguste Rodin's innovative, monumental sculptures, which rework Classical forms. In addition, artists of the twentieth century who were seen as revolutionary and modernist continually revived images from the Greek world and placed them in new and challenging contexts; Pablo Picasso and Giorgio De Chirico are notable examples.

Idealized Images. Every subsequent reappropriation of Classical art inevitably contains much that is alien to the ancient Greeks. This development is due to the differences in social and historical contexts that separate them from those later ages that often re-created the Greeks to suit their own idealized image of themselves. Moreover, some of the uses to which Greek forms have been put are more palatable than others, and this situation has led to recent questioning and reappraisal of the once paradigmatic status of Greek art for Western tastes. Some interesting artistic developments have emerged; yet, even those who renounce the Greek legacy implicitly acknowledge this influence, since they consciously define themselves against it. Picasso and De Chirico are two modern artists who could see Greek art as a vehicle for further image-making, rather than a constraint to be shunned. The legacy of Greek art, then, has not of necessity been a stifling one but has remained a challenge and stimulus to later artists and architects for more than two thousand years.

TOPICS IN THE ARTS

ARCHITECTURE

Late Geometric Period: 800–700 B.C.E. Architectural materials of the 700s B.C.E. tended to be of mudbrick, thatch, and wood, but some temple foundations of reasonable size have been unearthed, including one to Hera on Samos that measured one hundred feet in length. A restored clay model from the same period found at another sanctuary to Hera near Corinth gives an indication of eighth-century architecture. It could represent the temple itself or the house of the person who made the offering. More enduring innovations in architecture followed in the next century, inspired to some extent by contacts with Egypt. Indeed, by the early 600s B.C.E. the visual arts in Greece were reponding to the arts of the Near East in ways that both developed and departed from the achievements and style of much Geometric Period art.

Early Archaic Period: 700-600 B.C.E. Architecture of the early seventh century developed the canonical forms of the Doric order, probably invented at Corinth, and the Ionic order. Early materials were wood, but stone was later employed and was needed to support the roof, now made of terra-cotta tiles instead of thatch. The more austere Doric order had twenty-two grooves along each column shaft, and featured triglyphs (vertical incisions) next to spaces called metopes (which sometimes were filled with sculptures) on the area above the columns. The Ionic order had taller, slender columns which were surmounted by two heavy volutes (or spirals); each column had twenty-four gooves along its length. The Ionic order did not include metopes or triglyphs, but had a continuous sculpted frieze above the colonnade.

Influence from Abroad. Egypt played a role in influencing Greek architecture and sculpture at this stage, particularly in the eastern Greek regions of Ionia. Political and trading contacts between Egypt and eastern Greek regions increased from about 660 B.C.E. onward under the reign of the Egyptian king Psammetichus, who hired Ionian mercenaries for his military campaigns and established a trading post with the Greeks at Naucratis. Ionian architects were supposed to have witnessed large-scale Egyptian stone architecture, and it is clear that some Egyptian forms were adapted to Greek temple styles. However, the Greeks were also familiar with large-scale architecture and sculpture from the Mycenaean Period (1600–1200 B.C.E.), so influences came from both local and international sources. Also, the inventions of the detail in Doric and Ionic forms, as well as roof tiling, are essentially Greek achievements. Temple sculptures were painted and decorated the open triangular pediments above the front and rear, and sometimes were included on the friezes of temples in Ionic style. Temples generally were surrounded by an outer colonnade (row of columns) on all four sides, often, but not always, comprised of a formula of a fixed number at the front and twice that number plus one more at the side (for example, six by thirteen). Large-scale temples to various gods appear at this time, notably to Poseidon near Corinth, to Apollo at Thermon in northwest Greece, and an enlargement of the temple to Hera on the island of Samos.

Middle and Later Archaic Periods: 600–480 B.C.E. Increasing prosperity enjoyed by many *poleis* (city-states) and their colonies, as well as familiarity with Eastern models, led to developments in large-scale architecture and sculpture in the sixth century B.C.E., especially Greek temples and sanctuaries. A notable example was the temple of Artemis at Ephesus—one of the Seven Wonders of the Ancient World, but now completely destroyed. At Corcyra a large temple to Artemis was constructed about 590-580 B.C.E., which featured impressive, but now fragmentary, pedimental sculptures depicting the Gorgon Medusa in the center, and her two children Chrysaor, and the famous

---

INSPIRATION

Strabo, a geographer of the first century B.C.E., writes:

And they recount this tradition about Pheidias. When Panaenus asked him what model he intended to employ in making the image of Zeus, he replied that it was the model provided by Homer in the following lines of the *Iliad* (1.528–530): "Thus spoke the son of Kronos and nodded his dark brow, and the ambrosial locks flowed down from the lord's immortal head, and he made great Olympus shake."

Source: Strabo, 8.3.30

Detail of the North frieze of the Siphnian Treasury, late sixth century B.C.E.
(Photo courtesy of Ecole Française d'Archéologie, Athens)

winged horse, Pegasus. Western colonies in southern Italy and Sicily, some governed by tyrants, expressed their civic power and prosperity in constructing large-scale temples in Doric style that competed in size and grandeur with many on mainland Greece. The remains of the temple to Hera at Paestum in southern Italy, built around 540 B.C.E., indicate something of its original imposing presence. In Attica the Acropolis underwent an extensive face-lift from about 560, which included a large temple to Athena, famous for its pedimental sculptures depicting the hero Heracles wrestling sea monsters. Although this building program probably began earlier, much of it is associated with the tyrant Peisistratus, who also built a Royal Stoa (or colonnade) and began a huge temple to Olympian Zeus that was finally completed under the Roman emperor Hadrian nearly seven hundred years later.

Treasuries. Secular architecture and sculpture also reached new heights at this time. Treasuries built by various poleis at Panhellenic centers like Delphi were competitive expressions of power and success, often funded by spoils won in war. This competitiveness could lead to a variety of architectural styles and ornamentation. The treasury of the Sicyonians at Delphi was built circa 540 B.C.E. in Doric style while adjacent to it was the Siphnian treasury, in Ionic fashion, circa 530. On the best-preserved east and north faces of the continuous frieze of the Siphnian treasury were depicted such scenes as the gods on Olympus, battles between heroes at Troy (Achilles and Memnon), and the famous battle between the gods and giants, called the gigantomachy. There were highly accomplished elements such as the use of overlapping in depicting figures, such as appeared on the Chigi vase; there was also fuller, more naturalistic rendering of bodies compared to the Daedalic style; and there were impressive three-quarter-angle views of certain heads such as that of the giant, being mauled by the lion. Heads were no longer restricted to being rendered frontally or in profile as before. Such interesting angles in depicting figures occurs on the Doric-style Athenian treasury built circa 500-490 B.C.E., whose metopes depicted Heracles' and Theseus's independent

labors. One shows Heracles capturing the Cerynian hind with the taut, muscled hero seeming to leap out of the background over the animal in a burst of energy.

Temple of Aphaia. Developments in the vitality of architectural sculptures can be seen on the pediment of the temple to Aphaia on the island of Aegina (now housed in Munich). The two pediments seem to have been sculpted about ten years apart (circa 500–490 B.C.E.), each depicting scenes of the sack of Troy with Athena at the center. The older west pediment still has some more Archaic elements to it; for instance, one figure still has the so-called Archaic smile and props himself in a relatively upright frontal pose when shot by an arrow. On the east pediment a dying warrior appears to sag under the pain of wounds inflicted in war, as his head drops and hand falls out of his shield; in addition, his gritted teeth and flared nostrils give a new sense of vividness to the depiction of a hero in the throes of death on a battlefield.

Early and High Classical Periods: 480–400 B.C.E. Much of the expansion in the arts at this time was heralded by Athens, whose wealth came from its empire and the tribute exacted from her subjects, who were once her allies in the Delian League. The confidence and wealth in the aftermath of victory over Persia is most famously expressed in the Acropolis, rebuilt under Pericles after 450 B.C.E. This renovation featured the work of the legendary sculptor Pheidias and his workshop, especially on the new Parthenon, the great temple to Athena, which ever since has become a potent symbol of the "glory days" of Athens. Before 450, however, the most famous and largest building in Greece was the temple to Zeus at Olympia. It was built circa 470–456 in the Doric style and funded by the people of Elis from spoils won in war against Pisa. The temple measured 64.12 by 27.68 metres, had the canonical six columns at the front and thirteen at the side, and included sculptures in its pediments of Apollo and the centauromachy at one end and Zeus presiding over the combatants in a chariot race at the other; the labors of Heracles were depicted on its metopes. Its most famous feature was the

A modern reconstruction of Pheidias's Athena Parthenos, of which the original was made in circa 440 B.C.E. (Royal Ontario Museum, Toronto)

great chryselephantine statue of Zeus by Pheidias, constructed circa 435 B.C.E. The Zeus figure was larger than the cult statue Pheidias made for the Parthenon, and was seated, holding a Winged Victory in his right hand and sceptre in his left. The throne was embellished with Graces, Sphinxes, mythological scenes, and heroic battles; the screen between its legs was painted by Pheidias's brother (or nephew), Panaenus, and represented some of Heracles' labors and Achilles' battles; the base depicted the birth of Aphrodite. Pheidias's Zeus became one of the Seven Wonders of the World, inspired stories as to its creation, and was an object of profound veneration.

Parthenon. Crowning the Athenian Acropolis was the Doric style Parthenon, built between 447–432 B.C.E. by the architects Ictinus and Callicrates. It measured 69.5 by 30.88 metres and had eight columns at the front and seventeen at the side, and contained sculptures in its pediments depicting the birth of Athena in one end and her contest with Poseidon for the role of Attica's patron deity in the other. Its metopes depicted the Sack of Troy, the battle with Amazons, gigantomachy, and centauromachy; it also had one continuous frieze depicting a cavalcade, the Olympian gods and a ritual procession. The taller, slender columns and inclusion of a frieze give the Parthenon some Ionic touches, even though it is ostensibly a Doric temple; such combinations of architectural styles in the one building were to be more common in later fifth- and fourth-century buildings. Further interesting refinements in the Parthenon are in the slightly convex, inward leaning columns and the upward curve of the stylobate;

---

these have been interpreted to have optical effects so as to appear straighter and firmer when seen from a distance. The chryselephantine cult statue of Athena by Pheidias was nearly forty feet high, helmeted with a triple-plumed crest, wearing a miniature aegis, and standing with a Winged Victory in her right hand; her left hand held a spear and shield also propped up by a serpent. Images of heroic battles against the Amazons, gods against giants, Lapiths and Centaurs adorned her shield and sandals, and the birth of Pandora was depicted on the statue base. The Parthenon seems to have been part of the same plan as the Doric style Propylaia, the grandiose gateway to the Acropolis. Designed by Mnesicles in 437–432 B.C.E., it also featured some interior Ionic columns and a picture gallery, which included works by Polygnotus, one of the great masters of fifth-century painting.

Other Temples. Athens' architectural embellishments, begun under Pericles, continued after his death in 429 B.C.E. Elsewhere on the Acropolis was the Erechtheum, built in 421–407, in a varied style on several elevations to fit on the uneven terrain. It housed cult relics and featured Caryatids on its south projection. Another Ionic temple was known as the temple of Athena Nikê to the west of the Propylaia, built in the late fifth century and famous for its elaborate sculptures on its balustrade. Some further novel features in late fifth-century architecture are found in the temple to Apollo at Bassai in Arcadia that had external Doric columns, Ionic in the interior, and one free-standing Corinthian column, which develops the Ionic style into a more vegetal form. In the agora of Athens a fine, well-preserved Doric temple to Hephaestus measuring 31.77 by 13.71 meters (and six by thirteen columns), was begun circa 449 B.C.E. Like the Parthenon, this temple contained certain Ionic elements such as a frieze in the *pronaos* (front porch) and *opisthodomos* (back porch). Its metopes depicted the labors of Heracles and adventures of Attica's own hero, Theseus.

Later Classical Period: 400–323 B.C.E. The fourth century B.C.E. may be viewed as a transitional period that witnessed violent political change in the Greek world from the era of city-states, often at war with each other, to the rise of the monarchy imposed by Philip of Macedon and his son Alexander. Much in art was a continuation of Classical trends, but there were significant innovations in all major areas which clearly ushered in the Hellenistic styles of succeeding centuries. There tended to be fewer temples built during this period, but at Epidauros the extensive sanctuary to Asklepios was given a new temple to the god, near the well-preserved theater, famous for its magnificent acoustics and also built in the middle of the fourth century.

Variations. Notable features in fourth-century temple architecture were variations in style and proportion of Doric and Ionic orders. For instance, the temple to Athena Alea at Tegea in the Peloponnese, designed by Scopas, had taller, more slender Doric columns than usual, low entablature and an elongated cella plan lined by Corinthian and Ionic columns close against the walls,

The Nereid Monunment, circa 400 B.C.E.
(British Museum, London)

instead of being a genuine colonnade. Monuments to individual rulers became conspicuous in the fourth century, such as the Nereid Monument (circa 400 B.C.E.) in Lycia; it featured Ionic columns and a pediment mounted on a podium with free-standing sculptures between columns, and a frieze depicting scenes of the life of Achilles. The most famous example of a monument to an individual of this time is the Mausoleum, or tomb of Mausolus, an eastern ruler, who governed in Halicarnassus in 377–353 B.C.E.; the monument was probably completed by the 340s. Mausolus employed famous Greek artists of the day to work on it, including Scopas and Praxiteles, among others. There are difficulties in reconstructing the Mausoleum, but ancient descriptions and the foundations indicate that its base was about thirty-six by thirty-six meters and was about forty–forty-five meters high. It had thirty-six Ionic columns mounted on a podium; atop the colonnade was a pyramid of twenty-four steps, surmounted by a charioteer group. There were free-standing statues between columns and figures on the base of the podium; two have been identified as Mausolus and his wife (and sister) Artemisia, but their identity is not certain. Its frieze, sixty centimeters below colonnade was thirty meters above ground and depicted the battles against Amazons and centaurs; thus, Mausolus showed further "Hellenising" trends in his choice of images, as well as employing Greek artists. Famous in antiquity, the Mausoleum was another of the Seven Wonders of the World, but the edi-

fice was felled in an earthquake in the 1200s and later quarried by the Knights of St. John at Rhodes.

Sources:

William R. Biers, *The Archaeology of Greece: An Introduction* (Ithaca, N.Y. & London: Cornell University Press, 1996).

John Boardman, *Greek Art* (London: Thames & Hudson, 1996).

Jeffrey M. Hurwit, *The Art and Culture of Early Greece, 1100–480 B.C.* (Ithaca, N.Y. & London: Cornell University Press, 1985).

Nigel Spivey, *Greek Art* (London: Phaidon, 1997).

COMEDY

Limitations. The origins of comedy as a formal genre of drama are even more obscure than those of tragedy. Aristotle's *Poetics* (after 335 B.C.E.) is vague enough about the origins of the latter but explicitly says that much less is known about how comedy developed because in its early stages it was not taken seriously enough to warrant proper records being kept. Originally the performers in comedies were volunteers, and only at a comparatively late date did the medium win state support comparable to that of tragedy. Another source dates the earliest comic victory to one Chionides in 486 B.C.E. (thus, well after the traditional date of Thespis's first victory in tragedy) and regular competitions in comedy are certainly established by 472 B.C.E., when an incomplete inscription recording dramatic victors in Athens begins. However, even this date is nearly fifty years before the first surviving comedy, so there is little information about what comedy was like when records began; a passing remark by Aristotle suggests that it may have been even more personally directed than the later, surviving comedy. All surviving comedies from Classical Greece were written by one man, Aristophanes, although there exist the names and fragments of more than fifty of his contemporary rivals, and thus any description of this comedy must be essentially based on his work.

Divisions. Ancient scholars had a tripartite division of comedy, dividing it into Old, Middle, and New. New Comedy, essentially domestic in focus, had enormous influence on Roman and thence later European comedy, but only one fairly complete play from it survives. Middle Comedy too has survived only tenuously, with the exception of the two final plays of Aristophanes. Only with Old Comedy is there a significant body of work on which to base generalizations; and it is best defined by its relationship to tragedy.

Qualities. By definition, tragedy is serious and comedy is funny. In the Greek context, the seriousness of tragedy is unrelieved by any of the sort of scenes which lighten even William Shakespeare's darkest plays: perhaps there is only one real joke in all surviving Greek tragedy. Whether or not there is a corresponding complete lack of seriousness in Old Comedy allows of no certain answer, but its overwhelming preference for humor marks its most obvious difference from tragedy. The humor expressed itself often in ways that further distinguish this form of drama from its more respectable relation. Often Aristophanes refers in a

TRAGEDY'S ONLY JOKE?

Hecuba, the queen of the defeated Trojans, has been trying to convince Menelaus to kill his unfaithful wife Helen, the cause of so much misery to them both:

Menelaus: Attendants! Bring Helen to the ships to sail home.

Hecuba: Don't let her sail in the same ship as you.

Menelaus: Why not? Has she put on so much weight?

Source: Euripides, *Trojan Women*, pp. 1047–1050

highly explicit and self-conscious way to drama, both comic and tragic, and even to the play being performed: nothing nearly as explicit is ever found in tragedy, which keeps the dramatic illusion always intact if occasionally strained. This fact seems related to tragedy's desire to be believed at some level, as if it can only achieve its goal if it somehow engages the sympathy of the audience, for which some kind of plausibility seems a prerequisite. Comedy, however, is manifestly not interested in being believed—as witnessed by its surreal plotlines.

Political Commentary. Much of the humor of Old Comedy is at the expense of political figures of the day, again marking a clear difference from tragedy. Tragedies are set in the distant past, or (exceptionally) in a faraway place; Old Comedy is set in the present and is peopled by the playwrights' contemporaries. Not only political figures, like Pericles and Cleon, felt the sting of abuse: philosophers such as Socrates and tragedians such as Euripides are also held up to ridicule. So too are dozens of other Athenians who today are only names to us; democratic Old Comedy did not restrict its attacks to the rich and famous. Although ancient politics tended to be based more on personalities than on abstract policy issues, Aristophanes' treatment of public figures does not concentrate solely on these personal elements. Whether attacking a politician or a poet, he takes account of ideological issues as well. However, the extent to which Aristophanes has anything really serious to say about political issues is a hotly debated subject. No doubt his chief concern was invariably to raise laughs, but there are certainly passages where he explicitly claims to be offering, and to have offered elsewhere, sound political advice. One school of thought would maintain that this claim to offer serious advice is itself humorous—and indeed it is sometimes presented in that light, such as when he claims that even the king of Persia was aware of the sensible advice he had been offering the Athenians! The trump card usually played by this school is the fact that Aristophanes' *Knights* (424 B.C.E.), a vitriolic attack on the contemporary politician Cleon, was successful in dramatic competition shortly before the Athenian democratic assembly elected him to

high office; the conclusion drawn is that the political elements were not meant seriously by the poet or taken as such by the audience. However, that conclusion is obviously only one of several possible ones. As the old saying goes, a week is a long time in politics; Cleon's status may well have changed quickly. Again, it is quite possible that the judges of the festival did not accurately reflect the opinions of most of the audience—there is a similar discrepancy occurring with Aristophanes' *Clouds* (423 B.C.E.) when the judges went against the audience's vote. The apparent contradiction between the success of *Knights* and Cleon's subsequent election to office means nothing definite as regards the political purpose or impact of Old Comedy.

Obscenity. The plethora of contemporary references in Old Comedy certainly distinguish the genre from Tragedy. Another striking difference is the role of obscenity, which is ubiquitous in Old Comedy but completely absent from the more respectable medium. Not only did the standard male costume include a visible phallos, or artificial penis, but the texts are richly embellished with references to bodily functions in a way that those of Tragedy are not, and these functions are described in language that is clearly vulgar slang. When philosophers and serious poets need to mention sex, for instance, they do so in language that is euphemistic and vague, and when contemporary medical writers need to be more explicit they use a different vocabulary from that found in Old Comedy. Some of the latter's language is precisely the equivalent of modern "four letter words" and is used in similar contexts of aggression and transgression. This indulgence—indeed celebration—of transgression has been seen by some as an essential feature of Old Comedy, and parallels have been drawn with "carnival" practices in other cultures.

Fantasy. Old Comedy not only transgresses the boundaries of normal social restraint, but of common sense and rationality as well. Compelled to make up their own plots rather than rely on traditional myth, comic playwrights developed a rich and surreal fantasy element. In *Wasps* (422 B.C.E.), where the chorus themselves are half-men and half-wasps, dogs put each other on trial, and even a cheese grater can be called to give evidence. Other plays show similar exuberance of imagination: a chorus of frogs sing of the joys of marsh life, the birds wage war against the gods by besieging the heavens and preventing sacrificial smoke from reaching them, and an ordinary citizen acquires a giant dung beetle on which he flies to Olympus to get Zeus to put an end to the Second Peloponnesian War (431–404 B.C.E.). The *Ekklêziazousai* is along these lines too—women actually exercise political power, which was for contemporary Athenian citizens nothing short of a ludicrous fantasy.

Stepping Forward. Structurally, the most important difference between Old Comedy and Tragedy lies in the presence of the *parabasis* (literally "stepping forward"), when the chorus addresses the audience directly, some-

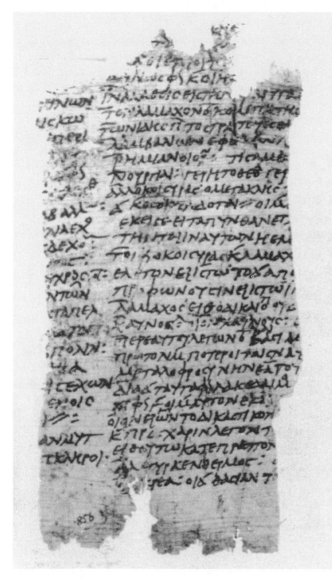

Fragment of a third-century C.E. papyrus commentary on Aristophanes' *Acharnians* (Brussels Mus. Roy. Inv. E. 5972)

mopolitan event and attracted fewer foreigners than the Great Dionysia and was also regarded as less important by the tragedians: two tragedians produced two plays each for any Lênaia festival, while the same number of comedians competed as in the larger festival.

Sources:

Kenneth J. Dover, *Aristophanic Comedy* (London: Batsford, 1972).

Arthur Wallace Pickard-Cambridge, *The Dramatic Festivals of Athens* (London: Oxford University Press, 1968).

DIDACTIC POETRY

Hesiod. Didactic poetry (from the Greek word *didaskô* or "teach") was always written in the same meter as epic (dactylic hexameter) and therefore not distinguished by the ancients from that grander genre. Nevertheless, the modern classification is well-established and convenient. There survives only one complete didactic poem from the period covered in this chapter, Hesiod's *Works and Days* (circa eighth century B.C.E.), and it was this poem which was to have great influence when a more scientific age revived the practice of didactic verse; there survive several such works from the Hellenistic (for example, Aratus) and Roman periods (especially Lucretius and Vergil).

THE ROOT OF ALL EVIL

Zeus punishes men for Prometheus's theft of fire:

"Son of Iapetos, clever above all others, you are pleased at having stolen fire and outwitted me—a great calamity both for yourself and for men to come. To set against the fire I shall give them an affliction in which they will all delight as they embrace their own misfortune." So saying, the father of gods and men laughed aloud; and he told renowned Hephaestus at once to mix earth with water, to add in a human voice and strength, and to model upon the immortal goddesses' aspect the fair lovely form of a maiden. Athene he told to teach her crafts, to weave the embroidered web, and golden Aphrodite to shower charm about her head, and painful yearning and consuming obsession; to put in a bitch's mind and a knavish nature, that was his instruction to Hermes the go-between, the dog-killer. . . . When he had completed the precipitous, unmanageable trap, the father sent the renowned dog-killer to Epimetheus taking the gift, swift messenger of the gods. Epimetheus gave no thought to what Prometheus had told him, never to accept a gift from Olympian Zeus but to send it back lest some affliction befall mortals: he accepted, and had the bane before he realised it. For formerly the tribes of men on earth lived remote from ills, without harsh toil and the grievous sicknesses that are deadly to men. But the woman unstopped the jar and let it all out, and brought grim cares upon mankind. Only Hope remained there inside in her secure dwelling, under the lip of the jar, and did not fly out, because the woman put the lid back in time by the providence of Zeus the cloud-gatherer who bears the aegis.

Source: Hesiod, *Works and Days*, pp. 54–68, 83–88.

times in the persona of their own character (as wasps or birds), other times speaking directly for the poet in the first person. Frequently political and literary references occur in this context, both of which also distinguish the two genres. However differences also existed in production: a comic chorus had twenty-four members (versus twelve then later fifteen for tragedy), and comedy was also able to make use of four speaking actors at once (versus three for tragedy).

The Lênaia. Comedy played a subordinate role in Athens' main drama festival, the Great (or City) Dionysia, in which five playwrights each offered a single comic play for competition. (Meanwhile there were a total of twelve plays written by three tragedians.) Yet, comedy had the major role in another Athenian festival from about the middle of the fifth century B.C.E., the Lênaia. Held in the middle of winter, this festival was a less cos-

Moral Fervor. Addressed to his brother Perses, Hesiod's poem is less concerned with the technicalities of its predominant subject matter, agriculture, than with questions of correct behavior and justice, in which it seems that his brother was rather deficient. This moral fervor was something that Roman didactic was later to cultivate. Popular also in later examples of the genre was the use of mythology, and here Hesiod set the example; in trying to explain why the world is so constructed that hard work is necessary just to survive, he offers an explanation based on the story of Pandora, the woman who brought all the trouble into the world, and then later the completely inconsistent story of the degenerating races of mankind. Apart from agriculture, Hesiod also advises on seafaring, and (in the last section of the poem) on the proper days for particular activities—the eleventh and twelfth days of the month, for instance, are suitable for shearing wool and picking fruit.

Source:
Peter Toohey, *Epic Lessons: An Introduction to Ancient Didactic Poetry* (London & New York: Routledge, 1996).

ELEGY AND IAMBICS

Theognis. The elegiac and iambic metrical schemes, were both unsung, and both form more regular metrical patterns than lyric. Achilochus of Paros, active in the late eighth or early seventh century B.C.E., practiced both, and his voice emerges as one of the most distinctive in Greek literature: a tough cynical soldier with a taste for obscenity, he also shows a pride in his poetic gifts. A much less complex character emerges in the seventh century Spartan elegist, Tyrtaeus, whose verse is full of exhortation to bravery on the battlefield and who upholds this as true excellence in a man. However, the largest body of extant elegy from the period under consideration is that composed for the symposium attributed to the poet Theognis, of the seventh or sixth century B.C.E. In fact, the verses clearly range over a wide chronological period and should be seen more as collection than as the work of a single man. Aristocratic in tone, they extol the pleasures of the feast and the love of youths, while complaining about the social turmoil as the "better" people find themselves displaced in the new order of things.

Hipponax and Solon. The range of poetry produced in iambic meter can be vividly illustrated by the works of Hipponax and Solon. The former, an Ionian poet of the late sixth century B.C.E., wrote monologues presenting himself as one who lived low life to the full, an enthusiast of burglary, sex, and drink. Yet, at the other end of the century Solon, chief magistrate in Athens 594–593 B.C.E., used the meter to write poems justifying his social policy, particularly his cancellation of debts. Iambic meters became in the fifth century the dominant spoken meters of tragedy and comedy; Aristotle claims that the iambic is the meter closest to natural speech.

Source:
Cecil Maurice Bowra, *Early Greek Elegists* (Cambridge, Mass.: Harvard University Press, 1938).

EPICS

Homer. Although the Archaic Period (700–480 B.C.E.) produced many epic poems, only the *Iliad* and the *Odyssey* (both composed circa eighth–seventh centuries B.C.E.) have survived intact, and these two poems must dictate what is known of the epic genre in the period. Both poems were attributed to Homer, but even in the ancient world there were those who denied that these two different poems were the work of one man; many modern scholars have gone much further and doubted whether authorship of either poem can be meaningfully attributed to one individual at all. In any case, it is certain that any poet to whom we might attribute the shaping of either poem in its current state drew exhaustively on a long tradition of heroic stories and highly polished technical skill in telling them.

Personal Background. The accounts of Homer's life found in ancient writings are entirely false and indicate that no genuine information about the author(s) of the epics survived to be recorded; whatever value these accounts have is simply inference from the poems themselves. The poems do indeed suggest some things about the poet(s): the language, although highly artificial, is predominantly Ionic, which suggests that the poems were composed on or near the coast of Asia Minor, and references to the geography of that area have been detected in the poetry and thought to confirm this origin. It is not surprising then that Chios and Samos were the two places most commonly claiming the honor of being Homer's birthplace.

Date of Composition. The date of the poems' composition is also uncertain, and in antiquity various guesses differed by several centuries. However, modern scholarship can take advantage of the not always unambiguous tool of archaeology, and several interesting facts emerge that are relevant to the date of the Homeric poems. In the first place, it would appear that Homer knows of things (such as types of armor) which had been out of use for centuries before other things that he writes about appeared. This fact indicates that it will not be possible to fix any clear date for the whole of the poem—rather, we must be dealing with an inherited tradition. Yet, a more precise indication of possible dating appears in two highly significant cultural practices, both of which date to around the middle of the eighth century. Belonging to this time are the earliest alphabetic Greek inscriptions to have been found, and also the earliest evidence for widespread continuous worship of heroes at their tombs. Both phenomena seem related to Homeric poetry, but in both cases the nature of the relationship is unclear. In the case of the latter, the two epics look back to a time when men were greater and much closer to the gods; it is possible that this attitude was inspired by what was beginning to happen around long-abandoned tombs. However, Homer does not mention such cults, and it is at least as plausible that the decisive push for these practices was the appearance of a massive poem (or several of them) dealing with the distant past and those ancestors who were but dimly remembered by the poet's contemporaries. (Admittedly, a third possibil-

The theater at the sanctuary of Asclepius in Epidaurus, dating from the fourth century B.C.E.
It is one of the best surviving examples of a Classical Greek theater (Scala)

ity needs to be considered: hero cults and Homeric poetry may be not so much causally connected as both cultural products of a shift in general Greek attitudes to the dead.)

Relationship with Writing. The vast size of the *Iliad* and the *Odyssey* immediately raises the question of the poems' relationship with writing. There is only one apparent mention of writing in the Homeric poems (*Iliad* 6.168–169), and even it is ambiguous. Since the pioneering work of the American scholar Milman Parry, it has been clear that the techniques of the Homeric poems are essentially those of oral poetry. Using the internal evidence of the poems' rich variety yet severe economy of noun–epithet formulas, Parry postulated a traditional system of storytelling which relied on the memorization of phrases, rather than of set texts, and he found parallels for this system in the contemporary singers of Yugoslavia; the use of language by literate poets, even when superficially imitating oral poetry, is shown to be profoundly different. Yet, the parallels Parry produced were nowhere able to match the massive scale and architectural construction of the Homeric poems: contemporary singers (like indeed the singers described in books 1 and 8 of the *Odyssey*) seemed capable of producing only comparatively short pieces. So it has been argued that the appearance of writing was the catalyst for the production of the Homeric poems in all their sprawling glory at a particular moment in history when the

tradition of oral poetry was still alive but the new technology of writing opened up great possibilities of narrative complexity and structure. Yet, in fact, as with the ambiguous relationship with tomb cult, the direction of influence is not certain; for it has recently been argued that the Greek alphabet was actually invented for the express purpose of recording epic poetry.

Bards. If the ancient biographers of Homer based their ideas simply on what they inferred from the poems themselves, it must be said that we must do the same when trying to understand the position of the bards who produced the poems. It is a reasonable assumption that the presentation of professional singers in the *Odyssey* (there are none in the *Iliad,* the poem of war) somehow reflects the reality of the tradition to which the Homeric poems belong. The bards in this poem sing to royal audiences, usually as dinner-time entertainment, and provide pleasure to their listeners—with the notable exceptions of Penelope and Odysseus, who weep on hearing stories precisely because they are true and remind them of their own situation. The poems are explicit that the bards are highly honored, but some details of the narrative simply do not harmonize with that claim: among the Phaeacians, for instance, Odysseus is so moved by the bard's song that he gives him a portion of his own food. This act is supposed to be a sign of honor, but the poem seems to let slip that

But Odysseus of many wiles,

At once when he raised the great bow and viewed it on all sides—

As when a man skilled at the lyre and at singing

Easily stretches a string over a new peg,

Tying at both ends the flexible gut of the sheep—

So without effort did Odysseus string the great bow.

He took it in his right hand and tested the cord.

It sang sweetly beneath like a swallow in its sound.

Source: Homer, *Odyssey* 21.404–411.

Achilles explains to Priam the meaning of life:

Such is the way the way the gods spun life for unfortunate mortals, that we live in unhappiness, but the gods themselves have no sorrows.

There are two urns that stand on the door-sill of Zeus. They are unlike for the gifts they bestow: an urn of evils, and urn of blessings.

If Zeus who delights in thunder mingles these and bestows them on man, he shifts, and moves now in evil, again in good fortune.

But when Zeus bestows from the urn of sorrows, he makes a failure of man, and the evil hunger drives him over the shining earth, and he wanders respected neither of gods nor mortals.

Source: Homer, *Iliad* 24.525–533.

the bard's position was closer to that of a beggar than an honored guest, who would naturally be given his own portion. Elsewhere too singers are described as being itinerant, thus contradicting the image of tenured security projected in other parts of the poem. So perhaps the *Odyssey* represents an attempt to present the bards as much more significant in the court life of the past than they were in the present—an ugly present that occasionally breaks through the narrative. If the poems were actually the product of wandering minstrels, hangers-on of no great moment at the courts of the wealthy, the great themes of hospitality and kindness to strangers in the *Odyssey* can be seen in a new light, as the products of personal experience more than anything else. In addition, the presentation of that poem's hero as a disguised beggar is also consistent with his role as a pseudo-bard (especially the great embedded narrative of his adventures in books 9–12), culminating in the extraordinary simile when Odysseus strings his great bow at the climax of the work, doing it as easily, says Homer, as a bard strings a lyre.

Warfare. If the themes of peace, wandering, and hospitality in the *Odyssey* can give us some insight into the conditions under which that poem took shape, the same cannot be said for the relentless story of war that is the *Iliad*. It is well known that many aspects of Homeric warfare are as fantastical as Odysseus's adventures, and that they combine different tactics and weapons in a way that would not happen on any real battlefield (thus, chariots become glorified taxis, rather than the massed weapons that they had been in actual warfare): although familiar enough with violent death, the bards of the tradition will have had no clear memory of the sort of warfare they describe. The foreignness of the subject matter invited the use of similes, which are more frequent in this poem, and give an insight into what the poet and his audience may have been familiar with: scenes of everyday life are evoked to describe the imagined conflicts in a way which brings out the differences between the world of the heroes of the poem and the audience. For instance, the Homeric heroes, despite being encamped by the sea for ten years, eat fish only when starving, but the poet's use of fishing in his similes suggests that, as we would expect from known Greek history, fish must have formed a fairly important part of the diet of his audience. Above all the *ekphrasis* (literary description of a work of visual art) of the shield of Achilles shows a world in all its variety of celebration, litigation, war, agriculture, shepherding, and dance; for once martial conflict is put into a wider context, achieving on a grander scale something that the similes are also able to bring about.

Human Tenderness. The bleak austerity of the vision of life and death in the *Iliad* is softened by powerful scenes of human tenderness: Paris and Helen retiring to bed after the former's disgrace on the battlefield; Hector's farewell to his wife and child to take part in a struggle he knows is hopeless; and above all Achilles' meeting with Priam as the latter begs for the return of his son's body for burial. This final meeting in the poem presents a realization of the essentially tragic condition of humanity in an indifferent universe. The vision of the *Odyssey* is different: there the gods care about justice and human morality in general. From the outset it is stressed that humans bring suffering upon themselves by ignoring the advice of the gods, and the punishment of the rapacious suitors at its conclusion is presented as a vindication of this view. Could two such different outlooks have coexisted in the one poet? In antiquity it was thought that the *Odyssey* was the product of Homer's old age, more akin to a comedy than to the tragic *Iliad*.

History. The relationship of the events in the Homeric poems to real history is significant. No one in the ancient world doubted that there had been a Trojan War (twelfth or thirteenth centuries B.C.E.) involving Greeks led by a king called Agamemnon, but they had no other evidence than the Homeric and other early epic poems, and the modern age has been much more skeptical. However, the discovery by

Heinrich Schliemann in the nineteenth century of millennia of history beneath the Hellenistic city identified by the Greeks and Romans as Troy brought spectacular new evidence into play, although it is questionable whether this archaeological evidence has actually advanced the case for a Trojan War in anything like the form of the tradition. The discoveries have failed to produce the minimum required for supporting the tradition, which would be evidence for a substantial city destroyed by enemy action. Furthermore, not a single inscription has been recovered from the relevant strata of the excavation: we remain quite ignorant of the identity of the inhabitants of Troy during that time (some have even suggested that they were Greek!) as well as that of their enemies. There is no reason to believe that there was even a kernel of historical fact behind the story of the Greek expedition to Troy in Homer.

Epic Cycle. An important corpus of early Greek epic poetry, now lost, was the *Epic Cycle*. Apparently put together after the two Homeric poems, in order to fill out the stories of Greek myth from the creation of the world to the end of the Heroic Age, the poems were attributed to a variety of authors in the ancient world, among them Homer himself. Two cosmological epics, the *Theogony* (not to be confused with Hesiod's extant poem of that name) and the *Titanomakhia* told of the origin of the gods and their internal struggles; three Theban epics *Oidipodeia, Thebais,* and *Epigonoi* told the story of Oedipus, of his sons and the Seven against Thebes, and of the later and successful attempt to capture Thebes by the sons of the Seven. The Trojan epics, *Cypria, Aithiopis, Little Iliad,* and *Iliou Persis* (The Sack of Troy) told the story of the Trojan War, from its origins until the sack of Troy; in terms of its story, the extant *Iliad* fits between the first two of this group; some of the most famous incidents in the Greek myth of Troy, such as the death of Achilles and the Wooden Horse, are not narrated in the *Iliad*, but featured instead in these vanished epics. The final group was *Nostoi* (Returns) and *Telegoneia*, with the *Odyssey* fitting between. This set told of the aftermath of the Trojan War, coming to an end with the death of Odysseus.

Sources:

Geoffrey Stephen Kirk, *The Songs of Homer* (Cambridge: Cambridge University Press, 1962).

Ian Morris & Barry Powell, eds., *A New Companion to Homer* (Leiden, Netherlands & New York: Brill, 1997).

A.J.B. Wace & Frank H. Stubbings, eds., *A Companion to Homer* (London: Macmillan; New York: St. Martin's Press, 1962).

HISTORY

Father of History. Herodotus has been christened "the Father of History," but he had several predecessors, with whom he was not afraid to disagree, but who clearly paved the way for his work. Chief among these was Hecataeus who flourished around 500 B.C.E. and who was a native of Miletus, not far up the coast of Asia Minor from Herodotus's Halicarnassus. The fragments of Hecataeus indicate that he too had a great interest in geography, writing a systematic tour of the then known world around the coasts of the Mediterranean and Black seas. However, a separate

Fragment of a third-century-B.C.E. papyrus with the text of book 1 of Thucydides' history (Hamburger Staats- und Universitatsbibliothek)

historical work makes clear how different he was from Herodotus: the titles applied to it by the ancients—*Histories, Genealogies* and *Stories of Heroes*—indicate the subject matter of his *historiê* (enquiry). This impression is confirmed by the fragments, which are concerned with mythology. Also, although they show a healthy desire to rationalize the more-absurd elements of myth, the limitations of any enquiry about such a remote subject are fairly clear.

East Versus West. Herodotus certainly did not abandon the study of myth, but he usually approaches it only as background for the main focus of his study, the conflict between East and West. The last events he covered in detail—the Greek invasion and the defeat of the Persian king Xerxes—had happened within a generation or two of his recording them, and there will have been plenty of still fresh traditions and eyewitnesses on which to draw. Thucydides carries this even further by restricting himself to the coverage of a war in which he himself took part, and he is quite explicit that his work is lacking *to muthôdes* ("the mythical element").

Xenophon. A final word must be reserved for the third extant historian of Classical Greece, Xenophon. In fact, to call him purely an historian does him less than justice, as he wrote extensively on a broad range of subjects, including philosophy (the *Memorabilia* and *Symposium*, in which

Socrates takes the central role), the pursuits of a country gentleman (*Cynegeticus* and *Horsemanship*), and politics (*Constitution of the Spartans*). Yet, he is most studied now as an historian, and for two works in particular: the *Hellenica*, a history of Greece in 411–362 B.C.E., and the *Anabasis*, describing Xenophon's experience as a mercenary in support of a claimant to the Persian throne (401–399 B.C.E.). The *Hellenica* continues Thucydides' incomplete narrative and suffers in comparison; so too do Plato's writings provoke invidious comparison with Xenophon's philosophy. Above all, Xenophon's Socrates, the product of a deeply conventional writer (despite his varied and interesting life), is a smug bore in comparison with the charismatic figure portrayed in Plato. However, it is certainly possible that the historian has presented a more accurate picture of the real man than did Plato.

Source:
Michael Grant, *Greek and Roman Historians: Information and Misinformation* (London & New York: Routledge, 1995).

LYRIC

Alcman and Others. Lyric or sung poetry (the term does not include epic, which was not sung in the historical period at least) goes back well beyond the earliest records of the Greek world. Already Homer mentions choral song several times, and the occasions to which he ascribes these, such as funerals and weddings, continued to provide major opportunities for the formal performance of song in more literate ages. Perhaps the first lyric poet the reader can name is Alcman, a Spartan of the seventh century B.C.E., whose fragmentary work contains several *Partheneia*, or songs for choruses of maidens. Around the end of that century lived Sappho and Alcaeus on Lesbos, but their work was chiefly monodic rather than choral. The spread of Hellenism also produced contemporary lyric in the West: Stesichorus worked in Himera and composed a famous

Fragment of a second-century-C.E. papyrus text of Sappho's poems (Bodleian Library, Oxford)

Palinode, or retraction-song, in which (supposedly after being blinded after one poem) he apologized to the deified Helen and claimed that she never went to Troy (his sight was then restored). Ibycus, a generation or two later, also had a western origin but moved from his native Rhegium to the court of the tyrant Polycrates in Samos, where Anacreon of Teos also worked. The first half of the fifth century B.C.E. was the final flush of lyric poetry in its own right: during this time were active the two best preserved lyric poets, Bacchylides of Ceos and Pindar, both of whom wrote choral lyric, especially victory odes for the successful in the Pan-Hellenic games. Lyric lingered on past the end of that century, particularly in the form of the dithyramb, narrative choral lyric that formed part of the City Dionysia drama festival in Athens. However, these seem to have been events valued chiefly for their music and display rather than their poetry, and by this time tragedy, originally a derivative of dithyramb according to Aristotle, was giving every opportunity for lyric expression in its choral odes.

Source:
David A. Campbell, *The Golden Lyre: The Themes of the Greek Lyric Poets* (London: Duckworth, 1983).

ORATORY

Polished Literary Medium. The rise of prose as the dominant mode of expression in the late fifth and fourth centuries B.C.E. coincides with the increasing importance of oratory as a polished literary medium in its own right. It is not by chance that probably the earliest surviving Attic prose occurs in the *Tetralogies* of Antiphon, practice speeches about imaginary court cases, nor that prominent among early prose are similar practice speeches (such as those of Gorgias). The publication of genuine speeches, no doubt motivated partly by the desire of speechwriters to advertise their work, seems to begin around 420 B.C.E., with Antiphon named as the first to publish real speeches.

Sophists. Whether or not this Antiphon was the same as the Sophist (itinerant professor of higher education) of that name, the important role that these intellectuals played in the move away from poetry should be acknowledged. With the exception of Critias, the Sophists did not write poetry. They wrote much prose, but we know of only a single poem, and that a short one, that any undisputed Sophist wrote. The Sophists were above all interested in teaching the art of public speaking, and it is an art necessarily prosaic in its form.

Atticism. Much of the shape of the survival of ancient Greek literature was determined by the movement known as Atticism, which originated in the mid first century B.C.E., apparently in Rome. This movement placed the prose literature of the fifth and fourth centuries B.C.E. far above that of the Hellenistic Age (323–31 B.C.E.), and so influential was its agenda that little Hellenistic prose has survived. Yet modern readers are well supplied with Classical oratory, from the so-called canon (a modern term in this meaning) of ten orators (Antiphon, Andocides, Lysias, Isocrates, Isaeus, Lycurgus, Aeschines, Demosthenes, Hyperides, and Dinarchus). The first person to have put together this list is unknown, but it seems likely that it is a product of the Atticists. The surviving speeches reveal a great deal of historical and legal matter, but that has been of little concern for most of their survival: they were apparently preserved, and faithfully studied for millennia, simply because they afforded the best training in the study of the Greek language of what was considered the best period.

Source:
George A. Kennedy, *The Art of Persuasion in Greece* (Princeton: Princeton University Press, 1963).

PHILOSOPHY

Definition. The term *philosophy* first approaches what modern society means by the word in the fourth-century B.C.E. writings of Plato; before that time the Sophist (itinerant professor of higher education) was not distinguished from the philosopher, and even in his lifetime the ownership of what was becoming a prestigious word was hotly disputed: Isocrates, essentially a teacher of rhetoric, called his subject "philosophy," but he lost this battle with Plato. The term refers to a way of thinking, not a way of expressing.

Presocratics. The first Presocratic philosophers are imperfectly known to us through fragments. Anaximander of Miletus published the first prose work of a philosophical treatise on the ultimate origin of the universe, which he maintained was impersonal. The profundity of the subject matter points to prose as the natural medium of the doctrine: the poetic accounts before him are naturally based in myth, and (to judge by early philosophical poetry) there seems to be something in the nature of verse which calls on the poet to take up or invent personal forces in it. The writings of the Sophists, virtually all in prose, were more concerned with rhetoric than anything else, but also contained much that was philosophical even by Plato's definition: for instance, a consistently argued relativism (the belief that judgments must necessarily be made from a certain viewpoint, and that objectivity is unattainable); a serious questioning of the existence of the divine; and challenging views on the nature and possibility of knowledge. Such ideas seem to have been explored in passing as part of rhetorical or other exercises; and indeed there is some evidence that Protagoras, like earlier pre-Socratics, published collec-

The theater at Delphi (A.G.E. Fototstock)

tions of pithy aphorisms rather than continuous prose accounts of his philosophy.

Platonic Dialogues. Against this background Plato wrote his dialogues. Clearly indebted to the Sophists, yet keen to distinguish himself and his teacher Socrates from them, Plato often presents his master in a highly destructive role, questioning and disputing the claims of the Sophists without offering anything positive. The apparently early dialogues in particular have this approach, and an important element is their lively characterization, at times verging into caricature, of the participants in the dialogue. As a prose writer Plato stands supreme in the Greek language: with his great feeling for parody, his writing covers nearly as broad a spectrum as Aristophanes', and yet his special mixture of colloquialism and solemnity is unmistakably his own. The dialogue as a philosophical form was pursued by other pupils of Socrates as well, and there are extensive examples extant from Xenophon.

Aristotle. The impression of Aristotle as a prose writer has been distorted by the way his works have survived. The works meant for public consumption were widely praised for their elegance in the ancient world, but these works have all been lost. The surviving works were written for members of Aristotle's school—some have even thought that they are notes taken by his pupils—and, for all their intellectual power, show none of the charm and polish of the published works of his teacher, Plato.

Source:
W. K. C. Guthrie, *A History of Greek Philosophy* (Cambridge: Cambridge University Press, 1962–1981).

POTTERY, PAINTING, AND MOSAICS

Late Geometric Period: 800–700 B.C.E. The late Geometric Period coincided with the rise of the Greek city-state or polis, and the emergence from the Dark Ages. The resultant prosperity of this time was felt clearly in the art of pottery, which built on styles known as Protogeometric (900s B.C.E.) and Early Geometric (800s B.C.E.). As the name suggests this early painted pottery featured abstract designs such as parallel straight lines, circles and semicircles, meanders, triangles, checkerboards, swastikas, as well as large areas of black glaze. Such controlled designs articulate the shape of the vase and emphasize various parts, such as its neck, shoulder, or belly. Many of these vases were used in a funerary context, sometimes containing the ashes and bones of the cremated, or precious objects owned during his or her lifetime. Such pottery was particularly prominent in Attica, which led the way in further innovations in pottery shapes such as the *oinokhoê* (wine jug), and the appearance of animals in rows, or friezes, in identical poses.

Human Figure. Around 760 B.C.E. the human figure reemerged en masse in Geometric art and was depicted in funeral scenes on huge vases (sometimes over 1.6 meters high), which functioned as grave markers for the aristocratic dead. A famous example is the Dipylon Vase, from the Kerameikos cemetery in Athens. This huge vase not only has a great range of Geometric designs, but contains

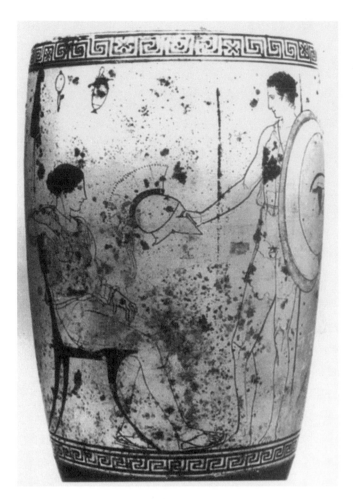

An Athenian white-ground *lekuthos* attributed to the Achilles painter (late fifth century B.C.E.) showing a warrior departing from home (National Museum, Athens [1818]/photo TAP)

two animal friezes on the neck, and, most importantly, a funeral scene between the handles, where the vase is widest. This vase was a grave marker for an aristocratic woman who is depicted lying in state (*prothesis*), while mourners raise their hands to their heads in a gesture of grief. The triangular torsos, seen frontally, emphasize their geometric origins, but the figures' legs in profile seem relatively organic and fleshy by comparison. The corpse itself lies under what is probably a shroud to be placed over it, and is presented to us in a stylized way upturned on its side. Such presentation underlines an important concern for the painter and his public: the need to understand what is being depicted. There is no attempt at perspective, variety of colors, shading, or overlapping, so the painter presents objects not as they would appear, but as how they can be best understood within the limits of his medium.

Wealth and Fame. Similar techniques apply in another Attic funerary vase or *kratêr* (bowl) from about 740 B.C.E. This example has a mourning scene which involves bringing the dead out for burial (*ekphora*) and a chariot procession on a lower level which may reflect the dead man's wealth and interests during his lifetime; in another contemporary funeral *kratêr* from Attica battle scenes are

A Corinthian *puxis*, circa 600–575 B.C.E. (Ashmolean Museum, Oxford)

depicted, which suggests the deceased may have been a warrior or had heroic aspirations. Interesting in these two *kratêres* is the increased area occupied by the human and animal figures, and slight variations such as the inclusion of the eye, and the depiction of the body in action. The increased interest in the human figure is an important step in Geometric art, and is felt in vase painting from the late eighth century. In some instances the decoration is kept to a minimum and the focus is on human action, whether it be warriors confronting lions, or a couple about to embark a two-tiered ship on a *kratêr* from Thebes of about 730 B.C.E. The size of this couple emphasises their importance, and some have suggested it may be Paris and Helen elop-

ing, or Theseus fleeing Crete with Ariadne; but their identity remains a mystery.

Early Archaic Period: 700-600 B.C.E. During the seventh century Corinth prospered under tyrants and enjoyed commercial success especially in pottery. Corinth developed new pot shapes such as the *aruballos* (a round, narrow necked jug for perfume) and *olpê* (a jug with a sagging belly). As for painting, Corinth broke with the rigid Geometric forms, and included more floral patterns, especially rosettes, as well as more animal imagery ranging from panthers to sphinxes to barnyard animals. Also, Corinthian painters used a range of colors such as red, purple, black, white, brown and orange; moreover, incision was now being used which gave scope for more complex images with overlaps than could be found in the Geometric silhouette technique. Much Corinthian pottery painting was of a miniaturist and precise nature. These new techniques are found on the Chigi Vase, discovered in Veii in northern Italy, dated to about 650 B.C.E. Three levels of activity are depicted on this vase: 1) the Judgement of Paris; 2) a hare hunt, cavalcade, and lion hunt; 3) ranks of overlapping heavy-armed warriors (hoplites) going into battle, accompanied by a piper. Use of incision and polychromy (many colors) adds to the vividness and compact design of these images, especially the hoplite scene, and the piper is expertly rendered in full profile while the warriors have frontal torsos, but legs and heads in profile. Large-scale fresco painting in Corinth flourished at this time, and this vase painter may have worked in that medium too.

Eastern Influence and New Styles. In Attica Orientalizing tendencies were felt in the works of the so-called Analatos painter, who included sphinxes, spirals, rosettes and even some incision in some of his works, such as an amphora of about 680 B.C.E. Much in the painting also owes much to the Geometric style, so it seems a transitional phase. By about 650 Attica had developed the so-called "Proto-Attic" style, which featured on many large-scale funerary vases, four feet high or more. Scenes from myth are often depicted in this style, such as the Blinding of Polyphemus, or Perseus fleeing the Gorgons on the Eleusis Amphora of about 650 B.C.E. In the Polyphemus scene the artist has used shading for the legs of Odys-

seus and the Gorgons—a technique not seen again on vases for over a century. Interestingly, the narrative of Polyphemus' drunkenness and blinding, known also from Homer's *Odyssey* (circa eighth–seventh centuries B.C.E.), has been compressed into one moment. Homer tells of how Odysseus and his men, on their way home from Troy, are washed ashore on the island of the one-eyed giants, the Cyclopes. The sailors become trapped in the cave of the most brutal of them all, Polyphemus, who proceeds to eat some of Odysseus' companions. Odysseus cunningly decides to get the Cyclops, who has never tasted wine before, into a drunken stupor, so that he can blind him and escape. On the Eleusis amphora this sequence of events is presented as one image: the wine cup the giant holds alludes to his inebriated state. This interest in narrative is a feature of Attic vase-painting but lacking in much seventh-century Corinthian pottery. Narrative is evident elsewhere, in an Orientalizing plate from Rhodes of about 630 B.C.E. which depicts the Greek Menelaus fighting the Trojan Hector (their names are inscribed); and a storage vase from Mykonos of about 650 B.C.E. has relief sculptures of the Greeks emerging from the Wooden Horse and sacking Troy.

Middle and Later Archaic Periods: 600-480 B.C.E. The art of vase painting from 600–480 B.C.E. underwent many important changes, with Attica often leading the way. After the innovations and success of the Corinthians in the seventh century, Attic potters and painters must have felt a need to compete, and answered the challenge with new pot shapes and developments in the "Black figure" style. In contrast to the miniaturism of a lot of early Corinthian pottery increased vase sizes, especially from Attica, allowed more scope for image making and mythic narratives on the neck and body. Incision was used to good effect and female figures were rendered white in contrast to the usual black for males. An early example is from about 610 B.C.E., depicting on the neck a furious Heracles killing the centaur Nessos whose knees buckle under the force of the hero's attack, while the belly of the vase shows the Gorgons in pursuit of Perseus. The Attic painter's interest in narrative is attested in the François Vase (circa 570 B.C.E.) which was

An Athenian amphora from the late sixth century B.C.E. showing Achilles slaying Penthesileia, the Amazon queen (British Museum, London [B210])

exported to Etruria in antiquity. This large vase is a volute *kratêr* used at parties where its images would be seen at eye level by the reclining revellers; it was made by Ergotimos and painted by Kleitias, whose signatures indicate the pride and opportunity for self-advertisement craftsmen took in their work. The vase depicts several myths on different levels such as episodes from the life of Achilles, the hunt for the monstrous Calydonian boar, Hephaestus' return to Olympus, among others; its central panel depicts the marriage of Achilles' parents, Peleus and Thetis, attended by the gods in a procession. Interestingly, many figures are labeled, which allows scholars to identify the myths involved. While it is known that contemporary poets such as Stesichorus and Alcaeus dealt with some episodes that appear on the vase, it is not certain that the vase alludes to these specific poems; its makers may have known the stories from a common tradition that became manifested independently in art and literature.

Regional Variations. By the mid-sixth century other regions such as Lakonia produced their own competent versions of Black figure painting for export. As well, Caere in central Italy had a distinct figural style at this time, using polychromy and white for male figures; a *hudria* (water jug) found in Etruria, dated to circa 550 B.C.E., injects humor into pictorial narrative by showing Heracles' overlord Eurystheus cowering in a bronze jar as the hero brings back the three-headed dog of the underworld, Cerberus—the last of his labors ordered by the king. Attica had many fine exponents of the black figure technique around 550–520 B.C.E., including the Amasis Painter (so-called because he painted for

The François Vase, an Athenian Black Figure *kratêr* made by Ergotimos and painted by Kleitias, circa 570 B.C.E. (Museo Archeologico, Florence)

a potter of that name) and Exekias, who both painted large amphorae with figures to match. The Amasis Painter is noted for depicting the wine god Dionysos with his followers, the satyrs and maenads, on wine pourers used at a drinking party, or symposium. Often there is meticulous attention paid to details of dress and musculature in these convivial, generic scenes. Well-known examples of Exekias' works depict heroic themes such as Achilles' killing of Penthesileia or the Suicide of Ajax (circa 540-530 B.C.E.). In the former, Exekias uses a complex composition involving an overlap of figures that emphasizes Achilles' superiority over the crouching Amazon. The two were said to have fallen in love at this rather inconvenient point, and Exekias seems to imply this in the rendering of each character's eye. His Ajax similarly has an element of pathos about him as he prepares to throw himself on his sword after losing to Odysseus in the contest for the dead Achilles' arms, and attempting to kill the Greeks during a fit of mad-

ness afterwards. Exekias brings out well the hero's isolation; his crouching posture is rendered in full profile against a stark background balanced by a wilting tree and an almost ghostly set of armor. One can even detect something of his inner torment by the incised lines on his forehead and cheeks. Unlike others who had depicted the hero already impaled on his sword, Exekias chooses the moment immediately prior, and movingly presents Ajax's plight, as Sophocles was to do in a tragedy on the same theme in the next century.

Red Figure. By about 520 B.C.E., "Red figure" vases begin to appear in Attica, where the technique was pioneered by painting the background black so the figures would be of the same color as the unpainted vase. Thus, the painter was no longer restricted to incision for details as had often been the case with Black figure. Now there were new pictorial methods at hand, such as a choice of brushes of varying thicknesses for depicting contour and relief lines

An Athenian Red Figure kalyx *kratêr* (wine mixing bowl) by the Niobid Painter, mid-fifth century B.C.E.
(Musee du Lourve, Paris [G341]/ photo Réunion des Musées Nationaux)

of the human body; different colors and washes could be used over the figures; effects of shading by color gradation could also be attempted; overlapping figures could be rendered more economically. It is possible that some of these techniques were influenced by large-scale frescoes of the time, but unfortunately these have not survived. Black figure continued to be used into the fifth century on, for instance, amphorae commemorating victories at the Panathenaic Games; and many early examples of Red Figure appear on so-called "bilingual vases" which had black and red figure designs of the same image. An amphora by the Andocides Painter of Attica (circa 520 B.C.E.) shows Achilles and Ajax playing a board game, rendered in both methods. Red figure soon became the favored medium of pot painters, and by the late sixth century more vivid images of the human body were being produced. For instance, the image of Heracles wrestling the giant Antaeus

on an Attic kalyx kratêr of circa 510 B.C.E. by Euphronius includes detailed anatomical musculature and some shading on the giant's belly. His rival, Euthymides, deftly depicted three revellers (or symposiasts) dancing in a variety of poses on an Attic amphora of circa 510–500 B.C.E.; here he employed the three-quarter view, most notably on the central figure whose back is seen in mid-turn. Evidently proud of his achievement, Euthymides wrote down the side of this image: "As Euphronius never did." While images of myth are found on Red figure vases by, for instance, the Kleophrades painter (active circa 490–470 B.C.E.), or Douris (active circa 490–480 B.C.E.), several scenes depicting symposia are found, as might be expected from such pottery which would be used in such an environment; Dionysus and his entourage are also widely depicted. On one Attic amphora by the Berlin painter, dated circa 490, there is an image of Hermes, a satyr and a fawn, done

An Athenian amphora with a painting of dancers performing for Dionysus; attributed to the Amasis Painter, mid-sixth century B.C.E. (Cabinet des Médailles, Bibliothèque Nationale, Paris [222]/photo Hirmer Verlag GmbH, Munich)

against a black background with minimal decoration; the striking setting and the expert overlapping of the figures, with its economy of outline, indicate new possibilities opened up by the red figure technique.

Early and High Classical Periods: 480–400 B.C.E. Although there are no surviving examples, major advances in large-scale painting, such as *skiagraphia* (shading), are known to have occurred in the fifth century. This practice was pioneered by Apollodorus by the 420s, and developed by Zeuxis,

Parrhasius, and others who seem to have rendered their figures more naturalistically and with a greater "deceptive" realism than before. Prior to this time, Polygnotus had achieved fame with his frescoes, which decorated public buildings such as the Stoa Poikilê in Athens and the Cnidian clubhouse in Delphi. Pausanias' description of the works at Delphi in which characters are often depicted on various levels in contemplative poses suggests that Polygnotus' style had something in common with that of the Niobid Painter, whose kalyx *kratêr* of circa

460 may copy a large-scale fresco. Pottery painting from 480–400 built on the technical innovations of the late sixth century, and at times shares some features with idealising forms of sculpture (and maybe Polygnotus' painting style) in depicting characters such as Achilles on the amphora by the Achilles painter (circa 440). One should note here the *contrapposto* pose of both Herakles (on the Niobid Painter's vase) and Achilles. The white-ground *lekuthos,* sometimes featuring polychrome decoration, became a popular funeral offering by circa 450 B.C.E. Many of its themes lent themselves well to the solemnity and dignity of much high classical Greek art, such as scenes of a warrior's departure on an amphora attributed to the Achilles painter of about 440. Fewer mythological scenes are known from this period (though many may be lost); but notable is the appearance of more decorative scenes such as those by the Meidias painter that emerge later in the century with soft figures in ornate drapery often gesturing delicately, as on a hudria of circa 410 B.C.E. Some see in such florid images a form of escapism, as Athens' defeat in the Second Peloponnesian War loomed ever closer, but the style was to continue after Athens had recovered to some extent in the next century.

Later Classical Period: 400–323 B.C.E. During the fourth century, painting is held to have reached it highest stage with greater techniques in particular of shading for more convincing illusionistic effects. Certain philosophers, such as Plato, were at times suspicious of such deceptive illusionism, which supposedly played tricks on the senses. However, many famous artists enjoyed success and some friendly rivalry during the fourth century in which advances in technical virtuosity were self-consciously displayed by competing painters such as Apelles and Protogenes. A recently discovered royal tomb at Vergina has yielded rich finds including much gold metalwork in the form of caskets and wreaths, iron and gold armor, and elaborate frescoes of mythological and hunting scenes. Some scholars claim this is the tomb of Philip II of Macedon who died in 336 B.C.E., while others date it towards the end of the century. One of the tombs contains a painting of Hades, god of the Underworld, carrying Persephone off to his domain. Here a variety of colors, applied with swift, confident strokes was employed to depict this frenetic scene, in a flamboyant fashion emphasized by the hand gestures, flowing hair and drapery, and emotive facial expressions of the two figures. The general loss of large-scale painting from this era makes it difficult to understand its style satisfactorily, but something of fourth-century figured style can be gleaned from these sorts of frescoes (which may echo the style of Scopas) as well as surviving pottery and some brilliantly colored mosaics. In a hunt-scene mosaic, framed by elaborate vegetal decoration from the Macedonian capital, Pella, the figures are rendered frontally and in three-quarter view; the musculature of animals and men is well-highlighted by gradations of colour in the stones that are more closely packed than earlier for subtle effects. Many fourth-century pots continued the decorative style of the Meidias painter of the late fifth century, and often involved crowded scenes with figures gilded and painted in white, red, or yellow. In southern Italy scenes from Greek drama become popular. Images on coins continued fifth-century trends in a naturalistic direction, although Athens was not even in a position to mint silver until 393 B.C.E. Developments are evident in more minute attention to details, such as in the image of Zeus from Elis in the fourth century B.C.E.

Sources:

William R. Biers, *The Archaeology of Greece: An Introduction* (Ithaca, N.Y. & London: Cornell University Press, 1996).

John Boardman, *Greek Art* (London: Thames & Hudson, 1996).

Jeffrey M. Hurwit, *The Art and Culture of Early Greece: 1100–480 B.C.* (Ithaca, N.Y. & London: Cornell University Press, 1985).

Nigel Spivey, *Greek Art* (London: Phaidon, 1997).

RHETORIC

Speech and Argument. People trying to convince others must always have used, however unconsciously, regular techniques of speech and argument. To that extent, rhetoric—the study of persuasive speaking—must far predate the earliest Greek texts. Yet, as a more formal discipline, with defined teachers and a consciously formulated body of knowledge to transmit, scholars can trace its beginnings to Sicily in the first half of the fifth century B.C.E. Aristotle tells us that, with the end of the tyrannies there at that time, and the subsequent rush of litigation in courts that were now free, the first teachers of rhetoric began to offer their services to citizens who wished to learn public speaking (by Greek law litigants were obliged to represent themselves in court). Aristotle actually regarded the philosopher Empedocles of Acragas as the founder of rhetoric, while other sources name the shadowy figures Tisias and Corax of Syracuse as among the first to be involved in the new discipline. More is known about the Sophist Gorgias of Leontini, whose famous visit to Athens in 427 B.C.E. has been regarded by ancient and modern scholars alike as a real watershed in literary history, and whose distinctive style, with its wordplay and concern for balance, evidently influenced Athenian literature of this period.

Impact. Gorgias brought with him a theory as well as a practice, although it is not clear how far it is correct to separate the two in the fifth century; his instruction may have been based on little more than getting his pupils to learn set speeches of an easily adaptable nature. Indeed, it has even been maintained that rhetoric as a word and concept belongs to the fourth century, not the fifth. Even if that were so, it would still be the case that what we regard as formal rhetoric begins to have an enormous influence on the field of literature in the last quarter of the fifth century B.C.E. in Athens. Then the first publication of speeches in written form took place, after which the requirements of the court and the assembly began to dominate much literary art, especially tragedy: no tragedies from the fourth century survive, but Aristotle's passing remarks in his *Poetics* (after 335 B.C.E.) make it clear that this tendency was strengthened in them. In the end, it can be argued that rhetoric ultimately damaged Greek literature, in particular poetry, just as, centuries later, it was to alter Latin literature radically around the beginning of the first century C.E. However, this ignores two crucial facts: it is precisely the fourth century B.C.E., when rhetorical instruction was well established, that has been regarded as the high point of Greek prose; and rhetorical theory had a significant impact on the lit-

Beaten bronze figures of Apollo, Artemis, and Leto from the temple of Apollo at Dreros on Crete, circa 700 B.C.E. (National Archaeological Museum, Athens (1)/photo TAP)

erary theory of the fifth century. However unappealing its excesses, the theory and practice of formal oratory profoundly shaped much of Classical Greek literature.

Source:

George Kennedy, *The Art of Persuasion in Greece* (Princeton: Princeton University Press, 1963).

SATYR PLAYS

Origins. Aristotle implies that Satyrs—men dressed up as the mythical hybrids who combined human with animal features—were associated with the origins of Tragedy. However all available evidence suggests that Tragedy actually predates the Satyr play as a formal dramatic type. The first Satyr plays are attributed to the obscure figure of Pratinas of Phleius, who seems to have been a contemporary of Aeschylus; certainly, Satyr plays were fully established by the time dramatic records begin in 472 B.C.E. Those records indicate that, during the period of extant Greek tragedy, tragedians at Athens' major dramatic festival were required to present one Satyr play as well as three tragedies; in most cases these four plays were not related narratively to each other. Scholars know of only one exception to this requirement: in 438 B.C.E., Euripides produced for his fourth play the tragedy *Alcestis,* which admittedly handles a variety of themes which seem to have been common in Satyr plays. Only one complete Satyr play survives, Euripides' *Cyclops,* but there are several hundred lines—perhaps about half—of Sophocles' *Trackers,* and many fragments of other plays.

Mythological Setting. The defining quality of the Satyr play was a chorus of twelve Satyrs, led by their father, Silenus, who seems to have had a freedom on stage unknown to members of tragic choruses. Often these choruses were transported to mythical scenarios in quite original ways: the *Cyclops* is loosely based on Book 9 of Homer's *Odyssey* (circa eighth–seventh centuries B.C.E.), featuring Odysseus' famous meeting with that monster, but in which there is no hint of the presence of the Satyrs who are central to Euripides' play. This regular mythological setting distinguishes Satyr plays sharply from contemporary comedy, and brings it closer to tragedy, which invariably dealt with myth. In fact, the relationship with tragedy is another characteristic feature of the genre, and one ancient critic went so far as to describe Satyr drama as "Tragedy at play." Essentially, Satyr plays set up a simple contrast between the subhuman chorus of satyrs and the actors, who seem to be drawn rather from the serious and (in some ways) noble world of tragedy.

Pronomos Vase. This contrast is evident in the first place in the quite different appearances of the two groups. The best illustration of fifth century B.C.E. drama, the Pronomos Vase (so called after the named central musician on it), is in fact an illustration of the cast of a Satyr play, and lets one see immediately the difference between the stage-naked Satyrs, equipped with animal tails and erect phalloi, and the ornately dressed actors. Again, the masks on the vase have a story to tell: the members of the Satyr chorus have characteristically ugly masks, with snub noses and pointy ears (in marked contrast to the real faces of the chorus members), while those of the actors are dignified and seem to be similar to those of contemporary tragedy. The contrast shows itself linguistically as well: in *Cyclops* the language of Odysseus is the language of tragedy, both in meter and vocabulary, while the other characters use colloquialisms and metrical freedoms found in comedy. Yet, perhaps the most important contrast is in his behavior, which is deliberately emphasized as being of a "noble and tragic" kind. Several times in the play Euripides goes out of his way to have Odysseus voice concepts of honor that clash ludicrously with the general baseness of the satyrs, who show enthusiasm mainly for sex and drink, and exhibit cowardice and treachery in the course of the play.

Hospitality and Morality. *Cyclops* seems to have been quite typical of Satyr plays in the sort of themes it handled. The presence of an ogre, the oppression and ultimate liberation of the satyrs, the importance of hospitality—all these crop up regularly in the fragments of other Satyr plays. The themes are simple ones, and the genre seems to have been a pretty simple one too, with an uncomplicated morality and a generally rollicking tone, well suited to one side of its most common hero, Herakles. Not only did these plays remind Athenians where Tragedy had originated, but they provided a pleasing contrast and relief after the solemnity and angst that characterize the far more complex world of tragedy.

Source:

David F. Sutton, *The Greek Satyr Play* (Meisenheim am Glan: Hain, 1980).

SCULPTURE

Late Geometric Period: 800–700 B.C.E. Human and animal figures are found in sculpture of the late Geometric period, often in either a funerary context or as dedications made at Panhellenic sanctuaries at Olympia and Delphi. Elegant ivory figures are known, such as an Attic model from the Kerameikos cemetery of about 720 B.C.E., which modifies rounder, fatter Eastern prototypes. Small bronze images have been found, which sometimes echo the style of Geometric vase painting in their elongation and stylized proportions, such as a horse dedications found at Olympia, or various warrior figures. As may be the case with Geometric painting, the impact of myth is felt in some of these figurines; encounters between male figures and monsters such as a centaur or the minotaur are known. Metalwork of a different kind also existed during this period, namely bronze tripods (three-legged cauldrons) dedicated at Olympia; and in Attica gold earrings, brooches, and decorative bands have been found in graves dating to the 800s B.C.E.

Early Archaic Period: 700–600 B.C.E. Of the changes that took place in Greek art during the seventh century, so many have been linked to the influence of areas like Assyria, the Levant, and Egypt that the first fifty years is known as the Orientalizing period. There were important developments such as the return of large-scale stone sculpture and architecture, and new, fantastical images in painting and metalwork in Greek art at this time. Corinth, which did not have a strong local tradition of Geometric painting, emerged as the leading innovator and exporter in pottery, and was only replaced by Attica towards the end of the century. Among the new images of Eastern origin is the griffin—a winged creature that has a bird-like head, serpent's neck, and lion's body.

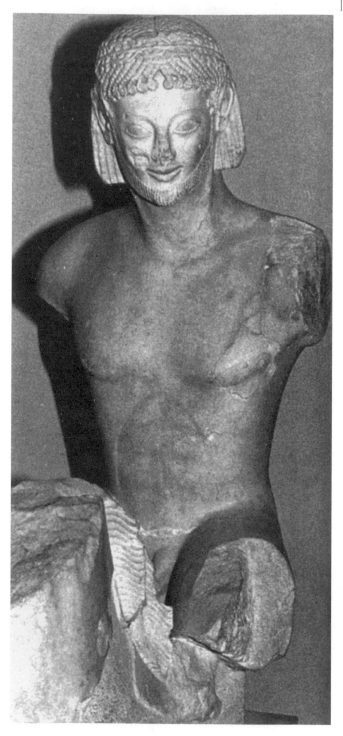

The Rampin Horseman, circa 540 B.C.E. (Acropolis 590, head in Louvre, 3104. Photo: Jeffrey M Hurwit)

Bronze griffin-heads, once connected to cauldrons dedicated at Olympia and made in the early 600s, have been discovered as well as griffin-headed pitchers from the Cyclades.

Bronze Statuettes. Innovations in sculpture are evident in three bronze statuettes from Dreros in Crete, found at the temple of Apollo. The tallest figure is the male, usually identified as the god, which stands eighty centimeters high, and is significantly larger than eighth-century figurines. Two female figures with him are understood to be the god's mother, Leto, and his sister, Artemis. The figures were made by a method known as *sphyrelaton*, which means they were hammered from separate sheets of bronze that were then nailed to a wooden core that defined their shape. Here they contrast to other known figurines that were made from molten bronze poured into hollow casts. According to ancient sources, early cult statues of gods, called *xoana*, were made of wood and may have been life size as early as the eighth century B.C.E.; but none have survived. Early seventh-century sculpture, however, sometimes attained life-size dimensions in durable material like stone. The Nikandre statue is an early example from Delos from about 660 B.C.E., and it has a dedicatory inscription. Although her features are badly worn, she has characteristics known as "Daedalic"—named after the first human artist of Greek mythology, Daedalus. (Such features are clearer on a smaller statue of about 640 B.C.E., known as the Auxerre goddess after where she was found.) Daedalic characteristics include a frontal pose, a U-shaped face, low forehead, and heavy wiglike hair that often falls into four tresses or is lined horizontally. These statues were painted brightly (traces have been found on the Auxerre goddess), and many were relief statues—attached to a background such as a building or altar. Over time these features varied and led to the famous style of Archaic statues of youths and maidens.

A HOMERIC SIMILE FOR AN ARTISAN

When Athena rejuvenates and embellishes Odysseus for his first meeting with Nausicaa, the goddess's handiwork is compared to that of a skilful artisan:

Then Athena, daughter of Zeus, made him seem taller for the eye to behold, and thicker, and on his head she arranged the curling locks that hung down like hyacinthine petals. And as when a master craftsman overlays gold on silver, and he is a clever one who was taught by Hephaestus and Pallas Athena in art complete, and grace is on every work he finishes, so Athena gilded with grace his head and shoulders, and he went a little aside and sat by himself on the seashore; and the girl looked on him in wonder.

Source: Homer, *Odyssey* 6.229–237.

The figure of a seer from the east pediment of the temple of Zeus at Olympia, circa 460 B.C.E.
(Photo: Hirmer Verlag GmbH, Munich)

Middle and Later Archaic Periods: 600–480 B.C.E. One of the most important legacies of Archaic Greek art is the development of free-standing sculptures of aristocratic youths and maidens, known as a *kouros* and *korê* respectively. Sometimes accompanied by inscriptions in poetic meters, these statues were often funeral markers, or else were public dedications made at a sanctuary to celebrate the subject's achievements. The making of the *kouros* type in stone and marble was a slow and expensive business aimed at an aristocratic clientele. It begins around 600 B.C.E., one example being the so-called "New York *kouros*" from Attica, whose stiff frontal pose, with arms his hanging down at the sides sets the pattern for later *kouroi*; bronze was also used toward the end of the sixth century. This style clearly owes something to Egyptian models, but there are some important Greek innovations here. Firstly the Greek statue is free-standing and seems to suggest the potential for walking, while the Egyptian is still embedded in its block; second, the *kouros* is naked (although sometimes might wear a choker); and third, the *kouros's* arms are usually carved free of his body, suggesting the potential for movement or variety of pose which eventually takes place in Greek sculpture. The musculature of the early *kouros* is initially not as naturalistic as that of his Egyptian predecessors, but becomes more so over time. Differences in rendering of the physique over time are clear when one compares the New York *kouros* with the Anavysos *kouros* (called Kroisos), made circa 530 B.C.E., and the *kouros* known as

Aristodidos, made about 500 B.C.E., whose arms are partly raised. Proportions of the body are altered, and sometimes appear less schematic and more naturalistic in an idealized sense. As celebrations of aristocratic virtue these statues tended to stick to a formula in showing the youth in an idealized beauty and pose, with the typical "Archaic smile." However, others show their subjects riding horses, such as the Rampin Horseman, dedicated on the Athenian Acropolis; made circa 540, this style introduces some action and breaks the strict frontality of the pose.

Maidens. *Korai* also had aristocratic associations, being made from similarly expensive materials such as marble. These maidens, however, wore clothes painted in bright colors, sometimes had head gear, stood with their feet together, and sometimes offered the viewer an object such as a pomegranate. Facial features become less schematic over time, although the Archaic smile is evident in many. Also figures sometimes become fuller, and sculptors show variation in the depiction of drapery and clothing, as evident when comparing the Berlin *Korê* of circa 570 with the Peplos *Korê* of circa 540 and the Euthydikos *Korê* of circa 490, whose pouting expression differs from the smile of other *korai*. Both *kouroi* and *korai* were widely produced in Attica; but, as democracy replaced the tyranny in the region in 509–508 B.C.E. and older aristocratic values were challenged, their production is rarer late in the sixth century, and seems to stop around 480 B.C.E.

Korê from the Acropolis, circa 490 B.C.E. (Akropolis Museum, Athens)

Early and High Classical Periods: 480–400 B.C.E. In free-standing sculpture from the early fifth century the sense of movement and implied vitality is enhanced through the *contrapposto* pose where weight is shifted onto one leg in figures such as the Kritian Boy, a dedication of circa 480 B.C.E., which seems more rounded than earlier kouroi. Implied movement becomes more obvious in some early Classical sculptures such as the splendid bronze god (Zeus or Poseidon) hurling his weapon, dated circa 460 B.C.E. found off Artemisium. Although his sweeping arms and slightly bent legs convey a sense of motion, his musculature does not fully reflect the nature of his action; the same seems to apply to Myron's famous "Discus Thrower," and to some of the metopes on the temple of Zeus depicting Heracles at his labors. This new approach has led to such sculpture being known as part of the "Severe Style," where there is some apparent attempt at restraint or idealism in depicting the figures. Some groups of sculptures from this time combine various attempts at such restraint with more realistic touches, such as the pedimental sculptures of the temple of Zeus at Olympia. In some instances one sees Lapiths grimacing in pain when attacked by centaurs, or remaining relatively unperturbed, while Apollo remains serenely in command at the center; on the other

pediment one sees an old man, vexed with foreboding, as he gazes on Pelops and Oenomaus, who are about to embark on a deadly chariot race.

Famed Sculptor. Polyclitus of Argos is, after Pheidias, the most famous Greek sculptor active in the second half of the fifth century B.C.E. Some trends evident in the Severe Style are taken further by Polyclitus, most notably in his "Spear-bearer" or *Doruphoros,* known to us only in copies, but originally a bronze, of circa 445 B.C.E. The statue depicts a young man of toned, muscular physique in a fully balanced *contrapposto* pose in which his left leg and right arm are relaxed, and right leg and left arm tensed; this is further emphasized in diagonals formed by his knees, hips and shoulders. The details of this pose became enormously influential throughout antiquity. Polyclitus wrote a treatise called the *Canon,* probably in relation to the statue, which outlined a series of numerical proportions for the body so that each part related to the other (finger to palm, palm to wrist, these to forearm, etc.) as a way of attaining "perfection." It is interesting to compare the *Doruphoros* to two original Greek bronzes of roughly the same period, known as the Riace bronzes, depicting two warriors, possibly from a victory monument; some even ascribe them to Pheidias. While there are similarities in pose, the more animated

"Hermes and Infant Dionysus," a sculpture attributed
to Praxiteles, but possibly a fourth-century B.C.E.
copy (Archaeological Museum, Olympia)

metopes. Some figures appear reminiscent of the Severe Style in the musculature and impassive facial expressions of Lapiths, while others show more advanced treatments of anatomy, and include flourishes such as elaborately carved drapery that gives certain figures an almost balletic appearance. The Parthenon frieze is special not only in spanning over 160 meters, but in showing humans in procession on the same level with gods, rather than mythological scenes. Interpretations remain conjectural, but the scene is usually read as some statement of civic pride, in which the Athenian citizenry is comprised of fine physical specimens, mostly in their youthful prime with uniformly solemn facial expressions; it again underscores the idealizing nature of the images. Of the pedimental sculptures the eastern figures are better preserved where the birth of Athena is depicted in the company of the Olympians. A sense of unity to this event is neatly achieved by having the heads of the horses and charioteer of the rising sun emerge in the left corner, while the moon and her horses sink in the right. The reclining figure at the left, usually identified as Dionysus or Herakles is rendered with greater naturalism and monumentality than, for instance, the old man on the temple of Zeus at Olympia; and in the female figures to the right spectacular effects in their drapery have been achieved by cutting more deeply into the marble than usual to suggest volume and complex folds. Such features further testify to the grand conception of the Parthenon, largely achieved through meticulous attention to detail. The influence of the style of the Parthenon sculptures is evident in parts of the frieze of the temple to Apollo at Bassai which depicts the centauromachy, and some relief-sculpture funerary monuments which appear late in the fifth century.

Later Classical Period: 400–323 B.C.E. Fourth-century sculpture is not radically different from High Classical in style, but tends to involve different subjects, such as personifications of "Peace" by Cephisodotus or "Opportunity" by Lysippus. Children are also rendered more naturally, and the gods appear less monumentally grand than before. One example is the marble "Hermes and Infant Dionysus" by Praxiteles (active circa 370–330), which may be an original by the master himself, or reworked in the Roman era, as the lower legs have been reconstructed. As an infant, the wine god is depicted with greater realism and not so much as a miniature adult; the folds in the robe beneath him are deeper and more complex than is usual in fifth-century sculpture, but clearly owe much to the deeply cut robes on some Parthenon pedimental figures. Hermes' pose develops the contrapposto pose to be now more languid and relaxed, to involve what is known as the Praxitelean "S" curve, with head, torso, and legs inclined at different angles, as in another statue by him, called "Apollo the Lizard Slayer." One of the most famous of all ancient statues was Praxiteles' Aphrodite of Cnidus, which depicted the goddess nude, emerging from her bath, and was designed to be seen from all possible angles in a circular shrine; the "frontality" and even four-square views of earlier sculpture was

facial gestures of the warriors and their thick beards give them a more forceful presence than the idealized *Doruphoros;* this description seems especially so for the tautly muscled Riace A, whose grimace and woolly hair make him comparable to a centaur. Idealization and serenity of expression were not necessarily universal aims in Greek sculpture of this time, and certain fifth-century writers speak of the emotive powers that large-scale artworks were perceived to have on the viewer.

Parthenon Sculptures. Variety of style is evident in the Parthenon metopes depicting the fight between Lapiths and centaurs that survive more abundantly than its other

The Acropolis in Athens: the Parthenon is the large structure to the right, while the Propylaia, the grandiose entrance, is on the left. The temple of Athena Nikê is in front of the Propylaia (Archivo Iconografico SA)

well and truly broken by this time. She is less languid than the Hermes but still shown almost as if in an unguarded moment. The statue made a great impact as one of the first monumental nude female sculptures, and, although the sensuality of the original is probably lost to us, it became the subject of many stories in antiquity about young men who became desperately besotted with it. A particularly emotive style in sculpture is associated with Scopas, who was architect of the temple of Athena Alea at Tegea, and one of the sculptors who worked on the Mausoleum. Pedimental sculptures of this temple have been found which seem to conform to the style attributed to Scopas by ancient writers, which often involved twisting torsoes and deep set eyes and agitated expressions. Many significant innovations were brought to fourth century sculpture by Lysippus (active circa 370–320 B.C.E.), whose works are mostly known to us through Roman copies. The proportions of the human figure and block-like features typical of Polyclitus's sculpture, were varied by these innovations of Lysippus, as in his famous, originally bronze, "Apoxuomenos" (or "Athlete scraping oil from himself") where the figure is taller and leaner and extends his arm out boldly into the viewer's space. As Alexander's official court sculptor, Lysippus' style was distinctive for depicting the king gazing intently under a mane of leonine hair. A couple of fourth-century male bronzes have survived, which seem to parallel features of Lysippus' and Praxiteles' styles; for instance, "The Marathon Boy" in his languid pose, softly moulded physique, and in the action of his arms which adds to the three dimensionality of the figure. Grave monuments of the fourth century show noteworthy developments in being more deeply cut than fifth-century models, with emotive pathos suggested by various means. In the Ilissos relief of circa 340 the central figure gazes out directly at the viewer, accompanied by the young boy crouching and weeping behind him,

A metope from the south side of the Parthenon showing Lapiths battling a centaur, 440s B.C.E.
(British Museum, London)

while he is contemplated by a mournful old man, perhaps his teacher or father.

Sources:
William R. Biers, *The Archaeology of Greece: An Introduction* (Ithaca, N.Y. & London: Cornell University Press, 1996).

John Boardman, *Greek Art* (London: Thames & Hudson, 1996).

Jeffrey M. Hurwit, *The Art and Culture of Early Greece: 1100–480 B.C.* (Ithaca, N.Y. & London: Cornell University Press, 1985).

Nigel Spivey, *Greek Art* (London: Phaidon, 1997).

TRAGEDY

Origins. The origins of tragedy were much debated by the ancient Greeks themselves. The Greek word *tragôidia* means literally "goat-song." Some scholars believe this term was used because tragedy originally involved a competition for the prize of a goat, or that tragedy was originally performed by humans who dressed as goatlike creatures. The latter explanation seems to be the one favored by Aristotle, who implies that tragedy began as a dithyramb (a type of choral song) sung by men dressed as satyrs. Mere choral singing, however, could never be equated with drama as such, and while there is some evidence that these choirs began in the Peloponnese, it was in Athens that the decisive move was made which established European drama. Tradition gives the name of the first individual actor, who stood out as separate from the chorus, as Thespis, and ascribes his first success to around 534 B.C.E. Thespis remains an extremely shadowy figure, but his status as the first actor was taken for granted in the ancient world; the Greek word for actor, *hupokritês* (hypocrite), indicates either "interpreter" or "answerer," thus showing that the actor was a feature added to something—a

---

THE SEDUCTION

The fifth-century Sophist Gorgias of Leontini, contemporary with many great developments in painting and sculpture, refers to the seductive power of artworks to explain Helen's attraction to Paris:

But when painters perfectly complete out of many colours and many objects a single object and form, they delight the sight. The making of figures and the fashioning of statues provides something pleasant for the eyes. Thus some things naturally give distress and others pleasure to the sight. Many things create in many people love and desire of many actions and bodies. So, if Helen's eye, pleased by Paris' body, transmitted an eagerness and striving of love to her soul, what is surprising?

Source: Gorgias of Leontini, *Praise of Helen*, pp. 18–19.

chorus—already there. The common question "What was the chorus in a Greek tragedy for?" wrongly approaches ancient drama from the modern practice and treats the actors as the essence of it; it is rather the presence of actors on the ancient stage that needs to be explained.

Essential Features. Not until about sixty years after Thespis' successful debut was there any real knowledge of the form of tragedy. The oldest surviving Greek tragedy is Aeschylus' *Persians*, produced in 472 B.C.E. Remarkably for a tragedy, this play takes as its subject matter not mythology, but recent history—the defeat of the Persian expedition sent against Greece a mere eight years before. Yet, its setting in the Persian capital, far remote from Athens, arguably gives it a distance from the audience that is usually accomplished by a story set in mythical times in Greece itself. Aeschylus' *Persians* shows already all of the features that we regard as typical of Greek tragedy, but this is perhaps not surprising, as all of the surviving Greek tragedies were written within a period of one man's lifetime (less than seventy years), and all were written by Athenians.

Structure. Tragedies typically begin with a *prologos* (prologue), which includes everything up to the entry of the chorus. The initial choral ode was called the *parodos* (entry). Subsequent choral odes were called *stasima* (standing songs)—not that the chorus stood still for these, but because they were sung after the chorus had reached their positions in the theater. The parts of the play between these stasima were called *epeisodia*—whence our word *episode*—which means "additions." The final part of the tragedy, that is everything between the last stasimon and the exit of all performers was called the *exodos* (exit). Two final pieces of terminology relate to singing by actors rather than the chorus. A *monôidia* is a solo song, and a *kommos* is literally a dirge but is used more generally in a loose sense of singing that is shared between the chorus and an actor.

Relationship. Formally, the most striking thing about Greek tragedy is the relationship between the chorus and the actors. The chorus typically represents a community over which one of the actors has power, invariably of a political kind. In *Persians* choruses naturally represent the citizens left behind when the army marched against Greece, and their defeated king, Xerxes, is the main actor of the tragedy. In Sophocles' *Oedipus Rex*, the chorus stands in the same relationship of subjects to the protagonist, while in his *Ajax* the chorus represents the sailors serving under the eponymous hero's command. In some of Euripides' plays such as

A detail from a fourth-century B.C.E. vase showing a scene from the *Eumenides*, the tragic play composed by Aeschylus (British Museum, London)

Alcestis (438 B.C.E.) and *Bacchae* (after 406 B.C.E.) the chorus is the political subordinate of one of the main characters, but many have felt that his essentially domestic interest in the heroes of mythology renders this political relationship less organically connected to his tragedies.

Role of the Chorus. Given this position of the chorus members, it is not surprising that their usual role is to react and to comment on their superiors; it is unusual for them to initiate action, and their helplessness is one of the things which marks out Greek tragedy as a nonrealistic medium. This essentially reactive and emotional role of the chorus is also expressed in performance by the restriction of united choral utterance to the sung (or at least chanted) rather than the spoken word. The sung/ spoken dichotomy by no means corresponds with a simple chorus/actors one, for actors themselves sometimes sang monodes, but all utterances of the chorus as such were sung or at least chanted to music. Their participation in the less elevated poetry of spoken drama was achieved usually through a single representative speaker, the *koruphaios*. The same situation occurs with dance— individual characters seem to have performed occasional dances in Greek tragedy, but this form of expression was far more commonly used by the chorus. The regular choral odes that punctuate every Greek tragedy were delivered by a chorus that danced as well as sang, although we have no knowledge of the choreography and hardly any of the music. Only the words of these songs survive, but they can be distinguished from the spoken dialogue of the plays by several signs. They are arranged, for instance, in quite different metrical patterns, they allow some features from the Doric dialect, and they also allow greater grammatical freedom than the spoken poetry. However, it is essentially a matter of degree: the spoken poetry of tragedy itself was already quite distinct from the language of prose and everyday conversation. The conventions of Greek tragedy allow situations to be presented from two quite different perspectives—the emotional, lyric perspective of the sung word, and the more rational medium of what was spoken. In fact, many passages show just this contrast, and it is a mistake to think that a character's change of mood is always due to a realistic representation by the poet of fickleness in the character; often, what has been presented is the character's own reaction to a situation, first emotionally (through lyric), and then rationally (through speech).

Interaction. Distinctive as the relationship between chorus and actors is, nevertheless, the interaction between the actors dominates the action in tragedy from the second half of the fifth century, that is to say, the tragedy of Sophocles and Euripides. Deeply imbued with contemporary philosophy and rhetoric, these playwrights produced dramas which opened themselves up as foci for debate about urgent issues which still matter to us today—above all questions of family obligation, of

justice in the state, and of humans' relationship to the supernatural. The format of tragedy allowed exactly balanced speeches to be presented, arguing opposite sides of a particular case. So interested were the tragedians in these abstract debates that what we regard as considerations of character are often ignored: the challenge seems to have been to write the most convincing speech possible, not to make its utterance by any particular person believable. At a more basic level, considerable doubt has been thrown on the idea that our modern notion of character really corresponds to ancient Greek perceptions of human behavior.

Production and Finance. In the fifth and fourth centuries B.C.E. in Greece, the production of tragedy formed part of a regular cycle of religious festivals; there were never more than a few days a year, even in Athens, when one could attend the theater. The most important dramatic festival in Greece, for which all the surviving Greek tragedies were written, was the Great Dionysia in Athens. Held over a few days in early spring, the festival involved production of tragedies, comedies, and of choral songs for dithyrambs. The tragedians produced three tragedies each, as well as a satyr play (a sort of comic postlude with a chorus of satyrs), and the plays did not need to be narratively related to each other. The festivals were intensely competitive, and tragedians were judged by a panel of citizens on the basis of their four works, not for any particular one of them. Prizes for the playwrights were paid for by the state, as was the cost of the actors; the more significant cost of equipping and training the chorus, however, would be met as a form of taxation by a wealthy citizen, who stood to gain kudos and (importantly in a democracy like Athens) popularity for successful productions.

Outdoor Theaters. The actual productions had many features distinguishing them from their distant descendants in today's theaters. The theaters were often vast (for instance, tens of thousands could fit into the main theater at Athens), always outdoors, and only used when daylight permitted. In the great age of drama in the fifth century B.C.E., Athens did not have a stone theater, and the audiences sat on wooden benches, surrounding a circular *orkhêstra* (dancing area). Here the chorus performed during the plays. The actors themselves must have used the orchestra as well for at least some of the time, although there may have been a slightly raised stage for them on the other side of the orkhêstra from the audience; it is certainly out of the question that there was any high stage at this point in history. Behind the actors was a wooden stage building with at least one door, usually representing a palace, through which actors (perhaps also the chorus on occasion) could enter and exit the acting area.

Face Masks. Both chorus and actors wore full face masks. Whatever their origin, masks had several practical advantages for ancient drama. They rendered the identity of characters more visible from a distance, and

OEDIPUS BLINDS HIMSELF

He rips off her brooches, the long gold pins
holding her robes—and lifting them high,
looking straight up into the points,
he digs them down the sockets of his eyes, crying, 'You,
you'll see no more the pain I suffered, all the pain I caused!
Too long you looked on the ones you never should have seen,
blind to the ones you longed to see, to know! Blind
from this hour on! Blind in the darkness—blind!'
His voice like a dirge, rising, over and over
raising the points, raking them down his eyes.
And at each stroke blood spurts from the roots,
splashing his beard, a swirl of it, nerves and clots—
black hail of blood pulsing, gushing down.

Source: Sophocles, *Oedipus Rex,* 1268–1279 (translated by Robert Fagles)

above all they allowed an actor to play more than one role. For Greek tragedy restricts itself to the use of three actors—that is to say, there are never more than three speaking actors on stage at any point in the drama, but one actor may well play several roles in any particular play. No masks survive from this period, but contemporary vase illustrations indicate that tragic masks were simple and unexpressive.

Stage Machinery. The general and unsurprising lack of technical sophistication in the production of Greek tragedy in the Classical Period (480–323 B.C.E.) is also illustrated by the stage machinery involved. Foremost were the *mêkhanê* (crane), sometimes used for the appearance of deities from on high, and the *ekkuklêma* (trolley), which was used to display corpses, the result of violent action offstage. It is a peculiarity of Greek tragedy that violent death is hardly ever portrayed in front of the audience; rather, the convention is for violence to be reported (sometimes in gruesome detail) by a messenger, and then for the resultant corpses to be displayed to the audience. With such limited means at their disposal, modern readers may well wonder how moving and entertaining were the performances of ancient tragedy. The truth seems to be that their real power lay in the scripts themselves, written in the one form of poetry in which Athens really excelled. The scripts of the plays were studied intensively for centuries after any thought of performing them had disappeared, and even during the Classical Period Aristotle, who must have witnessed countless performances himself, declared that the proper effect of tragedy could be experienced just through reading.

Source:

John Ferguson, *A Companion to Greek Tragedy* (Austin: University of Texas Press, 1972).

Arthur Wallace Pickard-Cambridge, *The Dramatic Festivals of Athens* (London: Oxford University Press, 1968).

SIGNIFICANT PEOPLE

AESCHYLUS

525/4-456/5 B.C.E.
TRAGIC DRAMATIST

Claim to Fame. Aeschylus is the earliest of the three Greek tragedians, whose work has survived in more than fragmentary form, and so is the first extant European dramatist. If he was not the first tragedian, he seems to have been the founder of what is recognized as the distinctive genre of tragedy, in respect of its production and its dramatic possibilities. Born of an aristocratic Athenian family, he took part in the battles of Marathon (490 B.C.E.) and Salamis (480 B.C.E.) against the invading Persians. The report and consequences of the Greek victory at Salamis are the focus of his first surviving play, *Persians* (472 B.C.E.). His other surviving plays are *Seven Against Thebes* (467), *Suppliant Women* (463), and a trilogy consisting of *Agamemnon, Libation Bearers,* and *Eumenides* called *Oresteia* (458). The authenticity of a seventh play, *Prometheus Bound,* is in dispute. The last two years of his life were spent in Sicily, at the court of the tyrant Hieron; the ancient biographical tradition imagines this move as occasioned by feelings of rejection at the hands of the Athenians, but it can be explained simply by a desire for honor and more concrete recognitions of his genius. According to the traditional account, Aeschylus died after a passing eagle dropped a tortoise on his head.

Distinctive Art Form. The ancients recognized in Aeschylus the true founder of tragedy as they knew it: the grandeur which he seems to have introduced, and his crucial innovation of a second speaking actor (thus allowing interaction between individuals, not just between one individual and a chorus), made possible all the most distinctive features of the art form. Although by the end of the fifth century B.C.E. he seemed already formal and remote, his poetry retained (and still retains) a solemn grandeur and power unequalled in ancient lit-erature. Moreover, his dramatic skill in the arrangement of scenes and introduction of characters has been rightly recognized as an essential part of his talent, although details of this ability are often only conjectural (for no stage directions from ancient plays survive). However, both his poetic and dramaturgical skill are always at the service of the great moral themes that bind his plays together, nowhere more impressively shown than in his *Oresteia* trilogy, in which the eternal questions of justice, human freedom, and destiny are worked out over several generations of the family of Agamemnon. The narratively connected trilogy—which was often used by Aeschylus but perhaps never by Euripides and Sophocles—allowed the playwright to examine the slow working out of these issues and to keep his focus on these themes, rather than on the particular stories of the individuals involved.

Sources:

John Herington, *Aeschylus* (New Haven: Yale University Press, 1986).

Marsh H. McCall, *Aeschylus: A Collection of Critical Essays* (Englewood Cliffs, N.J.: Prentice-Hall, 1972).

APELLES OF COLOPHON

FLOURISHED FOURTH CENTURY B.C.E.
PAINTER

A Royal Favorite. Apelles of Colophon was taught by Ephorus and Pamphilus of Sicyon, who put painting and drawing at the head of the educational curriculum of free-born boys, an innovation later followed by other Greek *poleis* (city-states). Apelles was the most celebrated of all ancient painters, at least by Pliny. He produced two volumes of written work on painting; and, while nothing of these survives, it is likely that Pliny used them as a source in his account of Apelles' achievements. As did Lysippus, Apelles enjoyed the unique patronage of Alexander, and only he was permitted to paint the royal portrait; he also painted Alexander's father, Philip II. Anecdotes connect him as well with fellow painter Protogenes, and Ptolemy I (one of Alexander's generals and successors). His image of Alexander wielding a thunderbolt in the temple of Artemis at Ephesus became famous, but seemed to have incurred the disapproval of Lysippus; other depictions by Apelles of Alexander included a triumph in which the king leads a personification of War as a bound captive, and another showing him with Victory, Castor, and Pollux. Other generals of Alexander painted by Apelles include Neoptolemos, Antigonos, and Archelaos.

Nature. He was reputed to be such a fine painter of horses that they neighed only at his paintings, and his *Nude Hero*, says Pliny, challenged Nature herself. His painting of *Calumny* is described at length in ancient accounts, and is said to allegorize his own experience in being slandered at the court of Ptolemy and nearly losing his life for it. (The ancient description influenced Botticelli to paint a version in the Renaissance.)

Aphrodite. Apelles' most famous work was *Aphrodité Anaduomenê* (Aphrodite Rising from the Sea), painted in Cos, then moved to Rome and universally admired; according to some, Phryne, Praxiteles' mistress, was the model. His attempt to repeat the image was cut short by death, brought on, it was said, by the envy of Nature herself. Apelles prided himself on the *kharis* (grace) of his works which outdid even those of his rivals whose works he admired; and he claimed to know, unlike Protogenes, when to cease working on a picture. As a result of considerable theoretical calculations he was able to cover his paintings in the finest black glaze that muted excessively bright colors and accentuated the reflection of others.

Sources:
Franciscus Junius, *The Literature of Classical Art*, 2 volumes, edited and translated by Keith Aldrich, Philipp Fehl, and Raina Fehl (Berkeley: University of California Press, 1991).

J. J. Pollitt, *The Art of Ancient Greece: Sources and Documents* (Cambridge & New York: Cambridge University Press, 1990).

ARISTOPHANES

CIRCA 446–CIRCA 386 B.C.E.
POET

Comedy. The works of Aristophanes are the only surviving examples of fifth-century Attic comedy known as Old Comedy. His first play *Banqueters* was produced in 427 B.C.E., but is nonextant. The titles of his extant works are *Acharnians* (425), *Knights* (424), *Wasps* (422), *Peace* (421), *Birds* (414), *Lysistrata* (411), *Thesmophoriazousai* (411), *Frogs* (405), *Assemblywomen* (392), and *Wealth* (388); there is also *Clouds*, an incompletely revised and never performed version of his comedy of 423 B.C.E. The first two and *Frogs* are known to have won first prize in the Lênaia, and indeed *Frogs* was given the exceptional honor of a second performance and earned its author the prestige of a crown of sacred olive for its sage political advice. Although it is difficult to determine whether Athenians expected anything at all serious in the way of advice from Old Comedy, the reception of *Frogs* must count as some evidence that they were prepared to listen on occasion. The same judgment may be deduced from the traditions of legal action taken against comic poets in general and Aristophanes in particular. The suit brought by Cleon, the target of Aristophanes' lost second play, *Babylonians*, and extant *Knights*, only makes sense if the medium was not regarded as simply one for clowning.

Favorite Targets. The first nine plays were written during the catastrophic Second Peloponnesian War (431–404 B.C.E.) between Athens and Sparta, and Aristophanes consistently argues for peace in them: the parabasis allows the playwright a direct utterance of views not afforded to tragedians (who in any case did not deal with contemporary events). Elsewhere, favorite targets include populist politicians (such as Cleon), corrupting philosophers (Socrates in *Clouds*), and new-fangled tragedians (above all Euripides in *Thesmophoriazousai* and *Frogs*). Although he is superficially a conservative in his depiction of the triumph of simple, old-fashioned heroes (often to the discomfort of more sophisticated characters), he is, in one scholar's words, a playwright "deeply imbued with irreverence," and he frequently ridicules traditional views and values too. The surface hostility to innovation masks a profound debt to it: a contemporary comic poet coined the verb *euripidaristophanizein*—"to behave like Euripides and Aristophanes"—to suggest the identity of the comedian's targets and models. Later and friendlier critics also emphasized his innovation by presenting him as a writer who had advanced Old Comedy beyond the crude simplicity of his predecessors early in his career and, at its end, laid the foundation for New Comedy.

Source:
Angus Bowie, *Aristophanes: Myth, Ritual and Comedy* (Cambridge: Cambridge University Press, 1993).

EURIPIDES

CIRCA 484–407/406 B.C.E.
TRAGIC PLAYWRIGHT

Limited Popularity. Euripides is the youngest of the three surviving Greek tragedians. His work had far more influence on later drama than did the plays of Aeschylus and Sophocles, and survives in much greater quantity. He started to produce plays in 455 B.C.E., and first achieved victory in a dramatic contest in 441 B.C.E., but compared with Sophocles his plays were generally not popular in his own lifetime (he won only four other competitions), and the surly figure he cut in the ancient biographical tradition seems to be a reflection of this lack of affection felt for his work. A total of nineteen plays under his name have been preserved, including the only complete Satyr play, *Cyclops*. Of these works, the ones that can be dated are *Alcestis* (438 B.C.E.), *Medea* (431 B.C.E.), *Hippolytus* (428 B.C.E.), *Trojan Women* (415 B.C.E.), *Helen* (412 B.C.E.), and *Orestes* (408 B.C.E.). Little is known about the details of his life: he played a smaller role in public life than Sophocles, and the domestic anecdotes about marital unhappiness are clearly just inferences from his plays. Although he is frequently mentioned in the works of his contemporary Aristophanes, it is doubtful if anything factual about his life can be unearthed from that source, as the comic poet is clearly far more interested in the tragedies than the tragedian. Toward the end of his life he left Athens for the court of Archelaus of Macedonia and died there, according to an implausible story, after being attacked by a pack of royal hunting dogs.

Death of Tragedy. Euripides' work is harder to characterize than that of his fellow tragedians not only because it is much more extensively preserved, but also because it is far more rhetorical. As such it shows the influence of Euripides' contemporaries the Sophists, itinerant intellectuals who taught the art of rhetoric and fostered a sceptical and relativistic outlook. Euripides, "the philosopher of the stage" as he was known in the ancient world, often launches into dramatically inappropriate speculation (a peasant farmer in the *Electra* expatiates on the difficulty of picking the truly virtuous) which seems more at home with them. This overintellectualization of drama was the reason Aristophanes blamed Euripides for the "death of tragedy." Yet, some of the plots of his tragedies such as *Bacchae* (after 406 B.C.E.), *Hippolytus*, and *Medea* show an awareness of the wild, impersonal forces at work in human lives, which cannot be held in check by mere reason. He has been called both a rationalist and an irrationalist, both with justification.

Source:
David Kovacs, "Euripides," in *Ancient Greek Authors, Dictionary of Literary Biography,* volume 176, edited by Ward W. Briggs (Columbia, S.C.: Bruccoli Clark Layman/Detroit: Gale Research, 1997), pp. 146–155.

HERODOTUS

CIRCA 484–CIRCA 420 B.C.E.
HISTORIAN

Acute Observer. Regarded as the "Father of History," Herodotus wrote the first surviving work of history, a sprawling work essentially on the conflicts between Greeks and Persians, but containing a great deal of discursive material as well. Born in the cosmopolitan city of Halicarnassus on the Carian coast of what is now Turkey, Herodotus left for Samos due to political trouble and may not have returned. He was an inveterate traveller, visiting Egypt, Babylon and Thrace, and was always interested in recording foreign customs and beliefs. He visited Athens and seems to have been well received there: Sophocles wrote a poem for him, and his work left its impact on contemporary drama, both tragic and comic. He was one of the settlers of the panhellenic colony of Thurii in southern Italy (444/443 B.C.E.): events from 430 B.C.E., recorded in his history, give a *terminus post quem* for his death.

Inquiry. The Greek word *historiē*, with which Herodotus described his work, means "inquiry" rather than "record of past events." Motivated though he be by an almost Homeric desire to record the great deeds of the Greeks and barbarians, there is no hint of divine inspiration as the source of his *History of the Persian Wars* (circa late fifth century B.C.E.): the information is hard won, the result of relentless questioning and listening. Often he will not give his opinion on a question, but will record what accounts different sources give: in this respect he differs markedly from his successor Thucydides, but precisely for this reason his writing can be a more useful and transparent source for further investigation than that of the more scientific historian. The digressionary style of the narrative, which is constantly interrupted by entertaining anecdotes, is shown at its most extreme in his long discussion of Egypt in book 2, most of which is at best of tangential relevance to its supposed motivation, the Persian invasion of that country. Furthermore, although he delights in telling of military stratagems, he took no part in the battles he describes and shows no real understanding of warfare—again a contrast with Thucydides. Yet, the comparison, although inevitable, is not really fair: the political and military focus of so much historical writing, starting with the later historian, was clearly not Herodotus' main interest, and his ethnographical approach, his delight in the diversity and unity of humankind, does simply not allow such a narrow focus. Never afraid to step out of his own field of expertise, he seems to have been occasionally taken in by his guides and informants, and the impression of naiveté this leaves is reinforced by a faith in religious phenomena, such as clearly manipulated oracles, which often seems to modern readers (and must have seemed to some of his contemporaries) simpleminded. However, his achievement is impressive when one sees his religious views woven into the whole of his narrative, as for instance when the defeat of the Persian forces is presented as part of a coherent pattern of divine punishment for arrogance.

Sources:
J. Gould, *Herodotus* (New York: St. Martin's Press, 1989).

J. Redfield, "Herodotus the Tourist," *Classical Philology*, 80 (1985): 97–118.

HESIOD

FLOURISHED CIRCA EIGHTH CENTURY B.C.E.
POET

Significance. Along with Homer, Hesiod is the oldest extant Greek poet. Scholars have no clear evidence about his date, nor did the ancients: a much-debated topic was his chronological relationship with Homer, with many believing in Hesiod's priority. Yet, unlike Homer, Hesiod reveals something of his life and family in his poetry, and his is the first distinctively individual voice in European literature. Hesiod's father came from Cyme on the coast of Asia Minor and moved to the village of Ascra by Mt. Helicon in Boeotia. It was on the slopes of Helicon while he was shepherding that Hesiod claims the Muses appeared to him, gave him a laurel branch, and instructed him to sing. Of course he followed their command, and elsewhere tells us that he won a tripod in a singing competition held at a funeral at Chalcis. This story was later elaborated with the imaginative detail that his opponent on this occasion was Homer, and led to the composition, probably early in the fourth century B.C.E., of an account of the contest between the two great early poets of Greece. Hesiod had a brother called Perses, against whom he was engaged in some sort of litigation, perhaps on a matter of inheritance, and his pointed advice to his brother helps us see his social position as a poor peasant at the mercy of corrupt judges.

Truth. When the Muses told Hesiod that they could tell the truth as well as "lies like the truth"—a phase apparently lifted from Homer's description of Odysseus' words to his wife—they made it clear that there were different sorts of poetry, and that his job was to produce the true sort. The poems confidently ascribed to Hesiod—the *Theogony* and the *Works and Days*—differ radically from the Homeric *Iliad* and *Odyssey* (circa eighth–seventh centuries B.C.E.) in subject matter and in general outlook. The *Theogony* is an account of the creation of the world and the rise to power of the current generation of gods. Considerable similarity has been noted with Near Eastern "succession myths," some of which contain parallel motifs in the struggles between generations of gods and between the established gods and a monster. *Works and Days* is a didactic poem on farming, but contains much other material, not least on the nature of justice and the gods' concern for it. In this poem especially one gets a different viewpoint from the essentially aristocratic perspective of Homer: readers sense an ungallant misogyny, and learn about hard work, the weak position of the ordinary man in the face of corrupt power, and about a wavering faith in the divine justice that will set all this right.

Sources:

Richard Hamilton, *The Architecture of Hesiodic Poetry* (Baltimore: Johns Hopkins University Press, 1989).

Robert Lamberton, *Hesiod* (New Haven: Yale University Press, 1988).

Mary R. Lefkowitz, *The Lives of the Greek Poets* (Baltimore: Johns Hopkins University Press, 1981).

LYSIPPUS AND LYSISTRATUS

FLOURISHED FOURTH CENTURY B.C.E.
SCULPTORS

Brothers. Lysippus and Lysistratus were brothers from Sicyon, sculptors in bronze, and active circa 370-320 B.C.E. Lysistratus' main claim to fame was his innovative use of plaster casts from actual subjects as a basis for his portrait-making. Among his works was a famous statue of Melanippê. He also took casts of other statues, possibly for further use in his own workshop or as a saleable, easily reproducable commodity. Lysippus was prodigious in his output and made substantial innovations to standards of sculpture set by Polyclitus, by making his figures slenderer, giving them smaller heads, and aiming for a more naturalistic effect in rendering of details such as hair. His portrait of Alexander the Great with upturned penetrating gaze and head directed slightly to the left under a mane of wavy hair was so admired by its subject that Lysippus alone was given commission to sculpt the king's image.

Reproductions. Copies of bronze originals and detailed descriptions from ancient sources give an indication of his style. He sculpted many athletic and military figures which became dedications at Olympia and elsewhere; the Agias portrait, known to us today through a (possibly contemporary) copy, is a famous instance. Among his most well-known works was the *Apoxuomenos* (athlete scraping oil off himself), whose outstretched arms reaching out into the viewer's space broke with Polyclitan "block" statuary, and later became an object of obsession for the Roman emperor, Tiberius. In addition to various gods such as Dionysus, he sculpted Heracles many times, including a colossal form at Tarentum, a miniature (the so-called *Epitrapezios*, one-foot high), and the famous *Farnese Heracles* where the great hero leans exhausted on his club after completing his labours. His statue of *Kairos* (Opportunity) seems to have been allegorical, and depicted a lean youth with long hair in front and bald at the back, holding a razor to indicate his own fleeting presence. Lysippus' influence was particularly strong in the Hellenistic era (323–331 B.C.E.), and continued immediately in his school in the work of his sons and pupils, such as Euthycrates, Eutychides, Tisicrates, and Chares — the sculptor of the Colossus of Rhodes, another of the Seven Wonders of the World.

Sources:

Franciscus Junius, *The Literature of Classical Art*, 2 volumes, edited and translated by Keith Aldrich, Philipp Fehl, and Raina Fehl (Berkeley: University of California Press, 1991).

J. J. Pollitt, *The Art of Ancient Greece: Sources and Documents* (Cambridge & New York: Cambridge University Press, 1990).

PARRHASIUS

FLOURISHED FIFTH CENTURY B.C.E.
PAINTER

Animation and Emotion. Parrhasius was more famous for his meticulous outline drawing, rather than use of shade and color. Pliny says he was the first to give symmetry to painting and animation to faces. He painted an image of the Athenian people and was able to endow them with palpable emotional states. He was noted for depicting strong emotion in his rendering of suffering heroes such as Philoctetes, Telephus, and the *Feigned Madness of Odysseus.*

For his painting of Prometheus in chains he is said to have tortured an old slave to death and used him as a model. One ancient account tells of a conversation between Parrhasius and Socrates where the philosopher points out the ability of painting to render not only physical appearances, but emotional and psychological states of the subject. Like many practicing artists, Parrhasius himself wrote on painting, although the work is lost. Accounts that he was arrogant (wearing a golden crown and purple robes like a rhapsode, a professional reciter of epic poems, or sophist) seem confirmed in his boastful poems about his own prowess, similar to those of his great rival, Zeuxis. He seems to have been a self-professed dandy and another of his competitors claimed that his depiction of Theseus made the hero look like he had been fed on roses instead of meat. His work was important and influential, providing models for later artists in the Roman period.

Sources:
Franciscus Junius, *The Literature of Classical Art*, 2 volumes, edited and translated by Keith Aldrich, Philipp Fehl, and Raina Fehl (Berkeley: University of California Press, 1991).

J. J. Pollitt, *The Art of Ancient Greece: Sources and Documents* (Cambridge & New York: Cambridge University Press, 1990).

PHEIDIAS

FLOURISHED CIRCA 465-430 B.C.E.
SCULPTOR

Cult Statues. Pheidias was an Athenian sculptor most renowned for his colossal cult statues of *Athena Parthenos* (447-438) and *Zeus* at Olympia (circa 430). He became a close friend of Pericles and was in charge of the entire building program of the Acropolis from the early 440s. Other works included the statue of *Athena Promakhos* (The Champion) on the Acropolis (circa 465-456) and the *Lemnian Athena*, named after those who dedicated it. He also produced statues of Athenian tribal heroes set up at Delphi, funded by the spoils of Marathon, and some have claimed that the Riace Bronzes are two survivals of this monument.

Scandal. Ancient descriptions enable scholars to identify the general appearances of the *Athena Parthenos* and *Zeus* at Olympia which are confirmed in various smaller copies. Both statues were of ivory and gold over a wooden core, embellished in jewels, enamel and paint with various images and narratives attached to their apparel. Pericles' enemies charged Pheidias with impiously depicting himself and Pericles on the shield and with embezzlement of the statue's materials. According to one account, he died of poison in Athens, but it is more likely he made his way to Elea, through flight or exile, about 438 and produced the *Zeus at Olympia*. Here his workshop has been excavated (dated to the 430s), resulting in the discovery of a cup bearing his name. Pheidias' earlier troubles caught up with him, and several sources say he was put to death after completing the Zeus, possibly by his Athenian enemies or as a result of another charge of embezzlement brought by the Eleans. Nevertheless, for many in antiquity, Pheidias was the greatest of all sculptors, able to endow his works with a majesty and grandeur worthy of their divine and heroic subjects.

Sources:
Franciscus Junius, *The Literature of Classical Art*, 2 volumes, edited and translated by Keith Aldrich, Philipp Fehl, and Raina Fehl (Berkeley: University of California Press, 1991).

J. J. Pollitt, *The Art of Ancient Greece: Sources and Documents* (Cambridge & New York: Cambridge University Press, 1990).

PINDAR

CIRCA 518–CIRCA 438 B.C.E.
LYRIC POET

Court Favorite. Pindar is the most famous and easily the best-preserved of the lyric poets of Greece. He was of Theban aristocratic birth, connected to important families throughout the Greek world, and wrote poetry for a wide range of royal patrons, from Macedon to Cyrene and Sicily. In 476 B.C.E. he joined the court of Hieron of Syracuse shortly after that tyrant had taken power. The dates of most of his surviving works ranging from 498 to 446 B.C.E., can be fixed exactly as they celebrate sporting victories which were well known and sometimes form the basis of ancient chronology (as in the dating by Olympiads). Nevertheless, the detailed information offered by the ancient biographical tradition is not likely to be correspondingly accurate. In particular, modern scholars have questioned whether the first-person statements in the surviving odes (where the text talks about "I" or "me") can be taken as the genuine voice of the poet himself.

Victory Odes. Pindar left behind a large body of lyric poetry, but only the four books of *Epinicians* (victory songs) survive intact. The Epinician odes were gathered together on the basis of the location of the victories they celebrated; the four great games (Olympian [at Olympia], Pythian [at Delphi], Nemean [at Nemea] and Isthmian [at Corinth]) which made up the cycle of Greek athletic competitions thus form the organising principle. Pindar wrote the poems as commissions to celebrate victories in the games, and they were designed to be sung by choirs to welcome victors home. Often the victors were no more athletic than the average horse-breeder today, as equestrian events conferred the crown of victory simply on the owner of the winning horse. The poems portray an intensely religious bard, not afraid to alter traditional stories which reflected badly on the pantheon, and who believed that the moment of victory could unite humanity briefly with the eternal power and felicity of the gods. Pindar's odes are unashamedly aristocratic in bias, explicitly so in an age that saw the birth of democracy in Athens and increasing debate about the best form of government—yet even so he was able to acknowledge the great role Athens played in defending Greece against the Persians, against whom his own city of Thebes had shown no resistance. Above all he stresses the irreplaceable reality of inherited virtue against that which was merely learned. Difficult but brilliant in language as well as thought—the logical connections between the sections of these poems often evade readers—the odes are an important source of myths.

Sources:

C. M. Bowra, *Pindar* (Oxford: Oxford University Press, 1964).

D. C. Young, "Pindar" in *Ancient Writers I,* edited by J. T. Luce (New York: Scribners, 1982), pp. 157–177.

POLYCLITUS

FLOURISHED FIFTH CENTURY B.C.E.
SCULPTOR

Bronze Medium. Polyclitus the Argive sculptor worked almost exclusively in bronze. He made statues of victorious athletes in Panhellenic games; his colossal gold and ivory statue of Hera for her temple in Argos, though celebrated in antiquity, never attained the status of its Pheidian counterparts in terms of the admiration it inspired. Polyclitus's reputation chiefly rests on his *Doruphoros,* or Spearbearer, usually dated circa 445-440. Lysippus was said to have commented, perhaps with some irony, that this statue was his teacher. Polyclitus also wrote a treatise called the *Canon,* probably in relation to the statue, which outlined a series of numerical proportions for the body. Only a couple of fragments remain of this work, and it has been suggested that Polyclitus may have been working with slight deviations from such numerical formulae to achieve his desired effects. It is also believed that Polyclitus may have been incorporating Pythagorean elements into his artworks, since speculative interest in the nature of numbers and in all phenomena as reducible to numerical concepts was current at this time in the writings of Pythagorean philosophers such as Philolaos. However, such connections, while interesting possibilities, remain conjectural. In any event, Polyclitus's evidently meticulous conception of his work indicates strong idealising tendencies.

Sameness. Other famous works included the *Diadoumenos* (boy tying a fillet around his head) a Heracles, Hermes, and a prize-winning Amazon. His style remained influential well into the Roman period, and even though some complained of a certain sameness to his sculptures or considered his works lacking in Pheidian grandeur, he was greatly admired for the skill and beauty of his creations throughout antiquity.

Sources:

Franciscus Junius, *The Literature of Classical Art,* 2 volumes, edited and translated by Keith Aldrich, Philipp Fehl, and Raina Fehl (Berkeley: University of California Press, 1991).

J. J. Pollitt, *The Art of Ancient Greece: Sources and Documents* (Cambridge & New York: Cambridge University Press, 1990).

POLYGNOTUS

CIRCA 500-CIRCA 440 B.C.E.
PAINTER

High Honor. The son and pupil of Aglaophon, Polygnotus was born in Thasos, an island of the north Aegean Sea. He was said to have lived with Elpinike, sister of the Athenian politician Cimon, who was influential in the years 470–450. He painted the Stoa Poikile in the Athenian agora, including scenes such as the *Sack of Troy.* For doing this painting without charging a fee he is said to have been awarded Athenian citizenship; another source tells us his painting of *The Rape of the Daughters of Leucippus* in a sanctuary of Castor and Pollux in Athens earned him this honor.

Other Works. In the wings of the Propylaia, or gateway to the Acropolis, he painted such Homeric figures as Achilles, and the meeting of Odysseus and Nausicaa, and for Athena's temple in Plataea he painted *Odysseus After Slaying the Suitors.* Other famous works included another *Sack of Troy* and an Underworld scene for the Lesche, or Clubhouse, of the citizens of Cnidus at Delphi. Pausanias gives a lengthy description of the paintings in this building in which the distribution of figures on various levels "in space" seems reflected in contemporary vases such that as by the Niobid Painter.

Characteristics. An evident feature of Polygnotus' work was the depiction of characters in the aftermath or anticipation of an event, so that emotion is alluded to rather than made explicit. He was also noted for innovations such as the rendering of transparent robes, and for the liveliness of facial expression. Perhaps most significantly, Aristotle mentions the noble character, or ethos, with which Polygnotus imbued his subjects and made them "superior to us," like figures from tragedy and epic. Fuller development of techniques such as shading were to come after him, but he is considered the first great painter of the Western tradition.

Sources:

Franciscus Junius, *The Literature of Classical Art,* 2 volumes, edited and translated by Keith Aldrich, Philipp Fehl, and Raina Fehl (Berkeley: University of California Press, 1991).

J. J. Pollitt, *The Art of Ancient Greece: Sources and Documents* (Cambridge & New York: Cambridge University Press, 1990).

PRAXITELES

FLOURISHED 370-330 B.C.E.
SCULPTOR

Marble Medium. An Athenian sculptor, Praxiteles worked in marble and to a lesser extent in bronze. He was particularly interested in the surface finish of his works and apparently admired best his marble statues that had been painted over by

Nicias. He depicted several youthful gods such as Eros for the people of Thespiae and another at Parium, satyrs, nymphs, a languid young Apollo killing a lizard (*Sauroktonos*) and Dionysus, among others. The bronze *Marathon Boy* may be traceable to a Praxitelean workshop. The famous marble *Hermes Carrying the Infant Dionyus* at Olympia, long thought to be one of his works, may postdate Praxiteles, though others think it may be an original. According to Vitruvius, he also worked on the Mausoleum at Halicarnassus, another of the Seven Wonders, and collaborated with other sculptors on athletic pieces such as chariot monuments.

Public Sensation. By far his most famous work, and one of the most written about pieces of ancient art, was his *Aphrodite of Knidos* or *Knidia,* known from copies and traceable to reproductions on local coins. Though Aphrodite had been depicted in diaphanous drapery or in various states of undress earlier, Praxiteles created a sensation by sculpting a monumental, totally nude statue of her, to be placed in a circular colonnaded shrine to offer the viewer the maximum number of vantage points. He is supposed to have used his mistress, Phryne, as his model, who apparently modeled for him for other works also. Ancient sources tell anecdotes of young men so besotted with the Cnidia that they tried to make love to it (as had happened with Praxiteles' statue of Eros at Parium); Nicomedes, a king of Bithynia, even offered to buy the Aphrodite by paying the national debt of Knidos. The fame of the statue eventually turned Knidos into a tourist mecca and ensured that the Praxitelean style depicting the ideal female form became standard in ancient art.

Sources:
Franciscus Junius, *The Literature of Classical Art,* 2 volumes, edited and translated by Keith Aldrich, Philipp Fehl, and Raina Fehl (Berkeley: University of California Press, 1991).

J. J. Pollitt, *The Art of Ancient Greece: Sources and Documents* (Cambridge & New York: Cambridge University Press, 1990).

SAPPHO

CIRCA 620–CIRCA 550 B.C.E.
POET

Relationships. Known as the Tenth Muse, Sappho was the most celebrated woman poet of the ancient world. Born in Mytilene on Lesbos, her early exile in Sicily is evidence of the politically volatile world in which she lived; yet, it is remarkable that politics are almost entirely absent from her surviving work, particularly in view of their importance in the poetry of her contemporary Mytilinean, Alcaeus. Instead, her focus is on her relationships with her brother, daughter (for she was evidently married), and female companions. The nature of her relationship with these last has been the subject of much speculation, so that the term "Lesbian" has acquired (at least in modern times) a more

than geographical significance. By any reckoning her expressed feelings towards her young friends was passionate and clearly erotic rather than maternal; and in fact a fragmentary parchment found early in the twentieth century seems to show that sexual relationships with them were celebrated in her poetry. It would, however, be naive to conclude that such poems necessarily recorded the historical truth, or even to assume that the modes of sexuality practiced on Lesbos correspond to modern categories (several of Sappho's poems were celebratory wedding songs for her companions). One ancient story has her committing suicide for the love of a man.

Extant Work. There is only one complete surviving poem of Sappho, which takes the form of an address to Aphrodite, asking for her help in the pursuit of a girl. A large fragment of another poem describes with unprecedented vividness her feelings of helplessness and panic in the presence of a girl she loves. From this sort of evidence, then, it would seem that much of her poetry was devoted to the expression of feelings. However, mythological scenes also interested her, and one papyrus fragment describes with a rich sensuality the details of the wedding celebration of Hector and Andromache; but even here what some critics have described as the poet's "feminine qualities" are on display.

Sources:
Mary R. Lefkowitz, *The Lives of the Greek Poets* (Baltimore: Johns Hopkins University Press, 1981).

William Seaton, "Sappho," in *Anicent Greek Authors, Dictionary of Literary Biography,* volume 176, edited by Ward W. Briggs (Columbia, S.C.: Bruccoli Clark Layman/Detroit: Gale Research, 1997), pp. 347–350.

SCOPAS

FOURTH CENTURY B.C.E.
ARCHITECT AND SCULPTOR

Divinities. Scopas was an architect and sculptor from Paros who worked mostly in marble. Famous for his statues of divinities, he sculpted Aphrodite and a personification of Longing (Pothos) for her shrine at Samothrace and again for her temple at Megara, where he also made an image of Eros and a personification of Desire (Himeros). Pliny tells us his most renowned works were sculptures in a temple of Poseidon, later brought to Rome, which featured the god, Thetis, Achilles, dolphins, and minor sea dieties. He made a colossal, seated Ares, which was later moved to the Circus Maximus, as was another Aphrodite sculpted by him which Pliny considered superior to Praxiteles' version. Images of Apollo Smintheus (the mouse-god), Artemis, and Athena were also among his well-known works commissioned for areas as far apart as Asia Minor and Thebes. He worked on column drums for the temple of Artemis at Ephesus, and the sculptures on the east side of the Mausoleum along with other leading sculptors of his day. His new design for the Doric temple of Athena at Tegea in Arcadia, after the original burned down in 395, was considered by Pausanias to be the best Peloponnesian temple. Its interior combined Ionic and Corinthian orders and the external colonnade was Doric; its front pedimental sculptures depicted the Calydonian Boar Hunt, while the fight between Achilles and Telephus was on the rear pediment. Fragments of these that have been found are generally thought to reflect his emotive style, if not coming from his own hand. It is also possible that certain frescoes from the fourth century, such as those found at the royal tomb at Vergina, reflect something of his sculptural style. Scopas produced a maenad which was famous in antiquity for its expressive energy and liveliness; a statue of a raving maenad in Dresden is often taken to be a copy, or at least derived from Scopas's original.

Sources:

Franciscus Junius, *The Literature of Classical Art*, 2 volumes, edited and translated by Keith Aldrich, Philipp Fehl, and Raina Fehl (Berkeley: University of California Press, 1991).

J. J. Pollitt, *The Art of Ancient Greece: Sources and Documents* (Cambridge & New York: Cambridge University Press, 1990).

SOPHOCLES

497/6–406/5 B.C.E.
TRAGIC PLAYWRIGHT

Significance. With Sophocles tragedy reached what many in the ancient and modern world have felt to be its highest point. The second of the three surviving Athenian tragedians, he was born in Colonus, just outside Athens, a generation after Aeschylus. It is recorded that in 480 B.C.E. he was chosen to lead a choral celebration of the great victory over the Persians at Salamis, an event which begins his continued involvement with both the artistic and the civic aspect of Athenian life. In 468 B.C.E. he put on his first play and defeated Aeschylus, but the production dates of few of his other works are known. Seven of his approximately 123 plays survive, and two can be dated accurately: *Philoctetes* was produced in 409 B.C.E. and *Oedipus at Colonus* posthumously in 401 B.C.E. (There is some reason for thinking that *Antigone* was produced around 441 B.C.E., but the date cannot be determined exactly.) Besides writing plays with great success (he won 20 competitions), he took part in political office; he was treasurer of the Athenian empire in one year, twice a general, and a member of a special council during the grimmest time of the Second Peloponnesian War (431–404 B.C.E.) against Sparta. He held a priesthood in Athens and was widely known and liked for his easygoing disposition.

Character. Two surviving statements from Sophocles himself about his own work indicate that he was particularly interested in the presentation of character on stage. He distinguished his mature plays from the "grandeur and harshness" of Aeschylus (which he claims to have followed when younger), and contrasts his own style as "most expressive of character"; he also claimed that, while he represented people as they should be, Euripides represented them as they were. As

one critic put it, his protagonists are often people fiercely determined beyond argument, even with themselves; the minor characters serve their main purpose in providing a contrast with the play's hero (for example, Chrysothemis in *Electra* and Ismene in *Antigone*). Through the isolation and moral certainty that his great figures like Antigone, Oedipus, and Ajax experience, Sophocles brings us closer to Homer than he does to his predecessor Aeschylus, whose plays are built on family relationships as worked out through several generations and on ethical crises: his Orestes, in stark contrast to Sophocles', is wracked with uncertainty about the morality of avenging his father's death on his mother. However, it is interesting to note that in the twilight of his career the older poet could still learn from the younger. Sophocles' most important technical innovation was the introduction of a third speaking actor, and Aeschylus made use of this breakthrough to present three actors on stage in his surviving trilogy, the *Oresteia* (458 B.C.E.).

Sources:

R. D. Dawe, *Sophocles, The Classical Heritage* (New York & London: Garland, 1996).

G. H. Gellie, *Sophocles: A Reading* (Carlton, Australia: Melbourne University Press, 1972).

G. M. Kirkwood, *A Study of Sophoclean Drama*, Cornell Studies in Classical Philology 31 (Ithaca, N.Y.: Cornell University Press, 1958).

THUCYDIDES

CIRCA 455–CIRCA 395 B.C.E.
HISTORIAN AND GENERAL

Great Work. Thucydides, an Athenian historian and general, wrote *History of the Peloponnesian War*, which is widely regarded as the greatest historical work of the ancient world. He was born of a wealthy family with strong Thracian connections, but became a strong supporter of Pericles, the democratic leader whose figure overshadows all subsequent Athenian politicians in Thucydides' work. Thucydides caught the plague that ravaged Athens early in the war, but recovered. He was elected general but in 424 B.C.E. failed to prevent the Spartan general Brasidas from taking Amphipolis in Thrace. Exiled for this failure, Thucydides returned to Athens at the end of the war and seems to have died shortly afterwards.

Deeds and Words. Thucydides' account of the war is unfinished and ends in mid-narrative, describing the events of 411 B.C.E., but there are references in the work to Athens' ultimate defeat. Thucydides tells the reader that he began keeping notes from the war's outbreak, but the order and date of the composition of the various parts have been subject to endless scrutiny. As the work stands, it is divided as its author stated into deeds and words: the narrative description of the events of the war, and the various speeches of a highly concentrated and abstract nature, supposedly reporting the words of important players in the conflict: a Spartan envoy, an Athenian in the assembly, a general before a battle, and so on. The style of these speeches is exceptionally bracing and difficult (and was found so by Greek scholars in later antiquity), so it is hard to believe that anything in such a style could have been delivered before large audiences; but at a more basic level it is quite unclear whether it was Thucydides' intention to present what was actually said or what the most powerful argument on any occasion would have been. Either way, the speeches are amongst the finest documents to survive in Greek for their combination of intellectual rigor and passion, above all in Pericles' famous defense of Athenian democracy in his Funeral speech. The narrative of events, often written with an almost clinical detachment and absence of moral judgements, also manages to focus our attentions on human psychology and suffering in a way that shows the clear influence of tragedy. Indeed, for all the undoubted influence of contemporary intellectual forces such as scientific medicine and rhetoric on his work, the overwhelming influence of myth has been detected in its structure and story.

Sources:

Mortimer Chambers, "Thucydides," in *Ancient Greek Authors, Dictionary of Literary Biography*, volume 176, edited by Ward W. Briggs (Columbia, S.C.: Bruccoli Clark Layman/Detroit: Gale Research, 1997), pp. 381–389.

K. J. Dover, *Thucydides* (Oxford: Clarendon Press, 1973).

ZEUXIS

FIFTH CENTURY B.C.E.
PAINTER

Realism. A painter from Heraclea in Southern Italy, Zeuxis was known in Athens, and Aristophanes mentions a painting by him of the god Eros in his *Acharnians* (425 B.C.E.). Between 413 and 399 he decorated the palace of the Macedonian tyrant Archelaus, who also kept the company of the poet Timotheus and playwrights Agathon and Euripides. Zeuxis was famous for the heightened realism of some of his paintings, which could allegedly deceive birds, involving him in a famous contest with Parrhasius; he also developed techniques of shading pioneered by the Athenian Apollodorus, who apparently remarked that Zeuxis stole the art of his teachers and carried it off with him. His paintings included some unusual subjects, such as a centaur family in which the gradation of color from the human to animal body of the mother beast was praised in antiquity. He famously painted an image of Helen by combining the best elements from a number of beautiful models from Croton in southern Italy; he thus worked with a concept of ideal beauty made of composite form. He accompanied this image with some lines from Homer, implicitly equating himself with the great poet. He composed some short poems about his own artistic talents, but such boasts were not uncommon in the competitive world of the Greek polis. Aristotle considered him inferior to Polygnotus in rendering nobility of character, but Pliny praises his painting of Penelope as embodying morality itself, and his painting of Menelaus was famous for movingly depicting its subject drenched in tears. He also painted monochromes on white, but generally had a reputation for depicting fuller figures whose volume is suggested by shade and color.

Sources:

Franciscus Junius, *The Literature of Classical Art*, 2 volumes, edited and translated by Keith Aldrich, Philipp Fehl, and Raina Fehl (Berkeley: University of California Press, 1991).

J. J. Pollitt, *The Art of Ancient Greece: Sources and Documents* (Cambridge & New York: Cambridge University Press, 1990).

DOCUMENTARY SOURCES

Comedy

Aristophanes is the sole complete witness for the genre of comedy in the period. Eleven of his plays survive, the best of which are *Wasps* (422 B.C.E.), *Clouds* (circa 418 B.C.E.), and *Frogs* (405 B.C.E.).

Didactic Poetry

Hesiod composed *Theogony* and *Works and Days* (circa eighth century B.C.E.)—the former recounts the birth of the gods and establishment of current Olympian order; the latter gives agricultural and moral advice to a troublesome brother.

Elegy and Iambics

The best preserved corpus of elegy is that attributed to Theognis, more an ideology and a tradition than an individual author. Iambics are best represented in the fairly considerable fragments of Solon, whose qualities as a lawgiver seem to have surpassed his poetic gifts.

Epics

Homer is said to have composed *Iliad* and *Odyssey* (circa eighth–seventh centuries B.C.E.), two epic poems that are the beginnings of European literature. They tell of the rage of Achilles at Troy and the return of Odysseus from that siege respectively.

History

The great writers of History were Herodotus, Thucydides, and Xenophon.

Lyric

Only Pindar and Bacchylides survive in any quantity, and the vast bulk of their extant work are odes commemorating victories at Panhellenic games. Tantalizing fragments of great poetry by Sappho and many others give modern readers a sense of what they have lost.

Oratory

About a century of oratory is well represented in the surviving literature, from the last quarter of the fifth century to 323 B.C.E. Works by each of the ten orators of the canon (Antiphon, Andocides, Lysias, Isocrates, Isaeus, Lycurgus, Aeschines, Demosthenes, Hyperides, and Dinarchus) survive.

Philosophy

There is considerable, but frustratingly fragmentary, material of the so-called Presocratic philosophers. The first philosophy to survive in any state of completion is that of Plato, whose great artistic skills have made him as important a figure for students of literature as of philosophy. His *Republic* (circa 380–360 B.C.E.) is his magnum opus, but many readers prefer the livelier dialogues like *Protagoras* and *Gorgias*. Aristotle's surviving work, being not meant for a general audience, is likely to attract fewer readers; but all students of literature should read his *Poetics* (after 335 B.C.E.). Xenophon's considerable output contains many works featuring Socrates which should be considered under the heading of philosophy.

Tragedy

Seven plays each survive of the great output of Sophocles and Aeschylus. Euripides' work is much better represented with eighteen tragedies and the only surviving satyr play, *Cyclops*.

Visual Arts

Ekphrasis is a term which simply means "description" usually applied to a work of art, real or imaginary, in ancient writings. Examples are as old as Homer: the images on Achilles' shield made by the god Hephaestus (*Iliad*, book 18), Agamemnon's armor (*Iliad*, book 11), Heracles' belt (*Odyssey*, book 11), and Odysseus' broach (*Odyssey*, book 19). Descriptions of artworks and images on shields are also found in Greek tragedy such as Aeschylus's *Seven Against Thebes* (467 B.C.E.) and Euripides's *Electra* (circa 420 B.C.E.), *Ion* (circa 413 B.C.E.), and *Phoenician Women* (410 or 409 B.C.E.). Ekphrasis was a popular literary form throughout antiquity.

Various references, comparative analyses, and allusions to art and artists occur in many other writings at this time of great developments in painting, sculpture, and architecture. Often these writings concern not technical matters, but the effects of art on the onlooker, and its relation to other concerns such as psychology, rhetoric, perception of character, and ethics. In *Praise of Helen*, the fifth-century Sicilian orator sophist, Gorgias of Leontini, interestingly makes visual art a counterpart to the persuasive power of language in its effects on the onlooker. Plato seems to have had varying attitudes to painting and poetry. At times he makes favorable references to artists like Pheidias and Zeuxis, but his most notorious pronouncements are from book ten of his *Republic*, where he speaks of painting as producing false and deceptive images that appeal to our unintellectual instincts. Xenophon's *Memorabilia* is our source for Socrates' discussions with the painter Parrhasius and sculptor Kleiton on the abilities of visual art to express the emotional and psychological state of its subject. Aristotle does not seem to have a definite view of the visual arts, but can certainly see value in the works of a painter like Polygnotus, who endowed his images with a noble character as in *Poetics*. Indeed, he suggests in *Politics* (after 335 B.C.E.) that contemplation of Polygnotus's figures by young people should be encouraged, which suggests that, for him, art could have a valuable function in shaping the character of impressionable onlookers.

CHAPTER FOUR

COMMUNICATION, TRANSPORTATION, AND EXPLORATION

by WILLIAM E. HUTTON

CONTENTS

CHRONOLOGY

96

OVERVIEW

98

**TOPICS IN COMMUNI-
CATION, TRANSPOR-
TATION, AND
EXPLORATION**

Language 99
Spartan Vernacular 99
The Language of Pygmies 102

Means of Communication 102
Flames of Foreboding 105
A Herald's Curse 106
Patterns and Practices
    of Transportation 107
*The Highs and Lows of Merchant
    Life* 107
Spiteful Colonist 109
The Colonization of Cyrene 110
Travelers of the Archaic Age 112
Roads and Land Traffic 113
*Out and About with Pausanias:
    Descriptions of Greek Roads* . . 114
Greek Wagon Rides 115

Sea Transport 118
Odysseus Builds a Raft 119
Home to Ithaca 122

SIGNIFICANT PEOPLE

Sostratus of Aegina 124

**DOCUMENTARY
SOURCES**

125

Sidebars and tables are listed in italics.

IMPORTANT EVENTS OF 800-323 B.C.E.

800* B.C.E.	• The *pentekontor,* a type of oared warship, is developed. • The late Geometric Renaissance begins in which the Greek alphabet is developed and the poems of Homer and Hesiod are written.
750*	• Colonists from the city-states of Chalcis and Eretria establish a trading post on Pithecussae, an island off the western coast of Italy. Soon thereafter the colony of Cumae is also founded near present-day Naples.
734*	• The Corinthians colonize the island of Corcyra and begin a settlement at Syracuse on Sicily.
700*	• Corinthian pottery is a popular trade commodity. • The Greeks establish an *emporion* (trading post) at Al-Mina in present-day Syria.
660*	• The city of Megara establishes the colony of Byzantium on the straits that connect the Black Sea to the Aegean.
625*	• The trireme, a sleek warship propelled by oarsmen arranged in three tiers, is developed.
600*	• Egyptian rulers grant control of the port of Naucratis in the Nile Delta to Greek traders; its markets specialize in grain, ivory, ebony, and handicrafts. • The *Diolkos,* a stone-paved causeway across the Isthmus of Corinth, is built in order to facilitate the transportation of goods.
590*	• The Athenians publish the law code of Solon on *Kurbeis* (triangular wooden pillars) in the agora or market place.

** Denotes circa date*

525*

- The merchant Sostratus of Aegina operates a profitable trading business.

500*

- The Athenians begin to construct a temple to their goddess Athena and pave a roadway up Mount Pentele in order to obtain marble for the project.

490*

- The *hêmerodromos* ("day-runner") Pheidippides spreads the news of the Athenian victory over the Persians at Marathon.

323*

- A common dialect known as *koinê* is prevalent in the various Greek settlements throughout the Mediterranean world.

An inscribed bronze tablet recording a loan made by the Sanctuary of Zeus to the polis of Locri, circa 350-250 B.C.E. (Reggio Calabria, Museo Nazionale Cat. 346/I/photo credit: Andrea Baguzzi, Milano5)

OVERVIEW

Expansion. In comparison to other ancient cultures, one of the remarkable characteristics of Greek civilization is its mobility. While the Egyptian and Mesopotamian civilizations remained largely confined to the areas near the fertile river valleys in which they developed, the Greeks expanded from their humble beginnings in what is now Greece to places as distant as the straits of Gibraltar in the West and the shores of the Black Sea in the East. Greek merchants, travelers, and settlers plied the waters and trade routes from one end of the known world to the other, spreading Greek language and culture in their wake and bringing home not only overseas goods and products but new ideas as well. Many of the characteristics of the Greeks that are most admired, including their adaptability, inventiveness, and openness to new ways of thinking, can be ascribed in part to this traveling lifestyle.

Geography. To understand how transportation and travel became such important factors in the development of Greek civilization, it is important to know something about the geography and natural resources of Greece. Situated at the southern end of the Balkan peninsula, Greece is crisscrossed by rugged mountain ranges. These ranges break up the countryside and confine the territory suitable for habitation to small, isolated valleys. The mountains make access from one valley to the next difficult, and, as a result, the communities in these separate valleys never unified to form a single country, organizing themselves instead into independent, autonomous city-states such as Athens and Sparta. Greece also has no more than a handful of navigable rivers, so river traffic, one of the main avenues of transport employed by other ancient civilizations, was largely unavailable. These circumstances combined to make travel and transportation within Greece somewhat laborious and difficult.

Natural Resources. At the same time that the geography of the Greek mainland had an isolating effect on the people who lived there, the natural resources of Greece, or rather the lack of them, provided great incentive for the Greek people to search for richer lands and broader opportunities. Most of the other great civilizations of the ancient Mediterranean region achieved prosperity through the agricultural richness of the great river valleys they inhabited. In contrast, though the earliest permanent settlements in Greece were agricultural ones, the productivity of the Greek soil was seldom better than marginal. Had the Greeks relied solely on the capacity of their land to produce staple foods such as grain and beans, they would never have reached the level of prosperity that they did and would never have had as strong an impact on the history of Western civilization. In order to increase their standard of living, many Greeks had to abandon the sedentary lifestyle and become travelers. Inhabitants of Greece began plying the waters of the Mediterranean even as early as the Stone Age, and after 800 B.C.E. they began leaving their homeland en masse, either to establish colonies in more promising soil, to find work as artisans or mercenaries, or to engage in trade. Although most of the people of the Greek communities were farmers who lived off the produce of their own land, the activities of traders, travelers, and itinerant workers provided an increasingly important source of surplus wealth that the Greeks otherwise would not have had.

Middlemen. In this trend toward a mobile lifestyle the Greeks had two circumstances in their favor. First of all, there is the position of their land in relation to other parts of the inhabited world. Greece, located on the eastern and southern extremities of the European continent, stood on the frontier between the world of the great Near Eastern civilizations and the rich but undeveloped land of Europe. Greeks were thus well-situated to play the role of middlemen in the traffic of goods from Europe to the Near East, a trade that included gold, amber, timber, and metals. The prosperity of the Mycenaeans, the earliest large-scale civilization of mainland Greece, which flourished from 1600 to 1200 B.C.E., profited from the control and exploitation of these trade routes.

Maritime Culture. The other advantage the Greeks had was their relationship to the sea. The Balkan Peninsula, as it plunges southward into the Mediterranean, forms the western boundary of the gulf known as the Aegean Sea, the most sheltered arm of the Mediterranean. As the sea meets the mountainous landscape, it forms a remarkably complex and sinuous coastline that offers countless bays and harbors. The ridges themselves continue beneath the sea and at frequent intervals rise above the surface again to form the islands of the Aegean, which serve both to break up the strong currents of the open water and to provide stepping-stones for outward-bound explorers. These geological circumstances made the Aegean a perfect training ground for a maritime culture. There are few places you can stand on the shore of the

Aegean and not see islands receding toward the horizon. It must have been tempting and tantalizing for the earliest inhabitants of Greece to gaze across the relatively smooth waters of the Aegean Sea and wonder what treasures lay on those islands and in the lands beyond.

Technologies. In terms of the technologies involed in transportation and exploration, including shipbuilding, road building, and vehicle design, the Greeks were not great innovators. With the exception of oar-driven warships, the design and construction of the ships that the Greeks used changed little from the time of the Bronze Age, and were based on models first developed not by the Greeks but by the Egyptians and Phoenicians. Though they did not lead the way in the area of technology, the Greeks put the technical knowledge they learned from their neighbors to new and productive uses. This pattern of adaptation of new ideas and know-how is characteristic of Greek civilization, and one of the more important results of the Greeks' predilection for trade and travel.

Assessment. Intimate and repeated contacts with outsiders made the Greeks savvy denizens of the Mediterranean. Not only could they deal knowledgeably and skillfully with any of the people whose paths they crossed, the Greeks also learned from them and enriched their own culture with the best that their neighbors had to offer. Egyptian art and architecture, Phoenician writing and trading techniques, and Mesopotamian ideas in mathematics, geometry, and astronomy all gave important inspiration to the Greek achievements in these areas, and without the long familiarity with these cultures that was brought about by the Greeks' movable lifestyle, the course of Greek civilization would have taken a profoundly different path.

TOPICS IN COMMUNICATION, TRANSPORTATION, AND EXPLORATION

LANGUAGE

Indo-European Family. The Greek language is one of a group of related languages called the Indo-European language family. This family gets its name from the fact that it includes most of the languages of ancient and modern Europe, including Greek, Latin, and English as well as some languages of central and southern Asia as far east as the Indian Subcontinent. Hindi, Pashto (the main language of modern Afghanistan), and Farsi (Iran) are all members of the family. In ancient times Sanskrit (the language of sacred Hindu writings) and the language of the ancient Persians were Indo-European.

Origins. How related languages came to be spoken in such far-flung places is a mystery, since it is something that occurred in the prehistoric period, long before any of these languages had writing systems that might have been used to record the movements of the people who spoke them. Based on evidence from the earliest written records of non-Indo-European peoples, archaeology, and clues in the Indo-European languages themselves, linguists believe that the Indo-European family began as a single language, or set of related dialects, spoken by nomadic people who inhabited the plains of central Asia to the east of the Caspian Sea. Sometime in the late Stone Age or early Bronze Age, between 4000 and 2000 B.C.E., these people began migrating in all directions. Some of them went to the East and South and brought with them the ancestors of the Sanskrit and Farsi languages, while others moved West

SPARTAN VERNACULAR

In the play *Lysistrata* (411 B.C.E.) by Aristophanes, the Athenian woman Lysistrata has called a congress of women from all over the Greek world to discuss how they can stop their menfolk from fighting. When the representative from Sparta, Lampito, arrives, she speaks a comic version of the Dorian dialect. The translator has tried to replicate the effect this would have had on the audience by having her speak a caricature of hillbilly vernacular.

LYSISTRATA: And here's our lovely Spartan. Hel*lo*, Lampito dear. Why darling, you're simply ravishing! Such a blemishless complexion—so clean, so out-of-doors! And will you look at that figure—the pink of perfection!

KLEONIKE: I'll bet you could strangle a bull.

LAMPITO: I calklate so. Hit's fitness whut done it, fitness and dancin'. You know the step? Foot it out back'ards an' toe yore twitchet.

KLEONIKE: What unbelievably beautiful bosoms!

LAMPITO: Shuckins, what fer you tweedlin' me up so? I feel like a heifer come fair-time.

Source: Aristophanes, *Lysistrata*, translated by Douglass Parker (Ann Arbor: University of Michigan Press, 1964).

Alphabets of the various Greek city-states and regions (from Anthony Snodgrass, *Archaic Greece* [1980], p. 80)

The chart compares the letterforms of the following alphabets across the rows Alpha, Beta, Gamma, Delta, Epsilon, Vau, Zeta, Eta, Heta, Theta, Iota, Kappa, Lambda, Mu, Nu, Xi, Omikron, Pi, San, Qoppa, Rho, Sigma, Tau, Upsilon, Phi, Chi, Psi, Omega, and Punct.:

N. Semitic; Attica, Sigeion; Euboia; Boiotia; Thessaly; Phokis; Lokrides and colonies; Aigina, Kydonia; Corinth, Korkyra; Megara, Byzantion; Sikyon; Phleious, Kleonai, Tiryns; Argos, Mycenae; Eastern Argolid; Lakonia, Messenia, Taras; Arkadia; Elis; Achaia and colonies; Aitolia, Epeiros; Ithake, Kephallenia; Euboic W. colonies; Syracuse and colonies; Megara Hyblaia Selinous; Naxos, Amorgos; Paros, Thasos; Delos, Keos, Syros; Crete; Thera, Kyrene; Melos, Sikinos, Anaphe; Ionic Dodekapolis and colonies; Rhodes, Gela Akragas; Knidos; Aiolis.

and began to infiltrate Europe. These movements had a profound effect on the population and language of Asia and Europe, but it is incorrect to speak of an Indo-European race or people who managed to dominate all of this vast territory by conquest. Language and ethnicity, though often closely related, do not always go together. Modern Indo-European language speakers include people of all races, colors, religions, and ethnic origins, and the same was likely the case in antiquity as well. Under the proper conditions, a relatively small influx of newcomers speaking a different language can have very wide-ranging effects on the language spoken in any given area without having much of an influence on the population's genetic makeup.

Expansion. The exact date at which Indo-European speakers began to come into Greece is unknown. One famous archaeologist, Colin Renfrew, believes that they came in along with the practice of agriculture at the beginning of the Neolithic Period (6000–3000 B.C.E.), but most scholars place the date at around 2100 B.C.E. The spread of an Indo-European language into the entire territory known today as Greece was probably a gradual thing. The island of Crete, later populated by Greek-speakers, was controlled by the non-Greek-speaking Minoan civilization until late in the Bronze Age (3000–1100 B.C.E.). By the time that historical records begin to appear, however, Greek is the only language that is attested on the mainland, and if any islands other than Crete were non-Greek-speaking at the end of the Bronze Age they probably became Greek-speaking during the vast migrations and changes of population that occurred in the wake of the Mycenaean collapse.

Dialects. As the proto-Greek language spread into the various isolated valleys and islands that make up the Greek landscape, communities of speakers became separated from one another and began to develop dialects, that is, versions of the language which are not sufficiently distinct from one another to be considered separate languages in their own right. While speakers of different languages cannot understand one another, speakers of different dialects of a language can communicate, though variations in pronunciation, grammar, and vocabulary are capable of instantly marking a person out as being a member of a specific group. An example is the difference between American English and British English. Speakers of these two dialects of English pronounce many words differently and have different vocabulary to designate certain things: for instance, what the British call a "lift," Americans call an "elevator." British and American speakers of English rarely have trouble understanding one another's speech, but whenever the speaker of one dialect hears a speaker of the other, he or she immediately perceives the difference and uses that information to categorize the person as being foreign or different.

Four Groupings. Similarly, the Greek dialects were mutually intelligible, but the characteristic vocabulary and pronunciation of each marked its speaker as belonging to a specific group. There were almost as many dialects of Greek as there were city-states, but most of them have been traditionally grouped into four major categories: the Attic-Ionic group, which included the dialect of Athens and those of most of the Aegean islands and some major cities in Anatolia, including Ephesus and Miletus; the Doric Group, comprising the dialects of most of the Peloponnese, Crete, and southwestern Anatolia; the Aeolic groups, including the dialects of Boeotia, Thessaly, and Lesbos in the northern Aegean; and the Arcado-Cypriot group, which included members in Arcadia (the landlocked interior of the Peloponnese) and Cyprus. This last group is closest in

	Attic	*Ionic*	*Dorian*	*Aeolic*
Athena (goddess)	Athênâ	Athênê	Athana	Athanaa
Poseidon (god)	Poseidôn	Poseideôn	Poteidan	Poseidan
four	tettares	tesseres	tetores	pessures
shrine	hieron	ieron	hiaron	iaron
ever	pote	kote	poka	pota

many respects to what seems to be the dialect recorded in the Mycenaean Linear B tablets of the Bronze Age. The following chart illustrates the differences in pronunciation for some common Greek words in various major dialects.

Social Indicators. As is the case with modern English, the Greek dialects had more of an effect as social indicators than they did as barriers to communication. To the

ears of an Athenian, the Doric dialect connoted rustic simplicity, and whether this was a bad thing (implying ignorance and a lack of sophistication) or a good thing (honesty and traditional values) depended on the situation and the attitude of the listener. Yet, the Doric dialect was used in Athenian drama for the odes that the chorus sang between episodes. (Drama first arose in Doric-speaking areas.) The use of Doric in Athenian choral odes shows the familiarity of the idiom and suggests that the difference in dialects was hardly a barrier to communication between the Greek cities. Toward the end of the Classical Period (480–323 B.C.E.), a common dialect, called *koinê*, began developing all over the Greek world. The dialect resulted from the interaction of peoples in various cities. Since the Athenians and other Attic-Ionic-speaking peoples were at the forefront in this interaction, their dialect was the one that the koine most closely resembled. The common dialect develops mostly, as one might expect, among traders, members of the elite, and others whose business took them outside of their home territory on a more-than-casual basis. Those who spent their entire lives on their farms or within the confines of their native villages probably clung to their local dialects for centuries.

Foreigners. When scholars look at how the Greeks communicated with the non-Greek world, some surprises present themselves. Historians have no evidence that foreign language instruction was even an important part of a Greek education. Despite the fact that the overseas activities of the Greeks brought them into contact with dozens of non-Greek-speaking populations, they seem to have made little effort to learn the language of any of them, relying instead on either their trading partners learning Greek or on the presence of interpreters who could translate their dealings with foreign peoples. This impression of ignorance of foreign languages on the part of the Greeks, however, may be somewhat magnified by the practices of historians from the period. It seems to have been part of the Greek literary tradition to pretend that the problems of communication between languages did not exist. Even in the earliest literature, Homer's tales of the Trojan War, matters of language and culture were regularized on the Greek pattern. The inhabitants of Troy, a non-Greek city, speak Greek in Homer's writings. They also worship Greek gods and live in the same sort of society that the Greeks do.

Interpreters. Most travelers were probably assisted in foreign lands by hosts or other local contacts, people who somehow had learned their languages and who could act as interpreters. Historical sources also mention professional interpreters who were hired to serve that function. The historian Herodotus was not always conversant with the languages of the places he visited, and sometimes he relied on interpreters. When visiting Egypt, he saw a hieroglyphic inscription that his interpreter told him listed "the amount spent on radishes, onions, and leeks for the laborers" who

Herodotus traveled all over the non-Greek world in researching his expansive *History of the Persian Wars* (circa late fifth century B.C.E.). Although he occasionally acknowledged the existence of different languages, they were rarely allowed to impinge upon his collection and presentation of information. Reproduced here is a good example from Herodotus's account of Egypt. Many important questions are suggested in this passage. When Herodotus's Greek informants conversed with the Ammonian king, what language did they do it in? In what language did the Ammonian king converse with his Nasamonian visitors? Why does the Ammonian king, presumably a Libyan and not a Greek, have a Greek name, Etearchus (meaning "True Ruler")? All these questions are posed by the passage; none of them are answered. Herodotus and other Greek writers of the period seem to have had little interest in such problems. All the different nationalities mentioned in this passage except for the sub-Saharan pygmies give the impression of inhabiting an international Mediterranean community where problems of cross-language communication have been solved. Did they all know Greek? Egyptian? Libyan? Or was polyglotism, the knowledge of several different languages, common among the traveling classes in these various societies; so common that no comment about it is made in our sources?

At that point the river runs from west to east; beyond, nobody knows its course with any certainty, for the country is uninhabited because of the heat. I did, however, hear a story from some people of Cyrene, who told me that during a visit to the oracle of Ammon they happened, in the course of conversation with Etearchus the Ammonian king, to get on to the subject of the Nile and the riddle of its source. Etearchus told them that he had once had a visit from certain Nasamonians, a people who live in Syrtis and the country a little to the eastward. Being asked if there was anything more they could tell him about the uninhabited parts of Libya, these men declared that a group of wild young fellows, sons of chieftains in their country, had on coming to manhood planned amongst themselves all sorts of extravagant adventures, one of which was to draw lots for five of their number to explore the Libyan desert and try to penetrate further than had ever been done before. . . . After travelling for many days over the sand they saw some trees growing on a level spot; they approached and began to pick the fruit which the trees bore, and while they were doing so were attacked by some little men—of less than middle height—who seized them and carried them off. The speech of these dwarfs was unintelligible, nor could they understand the Nasamonians.

Source: *Herodotus: The Histories*, translated by Aubrey de Selincourt (Harmondsworth, U.K. & Baltimore: Penguin, 1954).

worked on the Pyramid of Cheops. No inscriptions recording such mundane details have ever been found in hieroglyphics, and it is likely that either Herodotus himself was making a joke or, more likely, that his interpreter was taking advantage of his ignorance.

Sources:

Stephen Colvin, *Dialect in Aristophanes and the Politics of Language in Ancient Greek Literature* (Oxford: Oxford University Press, 1999).

J. P. Mallory, *In Search of the Indo-Europeans: Language, Archaeology, and Myth* (New York: Thames & Hudson, 1989).

Leonard R. Palmer, *The Greek Language* (Atlantic Highlands, N.J.: Humanities Press, 1980).

MEANS OF COMMUNICATION

Linear B. There are two main ways in which verbal messages are communicated: in oral form and in written form. Of these two methods, the latter was unavailable to Greek speakers until the late Bronze Age (3000–1100 B.C.E.), when the rulers of the Mycenaean palaces instituted the first writing system used to represent the Greek language known as Linear B. In comparison with their neighbors, the Greeks were relative latecomers to the art of writing. Egyptian hieroglyphics and the cuneiform writing system used by various peoples in Mesopotamia and the Near East date to the fourth millennium, B.C.E. Linear B was adapted by the Mycenaeans from Linear A, the writing system used by the Minoan civilization on Crete (1800–1500 B.C.E.) to represent their non-Greek language. The earliest examples of Linear B are found on clay tablets baked hard by the fire that accompanied a destruction of the palace of Knossos in Crete in about 1375 B.C.E., a time at which Knossos and the other former Minoan centers were controlled by Mycenaean Greeks.

Three Types. In the history of writing, there are various types of writing systems. All of them can be broadly categorized into three types: logographic systems, in which each symbol represents an entire word or concept (for example, Chinese writing); alphabetic systems, in which each symbol represents a single vowel or consonant (like the writing system you are now reading); and syllabic systems, in which each sign represents a syllable or a combination of vowels and consonants. Linear B (like Linear A) falls into this last category: one series of symbols represent the simple vowels *a, e, i, o,* and *u,* and the other symbols represent open syllables consisting of a consonant followed by a vowel, such as *pa, do, ze, mi,* and *su.*

Syllabic Writing. Some languages can be represented efficiently and accurately by a syllabic writing system. Modern Japanese, for instance, uses a syllabic script without any difficulty, since the Japanese language consists mainly of open syllables, such as *ka-ra-te* and *O-sa-ka.* In fact, when the Japanese borrow foreign words into their language, they customarily insert extra vowels to make all the syllables into open ones; for instance the word *football* becomes, in Japanese, *fu-to-bo-ru.* In the absence of any real knowledge about the ancient Minoan language, linguists can only assume that it was similar to Japanese in this respect and that the Linear A writing system was therefore well suited to it. Greek, however, is a language with many consonant clusters and other phonological complications, and for this reason Linear B, which retained the syllabic

A Mycenaean Period (1600–1200 B.C.E.) Linear B tablet discovered at Knossos on Crete (from John Chadwick, *The Mycenaean World* [Cambridge: Cambrige University Press, 1976], p. 16. Reprinted by permission of the publisher).

character of Linear A, was an extraordinarily clumsy way of writing Greek. When two or more consonants come together in a Greek word, Linear B omits one or more of the consonants or expands the word with dummy vowels (as Japanese does with the word *football*). For instance, the Greek word *stathmos*, meaning "station" or "stable," is written as *ta-to-mo* in Linear B. In the initial consonant cluster *st* the *s* is simply omitted, and in the medial cluster *-thm-* is expanded to two syllables: *to-mo*. Note also that in Linear B there is no way to distinguish between *t* and *th* and no way to represent a final consonant like the final *s* in *stathmos*.

Literacy. For these reasons, Linear B seems never to have caught on amongst the general population of Mycenaean Greece. As far as scholars can determine Linear B was used exclusively by the scribes and bureaucrats who administered the Mycenaean economy, in which authorities collected commodities and products and redistributed them to manufacturers and consumers. Amongst these records keepers, who needed the script to record a finite number of facts about a finite variety of goods and materials, Linear B was a perfectly adequate and efficient writing system, but as a script for whatever a Greek speaker might want to express, it had severe limitations. So, while the palace scribes were writing Linear B, the rest of the Mycenaean population, including probably those members of the upper classes who had no direct involvement in the economic affairs of the palaces, remained illiterate, and after the fall of the Mycenaean palaces even that limited literacy was lost. Without any palaces to keep records for, there was no need for a records keeping script, which was largely the only role that Linear B played.

Greek Alphabet. In the aftermath of the Mycenaean period (1600–1200 B.C.E.), the Greeks remained illiterate for several centuries. Not until the period of the Geometric Renaissance (800–700 B.C.E.) did they recover the art of writing, but when they did so they created a new means of communication that was much more versatile and well-suited to the Greek language than Linear B. It was this new system of writing, the familiar Greek alphabet, that became the medium through which Greek history and literature was recorded, and this same alphabet became the basis for both the Roman alphabet (which is used by speakers of most European languages, including English) and the Cyrillic alphabet, in which Russian and other Slavic languages are written. It is certainly one of the Greeks' most important legacies to Western civilization.

Vowels. The alphabet was based on a West Semitic writing system that was also employed by the Greeks' trading partners, the Phoenicians. One crucial change that the Greeks instituted was the invention of vowels (the letters in the Semitic alphabets only represented consonants). This adaptation was necessary: the structure of words in Semitic languages allows them to be represented recognizably without vowels. Hebrew, for example, a Semitic language that uses a writing system based on the same ancient model as Greek, is written with no vowels. Greek, however, has many words with several vowels in sequence, and these would be difficult or impossible to recognize if written without vowels. For instance, the word *aaatos*, meaning "unharmed," would be represented merely as *ts* in a script without vowels. There are also various pairs of words in Greek that would be indistinguishable in the absence of vowels. For instance, the words *pais* (child) and *pous* (foot) would both be represented indistinguishably as *ps*. The Greeks took letters from the Semitic script that represented sounds that the Greek language did not have and reassigned their values to vowels. This change made the writing system more adaptable for other languages and enabled the Greek alphabet to spawn several other writing systems worldwide.

Ostraka. The earliest examples of Greek writing are found scratched on the surface of pottery shards dating to the eighth century B.C.E. The reason for this occurrence is probably that pottery lasts longer than other materials that were used as writing surfaces, not that pottery was the earliest or most popular writing medium. Nevertheless, pottery shards, or *ostraka* in Greek, were inexpensive and readily available, and they continued to be used for writing throughout antiquity. This practice has even given birth to a familiar word in English vocabulary: every year the Athenian people were allowed to vote in order to send a powerful politician into exile for a period of ten years. Each citizen would scratch the name of his least favorite politician onto an *ostrakon* and deposit it along with all the other ostraka in a specified place. If any one statesman received a set number of votes, he was exiled. This process, by which the Athenians hoped to prevent any one leader from amassing too much power, was called *ostrakismos*, from which the English word *ostracism* is derived.

A drawing of a chariot tablet found at Knossos on Crete (from John Chadwick, *The Decipher of Linear B* [Cambridge: Cambridge University Press, 1976], p. 108. Reprinted by permission of the publisher).

Deltos. Another inexpensive medium for writing was the *deltos* or *deltion*. The deltos consisted of a pair of small wooden tablets connected together at one edge so that they hinged open like the covers of a book. The interior faces of the tablets were coated with beeswax, and messages or accounts could be inscribed in the soft wax and erased when a new message needed to be recorded. The deltos was commonly used throughout the Mediterranean region; one was even found on the Bronze Age Ulu Burun shipwreck. The advantage of the deltos was that it was reusable, but since it could only hold a limited amount of text, it was not well-suited for recording and transmitting the great literary works of ancient Greece. For that reason, papyrus scrolls were the main medium.

Papyrus and Parchment. Papyrus was the most common medium for recording all sorts of writing. Papyrus is a paper-like fabric made from the internal pulp of reeds that grow in the Nile Delta region of Egypt. Sheets of papyrus were attached to one another edge-to-edge to form a continuous writing surface that could be rolled up into scrolls. Another material that was similarly used for extended texts was animal tissue. The laborious method of preparing hides and membranes for use in writing was known in the Archaic (700–490 B.C.E.) and Classical (490–323 B.C.E.) periods, but did not begin to rival papyrus in popularity until the third century B.C.E., when it became a major product of the city of Pergamum in Anatolia. From the name *Pergamum* the English word *parchment* is derived.

Need. Since papyrus came only from Egypt, it was a relatively expensive commodity, and as the literary arts flourished in Greece, it became one of the major imports. Athens in particular became for all intents and purposes an intermediary site for the processing of papyrus, importing the raw material from Egypt and exporting the finished product in the form of books to the rest of the Mediterranean world.

Stone Inscriptions. Stone was another important, though less mobile, medium upon which communication occurred. Stone inscriptions written in the Greek alphabet occurred early in the Archaic Period and increased in frequency throughout the Classical Period. Private citizens used inscribed stones to mark the boundaries of their property, to memorialize their dead, and to take credit for their offerings to the gods. Governments used them to record laws, decrees, treaties, accounts, and anything else they thought needed recording in a permanent, publicly accessible format. Inscribed stones, thousands of which have survived, provide historians with much important information about the functioning of ancient politics and economies, particularly in Athens where a relatively literate population and an open, democratic form of government produced many inscriptions.

Movement of Information. There are basically two ways to disseminate information: one is to send the information out to people by various means; the other is to post it in a central place and let the people come to it. The latter sort of dissemination occurred in many, if not most, Greek city-states on a regular basis. The typical Greek city had at its center a large open space, called an *agora*, which functioned as a central marketplace, a social gathering spot, and, quite often, a place for people to meet for political purposes. In such places the government could post laws, results of elections, levy lists for the military and other information, and rely on a significant percentage of the populace to see it and relay the information to the rest of the people. In Athens, for instance, the law code of Solon (circa 590 B.C.E.) was published on triangular wooden pillars called *kurbeis* in the agora. The *kurbeis* provided access to the law for the common people and served as a check on the power of the upper-class magistrates who otherwise might have been tempted to remember and interpret the law in self-serving ways.

Aggareion. For the communication of information farther afield, there were no regularly established institutions analogous to a modern postal service or news service, either within or between any of the Greek cities. Dissemination of news and transmission of messages was conducted on a largely informal and ad hoc basis. In this area the Greeks lagged behind their neighbors in the Near East, especially the Persians, who had a system of relay messengers, called the *aggareion*, manned by riders on horseback. This ancient version of the Pony Express allowed the Persian king to send and receive messages from far-flung parts of his enormous empire with a quickness that astounded the Greeks. The *aggareion* depended to a great extent upon the Persians' more sophisticated road system, the lack of which, together with the polit-

CLYTEMNESTRA:

The god of fire—rushing fire from Ida!
And beacon to beacon rushed it on to me,
my couriers riding home the torch.
From Troy
to the bare rock of Lemnos, Hermes' Spur,
and the Escort winged the great light west
to the Saving Father's face, Mount Athos hurled it
third in the chain and leaping Ocean's back
the blaze went dancing on to ecstasy—pitch-pine
streaming gold like a newborn sun—and brought
the word in flame to Mount Makistos' brow.
No time to waste, straining, fighting sleep,
that lookout heaved a torch glowing over
the murderous straits of Euripos to reach
Messapion's watchmen craning for the signal.
Fire for word of fire! tense with the heather
withered gray, they stack it, set it ablaze—
the hot force of the beacon never flags,
it springs the Plain of Asopos, rears
like a harvest moon to hit Kithairon's crest

and drives new men to drive the fire on.
That relay pants for the far-flung torch,
they swell its strength outstripping my commands
and the light inflames the marsh, the Gorgon's Eye,
it strikes the peak where the wild goats range—
my law, my fire whips that camp!
They spare nothing, eager to build its heat,
and a huge beard of flame overcomes the headland
beetling down the Saronic Gulf, and flaring south
it brings the dawn to the Black Widow's face—
the watch that looms above your heads—and now
the true son of the burning flanks of Ida
crashes on the roofs of Atreus' sons!
And I ordained it all.
Torch to torch, running for their lives,
one long succession racing home my fire.
One,
first in the laps and last, wins out in triumph.
There you have my proof, *my* burning sign, I tell you—
the power my lord passed on from Troy to me.

Source: Aeschylus, *Agamemnon*, translated by Hugh Lloyd-Jones (Englewood Cliffs, N.J.: Prentice-Hall, 1970).

---

ical fragmentation that hindered cooperation on any intercity institutions (including roads), precluded the Greeks from copying this Persian institution.

Heralds and Envoys. For the exchange of official messages, either between governments or between opposing armies on the battlefield, the Greeks employed heralds (*kêrukes*) or, at a higher level, ambassadors or envoys (*presbeutes*). While there is no firm distinction between heralds and envoys, the latter generally seem to have been empowered to negotiate with people, while heralds simply delivered messages. By a convention observed in most parts of the Mediterranean world, heralds and envoys were considered sacrosanct. Heralds carried a special staff, called a *kêrukeion*, which entitled them to hospitality and freedom from harassment. If a herald was mistreated or killed as he passed through enemy territory, it was considered a crime of the greatest religious consequence.

Skutalê. Hermes, who acted as the messenger of the gods in myth, was held to be the god of heralds and was usually portrayed carrying a divine, winged version of the *kêrukeion*. An interesting variation on the *kêrukeion* was the *skutalê*, a staff or a standard diameter carried by officials of the Spartan government. When the Spartans wished to send a message to their representatives abroad, they wound

a strip of leather around a *skutalê* and wrote the message upon it. The leather strip was then delivered to the Spartan representative in the field who wound it around his own *skutalê* to read the message. It is thought that the use of the *skutalê* was more of a symbolic gesture than an attempt to keep the message secret. If the leather strip fell into the wrong hands, its message could be easily pieced together even by someone who did not have a proper *skutalê*. Yet, the Spartan official who received such a message was at least assured that it had been written by someone possessing a *skutalê* of the requisite diameter, which made it less likely that an enemy could pass on to him forged instructions from his government.

Emergency Messages. Official communications traveled by the same means as people and trade goods. The chief overland method was on foot or, in the rare cases where conditions permitted, by horse. Emergency messages within the area of the Aegean were most often sent by sea. An illustrative example occurred in 427 B.C.E., during the Second Peloponnesian War, when the Athenians were engaged in punishing the people of the island of Lesbos for attempting to break away from Athenian control. The Athenian assembly first decided to put all the men of the chief city of Mytilene to death and to sell the women and children into slavery. A trireme was dispatched to Les-

According to Herodotus, when the Athenians and the Spartans killed some Persian messengers who had come demanding the submission of Greece to the will of the Persian king, divine punishment was the result.

To Athens and Sparta Xerxes [the Persian king] sent no demand for submission because of what happened to the messengers whom Darius had sent on a previous occasion: at Athens they were thrown into the pit like criminals, at Sparta they were pushed into a well—and told that if they wanted earth and water for the king, to get them from there. This time, therefore, Xerxes refrained from sending a request. Just what disagreeable consequences were suffered by the Athenians for this treatment of the king's messengers, I am unable to say; perhaps it was the destruction of their city and the countryside around it—though I do not myself believe that this happened as a direct result of their crime. The case is clear, however, with respect to the Spartans: upon them fell the anger of Agamemnon's herald Talthybius. . . . Now there was a long period after the incident I have mentioned above, during which the Spartans were unable to obtain favorable signs from their sacrifices; this caused them deep concern, and they held frequent assemblies at which the question "Is there any Spartan who is willing to die for his country?" was put by the public crier. Thereupon two Spartans, Sperchias, the son of Aneristus, and Bulis, the son of Nicoles, both men of good family and great wealth, volunteered to offer their lives to Xerxes in atonement for Darius' messengers who had been killed in Sparta. They were dispatched accordingly to Persia to meet their doom.

Source: *Herodotus: The Histories,* translated by Aubrey de Selincourt (Harmondsworth, U.K., & Baltimore: Penguin, 1954).

bos, situated on the opposite side of the Aegean, to deliver the verdict. The next day, however, the assembly repented and sent off a second trireme with orders to exact a more lenient punishment. The crew of the second trireme rowed as quickly as they could, ate their meals while seated at their oars, and slept only in shifts so that the vessel was under constant propulsion. They arrived at Mytilene just a few hours after the first ship, which had had a day-and-a-half head start, and just in time to prevent the horrific sentence from being carried out.

Day Runners. When emergency messages had to be carried over land, the Greeks employed long-distance runners, called *hêmerodromoi* (literally, "day runners"). The most famous of all hêmerodromoi was an Athenian named Pheidippides. In 490 B.C.E., when Persian invaders landed on the beach at Marathon in Athenian territory, the Athenians dispatched Pheidippides to Sparta to seek the assistance of the Spartans. He ran to Sparta, a distance of some 140 miles, much of it over bad roads and mountainous terrain (in crossing one mountain a vision of the god Pan appeared to him), and arrived with his message in less than

two days. His Herculean effort turned out to be in vain: the Spartans were celebrating an important religious festival and could not send troops until it was over. Nevertheless, the Athenians succeeded in repulsing the Persian assault, and Pheidippides ran the 26 miles from the battlefield to the city of Athens to announce the victory. After completing his run, he delivered the joyous news and promptly dropped dead. (Although the run to Athens is probably a legendary addition to the original story, this event has bequeathed to modern English the term *marathon* to describe a 26-mile footrace.) The fact that the Greeks used hêmerodromoi rather than horsemen for these sorts of missions attests to the poor quality of the interurban road system in Greece.

Beacons. One method of communication that did not depend on standard avenues of transport was telegraphy by means of fire and smoke signals. In this area too, the Greeks were not as advanced as their neighbors to the East. There is evidence that the Persians and other large Near Eastern empires controlled systems of beacon relays whereby signals could be sent from one end of the empire to another almost instantaneously. A description of such a system is preserved in the writings of the Athenian playwright Aeschylus. In the play *Agamemnon* (458 B.C.E.), the mythical queen of Argos, Clytemnestra, describes the fire signal sent to her by her husband, Agamemnon, to announce the capture of the city of Troy. The original beacon fire was lit in the vicinity of Troy, from where it was seen by lookouts on the neighboring island of Lemnos, who lit their own fire in turn and passed the signal on. In this manner the fireborne message traverses the entire periphery of the Aegean before arriving at Argos in southern Greece. Some scholars have thought that this mythical beacon system might reflect actual systems put in place by the Greeks during the period of the Persian wars, but it is more likely a simple reflection of a practice that the Greeks saw the Persians employing during those conflicts. In fact, it forms part of the playwright's ominous characterization of Agamemnon and Clytemnestra as overweening oriental-style dynasts.

Codes. Historical references show the Greeks' use of fire signals to be decidedly more modest. In most cases, no relay of signals was involved, and it was simply a matter of hilltop lookouts sending a fire signal (or a smoke signal during daylight hours) to a nearby city or army camp, usually to signal the approach of hostile forces. The amount of information that could be sent by such beacons was extremely limited: the sender and receiver decided beforehand what a lit beacon would mean, but in the Classical Period there is no evidence for a flame code or flame array being used to communicate a message more complex than "here comes the enemy." There is some evidence of a simple flame code being used on occasion: a lit torch waved back and forth indicated the approach of enemies, while a torch held steady signaled the approach of friends. More sophisticated uses of flame signals—involving relays and arrays of flames and the use of different burning times to send more complex information—were attested to during the later Hellenistic and Roman periods.

Private Messages. While official communications among the Greeks were not terribly advanced, private communications were even more rudimentary. Private citizens who wanted to send messages abroad had to do so by informal means. They could write their messages on papyrus, *ostraka*, and wax tablets, or even emboss them on strips of soft metal such as lead. To deliver the messages, however, in the absence of a regular postal service, they simply had to find someone, a merchant or a traveler, who was bound for the location of their addressee. Finding someone was usually possible in busy trading ports like Piraeus, the port of Athens, but the ultimate delivery of the message depended on the reliability and honesty of the person who was engaged to carry it. Prompt delivery of such messages could certainly not be counted upon.

Sources:

Sian Lewis, *News and Society in the Greek Polis* (Chapel Hill: University of North Carolina Press, 1996).

Roger D. Woodard, *Greek Writing from Knossos to Homer: A Linguistic Interpretation of the Origin of the Greek Alphabet and the Continuity of Ancient Greek Literacy* (New York: Oxford University Press, 1997).

PATTERNS AND PRACTICES OF TRANSPORTATION

Upheaval. Following the collapse of the Mycenaean civilization around 1200 B.C.E., Greece entered a period known as the "Dark Ages." All the great achievements of mainland Greek civilization vanished: the art of writing was lost; centralized government broke down; population declined drastically; and settlements devolved into isolated farming communities. Although some archaeologists are finding evidence for more prosperity, social complexity, and organization than they had previously expected, there is no disputing that this was a time of drastic reorganization of political and economic life in Greece. For one thing, the upheaval at the end of the Bronze Age (3000–1100 B.C.E.) disrupted the networks of exchange from which the Mycenaeans had profited, and Greece became more isolated from the outside world. At the same time, there occurred in this period the first recorded large-scale migrations of people from and within the mainland of Greece. Within the first two centuries following the fall of the Mycenaean palaces, many Greeks fled the upheaval on the mainland and sought new homes in overseas locations. It is at this time that the coastal region of western Anatolia became heavily populated with Greeks, and the island of Cyprus also received an influx of immigrants, laying the basis for the Greek-speaking community that remains the largest ethnic group on that island to the present day. These movements of peoples were symptoms of decline, rather than prosperity, but they set the stage for later expansion that would mark the Greeks' return to full participation in the Mediterranean trade economy.

Recovery. By 800 B.C.E., Greek fortunes had begun to recover, and in the century between 800 and 700 the pace of change was extraordinarily rapid. The Greeks regained the art of writing by inventing a new script, the familiar Greek alphabet, which they based on the writing system of the Phoenicians or one of their neighbors in the Levant. Agricultural productivity increased, perhaps in part because the introduction of iron tools and implements made farming more efficient, and as a result the population began to boom. The Greeks also started to rebuild their political organization. Villages within distinct geographical areas joined together, either willingly or by force on the part of the stronger communities, and established a common government and market for local goods. This development is the origin of the independent Greek city-states such as Athens, Corinth, and Sparta, which were to be hereafter the basis for political organization in Greece.

Borders. The boundaries of the Greek city-states were generally those provided by nature: the limits of the territory were defined by the nearest mountain ranges and seacoasts. This situation is unlike the one in the Bronze Age

---

THE HIGHS AND LOWS OF MERCHANT LIFE

According to Herodotus, in preparing for their colonization of Cyrene, the Therans took a scout named Corobius to the island of Platea off the coast of Libya and left him there to reconnoiter. When the Therans failed to return for him, he was aided by some Samian merchants, who then went on to have their own adventure.

They reached Platea and put Corobius ashore with enough supplies for a stated number of months, and then made sail again with all speed for home, to bring the news about the island. They had agreed with Corobius to be away a definite length of time; this period, however, was exceeded and Corobius was in distress from lack of supplies, until a Samian vessel bound for Egypt, under the command of a man called Colaeus, was forced by the weather to run for Platea. The Samians listened to Corobius' story, left him enough food to last a year, and resumed their voyage to Egypt, which they were anxious to reach. Easterly winds, however, prevented them from getting there, and continued so long that they were driven away to the westward right through the Pillars of Heracles [the Straits of Gibraltar] until, by a piece of more than human luck, they succeeded in making Tartessus. This trading port had not at that period been exploited, and the consequence was that the Samian merchants, on their return home, made a greater profit on their cargo than any of the Greeks of whom we have precise knowledge, with the exception of Sostratus of Aegina, the son of Laodamas—with him, nobody can compare.

Source: *Herodotus: The Histories*, translated by Aubrey de Selincourt (Harmondsworth, U.K. & Baltimore: Penguin, 1954).

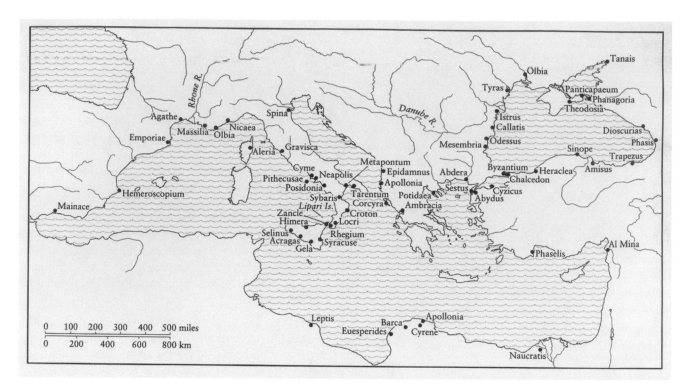

A map of Greek colonies founded between 750 B.C.E. and 500 B.C.E. (Sarah B. Pomeroy, and others, *Ancient Greece: Political, Social, and Cultural History* [1999]; used by permission of Oxford University Press)

when a single Mycenaean palace could have authority over an area far beyond the local region in which the palace was situated. The smaller scale of the city-states was a limiting factor in the development of roads and other facilities for overland transportation.

Tensions. Along with these positive developments, some negative ones occurred as well. The growth in population began to strain the resources of the Greek city-states and exacerbate class divisions within the population. Farmland, always in short supply in Greece, became more valuable and a source of conflict. Various contemporary documents surviving from 700 B.C.E. were written in the new Greek alphabet, so the events of this era, called the "Archaic Period" (700–480 B.C.E.), are known with somewhat more certainty than those of the preceding periods. Amongst the earliest events recorded in this era were the first major wars between city-states, and generally the issue in these conflicts was control of agricultural land. Heightened prosperity and population brought heightened tension in Greece.

Contacts. A reestablishment of Greek contacts with the outside world accompanied all these domestic developments and played a role in accelerating them. Probably through the activities of the Phoenicians, the Greeks were reintroduced to the Mediterranean trading networks. Recent archaeological excavations at Greek communities have yielded goods from overseas which demonstrate foreign influences in art and other aspects of culture. Greeks began to return to the widespread cultivation of the olive and the grape, and started taking advantage again of their value as export commodities.

Iron. A major impetus toward getting involved in trade again was probably the need for iron. As was true in the case of copper and tin, there were no plentiful sources of iron ore on the Greek mainland, and as demand for this useful metal increased, supplies of it had to be sought overseas. One of the major sources for it was the island of Elba, off the western coast of Italy. Initially, it was probably non-Greek merchants, chiefly Phoenicians, who acted as agents in bringing iron and other commodities to Greece and taking away Greek goods in exchange, but it was only a matter of time before the Greeks took an active role in overseas trade themselves.

Colonization. One of the earliest and most important manifestations of Greek mobility in the Archaic Period (700–480 B.C.E.) was the move toward colonization. In this area the Greeks once again were following the lead of the Phoenicians, who had established their own colonies in the Mediterranean, the most famous example being the city of Carthage on the coast of North Africa (in what is now Tunisia), around 750 B.C.E. At about the same time, Greeks from the city-states of Chalcis and Eretria set up a trading post on the island of Pithecussae off the western coast of Italy. This settlement was followed soon afterward by a full-fledged colony at the site of Cumae, near modern Naples. Much of the earliest Greek colonizing activity was directed toward the West. In around 734 B.C.E. the Corinthians established a colony on the island of Corcyra, off the northwest coast of Greece and astride the shipping lanes between Greece and Italy. Meanwhile, they also founded the colony of Syracuse in Sicily. Throughout the latter 700s and on into the 600s other

SPITEFUL COLONIST

In this passage from Herodotus, Dorieus, the son of one of the Spartan kings, cannot stand the thought of staying in Sparta and seeing his unworthy half brother Cleomenes take over the throne. He therefore leaves Sparta and establishes a new colony on the African coast. This passage illustrates how colonization could be used to avoid political trouble at home, and how it was not always undertaken as a result of sober strategic and economic calculation. Note the emphasis on the observance of religious formalities (or lack thereof). This excerpt also suggests that by the time Dorieus set out on his ill-fated expeditions (circa 520 B.C.E.), the number of places one could lay claim to in the Mediterranean without serious opposition were exceedingly rare.

Dorieus was the finest young man of his generation and confident that his merits would assure his succession. As a result of this he was naturally indignant when, on the death of Anaxandrides, the Spartans followed their usual custom and put the eldest son, Cleomenes, on the throne. Unable to bear the prospect of being ruled by Cleomenes, he asked the Spartans for a body of men and took them off to found a settlement elsewhere, without previously consulting the Delphic oracle on a suitable site, or observing any of the usual formalities: he just went off, in a fit of temper, to Libya, with some men from Thera to act as guides. Arrived there, he settled by the river Cinyps, on a piece of excellent land belonging to the Libyans. Within three years, however, he was driven out by the Macae (a Libyan tribe) and the Carthaginians, and returned to the Peloponnese. Here he was advised by a certain Antichares of Eleon, on the strength of the oracles given to Laius, to found the city of Heraclea in Sicily; for, according to this person, all the country of Eryx in Western Sicily belonged to the Heraclids, as Heracles himself was its original conqueror [the Spartan royal families claimed to be descendants of Heracles]. Dorieus, accordingly, went to Delphi to consult the oracle on his chance of acquiring the land which he was after, and was told by the Priestess that it would certainly be his, whereupon he fetched the band of settlers whom he had taken to Libya and sailed with them along the Italian coast. . . . They reached Sicily, but were defeated and killed, with all the men under their command, in a battle with the Phoenicians and the people of Egesta. The only one to escape was Euryleon, who collected the few survivors of the army and captured Minoa, a colony of Selinus, and helped the people of Selinus to free themselves from their ruler Peithagoras.

Source: *Herodotus: The Histories,* translated by Aubrey de Selincourt (Harmondsworth, U.K. & Baltimore: Penguin, 1954).

Greek city-states followed the lead of the Chalcidians, Eretrians, and Corinthians in planting colonies in Sicily and southern Italy, to the extent that these regions became dominated by Greek-speaking communities and would eventually come to be referred to as *Magna Graecia,* or "Greater Greece." As available land in this area filled up, other colonizing states turned elsewhere: to the northern coast of Africa; to the coasts of what is now France and Spain; to the northern coast of the Aegean (populated at that time by non-Greek tribes of Macedonians and Thracians); and to the Black Sea.

Byzantium. In about 660 B.C.E., the city of Megara founded the colony of Byzantium on the Bosporus, the more easterly of the two crucial straits that connect the Black Sea to the Aegean. Subsequently, Greek colonies were set up all along the coast of the Black Sea in what are now Turkey and the Ukraine. By the end of the Archaic Period in 480 B.C.E., Greek cities had been established from one end of the Mediterranean to the other, and it is likely that more Greeks were living in the colonies than in the mainland of Greece itself.

Means to an End. The establishment of a Greek presence in all of these places ensured that Greeks would take over the dominant role in Mediterranean trade from the Phoenicians. Unlike the colonization undertaken by European powers in the modern era, however, the main reasons for Greek colonization do not seem to have been economic ones, such as control of trade routes, access to foreign goods, or exploitation of native labor. Instead, the Greeks seemed to have viewed colonization mainly as a means to reduce tension at home. To counter the strife that could be caused by rising populations and the lack of adequate crop lands, the Greeks took to colonization as a safety valve. Excess population, and in particular disgruntled and divisive elements of the citizenry, could be shifted off to foreign lands where they could make a new life for themselves without draining the resources of the mother city. That the colonies were not founded primarily for economic reasons is also confirmed by the fact that when they were established they generally became independent city-states in their own right, with little or no political control exerted by the mother city, and with no obligation to grant her special economic concessions, as was required, for instance, of the American colonies by Britain in the days before the American Revolution.

Breadbasket. Nevertheless, when colonists departed from their homeland, they naturally chose places to settle that would provide them with the best economic opportunities. It is no accident, therefore, that the earliest Greek colonies were located along the western coast of Italy near good sources of iron. Likewise, colonies planted on the coasts of Africa and Asia Minor (on the Black Sea) were perfectly situated to become intermediaries in the exchange of goods between the Greeks and the people of those regions. Greek colonists, remembering the lessons of the difficult life they led in the mother country, avoided replicating the experience by seeking out localities where the crop lands were fertile and plentiful. Sicily, northern Africa, and the Ukrainian plains near the Black Sea

The following inscription in stone purports to record the actual text of an agreement the people of Thera (modern Santorini) swore to when they were sending off a colony to Cyrene in Libya, circa 600 B.C.E. (The stone was not inscribed with this text until the fourth century B.C.E., and some scholars doubt that it reproduces the text of the colonists' oath accurately.) The Therans claim that they decided to send the colony not because they needed land or raw materials but because the god Apollo told them to through an oracle. Participation in the expedition was not necessarily voluntary. Members were drafted from every family, and those who refused to go were liable to execution.

Since Apollo spontaneously told B[at]tos and the Therans to colonize Cyrene, it has been decided by the Therans to send Battos off to Libya, as Archagetes and as King, with the Therans to sail as his Companions. On equal and fair terms shall they sail according to family (?), with one son to be conscripted [a large gap in the inscription occurs here] adults and from the [other] Therans those who are free-born [small gap] shall sail. If they [the colonists] establish the settlement, kinsmen who sail later to Libya shall be entitled to citizenship and offices and shall be allotted portions of the land which has no owner. But if they do not successfully establish the settlement and the Therans are incapable of giving it assistance, and they are pressed by hardship for five years, from that land shall they depart, without fear, to Thera, to their own property, and they shall be citizens. Any man who, if the city sends him, refuses to sail, will be liable to the death-penalty and his property shall be confiscated. The man harboring him or concealing him, whether he be a father [aiding his] son or a brother his brother, is to suffer the same penalty as the man who refuses to sail. On these conditions a sworn agreement was made by those who stayed there and by those who sailed to found the colony, and they invoked curses against those transgressors who would not abide by it—whether they were those settling in Libya or those who remained. They made waxen images and burnt them, calling down [the following] curse, everyone having assembled together, men, women, boys, girls: "The person who does not abide by this sworn agreement but transgresses it shall melt away and dissolve like the images—himself, his descendants and his property; but those who abide by the sworn agreement—those sailing to Libya and those staying in Thera—shall have an abundance of good things, both themselves [and] their descendants.

Source: Charles W. Fornara, *Archaic Times to the End of the Peloponnesian War* (Cambridge: Cambridge University Press, 1983).

Regardless of the motivation behind this colonizing expedition, the colony of Cyrene was destined to become a rich source of grain for Greece. The following inscription from the fourth century B.C.E. records how Cyrene provided critical supplies of grain to various places in Greece during a period of famine:

[The following are] all those to whom the city gave grain, when the grain-shortage took place in Hellas. To the Athenians one hundred thousand [bushels]; to Olympias sixty thousand; to the Argives fifty thousand; to the Larisans fifty thousand; to the Corinthians fifty thousand; to Kleopatra fifty thousand. . . .

The list goes on for several lines. In all the Cyreneans "gave" (or more likely, sold at a bargain rate) 805,000 bushels in this year. That would correspond to the yield of approximately 8,000 acres of field cultivated with modern farming methods and techniques. The actual amount of Cyrenean land needed to produce this much grain must have been far greater.

Source: Phillip Harding, *From the End of the Peloponnesian War to the Battle of Ipsus* (Cambridge: Cambridge University Press, 1985).

beckoned with acre upon acre of rich, unoccupied land. Eventually these regions become the breadbasket of Greece. Population in the old Greek city-states continued to grow and, in many places, outstripped the capacity of the land to support it, so grain for everyday consumption became one of the top imports. The colonists gladly shared their surpluses, at a price, with their cousins in Greece and became wealthy in the process. So while the original reasons for Greek colonization might not have been to control trade routes, cut out the middlemen in their access to raw materials, and open new markets for Greek goods, these were certainly some of the most important effects. With much of the Mediterranean becoming a Greek lake, large amounts of materials were being transported back and forth from the colonies to the motherland and vice versa.

Greek Traders. Colonization and the presence of imported objects in the archaeological record of the Greek cities do not in themselves show that the Greeks were taking a more active role in trade. After all, there is no reason why the Phoenicians or other non-Greek traders could not have been the ones who were bringing foreign goods to Greek lands and carrying away Greek products in exchange. More significant in demonstrating the activities of the Greeks themselves is their establishment or participation in various *emporia* (trading posts) across the Mediterranean seaboard. These places were not colonies, in the sense of permanent independent communities with their own governments and laws. The Greeks and others came there not to settle but to trade.

Al Mina. A site in present-day Syria, known by the modern name of Al Mina, was one such *emporion*.

A model of the Ionian city of Priene (formerly Staatliche Museen, Berlin)

Excavators have uncovered evidence of a port, warehouses, and a large amount of Greek pottery from as early as the 700s B.C.E. The best explanation for the preponderance of Greek artifacts at the site is that Greeks were coming there regularly and bringing their wares to trade with people who had access to the wealthy trade routes of Asia. If traders from other lands were the ones who brought these Greek articles to Al Mina, one would expect them to have left behind more materials from places besides Greece. This trading post demonstrates that even at this early date, the Greeks were competing with the Phoenicians not only in the Aegean and in the West, but in the Phoenicians' own backyard.

Naucratis. Something in between an emporion and a colony was the Egyptian town of Naucratis. Situated on the Canopic branch of the Nile Delta, the westernmost of the main branches of the delta, Naucratis was given to Greek traders by the Egyptian pharaoh sometime in the late seventh century B.C.E. This settlement allowed the Greeks to have a foothold in Egypt (the Egyptians were large consumers of Greek olive oil) and a source of grain, ivory, ebony, and Egyptian handicrafts for Greek markets. It was also a means for the Egyptian authorities to control the activity of Greek traders. Merchants who landed anywhere in Egypt other than Naucratis were detained until they swore an

oath that they did not do so on purpose. They were then required to proceed to Naucratis, which eventually became more of a city than a trading post. Traders from many different Greek cities erected temples there, and a permanent community developed. Herodotus says that the pharaoh Amasis took as wife a Greek woman from Naucratis.

Trade Items. Greek exports in this period were roughly the same as they were in the Bronze Age, olive oil and wine being the chief articles. Fine pottery also was a trade item in itself. Greek vase painting was always among the best in the Mediterranean, and in this period first Corinthian vase painters, who covered their pots with harmonious bands of stylized animals and decorative patterns, and then the Athenians, who pioneered the representation of humans and narrative scenes on pottery, became highly popular throughout the Mediterranean world. Greek metalwork, including bronze and iron weaponry and bronze artwork, was also in demand. The city of Argos in Greece was particularly well-known for the quality of its metalworkers.

Carrying Trade. However, Greek traders did not traffic only in Greek wares. The holds of Greek merchant ships were typically full of goods from a variety of sources. Many Greek shipowners made the bulk of their income by acting as middlemen for other people's transactions and carried little or nothing from their

This inscription was scrawled by two Greek mercenaries on one of the legs of the great statues of Abu Simbel, in Egypt about 700 miles up the Nile River from the Mediterranean. It is one of many such graffiti that the Greek soldiers left while on an expedition for the Egyptian king around 591 B.C.E.

When King Psammetichos had come to Elephantine, this was written by those who sailed with Psammetichos, son of Theokles, who went as far upstream as they could—above Kerkis. Potasimto led the foreigners and Amasis the Egyptians. This was written by Archon son of Amoibichos and Pelekos son of Eudamos.

One of the earliest Greek poets whose writing survives, Archilochus of Paros (circa 650–600 B.C.E.) composed this pithy poem describing his life as a mercenary:

I depend on my spear for my kneaded bread; I depend on my spear for my wine
From Ismaria; I lean on my spear while I drink it.

The following story about the poet Arion illustrates the vulnerability of a lone traveler in this time, although the part about the dolphin is probably an embellishment.

Most of his time Arion had spent with Periander [ruler of Corinth], till he felt a longing to sail to Italy and Sicily. This he did; and after making a great deal of money in those countries, he decided to return to Corinth. He sailed from Tarentum in a Corinthian vessel, because he had more confidence in Corinthians than in anyone else. The crew, however, when the ship was at sea, hatched a plot to throw him overboard and steal his money. He got wind of their intention, and begged them to take his money, but spare his life. To no purpose, however; for the sailors told him either to kill himself if he wanted to be buried ashore, or to jump overboard at once.

Arion, seeing they had made up their minds, as a last resort begged permission to stand on the after-deck, dressed in his singing robes, and give them a song; the song over, he promised to kill himself. Delighted at the prospect of hearing a song from the world's most famous singer, the sailors all made their way forward from the stern and assembled amidships. Arion put on his full professional costume, took up his lute and, standing on the afterdeck, played and sang a lively tune. Then he leapt into the sea, just as he was, with all his clothes on.

The ship continued her voyage to Corinth, but a dolphin picked up Arion and carried him on its back to Taenarum. Here Arion landed, and made his way in his singing costume to Corinth, where he told the whole story. Periander was not too ready to believe it; so he put Arion under strict supervision, keeping the ship's crew meanwhile carefully in mind. On their return he sent for them, and asked if they had anything to tell him about Arion. "Oh yes," they answered, "we left him safe and sound at Tarentum in Italy." But no sooner were the words out of their mouths than Arion himself appeared, just as he was when he jumped overboard. This was an unpleasant shock for the sailors.

Source: *Herodotus: The Histories,* translated by Aubrey de Selincourt (Harmondsworth, U.K., & Baltimore: Penguin, 1954).

own native cities. Aegina, a small island off the coast of Athens with few natural resources or exportable goods, was apparently full of such entrepreneurs. The merchants of Aegina carried cargoes of oil, wine, iron, and slaves (a new import of growing importance to Greece), and they were active in Egypt, the West, and in the Black Sea area. By some accounts, the Aeginetans produced the first minted coinage in all of Greece, and their weights and measures served as the standard that many Greek city-states followed. The profits they sent back home made their poor little island a rich one and allowed it to support a population far in excess of what the land of the island could have fed on its own.

Mercenaries, Poets, and Teachers. Historical records and archaeological remains of the Archaic Period also reveal that the Greeks were traveling and moving about for many reasons other than colonization and trade. Many men who found farming difficult went abroad to serve as mercenaries. Through fighting one another the Greeks had become proficient at a type of heavily-armored infantry combat called hoplite warfare and were in high demand as paid soldiers among the kingdoms of the Near East and Egypt. Meanwhile, poets and teachers could find their services in demand from one end of the Mediterranean to the other. The poet Anacreon, for instance, was born in the Anatolian city of Teos but spent much of his career on the island of Samos and late in life moved to Athens at the invitation of that city's ruler. Sappho of Lesbos, Greece's most famous woman writer, spent part of her life in Sicily (a result of exile, not popularity). Another poet, Ibycus, was born in southern Italy and came to Samos at the same time that Anacreon was there. An especially interesting case is the poet Arion. Hailing from Methymna on Lesbos, he came to Corinth to be a court poet for the ruler of that city and left of his own volition to seek his fortune, successfully, amongst the Greek communities in Italy and Sicily. We can assume that less talented poets, who had a hard time keeping the same audience entertained for long, had to travel around even more.

Sources:

John Boardman, *The Greeks Overseas: Their Early Colonies and Trade* (London & New York: Thames & Hudson, 1980).

Robin Osborne Jr., *Greece in the Making, 1200–479 BC* (London & New York: Routledge, 1996).

Anthony M. Snodgrass, *Archaic Greece: The Age of Experiment* (London: Dent, 1980).

ROADS AND LAND TRAFFIC

Limitations. The main avenue of travel and heavy transport in ancient Greece was the sea. This fact was true in all of the Mediterranean lands, but was nowhere more the case than in Greece, where the waters were placid, the harbors plentiful, and the facilities for land transport limited. While overland roads certainly existed in Greece, they were in most cases rudimentary and were unsuitable for the transportation of large cargoes. In later centuries the Romans would earn themselves a reputation for road construction in the Mediterranean, but this art was one in which their Greek predecessors had little to teach them. It was not so much that the Greeks were incapable of competent road building; they could build a sturdy road where there was need for one, and many of the roads they built in the vicinities of cities and on the approaches to major religious sanctuaries were quite well constructed. Yet, road building on the scale of the Romans was something never seen in Greece until the modern era. The main reason for this situation was, once again, Greece's geography: formidable mountain ranges presented considerable engineering difficulties for any but the shortest roads. The political fragmentation of Greece also was an obstacle. Few individual city-states could muster the sort of manpower and financial resources to build and maintain a reliable network of highways, and the relationships between neighboring city-states was rarely cordial enough to encourage cooperation on such matters. Moreover, the convenience of transportation by sea, and the habits in that direction that the Greeks had long inculcated, made the effort of building and maintaining first-class roads a low priority.

Greek Roads. One indication of the poor development of Greek roads and the unsuitability of the terrain is the fact that centuries later, when Greece was actually part of the Roman Empire, even the Romans did not practice their vaunted road-building skills in the region. The closest thing to a major Roman highway in Greece was the Via Egnatia, which ran from the Adriatic coast in present-day Albania to the city of Thessalonike, on the northern Aegean Sea, and from there east to Byzantium. Farther south, Roman road engineering was employed only in a few sporadic cases. The antiquarian Pausanias, who wrote about his travels in Greece in the second century C.E., provided a valuable account of the state of Greek roads dating from the Roman Period. Although Pausanias lived much later than the period covered in this volume, it is a safe assumption that the condition of roads before the end of the Classical Period (480-323 B.C.E.) was little different from, and certainly not much better than, what he described.

Major Arteries. The routes mentioned by Pausanias were used for traffic between cities and sanctuaries. The road between Athens and Corinth was the only place in which Pausanias mentioned Roman road engineering in Greece. It was not only the most direct route between two major cities, but also the avenue for the majority of the traffic passing between the Peloponnese and central and northern Greece. Apparently in Classical times this road was a narrow and treacherous path along sheer seaside cliffs, probably suitable only for pedestrians and pack animals, and any wheeled traffic had to take a more circuitous inland route. It was only in Pausanias's own day that the Roman emperor Hadrian ordered the improvement of this road, widening it so that wheeled traffic could pass in both directions. (It seems that even the best roads in ancient Greece were wide enough only for a single vehicle to pass at a time, and this accounts for Pausanias's admiring comments on the width of Hadrian's road.) Another route singled out for praise by Pausanias passed between two major cities, Argos and Tegea, and would have also carried the bulk of traffic bound for Sparta, Olympia, and other major sites in the Peloponnese. It too was suitable for wheeled traffic.

Delphi. Pausanias also described the roadways around the major religious shrine at Delphi. Sacred to the god Apollo, Delphi was the chief oracular shrine in Greece, and people seeking insight into their futures were constantly visiting the site (except in the winter months, when traveling was worse and the god was said to vacate his shrine). Delphi is located in particularly mountainous terrain, within the folds of the enormous Parnassus massif, and the roads as described by Pausanias were generally difficult, even the route which probably carried most of the overland traffic to the shrine. Apparently not even an important and lucrative religious shrine warranted well-engineered roads for the convenience of its devotees. Of course, in the case of Delphi, the effort that the pilgrim had to make in getting to the site may have been viewed as a soul-cleansing aspect of his or her religious experience.

Clues. Because of the undeveloped nature of most ancient Greek roads, modern archaeologists often have difficulty locating them and distinguishing them from ones made in later periods. In many cases, moreover, the Greeks chose the most convenient route between places, with the result that later builders would choose the same courses for their more thoroughly engineered roads and in the construction process cover and obliterate the remains of the earlier avenues. There are some cases, however, where a route used by the Greeks can be identified with reasonable certainty, and for this reason scholars are able to make some general observations about Greek road-building techniques.

Construction Techniques. In many cases, Greek roads were little more than paths that were cleared and leveled by continual use. Some important routes seem to have been given no deliberate improvement at all, and in fact the path of the road was occasionally nothing more than a dry streambed. Flagstone and cobblestone paving has been found on some routes, but not frequently enough to make archaeolo-

The *stadion* was the standard Greek unit of large-scale distance measurement and was equivalent to a little more than two hundred yards. About eight stadia, or furlongs, make a mile.

[The coast road between Athens and Corinth] which is still named after Sciron, was first, they say, made passable for foot passengers by Sciron when he was war minister of Megara; but the Emperor Hadrian made it so wide and convenient that even chariots could meet on it.

The road from Tegea to Argos is an excellent carriage-road, and quite a highway.

From this point the road [one of the main overland routes to Delphi] grows steeper and more difficult for a man on foot.

The ascent [from Delphi] to the Corycian cave is easier for a man on foot than for mules and horses.

Tithorea is distant, I should guess, eighty furlongs from Delphi by the pass over Parnassus. The other road, which is not mountainous the whole way, and is even suitable for vehicles, was said to be some furlongs longer.

Lilaea is a winter day's journey from Delphi: the way lies across and down [Mount] Parnassus. We judged the distance to be one hundred eighty furlongs.

From Cleonae there are two roads to Argos. One, a shortcut, is a mere footpath: the other is over the pass of the Tretus, as it is called. The latter, like the former, is a narrow defile shut in by mountains on all sides, but it is better adapted for driving.

The road [from Sikyon] to Titane is sixty furlongs, and impassable for carriages by reason of its narrowness.

There is a pass into Arcadia from Argolis by Hysiae and over Mount Parthenius, debouching [(coming out)] in the territory of Tegea; and there are two other passes debouching in the territory of Mantinea, one through Prinus, as it is called, the other through the Ladder. The latter is the wider pass, and steps were formerly made in it to facilitate the descent. . . . The other road is narrower than the one I have described, and leads over Artemisius.

Source: *Pausanias's Description of Greece,* translated by J. G. Frazer (London: Macmillan, 1913).

such measures the grade of Greek mountain roads sometimes approached 30 percent, meaning that for every ten feet in length the road rose three feet in height. This gradient is steep—by comparison modern highways are generally engineered to avoid gradients over 10 percent—and would have made wheeled traffic difficult, though not impossible. Greek roads were often less than two meters (6.5 feet) in width and were rarely wider than three meters (10 feet). As a result, it is easy to see why Pausanias found a road in which carriages could pass each other abreast particularly remarkable.

Wheel Ruts. An expedient that the Greeks frequently employed to accommodate wheeled traffic over terrain that was particularly steep, rough, winding, or slippery was the cutting of wheel ruts. These grooves were carved into the roadway in which the wheels of vehicles would run, giving them improved traction and preventing them from sliding off to the side of the road. In some places, wheel ruts were the only improvements made to the roadway, and the areas between and alongside the ruts were left in their original rough and rocky state. The distance between ruts varied from road to road, but the average was 1.5 meters (about 5 feet). Makers of carts and wagons for cross-country traffic had to keep this fact in mind if they wanted to produce vehicles that could be used on these roads.

First-Rate Highway. One road that has been identified with some certainty by archaeologists is the one which Pausanias identified as "a first rate highway," the route between Argos and Tegea. This road, though it was used in the Roman Period, shows no trace of distinctively Roman engineering, so it can be taken as an example of the best that ancient Greek road builders could accomplish. It crosses a pass through a particularly tall and rugged range of mountains. The pass, known as Mount Parthenius, is not the lowest one in this range, but it provides the most direct access between the territories of Argos and Tegea, a fact that shows the builders were concerned more with minimizing the distance of the road than they were with making it as gentle a route as possible. Many of the best features of Greek workmanship are exhibited on this route: flagstone paving covers the road in many stretches and may have at one point run the entire length of the road. When the road runs along the sides of slopes, it is carefully terraced, and in the steeper parts it is equipped with zigzagging switchbacks. Wheel ruts have been found in some of the steeper stretches, and in one particularly steep place the paving is interrupted at intervals by rows of stones that stand up above the rest of the pavement, forming something analogous to speed bumps in modern streets. At first glance these barriers would seem to be an impediment to wheeled traffic, but in all likelihood they were put there in order to prevent carts and wagons from rolling backwards as they made their way up the hill. Despite all these improvements, some characteristics illustrate the limitations of the Greeks' road-building practices: even with switchbacks and terracing, the slope of the road sometimes

gists think that this was a common practice in cross-country road building. Deliberate leveling of the roadbed is detectable in some cases. It was usually accomplished by simply filling in rough places or, where the road ran along a slope, by building an earthen terrace held in place by a retaining wall. The steepness of roads that passed over mountains was often countered by the laying out of switchbacks that formed a zigzag pattern up the slope. Even with

In the following passage from Homer's *Iliad* (circa eighth–seventh centuries B.C.E.), King Priam of Troy is preparing to take a wagonload of riches to Achilles. The Greek warrior had killed his son, Hector, and Priam hopes to ransom Hector's body from Achilles so that he and the Trojans can give him a proper funeral. After berating his remaining sons, Priam commands them to get the wagon ready. The "carrying basket" is the wickerwork siding attached to the wagon platform. The wagon has a single pole that runs between two mules. On the yoke is a ring which the "peg" (the end of the pole) slips into. The yoke is then lashed in place by leather thongs ("yoke lashing") that are wrapped around the pole and around a knob on the yoke. Unmentioned here are the parts of the yoke that actually contact the mules: a pair of yoke pads that go between the yoke and their shoulders, two thick straps that wrap around the front of their necks, and leather thongs that run behind their front legs.

"Well then,
will you not get my wagon ready and be quick about it,
and put all these things on it, so we can get on with our journey?"

So he spoke, and they in terror at the old man's scolding hauled out the easily running wagon for mules, a fine thing new-fabricated, and fastened the carrying basket upon it.

They took away from its peg the mule yoke made of boxwood with its massive knob, well fitted with guiding rings, and brought forth the yoke lashing (together with the yoke itself) of nine cubits and snugged it well into place upon the smooth-polished wagon-pole at the foot of the beam, then slipped the ring over the peg, and lashed it with three turns on either side to the knob, and afterwards fastened it all in order and secured it under a hooked guard.

Then they carried out and piled into the smooth-polished mule wagon all the unnumbered spoils to be given for the head of Hektor, then yoked the powerful-footed mules who pulled in the harness and whom the Mysians gave once as glorious presents to Priam.

Source: Homer, *The Iliad,* translated by Richmond Lattimore (Chicago: University of Chicago Press, 1951).

Here is a famous story told by Herodotus that involves vehicular transport. By looking beneath the moralizing lesson of the story and focusing on a more mundane level, one can see that a well-to-do household apparently did not have enough oxen both to take care of the plowing and to carry the apparently infirm matron of the family around on her cart. It also shows that such a family could have a single vehicle that would have to serve all their transportation needs. An oxcart would have been a heavy vehicle, built for heavy loads, not for ferrying one old lady to a festival. This story, to the extent it has any basis in fact, is dated to the late seventh or early sixth century B.C.E.

Two young men of Argos . . . Cleobis and Biton . . . had enough to live on comfortably; and their physical strength is proved not merely by their success in athletics, but much more by the following incident. The Argives were celebrating the festival of Hera, and it was most important that the mother of the two young men should drive to the temple in her ox-cart; but it so happened that the oxen were late in coming back from the fields. Her two sons, therefore, as there was no time to lose, harnessed themselves to the cart and dragged it along, with their mother inside, for a distance of nearly six miles, until they reached the temple. After this exploit which was witnessed by the assembled crowd, they had a most enviable death—a heaven-sent proof of how much better it is to be dead than alive. Men kept crowding round them and congratulating them on their strength, and women kept telling the mother how lucky she was to have such sons, when, in sheer pleasure at this public recognition of her sons' act, she prayed the goddess Hera, before whose shrine she stood, to grant Cleobis and Biton, who had brought her such honour, the greatest blessing that can fall to mortal man.

After her prayer came the ceremonies of sacrifice and feasting; and the two lads, when all was over, fell asleep in the temple—and that was the end of them, for they never woke again.

Source: *Herodotus: The Histories,* translated by Aubrey de Selincourt (Harmondsworth, U.K. & Baltimore: Penguin, 1954).

approaches 25 to 30 percent, and at times the road narrows to less than two meters—wide enough for a single cart but not for two going in opposite directions.

Diolkos. The Greeks demonstrated the ability to engineer roads that could be used to transport extremely heavy freight. In the early sixth century B.C.E., the people of Corinth built a pathway paved with massive stones all the way across the six-mile-wide Isthmus that serves as the only land link between the Peloponnese and the rest of Greece. The Corinthians had become a wealthy and powerful city thanks in no small part to their control of the Isthmus. All land traffic between the Peloponnese and the more northerly parts of Greece had to go through this neck of land, and Corinthians were in a position to control that traffic and to exact duty and tolls from those who passed through their territory. The Corinthians had ports on both

The Panathenaic Way, the main thoroughfare by the
agora of Athens (David Hurn/Magnum, Paris)

by being able to charge an even more handsome fee for each boatload. In the event of war the *diolkos* could also be a strategic benefit for the Corinthians and their allies, since they could use it to transfer their warships more quickly and safely between the eastern and western theaters of war. Exactly how the Corinthians managed to move ships across the *diolkos* is not known with certainty. Large wheel ruts ran down the middle of the track, so it is likely that the ship was pulled onto an oversized wheeled sled and towed across by a large team of oxen or mules. In modern times a function similar to that of the *diolkos* is served by a canal cut through the Isthmus almost along the same line of the dragging route. Many attempts were made in antiquity to dig a canal through the Isthmus, but none of them got far past the planning stage.

Quarry to Temple. Another example of a heavy-freight roadway in ancient Greece comes from Athens. In the early fifth century B.C.E., the Athenians decided to build an enormous new temple for their patron goddess, Athena, on the acropolis (citadel) of the city. This temple, the forerunner of the famous Parthenon, was to be built of marble from Mount Pentele, some ten miles to the northeast of the city. Since some of the architectural elements of the temple, such as the column drums and capitals for the exterior colonnade, were of gargantuan size, sometimes ten tons or more, transporting them from the quarries to the city was a problem. The Athenians solved the problem by constructing a marble-paved track all the way up the side of the mountain to the quarries themselves. Blocks were laboriously winched and levered out of the quarries up to the track, where they were put on wooden sleds and carefully lowered down. Since the way was all downhill, no propulsion was necessary. In fact, the problem was not getting the marble blocks going but keeping them from sliding down too quickly and getting out of control. To prevent this dangerous situation from occurring, the Greeks dug large postholes at regular intervals beside the track. Thick wooden posts were inserted in these holes, and stout ropes were tied to the block and wrapped around the posts. As gravity pulled the block downhill, the ropes were gradually released, and the descent of the block was controlled until it reached the level of the next set of posts where the process was repeated. After the block reached the base of the mountain, the road to Athens was no longer uniformly downhill, so the block had to be loaded on special large wagons pulled by teams of mules the rest of the way to the city. The process involved in transporting these large stones is revealed partly by archaeological remains—the paved trackway, for instance, is still visible in some places along the mountain—and partly by inscriptions relating to the finances of the building of this temple and other subsequent temples. The original Athena temple was only partly complete when it was destroyed by the invading Persian army in 480 B.C.E. The same methods, however, were employed in building the Parthenon a few decades later.

Foot Travel. Because of the nature of Greek roads, the most common way to travel along them was on foot. It is

sides of the Isthmus and thereby had easy access both to the Aegean and to the western sea routes that led to Italy and Sicily, a fact that made them almost automatically one of the leading maritime states in all of Greece. Most importantly, even for non-Corinthian merchants carrying cargo from the Aegean to the West or vice versa, it had long been the practice to sail up to the Isthmus, unload the cargo onto mule- or oxen-driven wagons (owned and operated, no doubt, by Corinthians who charged a handsome fee for the service), and carry it across to the other side where it would be put into different ships for the rest of the journey. In this way the merchants could avoid risking their cargoes on the open seas of the Mediterranean. Some of the most treacherous winds and currents in the sea were in the waters off Greece's southern tip, and the only practical way for merchants to avoid them was by the trans-Isthmus service provided by the Corinthians. The stone track that the Corinthians built was an improvement on this service. Called the *diolkos* ("drag-across"), the track allowed the Corinthians to convey not just the cargo but the entire ship across the Isthmus. In this way the merchants who used the service benefited by being able to use the same ships for the entire journey, and the Corinthians benefited

A relief detail of Hermes and one of the Kharites (Louvre, Paris)

clear from Pausanias's descriptions that he did most of his traveling through Greece as a pedestrian, and other descriptions of travel confirm that this mode of locomotion was used far more frequently than any other. Many vase paintings depict the travelers' god Hermes wearing special garments. Travelers' clothing consisted of sturdy footwear, a broad-brimmed hat to protect the person from the Mediterranean sun, and, for men, a shorter garment than they were accustomed to wearing around town, leaving more room for their legs to move. For particularly strenuous walks, men would hitch up their garments even further and travel "well-girt." A traveler planning on an overnight stay carried with him a sack containing bedding in addition to food and extra clothing. The Greeks were accustomed to traveling in this manner and made good time in doing so. Pausanias measured his routes both in terms of distance and time, allowing his readers to calculate how quickly he walked. (It works out to a little less than three miles per hour, which, over difficult terrain, and figuring time for rest and for meals, is a fairly respectable pace.) There is

some evidence that when goods needed to be transported overland they would sometimes be carried on foot by people using packs or shoulder braces. However, the average person could not haul more than fifty pounds over great distances, so no large-scale movements of goods were likely to have been undertaken in this manner.

Domesticated Animals. The Greeks possessed various domesticated animals that were used for overland transport, including horses, mules, donkeys, and oxen. Of these animals, donkeys and mules were the most versatile and commonly used. They were either ridden, hitched to wheeled vehicles, or used as pack animals capable of carrying three or four times as much cargo as a human. Horses were employed much less frequently because they were expensive to obtain and raise; they were a privilege indulged in by the upper classes and used chiefly for racing and, to a lesser extent, warfare. Although far more fleet of foot than donkeys or mules, horses were difficult to control, more temperamental, less surefooted on mountain roads and tracks, and prone to injury. One clear indication of the uselessness of horses for overland transport in Greece was the fact that when a message needed to be sent quickly over a long distance, the Greeks used runners rather than riders on horseback or horse-drawn chariots. Oxen were useful as draft animals when large loads had to be transported. They had greater pulling power and could be harnessed more efficiently than either horses or mules. The drawbacks to oxen were that they were slow (averaging about one mile per hour versus three miles per hour for mules), and they were also rare and expensive compared to donkeys and mules.

Wheeled Vehicles. Aside from local traffic, the usefulness of wheeled transport was considerably limited by the nature of the terrain and the deficiencies of the roads. Perhaps for this reason, the Greeks made few if any innovations or improvements in the realm of wheeled vehicles. Literary and artistic representations show that the Greeks had two-wheeled and four-wheeled carts that carried people or light cargo. These vehicles were generally pulled by donkeys or mules. Larger four-wheeled wagons, pulled by mules or oxen, were used for heavier loads. The basic Greek cart or wagon seems to have been little more than a wooden platform to which wooden or wickerwork sides were attached in order to keep the cargo from falling out. The wheels and axles were usually made of wood, and the heavier vehicles generally had solid wooden wheels, whereas chariots and lighter carts tended to have four-spoked wheels.

Location of Cities. Wheeled vehicles were essential for transportation in and around the cities. Few Archaic or Classical Greek cities were located right on the water. Fear of piracy and hostile raids led the Greeks to fortify places at a safe distance from the shores, and habitation tended to cluster around the citadels. Athens, for instance, was four miles inland from its port, Piraeus; Corinth was similarly distant from its two harbors; and Sparta, the least maritime of all major Greek cities, was twenty miles from its port, Gutheion. Even a city that sent and received much cargo by sea still had to manage to bring goods from the port to where people lived, and wheeled traffic clearly did most of that kind of moving. Wagons and carts were also put to good use by the farmers in the Greek countryside, particularly for bringing their goods to market. One effect of the formation of the city-states out of scattered farming villages was the concentration of population and commerce into a single, central area, although farmers in the hinterlands had to make longer trips to the market. Within the territory of the city, wagon roads were probably reliable enough (when the weather was dry and rain did not turn the pathways into rivers of mud) for wheeled conveyance to be put to good use. In limited circumstances, then, land transportation was an important part of Greek life and economy, but for long-distance transportation of people and large cargoes, there was no real alternative to the sea.

Sources:

Robert James Forbes, *Studies in Ancient Technology, Volume II: Transport and Road Building* (Leiden, Netherlands: E. J. Brill, 1955).

Manolis Korres, *From Pentilicon to the Parthenon* (Athens: Melissa, 1995).

William Kendrick Pritchett, *Studies in Ancient Greek Topography, Part III: Roads* (Berkeley: University of California Press, 1980).

Pritchett, *Studies in Ancient Greek Topography, Part IV: Passes* (Berkeley: University of California Press, 1982).

SEA TRANSPORT

The Ulu Burun Wreck. In many respects scholars know more about the construction of the ships of the Greeks than they do about their land vehicles. Few carts and wagons were buried intact for later archaeologists to discover. Land vehicles, once they had outlived their usefulness, were abandoned in a field to decay or were broken up for firewood and scrap metal. In contrast, as a result of storms, faulty navigation, and hostile activity many ancient ships met their end by settling, cargo and all, on the protective sand and mud of the Mediterranean sea floor. There they remained for generations, decaying slowly, until in the present century they became accessible to the relatively new science of underwater archaeology. For example, the Ulu Burun ship went down around 1300 B.C.E. off the southern coast of Turkey in 150 feet of water. It was discovered in 1982, and although the superstructure of the ship had disintegrated, the items in the hold, and the planking of the hull underneath them, were remarkably well preserved. Archaeologists retrieved ingots of copper, gold jewelry, amber, glass, ebony, ivory, tin, pottery, drinking vessels, and bronze weapons. Similar wrecks have given scholars valuable insight into seafaring and waterborne commerce in later periods. Other information about Archaic Period (700–480 B.C.E.) and Classical Period (480–323 B.C.E.) sea activity comes from literary descriptions and artistic representations. These sources, however, tend to be problematic: literary descriptions are usually somewhat sketchy and difficult to interpret, since the authors were generally more interested in what the ships were doing than in the ships themselves. Artistic representations tend to be stylized and inexact and fraught with the problems that any two-dimensional representation of three-dimensional objects entails.

Ship Design. From this combination of sources, classicists have determined that Greek ships tended to be rather conservative in design, preserving the same basic layout and construction methods that were used by the Egyptians and other Mediterranean peoples since the early Bronze Age (circa 3000–1100 B.C.E.). All ships appear to have been constructed by the "shell-first" method visible on the Ulu Burun wreck in which the hull is formed with a series of tight-fitting planks before being attached to the ship's frame. Moreover, the vessels seem to fall into two basic classes: long, narrow galleys powered both by oar and sail power, and shorter, wider merchant ships driven solely by the wind. For both types of ship the sails and rigging were similar: a single large sail, rectangular in shape, was mounted amidships. In the Classical Period it became more common to mount a smaller rectangular sail in front of the mainsail for additional power and directional control.

Specialization. In the Classical Period and later, these two types of ships became specialized for separate uses: the long, oar-driven galleys were used mainly for warfare and the rounder sail-driven ships were used for carrying cargo. Scholars often assume that the same division of labor was present in the Archaic Period and earlier, but there is some reason to doubt that assumption. The simple sails and rigging of ancient Mediterranean ships put them at the mercy of the winds to a considerable extent, while oar-driven ships were relatively independent of wind direction. Proceeding under sail against the wind is a difficult process and one which the early Greek mariners may not have mastered right away, a fact that would have caused trouble for merchants who had to deliver their cargoes to certain ports within a specific amount of time. For this reason, some historians believe that in the early period all seagoing ships were oar-driven, and that it was only after the art of sailing had advanced further that the oar-driven merchant ship was abandoned. This hypothesis has the advantage of explaining why in the midst of dozens of artistic representations of oared galleys from the early Iron Age (circa 1100–700 B.C.E.) and the Archaic Period, sail-only ships do not appear until late in the sixth century. At the same time, however, there is no evidence whatsoever that the Ulu Burun wreck, unquestionably a cargo ship, was driven by oars. This fact indicates that if the early Iron-Age and Archaic Greeks could not manage a sail-driven merchant ship, then this art was temporarily lost with the end of the Bronze Age. Whenever it occurred, the development of sail-driven merchant ships was definitely a boon to commerce. The area taken up by twenty or thirty oarsmen and their gear and provisions was space that could be more profitably filled with cargo. The additional capacity of sail-driven ships more than made up for the loss of speed and directional control.

Winds and Rigging. Although sailing the waters of the Mediterranean was never as hazardous as sailing on the Atlantic Ocean, the ships of antiquity were not as large or as sturdily built as the great oceangoing vessels of more modern times, so ancient mariners avoided putting to sea at times when the weather was threatening. Prime sailing season was considered to run from late spring to early fall, when storms and high winds occurred only sporadically, and between the months of November and March practically no sailing occurred at all. During the sailing months the direction of the prevailing winds was relatively constant and predictable. In the Aegean area, winds generally came from the northwest at the beginning of the sailing season and gradually swung around to the north as the summer months progressed. Under such conditions, the ability to sail contrary to the wind was crucial to sail-driven ships, since without that ability all trips would be one-way. The simple rectangular sail on ancient Mediterranean ships was typically hoisted up the mast on a horizontal beam called a yard. The yard was loosely attached to the mast so that it could be pivoted by means of ropes attached to either

ODYSSEUS BUILDS A RAFT

This account from Homer's *Odyssey* (circa eighth–seventh centuries B.C.E.) is one of the best literary descriptions from antiquity of the "shell-first" shipbuilding construction method. In this story the goddess Kalypso, who has been detaining the hero Odysseus on her island for seven years, is ordered by the other gods to let him go and find his way home. She reluctantly complies and furnishes him with the tools and materials he needs to build himself a simple ocean-going vessel. Although Odysseus was a man of many talents, it is unlikely that a nonprofessional could accomplish the boat-building job he does here. Shell-first construction was a job for a master carpenter: the planks of the hull had to be joined so tightly and closely that when they swelled upon contact with the water they formed a watertight seal. The ancients used no caulking or other form of waterproofing on their hulls.

But when she had shown him where the tall trees grew, Kalypso, shining among divinities, went back to her own house while he turned to cutting his timbers and quickly had his work finished.

He threw down twenty in all, and trimmed them well with his bronze ax, and planed them expertly, and trued them straight to a chalkline.

Kalypso, the shining goddess, at that time came back, bringing him an auger, and he bored through them all and pinned them together with dowels, and then with cords he lashed his raft together.

And as great as is the bottom of a broad cargo-carrying ship, when a man well skilled in carpentry fashions it, such was the size of the broad raft made for himself by Odysseus.

Next, setting up the deck boards and fitting them to close uprights he worked them on, and closed in the ends with sweeping gunwales.

Then he fashioned the mast, with an upper deck fitted to it, and made in addition a steering oar by which to direct her, and fenced her in down the whole length with wattles of osier to keep the water out, and expended much timber upon this.

Next Kalypso, the shining goddess, brought out the sail cloth to make the sails with, and he carefully worked these also, and attached the straps and halyards and sheets all in place aboard her. And then with levers worked her down to the bright salt water.

end. In this way the sail could be made to face almost any direction; it might start out on a journey standing perpendicular to the long axis of the ship and be turned, if conditions warranted it, so that it was almost perpen-

A drawing of an Etruscan merchant vessel taken from a painting discovered in a tomb at Tarquinia, Italy, circa early fifth century B.C.E. (photo courtesy of Mario Moretti)

dicular to the short axis. The bottom of the sail was held in place by ropes at both corners so that it too could be moved as the yard changed position and could also be set in different positions relative to the yard. Along the bottom of the sail another series of ropes called brails was attached. These ropes ran up and over the yard and back down to the deck. Sailors could pull down on any or all of these ropes to draw the sail up, making its open surface smaller or changing its shape. By these means experienced seafarers could optimize the shape and position of their sail in response to the strength of the wind and in accord with the direction in which they wanted to travel. With such capabilities ancient mariners were able to make headway against the wind. No sail-driven ship can sail directly into the wind, but by positioning the sail so that the wind hits it side-on rather than head-on, it is possible to make progress in a direction that is less than ninety degrees off the direction of the wind. For example, if the wind was coming directly from the north, a competent Greek sailor could set his sails so that his ship moved in a direction that was slightly to the north of west or slightly to the north of east. By proceeding to the northeast for a while and then turning to the northwest, the ship could make overall progress in a northerly direction. This laborious zigzagging process is known as tacking, and in this way the ancient Greeks (and other Mediterranean peoples) overcame the tyranny of the winds.

Coasting. Navigation was also more problematic for ancient mariners than it is for modern ones. The only maps that existed in the Archaic and Classical periods were rudimentary and, in all likelihood, highly inaccurate. In addition, even if ancient sailors had accurate maps, there was no good way for them to tell where they were in relation to their destination. Latitude and longitude were concepts unknown to them, and the compass, sextant, and chronometer were centuries away from being invented. In the absence of such aids, the surest way for an ancient sailor to get where he wanted to go was by following visible landmarks. For this reason as well as for the sake of safety, mariners avoided sailing out of sight of land. This method was easy to do in the Aegean, with its profusion of islands. In the open waters of the Mediterranean, however, it led to a practice known as coasting. If a ship headed out from Sicily bound for Corinth, which is roughly on the same latitude, it would not head directly east over the open water. Instead, it would proceed northeast along the southern shore of Italy, cross the narrow strait between the heel of Italy and the Balkan Peninsula, and then proceed south along the western coast of Greece until it

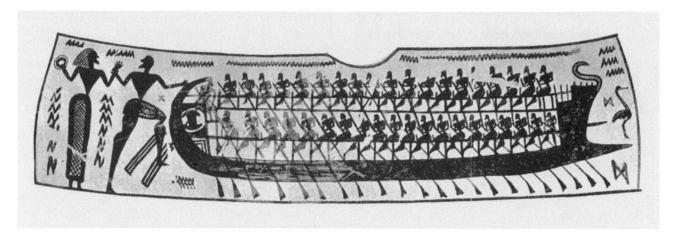

A painting of a two-banked warship found on a Theban bowl, circa late eighth century B.C.E. (from John Sinclair Morrison, *Greek Oared Ships, 900–322 B.C.* [1968], plate 19)

reached the Gulf of Corinth. Such a course took far more time than the direct route, but it allowed the pilot of the ship to navigate by known landmarks. It also kept the ship in easy reach of refuge should inclement weather or some other emergency arise. Mediterranean merchants did make journeys over open water in some instances—for instance, on the route between Crete and Egypt—but they preferred not to and only did so when there were immediate and substantial benefits in taking the more direct route. On the open water the only means a navigator had for determining position and direction were the position of the sun or, at night, the stars. That situation, combined with the instinct for time, distance, and direction that a sailor develops over years of experience, enabled them to cross the seas effectively when they had to, but coasting was always the preferred practice.

Trade Routes. The steadiness of the prevailing winds and the predilection for coasting had definite effects on the interaction of various peoples of the Mediterranean and on the development of trade. Since the winds were usually northerly, sailing from Europe to Africa was relatively easy, but sailing in the opposite direction was not. For this reason, traffic from Libya and Egypt generally took the coastal route around the eastern end of the Mediterranean, passing by Phoenicia and Cyprus before reaching the Aegean and the rest of Europe. The success of the Phoenicians as traders can be explained in part by these circumstances. Not only were they positioned to dominate the passage of goods from the interior of Asia to the Mediterranean, they also were straddled the path by which most seaborne traffic from Africa made its way to Europe. A similar explanation lies behind the success and prosperity of places such as Corcyra, located far away from the centers of civilization but directly on the coasting route for sea traffic between the eastern and western Mediterranean.

Ship Size. Sail-driven merchant craft varied significantly in size, according to whether they were to be used for long or short runs and according to the financial resources of the people having them built. Ancient documents make little reference to ships having a capacity of less than fifty tons of cargo. A more typical size was one hundred to two hundred tons, and there was a tendency toward larger ships, capable of carrying five hundred tons or more, in the Classical Period. These cargoes were small by the standards of later antiquity. Roman grain ships that plied the waters between Italy and northern Africa typically had a capacity in excess of one thousand tons. When merchant ships had room for extra cargo, it would often take it on in the form of paying passengers. In the absence of any services strictly for passenger traffic (with the exception of short-distance ferry runs), the only way for someone not on commercial or state business to sail from one place to another was to go down to the nearest port and find a merchantman going in the right direction. For example, the poet Arion tried to return from Sicily to Corinth aboard a merchant ship. The speed that a merchant ship could attain varied with size and load, and was also significantly affected by wind conditions. Based on ancient accounts, a typical speed for a merchant ship was four to five knots with a following wind and no more than one or two knots in the windward direction because of the zigzagging necessary for tacking. Crossing the Aegean, even under favorable conditions, took a good two or three days for a merchant ship; crossing from Africa to Europe could be a matter of weeks or even months. As may be expected, oared ships did much better.

The Kyrenia Wreck. A good example of what is presumed to be a Greek merchant ship was found off the northern coast of Cyprus (along the same trade route plied by the Ulu Burun vessel) near the site of Kyrenia. This ship went down with its cargo sometime shortly after 300 B.C.E., and it was quite an elderly ship when it succumbed to the sea. Carbon-14 dating showed that the wood from which the ship was made was around eighty years older than the cargo that it was carrying. Whether such longevity was typical for ships of this time is impossible to say, but it still speaks well for the

In this passage from Homer's *Odyssey* (circa eighth–seventh centuries, B.C.E.), the Phaeacians prepare to convey Odysseus home to Ithaca, along with an enormous pile of gifts they have given him in token of their friendship.

But when they had come down to the sea, and where the ship was, the proud escorts promptly took over the gifts, and stowed them away in the hollow hull, and all the food and the drink, then spread out a coverlet for Odysseus, and linens, out on the deck, at the stern of the ship's hull, so that he could sleep there undisturbed, and he himself went aboard and lay down silently. They sat down each in his place at the oarlocks in order, and slipped the cable free from its hole in the stone post.

They bent to their rowing, and with their oars tossed up the sea spray, and upon the eyes of Odysseus there fell a sleep, gentle, the sweetest kind of sleep with no awakening, most like death; while the ship, as in a field four stallions drawing a chariot all break together at the stroke of the whiplash, and lifting high their feet lightly beat out their path, so the stern of the ship would lift and the creaming wave behind her boiled amain in the thunderous crash of the sea. She ran on very steady and never wavering; even the falcon, that hawk that flies lightest of winged creatures, could not have paced her, so lightly did she run on her way and cut through the sea's waves.

Source: Homer, *The Odyssey*, translated by Richmond Lattimore (New York: Harper & Row, 1967).

Greek boat-builder's craftsmanship. The Kyrenia wreck was small as far as merchant ships go, measuring approximately fifty feet from stem to stern and fifteen feet from side to side, and having a capacity of less than one hundred tons. The hull was constructed by the typical shell-first method, but the builders added an innovation of the late Classical Period: a thin sheeting of lead on the lower portion of the hull. Marine archaeologists believe that the purpose of the lead was to prevent infestation of the wood by seaborne parasites that would eventually cause it to rot away. In the hold of the ship divers found a cargo that was not as diverse as that of the Ulu Burun ship, but was still interesting and informative. At the bottom were a set of twenty-nine heavy stone grain mills, which were either part of the merchant's cargo or were placed there to provide ballast (stabilizing weight). Stored above these millstones were over four hundred amphorae (oval-shaped jars and vases), which originally would have contained commodities such as oil or wine. Also found scattered over the whole cargo area was a large quantity of almonds. These were probably being transported in cloth sacks that did not survive the centuries. Perhaps the most interesting aspect about the Kyrenia ship's cargo is the provenance

of the various goods. The amphorae that it had on board were of various types, some in styles that were common of Rhodes and Samos, two islands known for their wine production. So it seems that like the Ulu Burun ship the Kyrenia vessel called at various ports, adding local wares from each to the collection of diverse commodities stored in its hull.

Oared Ships. Oared galleys appear in Greek art from an early date, and they are also referred to in the earliest Greek literature. Even in the Bronze Age, amongst the Egyptians, Phoenicians, and other Aegean peoples, ships of this type were used for naval warfare, and for the Greeks of the Classical Period that was almost their sole function. As was mentioned above, however, there is some reason for thinking that they were used more generally for all seagoing activity during the early Iron Age.

Design. In the earliest Greek representations of oared ships from the ninth century B.C.E., they exhibit a fairly uniform appearance: long and slender, they have a sleek, graceful hull that curves upward in the stern, often curling back onto itself to form a covered area at the back of the ship. In the front, ahead of an upright stempost that also sometimes curls back over the deck, the hull tapers to a fine point at the waterline. In later manifestations of this type of ship, this projection is armored with bronze and used as a ram. Whether this design feature was also the case in these early ships is difficult to ascertain; no mention of a ram is made in literary descriptions until later in the Archaic Period. In the rear of the ship the helmsman stands, steering the ship's course by means of one or (more frequently) two rudder blades. If the ship has a sail (which not all do in these early representations), it is of the standard rectangular type. Some of the ships seem to be open in the interior, while others have a decking that is supported on posts above the level of the gunwale (the topmost row of the hull's planking). The oarsman in the earliest depictions all sit on the same level facing the stern, with their oars projecting over the gunwale. Their numbers vary from five or six to upwards of twenty to a side. In his poems Homer described large vessels mainly used for transporting warriors to the site of the battle. Since Homer's works are a mythical reflection of a bygone age, scholars do not take his descriptions as completely accurate.

Propulsion. The most important innovation in the design of these ships was the number and the placement of the oarsmen. Depictions of ships from the late ninth century show two rows of oarsmen on each side. This arrangement is something seen both in Greek and Near Eastern ships, and where it developed first is uncertain. In some of these double-oared ships the bottom row of oarsmen are shown sitting at gunwale level, while the upper row sits at the level of the raised deck; in others it is the top row that rides at the gunwale, while the lower row's oars project through oarholes in the hull closer to the water line. The advantage of the two-level arrangement was that more oarsmen could be accommodated

A modern reproduction of a Classical-era trireme (Paul Lipke/Trireme Trust, Montague, Mass.)

without increasing the length of the hull, a thing which was to be avoided since an overly long hull would tend to be flimsy and unstable. Galleys of this type could fit as many as twenty to twenty-five oarsmen on each side, and it is probably this sort of ship that is referred to when ancient sources describe the *pentêkontoros* (fifty-oar ship), the main type of warship used in the early Archaic Period.

Trireme. The apex of this line of development occurred some time in the latter seventh or early sixth century when a third row of oarsmen was added. Although this innovation occurred simultaneously in both Greece and Phoenicia, many scholars think that it originated with the Greeks. The three-row galley is referred to as a *trièrês* (trireme or triple-oared ship). In the Greek version, the third row was added by building a platform that projected outward above the gunwale. The topmost rank of oarsmen sat at the level of this platform, while the lower two occupied benches at the gunwale and the mid-hull levels. The oarsmen were staggered so that none was seated directly on top of another, allowing the three rows to be accommodated without increasing the hull's profile to unstable heights. The trireme became the standard ship of war in the entire eastern Mediterranean throughout the late Archaic and Classical periods. The Classical Greek trireme had one hundred and seventy rowers, eighty-five on each side, and

was built for speed: at a length-to-width ratio of approximately 8:1 (about 120 feet in length and 15 feet in the beam) they resemble modern racing sculls. The success with which they operated was a remarkable accomplishment of training and coordination. A well-trained and experienced crew of oarsmen could propel their ship at a speed upward of ten knots under favorable conditions, and they also became adept at timing their oarstrokes in ways that allowed the ships to perform complicated battle maneuvers.

Military Use. The use of the trireme and its predecessors in wartime is variously described in ancient sources. In the surviving artistic representations the ships are depicted as clashing with one another with armed warriors on board. The goal in such fighting was either to overtake the enemy ship and board it or to use one's own ship as a platform from which to hurl spears and other projectiles at the foe. It was not until the late Archaic Period that oared galleys were used in formation with maneuvers and tactics that were analogous to infantry battles on land. In such fighting the main offensive weapon was the ship itself with its five hundred pound ram, and the objective was to come at enemy vessels from the side in order to shatter the planking of their hulls. Even in the Classical Period, however, there were other modes of employing the trireme. They were capable of carrying a complement of armed warriors for making raids on enemy territory and for boarding enemy ships or assailing them with missiles. The number of rowers could also be reduced to turn the ships into troop or cavalry transports. Triremes were also used on occasion to convey important military or governmental messages over long distances.

A Working Model. No trireme wreck has been excavated, or even discovered, in the Mediterranean. Riding high in the water, and with no heavy cargo weighing it down, a trireme would have been next to impossible to sink. When the hull was breached, instead of drifting to the bottom, the trireme would have simply broken up and floated away, its wooden components ending up scattered on beaches wherever the current took them. What scholars know of the trireme comes solely from literary sources and artistic representations. Based on these sources, however, a team of scholars and scientists from Britain, Greece, and other countries succeeded in building a working replica of a Classical Greek trireme. Many of the features of the *Olympias* are hypothetical, but in a series of trials in the late 1980s and early 1990s, crews of volunteer rowers achieved enough efficiency and coordination to closely approximate the speed and maneuverability of its ancient counterparts.

Sources:
Lionel Casson, *Ships and Seamanship in the Ancient World* (Princeton: Princeton University Press, 1971).

John Sinclair Morrison and Roderick Trevor Williams, *Greek Oared Ships 900–322 B.C.* (London: Cambridge University Press, 1968).

H. T. Wallinga, *Ships and Sea-power before the Great Persian War: The Ancestry of the Ancient Trireme* (Leiden, Netherlands, & New York: E. J. Brill, 1993).

SIGNIFICANT PEOPLE

SOSTRATUS OF AEGINA

FLOURISHED SIXTH CENTURY B.C.E.
MERCHANT

Reputation. Sostratus is one of the few ancient Greek merchants that is known by name. Originally from the island of Aegina, he became famous as a transporter of other people's goods in the latter part of the sixth century B.C.E. The historian Herodotus commended him on the profits he made on his cargoes: "with him, nobody can compare." He is also one of the elite class of individuals of this period whose existence is attested both in literature and in archaeological remains: many pots and pot shards, mostly of Athenian workmanship, have been found in Italy bearing Sostratus's mark, along with an offering of a stone ship's anchor that he made to the god Apollo. Sostratus was the foremost of what must have been a large number of Aeginetan entrepreneurs who made the island wealthy and powerful in the latter part of the Archaic Period.

Source:
John Boardman, *The Greeks Overseas: Their Early Colonies and Trade* (London: Thames & Hudson, 1980).

DOCUMENTARY SOURCES

Aristophanes, *Acharnians* (425 B.C.E.); *Lysistrata* (411 B.C.E.); and *Frogs* (405 B.C.E.)—comic plays rich in real-life details. The first two have interesting sections of dialogue in dialect.

Demosthenes, *On the Navy Boards* (354 B.C.E.)—a speech advising a naval building program in order to counter the threat from the Persians. The navy boards were the associations of citizens responsible for building, equipping, and manning warships.

Herodotus, *History of the Persian Wars* (circa late fifth century B.C.E.)—this text is the best historical source for the Archaic Period (700–480 B.C.E.). It is rich in detail on many aspects of communication and transportation.

Hesiod, *Works and Days* (eighth century B.C.E.)—a priceless poetic handbook on farming. It includes information on transportation and communication. Hesiod's view of seafaring, written at a time when many Greeks were beginning to travel by water, is rather bleak.

Homer, *Iliad* and *Odyssey* (circa eighth–seventh centuries B.C.E.)— these epics are full of vivid portrayals of seafaring, land travel, and communication techniques, as well as everyday life. Caution should be used with these sources because they are based on legends and so their accuracy is debatable.

Thucydides, *History of the Peloponnesian War* (circa 455 B.C.E.–circa 395 B.C.E.)—written at the time of the conflict (431–404 B.C.E.), it provides expert details on sea battles and military logistics. Thucydides was a general in the Athenian army before being sent into exile.

Xenophon, *Anabasis* and *Hellenica* (both written circa 430 B.C.E.–circa 356 B.C.E.)—the *Anabasis* is Xenophon's firsthand account of an ill-fated expedition he participated in as a mercenary in the year 401 B.C.E.; the *Hellenica* is his continuation of Thucydides' history. Both texts are full of accurate, sober detail regarding military transport and communication as well as Greek contacts with non-Greeks.

An Athenian cup (circa late sixth century B.C.E.) with a painting of a pirate ship chasing a Greek merchantman
(British Museum)

A Greek road in southern Italy that later became the Roman Via Appia (A. F. Kersting)

CHAPTER FIVE

SOCIAL CLASS SYSTEM AND THE ECONOMY

by BORIMIR JORDAN

CONTENTS

CHRONOLOGY
127

OVERVIEW
131

TOPICS IN SOCIAL CLASS SYSTEM AND THE ECONOMY

Archaic Period: Social and
  Agricultural Crisis 133
Athens 134
Boeotia. 138
Classical Period: Economic
  Crisis 138

Colonization 140
Corinth 141
Economic Activities 143
Ionia and The Aegean
  Islands 144
Sicily and Southern Italy 146
Social Organization 147
The Alcmaeonids 147
Sparta 148
Technological Advances
  and Innovations 151
Athenian Coins 152
Thessaly. 153
Trading Posts 153

Transportation and Exchange
  of Goods and Services. 155
The Tyrants 156

SIGNIFICANT PEOPLE

Hippias 158
Periander 158
Polycrates 158

DOCUMENTARY SOURCES
159

Sidebars and tables are listed in italics.

800 B.C.E.

- The Euboeans and Ionians establish a trading post at Al Mina on the mouth of the Orontes River in present-day northern Syria. It quickly becomes an important link in the Greek trade routes to the East.

775

- The Euboeans set up a trading post at Pithecusae on the island of Ischia in the Bay of Naples.

750*

- The Euboeans settle Cumae in Italy and develop a lively metal trade with the Etruscans.

734

- The Chalcidians settle Naxos, the first Greek colony in Sicily.

733

- Corinth colonizes Syracuse and the island of Corcyra.

720

- The Achaeans settle the town of Sybaris. Located in southern Italy on the Gulf of Tarentum, Sybaris becomes noted for its luxury and eventually boasts a large population.

706*

- Spartan colonists settle at Tarentum (also known as Taras) on the Gulf of Taranto, southeast of present-day Naples, Italy. The inhabitants of this port city engage in growing olives, raising horses, manufacturing pottery, fishing, shipbuilding, and dye-making.

664

- Greek mercenaries and traders begin to penetrate the interior of Egypt.

650*

- Coins come into use in Lydia and Ionia and soon spread to the city-states in Greece. These earliest coins are made of electrum, an alloy of gold and silver. They are stamped with the heads of a lion and a bull and weigh roughly seven to eight grams apiece.
- Greek settlements begin to arise along the shores of the Black Sea.

*Denotes circa date

630
- The Greek colony of Cyrene is founded in North Africa.

625-585
- Periander is tyrant of Corinth, and under his rule the city flourishes. He orders the construction of a portage across the Isthmus of Corinth to facilitate trade, and during his reign the government is funded largely by import duties.

600
- The Phocaeans, a group of Ionian Greeks, settle Massilia (present-day Marseilles, France).

594
- The Athenians elect Solon archon during a period of acute economic distress. Solon immediately institutes a series of constitutional and financial reforms, including dividing the population into four income groups, banning the enslavement of citizens for debts, and prohibiting grain exports.

546-522
- The tyrant Polycrates reigns in Samos. His fleet dominates the trade routes of the eastern Mediterranean and commits various acts of piracy.

525
- Cleisthenes becomes archon of Athens. Regarded as the founder of Athenian democracy, he devises a new political organization based on locality rather than the family and clan.

500*
- Athenian pottery replaces Corinthian pottery in popularity throughout the Greek world.

482
- A new vein of silver is discovered at Mount Laurium in Attica, about twenty-six miles southeast of Athens. The profits are enormous and are used to help finance the construction of a new Athenian fleet.

480*
- Athens has a population of approximately 250,000 people divided into three classes: citizens, *metics* (resident aliens), and slaves.

- Sparta has a population of around 70,000 people divided into three categories: Spartiates (equals or peers), *Perioikoi* ("Dwellers Around"), and Helots (serfs or slaves). The social system of the city-state is based upon the one advanced by the lawgiver Lycurgus, emphasizing the virtues of austerity, education, and discipline.

465

- Athens attempts to establish a colony in Thrace to exploit the timberlands of the region; the settlement fails in part because of Macedonian opposition.

450*

- Athens confiscates allied lands in Lemnos, Naxos, Andros, and Carystos and sends colonists known as "plot holders" to those areas. Over the span of the next four years, settlers are also dispatched to Thracian Chersonese, Chalkis, and Eretria.

443

- The Athenians settle Thurii in southern Italy.

437

- Athens finally establishes a colony in Thrace at the timber-rich site of Amphipolis. The Spartans capture the settlement in 424.

421

- Athenian workers begin construction of an Ionic temple of Athena on the Acropolis. Known as the Erechtheum, it is completed in 405.

413

- Approximately twenty-thousand Athenian slaves flee the city during a Spartan blockade. The Boeotians capture most of the runaways and resell them.

400*

- The *Trapezites*, or money changer, in the major Greek city-states lends money to merchants at interest rates varying from 12 to 30 percent.

OVERVIEW

Great Migrations. Several centuries of unsettled conditions and regress followed the collapse of the Bronze Age (3000–1100 B.C.E.) civilization in Greece and the Aegean region. This so-called Dark Age (1000-800 B.C.E.) was a time of movement throughout the eastern Mediterranean. In Greece proper mass migrations took place from the north to the south and from the west to the east. The Dorian Greeks moved into Greece from the north, traversed the peninsula, and finally settled in the Peloponnese. Meanwhile, an overflow of Dorians from the Peloponnese colonized some of the southern Cyclades islands, Crete, Rhodes, and the southwestern corner of Asia Minor. The Aeolians came from Thessaly and settled on the island of Lesbos and in the northwestern corner of the Asiatic mainland. A third group called the Ionians came from south central Greece, chiefly Attica and the island of Euboea, and established themselves on most of the Cyclades and on the coast of Asia Minor. This coastal strip, called Ionia, eventually gave its name to all the Greek settlements in Asia Minor.

Causes. The exact causes of these early migrations are unknown. What available evidence there is consists of archaeological finds and a literary tradition the reliability of which is difficult to assess. Some ancient sources speak of the "return of the Heraclidae," meaning the movement of the Dorians at the end of the Bronze Age, which may somehow have caused the migrations to the east. During the tenth and ninth centuries B.C.E. there was a general decline in the standard of living along with considerable depopulation. Yet, population pressures cannot explain the great migrations.

Emergence of the Polis. Between 800 and 700 B.C.E. a gradual improvement in living conditions took place, and the population of Greek lands began to increase apace. The first and most important achievement of the Archaic Period (700–480 B.C.E.) was the creation of the polis, or city-state, comparatively small territories dominated by proportionally large urban centers. Just how the city-state came into being is not known. All that scholars know is that around the middle of the eighth century city-states existed in many parts of Greece. The proof of their existence is that at that time several of them established overseas colonies, the foundation of which can be dated securely to the eighth century. An inscription from the town of Dreros on the island of Crete, which regulates appointments to a magistracy, is dated to 650–600 B.C.E. This document, engraved on stone, provides firm evidence that in the second half of the seventh century the city-state had been in existence for quite some time.

Growth and Development. Once it came into existence, the city-state grew, albeit at a slow pace. Some interior towns, most notably Sparta, never became full-fledged cities like Athens or Corinth, for example, but remained conglomerations of villages for most of their independent lives. The central towns generally grew up around a hill or an outcropping of rock located at some short distance from the seashore. The distance from the sea reduced the danger of water-borne attacks by enemy city-states, pirates, and other marauders. The hill or rock, called the acropolis, in times of crisis served as a place of refuge for the townspeople and the farmers from the nearby countryside. The arable land in the city-state was owned by private persons. The rest of the city-state's territory, which in Greece is almost always hilly or mountainous, was probably communal land used as pasture and, if wooded, as a source for timber and firewood, at least during the earlier eras in the history of the Greek peninsula, when many of its forests were still standing.

Topography. The fragmentation of Greece into independent states of varying sizes no doubt has a partial explanation in the topography of the peninsula: valleys and plains were separated from each other by mountains. There were, however, regions that, although they were geographic units, nevertheless failed to become united territories. This situation was true of Boeotia, for instance, which always contained several autonomous cities. Attica, on the other hand, which its mountain ranges divide into distinct parts, did become one state. Another possible explanation might be the fact that some new communities grew up around Bronze Age settlements.

Typology. Two types of city-states came into being and developed in the course of the Archaic Period. One type was a state having an urban center and a territory that varied in size. Examples include Athens in Attica; Thebes, Orchomenos, and Coroneia in Boeotia; and

Chalcis and Eretria on the island of Euboea. Another type had no central city; people lived in villages and hamlets that were not held together in a strong political union by a central government operating from the city-state's capital. With some exceptions these city-states had the larger territories, as, for example, Thessaly in northeastern Greece and Aetolia and Acarnania in the west. Insofar as these states had a certain cohesion, it was provided by the common ethnicity of the inhabitants: they were Thessalians, Aetolians, and Acarnanians, and therefore the cities are called "ethnicity" or "ethnos" states.

Cosmopolitan Character. The states without a dominant urban center preserved their early political and social structures; in this respect they remained states of the Archaic Period throughout their history. In contrast, the states with a capital city and a central government represented a more advanced political and social development. Whereas the unincorporated states remained entirely agrarian and had few foreigners among the population, the more "modern" states, except for the special case of Sparta, gradually acquired a cosmopolitan character by admitting within their borders foreign residents and acquiring slaves from abroad.

Exception. Sparta controlled a large territory with some of the best agricultural land in it. It was therefore self-sufficient in all the essentials of life and did not need to rely on outside contacts like trade; imports to Sparta stopped completely in the sixth century. The Lycurgan constitution turned the Spartans into such formidable fighters that they could defend their country without the aid of fortifications—there was no acropolis in Sparta and no wall surrounded the town. Except for a certain amount of unrest on the part of the Helots (serfs or slaves), Sparta, even after military reverses in the fourth century, did not experience, until a later age, the internal upheavals and civil strife that afflicted Athens.

Symbiotic Relationship. By the beginning of the fifth century the urban centers of the more important states had increased in size and population and had developed a symbiotic relationship with the agrarian hinterland. The rural countryside produced the food; the city housed the administration of the state, the more important religious cults and the buildings belonging to them, and the cultural and commercial institutions necessary for a truly civilized life. Besides these services, the city repaid the country for the produce it drew from it by returning as much as possible of the rents and taxes that the countryside had paid.

Colonization. The colonization that began in the early Archaic Period and continued into the fifth century had little, if anything, to do with a dramatic increase in manufacture and trade in the Greek world. It was dictated in the main by the negative economic factor of land hunger. The first purely commercial settlements were few, but trade between mother cities and colonies gradually increased. Other motives for colonization were the needs for raw materials and easily accessible fuel.

Economic Activities. In ancient Greece the three main economic activities—agriculture, religion, and warfare—occupied a much more important position than they do in the developed economies of the modern world. Commerce and industry played a correspondingly lesser role. Agriculture remained the chief economic activity for all of antiquity. Cults generated wealth for city-states in the form of gifts to the gods and festivals, while warfare allowed for the acquisition of enemy booty.

Tyrants. Whatever their faults, under the rule of the strongmen most of ancient Greece prospered. In fact in the sixth century, a time of vibrant economic activity, the foundations for the great achievements of the Classical Period were laid. Peisistratus, Periander, Polycrates, and other tyrants all increased the wealth and prestige of their respective city-states.

TOPICS IN SOCIAL CLASS SYSTEM AND THE ECONOMY

ARCHAIC PERIOD: SOCIAL AND AGRICULTURAL CRISIS

Solon. Despite the rise in economic well-being and the growth of nonagricultural jobs during the Archaic Period (700–480 B.C.E.), there is no indication of the advent of a new social class based on the newer occupations provided by manufacture and commerce. Agriculture remained the foundation of the economy, a fact confirmed by the work of the Athenian legislator and reformer Solon, who, in dividing the population of Attica into four classes, used as his criterion the amount that a citizen's land could produce.

Land Problems. The appearances of Solon and of his legislation on the historical stage were due to a crisis that occurred in some places during the last century of the Archaic Period. The origin and development of the crisis and the solution to the problems it created cannot be followed with much accuracy and detail, except in the better-documented states, such as Athens, and even there not everything is clear. Apparently the problems were connected with the land. Despite the considerable exodus to the colonies, Greece in the sixth century continued to be faced with overpopulation. As living conditions improved, the mortality rate declined; archaeological discoveries show an increase in the number of settlements and the presence of a denser population. The insufficiency of the land to feed a growing population, a phenomenon observable also in some parts of Ionia, induced some city-states to import grains.

Sixth-Sharers. Nevertheless, food shortages did not cause farm income to rise. As the soil was being overused, while, despite countermeasures, the practice of dividing farms between several heirs continued, the farmers found it difficult to make ends meet and began to fall into debt to a relatively small number of wealthy owners of large estates. To pay off their debts small farmers became something resembling sharecroppers: they turned over one-sixth of their produce to their creditors and became known as *hektêmoroi* ("sixth-sharers"). If a debtor defaulted on his loans, the creditor could sell him as a slave, an outcome made possible by the practice of making loans on the security of a person's body. Some Attic farmers apparently deliberately chose to become dependent on the large landowners, becoming in effect their slaves, in order to find protection from their creditors. This development was favorable to the landlords, who thereby substantially increased their labor force.

Slavery. The gradual enslavement of the population was intolerable. Solon received the task of finding a remedy. He was not opposed to the institution of slavery, and his reforms did not affect the chattel slaves. Instead, he took steps to stop the enslavement of free citizens. He abolished the status of sixth-sharers, canceled all debts, and prohibited the enslavement of citizens in the future. The Athenians who had been sold into slavery abroad were brought back. Solon also promulgated some other reforms, including a prohibition to export grain and all other agricultural products except olive oil.

Census Classes. Modern historians are in general agreement that Solon did not redistribute the land among the farmers who had been dispossessed by the large landowners. Solon himself clearly says in his poems that he did not do so. He is supported by Aristotle, who says that the commoners were disappointed in their hope of land distribution. However, Aristotle also says that before Solon's reforms all the land of Attica was in the hands of the few. There is a fundamental contradiction in the sources on this point, for if all or most of the land was owned by a few landlords, it is hard to see how Solon could have defined his census classes on the basis of land yields "in wet and dry measure," that is, in grain, oil, and wine. Thus, the highest class obtained a yield of 500 bushels and hence were called "500 Bushels Men." The next class, the "Knights," owned sufficient land to yield 300 bushels, an income allowing them to keep horses. The land of the third class produced 200 bushels. These men could only afford a pair of oxen with which they plowed and were called "Men of the Yoke." Even the lowest class, whose members were called "Laborers," and who may or may not have owned land, was defined in terms of a farm income of less than 200 bushels. According to the best estimates, 30 acres were needed for a yield of 500 bushels; some 18 acres for 300; and something above 12 acres for 200 bushels. Yet, with the land in the hands of a few landlords, Solon's criteria for his census classes became meaningless. One resolution of the difficulty in the evidence is to assume that Solon carried out

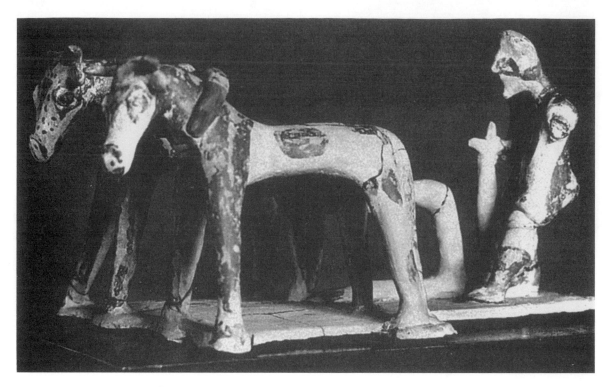

A Boeotian terracotta of a plowman with his horses (Musée du Louvre, Paris, France)

at least some land distribution. It is also possible that the liberation of the sharecroppers from debt-bondage automatically brought about their transformation into small farmers, but evidence for this is lacking.

Other Opportunities. A third possibility is that under Solon's new order landless farmers could turn to work in the metropolis, as craftsmen, small businessmen, and shopkeepers. That Solon's reforms opened up avenues to non-agricultural employment is supported by the fact that laborers and craftsmen of various kinds obviously found employment in the great building and improvement programs initiated by the tyrants.

Sources:
Antony Andrewes, *The Greeks* (New York: Knopf, 1967).

M. M. Austin and P. Vidal-Naquet, *Economic and Social History of Ancient Greece: An Introduction,* translated by Austin (Berkeley: University of California Press, 1977).

Nicholas F. Jones, *Ancient Greece: State and Society* (Upper Saddle River, N.J.: Prentice Hall, 1997).

Anthony M. Snodgrass, *Archaic Greece: The Age of Experiment* (London: Dent, 1980).

ATHENS

Archaic Period. In Athens during the Archaic Period (700–480 B.C.E.), Solon divided the Athenians according to their income, while at the end of the sixth century another legislator, Cleisthenes, divided them according to their places of residence. Villages and hamlets became the basic unit of the state, and Cleisthenes created ten separate bodies of people, or "tribes." In the course of the sixth century some rules were established as to which Solonian income class could hold what public office, while the new Cleisthenic system made the selection of individuals orderly. As might be expected, the most important offices were reserved for the highest income class; lesser offices were filled by the next two income classes. No office carried pay. The lowest class could only sit in the assembly and serve as jurors in the courts. All four classes had the right to appeal to a court of last resort instituted by Solon. These measures affected only the citizens.

Classical Period. The social classes into which the residents of Athens and Attica were divided in the Classical Period (480–323 B.C.E.) were three: citizens, *metics,* and slaves. The political and legal rights and the social status of these groups did not coincide. Only the citizens, who throughout the Classical Period constituted a homogenous group, had full rights, including the right to own land. It is estimated that at the end of the fifth century, three-fourths of the citizens of Athens owned land in some form or another. Until the beginning of the Second Peloponnesian War in 431 B.C.E., the political leaders of Athens were landowners. During the war men who had made money in trade and manufacture began to rise to power, but owning land continued to carry prestige, and commercial nouveaux riches met with criticism and ridicule, examples of which are found in the comedies of the era.

Land Ownership. As at Sparta, the question of the inalienability of land is difficult to decide. It probably could be bought and sold in the fifth century; certainly it was possible to do so in the fourth century. However, real estate was not commercialized as it is in the modern world. Mortgage was regarded as a bad thing and was used only in emergencies. It does not seem to have been used to raise money for other purposes; for example, to invest in business.

Agriculture. The basis of the Athenian economy in the fifth and fourth century remained farming. Much of it was subsistence farming rather than market farming, since only the farmers in the neighborhood of Athens could bring their produce to market in the city; even there most of the activity was exchanges in kind, rather than for cash. Some "heavy industry" in the form of mining also existed. The state leased the silver mines at Laurium to private entrepreneurs, who were generally citizens, for exploitation. Other citizens are known to have owned factories. The father of the orator and politician Demosthenes owned two enterprises, which might be described as "large-scale industry," one manufacturing beds and employing twenty slave carpenters, and another, a cutlery, employing thirty workers. Citizens also worked in such professions as lawyers, architects, and sculptors; the citizens at the bottom of the social scale were employed in various trades, such as carpenters, painters, sawyers, masons, blacksmiths, and sailors.

Metics. Resident aliens residing in Athens were known as *metics,* which means "those who have changed their place of residence." Solon encouraged the immigration to Athens of citizens of other Greek states as a way to increase trade and manufacture. The foreigners who established themselves as tradesmen and craftsmen in Athens in the course of the sixth and fifth centuries certainly did invigorate the Athenian economy with their skills and talents. The metics in the fifth century were mostly Greeks; in the fourth century a great variety of nationalities was represented among them: Thracians, Lydians, Carians, Phoenicians, and Egyptians lived and worked in Athens. Toward the end of the fourth century the metic population was probably about one-half that of the citizens. The institution was not peculiar to Athens; metics lived in many other Greek cities.

Origins. The attitude toward land and farming no doubt had something to do with the origins of this class. Historically, agriculture was the earlier economic activity; custom and tradition kept it in the hands of citizens. Along with this attitude went the low opinion that citizens had of what they regarded as demeaning work, which included almost all occupations except agriculture. Once the metic system was established, it was found to provide in the persons of the foreigners a reliable class of people who would do what the full citizens refused to do. The metic system, in other words, ensured the presence of a population that could take care of the economic life of the state.

Occupations. Since they could not own land, the metics naturally turned to those economic activities that were open to them: manufacture, commerce, and banking. Most of the small businessmen in Athens and Attica were metics. Many metics also worked as skilled journeymen and artisans, and some were extremely successful. In the largest manufacturing enterprise known to have existed in Classical Athens, the metic family of Cephalus owned an arms factory employing 120 slave workmen, who made shields.

Political Rights. The metics had no political rights and no voice in the government of the state. They were not eligible to sit in the popular assembly, or the senate, of Athens, or hold any public office. They did enjoy the passive protection of the laws, but at first could not sue or defend themselves in person before the court. All metics were required to have a guardian or patron who was a citizen, and they depended on this patron to represent them in court. The inability to appear personally in court fell into abeyance early; already in the fifth century there were instances of foreign residents engaged in litigation without the interjection of a patron. The restriction, too, on metic ownership of land was gradually eased until it became merely theoretical.

Taxes. A metic's obligations were the payment of a special tax, which, at twelve drachmas for men and six drachmas for women, was low; another tax was imposed on them for the privilege of trading in the marketplace. Deserving metics could be granted an exemption from the annual metic tax and so be put on the same level as the citizens, who did not pay a tax on their persons, but only on their property. In addition to these obligations, the metics were also liable to the taxes and duties incumbent upon the citizens. They had to undertake the so-called liturgies, that is, the financing and supervision of certain public activities, such as paying the expenses for a warship and its crew, and if qualified to do so, serving as the ship's captain. Like the citizens, the metics served in the army and navy and were subject to the payment of a special tax that was raised in time of war or great emergencies.

Wealth. The basis of the metics' social position was wealth; some were poor, while others were extremely rich. Apart from some rare prejudice toward them motivated by snobbery or xenophobia, the rich metics were accepted by the citizens, and even by the aristocrats among them, as their social equals. The sons of Cephalus were counted among the wealthiest Athenians, belonging to the social and intellectual elite.

Contributions. Although they were resented occasionally as upstarts, the metics were not regarded as economic rivals of the citizens. On the contrary, their contributions to the economic life and well-being of the state were welcomed by the citizens. The metics, for their part, accepted the order under which they lived, for it enabled them to live in peace and enjoy the material prosperity, power, and prestige of Athens. Many of them became fully assimilated, and, as a whole, the metics never formed a separate, much less a hostile, group against the citizens. In times of internal conflict they favored the democracy against the party of the oligarchs.

Slaves. A third legal class at Athens comprised the slaves, both public and private. Although they were legally property, like inanimate objects, slaves were granted a certain protection of the laws. They could not be beaten, wounded, or killed. Apart from that, slaves had no legal personality; they could not go to law, and it was up to their owners to protect them from injury. They

A view of the northwestern side of the agora of ancient Athens (Photo: Ekdotike Athenon SA, Athens)

could testify in court, but their testimony was valid only if given under torture. Like the metics, the slaves belonged to different nationalities from various parts of the eastern and northern neighbors of Greece such as Asia Minor, Thrace, and Scythia, in present-day southern Russia. There were also Greeks among them. Men became slaves through war or through piracy, as prisoners who were then sold into slavery. Women and children of towns and cities captured by the enemy were regularly enslaved. Given the frequency of warfare and the unsafe sea lanes, anyone could become a slave. In fourth-century Athens non-Greek slaves predominated.

Mining. Slaves did the same sort of work as the members of the free workforce and were to be found in every sector of economic life: in farming, commerce, manufacture, domestic service, and in the navy, as oarsmen on the warships. Only mining was regarded as specifically slavish work, although occasionally freemen worked in the silver and lead mines located at Laurium, a district in southern Attica.

Working Conditions. The conditions in which slaves lived and worked varied considerably. The type of work that a slave did determined his social status and his standard of living, in a manner similar to that of the metics. At the bottom of the scale were the slaves working in the mines under harsh conditions in narrow tunnels, without much hope of gaining their freedom and with a short life expectancy. As far as the rest of the slaves were concerned, the differences between free and slave labor were few. One difference was that the free worked for themselves, while the slaves worked for someone else, although here, too, there were exceptions. A second difference was that slave labor was more likely to be employed in the larger "factories," and free labor in the smaller, family businesses. On top of the slave hierarchy stood the public slaves—scribes, secretaries, and assistants working in the political, administrative, fiscal, and other committees that constituted the large bureaucracy of democratic Athens. Another group of public slaves formed the police force of Athens. The public slaves enjoyed a privileged position and considerable personal freedom.

Pasion. Another privileged group consisted of slaves who lived apart from their owners, with the consent of the latter. These "separately domiciled" slaves worked in all sorts of occupations as independent operators, but on condition that they turned over a portion of their earnings to their masters; by saving up some of the rest of their income they could buy their freedom and rise to the status of metics. The independently working slaves did not differ much from the free artisans and craftsmen; there is even some reason for thinking that they had some legal standing that allowed them to seek the protection of the courts. A slave could advance himself considerably. The banker Pasion, for example, began his career as a slave in a banking firm, then became a freedman, and eventually an Athenian citizen. Pasion was the wealthiest banker and manufacturer of his time, and at his death was a multimillionaire in modern terms.

Erechtheum. Inscriptions on marble show that citizens, metics, and slaves worked side by side as craftsmen and laborers. In one instance an inscription records the trades, social class, and pay of the workers completing the construction of the temple of Athena, known as the Erechtheum in the last decade of the fifth century. Much of the temple still stands today on the Athenian Acropolis. Many professions and trades are listed; among them are 2 architects and their secretary, 44 masons, 19 carpenters, 9 sculptors, 7 wood-carvers, 3 painters, a pair each of sawyers and wax modellers, 1 joiner, lathe worker and gilder, and 7 men whose trade is unknown. Of the total 107 workers, 24 were citizens, including the architects and their secretary, 42 were metics, and 20 were slaves. Sixteen slaves worked in the specialized trades of masonry and carpentry; no slave worked as a common laborer, while six freemen did. Later sources add coppersmiths, engravers, wagon masters, drivers, ropemakers, weavers, and leather workers to the work force on the Acropolis. On the whole these men did the same kind of work and were paid the same wage. The only distinctions made were that the architects and their secretary were under contract for one year and received a salary, two distinct advantages. The rest of the workers, depending on the type of work they did, were paid either by the day or by their production rate. Slaves also regularly served in the navy of Athens as oarsmen, side by side with citizen and metic shipmates; in fact, the majority of the rowers in the warships were slaves.

Assimilation. Through the work that they did the slaves of Athens became assimilated with the lower classes of the free population. They did not constitute a separate social class, nor did they compete with the citizens for employment. The modern view that slave labor made worse the economic position of the free workers is mistaken. Nowhere in the ancient sources is there any indication of antagonism against slave workers; on the contrary, free workers regarded the slaves as "working companions," rather than as economic rivals.

Slave Revolts. At the height of the Peloponnesian War in 413 B.C.E., the Spartans blockaded Athens, and twenty thousand slaves ran away. Many of them were probably miners escaping their harsh working conditions. They fell into the hands of the Boeotians, who sold them for a good price. The deserters did not intend to start a slave war against Athens. Apart from a few revolts by the helots at Sparta, there were no slave uprisings of the kind that occurred later in Roman Italy. The differences in nationality and in their social and economic circumstances prevented slaves in Greece from developing a class consciousness and so from uniting to form a program of common action.

Imperialism. For fifty years after the Persian Wars, Athens was the most prosperous Greek state, mainly because it was now an imperial power. The old belief that war was a legitimate means of enriching oneself remained alive, but in the Classical Period it took on the more subtle form of imperialism, which may be defined as the imposition by a superior power of demands on others, in this case demands for the payment of tribute. It had been agreed originally that the moneys paid into the treasury on Delos were to be used in prosecuting the war against Persia; however, it was probably inevitable that some of the tribute from the dozens of city-states should eventually come to be used for the benefit of Athens alone. The increase of Athens's wealth from this source explains how that country, having only mediocre farmland and few natural resources except silver, could become the wealthiest city-state in the Greek world, building public buildings on a magnificent scale, maintaining large war fleets, and waging war, all at the same time.

Plot Holders. No voice was raised in Athens to defend the interests of the states subjected to Athenian rule. One politician, Thucydides, the son of Milesias, raised the question of the tribute paid by the states for the construction of new public buildings, but he did not really champion the cause of the subject states. The Athenians were fully satisfied with the benefits from their empire; besides the financial benefit from the tribute, they held control of foreign sources of various commodities. As virtual dictators over their vassal states, the Athenians could confiscate allied lands and settle on them as so-called plot holders. Having such holdings in the Aegean region was not enough for them; in 415 B.C.E. they began a war against Sicily for more such free land.

Rivals. The Athenians were not the only imperialists. Other states also built empires, not for financial gain, but for political and military reasons. The Spartans, for instance, did not force the members of the Peloponnesian League, of which they were the leaders, to pay tribute. Nevertheless, the members of the League did contribute some of their wealth by paying for the maintenance of the military forces of the League. Corinth also practiced a form of imperialism. She maintained links with her colonies, requiring some of them to grant special privileges to the mother city.

Imports. In the Classical Era the chief concern of Athenian authorities was feeding the population, which was large for its time, probably numbering around 250,000 people. During this period Athens regularly had to import two-thirds of its grain from abroad. Its leaders accordingly followed a policy of keeping the sea lanes open to grain cargoes bound for Athens and of controlling the Dardanelles, the vital passage to the grain regions along the Black Sea. Sicily, too, was a source; early in the Second Peloponnesian War the Athenians sent warships to Sicily to intercept grain transports sailing for the Peloponnese.

Timber. Athens kept control of the sea with her powerful navy, but the navy in turn stood in constant need of raw materials with which to build new ships and maintain the old. The greatest need was timber, the main sources of which were the hinterlands of the Thracian coasts, southern Italy, and Sicily. In 465 B.C.E. Athens made an attempt to establish a settlement in Thrace, with a view to obtaining timber there, but attacks upon the settlers by the native tribes and opposition from the kings of Macedon frustrated the operation. After another unsuccessful venture in 445 the Athenians turned to the west, making treaties with various Sicilian and south Italian towns. Two years later a colony was established at Thurii in south Italy. In 437 Athens finally gained a foothold in Thrace with the foundation of Amphipolis, but it lost the town in 424 to the Spartans.

Self-Sufficiency. Other commodities needed for both military and civilian purposes also had to be imported throughout the Classical Period. They included various metals, flax for sails, and pitch and ruddle (vermillion or cinnabar) for the hulls. For these commodities, as well as papyrus and leather, Athens had to rely entirely on imports. Athens was self-sufficient only in honey, wine, and olive oil; it also had natural resources of silver, marble, and potting clay.

Profits. The Athenians could not pay for all these imports with money earned by export. Neither the export of olive oil, Attic wine, nor manufactured goods was able to generate substantial profits. In the fifth century Athens was rich from the tribute paid by the subject states and could pay for its imports. In the fourth century it had to rely on the export of silver, taxation, and the revenue from duties and tolls levied on the maritime traffic in its ports. Increasingly Athens also attracted visitors eager to participate in her intellectual life, and also ordinary tourists, whose money was beneficial to the economy.

Second Peloponnesian War. The major changes in the wake of the Second Peloponnesian War (431–404 B.C.E.) were political. Sparta replaced Athens as the dominant power and was itself replaced by Thebes. Intermittent warfare continued down to 338, devastating fields and dislocating farmers. Farmers and veterans of the war sought employment as mercenaries. The collapse of the Athenian empire at the end of the fifth century added to the unemployment: the craftsmen, artists, and builders whom Athens had employed with the money extracted from the empire sought work in more stable states in Asia or in Sicily and Italy. Colonization like that in the Archaic Period could no longer provide a safety valve for overpopulation.

Lean Times. In Athens itself there was a certain physical recovery from the devastation of the countryside during the long Peloponnesian War. Nonetheless, the early fourth century was a period of lean times financially, and for the remainder of the century the Athenians were less prosperous than they had been during the days of their great empire. The problems of the preceding era remained, but in a more acute form, the overriding among them being the need to feed a population that had decreased somewhat but was poorer. A declining capacity to import grain and other vital commodities, despite the organization of a new maritime league, meant that Athens no longer had the same control of the sea as in the preceding century.

Survival. Despite these problems, there was no permanent crisis of the kind alleged by Marxist historians, either in the farmlands or in urban society. No landgrabbing by big capitalist proprietors took place, either in Attica or in Greece in general. Attica continued to be a land of small estates, which on the whole managed to sustain themselves. On the "industrial" side there is some evidence of an increase in entrepreneurial activity, chiefly in the mining of silver.

Sources:

Antony Andrewes, *The Greeks* (New York: Knopf, 1967).

M. M. Austin and P. Vidal-Naquet, *Economic and Social History of Ancient Greece: An Introduction*, translated by Austin (Berkeley: University of California Press, 1977).

Moses I. Finley, *The Ancient Economy* (Berkeley: University of California Press, 1973).

Simon Hornblower, *The Greek World 479–323 BC* (London & New York: Methuen, 1983).

Nicholas F. Jones, *Ancient Greece: State and Society* (Upper Saddle River, N.J.: Prentice Hall, 1997).

Russell Meiggs, *Trees and Timber in the Ancient Mediterranean World* (Oxford: Clarendon Press, 1982).

J. Perlin and Borimir Jordan, "Running Out: 4,200 Years of Wood Shortages," *Co-Evolution Quarterly*, 37 (1983): 18–25.

Anthony M. Snodgrass, *Archaic Greece: The Age of Experiment* (London: Dent, 1980).

BOEOTIA

Cattle Lands. A region in central Greece bordering on Attica, Boeotia was named after its large cattle pastures. The area consisted of the two plains of Orchomenos and Thebes, both of which were good wheat land. In the second half of the sixth century, a Boeotian League of many small towns came into being and issued a common coinage. In the Classical Period (480–323 B.C.E.) the number of cities and towns had shrunk to about a dozen, controlled in varying degrees by the largest city, Thebes.

War Prosperity. On the whole the Boeotians were a self-contained agricultural people who did not share the overseas expansion of Greece. Boeotian farms were prosperous, and the land was regarded as rich. The Boeotians profited from the economic difficulties of Athens, their neighbor to the southeast, during the Second Peloponnesian War (431–404 B.C.E.), when the Spartans occupied the Attic plain, making it possible for Athenian slaves to desert to Boeotia. The Boeotians made money by selling the slaves; they also made inroads into Attica, capturing quantities of military equipment and looting the estates of the wealthier Athenians. The pillaged property, combined with a sound agricultural economy and the acquisition of the city of Plataea from Athens, created a considerable prosperity and a rise in the population in the fourth century.

Source:

Simon Hornblower, *The Greek World 479–323 BC* (London & New York: Methuen, 1983).

CLASSICAL PERIOD: ECONOMIC CRISIS

Food Supply. During the Classical Period (480–323 B.C.E.), the city-states were primarily centers of consumption, and the first task of their governments was to provide their people with the commodities essential for survival, imported grain being the most important of them. Athens was not the only state in need of foreign grain; several other states in Greece proper and in Ionia also had to rely on regular imports. Insofar as the city-states could be said to have had an economic policy, that policy consisted in ensuring the supply of food and finding the means to pay for it. The solution of these two problems overrode all other economic concerns; in effect, a state's economic policy was, in reality, based upon imports, and its financial goals consisted in little more than the raising of taxes.

A bowl painting of agricultural laborers on the road to market (Musée du Louvre, Paris, France)

Exports. Because governments considered their people only as consumers and not as producers, they did not devise export policies either. Exports were left entirely to private operators, although sometimes a government forbade foodstuffs from leaving the city-state. In any case cities and states seldom had a surplus of goods to export, and when they did, they could not always sell them. Athens, for instance, could not derive a significant revenue from the export of olive oil, because there were no foreign markets for it: virtually the entire Mediterranean region produced its own olive oil in sufficient quantities to satisfy domestic demand. Athens produced some of the finest decorated pottery, but the market for it was small, and its exports did not generate enough income to balance the cost of imports. In short, the combined revenue from agriculture and manufacture was quite insufficient to cover the cost of imported consumer goods.

Land Transport. A second problem besetting all states was the difficulty and cost of land transport. The chief beasts of burden were the ox, mule, and donkey. Both the cost of feeding the animals and their slow movement on bad roads made land transport far more expensive than water travel. It has been calculated that moving a cargo of grain from one end of the Mediterranean to the other cost less than moving it seventy-five miles on land. A city or town could afford to be supplied with food grown, at most, four to five miles away from it. In times of a bad harvest an inland city, which was not particularly affluent and was without the possibility of water transport, faced starvation since it could not import food from farther away. Only the richest and most powerful cities could afford to move the commodities necessary for life by land. Cities on the coast or on navigable rivers could import much of the necessary grain and did not have to rely on the produce from their own distant hinterland. Easy access to waterways was therefore a precondition for the growth of populations in the cities; their absence perforce limited such growth considerably. The Greeks may have planted colonies on the coasts of the Mediterranean Sea not only to relieve population pressures, but also to have a way of importing grain by sea. A small group of colonists in an exceptionally fertile region could grow large amounts of grain, which could then be shipped to Greece at a relatively small cost.

Other Expenses. Thirdly, Greek states had to pay not only for food: money was required also for defense, the construction of public buildings, and for the salaries of officials. In some states citizens expected handouts of public money. Athens, for example, regularly paid subsidies to its citizens, such as the price of admission to the theater, jurors' pay, and subventions to attend meetings of the popular assembly. There was also the custom of offering free meals for life at public expense to deserving people. Yet, despite the need to raise and spend money regularly, Greek states had no fiscal policy in the modern sense and no budgets; there was no such thing as a balance sheet listing expenditures and revenues. Nor was there any economic planning or accumulation of reserves. Nevertheless, there were exceptions. Themistocles persuaded the Athenians to accept his plan of spending the revenue from the silver mines at Laurium for the construction of warships instead of distributing it among the citizens. Athens also accumulated a reserve in the fifth century with the help of the resources of her empire.

Raising Revenue. Whatever fiscal policy that existed, was of the crudest kind and was concerned only with raising revenues. Greek states generated most of their income by levying taxes on individuals. Port cities raised revenue from the maritime traffic in their harbors by collecting fees for services to ships and by imposing harbor dues, tolls, and dock charges. Whatever export of agricultural and manufactured goods took place was also taxed; but as such exports were limited, the revenues from them were correspondingly small. Where no farming and manufacturing were carried on, as on some smaller islands, fishing and ferrying were possible sources of revenue. States fortunate enough to have gold or silver mines in their territory relied on a steady source of income until the ore was depleted. A vigorous exchange of goods with other countries might have increased the revenues from taxes levied on business. Yet, the growth of business was limited by the lack of most business practices known to the modern world. There were no financial instruments, and the extension of credit for business purposes was unknown. Loans were a regular practice; however, they were not really a form of credit, but an insurance policy against the great risk of losing ships and cargoes at sea.

Vassals and War Booty. For imperial states tribute from subject and vassal countries was another source of income. Related to the revenue from imperialism was income from the sale of booty captured in war, a method of enriching oneself that was accepted as normal.

Tourism. As a final source of income, at least for those states that attracted visitors, there was always tourism. As a center of learning, literature, and art, Athens in the Classical Period received visitors from abroad, including students at the philosophical schools. The places that hosted major religious festivals, especially those offering athletic and cultural spectacles, also attracted large crowds of visitors. As these festivals took place regularly, the tourist money spent at them was a dependable source of considerable income for the host locality.

Sources:
M. M. Austin and P. Vidal-Naquet, *Economic and Social History of Ancient Greece: An Introduction,* translated by Austin (Berkeley: University of California Press, 1977).

Moses I. Finley, *The Ancient Economy* (Berkeley: University of California Press, 1973).

COLONIZATION

Expeditions. The population movements of the Archaic Period (700–480 B.C.E.) differed greatly from the mass migrations of the Dark Age (1000–800 B.C.E.). This time the emigrants departed under the aegis of the mother city and sometimes at her behest and with the sanction in the form of an oracular pronouncement of a god, usually Apollo. The metropolis also organized the colonizing expedition and appointed its leader. The colony that the emigrants founded at their place of destination was a regular city-state right from its inception. In organizing the new settlement the colonists generally replicated the civic and religious institutions of their mother city.

Settlements. Among the earliest settlements abroad were the colonies in Sicily and southern Italy, as far north as the Bay of Naples. Most of these colonies date to the eighth century B.C.E. Other regions colonized include the northern and eastern shores of the Aegean along the coasts of Thrace and Asia Minor. The number of the settlements in these areas grew until the entire Aegean littoral was Greek by the beginning of the fifth century. Meanwhile, the coasts along Dardanelles, the Sea of Marmara, and the Bosporos had also been settled by Greeks, while other colonies had sprung up at various spots around the Black Sea and along the southern coast of Asia Minor. Greeks also settled the island of Cyprus and established a colony at Cyrene in North Africa. There were Greek colonies in the far west on Corsica and the Balearic Islands, along the coast of Spain, and in the south of France near present-day Nice, Antibes, and Marseilles.

Social and Economic Causes. Until recently many economic historians believed that the motive for colonization was commerce. An economic revolution in old Greece, beginning in the eighth century, was the cause of a great increase in agricultural production and in the manufacture of durable goods, and so the need to export both increased also. The foundation of colonies overseas had in part the purpose of establishing new markets for the surplus production of the home states. The social and political consequence was the rise of a new class of wealthy manufacturers and merchants who demanded, generally unsuccessfully, equal political rights with the old landed aristocrats controlling the governments of the archaic states. The demands of the nouveaux riches were eventually met by the so-called tyrants, sole rulers, who came to power as the champions of the new mercantile class. In the meantime the emerging commercial world required an easy means of exchange and found it in the invention of coinage. The use of money, however, benefited only the rich and caused the small farmers to fall into debt.

Modern Model. In large part the model for this reconstruction was the industrial and mercantile world of modern times. The ancient evidence on which it rests is of necessity chiefly archaeological, that is, the distribution of pottery, since whatever written evidence scholars have is not detailed and mostly records political events. Pottery was widely used, and great amounts of it have been found throughout the Mediterranean region. It is not, however, an accurate indicator of the scale either of manufacture or of trade. First of all, only the fine, painted pottery has been studied extensively. Second, the manufacture of painted pottery was a luxury industry. Decorated vases were owned only by the rich; hence, the demand for them and the quantities produced and sold were small. Third, the fine ware also tended to be small in size and was therefore not used as containers of exportable goods, such as wine or oil. Finally, the majority of Greek states did not produce and

A black-figure amphora painting of merchants weighing grain, circa 550-530 B.C.E. (Metropolitan Museum of Art, New York)

export painted pottery, while some of the overseas colonies such as on Sicily and near Marseilles that might be expected to import ceramics from the mother city made their own instead.

New Explanations. The results of recent archaeological research and the reexamination of the literary evidence have provided a different and better understanding of economic activity in ancient Greece. In this new picture the manufacture of pottery and trade with it, the backbone of the older reconstruction, plays a comparatively small part. The second large movement of people out of mainland Greece was caused by economic problems, or more exactly by overpopulation and consequently, scarcity of land. The population of many states and cities had been on the increase since the end of the Dark Age, while the supply of food had not. Greece and all other ancient states, like those of preindustrial Europe, were agrarian societies. The annual yield of a harvest, as in most parts of Europe today, was of only three or four times the seed grain. With such meager yields, even from a good harvest, grain became so scarce during the worst months of winter that bread was rationed; when the harvest was bad, there was starvation. This situation was made worse in Greece by the custom of dividing estates between all the male and, occasionally, female heirs. Disposing of an estate in this manner meant that smaller farms were the rule and large estates an exception.

Solutions. Efforts were made to limit the number of people living off a farm. One way was to delay marriage and procreation. According to the poet Hesiod, who wrote around the end of the eighth century, the right age for a man to marry was thirty. More than a century later the Athenian legislator Solon set the right age at twenty-nine to thirty-five years. Since males in ancient Greece were considered old enough to marry and have children at eighteen, clearly marriage was either being postponed deliberately. This scenario means that, given the life expectancy in that era, the son married when his father was near the end of his life or dead, so that a farm did not have to support the older generation as well as that of the son. Another consequence of a delayed marriage was that men between the years of eighteen and thirty would probably not have children; moreover, some men did not live to reach the age of thirty. Hesiod also recommended having only one son, which implies sexual abstinence in marriage. This recommendation and the pressure to marry later in life encouraged prostitution, well attested in the Archaic age, and the tolerance of homosexuality. Other ways of dealing with overpopulation were infanticide and exposure of newborns, and, if there was no dowry for her, marrying one's sister rather than bringing another woman onto the farm.

Sharers of Land. The driving force behind this great wave of colonization was keeping population growth in check at home and satisfying the hunger for land by establishing colonies abroad. Finding new good land for agriculture was the aim of the emigrants. The colonists most often settled in regions that were the most fertile in grains. The first settlers of Syracuse in Sicily called themselves *gamoroi* ("sharers of land"), while the colony at Metapontum on the Gulf of Taranto struck coins that bore as the city's symbol an ear of wheat.

Safety Valves. The Greeks took for granted that the colonies were primarily agricultural foundations providing safety valves against overpopulation in the mother country. They applied different terms to settlements abroad in order to distinguish an agricultural settlement from a commercial settlement. When a colony, often led by an aristocrat, was founded, it was called an *apoikia* ("house away from home"). A commercial foundation, on the other hand, was termed an *emporium* (trading post).

Sources:

Antony Andrewes, *The Greeks* (New York: Knopf, 1967).

John Boardman, *The Greeks Overseas* (Baltimore: Penguin, 1964).

Thomas James Dunbabin, *The Western Greeks: The History of Sicily and South Italy from the Foundation of the Greek Colonies to 480 B.C.* (Oxford: Clarendon Press, 1948).

Antony M. Snodgrass, *Archaic Greece: The Age of Experiment* (London: Dent, 1980).

Chester G. Starr, *The Ancient Greeks* (New York: Oxford University Press, 1971).

CORINTH

Fertile Lands. As did other places in the ancient world, Corinth had agriculture as its fundamental economic activity, especially in the Archaic Period (700–480 B.C.E.). Corinth's territory was smaller than that of Athen's. Its agricultural land was therefore limited; moreover, it was divided into many small farms, which probably for that reason were less productive. On the other hand, the Corinthian land was more fertile than the land of Attica.

Crossroads. From an early time the commercial element in Corinth was stronger than elsewhere in Greece. This situation was only natural, given the city's location at the crossroads of land and sea routes. The historian Thucydides wrote that "Corinth was an emporium from most ancient times. At first it collected tolls from trade moving by land from and into the Peloponnese, then from trade by sea. The Corinthians built a navy, put down piracy, and used their naval power to increase their revenues." Another ancient author says that Corinth became wealthy because of its ports of trade. It had two harbors, one on the Aegean Sea and facing Asia, the other on the Corinthian Gulf looking toward western Italy. The income generated in the harbors was of two kinds. The first type consisted of the tolls and duties imposed upon maritime and land traffic moving across the land bridge. Masters of cargo vessels preferred the transshipment from one side of the Isthmus to the other as opposed to the dangerous rounding of the southern tip of the Peloponnese. The other kind of revenue came from the trade that Corinth carried on in her own right in her harbors. Corinthian pottery was exported widely: it has been found in some quantity on sites in Italy and Sicily, where Corinth established its only significant colony, Syracuse. At the end of the sixth century Corinthian

The site of ancient Corinth, with the remains of the sixth century B.C.E. temple of Apollo in the foreground (National Tourist Organization of Greece, Photo V. and N. Tombazi)

pottery began to be displaced in the markets by pots made in Athens. Nonetheless, Corinth continued to be a lively manufacturing sector, and although few if any ancient states survived from manufacture alone, the city must have derived at least a part of its revenues from making and exporting commodities.

Isthmia. Another source of income, perhaps as productive as trade, was the festival held every two years in honor of Poseidon on the Isthmus of Corinth. Recent archaeological research has established that the cult of Poseidon began during the transition from the Bronze Age (3000–1100 B.C.E.) to the Iron Age (1100–700 B.C.E.), while the Isthmia (the site of the sanctuary of Poseidon) was a center of production of terracotta ware as early as 800 B.C.E. From an early date the Isthmian Games attracted athletes, spectators, and pilgrims from all parts of the Greek world; by the beginning of the fifth century the festival had become popular, offering not only sport spectacles, but also such entertainment as plays, concerts, dance performances, and literary recitals in prose and verse. Audiences and spectators spent handsomely while attending the Games; money was also spent by the performing artists, while the official delegations of various states enriched the sanctuary of Poseidon with the valuable gifts that they dedicated to the god. Visits to nearby Corinth by many in the large crowds gathered at the Isthmia added to Corinth's revenues.

Grain Imports. The general prosperity of Corinth led to an increase in population and so to a growing need for grain of which Corinth became the prime importer in the Peloponnese. Athenian naval activity during the Second Peloponnesian War (431–404 B.C.E.) kept Sicilian corn shipments from reaching the Peloponnese. In the later fourth century Corinth received grain from Cyrene in North Africa.

Decline. Corinth suffered much from the Peloponnesian War: its commerce was eroded, and its small businesses declined. A sign of impoverishment and unemployment in the overpopulated city-state was the emigration of many Corinthians to Sicily in the second half of the fourth century. After that time Corinth never again was a major power in the history of antiquity.

Sources:
Antony Andrewes, *The Greeks* (New York: Knopf, 1967).

Moses I. Finley, *The Ancient Economy* (Berkeley: University of California Press, 1973).

Borimir Jordan, "Isthmian Amusements," *Classics Ireland,* 8 (2001): forthcoming.

ECONOMIC ACTIVITIES

Farming. The basis of the Greek economy, and of the ancient world in general, from first to last remained agriculture. In the main it took the form of subsistence farming; market farming, even after the introduction of coins, was limited. The typical farmer's market was a place where farmers from a few miles around met to exchange produce with each other: in agriculture as in

manufacture during this period there was no genuine mercantile element. Moreover, there was no exportation of agricultural produce. The vast majority of the colonies were self-sufficient agricultural settlements. The colonists for the most part worked their land themselves. Some relied on the labor of the neighboring non-Greek population, whom the settlers enslaved. Examples of such enslavement were the Killyrioi who were subjected by the settlers of Syracuse in Sicily, and the Mariandynians who became slaves of the citizens of Heraclea Pontica in Asia Minor.

Religious Cults. There were some other activities that, although they were not deliberately planned to do so, nevertheless contributed to economic life. One of these was religion. The polytheistic Greeks worshipped major gods and minor divinities in many places. Throughout Greece there arose large sanctuaries containing many buildings and various smaller sacred precincts. The best known were the sanctuaries where the great Panhellenic athletic festivals took place: Olympia, Delphi, the Isthmus of Corinth, and Nemea. The construction of temples, smaller shrines, ancillary buildings, and in time of theaters and stadiums provided work for many craftsmen and architects, who traveled to the sanctuaries to fulfill their commissions. The acquisition of building materials—stone, metals, wood—also stimulated economic life.

The Dedications. The custom of offering gifts to the gods in the form of dedications also had an effect on the economy. The dedications consisted of pottery, sculpture, decorated marble slabs, and other artifacts, all of which were commissioned and paid for by both private persons and state governments. Objects made of the precious metals and of the less valuable bronze, as well as ingots of all these metals, were offered up as gifts to the gods, not only by the Greeks, but also by foreign potentates. Two kings of Lydia in Asia Minor, Gyges and Croesus, sent such gifts to the sanctuary of Apollo at Delphi. Most of the silver there came from Gyges; he also gave many golden vessels, including six golden bowls weighing nearly 2,500 pounds each. Croesus sent to Delphi 117 ingots, each eighteen inches long, nine inches wide, and three inches thick. Four of them were refined gold weighing 142 pounds each, the rest were electrum, an alloy of gold and silver, weighing 114 pounds each. He also sent a statue of a lion made of pure gold, and standing on a base of gold bricks were two huge bowls, one golden, the other silver.

Financial Centers. The gifts from the rich Lydian kings were of course exceptional, but the point is that in the Archaic Period the sanctuaries began to amass great wealth. Dedications of the Lydian type were not the only source of the sanctuaries' wealth. More-modest gifts from ordinary but well-to-do people added to the wealth. It was also customary to give to the gods a portion of the booty captured in war, so that in the course of time the sanctuaries acquired huge quantities of valu-

The stadium at Delphi for the Pythian Games (Melia)

able goods looted from defeated countries. Thus, the religious centers of archaic Greece came to resemble modern financial centers, although it is not fully clear in what way the capital assembled there had an impact on the economy. In the fifth century it was possible to borrow with interest from the treasury of a deity to defray the state's expenses. Around the middle of the fourth century the Phocians, a people in the vicinity of Delphi, plundered the sanctuary of Apollo and melted down many of the gold and silver votive offerings to pay for expenses they had incurred in war. On this occasion at least and in such a crude way, the capital of Delphi was spread around and no doubt spurred on some economies. Whether Delphi and other rich sanctuaries lent money in earlier times is not clear but quite possible.

First Fruits. Religious cults and the various activities connected with them contributed to the economy in yet another way. At the sites of the great international festivals and local religious celebrations and games there gathered during the holidays large crowds of worshippers, spectators, athletes and their trainers, and artistic performers and their coaches. The crowds, which could number in the thousands at Olympia, Delphi, Isthmia, and Nemea, had to pay for food and drink and whatever other services they required. The customary sacrifices offered to the gods, consisting of the choicest farm produce and termed "first fruits," involved expenditures, as did the ritualistic communal meals. The various artistic and cultural activities such as dancing, singing, and plays required more outlays, as did ceremonial processions and initiations into cults. Some of these events and practices were so expensive that they were financed by a state or by smaller bodies such as cult associations and other corporate entities, and sometimes by wealthy individuals.

War. Only one-tenth of the booty from warfare went into the coffers of the sanctuaries; the rest of it remained in the communities of the victorious city-state. As a result, warfare had a sizable impact on the economy.

Aristotle observed that war is a way of acquiring property, and his observation was based on practical experience: he observed victorious states acquiring the arable land of their enemies. While on campaign, armies maintained themselves from the crops of the territory they had invaded and from pillaging the inhabitants' property.

Sources:

Moses I. Finley, *The Ancient Economy* (Berkeley: University of California Press, 1973).

William Kendrick Pritchett, *Ancient Greek Military Practices. Part I* (Berkeley: University of California Press, 1971).

Anthony M. Snodgrass, *Archaic Greece: The Age of Experiment* (London: Dent, 1980).

IONIA AND THE AEGEAN ISLANDS

Rich Colonies. The Greek settlements up and down the coastal strip of Ionia were quite prosperous in the sixth century B.C.E. They had sufficient wealth to pay for the construction of considerable buildings, some of them of a colossal size. Examples are the huge temples of Hera (in her large sanctuary on Samos), Artemis (at Ephesus), and Apollo (on Lesbos and at Didyma). More-modest temples were built on Chios, at Mytilene, and in Phocaea. Early in the Archaic Period (700–480 B.C.E.) Samos and Miletus were rich enough to give assistance to the cities in Euboea at war with each other. Further evidence of the Ionians' prosperity is the large number of ships that they were able to build during the Ionian revolt against Persia in 494 B.C.E. Miletus, which had reached the height of its prosperity at that time, together with Samos and Chios provided 240 ships among them. Polycrates, the tyrant of Samos in the sixth century, was wealthy enough to fund the construction of a one-mile-long aqueduct through an entire mountain.

Persian Rule. The prosperity of Ionian Greece did not diminish after its cities had passed under Persian rule in the second half of the sixth century. The Persians demanded payment of tribute, but they permitted considerable autonomy to the Greeks, including the right to grant tax exemptions as they saw fit. The population of the coastal strip was not Greek exclusively: Persians and other Asiatic nationals had settled among the Greek colonists, with whom they lived on good terms. The reason for the Ionians' revolt against Persia was not economic, for they continued to prosper; it was the desire to be free. The Ionian Greeks preferred self-government to good but alien government, and regarded having to pay tribute and to serve in the Persian military as restrictions on their freedom.

Athenian Rule. After the Persian Wars the Ionians became members and then subjected states in the alliance dominated by Athens. The Athenians, too, demanded the payment of tribute, but were perhaps not as insistent on using force as the Persians in cases of nonpayment.

Buildings. It is the standard view among classicists that Ionia in the fifth century was in an economic decline because expensive public and religious buildings were no longer being built. However, while such construction is an indication of wealth, its absence does not necessarily indicate an economic eclipse. For one thing,

The Avenue of Lions on the island of Delos (Photo: Robert Tobler, Lucerne)

not all communities built colossal temples in the sixth century. Only the largest towns built them, when the importance of the cults demanded the construction. Next, the buildings constructed earlier may have been adequate, and in any case, some construction can be shown to have occurred in several Ionic cities. Thirdly, the analogy with Athens, which contributed to the view of economic decline, is not pertinent. Athens could build on a grand scale because it had at her disposal the tribute from her empire. There is, on the other hand, positive evidence for Ionian prosperity: a few states were rich enough to furnish ships to the Delian League; some construction did take place, albeit on a smaller scale; the Ionian states could pay tribute both to Athens and to Persia at the same time; and, finally, the island of Chios possessed more slaves in the Classical Period (480–323 B.C.E.) than any other Greek state.

Source:
R. Osborne, "Archaeology and the Athenian Empire," *Transactions of the American Philological Association,* 129 (1999): 319–332.

SICILY AND SOUTHERN ITALY

Syracuse. When the Greeks colonized Sicily, they became the neighbors of three native peoples, the Sicani, Siculi, and Elymi. Throughout their history there the Greeks also had to reckon with the Carthaginians to the south, who established colonies in western Sicily, and the Etruscans to the north, who also had designs on the island. The Greek colonists arriving from the eighth century onward ejected the natives from the best sites of the island; in Syracuse, the island's largest city, they reduced them to a dependent status similar to that of the helots in Sparta.

Riches. The colonists were attracted by the fertility of the island; it produced wheat, wine, oil, cattle, and horses. In later times Sicily became a chief supplier of grain to the Romans as well. Early commercial contacts with old Greece are indicated by Corinthian and Rhodian pottery found at Sicilian sites. In short, Sicily was a wealthy place. The temples built there in the sixth century attest to this wealth: they were in every way as imposing as those in Greece.

Sybaris and Tarentum. In southern and western Italy the Greek settlements were also successful economically. Sybaris (founded 721 B.C.E.) became proverbial for its wealth and luxurious way of life. Tarentum, settled by Spartans in 705 B.C.E., owed its prosperity to its rich soil and a thriving fishing industry. Handicrafts, especially the textile industry, also flourished there, while its harbor was a convenient port of call.

Timber Lands. From the early fifth century onward Athens began to show great interest in Sicily and southern Italy not only because of their agricultural products, but also because of their timber. Themistocles, who built up the Athenian navy, was interested in

The temple at Segesta, in the north-western part of Sicily (Photo: Leonard von Matt. Buochs)

the region, and it was still virgin land when new arrivals began to appear. The native peoples and the Carthaginian and Greek settlers had not deforested the region nearly as much as the Bronze Age (3000–1100 B.C.E.) inhabitants and their successors had decimated the woods of Old Greece. Homer represents the Mediterranean west as heavily wooded, and it is significant that Corinth, the city credited with the earliest interest in seafaring and with the invention of the Greek warship, founded Syracuse in the eighth century (733 B.C.E.), the traditional lifetime of Homer.

Instability. For much of the Classical Period (480–323 B.C.E.) conditions in western Greece, especially Sicily, were unsettled. There was pressure from Carthage and racial friction between the different ethnic groups. The Athenian invasion in 415–413 B.C.E. exhausted Syracuse financially; soon afterward the tyrant Dionysius I, who restored prosperity and power to the city, nonetheless barely managed to repel Carthaginian attacks. After Dionysius there was chaos: petty tyrants established themselves in many places, and a great decline set in. The ancient reports speak of public spaces in the cities covered with vegetation and of wild boars, deer, and other wild animals roaming in them. In the second half of the fourth century the Corinthian Timoleon resettled Sicily with new colonists and refounded Syracuse. However, his new order did not long endure, and Sicily did not see permanent peace until it became a Roman province.

Sources:

M. M. Austin and P. Vidal-Naquet, *Economic and Social History of Ancient Greece: An Introduction,* translated by Austin (Berkeley: University of California Press, 1977).

Thomas James Dunbabin, *The Western Greeks: The History of Sicily and South Italy from the Foundation of the Greek Colonies to 480 B.C.* (Oxford: Clarendon Press, 1948).

R. Osborne, "Archaeology and the Athenian Empire," *Transactions of the American Philological Association,* 129 (1999): 319–332.

SOCIAL ORGANIZATION

Two Categories. The ancient Greek states fell into two categories. The first group was composed of loosely confederated regions without a main urban center; these tended to be completely agricultural, somewhat backward, and inhabited by a homogenous people, without a significant admixture of foreigners. In the second group there were more-advanced states in which urban centers exercised political control, set the tone in social relations, and gave rise to an urban "middle class" of craftsmen and tradesmen. Such states also contained free foreign residents. The two types of states had in common a population of slaves.

Social Hierarchy. The traditional social order of the free population continued to be divided into aristocrats and commoners. The tyrants were not well disposed toward the aristocrats—after all, they had succeeded to power in order to end their misrule—but they could not destroy the nobility's influence altogether. After the

THE ALCMAEONIDS

The Alcmaeonid family had a powerful influence over Athenian politics for two centuries and developed a reputation for intrigue, opportunism, and violence. In circa 625, one of its members, Megacles, orchestrated the murder of the usurper Cylon and his followers at an altar sanctuary. The populace accused the family of sacrilege and murder, and the stigma of bloodguilt plagued the Alcmaeonids thereafter. The family was expelled from the city but returned in the early sixth century and accepted the reforms of Solon.

When Peisistratus attempted his first seizure of power in 560, the Alcmaeonids allied themselves with the conservative faction, and the family was exiled again. They returned to Athens when one of their members, Cleisthenes, became archon in 525, but the tyrant Hippias expelled them once more following the murder of his brother Hipparchus in 514. The following year Cleisthenes staged an unsuccessful invasion of Attica from the family's base in Boeotia.

In 510 the family gained popular support by funding the rebuilding of the temple of Apollo at Delphi, damaged when the Spartans drove out Hippias. The subsequent constitutional reforms introduced by Cleisthenes also met with wide acceptance. During the Persian wars, the Alcmaeonids were suspected of secret dealings with the enemy and gradually lost their prominence. The mothers of both Alicibiades and Pericles were from the Alcmaeonid family.

Source: Michael Grant, *The Rise of the Greeks* (New York: Scribners, 1987).

demise of the tyrants, aristocrats again became the ruling class in most city-states. Below the nobility and the commoners there existed a large class of slaves. Slavery was ubiquitous in the entire ancient world, including the countries of the Near East and North Africa.

Slave Labor. Ancient society depended on slave labor in large part because the citizens regarded manual work as unworthy of freemen. A similar attitude was adopted by the free toward other occupations such as retail buying and selling. Even manufacturing and trading on a large scale were regarded as social and political disqualifications. The availability of slave labor only encouraged this attitude; whenever possible, all menial work was left to slaves, and as a result slave labor became more necessary.

Types of Slaves. In Greece slavery was present in two categories. One category consisted of slaves bought and sold as a commodity on the open market. These chattel slaves could be Greeks from other states and non-Greeks from the so-called barbarian lands to the east and north. The other category was made up of native populations that had been subjugated by the

A terracotta figurine of a reveller and his young slave
(British Museum, London)

Greek newcomers. At Sparta the enslaved population was called helots, and on Crete, Klarotai. In Thessaly the Penestai were the subjected people, and in Eastern Locris, the Woiki-atai. When the Corinthian colonists founded the city of Syracuse in Sicily, they enslaved the native Killyroi in the vicinity of the new town and used them as farm workers. A similar fate befell the Mariandynians on the southern shore of the Black Sea at the hands of the colonists of Heraclea Pontica.

Native Slaves. Few details are known about any of these subjected people, except for the helots, who were an integral part of the Spartan state. As natives their class was self-perpetuating, and so differed fundamentally from the chattel slaves. Moreover, they were employed mainly as laborers on the farms of their masters and as domestic servants. They are often called serfs in modern studies, which is misleading because the special reciprocal relations between a medieval lord and his serf did not exist in antiquity.

Sources:
Moses I. Finley, *The Ancient Economy* (Berkeley: University of California Press, 1973).

Nicholas F. Jones, *Ancient Greece: State and Society* (Upper Saddle River, N.J.: Prentice Hall, 1997).

Anthony M. Snodgrass, *Archaic Greece: The Age of Experiment* (London: Dent, 1980).

SPARTA

Distinct Characteristics. Sparta differed markedly from all other Greek states in several crucial respects. First, it remained a monarchy of a peculiar kind: two kings ruled at the same time during Sparta's entire history as an independent state. Secondly, Sparta was never governed by tyrants. Thirdly, the social and economic system attributed to Lycurgus was unique in the Greek world, and in fact in all of recorded history.

Backward Region. Sparta was a hybrid of the Archaic "ethnos" or unincorporated state and city-state, sharing some features of both. The territory of Sparta, including Messenia, was one of the largest and among the most fertile in Greece. Its economic base was agriculture, without even the smallest admixture of export and import trade, at least in the Classical Period (480–323 B.C.E.), or of manufacture beyond what was needed domestically. In this sense Sparta remained backward for most of the fifth and fourth centuries. Like some ethnos-type states Sparta was not a great colonizer, the only place of some significance founded by her being Tarentum in southern Italy. Sparta was also not receptive to foreigners, and in fact was quite xenophobic. On the other hand, Sparta resembled a city-state like Athens; she had a central government, was the head of a military and political alliance, the Peloponnesian League, and played a dominant role in the politics and history of Greece.

Three Categories. With respect to its social structure the Spartan population was divided into three main categories. At the top stood the Spartans proper, full citizens who called themselves equals or peers and who were also known as Spartiates, to distinguish them from other Spartans like the "Dwellers Around." The Spartiates were not all exactly equal; a small minority of them formed an aristocracy whose members were wealthier than the rest of the equals and had more social and political clout. Another segment of the Spartiates were called the "inferiors," perhaps because their income, for whatever reason, was less than that of the other peers. Nevertheless, as a body the peers constituted an egalitarian elite, whose members owned all the land. They did not, however, work their land themselves, nor did they work at any other productive occupations. Instead, they spent all their time in physical exercise and military drill, and also in the governance of the state, as members of the Spartan assembly and senate. The Spartiates furnished the executive of the state, the two kings who were the commanders in chief of the army and were the chief religious officials of Sparta, and the five Ephors or "Overseers," who ran the state from day to day.

Perioikoi. Below the elite Spartiates stood a class known as *Perioikoi* ("Dwellers Around"). The Perioikoi were true Spartans: together with the Spartiates they constituted the entire free Spartan folk. Both groups spoke the same Greek dialect and were included in the official designation of the Spartan state, the Lacedaemonians. The *Perioikoi* were in no way the subjects or dependents of the Spartiates. Like the Spartiates, they served in the army as heavily armored infantry, or hoplites, and they could participate in the Olympic Games, to which only free citizens were admitted. One of "the Seven Wise Men," Cheilon, came from a Perioikic town, while the poets Xenodamus and Philoxenus came from the Perioikic island of Cythera.

Poor Lands. The mass of the *Perioikoi* were small landowners: after they occupied Laconia the Spartiates assigned the less productive land to them, while keeping the best fields for themselves. Forcing their weaker fellows to live on the poorer land was the Spartan version of colonization due to overpopulation: instead of being sent to live in new settlements overseas the *Perioikoi* were relegated to land in the hills or on the periphery of the country.

Differences. There was, however, an essential difference between Spartiates and *Perioikoi*. The *Perioikoi* had no political rights; they could not attend the popular assembly or hold political office. In all matters of domestic and foreign policy they had to abide by the decisions of the Spartiates. The political disqualification is probably to be explained by the fact that the distances between their homes and the political center of Sparta made it difficult for the *Perioikoi* to attend the assembly until they eventually lost their political rights through default.

Helots. The third large class of people living in Sparta, the helots, were the descendants of the Bronze Age (3000–1100 B.C.E.) or Mycenaean Age (1600–1200) Greeks, whom the Dorian Spartans subjugated when they occupied Laconia. The Greeks regularly referred to them as slaves, but the helots were quite different from the chattel slaves in other states. They certainly were not freemen, but they were not, strictly speaking, the property of individual Spartans, who were not allowed to buy or sell them. Nor could they be freed, except by the state. The helots, in short, belonged to the whole community. As an indigenous people not imported from outside, the helots were self-perpetuating: they had their own families and their own possessions, which were handed down from generation to generation. Equally importantly, the helots had their own religious cults and celebrated at least one religious festival of their own. In sum, the Helots possessed all the normal human institutions except freedom. As a result they were a privileged group as servile classes go; the ancient sources quite correctly describe their condition as "between slavery and freedom."

Farming. The main activity of the helots was the cultivation of the farms belonging to their masters: they were the food producers of the Spartans, to whom they delivered a fixed quota of their crops. Beyond that the helots formed the labor force of craftsmen, vendors, fishermen, and transport workers who produced the other necessities of life, as for example the shoes known for their high quality throughout Greece. Finally, the helots also served in the Spartan army, at times forming sizable contingents in expeditionary forces.

Lycurgan Social Order. The entire population of Sparta was most profoundly affected by a regime, instituted at some time in the seventh century and attributed to the lawgiver Lycurgus, which governed daily life with a strictness and regularity unknown elsewhere in history. This regime, which determined the economic and social structures of Sparta for centuries to come, consisted of three parts: austerity, education, and discipline.

Austerity. The main component of Lycurgus's austerity program was the regulation of consumption. Spartans were required to eat moderately; in effect they were put on strict rations of what was generally unappetizing food. Occasionally, as a relief from their dreary diet, the citizens were allowed to supplement it with venison from hunting expeditions. More abundant fare was also available during religious festivals. To ensure against overindulgence in food Lycurgus instituted the so-called common messes. Spartan men were required to contribute a ration of food to the mess and to take their meals there together for most of their adult life. The consumption of alcohol was also rationed. Drinking to excess during meals and at *sumposia* (drinking parties) was greatly frowned upon. Besides limiting consumption the common messes also had the purpose of maintaining the solidarity and morale of comrades in arms. At times they were also a venue for entertainment after dinner.

Dress Code. A series of rules regulated the dress of children and women and the personal appearance of the men. Adult males were expected to wear a standard type of garment made of coarse wool having the same color. Any attempt to decorate the drab cloak was met with the severest public censure. Specific rules regulated the heads of hair and beards of all adult males. The Spartans, in effect, had to wear a uniform; an adult male could always be recognized by his clothes and appearance alone. Women were required to obey certain specific regulations prohibiting the use of such things as cosmetics, perfumes, and dresses, appropriate only for prostitutes.

Property. A Spartan could not build a sumptuous house for his family. In addition, he was forbidden to make free bequests or gifts of land and to own silver and gold. The possession of money was frowned upon; Sparta resisted the introduction and use of coinage longer and more stubbornly than any other Greek community. One or two of the rules about personal property proved untenable in the long run and were repealed in the fourth century. If the purpose of the rest was to prevent the accumulation of great wealth, they were ineffective. It was especially the women who became rich by inheriting from their parents and, when widowed, often from more than one husband.

Education. Young Spartans had virtually no family life. At age seven or eight boys had to leave their families and came to live together in barracks, where they underwent the training and instruction known as the *agôgê*. While in

The ruins of Sparta

the *agôgê* the young Spartans were divided into several age groups, each supervised by a person who was somewhat older than his charges. The Spartans had discovered an important truth: young people accept instruction and orders more willingly from someone close to them in age than from older men; they also more readily take a younger supervisor as their role model than an older one. During the years of their training the boys and teenagers were kept on a strict diet. Their rations were so small that they were encouraged to supplement them by stealing, an activity in which they learned stealth, slyness, dexterity, self-reliance, and endurance, all qualities highly prized by the Spartans and believed by them to foster self-discipline and self-control in a person. If they were caught stealing, the boys were beaten. Any violation of the discipline of the *agôgê* was punished promptly, usually by a thrashing. Flogging, especially of the young males, was commonplace at Sparta. Not all of it was punishment; ritualistic beatings of youngsters was a part of a religious festival in honor of the goddess Orthia, who is identified with Artemis.

Dress Code. A dress code was prescribed for members of the *agôgê;* it varied according to the age group. Younger boys were required to play in the nude, walk barefoot, and to have closely shaved heads. Later they were allowed only one garment, both in summer and winter. The Ephors inspected the dress of the youngsters daily and punished an improper appearance with a beating. Girls and young women, too, had to abide by a dress code, which appears to have been a little less rigorous. Both sexes were required to exercise; much of their day was spent in physical training. The educational program included choral singing and dancing; youngsters were taught to recite and sing from memory. They also learned the skill of making brief but incisive observations on any topic and to respond to remarks with brief and witty repartees. The males finished their education at age twenty and entered the ranks of the army. They remained on active service, living in army barracks, until they reached the age of thirty. At that point the Spartiate could live at home with his wife, but he was expected to continue taking his meals in the common messes.

Discipline. The lessons that the Spartans learned in the agoge laid the foundation of the famous discipline of the adult Spartans. The training of Sparta's youth is regarded by most modern students of Spartan society as having the object of producing militarists slavishly devoted to the autocratic state. Although there is some truth in it, this judgment is an exaggeration. Their schooling did turn the young into strong soldiers obedient to authority and loyal to the state. However, it achieved a host of other beneficial effects as well. The habits ingrained into them in the agoge remained with the Spartans for life. They continued to practice moderation in food and drink and to engage in regular physical exercise well into old age. As a result the Spartans were the healthiest people in Greece, and so capable of enduring great hardships. These two habits, moderation and exercise, formed one of the cornerstones of the discipline. The other cornerstone was their intellectual training. It taught them to be prudent in their domestic affairs and deliberate and cautious in foreign policy. Calm in the face of misfortunes, the Spartans were slow to act, but once embarked on a course of action they became determined and persistent.

Attributes and Flaws. The Lycurgan social and economic organization had yet another salutary effect. It masked the differences and distinctions of wealth and pedigree existing among the Spartiates, who could call themselves each others' peers with a great deal of truth.

Although their equality was not absolute, it reduced rivalry and contentiousness among the peers; seldom, if at all, were there power struggles among them of the sort that occurred in other city-states, including the Athenian democracy. As a result Sparta never experienced tyranny or civil war; for several centuries its political, social, and economic systems proved remarkably stable. Yet the regimentation that achieved this stability came with a price: Sparta produced no philosophers, dramatists, and only a few poets, although her way of life was admired by some Greek thinkers. Spartan frugality also precluded the construction of magnificent temples and public buildings of the sort that many other Greek states were able to build. There was, furthermore, a somewhat darker side to the Lycurgan order than the absence of a vigorous cultural and intellectual life.

Food Consumption. As the farmers supplying food to the Spartiates, the Helots had larger quantities of food at their disposal than their masters. Yet the Helots, like the Spartiates, were required to limit their consumption, for several reasons: first, so as to conform to the official regime of austerity and not arouse envy and indignation in their masters; second, for the reasons of health noted above; and third, because lean, tough people make much better workers and soldiers than soft and corpulent ones. Accordingly the Spartans executed those helots who became overweight. This cruelty and other indignities inflicted on them have been explained as deliberate expressions of contempt for the helots on the part of their powerful masters, who thereby wished to demonstrate to the helots that they were indeed slaves, and as such a separate and inferior people, who must be kept segregated from the society of the Spartans.

Integration. In reality the restrictions of food and most other measures against the helots had exactly the opposite aim: to integrate them into the heavily regimented Spartan society. Like the Spartans themselves, the helots were required to wear garments and caps of animal skin, which amounted to a uniform. Again like their masters the helots were beaten, except that while the Spartan young could receive a thrashing at any time, the helots had to submit only to an annual beating. The daily freedom of movement and action of the helots was also restricted. Just as the Spartans had to be present at all times either in the barracks, the gymnasium, drill square, or mess hall, so also were the Helots required to be at work during the day, and inside their houses after nightfall. Those who violated the curfew were killed if they were caught.

Military Service. These arrangements illustrate that the Helots were subjected to a similar austerity and discipline as the free Spartans. As they also served in the Spartan army, their situation appears to have been similar to that of the Perioikoi: the helots took part in some version of the Spartan agoge, perhaps as low-ranking members of it.

Significance. The Helots were loaded down with a double burden: they had to endure the hardships of slavery while at the same time they were subjected to the rigors of regular Spartan society. The double form of servitude

explains an ancient judgment that in Sparta "the slave is most slave." On the other hand, as participants in the regime of austerity and discipline the helots were treated like the Spartans, and so were regarded as being "between slavery and freedom."

Classical Period. Sparta's social and economic system remained fundamentally the same in the Classical Period (480–323 B.C.E.), but there were some changes. Beginning at some time during the Second Peloponnesian War (431–404), and perhaps because of the casualties suffered in it, Sparta experienced manpower shortages; in the fourth century the number of Spartan soldiers had been reduced considerably. There were other changes as well. Earlier most land had been inalienable, but in the fourth century a Spartan could pass on land owned by him to another person as a bequest or as a gift. Now citizens also had permission to own gold and silver. Estates grew larger, and quite a few of them came to be owned by women. The women were free to marry whom they liked, they could inherit wealth, and they were free from restrictions on property. As land came to be owned by fewer people, some Spartans were forced from their farms and fell into debt. Those who could not afford to pay their share to the common messes were downgraded socially; others, unable to support a wife, refused to marry, thus contributing to the decline in population.

Spartan Empire. Despite these problems Sparta succeeded Athens as the dominant imperial power in Greece after the Second Peloponnesian War, governing an empire that extended well beyond her traditional vassal states in the Peloponnese. However, her empire, like that of Athens, did not endure. The shortage of soldiers weakened Sparta's military power; she lost the battle of Leuctra in 371 B.C.E. to the Thebans, and with it her empire, including her prize possession, Messenia. Yet Sparta did not experience any social revolutions in the fourth century; there was only one conspiracy, and that was detected early and suppressed in time. After Leuctra the Thebans liberated those helots who had become their prisoners of war, but the system of helotry as a whole endured into the Hellenistic period. Despite the loss of the fertile Messenian plain, Sparta continued to be self-sufficient in food and most other commodities vital for daily subsistence.

Sources:

Simon Hornblower, *The Greek World 479–323 BC* (London & New York: Methuen, 1983).

George Leonard Huxley, *Early Sparta* (Cambridge, Mass.: Harvard University Press, 1962).

A. H. M. Jones, *Sparta* (Cambridge, Mass.: Harvard University Press, 1967).

Humfrey Michell, *Sparta* (Cambridge: University Press, 1952).

Anton Powell and Stephen Hodkinson, eds., *The Shadow of Sparta* (London & New York: Routledge for the Classical Press of Wales, 1994).

TECHNOLOGICAL ADVANCES AND INNOVATIONS

Coinage. The introduction of coinage represented a great advance of the Archaic Period (700–480 B.C.E.). Coins began to be minted in Lydia at the end of the sev-

ATHENIAN COINS

8 copper pieces = 1 iron or bronze obol

6 obols = 1 drachma

2 drachmas = 1 gold stater

100 drachmas = 1 mina

60 minas = 1 talent

Source: Will Durant, *The Life of Greece, The Story of Civilization: Part II* (New York: Simon & Schuster, 1939).

enth century. They came into use among the Greeks around twenty-five years after their invention, first in the Greek settlements along the Asiatic coast, and then in Old Greece. The introduction of coinage and its spread do not appear to have been due to the requirements of trade and commerce, that is to say, to facilitate the exchange of goods, and despite the usefulness of coinage as a commercial tool, most of the economic activities of the time were conducted without the use of money. Early coins occurred in large denominations; stamped of the costly electrum (an alloy of gold and silver), they were not useful in retail trade. The rare incidence of smaller denominations suggests that at first coins were not meant for internal use in local trade. Money played no great role in international trade either: the large denominations did not circulate much outside the state that issued them. Only late in the Archaic Period did Athens and some of the Greek colonies along the Thracian seaboard begin to use coinage in foreign trade. Both regions owned silver mines, and their coins have been found in the Levant and in Egypt. However, they seem to have been exported to these places for the value of the silver, not as money proper. It is significant, too, that even during this later period the circulation of coins and goods do not overlap. In short, the motive for the introduction of money was not commercial; the advent of currency did not signal the advent of a money economy in Archaic Greece.

Initial Use. Originally the introduction of coinage had a political purpose: to assert the authority and the independence of the state that minted them, and to spread the reputation of that state as much as possible; in effect the coins functioned as advertisements and a kind of propaganda. However, at the same time, coinage helped to establish norms. The second half of the Archaic Period was a time of standardization and classification of values, laws, and social strata. Draco and Solon in Athens and other lawgivers codified statutes and defined socioeconomic groups with some precision. The systematization of laws served to define right and wrong and thus to do away with arbitrary judgments. Coinage similarly defined values, and in so doing proved of benefit in the exchange of goods. Even if no money changed hands, in commercial transactions, especially those on a large scale, the relative values of commodities had to be expressed in some way, and currency made this possible: it was no accident that the larger denominations of Greek money began as measures of weight.

Means of Exchange. Once it came into more general use, money helped states acquire the means to pay for their national defense, the building of warships, or for hiring mercenaries. A state was also able to accumulate surpluses and distribute them to its citizens, who in ancient Greece always expected handouts from the public treasury. On the whole, however, coinage served a political purpose and its effect on the economy in general was slight. Centuries after coins appeared, people still used various objects, such as iron spits, tripods, and even animals, as a means of exchange.

Construction. Coinage was not the only invention that the Greeks took over from their neighbors to the east. From the Assyrians and the Egyptians they learned to hoist heavy blocks of stone by means of ramps, a technique that they applied in the construction of their large temples. During the sixth century, however, the Greeks replaced this laborious method with their own invention of hoists and pulleys. The new technique allowed them to build with smaller blocks, which made the work easier and less time-consuming. The boom in construction in this period, as it may rightfully be called, was in no small measure due to the new invention.

Shipbuilding. Between 650 and 500 B.C.E. considerable advances were taking place in ship construction, and merchant ships moving under sail and carrying heavy cargoes made their appearance. At some time between the ends of the seventh and the sixth centuries the trireme was invented. The main propulsion of the triremes was oars, but they were also equipped with masts and sails. The triremes became the standard Greek warships down to the end of the Classical Period (480–323 B.C.E.) and were still in use, along with newer types, after the time of Alexander the Great.

Military Innovations. Changes took place in armies as well. A new form of fighting appeared at the beginning of the seventh century: heavily armed and armored foot soldiers called hoplites were grouped in a battle formation known as a phalanx. Gradually the hoplite's equipment was improved. A new type of composite body armor combining leather and metal replaced the heavier bronze plate armor; this innovation made soldiers more mobile. They wore one-piece helmets and fought with a new type of two-edged sword. Archers were not used except by the people of Crete; in the second half of the sixth century they were introduced in a few other regions. There was no improvement in the cavalry, which was never the principal military arm of Greek armies.

Significance. These innovations and advances were both the manifestation and the cause of an improvement in economic conditions, which had taken place by the second half of the sixth century and which continued to get better in the next century. The changes in military hardware undoubtedly gave more employment

Greek coins (British Museum, London)

to craftsmen, as did the construction of ships. In virtually every region of the Greek world, and especially in the rich colonies in Sicily and Italy, sacred buildings were being built, some of them of colossal size. There was a marked increase of offerings to the gods; the archaeological finds from the period were richer and more varied and included more luxury items. Another sign of a growing prosperity was the development in manufacture, especially of ceramic ware, although, as has already been said, pottery is not an accurate index and does not permit the inference of a corresponding upswing in the export of goods. In these more favorable conditions urban populations were increasing as well. It was becoming possible in some degree to live from occupations other than agriculture. These professions included a certain amount of trade, which increased the income of some communities, such as Corinth, which profited from its role as an emporium near the Isthmus of Corinth.

Sources:
M. M. Austin and P. Vidal-Naquet, *Economic and Social History of Ancient Greece: An Introduction,* translated by Austin (Berkeley: University of California Press, 1977).

Lionel Casson, *Ships and Seamanship in the Ancient World* (Princeton: Princeton University Press, 1971).

William Kendrick Pritchett, *Ancient Greek Military Practices. Part I* (Berkeley: University of California Press, 1971).

Anthony M. Snodgrass, *Archaic Greece: The Age of Experiment* (London: Dent, 1980).

THESSALY

Pastures. Ruled by its aristocratic families, Thessaly was a land of great fertility. It had large tracts of productive farmland, which yielded a surplus of wheat that the Thessalians exported to their neighbors. Its pasturelands ensured that Thessaly had the best cavalry in Greece. Below the aristocratic families there was a large class of citizens rich enough to keep horses; this class provided the cavalry, which was the backbone of the military force. At the bottom of the ladder stood a class of people called *penestai,* who like the helots in Sparta were a subjected people neither free nor fully slaves, but somewhere in between. No "middle class" comparable to that in Athens existed in Thessaly.

Forests. In the late Archaic (700–480 B.C.E.) and early Classical (480–323 B.C.E.) eras, Thessaly apparently still possessed large tracts of forests, for there existed magistrates called forest wardens. If a part of their duties was to protect the land from deforestation, this protection may have been the reason why maritime states like Athens looked to Macedonia and Thrace for their timber, and not to Thessaly.

Source:
Simon Hornblower, *The Greek World 479–323 BC* (London & New York: Methuen, 1983).

TRADING POSTS

Emporiums. Although trade and commerce were not the principal motives for planting colonies, they were still important activities in the Archaic Period (700–480 B.C.E.). Once they came into existence the colonies no doubt gave a certain impetus to the international exchange of goods. However, more trade was carried on at the emporiums or trading posts.

Al Mina. An early trading post was Al Mina on the northern Levantine coast of Syria. It was founded around 800 B.C.E.; its Greek name has not survived. Al Mina shares a feature with most emporiums of the early Archaic Period, its great distance from the homeland. Ampurias was on the distant northeastern coast of Spain, and other trading posts were planted in similarly remote places: on the northwest coast of Sicily, on the Sea of Azov in south Russia, and in the Nile delta. Naucratis, an emporium in Egypt, was founded at the end of the seventh century; like the earlier Al Mina it was not a state-sponsored colony, but simply a place where Greek traders, most of them from the island of Aegina and from Asia Minor, lived and worked along with the native Egyptians. The traders depended on the good will of the pharaoh, who exercised strict control over the Greek section of Naucratis, which was separated from the Egyptian. The Greeks needed permission from the pharaoh to build temples to their gods; intermarriage between Greeks and Egyptians was

A view of the site of Al Mina, with Mount Kasius in the background

prohibited. Yet, as at Al Mina, the Greeks at Naucratis lived peacefully with their non-Greek neighbors; at any rate there is no evidence of conflict between the Greek settlers and the local population.

Facilitation of Trade. Another sign of peaceful commercial interaction between the Greeks and their neighbors living along the shores of the eastern Mediterranean Sea was the creation of a true alphabet. The Greeks derived their letters from the Phoenician, adapting some of the consonants in the Phoenician model to fit the vowels of the Greek language. Although there is no absolute proof for it, it is virtually certain that the alphabet was invented in order to keep records of goods bought and sold. There is likewise little doubt that traders from the island of Euboea devised and imported the alphabet into Greece from Al Mina at some time before 750 B.C.E. The new literacy followed the trade routes, reaching Euboea at an early date and spreading from there to Athens and other Greek regions. It can hardly be a coincidence that Euboean pottery of about 800 B.C.E. is among the earliest artifacts found at Al Mina and that some luxury objects from the east reached Euboea about that time, probably via Al Mina.

Bronze Town. There was a third type of colony besides the agricultural settlements and the trading posts. Some colonies were sent out neither in search of good land nor to establish trading posts, but to find raw materials. This task may well have been the reason behind the settlement at Al Mina. The settlers there came from the Euboean town of Chalkis or "Bronze Town," which was known for its metal-work, and it is quite likely that the Euboeans were looking for metal when they arrived at Al Mina. The metal was not shipped back to Euboea, but worked into marketable objects in the settlement. This practice occurred in other places as well. Early Euboeans settled at Cumae on the Bay of Naples in order to trade in metals with the Etruscans to the north; they also settled the nearby island of Ischia, which had metal deposits of its own. The excavations at Pithecussae, the main town of Ischia, have revealed that the settlers smelted the local ore in their foundry; the iron thus produced was worked into objects on the same spot by a smith, whose workshop was found right next to the foundry. The finished objects were then exported. The same arrangement of a smelter with a blacksmith's forge next to it was found at Motya in Sicily and in the remote mountains of Arcadia at Bassae. Not only metal objects, but, as we will see, objects of stone, too, were manufactured at the places where the raw material was readily available. The archaeological findings thus tend to disprove the unanimous view of earlier modern economic historians that ancient Greek cities, like modern industrial states, lived from the export of goods manufactured in them.

Fuel. There was another consideration besides the presence of iron ore or stone in selecting remote places for the production of objects: easy access to the necessary fuel. By the end of the Bronze Age people had been using wood in construction, manufacture, and above all as fuel for more than a millennium, causing considerable deforestation throughout Greece and in some other parts of the ancient world as well. The Bronze Age may in fact have come to an end when the supply of wood for fuel in copper-producing regions such as Cyprus began to run out. The shortage of fuel for smelting and forging made it necessary to search for metallic ores in wooded regions affording accessible fuel; when iron ore was discovered in such places, that metal began to supplant copper. Remote places such as Ischia and Bassae were still wooded in the Archaic Period, making fuel easily available.

Sources:

M. M. Austin and P. Vidal-Naquet, *Economic and Social History of Ancient Greece: An Introduction,* translated by Austin (Berkeley: University of California Press, 1977).

B. F. Cook, *Greek Inscriptions* (Berkeley: University of California Press / London: British Museum, 1987).

J. Perlin and Borimir Jordan, "Running Out: 4,200 Years of Wood Shortages," *Co-Evolution Quarterly,* 37 (1983): 18–25.

Anthony M. Snodgrass, *Archaic Greece: The Age of Experiment* (London: Dent, 1980).

TRANSPORTATION AND EXCHANGE OF GOODS AND SERVICES

Raw Materials. Much of the activity that can be described as trade in the Archaic Period (700–480 B.C.E.) consisted in the movement of raw materials, such as marble, metals of various kinds, and finished objects made of gold, silver, bronze, and iron. Archaeological research has established a fairly wide distribution of these commodities, meaning that there existed an extensive maritime network in the Greek world. The transport of marble from various quarries in particular implies the presence of ships capable of carrying heavy cargo. Such vessels made their appearance in the second half of the sixth century, replacing the lighter warships that had been used earlier because of the danger of losing valuable cargoes to pirates.

Travels. The merchantmen were owned by independent shipmasters whose travels took them to Etruria (present-day Tuscany), Cyrenaica in North Africa, Egypt, and the Spanish coast west of Gibraltar. Generally the traders were citizens of their city-states; occasionally they were aristocrats. Some of them made a great deal of money from maritime trade; Sostratus of Aegina and several merchant captains from the island of Samos amassed large fortunes.

Skilled Workers. The stone, chiefly marble, intended for construction was not shipped in its rough state; stone masons dressed it into nearly finished building blocks in the quarries where it was found, before it was transported to the construction sites. Like the stonemasons and the metalworkers on Ischia and elsewhere, sculptors, too, did much of their work in the quarries. They then traveled to the places where public buildings were being built and readied the sites to receive the sculptural decoration that they were creating. Archaeologists have found unfinished statues and half-hewn building blocks in several ancient quarries. There are recorded instances of Creten sculptors at Tegea, while Corinthians worked in Etruria and Athenians in Ionia. To earn their living architects also traveled

A stone quarry used by the ancient Greeks in Italy (National Archaeological Museum, Athens. Photo: Jean Mazenod)

to the sites of construction. The architect who designed the sixth-century temple of Apollo at Delphi almost certainly came from a place other than Delphi. One of the sculptors who fashioned some of the statuary in the temple certainly did: he was an Athenian named Antenor. Most Greek states gave money for the building of the temple; the noted Athenian family of the Alcmaeonids paid for the marble plates from the island of Paros that covered the frontal facade. The transport of the plates must have been not only difficult but expensive as well, in view of the location of Delphi in the mountains high above sea level.

Impact. All these activities, smelting and forging, quarrying, producing sculpture and pottery, erecting large edifices, and building ships, had a certain impact on the overall economy of Greece and its colonies. Laborers, semi-skilled workers, specialized craftsmen, architects, and artists were paid in some form, and they spent to support themselves. The wealthy traders and shipowners also spent. However, the effect that production, commerce, and transportation had on the Archaic Greek economy as a whole was only moderate.

Friendship and Gifts. Moderate, too, was the impact of a well-developed system of exchanging goods and services by both individuals and small enterprises such as farms. A special form of the exchange of services was the so-called guest-friendship, an arrangement whereby individual persons entered into an agreement of reciprocal hospitality, which made commercial travel possible in a time without hotels and restaurants. A network of gift-exchanges was also developed, examples of which are present in the epic poems of Homer. Both private persons and heads of government exchanged gifts with each other, although it was only the wealthier in both categories who could afford gifts of economic importance. Gifts from statesmen or kings to the sanctuaries of the major gods did have such a significance.

Source:
Anthony M. Snodgrass, *Archaic Greece: The Age of Experiment* (London: Dent, 1980).

THE TYRANTS

Position of Power. Tyranny was a nearly universal phenomenon in the more significant states of Greece during the Archaic Period (700–480 B.C.E.). The tyrants were sole rulers, autocrats or dictators, but the title did not carry the odious connotation of the modern usage. Tyrants were found in the Peloponnese, Athens, the Aegean islands, Ionia, and Sicily. The older view that the tyrants came to power as the champions of a new manufacturing and commercial class has lost its validity in the light of more-recent research. Another position, namely that as the gap between rich and poor widened the tyrants took the side of the discontented poor and promised to improve their condition, has also lost ground. The tyrants did come to power with the support of the commons, but for a different reason. They assumed power because the ruling aristocratic families proved incapable of maintaining law and order. The more-powerful nobles were engaged in constant struggles with each other for control of the government, ignoring the needs of their fellow citizens. Unable to keep order within their own ranks, these regimes brought their communities near to internal collapse. A graphic example of the infighting is the coup d'état attempted in late-seventh-century Athens by one Cylon, a nobleman and Olympic victor. The attempt was put down by the aristocratic government in power, which executed Cylon without a trial.

Law Codes. This illegality, which was also a sacrilege, provoked a demand for declarative laws setting forth which acts were crimes and specifying the appropriate punishment for each. At Athens a man called Draco promulgated a law on homicide soon after the failed revolution of Cylon. Lawgivers appeared in other states as well, and their law codes were published in order to make them known to all, and so to eliminate arbitrary interpretation. Greece, in short, entered upon an age of codification of laws and the establishment of social norms, in the same way that coinage began to define the value of things. These processes formed a fundamental tendency of the Archaic Period. Without the work of the lawgivers, the

A Roman copy of a monument to the tyrannicides, which stood in the agora at Athens (Naples, Museo Nazionale)

principal agents of this tendency, the life of the civic community could not be imagined. Draco and Solon at Athens were not the only legislators; there was the semilegendary Lycurgus at Sparta, Zaleucus in Italian Locri, Andromachus at Rhegium, and Charondas in Catana in Sicily. Despite their efforts the reformers and lawgivers were not entirely successful in ridding the polity of the anarchy created by the mismanagement of the oligarchs. While some people accused them of going too far, others maintained that they had not gone far enough.

Corinth. Thus, tyranny became the answer to the troubled conditions in many places. Although it did not prove permanent everywhere, the installation of strongmen reestablished order, and with order came an economic upswing resulting in greater prosperity. Corinth became a considerable exporter of goods, especially pottery, under its tyrants. The construction of a causeway across the Isthmus in the reign of the tyrant Periander (circa 625–588 B.C.E.) allowed the imposition of tolls on cargo hauled from the Aegean to the Gulf of Corinth. Such imposts added to the revenue of the city and remained a source of income for Corinth in the centuries to come. The Corinthian tyrants

A view of the tunnel built by the engineer Eupalinus on Samos, circa 530 B.C.E. (Deutsches Archäologisches Institut, Athens)

employment to many people for an extended period of time. Like his Corinthian counterpart, Polycrates took a strong interest in trade with Egypt, concluding a treaty with the pharaoh Amassis. The construction in stone of the colossal temple of Hera in the goddess's sanctuary, like the tunnel of Eupalinus, also gave work to many, as did a naval building program.

Miletus. Little is known about the policies of Thrasybulus, tyrant of Miletus between 625 and 600 B.C.E. His successor Histiaios acquired Myrkinos, a place in Thrace, which the Persians gave him as a reward for collaborating with them. Histiaos may have been interested in the silver mines and the still abundant timber in Thrace.

Argos and Athens. In mainland Greece Pheidon of Argos fits the mold both of a strongman and of a regulator; he is reputed to have established standard weights and measures in the seventh century. More information is available about the Athenian tyrant Pisistratus and his sons Hippias and Hipparchus who ruled in the second half of the sixth century. The government of the Pisistratids proved beneficial to the economic development of Athens. Pisistratus retained the Solonian reforms and took steps to increase the socioeconomic well-being of his subjects. He improved the water supply and the road system of Athens, and made loans available to needy farmers to enable them to continue making a living from the land. As a result, landless residents in the city could return to the fields in rural Attica. As agricultural production increased, Pisistratus taxed it to gain more revenue. A more fair administration of local justice allowed farmers to settle disputes without losing time by going to court in the city.

Building Program. Equally beneficial was Pisistratus's building program. Projects such as the construction of the huge temple of Olympian Zeus near the Acropolis provided work and wages for the dispossessed farmers in the city. (The remains of that temple and of some other edifices indicate that flourishing building trades existed in late sixth-century Athens.) Growing apace, too, were the production of sculpture and of fine pottery, especially the high quality Athenian black-figure vases.

Sources:

Antony Andrewes, *The Greek Tyrants* (London: Hutchinson's University Library, 1956).

Andrewes, *The Greeks* (New York: Knopf, 1967).

Nicholas F. Jones, *Ancient Greece: State and Society* (Upper Saddle River, N.J.: Prentice Hall, 1997).

also sought to promote trade relations with Egypt; it is probably no accident that Periander's nephew and successor in the tyranny was named Psammetichus, after an Egyptian king.

Samos. On the island of Samos the tyrant Polycrates built up the harbor of the city for the benefit of the navy and merchant fleet. He commissioned an aqueduct to carry water to the city of Samos. Around 530 B.C.E. his engineer Eupalinus cut a tunnel through an entire mountain, an engineering feat of the first order, which must have given

SIGNIFICANT PEOPLE

HIPPIAS

DIED 490 B.C.E.
TYRANT OF ATHENS

Revenge. One of the sons of Pisistratus, Hippias ruled Athens as a tyrant from 528 to 510 B.C.E. The city-state prospered under the early part of his reign, and Hippias was considered to be a patron of artists and craftsmen. However, following the assassination of his brother Hipparchus in 514, Hippias used severe measures against his political enemies. Four years later the Spartan king Cleomenes I invaded Attica and expelled Hippias and his followers. Taking refuge with the Persians, he returned to Greece with the army of Darius I in 490 and supposedly advised the landing in the bay of Marathon. He died at Lemnos soon afterward.

Source:
Michael Grant, *The Rise of the Greeks* (New York: Scribners, 1987).

PERIANDER

DIED 588 B.C.E.
TYRANT OF CORINTH

Commercial Prosperity. Periander was the tyrant of Corinth from circa 625 to his death in 588 B.C.E. Although he treated the Corinthian nobility harshly, he was an effective ruler who encouraged the commercial activities of his city-state and built the portage across the Isthmus of Corinth. During his reign import duties accounted for almost all government revenues. He founded colonies at Potidaea in Chalcidice and at Apollonia in Illyria as well as conquered Epidaurus and Corcyra. Nevertheless, his land aggrandizements did not prohibit Periander from maintaining friendly relations with Thrasybulus, tyrant of Miletus, as well as the kings of Lydia and Egypt. A patron of the arts, Periander composed a collection of two thousand maxims and is considered by some scholars to be one of the Seven Wise Men of Greece.

Source:
Will Durant, *The Life of Greece, The Story of Civilization: Part II* (New York: Simon & Schuster, 1939).

POLYCRATES

DIED 522 B.C.E.
TYRANT OF SAMOS

Naval Dominance. The tyrant Polycrates ruled the island of Samos from circa 546 to 522 B.C.E. He initially took control of the city of Samos during a festival and quickly eliminated his two brothers who had aided his ascension to power. His domestic building programs included an aqueduct and a temple. Polycrates commanded a fleet of one hundred vessels, which dominated the eastern Aegean Sea and committed various acts of piracy throughout the region. His attempts to gain control of the Greek Ionian colonies caused him to seek alliances with major powers and then to change sides whenever it was politically expedient. For example, in 525 B.C.E. he abandoned his Egyptian allies and loaned a squadron of ships to the Persian fleet. Soon afterward his political opponents, with the aid of Sparta, attempted to remove him from power but failed. Three years later Oroetes, the Persian governor of Sardis, lured him to Asia Minor and had him crucified. Like many other Greek tyrants, Polycrates was a patron of artists and poets.

Source:
Will Durant, *The Life of Greece, The Story of Civilization: Part II* (New York: Simon & Schuster, 1939).

DOCUMENTARY SOURCES

The Greeks did not recognize economic and social history as an autonomous subject of study separate from politics and political theory, and did not write treatises on economics in the modern sense of the word. Of the two essays with the titles of *Oikonomikos* and *Ways and Means* (both written circa 430–circa 356 B.C.E.) by the historian, essayist, and biographer Xenophon, the first mainly praises agriculture, contrasting it unfavorably with manufacture; the overriding concern of the second is how to increase public revenue by various means. Another piece titled *Oeconomica* by a writer of the school of Aristotle repeats much of Xenophon's *Oikonomikos* and proposes stratagems to increase a state's income.

The rest of the surviving information is scattered over practically all of Greek literature, including the poets and dramatists. Among the sources are Herodotus, *History of the Persian Wars* (circa late fifth century B.C.E.); Thucydides, *History of the Peloponnesian War* (circa late fifth century B.C.E.); and Xenophon, *Agesilaus, Anabasis, Hellenica*, and *Constitution of the Lacedaemonians* (all written circa late fifth century B.C.E.). There is also Plato's *Laws* (circa 355–347 B.C.E.), Aristotle's *Politics* (circa 335 B.C.E.), the speeches of the politician Demosthenes and legal experts Lysias and Isaeus, as well as the essays of the pamphleteer Isocrates.

Aside from inscriptions on stone, another source of authentic record is archaeology. Archaeological discoveries and research provide the main evidence for the Archaic Period (700–480 B.C.E.) for which the literary evidence is exiguous, consisting of little more than the *Works and Days* (circa eighth century B.C.E.) of the poet Hesiod, which is a kind of farmer's almanac, and the poems of Solon in which he mentions his reforms.

A storage jar from Chora, Mykonos, mid-seventh century B.C.E.
(Archaeological Museum, Mykonos)

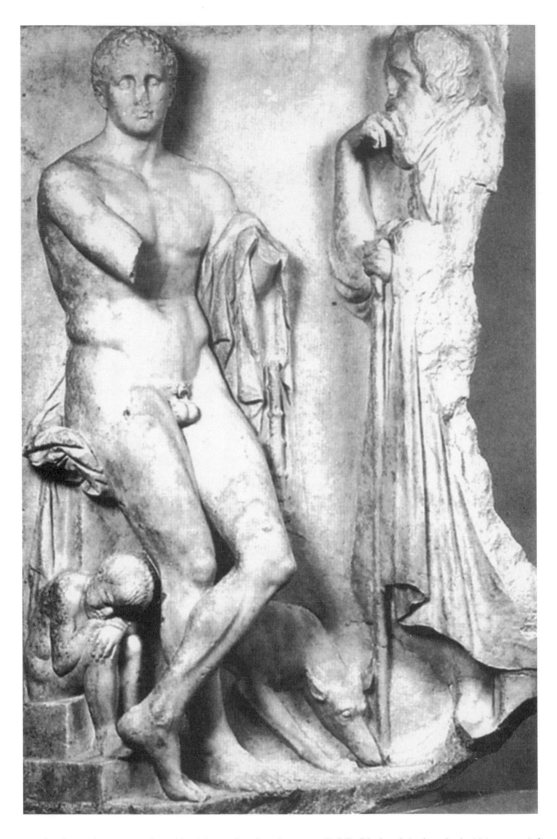

A grave stele of an unknown man found in Athens, circa fourth century B.C.E. (National Archaeological Museum, Athens (869)/ photo TAP)

POLITICS, LAW, AND THE MILITARY

by DAVID C. MIRHADY

CONTENTS

CHRONOLOGY

162

OVERVIEW

172

TOPICS IN POLITICS, LAW, AND THE MILITARY

The Archaic Greek World ... 174

A Homicide Trial in The Homeric World 175

Athens and Sparta 176

The Spartan Constitution 177
The Law Code of Draco 179
The Battle of Marathon 181
The Macedonian Art of Warfare 182
Oratory and Rhetoric 183
The Persian Menace 184
The Polis in Decline 187
Uncertainty after Mantinea 189
Political Assemblies of Athens . .190
Punishment 191
The Second Peloponnesian War .192
War Engines: Land and Sea ...195
Weaponry 196

SIGNIFICANT PEOPLE

Alcibiades 198
Alexander The Great 198
Demosthenes 201
Pericles 201
Philip II 202
Solon 203
Themistocles 204

DOCUMENTARY SOURCES

204

Sidebars and tables are listed in italics.

750 B.C.E.

- The hoplite makes an appearance for the first time on Greek battlefields. This type of infantryman receives his appellation from the *hoplon* (round shield). He wears a helmet and face mask, plate armor on his chest and back, and metal greaves to protect his shins and knees. His armaments include a long spear and iron sword. Hoplites fight in a close-packed formation known as a phalanx.

734

- The War of the Lelantine Plain begins. Many of the fledgling *poleis* from throughout the Greek world take sides in a war between Chalkis and Eritrea over the Lelantine plain, which separates them. The war ends in 680.

730

- The First Messenian War begins. Over the course of the next twenty years, Sparta conquers Messenia and the inhabitants of the region are relegated to slave status; the Spartans call them *helots*.

675

- The legendary lawgiver Lycurgus is said to devise a system of military education that renders Spartan hoplites the premier fighting force in Greece. Boys are removed from their families at age seven or eight and subjected to years of a rigorous state-controlled curriculum of athletics and military training.

669

- A Spartan army attempting to conquer the northern city-state of Argos meets with defeat at the Battle of Hysiae.

650

- The Second Messenian War begins and lasts for thirty years. Meanwhile, a one-hundred-year period of tyranny begins in Sicyon, Corinth, and Miletus when individual aristocrats, with popular support, seize power from the other wealthy citizens by unconventional means.

632

- In the Conspiracy of Cylon, an attempt to seize power by a would-be tyrant in Athens is brutally suppressed. Cylon and many of his followers are murdered by a member of the aristocratic Alcmaeonid family.

* Denotes circa date

621

- Draco promulgates the first written laws in Athens; these laws are known for the severity of their punishments. The Law Code of Draco provides a definition of homicide, distinguishing between murder and accidental or justifiable manslaughter.

594

- The Athenian moderate Solon brings in wide-ranging reforms in order to defuse strife between the rich and poor of the city. Among the changes he implements are canceling all debts for which personal freedom is used for security.

566

- Over the course of the next fifty-five years, the tyrant Peisistratus and his sons seize power three times in Athens, promoting unity and commerce. Peisistratus helps farmers by creating a state loan fund financed by a duty on produce and trade items. He also limits the jurisdiction of local aristocrats by establishing a circuit-court system.

560

- Croesus of Lydia begins a campaign to subdue the Greek cities of Asia Minor. He captures Ephesus and other cities in western Anatolia. Afterward, he conciliates the Greeks by making rich gifts to the oracle at Delphi.

546

- Persian king Cyrus II the Great conquers Lydia by defeating Croesus at Sardis and gains control of the Greek settlements in Asia Minor.

510

- Spartan king Cleomenes I attacks Athens and drives out the tyrant Hippias, the son of Peisistratus. He later supports Isagoras and the aristocratic party in Athens.

508

- Cleisthenes implements constitutional changes to relieve regional tensions in Athens and in the process forms the basis of Athenian democracy.

499

- The Ionian Rebellion begins when the Greek settlements of Asia Minor rise up against Persian rule. After five years, the Persians finally suppress the insurrection, killing many of the male settlers and enslaving the women and children.

493

- Themistocles begins his one-year term as archon (magistrate) of Athens; he will later take steps to increase the fleet and develop the port of Piraeus.

490

- In one of the greatest battles in world military history, an Athenian army under Miltiades repulses a Persian invasion at the bay of Marathon, about twenty-six miles north of Athens.

487

- Ostracism is used for the first time in Athens as a means of banishing prominent politicians who might destabilize the democracy.

480

- At the narrow coastal pass of Thermopylae, King Leonidas and three hundred Spartans make a heroic stand against a massive Persian army under Xerxes. Afterward, the Persians march eighty miles southward and sack Athens.

- Off the island of Salamis, Greek ships encounter a much larger Persian fleet. After seven hours in which the Greek ships engage the enemy with ramming tactics, the Greeks win a stunning victory, losing only forty vessels as opposed to two hundred for the Persians. As a result, Xerxes leads most of his two hundred thousand troops back to Asia Minor.

479

- A Spartan army led by Pausanias defeats the Persians under Mardonius at Plataea in Boeotia. Meanwhile, a daring Greek expedition destroys a beached enemy fleet at Mycale. In the aftermath of these Greek victories, the Ionians join their brethren in the war against Persia.

478

- Athens becomes the leader of the Delian League (so named because the treasury is on the sacred island of Delos) to counter Persian aggression. This voluntary alliance of Greek city-states includes the Ionians, and its strength is primarily naval.

474

- Cimon, the son of Miltiades and a hero of the Battle of Salamis, becomes the leading statesman in Athens. He encourages Athens's leading role in the Delian League and continues to expand the city's naval forces.

471
- Themistocles is accused of treason and flees to Persia, where he becomes a provincial governor under King Artaxerxes I.

467
- In the battle of the Eurymedon River in Pamphylia in southern Asia Minor, Cimon wins a major victory, thus effectively ending the Persian threat to Greece.

465
- The northern island of Thasos rebels against the Delian League, but Cimon puts down the uprising within two years. This action leads to a deterioration in relations between Athens and Sparta.

464
- A helot revolt begins in Sparta and lasts for ten years. Athenian offers to help quell the insurrection are met with suspicion by Spartan authorities.

462
- Ephialtes, leader of the democratic faction in Athens, abolishes the power of the Areopagus (senate) and transfers its judicial powers to the Assembly.

461
- Ephialtes is assassinated by an agent of the oligarchs and is replaced by Pericles. The new city leader orchestrates the ostracism of Cimon, who loses favor with the democratic faction following the failed effort of Athenian forces to suppress the helot revolt in Sparta.
- The First Peloponnesian War begins, pitting Athens against the Peloponnesian League led by Sparta. The origins of the conflict are found in Athenian naval dominance in the Aegean Sea that make many city-states look to Sparta for protection.

458
- The Athenians begin building the Long Walls, a series of parallel fortifications connecting Athens and its port of Piraeus five miles away. Meanwhile, Athenian land forces conquer Boeotia.

457
- A revolt in Aegina fails after Pericles orders an Athenian army to crush it.

POLITICS, LAW, AND THE MILITARY

454
- The treasury of the Delian League is moved to Athens for safekeeping.

451
- Athens and Sparta agree to a five-year truce. Meanwhile, Pericles's law defining citizenship is passed in Athens.

449
- The Peace of Callias formally ends hostilities between Athens and Persia.

447
- The Boeotians and Spartans defeat the Athenians at Coronea.

446
- The Athenians crush a revolt on the island of Euboea.

445
- Athens and Sparta agree to the Thirty Years' Peace. The treaty officially recognizes the existence of an Athenian naval empire, although Athens must relinquish control of the territory it conquered during the war, especially Boeotia.

440
- A revolt in Samos, a subject ally of Athens, is quickly suppressed.

435
- Diplomatic relations sour between Corinth and Corcyra over control of the Adriatic seaport of Epidamnus, founded by both city-states in the seventh century B.C.E. As a result of the conflict, Athens and Corcyra form an alliance two years later.

432
- Potidaea revolts from Athens. Pericles sends an army to besiege the city, but the inhabitants resist for two years and seriously weaken the military resources and prestige of Athens.

431

- The Second or Great Peloponnesian War begins, pitting an Athenian-led alliance against a group of city-states headed by Sparta. The Athenian alliance includes most of the island and coastal states of Greece, while the Spartans lead states of the Peloponnese and central Greece, as well as the sea power Corinth.

430

- A plague lasting for nearly three years breaks out in Athens and kills one-fourth of the soldiers and a great number of citizens. One of its victims is Pericles, who dies the next year.

427

- The Spartans capture the strategic city of Plataea. On the island state of Lesbos the Athenian general Paches suppresses a revolt and sends one thousand leading citizens to Athens for execution.

425

- The Athenians fortify Pylos in the western Peloponnese and capture several hundred full-Spartan citizens on the nearby island of Sphacteria.

424

- The Boeotians defeat the Athenians at the Battle of Delium. Meanwhile, the Athenian Assembly votes that the taxes of subject cities would be raised in order to finance the war.

423

- A one-year armistice between Athens and Sparta goes into effect.

421

- The general Nicias persuades the Athenians to accept a Spartan overture for peace. The Peace of Nicias lasts for six years and is a tense period of diplomatic maneuverings in which each major power attempts to win the smaller states over to its side. Both Athens and Sparta still conduct small-scale military operations.

418

- The Spartans defeat an Athenian-Argive army at the Battle of Mantinea.

416
- Athens makes an unprovoked attack on the island of Melos and enslaves the inhabitants. The city of Segesta sends envoys to Athens warning that Syracuse intends to subjugate all of Sicily as well as send food and money to Sparta if the war is renewed.

415
- Athens sends a military expedition under Alcibiades to Syracuse in Sicily. Alcibiades, however, is accused of mutilating the statues of the god Hermes, and instead of returning to Athens, he offers his services to Sparta.

413
- Sparta builds a permanent fort in Attica at Decelea. Meanwhile, the Athenian forces in Sicily are defeated.

412
- The allies of Athens revolt, and Persia declares war on the city.

411
- The aristocrats in Athens stage a successful revolt but are then overthrown by the more moderate regime of the Five Thousand led by Theramenes.

410
- Alcibiades returns to the Athenian side after losing the confidence of the Spartans. He is again appointed general and wins a naval victory at Cyzicus.

409
- Alicibiades captures Chalcedon and Byzantium, ensuring a reliable food supply for Athens from the Bosporus.

407
- Alcibiades is dismissed from Athenian service after one of his lieutenants loses the Battle of Notium. Fearing for his life, Alcibiades flees to Bithynia.

405
- The Athenian fleet suffers a decisive defeat at Aegospotami.

404
- The Second Peloponnesian War ends when Athens capitulates and an oligarchic government is installed by King Lysander of Sparta. The "Thirty Tyrants" rule for one year before the restoration of a democratic government.

401
- Cyrus the Younger leads an expedition of ten thousand Greek mercenaries against his brother, Artaxerxes II of Persia. Cyrus wins a victory at Cunaxa in Mesopotamia but is killed in the battle and his soldiers march back to the Black Sea and safety.

395
- In the Corinthian War, Corinth, Thebes, Argos, and Athens unite with Persia to contain Spartan imperial ambitions.
- Athens rebuilds its Long Walls.

394
- At Cnidus, off the southwest coast of Asia Minor, a Persian fleet under the Athenian Conon defeats a Spartan navy.

386
- The Peace of Antalcidas, or the King's Peace, ends the Corinthian War and determines that Asia Minor belongs to Persia while the Greek city-states should be autonomous.

378
- The Second Athenian League, which includes Thebes, is formed to thwart Spartan hegemony in Greece.

371
- At the Battle of Leuctra, the Thebans under Epaminondas defeat the Spartans and put an end to their military dominance. Epaminondas achieves this stunning victory by reforming the standard hoplite phalanx.

362
- Thebes defeats Sparta at the Battle of Mantinea, but Epaminondas is mortally wounded during the fighting.

359

- Philip II becomes king of Macedon and quickly begins a reorganization of the military.

357

- Several important allies of Athens revolt, leading to a significant loss in Athenian power after a two-year struggle known as the Social War.

355

- The Phocians seize the Panhellenic sanctuary at Delphi and provoke the Sacred War, a nine-year struggle in which Philip of Macedon becomes heavily involved in Greek affairs.

338

- At the Battle of Chaeronea, Philip of Macedon defeats an army of Greeks, ending the age of the *polis*. A congress of Greek states accepts Philip as ruler of Greece and approves a draft of troops for his planned invasion of Ionia.

337

- Philip of Macedon establishes the Corinthian League of Greek states, which declares war on Persia.

336

- Philip of Macedon is assassinated and his son Alexander assumes the throne, reaffirming his father's pledge to attack the Persians. Meanwhile, Darius III becomes king of Persia.

335

- In order to maintain control of the Macedonian kingdom following his father's death, Alexander suppresses several small revolts and sacks Thebes.

334

- Alexander the Great crosses over into Asia Minor and defeats the Persians at the Battle of the Granicus River.

333

- The Macedonians defeat the Persians at the Battle of Issus and gain control of Ionia.

332

- The ports of Tyre and Gaza fall to the Macedonians who now hold present-day Syria, Lebanon, Israel, and Egypt, where the city of Alexandria is established.

331

- Alexander defeats Darius at the Battle of Gaugamela (also known as Arbela) and takes Mesopotamia. Later in the year, he enters Babylon and Pasargadae and burns the palace of the Persian kings at Persepolis.

330

- Darius is murdered by his army officers, and Alexander declares himself to be the new Persian king before beginning a two-year campaign in Bactria and Sogdiana.

327

- Alexander and his army enter India. The next year they cross the Indus River and defeat King Porus at the Battle of Hydaspes River. Afterward, Alexander conquers Punjab.

324

- The Macedonian army returns to Susa in Mesopotamia, where it celebrates its victories.

323

- Alexander the Great falls ill and dies of a fever at the age of thirty-two in Babylon; his principal generals divide the kingdom among themselves.

OVERVIEW

Polis. The Greeks' greatest accomplishment in the area of politics was the polis (self-governing city-state) itself. It so dominated the lives of the Greeks during the Archaic (700–480 B.C.E.) and Classical (480–323 B.C.E.) periods that Aristotle, one of the greatest philosophers of all time, assumed that a human being was by nature a political animal; the polis was for him the natural way for humans to live. There were hundreds of city-states scattered around what is known today as Greece, as well as the western coast of Turkey, the Black Sea, North Africa, Sicily, Italy, and even southern France.

Environment. As early as 2000 B.C.E., the Greeks settled a mountainous country with a jagged coastline in which arable land was largely confined to limited areas capable of sustaining only small settlements. Mountain passes within Greece were largely impassable, except by foot and pack animal, and each settlement developed a keen sense of independence. Few were far from the sea, and the Greek desire to supplement their meager food production from vines, olives, and cereals, as well as their need for metals and timber, led them to trade far beyond the confines of Greece itself, mostly to the Black Sea, Egypt, and Sicily. Most of the settlements extended over a combination of coastline, arable land, and hillside or mountain, many of the people migrating through the year from one area to another. Many families came to possess a combination of small parcels of land at different elevations and with differing climatic conditions; this diversity lessened the risks associated with varying weather conditions from year to year. In some settlements, however, where people migrated less, divisions were created among coastal people, farmers, and mountain herdsmen.

Legends. When the Greeks looked back from the historical period (after 800 B.C.E.) to the legendary origins of their own civilization, they could trace a few vestiges of the Minoan civilization of the second millennium B.C.E. in the stories of King Minos, his labyrinthine palace at Knossos on the southern island of Crete, and the half-man/half-bull monster, the Minotaur, that dwelled in it. Perhaps they also had some access to remains of the art of the Minoans, in which the bull is prominent. However, most of the stories of early Greek legend take place on the Greek mainland at places like Argos, Mycenae, Tiryns, Thebes, and Athens. The greatest legend of all, that of the Trojan War, focused

on a city from across the Aegean Sea, Troy. The stories include Heracles, who was born in Thebes to a family from Argos, and his Twelve Labors; Perseus of Argos and his quest to slay the Gorgon; Oedipus of Thebes and his tragic involvement with his mother and father; and, of course, Theseus of Athens, who slew the Minotaur.

Symbolism. Heracles fought with the club and bow and arrow, protected by an invincible lion skin draped over his head and back. His traditions thus go back probably to a time before the use of bronze, which was used for the earliest swords and spears. He was the individualistic hero who fought alone, not as part of, or even at the head of, an army. Perseus's far-flown adventures against the Gorgon take him to several locations in the Near East and reveal influences from these areas. After the revelation of Oedipus's killing of his father and incestuous marriage to his mother, his sons, Eteocles and Polyneices, fought over the kingship of Thebes and assembled other kings with their armies from various parts of south and central Greece to fight over the fortified walls of Thebes. Like the fortified walls of Troy, this image of large fortification walls protecting a central citadel is one that can be witnessed as remains of the Mycenaean civilization of 1600–1200 B.C.E. Theseus's triumph over the Minotaur may be symbolic of the triumph of mainland Greek civilization over the Minoans. The archaeological record bears out the fact that the mainland Greeks overcame the Minoans, even though they adopted many of the advanced aspects of their civilization. These legendary events recall in a vague way the events of the Greek Bronze Age (3000–1200 B.C.E.) that came to a sudden end about 1200 B.C.E., after which Greece spent four centuries in what are now called the Dark Ages.

Hoplites. Inspired by the acquisition of writing from the Near East, the polis emerged with Greek civilization itself. The indomitable pride that the Greeks took in the economic and political autonomy of their poleis stemmed not only from their geography, which isolated many settlements on the Greek peninsula, but also from the pride that each individual Greek took in owning his own land, working it, and defending it. The coming of the Iron Age in Greece in the eighth century B.C.E. enabled individual farmers to bring more land under cultivation and thus to provide more wealth. It also allowed them to arm themselves with *hopla* (iron weapons) that made them a fighting force surpassing the aristocratic chieftains who had done the fighting before and had thus dominated the rest of the people. Soon it was discovered, moreover, that the hoplite soldier fought most effectively in a tightly packed formation, a phalanx.

Foundation of Spears. The phalanx became the basis for political organization in Greece. The soldiers who donned their armor and defended their city-state could not be denied political rights. Because everyone in the phalanx was tightly linked together and shared equal responsibility for its success, equality was an essential idea for the Greek polis. Different cities developed this system in different ways, however, and Greece saw aristocracies, oligarchies, tyrannies, and democracies, all based on differing notions of equality. The Spartans, for instance, who faced a native slave population, devoted themselves almost entirely to hoplite training as a means to ensure their security. The Athenians, on the other hand, found room for their own lower classes, eventually, by finding them a significant military role in the manning of their fleets of triremes, which were the basis of their naval empire. Even without the financial means to own armor, the rowers won political rights for themselves, which gave Athens the most thoroughgoing democracy the western world has ever seen. Although Athens had slaves and women who enjoyed only limited political rights, the Athenian experiment in direct voting in both the assembly and popular law courts and the distribution of administrative responsibilities through lotteries went further in empowering the people than any modern system ever has.

Law Codes. The constitutional arrangements of the early Greek poleis gave rise to a generation of lawgivers, some of them legendary, with whom the particular characters of the Greek poleis were associated. These men included Lycurgus of Sparta, Solon of Athens, Zaleucus of Locri (in Italy), and Charondas of Catana. They composed the first prescriptive codes of law in the world and took special steps to see to it that their laws were followed. The Greeks thus came to be a people governed by the idea of the rule of law, which superseded the whims of individuals and even democratic assemblies. Scores of speeches composed for delivery before the law courts of Classical Athens attest to the Athenians' sophisticated understanding of the legal issues surrounding homicide, assault, contracts, wills, adultery, and theft. Even the great philosopher Socrates had to present a defense speech before an Athenian court on a charge of impiety and corrupting the young: he lost and was sentenced to death in 399 B.C.E.

The Persians. Beginning in the sixth century B.C.E., the Greek cities encountered a serious threat to their autonomy in the form of Persia. Cyrus the Great came to power around 557 and immediately embarked upon a policy of expansion. Although the Greek settlements in Asia Minor were subdued, an Athenian-led force won a decisive victory over a larger Persian army at Marathon in 490. Greek naval victories at Salamis (480) and Mycale (479) ended the Persian threat to the poleis for the time being.

Greek Wars. These stunning victories instilled in the Greeks a sense of confidence and pride in their cities and forms of government. However, the unity that they exhibited in their conflict with Persia soon gave way to petty squabbles and jealousies and resulted in the Greek world being divided into two spheres of influence, one dominated by Athens and the other by Sparta. Beginning in 461, these two cities and their respective allies fought the First Peloponnesian War. The Thirty Years' Peace of 445 ended the conflict and gave formal recognition to an Athenian Empire but did little to soothe the animosity of the contending sides. In 431 the Second, or Great, Peloponnesian War began when the Spartans invaded Attica, the Athenian homeland, following disputes over Corcyra, Megara, and Potidaea. Attempts to sustain a peace agreement of 421 ultimately failed, and the war continued with Athens's slowly losing ground. A major defeat at Syracuse in 413 reduced the power and prestige of Athens, provoked its allies to desert, and brought the Persians into the conflict on the side of Sparta. In 404 the war ended with the surrender of Athens. The masterful account of this war by the contemporary historian Thucydides has made it one of the most renowned conflicts in history.

Weakened Cities. Although Sparta and its allies won a hard-fought victory, the defeat of Athens did not bring peace. In fact, the rivalry between the Greek cities continued to grow and fester. The two old enemies, along with the rising city of Thebes, engaged in political machinations that weakened all the Greek cities and left them vulnerable to Macedon, their monarchical neighbor to the north. Philosophers such as Plato and Aristotle thought long and hard about the nature of the polis. In his famous work, *Republic* (circa 380–360 B.C.E.), Plato criticized the *poleis* of his own time and championed the idea of a polis run by philosopher-kings. In his *Politics* (circa 335 B.C.E.), Aristotle also speculated about a utopian polis that could overcome the degradations of the poleis of his own time.

Macedon. Worn down by internecine warfare, particularly the Sacred War of 355–346, the Greek poleis stood by indecisively as a new power increased its strength. In 338 B.C.E. a Macedonian army under Philip II defeated a combined Greek force at Chaeronea in Boeotia. Philip had created a well-trained, professional army, but his first son, a former student of Aristotle, Alexander III, later called Alexander the Great, perfected this military machine and created a vast empire that stretched from Greece to the Indus Valley. Alexander set the stage for the Hellenistic Age (323–331 B.C.E.), in which Greek culture and learning spread throughout the eastern Mediterranean and Middle East, but the Macedonians also brought to an end the dominance of the polis as the primary form of political organization for the Greeks. Like the Persians they had helped defeat, the Greeks were now ruled by kings. Instead of a political identification, the world, the *kosmos* or *oikoumenê*, gave them a new, cosmopolitan identity.

TOPICS IN POLITICS, LAW, AND THE MILITARY

THE ARCHAIC GREEK WORLD

The Politics of Homer. During the Archaic Period (700–480 B.C.E.) Greece went through a political and social renewal. The epic poetry of Homer, composed toward the end of the eighth century, indicates some of the changes that occurred. For several generations before, oral poets had composed and sung epic poems celebrating various aspects of the legendary war against Troy. Now two parts of that epic cycle took shape through the skill of a poet, or poets, whom we call Homer. The first, the *Iliad*, focuses on the anger of Achilles, the greatest fighter among the armies amassed against Troy. This anger, which is directed at Agamemnon, the expedition's commander, leads to Achilles' petulant withdrawal from fighting, with disastrous consequences for his friends and allies, including his best friend, Patroclus, whose death leads Achilles to rejoin the fight and kill the Trojans' leading warrior, Hector, in the climax of the epic. The second story, the *Odyssey*, relates the ten-year voyage home of Odysseus, the craftiest of the fighters among the armies amassed against Troy, and the struggles of his family anxiously awaiting his return. Along the way he has fantastic adventures, loses all his ships and crew, and arrives to find his home under siege by men who want to take his place.

Inspiration. The poems of Homer were inspired by events from a different world. To the extent that their legendary stories do reflect historical events, these must be from the time of the Mycenaeans. Not since that time had the Greek world been organized into the sort of fortified palaces that Homer describes. In fact the archaeological record has even borne out Homer's description of a palace at the site of Troy; however, the details of Homer's story can hardly extend back five hundred years. They are probably descriptions inspired by the social and political organization from Homer's own time, and from that of the oral poets from whom he inherited so much of his material.

Hesiod. During the same time that Homer was composing his poetry, Hesiod employed the same metrical pattern in composing two poems with an altogether different focus. In the *Theogony* he adapted several stories from Near Eastern traditions in order to systematize and explain the origins of the Greek gods. In his *Works and Days* he reuses

A bronze statuette of a hoplite, circa late sixth century B.C.E. (Peter Newark Military Pictures)

some of these myths in an elaborate lesson in morals addressed to his disloyal brother.

Written Language. In order for the poetry of Homer and Hesiod to be preserved in a set form (and in the case of Hesiod, perhaps, even for it to be composed at all) there had to be writing. The syllabic Linear B script of the Mycenaeans had died out with them. The epic poetry of Homer had been developed by oral poets, but with Greek contacts with the Near East came the adoption of an alphabetic writing system. There are debates about where exactly the transmission of the alphabet took place and who was involved, but it is clear that once the transmission was made, the alphabet spread quickly throughout the Greek-speaking world, from southern Italy to Cyprus. Unlike Linear B, which was apparently used largely only for administrative reasons and for trade, the new Greek alphabet shows signs of having been devoted largely to poetry, especially epic. One of the earliest samples, from Pithecussae, an island off southern Italy, makes a reference to Nestor, one of Homer's characters, and to Aphrodite, the goddess of love. It seems likely that drinking parties included the recitation of Homer's poetry.

Mixture. The social and political organization in Homer's poetry is a mixture of institutions, some of which extend back to the Mycenaeans while others reflect his own times. For one thing, Homer did not know anything about "Greeks" (Hellenes), the people of later times who were united by language and religion. The collected armies that attack Troy are variously called Achaeans, Argives, or Danaans, and individual groups among them are identified from their home areas, such as Crete, Sparta, or Salamis. However, they speak the same language and worship the same gods as their enemies the Trojans and many of the Trojans' allies, though some of the latter, like the Carians, are foreign speakers.

Leaders. The army consists of a collection of groups led by individual noblemen, called *basileis* (kings). Homer also uses the Mycenaean term *wanax* (lord) but it is not used by any other sources from that time. Agamemnon as *wanax* is the commander in chief, but in some ways he is simply a first among equals. He has the greatest wealth and the most soldiers and ships of any of the Argive commanders, but they are all more or less free to follow his leadership or

not. They are there to serve their own interests and as a favor to him, not because he can compel them. They have meetings before the assembled armies in which various leaders take up a scepter, which signifies the right to speak. They want to achieve a consensus, but because of the size of Agamemnon's army, what he himself ultimately decides carries great weight. Nevertheless, a commander such as Achilles can disagree with him vehemently and go off to sulk without Agamemnon's being able to coerce him. On the other hand, when Thersites, an upstart commoner without the support of an army, tries to dress down Agamemnon and the other Argive leaders, he is silenced with a box around the ears. Free speech had its limits in the Homeric world.

Justice. In the *Odyssey*, Odysseus marks the midafternoon by saying that it is "when a man rises from the *agora* (the assembly place) for dinner after deciding disputes of young men seeking judgment." The public day was then over. Judicial activity played such a large role in the public life of Homer's time that he used it as a way to establish the time of day. In the *Iliad*, when the god Hephaestus decorates a new shield for the hero Achilles, he inscribes two poleis, a city at war and a city at peace. In the city at peace he illustrates two scenes, one a wedding procession and the other a judicial scene, further confirmation of the centrality of justice for early Greek civic life.

Homicide. In the modern world homicide is a criminal matter and prosecuted by the state. In Homer's world it is a matter between the killer, who seems in the shield scene to have accepted blame for the man's death and wants to make reparation (rather than go into exile), and a survivor of the dead man, who has up to now refused any compensation, or blood-price. There is no question of his trying to take vengeance on his own. In cases where the killer was really evil and considered a threat to the community, it would not have been a judicial matter at all: the man would simply have been driven out or killed. Here the men have been unable to reconcile their differences, but they both seek out a third party in the assembly place to render a judgment and bring their dispute to an end. Although the procedure seems to be recognized by all, there are no laws to govern what should be done. The tradition of paying a blood-price might have played a role, but it did not determine the situation. Instead, a group of elderly aristocrats each propose their own judgment. The two men in dispute have each contributed a weight of gold, and they themselves will decide which of the judgments they can both live with.

Greek Expansion. As the economy and population of the Greek world grew in the eighth and seventh centuries, various changes occurred in the political landscape. Increasing population created pressures on the land base, and increasing economic activity created a wealth of various goods for trade, as well as a hunger for new goods and raw materials. Despite the Greek determination for self-sufficiency, the economic activity of the individual household, or *oikos*, no longer satisfied the needs of its members. There was thus more trade between households and an increased

A HOMICIDE TRIAL IN THE HOMERIC WORLD

The people were gathered together in the assembly place, and there a dispute had arisen, and two men were disputing about the blood-price for a man who had died. The one made a claim to pay back in full, declaring publicly to the village, but the other was refusing to accept anything. Both were heading for an arbitrator to get a limit; and the people were speaking up on either side to help both men. But the heralds restrained the people, as meanwhile elders were seated on benches of polished stone in a sacred circle and took hold in their hands of scepters from the heralds who lift their voices. And with these they sprang up, taking turns, and rendered their judgments and in their midst lay on the ground two weights of gold, to be given to the one among them who pronounced a judgment most correctly.

Source: *Iliad* 18.497–508.

specialization of trades. The need for a central, urban market where these new, specialized goods could be traded gave rise to an urban population and thus an identification with a particular urban center. The Greek *polis* was born, an autonomous population based on an urban core, what one usually understands as the "city-state."

Agora. The principal characteristic of the *polis* was the *agora*, the gathering place or market. It was normally located close to a religious sanctuary, where people gathered for festive occasions also. The original function of the *agora* was as a gathering place for trading between households and for discussion of common points of interest. It was essentially an open area upon which various temporary structures might be set up, like tables and booths for trading or a tent structure for dramatic presentations or festive dancing. It had to remain open, however, for common use. Any privatization would frustrate its function as a communal gathering place. Manufacturing was also done close to this area, where bronze, iron, ceramics, and leather might be worked more economically than they could be in an individual house.

Settlements. Rising population levels and interests in trading led many Greek cities to resettle parts of their populations away, in less populated areas on the fringes of the Greek world, on the borders with other peoples, in North Africa, Sicily, France, Spain, and the Black Sea. These were not colonies on the later Roman model, in which the new settlements were largely governed by the home cities. Each new settlement immediately became an independent polis. It certainly had ethnic and traditional ties with its mother city, but in general these were quickly forgotten if the interests of the new settlement were contrary to those of its parent. The methods of selection for the settlers and the way they organized their settlements could vary a great deal. The settlements thus offered an area for experimentation in the way that the polis was governed. For instance, the privileges of large, landed wealth that tended to keep power in the hands of relatively few aristocrats in the original cities were not present in the new settlements, where land tended initially to be divided evenly. Those with ability and leadership skills could rise to the top more easily.

Greek Identity. Another consequence of the resettlement movement was that as the Greeks came into contact increasingly with non-Greek-speaking peoples, they gained a heightened sense of their own Greek identity, their language, religion, and cultural commonalities. The oracular shrine of the god Apollo at Delphi was regularly consulted about where new settlements should be located. Since Greeks considered Delphi the center of the world and gathered there for consultation about many issues, the oracle could serve as an important clearinghouse of information. Greek self-consciousness gave an added boost to the great festival games also. Participants in the Olympic Games, which were held every four years at Olympia in the northwest Peloponnese from 776 B.C.E. onward, had to speak Greek and worship the Olympian gods.

Warfare. The political structure of the *polis* was also greatly transformed by the technology of warfare. The affordability and strength of the new weapons meant that every Greek farmer of moderate means could own his own weaponry. The aristocrats who had formerly dominated because only they could afford durable weaponry now found that their advantage was neutralized. Moreover, the new middle-class farmers who owned their own weapons, the hoplites, found that they could fight most effectively when they were tightly massed in a phalanx formation, their overlapping shields providing maximal mutual protection. With military force came political demands: the hoplites demanded a say in government.

The Tyrant. In many of the most economically active cities, where social and economic mobility most undermined the traditional political power structure, the way was opened for a particularly ambitious person, usually one of the aristocrats, to champion the cause of this new class against the aristocrats. The experience of Cypselus at Corinth was typical. Corinth was thriving as a result of its strategic trading location on the isthmus between central Greece and the Peloponnese. Travelers by land and sea used the isthmus, and the Corinthians developed strong trading relationships. Cypselus used his position as a military leader to topple the domination of the city by his mother's family, the Bacchiads. Like Pheidon of Argos, Cypselus took power in an unprecedented way and earned the designation "tyrant." Yet, he was a champion of the people and was able to concentrate the city's resources on public enterprises, public works, and festivals. In time, the usefulness of the institution of the tyranny as a protector of the popular interests wore out. The tyrant, or his son or grandson, had to spend more time protecting his own power than doing truly useful things for the people. He often resorted to cruel means, which left the Greeks with a bad view of tyrants; however, tyrants usually had popular support at the beginning.

Sources:

Antony Andrewes, *The Greek Tyrants* (London: Hutchinson's University Library, 1956).

John Boardman, *The Greeks Overseas: Their Early Colonies and Trade* (London: Thames & Hudson, 1980).

Michael Grant, *The Rise of the Greeks* (New York: Scribners, 1987).

Anthony Snodgrass, *Archaic Greece: The Age of Experiment* (London: Dent, 1980).

ATHENS AND SPARTA

Two Cities. Athens and Sparta came up with different solutions to the challenges facing the early Greek *poleis*. In the eighth century B.C.E. the two were in many ways similar, both dominated by aristocratic families who led the cities both militarily and culturally; however, the two cities had differences, too. The Attic countryside surrounding Athens was accessible from the outside, and the political identification of its citizens was fairly weak. Despite the *sunoikismos*, the political unification of Attica under the legendary Theseus, only the ancient religious ties to Athena and her sanctuary on the Acropolis drew

Two ostraka of Themistocles, circa 480 B.C.E. (Agora Museum, Athens)

the Athenians together. Economic inequalities among those living along the coast, on the larger inland plains, or in the hills seemed more important than Athenian identity and unity. Sparta, on the other hand, was in Laconia, an out-of-the-way corner of the Peloponnese, the large peninsula that forms southern Greece. It had a large, indigenous population of slaves, the Helots, whom the Spartans had suppressed in their earliest history and on whose labors they depended for their livelihood. Although Laconia is relatively large, only those living in the few closely neighboring settlements in its center on the Eurotas River were recognized as Spartans. The people inhabiting the surrounding areas were referred to as *perioikoi*, "those living around."

Military State. In the course of the eighth and seventh centuries, instead of sending out settlements abroad in order to alleviate population pressures and develop trading opportunities, the Spartans took another strategy. They conquered the neighboring area of Messenia, on the western side of Mt. Taygetus, in a war that lasted twenty years (740–720 B.C.E.). However, when they attempted to overpower their northern neighbors in Argos, the Spartans lost a disastrous battle at Hysiae in 669 B.C.E. They lost so many men that they were almost powerless when Messenia revolted, and they were forced into another war, which lasted thirty years, against the Messenians (650–620 B.C.E.), during which they committed themselves to military pursuits in an extraordinary way. Sparta became a closed society, intensely jealous of its security and suspicious of outside influences.

Equals. The Second Messenian War also brought political reforms. The land of Messenia, which had originally been allotted only to the wealthy, was now allotted equally to every male Spartan at birth. They considered themselves *homoioi* (equals). There were no doubt still inequalities, which became painfully clear in times to come, but equality among the Spartans was the great idea of the Spartan political system. As in other Greek *poleis*, it stemmed from the idea that within the Spartan hoplite phalanx each man was equal. Each Spartan male was assigned to one of several eating clubs, *sussitia*, to which he made contributions from his land allotment, and he identified himself more with them than with his family or geographical area.

Legendary Lawgiver. Sparta's constitution was ascribed to a legendary lawgiver, Lycurgus, who was inspired by an oracle of the god Apollo. The ancient sources differ widely over when Lycurgus lived and what exactly he did, but Plutarch provides the text of an early document, known as the Great Rhetra, which seems genuine, if not altogether clear. To Lycurgus was traced the Spartans' pride in *eunomia*,

---

THE SPARTAN CONSTITUTION

"**H**aving established a sanctuary of Syllanian Zeus and Athena, having 'tribed tribes and obed obes,' and having established a Gerousia (Senate) of thirty members, including the (two) chief leaders (kings), from season to season, they are to hold Assemblies between Babyca and Knakion in order to introduce and reject measures. And the *damos* is to have lordship and power." Later a clause was added: "if the *damos* takes a crooked decision, the elders and chief leaders are to be removers."

Source: Plutarch, *Life of Lycurgus* 6 (circa 46–circa 120 C.E.)

good government, or more literally, a good legal system. A Spartan saying was "good men need few laws." Because of their homeland, the Spartans were called Laconian, or simply "laconic," which in English means someone who uses few words.

Good Government. Sparta had a mixed constitution. Within groupings of tribes and *obes*, the specific configurations of which remain a mystery, their constitution had royal, aristocratic, and democratic elements. Its two kings, who came from the same two families generation after generation, the Agiads and Eurypontids, provided the royal element. They led Sparta's armies in war and were given various other privileges. The Gerousia, or senate, had twenty-eight members, besides the kings. They were all over sixty years of age and elected for life by the assembly from the most noble households. In providing the aristocratic element, the Gerousia prepared measures for discussion before the assemblies. It also heard criminal cases and in time gained the power to overturn decisions of the assembly. So the democratic element (*damos* is the form of *dêmos* in the Spartan dialect, which is called Dorian), which was originally sovereign, later had its powers checked. All male Spartan citizens over thirty who had completed Sparta's famously rigorous training and education, known as the *agôgê*, and were members of one of the *sussitia* formed the assembly. The assembly met in remote locations such as Babyca and Knakion so that there would be no distractions. The assembly did not officially discuss the measures presented to it by the Gerousia; it only voted for or against. Some informal discussion, however, must have taken place.

Overseers. Missing from the Great Rhetra, but well known in the historical period, was the annually elected board of five *ephors*, who were overseers of the kings. Each month they exchanged oaths with the kings to uphold their rule so long as the kings reigned according to the laws. Most scholars believe that the ephors were established sometime later than the Great Rhetra; however, their office may have existed from the beginning, but many have been seen originally only as an accessory to the kingship, as a sort of unofficial means of communication between the kings and the deliberative bodies in executive matters.

Rival. Athens grew more slowly than many other Greek states, including Sparta, but once its development gathered momentum, the size of its population and landmass led it to become one of the most dominant *poleis*. Evidence from the clearing of graves from the Athenian *agora* (gathering place or market) suggests that the identity of Athens as a civic center was increasing about 700 B.C.E. At some point, alongside or in place of the traditional office of *basileus* (king), there developed that of the annually elected *arkhôn* (ruler or magistrate), who had executive responsibility. Originally elected for life, but then later for ten years, the archonship became an annually elected office by 682 B.C.E. In time, Athens selected three such annually elected archons: the eponymous archon, who gave his name to the year in which he served; the archon basileus, who took over

many of the traditional and religious roles of the king; and the *polemarch,* who had responsibility for war. Only members of the wealthiest families could be elected to these offices. They were the Eupatrids, "sons of good fathers." After their year of elective office, the archons joined the Areopagus Council, which ruled the city. Later, six more annually elected magistrates were added, the *thesmothêtai,* whose name suggests that they originally had some responsibility connected with recording laws or judicial decisions.

Social Classes. Besides their geographical divisions, Athenians were also divided ethnically into four tribes that were common to all Ionian Greeks. Athens had no indigenous slave population like the Spartan Helots, so there was social stratification only among the Athenians themselves. Some Athenians were enslaved to others. The slaves were referred to as *hektêmorioi* or "sixth-parters," though the exact meaning of this term is unclear. Presumably they paid a rent of one-sixth, or perhaps five-sixths, of the harvest on the land they worked. If they got behind, they could be sold as slaves, even away from Athens.

Conspiracy of Cylon. Athens was also being challenged by its neighbors, such as Megara, and had a need for the sort of hoplite soldiers that could only be supplied by a thriving middle class. This situation created tensions of the sort that were being resolved in many *poleis* by the seizure of power by tyrants, who championed the causes of the common people against the aristocrats. In Athens, about 632 B.C.E., an aristocrat and Olympic victor named Cylon, who was married to the daughter of the tyrant of Megara, tried to seize power by taking control of the Acropolis. After the coup had failed, Cylon's supporters sought refuge as suppliants, invoking the protection of the gods. They were told by magistrates of Athens that their suppliancy was recognized and that they should come down from the Acropolis. However, when they did so they were massacred. A trial was held and the eponymous archon Megacles and his entire family, the Alcmaeonids, were banished from Athens in order to rid the city of the religious pollution, or miasma. Even the family's graves were dug up and their contents removed from Athenian territory. In time the Alcmaeonids returned to Athens, and many of Athens's most illustrious leaders, including Cleisthenes, Pericles, and Alcibiades, belonged to this family, which was nonetheless haunted by the miasma.

Draco. One consequence of Cylon's attempted coup was the setting down for the first time a set of laws for Athens, the so-called Constitution of Draco. This now written form of Athenian traditional laws was a major step in the administration of justice and might have lessened the power of the aristocrats, but the laws were later regarded as having been harsh (which resulted in the English word *draconian* referring to harshness). Draco's laws did little to alleviate the tensions that Athens faced. Only one part of his law code survived, that concerning homicide, a part of which was later inscribed during a reorganization of Athenian laws.

Athenian Lawgiver. As tensions continued to rise, relief was sought finally in 594 by turning the city over temporarily to a single man who served as both archon and reconciler. This man was Solon. He used poetry to communicate his ideas about the nature of Athens's problems and his solutions for them. Much of this poetry survives, and in it, Solon talks about the *horoi* (marker stones) that indicated that land was "enslaved," about Athenians who were enslaved and sold abroad, and about the "crooked judgments" that led to this enslavement. His principal methods of solving the problem were the *seisakhtheia*, the "shaking off of burdens" by which he presumably canceled debts; the reorganization of the class system by wealth rather than birth; and the empowerment of the courts as a check against the power of the magistrates.

Four Classes. The seisalchtheia forbade the enslavement of Athenians that resulted from debt, and it freed and repatriated many who had been enslaved. The reorganization of Athens's classes broke down some of the antiquated power structures and gave recognition to the upwardly mobile members of the new mercantile and manufacturing classes. According to Solon's system, the Athenians were divided into four classes by wealth. The *Pentakosiomedimnoi*, or five-hundred-bushel class, were the wealthiest. The *Hippeis*, or Knights, could produce at least four hundred bushels from their land. The *Zeugitai*, or Yoke Class, could produce two hundred bushels, and the *Thetes*, or Laborers, were the lowest, and most numerous class. Although only members of the highest classes could be elected to office in Athens, Solon allowed anyone who wished (not just the victim) to seek restitution for injustices. He also allowed for appeal of any decision to the law courts, in which all the classes participated, and he gave many more rights to the lower classes. In the law courts, the poorer classes could use their numbers to check the power of the rich.

Geographical Inequalities. Solon might have used his enormous powers to become a tyrant, but he consciously resisted that temptation. After reforming Athens's political system, he left the city for ten years. Despite the breadth of Solon's reforms and the huge respect that his name was given in later generations, however, Athens's political strife, or *stasis*, continued, based mainly on geographical inequalities. In some years no chief magistrate was elected. One archon who was elected to the annual office attempted to stay on and did so for three years before he was removed. In 580 B.C.E. a temporary solution was found through the appointment of a board of ten, who served jointly as archon. The board consisted of five aristocrats, three farmers, and two laborers. The three groups represented not only economic divisions but also Athens's geographical divisions: the central plain, where the wealthiest landowners were; the shoreline, with its less wealthy farmland; and "beyond the hills," whose leaders likely came from the towns beyond the ring of mountains surrounding Athens itself. The last group actually included a wide range of people—

laborers, tradesmen, those freed from slavery by Solon's cancellation of debts, and recent immigrants. Many were refugees from the prosperous and advanced coastline of Asia Minor, which was coming under the control of the Lydians, and, after 547 B.C.E., the Persians.

A New Tyrant. Peisistratus's rise to power as tyrant was by no means smooth. He rose first through a bit of political chicanery, staging an assault on himself to justify getting bodyguards and then using them to seize power in 561 B.C.E. After five years he was thrown out, but he soon returned with the help of a marriage alliance with the daughter of the leader of the shore group. When he refused to consummate the marriage after six years, however, he was again driven out. He returned finally in 546 B.C.E. at the head of an army of friends and mercenaries and drove out his opponents. During his ten years away from Athens, Peisistratus had fostered many connections throughout Greece, which he continued to utilize during his tyranny.

Political Identity. The Peisistratid tyranny, that of Peisistratus and his sons Hippias and Hipparchus, who succeeded on his death in 527, was obviously not a time in which Athens's politics could develop at an institutional level. Peisistratus and his friends and family were in control, even though he allowed the normal mechanisms instituted by Solon to function. The archons were always elected under their supervision and usually from their ranks. This situation meant that the Areopagus Council, which had effective legislative control, was gradually filled up with Peisistratus's people. However, in less obvious ways their tyranny was crucial for the development of Athens's democracy. Peisistratus imposed a tax of 5 percent on all produce and used the proceeds to finance a large public works program. This tax served

---

THE LAW CODE OF DRACO

Even if a man kills another unintentionally, he is exiled. The kings are to adjudge responsible for homicide either the actual killer or the planner; and the Ephetai are to judge the case. If there is a father or brother or sons, pardon is to be agreed to by all, or the one who opposes is to prevail; but if none of these survives, by those up to the degree of first cousin, if all are willing to agree to a pardon; the one who opposes is to prevail; but if none of these survives, and if he killed unintentionally and the fifty-one, the Ephetai, decide he killed unintentionally, let ten phratry members admit him to the country and let the fifty-one choose these by rank. And let also those who killed previously be bound by this law. A proclamation is to be made against the killer in the agora by the victim's relatives as far as the degree of cousin's son and cousin. The prosecution is to be shared by the cousins and the cousins' sons and by sons-in-law, fathers-in-law, and phratry members.

---

to increase the role of the polis in Athens's economy, to provide a new sort of employment, and to achieve a great degree of economic stability and prosperity. Peisistratus also cleared Athens's *agora* (gathering place or market) of private dwellings in order to achieve a proper civic center. He began the minting of Athenian coinage, and he also used legislation and loans at especially good rates to keep all agricultural land under production in the most effective ways. Under his leadership Athens's farmland shifted somewhat away from grains and into olives, whose oil could be processed and sold abroad at a much higher added value. He also sent out traveling courts through the countryside of Attica, so that the polis took over judicial functions from local aristocrats. Besides building programs on the Acropolis and in the central agora, Peisistratus and his sons also put polis money behind the large festivals, like the yearly Panathenaia, which was celebrated with pomp every fourth year, and the Dionysia, where Athens's theatrical traditions were born. Besides making him popular, these actions fostered a stronger sense of Athenian identity than had existed before. Instead of relying on the aristocrats, Athenians now relied on their polis to pursue prosperity.

Tyrannicide. In 514 B.C.E. Athens's tyranny changed. One of the sons of Peisistratus, Hipparchus, was assassinated, and as a result, his brother Hippias imposed harsh measures on the Athenians, harsh enough for the Athenians ever after to condemn even the notion of tyranny. The family of Alcmaeonids, which had led the shore group in Athens before being driven out by Peisistratus, managed to persuade the Spartans to rid Greece of tyrants, so the Spartans marched on Athens and eventually forced Hippias to withdraw. He went to Asia Minor and enjoyed the protection of the Persians.

Father of Democracy. In Athens, with the withdrawal of the Peisistratids, Athens's old regional conflicts began to resurface. Legislation was introduced to outlaw "those of impure descent," which meant the immigrants from Asia Minor and the Alcmaeonids, whose family still suffered from the miasma associated with the massacre of the followers of Cylon more than a century before. The legislation was resisted, but tensions remained, principally between the Alcmaeonids and the other old aristocrats. These tensions were resolved when Cleisthenes, the leader of the Alcmaeonids, "brought the demos into his *hetairia*." (In this context, demos refers to the mass of citizens in the lower classes; hetairia refers to the aristocratic social clubs that formed the basis of political alliances in Athens.) The demos had been the backbone of the Peisistratids' support until their tyranny became despotic; now it would govern itself.

Power of the People. Despite attempts by aristocrats to reenlist the Spartans to drive out the Alcmaeonids, the demos insisted on its independence, and after shedding some aristocratic blood and besieging the Spartans on the Acropolis, they allowed the Spartans to withdraw

and won their democracy. Cleisthenes was the reformer who gave Athens's democracy its definitive shape, although little is known about his life, especially after he was elected archon in 508. His most important step was to redefine Athenian citizenship. From now on, the Athenians would be no longer divided by the traditional divisions into four tribes, which were dominated by the aristocrats with their brotherhoods, or *phratries*, and their control of many of Athens's priesthoods. Instead, the Athenians now had ten tribes, membership in which depended entirely on geography, on which demos (town or area) they lived in. (The word for town was also *dêmos*, but modern scholars call these towns or areas *demes* [pronounced "deems"] in order to distinguish them from the *dêmos*, which became either the mass of citizens of the lower classes or the entire citizen body. Since Athenian politics increasingly worked on the principle of one man/one vote, and the lower classes greatly outnumbered the upper classes, these two meanings were not that distinct in practice.) To cut through Athens's geographical strife, Cleisthenes constructed each of his 10 tribes from the 139 or so demes in the city center, along the shore, and from the rich plains areas. Each tribe consisted of demes from each of these three areas. To cut across Athens's old family squabbles, Athenians began to identify themselves not with their patronymic or father's name, which identified their family, but with their demotic name, which identified their deme.

Military Service. At eighteen years of age, every Athenian male was taken by his father before his local deme assembly, which voted on whether to accept him as a member. Once accepted, he spent the next two years in military training and on garrison duty with the other members of his tribe, drawn from all three of Athens's regions. The sort of close male bonding that this arrangement encouraged, which was maintained through entire lifetimes, served to break down Athens's geographical tensions.

Governing Bodies. Each of Athens's ten tribes elected fifty members to Athens's Council, or *Boulê*, which was expanded from four hundred to five hundred members. To make up the fifty, each deme elected a specific number of Council members each year. This Council met regularly and oversaw the administration of the polis, as well as preparing motions to go before Athens's Assembly, or *Ekklêsia*, which was the sovereign body, making all the important decisions. All Athenian males over eighteen took part in the Assembly. The political year was divided into ten "months," during each of which the Council members from each tribe formed an executive body, a *prutanis*, which governed the city. Each day one of the fifty would officially be "president."

Court System. Athens's courts were also selected by tribes. Each year six thousand Athenians took the Heliastic oath to serve as judges, and each day the courts sat, up to five thousand of them being called to serve in courts that could number from hundreds to thousands. An elaborate lottery system was used for the selection of *dikastai* (judges) immediately before they heard and decided their cases. This procedure, and the great numbers involved, ensured that the judges could not be bribed.

Ostracism. Cleisthenes is also said to have introduced ostracism, no doubt to prevent the return of tyranny. Each year at the same time, the Athenian assembly voted whether to conduct an ostracism. If the vote passed, then one month later every Athenian citizen went to the agora and deposited a piece of broken pot, an *ostrakon*, on which he had written the name of someone he wanted to see ostracized. If enough votes were cast, then the "winner" was required to leave Athens for a period of ten years. He need not have done anything wrong. In fact, some sources report that the individual was ostracized simply because his greatness disturbed the political balance of the democracy. Except for the period 480–450 B.C.E., few people were ever actually ostracized in Athens, but the potential for the use of ostracism was thought to be an indication of the strength of Athens's democracy.

Equality. In the early years of Athens's Cleisthenic democracy, much power must still have been in the hands of the Areopagus, whose members, as former magistrates, all belonged to the wealthiest classes. Its role was to protect the constitution, which could give it quite far-reaching powers. The power of the *dêmos,* although officially sovereign through the assembly of all Athenian citizens, still had to establish itself in practice. Yet, the label that Cleisthenes's reforms took, *isonomia* ("equality before the laws" or "a legal system based on equality"), laid the foundation for Athens's dêmos to achieve its sovereignty in practice as well as formally.

Sources:

Moses I. Finley, *Democracy Ancient and Modern* (New Brunswick, N.J.: Rutgers University Press, 1985).

J. T. Hooker, *The Ancient Spartans* (London: Dent, 1980).

Chester G. Starr, *Individual and Community: The Rise of the Polis, 800-500 B.C.E.* (Oxford: Oxford University Press, 1986).

David Stockton, *The Classical Athenian Democracy* (New York: Oxford University Press, 1990).

THE BATTLE OF MARATHON

Background. In 499 B.C.E. the Ionian Greeks, those residing on the coast of Asia Minor and various islands in the Aegean Sea, rebelled against their Persian overlords. Some of the Greek city-states were sympathetic to the plight of the rebels during these early Persian Wars, and Athens and Eretria sent military aid in the form of warships. Nevertheless, the Persian king Darius I crushed the rebellion by 494 and then decided to chastise the interfering Greek city-states. In the case of the Athenians, he wished to reimpose on them the rule of the tyrant Hippias, who had been forced from Athens twenty-one years before. In the summer of 490

B.C.E. a Persian army of approximately 26,000 men landed in Greece; while one-half of the force laid siege to Eritrea on the island of Euboea, the remainder bivouacked twenty-six miles north of Athens at Marathon.

Persian Forces. The army of Darius I was composed of troops from many regions of the Persian empire. The regular professional soldiers were the Medes, Elamites, and a group of royal guards known as the Immortals. They were armed with bows and would fire arrows at their enemies before engaging in close combat with short spears and daggers. Although they had wicker shields, they wore no protective armor, as did the Greek heavy infantry. The Persian cavalry, made up of excellent horsemen such as the Medes, Elamites, Bactrians, and Sakai, also was armed with bows, although the Sakai carried axes as well.

Greek Forces. The Athenians gathered an army of ten thousand troops, including one thousand Plataeans, and placed them under the command of an experienced general, Miltiades. Although the Spartans were invited to join with their highly trained soldiers, they hesitated to send any aid. The Greek infantrymen who participated in the Battle of Marathon were called hoplites, so named because they carried round shields known as *hopla*. The hoplites were heavy infantrymen, meaning that they carried long thrusting spears (eight to ten feet in length) and iron swords and wore plate armor and helmets. Hoplites fought in a phalanx, a large rectangular formation which had between six and eight ranks. Troops in a phalanx relied on shock action to defeat enemy forces. As the soldiers moved closer to the enemy, the first few ranks would level their spears while interlocking shields to protect the formation.

The Engagement. In late September 490 Miltiades and his men formed for battle on the heights above the Persian encampment on the bay of Marathon. The Athenian phalanx attacked so swiftly that the Persians, their backs to the sea, had little time to react and use their bows before being overrun by the hoplites. In a stunning victory, the Greeks roundly defeated the Persians and killed thousands of the invaders. Marathon was the first time that a Western army had beaten an Eastern army, and it proved the military worth of hoplites over lightly armed troops.

Sources:

Larry H. Addington, *The Patterns of War through the Eighteenth Century* (Bloomington & Indianapolis: Indiana University Press, 1990).

Peter Green, *The Greco-Persian Wars* (Berkeley: University of California Press, 1996).

Herodotus, *The Histories,* translated by W. Blanco and J. Roberts (New York: Norton, 1992).

Malcolm F. McGregor, *The Athenians and Their Empire* (Vancouver: University of British Columbia Press, 1987).

Russell Meiggs, *The Athenian Empire* (Oxford: Oxford University Press, 1972).

Richard A. Preston, and others, *Men in Arms: A History of Warfare and Its Interrelationships with Western Society* (Fort Worth, Tex.: Holt, Rinehart & Winston, 1991).

A vase painting of a messenger reporting news of Persian defeat to King Darius I
(NAM, Naples; Photo: Soprintendenza alle Antichità di Napoli)

THE MACEDONIAN ART OF WARFARE

The Outsiders. To many Greeks, Macedon was not part of the Greek world. Most of the Macedonians did not speak Greek, and their social organization was closer to that of the Homeric world, with its hereditary kingships and clan chiefs, than it was to the contemporary world of the Greek *polis*. Macedon was an area rich in timber and metals. As far as the Greeks were concerned, its people simply provided a buffer between themselves and the even less civilized people who lived beyond Macedon. However, a Macedonian, Philip II, organized a formidable army that not only conquered the Greek city-states but also represented one of the most powerful military machines in Western society before the advent of firearms.

War Machine. As a young boy, Philip of Macedon lived in Thebes and observed how military power functioned. He was a great admirer of the strategic and tactical ideas of the general Epaminondas, including his use of the hoplite phalanx. During the early part of his reign, Philip devoted himself to reorganizing his army, instilling greater discipline, and modifying its fighting

style and equipment. First of all he introduced selective conscription for set periods of time that allowed him to conduct year-round campaigns. Besides the deeper phalanx (sixteen ranks), Philip introduced the use of the sarissa, a much longer spear (approximately fifteen feet long) than that used by the other Greek hoplites. It gave his men the advantage of striking their opponents first as their phalanxes clashed. The sarissa required both hands, however, so Philip's soldiers had to use a different sort of shield, one that rested on the upper left arm without needing the left hand for support. His soldiers had no breastplate. By combining the best attributes of the hoplite and the peltast (a lightly armed soldier), Philip blurred the lines between citizen and noncitizen soldier. His soldiers could also be much less expensively armed.

The Companions. Since Macedonia was a much wider, more open area than most Greek centers, there were also many more horses available for cavalry. The Companions were elite cavalrymen composed of some two thousand landholding aristocrats; they represented the main striking force of the army. Other units in the

A detail from a mosaic (circa 300 B.C.E.) found in Pompeii and showing Alexander the Great at the Battle of Issus in 333 B.C.E. (Naples, National Museum; Photo: Andre Held)

Macedonian army included mercenary cavalry from Thessaly and slingers and javelin throwers from Crete. Philip also employed the torsion catapult, a missile weapon capable of throwing a sixty-pound stone four hundred yards.

Integration. Philip integrated all these different elements into a fighting force not seen since the Assyrians. Units of the Macedonian army acted in close coordination: while the phalanx engaged the enemy head-on, the cavalry and light troops would attack the rival army's flanks and rear, weakening its resistance until it fled the field.

Logistics. The Macedonian army could also travel farther than other armies. Philip reduced his army's dependence on wagons and carts by making his men carry their own arms, armor, personal possessions, and rations. Only one pack animal was allowed for every fifty soldiers, and as a result, the soldiers could make longer strategic marches.

Victories. The Macedonian military machine developed by Philip enabled him by 346 B.C.E. to gain control of Thessaly, Thrace, the straits at the Bosphorus, and the strategic pass at Thermopylae. He invaded Boeotia in 338 and won his most famous victory at Chaeronea, defeating a combined Athenian-Theban army and becoming ruler of all the Greek city-states.

Alexander the Great. Philip was planning to liberate Ionia from Persian rule when he was assassinated in 336.

His son, Alexander III, or Alexander the Great, accomplished that feat in his stead. In fact, Alexander, in many regards, perfected the army created by his father. He defeated the Persians in a series of battles at the Granicus River (334), Issus (333), and Gaugamela (331), and campaigned as far east as Parthia, Margiana, Sogdiana, and Bactria (present-day Iran, Afghanistan, and Uzbekistan).

Sources:
Larry H. Addington, *The Patterns of War through the Eighteenth Century* (Bloomington & Indianapolis: Indiana University Press, 1990).

Eugene N. Borza, *In the Shadow of Olympus: The Emergence of Macedon* (Princeton: Princeton University Press, 1990).

A. B. Bosworth, *Conquest and Empire: The Reign of Alexander the Great* (Cambridge & New York: Cambridge University Press, 1988).

George Cawkwell, *Philip of Macedon* (London & Boston: Faber & Faber, 1978).

John R. Ellis, *Philip II and Macedonian Imperialism* (London: Thames & Hudson, 1976).

Donald W. Engels, *Alexander the Great and the Logistics of the Macedonian Army* (Berkeley: University of California Press, 1978).

Richard A. Preston, and others, *Men in Arms: A History of Warfare and Its Interrelationships with Western Society* (Fort Worth, Tex.: Holt, Rinehart & Winston, 1991).

ORATORY AND RHETORIC

Public Speaking. The participatory nature of Athens's democracy required its citizens to be proficient public speakers. Although some leading figures clearly spoke more than others, every citizen had to be able, in theory at least, to promote and defend himself and his positions, whether in the assembly, the courts, or at the village meetings. Oratory was clearly of critical importance in Athens. Beginning in the fifth century B.C.E., Athens attracted many professional intellectuals, or sophists, such as Protagoras and Gorgias who, among other things, taught public speaking for a price. Many leading citizens led the community both as speakers and generals; examples include Themistocles, Aristides, Nicias, Alcibiades, Cleon, and Pericles.

Specialization. In the fourth century, an era of specialization began when the military leaders were no longer the prominent speakers. New laws recognized distinct roles for generals (*stratêgoi*) and public speakers (*rhêtores*). The philosopher Plato used (and possibly coined) the term *rhetoric* to characterize, negatively, the art by which the new class of speakers dominated Athenian politics and manipulated the public assemblies. Sophists composed handbooks on specialized forms of argumentation, delivery, and style. Athenian citizens and foreigners who had a knack for composition earned money as *logographoi* (speechwriters) for those lacking the ability, or confidence, to compose speeches for themselves. The best of these men such as Lysias, Isocrates, Isaeus, and Demosthenes collected their compositions, which served as models for school children for centuries. Many of these speeches survive today and were composed for delivery in the Athenian courts, Assembly, and Council and for various ceremonial occasions.

Aristotle. In response to Plato's rather negative portrayal of rhetoric a generation earlier, the philosopher Aristotle composed a treatise on rhetoric that brought together the ideas of many of the previous handbooks and gave them a philosophical rationale. For instance, he saw three kinds of speeches distinguished by time and who the listeners were: deliberative speeches were about the future and are heard by members of the assembly; judicial speeches were about the past and are heard by members of a court; and display, or "epideictic," speeches were about the present and are heard by listeners at ceremonial occasions.

Sources:
George A. Kennedy, *The Art of Persuasion in Greece* (Princeton: Princeton University Press, 1963).

Josiah Ober, *Mass and Elite in Democratic Athens: Rhetoric, Ideology, and the Power of the People* (Princeton: Princeton University Press, 1989).

THE PERSIAN MENACE

Marathon. In 490 B.C.E. at Marathon, on the northern coast of Attica, the Athenians repulsed an army of Persians intent on gaining their submission and on reimposing on them the rule of the tyrant Hippias, who had been forced from Athens twenty-one years before. That Athens could block both the Persians and the return of tyranny gave a tremendous morale boost to its still budding democratic constitution. The Athenians had adopted it in 506, but they still had concerns about those who might aim at tyranny. That they won this victory without the help of the Spartans, the foremost warriors of the Greek world and the leaders of the Hellenic League, helped establish the Athenians' own claim to be an effective, independent fighting force. Athens was clearly the leading city among the Ionian

Greeks, who lived on the central islands of the Aegean and on the coast of Turkey, and the Athenians had already established influence around the Hellespont and on Lemnos. However, they had lacked confidence in themselves in comparison to the Spartans, their superior Dorian cousins. After Marathon they were much more confident.

Thermopylae. In 480 the Persians attacked again, this time with a much larger force. There were questions among the Greeks about where to meet them in battle. Many from the Peloponnese thought that the Greeks should withdraw to their southern peninsula and block the Persians at the isthmus. However, this course of action meant abandoning Athens and many other poleis to the enemy. As a result, the Spartan king Leonidas heroically led his elite bodyguard of three hundred experienced hoplites north to Thermopylae, a narrow pass between north and central Greece. If he were killed, he thought, the Spartans would fight to the end to avenge him. For a time Leonidas's force, with contingents from several other poleis, managed to block the enemy advance, but after several days the Persians found a way around the pass. Leonidas sent the other Greeks away while he and the Spartans made a desperate stand against the Persians, sacrificing themselves for Greek unity.

Salamis. Afterward, at the island of Salamis, near Athens, a combined Greek navy managed to defeat a much larger Persian fleet. Although Sparta technically commanded the Greek fleet, it was recognized as a united fighting force. The Athenians had provided the most ships, and the tactical guile of one of their commanders, Themistocles, contributed in large part to the victory as well as to maintaining Greek unity in trying circumstances. The fact that the Athenians first abandoned their city to the ravages of the Persians and then still fought alongside the rest of the Greeks gave them even more respect; they put Greek interests before their own.

Final Victories. In 479 the Greeks met and defeated the much larger Persian land forces at Plataea, on the border between Attica and Boeotia. Here again the Greek forces worked effectively together, the Athenians showing themselves to be every bit as competent on the field as the Spartans. At almost the same time, across the Aegean at Mycale, the Greek fleet again defeated the Persians. While the Persians could still dominate the many Greek cities along the coastline of western Turkey, they would never again attempt an assault on the Greek mainland.

Reflection. At the next Olympic games, in 476, which were the preeminent event to be shared by the entire Greek-speaking world, everyone applauded Themistocles as the person behind the Greek victory. There were criticisms only against the poleis that had refused to participate in the combined Greek forces, such as Corcyra and Syracuse, and those cities that appeared to have given up to the Persians without an adequate fight, such as Thebes.

Panhellenism. The stage seemed to be set for a period of prosperous Panhellenism, the idea of a united Greece.

Historians discern that these united accomplishments held a strong psychological grip over the Greek world. Long after there would be references to "the Marathon men" who had repulsed the Persians. The Athenian Acropolis, whose monumental buildings had been destroyed by the Persians, was not rebuilt for a long time in commemoration of what "the barbarians" had done. Even when its edifices were renovated, conscious memorials of the conflict with the Persians were included. The columns of the old Parthenon were embedded in a prominent place on the side of the Acropolis, and 192 figures were included in the new frieze, one for each of the Athenian dead at Marathon. The metope sculptures celebrate the battles of Greek heroes against monsters, forces of savagery that represent the barbarian threat. Persia had become a point for comparison for the Greeks: the world was divided into Greeks and non-Greeks, or barbarians, who were understood to be the Persians. The Greeks gained a sense of their homeland Hellas and what it meant to be Hellenes.

Imperialism. The Athenians in the fifth century reached the peak of their cultural development, which has made their achievements, whether the Parthenon or the tragedies of Sophocles, the "classical" models on which so much Western art, architecture, and literature have been based. Especially exciting is the fact that these were the achievements of the world's first democracy. Yet, Athens was not only a democracy, it was also a slave-owning society, and in this period whose accomplishments have been so celebrated, Athens was considered a "tyrant city" by many Greeks, including some Athenians.

Disunity. After the Greek victories at Plataea and Mycale, the Hellenic League was poised to pursue a vendetta against the Persians and drive them out of the Greek world entirely. The Athenians then organized the Delian League, which united the Ionians of the Aegean Islands and the coast of Asia Minor. Sparta and its Peloponnesian allies, who were mostly Dorian, did not join. The Hellenic League continued to exist until 462 B.C.E., but the Delian League took over the fight against Persia, and Athens was its *hêgemôn* (leader).

Delian League. Athens had no political parties, so it is impossible to look for a cohesive policy with which any group can be identified. Yet, in the early years of the Delian League there were at least four areas in which Athenian views diverged. The first was in regard to pursuing antagonisms against Persia. Sparta, with its large Helot population to control at home and its commitment to land-based hoplite warfare, had allowed Athens to assume leadership in this area. Following Aristides, the Athenians accepted Greek hegemony, or leadership, against the Persians without exception. However, there were nuances to this role: some states in 480 had gone over to the Persian side; were they to be excluded from the Greek councils? One of these was the Amphictyonic Council, which administered the sanctuary and oracle at Delphi. The Spartans wanted to expel the "medizers," those who had collaborated with the Medes (Persians), from this Council. Themistocles

A modern statue of the Spartan king and general Leonidas near the battlefield at Thermopylae (Sonia Halliday Photographs)

opposed the Spartans on this point and quickly lost good standing with them.

New Fortifications. The second area for divergence was with regard to Sparta and the Greek alliance. The Persians had sacked Athens twice, in 480 and 479, and the city had been in ruins. Although the Acropolis was left largely unrestored as a memorial of the Persian destruction, which the Spartans encouraged, Themistocles took a leading role in refortifying Athens despite Spartan opposition. He also suggested burning the Greek fleet in order to ensure Athenian naval dominance. This proposal caused his sometime political rival Aristides to stand against him. Moreover, Sparta soon withdrew from involvement in the Greek alliance because its regent, Pausanias, misbehaved and discredited the Spartans.

Miltiades. A related area involved attempts by Athens to achieve influence beyond its borders. Even before the Persian incursions, the Athenian Miltiades established a principality in the Chersonese. Miltiades then won great acclaim by leading the Athenians at Marathon. Nevertheless, his further attempts at expansionism at Paros had been a failure, and he died in disgrace in 489.

Politics. The fourth area of divergence was in politics at home. In the aftermath of Salamis, the aristocratic council of the Areopagus, consisting of former archons, had the upper hand. Its leadership had proved decisive in organizing the Athenian resistance to the Persians, but there was a change in the offing. In 487 the selection of magistrates was changed from election to selection by lottery. This situation meant that although the older members of the Areopagus had all enjoyed sufficient popularity, at least at one time, to have been chosen to lead the Athenians, the more-recent members held their positions only by the luck of the draw. They had no political capital upon which to base their Council's authority. On the other hand, Athens's new naval dominance gave its rowers huge new political importance. Democratic politicians, such as Themistocles, made use of this new political force. They had to act through the mechanisms of the *polis,* since they had no money of their own. Aristocratic politicians could dispense largesse as they wished, and they could themselves finance ships for Athenian fleets.

Cimon. After organizing the Delian League, Aristides faded quickly from the scene, and Themistocles held the upper hand; however, his arrogance toward the other Greeks and his lack of a pure Athenian aristocratic pedigree quickly led to a loss of political support, especially in a city still dominated by the aristocratic Areopagus. The new political and military star was Cimon, the son of Miltiades, who had impeccable aristocratic credentials and ambitions for Athens and the Delian League. After expelling the Spartan renegade Pausanias from Byzantium, he had captured Eion in northern Greece and then the island of Skyros, near Euboea. These two places had been pockets of pro-Persian sympathizers. Nevertheless, they were Greek states, and there was some unease about the Greek alliance attacking other Greeks. Then Cimon moved against Carystos and finally Naxos, which revolted in the early 460s. The first great battle against the Persians after Mycale in 479 did not occur until the naval battle of the Eurymedon River in 467, but the possibilities of exploiting this victory were forestalled. The Greek fleet turned back to suppress a revolt by the island of Thasos in 465.

Exile. Themistocles was ostracized sometime in the mid 470s, just as he had had Aristides ostracized some years before. Once out of the city, he was powerless to act against those at home who brought charges against him. The playwright Aeschylus produced his *Persians* in 472, celebrating Themistocles's moment of triumph at Salamis. But it was not enough. Themistocles was forced to flee from his sanctuary at Argos, and after an epic chase across the Greek world in search of refuge, he finally ended up in the Persian king's court.

Intrigue. Cimon had rock-solid support among Athens's upper classes. He was one of them; he was enormously successful as a general; and he managed to allay the tendencies of some in the state to provoke the inevitable confrontation with Sparta over the manner of Athens's leadership role. Sparta was not pleased when Cimon led the Delian fleet against Carystos and Naxos, but it was powerless to do anything. However, when Cimon and the fleet besieged Thasos in 465 and the island's inhabitants appealed to Sparta for help, the Spartans secretly offered to invade Attica, which would have forced Cimon to break off his attack. Thus, one pillar of Cimon's support was undercut because his leadership no longer excluded the possibility of Spartan aggression. The small landowners in the Attic countryside, the backbone of Athens's hoplite class, protested loudly and started looking for someone to take a more militant line against the Spartans.

Disrespect. The Spartans were prevented from attacking Attica by a revolt of their Helot population at Ithome in Messenia, and by an earthquake. These events also gave Cimon an opportunity: he would lead the Athenians to Sparta's aid and thereby win back their goodwill. In their moment of distress, the Spartans invited him to come. Cimon led four thousand troops into Spartan territory, but the actual appearance of this unprecedented sight, Athenian soldiers in Spartan territory, frightened the Spartans, who were now, in any case, recovering on their own. The Athenians were a potentially subversive presence, and they were told to go home.

Reforms. The Athenian *dêmos* itself also became concerned, which caused a great change in policy. Alliances were forged with Sparta's rival Argos and with Thessaly. Antagonism with Megara, on the border with Attica and thus a potential buffer, came to an end. Cimon was ostracized. The Areopagus, which had championed Cimon, lost many of its political and legal functions, which were shifted to the Council and Assembly. Aeschylus, the playwright who had earlier celebrated the Athenian victory over Salamis in order to ease anger against Themistocles, now wrote about how the Areopagus was originally instituted as a homicide court, which was now the only function it had left. The Areopagus had had sweeping powers to preserve the constitution by hearing cases against magistrates and generals. These cases were now given to the more-representative assemblies as were the *dokimasia* and the *euthuna,* by which magistrates were scrutinized and audited at the beginning and end of their terms. In addition, the senior magistrates would no longer try cases; all legal proceedings would go straight to the popular law courts.

Pericles. The author of these democratizing reforms in 462 B.C.E. was Ephialtes, an aristocrat and a devoted democrat. Soon after his reforms, however, he was assassinated. His role as the champion of the democrats was taken over by Pericles, who went on to dominate Athenian politics for more than thirty years. One of Pericles' first reforms was to introduce payment for participation in Athens's juries. Unlike today, Athenian jurists could not be compelled to participate, so unless they received some compensation, only those who could afford to take time away from their other responsibilities could participate. With jury pay, Pericles saw to it that the lower classes could judge cases as well. In 457 he opened the holding of the senior magistracies to the *Zeugitai.* In 451 he introduced a law requiring that to be recognized as an Athenian citizen, a man had to show that both his parents had been Athenians.

War. Under Pericles' leadership, Athenian relations with Sparta continued to sour. Athens's assistance to Megara in severing its ties to the Spartans and the other Peloponnesians led to what is now called the First Peloponnesian War (461–445 B.C.E.). During this conflict, Athens built its Long Walls, which connected Athens with its harbor at Piraeus. In 458 the Spartans marched north into Boeotia in an attempt to shore up their allies in Thebes. The Athenians confronted them at Tanagra and were defeated, but the Spartan losses were also considerable and forced them to withdraw. Athens then retook Boeotia and dominated it for the next ten years.

Athenian Empire. Athens's hostility to Persia had not yet wavered. In 459 two hundred Athenian ships ventured to Egypt to support a revolt against the Persians. Like other revolts against the great Persian king, this one enjoyed temporary success, but in 454 it collapsed and Athens's entire expedition, including fifty more ships that had been sent out as reinforcements, were lost. It was a huge disaster, which led to two significant events. First, citing the possibility of a renewed Persian threat, Athens moved the treasury of the Delian League from Delos to Athens. Second, in about 450 Athens ended its hostilities with Persia with the so-called Peace of Callias. Despite the end of the war against Persia, however, Athens continued to insist that its allies contribute to the upkeep of its fleet. The Delian League had become the Athenian Empire.

Peace Treaty. In 447 Athens's ambitions to maintain a hold over Boeotia and thus hold an empire on land as well as on the sea were ended when the Spartans again defeated them, this time at Coronea. Two years later a peace treaty was concluded, and Sparta was to lead the Greeks of the Peloponnese and Boeotia, while Athens was to have its naval empire. The peace treaty required that trials involving Athenians and its allies be held at Athens, and it imposed Athenian silver coinage, weights, and measures on all its allies. Those allies that were deemed recalcitrant could expect to have a colony of Athenian *clerychs*, stakeholders, placed nearby. The clerychs allowed the Athenians to keep an eye on things and provided a home for some of Athens's burgeoning population.

Sources:

Peter Green, *The Greco-Persian Wars* (Berkeley: University of California Press, 1996).

Herodotus, *The Histories*, translated by W. Blanco and J. Roberts (New York: Norton, 1992).

Malcolm F. McGregor, *The Athenians and Their Empire* (Vancouver: University of British Columbia Press, 1987).

Russell Meiggs, *The Athenian Empire* (Oxford: Oxford University Press, 1972).

THE POLIS IN DECLINE

Reflection. While historians and other intellectuals of the fifth century B.C.E. took the polis for granted, the trauma of the Peloponnesian War led philosophers such as Plato to think beyond the political reality of the fourth century to speculate about a political utopia, a model for a polis that could achieve some permanence. As important as Plato's speculations have been for the history of philosophy, however, the political reality that he rejected was moving beyond the *polis* altogether. Government was needed that could encompass areas and populations greater than any one *polis*, and yet no city could achieve lasting dominance over the others.

Spartan Hegemony. The restoration of democracy in Athens in 403 had little effect in the rest of Greece, where Sparta's power was unchallenged. This period of time is referred to as Spartan hegemony. The word *hegemony* is based on the Greek word *hēgemonia*, which means leadership; however, hegemony is stronger than leadership, although it does not quite mean domination. Through the strategy of their commander Lysander, the Spartans inherited most of Athens's empire, with the contributions of its subject allies, to add to its own considerable holdings in the Peloponnese. Under Spartan *harmosts* (governors), councils of ten local citizens, called decarchies, ruled the affairs of the poleis in accordance with Spartan interests.

Diplomacy. Nonetheless, the Spartans had some decisions to make. In order to defeat the Athenians, they had sought and received help from the Persians in exchange for the Persians' receiving a free hand to dominate the Greeks who lived on the coast of Turkey. Would the Spartans abide by their agreements with the Persians, or would they renew their role as champions of the Greek world and pursue war against Persia? The obstacles to their plans were no less true in 400 B.C.E. than they had been in 479 B.C.E. The basis of their livelihood was still the labor of the large population of Helots, against whom the Spartans had to stay ever vigilant. The Spartan *agōgē*, or training, which produced such effective soldiers, also seemed to depend on the Spartans' living only within their controlled lifestyle at home. Outside influences could quite easily corrupt. Spartans, dealing with money for the first time, succumbed to the temptation to steal. Harmosts given command over foreign populations for the first time quickly became tyrants. However, the involvement of many Greek mercenaries in a rebellion led by Cyrus the Younger in an attempt to seize the Persian throne from his brother Artaxerxes II in 401 showed the potential strength that a united Greek army might have against the Persians. Cyrus's mainly Greek force managed to defeat a Persian army at Cunaxa, deep in Persian territory in Babylonia. Only the death of Cyrus at Cunaxa prevented the ten thousand Greek mercenaries from asserting control.

Lysander. The successes of the Spartan commander Lysander became his own undoing. The personal loyalty that he enjoyed in so many of the cities he had captured was resented by the Spartans back home. Because he was not one of Sparta's two kings, his extraordinary personal power and prestige were viewed as a threat to Spartan government. He was recalled, and the citizens who formed the many local decarchies were dismissed as if they were his personal clients. In 397 B.C.E., however, Lysander returned to some prominence when his boyhood friend Agesilaus was able to become king after a disputed succession.

A modern monument on the site of the Battle of Leuctra, commemorating the defeat of the Spartans by Epaminondas in 371 B.C.E.

Initial Victories. Agesilaus had great plans to pursue war against the Persians. Modeling himself on Agamemnon and the legendary Greek expedition against Troy, in 396 he assembled an army in the same location in Boeotia where Agamemnon's fleet had disembarked. However, by this time Sparta's former allies were growing weary of Spartan hegemony, and the Thebans marched out and interrupted Agesilaus's preliminary sacrifice. The expedition set off, nevertheless, and won several victories in northwest Turkey.

Setbacks. Agesilaus's successes were cut short, however, by two developments. First, in 395 an Athenian general, Conon, who had escaped the disaster at Aegospotami in 405 by sailing to Cyprus, returned at the head of a Persian fleet and defeated the Spartans at Cnidus in the southeastern Aegean. Second, in Greece, the cities of Thebes, Athens, Corinth, and Argos put aside their differences and united against Sparta. Agesilaus had to be called home.

The King's Peace. Because so much of the fighting took place near the isthmus of Corinth in an attempt to restrict Spartan influence to the Peloponnese, the new war has been called the Corinthian War. Besides the four Greek poleis, the Persians also joined in opposing Sparta. Athens was the prime beneficiary of the Persian aid: it rebuilt its

Long Walls and refortified its port at Piraeus. Soon the Athenians reestablished their influence in many parts of the Aegean, especially in regaining a corridor to the Black Sea for its grain supplies. Their renewed power and imposition of taxes on all maritime trade by their allies made the Persians and the Thebans worried, however, and both these powers turned their support to Sparta. By 387 the Spartans had managed to block Athens's access to the Black Sea again, and the Athenians were forced to accept a peace brokered by the Persian king. Since it was dictated by the Spartan Antalcidas, it is variously known as the King's Peace or Peace of Antalcidas.

Betrayal. The terms of the King's Peace assured the Persians their control of the Greek cities in Asia Minor. As a result, it was seen by many as a betrayal of Greek interests. Within Greece, its guiding principle was autonomy: no polis was to impose itself on any other. This principle was directed mainly at the Athenians, but it also prevented the Thebans from dominating the other cities of Boeotia. It did nothing, however, to check Sparta's domination of Messenia. In fact, Sparta became the enforcer of the Peace. In 382 a Spartan commander on his way to northern Greece to break up a league of states loyal to Olynthus took the opportunity afforded by a religious celebration in

Thebes to seize the city's acropolis, which was known as the Cadmeia. The unprovoked nature of the attack and its transgression against religious customs led the Spartans to punish the commander, but they held on to the Cadmeia. This sort of Spartan highhandedness led the Thebans to join with the Athenians and many of Athens's former allies again to form what is now called the Second Athenian League. The terms of the League were carefully formulated to abide by the terms of the King's Peace: no polis would surrender its autonomy to another. Unlike the Athenian Empire of the fifth century, this League was governed not by the Athenian Assembly but by an independent *sunedrion* (congress). At its peak, the League had up to seventy members. Although the Athenians were clearly the strongest member, especially with their navy, they allowed the synhedrion a veto over their actions, and they did not impose any clerychies on their allies.

Defiance. Despite the pious sentiments of 378 B.C.E. establishing the Second Athenian League while preserving the autonomy of its individual member states, the tendency for the stronger states to dominate the weaker was impossible to escape. Thebes took advantage of its alliance with Athens to consolidate its hold over Boeotia through the Boeotian Confederacy, and Athens itself took greater advantage of its hegemony over the maritime poleis. The Spartans were intent on putting a stop to Thebes's ambitions. In 375, however, the Thebans under Pelopidas stunned the Greek world by defeating a relatively small force of Spartans in a battle at Tegyra. In 371, after a failed peace conference in which the Spartans had refused to

allow the Thebans to settle terms on behalf of all the Boeotians, the Spartans came north with a force of more than ten thousand hoplites to destroy the Boeotian Confederacy. The Thebans under Epaminondas met them for battle at Leuctra.

Leuctra. Epaminondas had revolutionized hoplite fighting. He massed his hoplite phalanx fifty men deep on his left, directly against the Spartan strength. An elite force, called the Sacred Band, was in the front ranks of Epaminondas's phalanx. By carefully timing his cavalry attack, and taking advantage of Spartan confusion at his unusual formation, Epaminondas charged the Spartans at the right moment, killing their king and forcing the enemy to withdraw with heavy losses. The Battle of Leuctra marked the end of Spartan military dominance in Greece. Economic problems in Sparta had led to a drop in population. Even if they had had the will, the Spartans could no longer field an army of sufficient size to dominate. Soon, other cities in the Peloponnese gained their liberation from Spartan hegemony.

Mantinea. The next year Epaminondas followed up his victory by invading the Peloponnese; however, instead of attacking Sparta directly, he led his forces to Messenia, the source of Sparta's economic prosperity. He freed Messenia and reestablished it as a unified polis. In subsequent years he invaded the Peloponnese repeatedly, while Thebes enjoyed its brief period of hegemony over the Greek world. Loosely following the model that the Thebans had adopted for their Boeotian confederacy, Epaminondas initially encouraged the development of the Arcadian Confederacy as a buffer to the Spartans. It had its capital at Megalopolis and included an assembly of ten thousand, a council, and magistrates selected according to the size of their home polis. Soon, however, the Confederacy became fragmented and its members, encouraged by Athens, began to resist Theban control. In 362, in an attempt to put down unrest in the Peloponnese, Epaminondas was killed in the Battle of Mantinea.

Athenian Resurgence. The historian Xenophon ends his *Hellenica*, a history of the period 411–362, by noting the uncertainty that followed the Battle of Mantinea. Sparta's time as a dominant military power had been finished after the Battle of Leuctra in 371 B.C.E. Now Thebes's period of hegemony had passed with the death of its most decisive leader. Athens was once again the leading Greek *polis*, but without ambitions to pursue a war against either a Greek power or the Persians. With no threat from any of these quarters either, its justification for maintaining an empire seemed to have gone. Nevertheless, the Athenians were increasingly interested in recovering Amphipolis, a strategic commercial and mining center on the north coast of the Aegean, but this goal would have served only the Athenians, not their allies.

UNCERTAINTY AFTER MANTINEA

In 362 the Thebans defeated the Spartans and their allies at Mantinea. However, the Theban victory was marred by the death of the general Epaminondas, and as a result Thebes gradually lost its power among the city-states.

When these things had taken place, the opposite of what all men believed would happen was brought to pass. For since well-nigh all the people of Greece had come together and formed themselves in opposing lines, there was no one who did not suppose that if a battle were fought, those who proved victorious would be the rulers and those who were defeated would be their subjects; but the deity so ordered it that both parties set up a trophy as though victorious and neither tried to hinder those who set them up, that both gave back the dead under a truce as though victorious, and both received back their dead under a truce as though defeated, and that while each party claimed to be victorious, [27] neither was found to be any better off, as regards either additional territory, or city, or sway, than before the battle took place; but there was even more confusion and disorder in Greece after the battle than before.

Source: Xenophon, *Hellenica*, 7.5.26–7.

The Social War. Discontent among Athens's allies grew until finally, in 357 B.C.E., Rhodes, Cos, Chios, and Byzantium revolted in what is now called the Social War, from the Latin word *socii* for "allies." These states were helped and encouraged by Mausolus, the king of Caria who acted as the Persian governor, or satrap, for the area. The two-year conflict certainly prevented the Athenians from thinking about pursuing a campaign against the Persians. The Athenian citizens had long enjoyed the revenues generated by the Second Athenian League to finance ships and mercenaries to fight on their behalf. They no longer had the heart to pursue a war to maintain an empire after their navy lost a major battle at Embata in 356. Moreover, the Persian king threatened all-out war if the Athenians did not restrain their general Chares. Although Athens kept a remnant of its League intact, the loss of four of its major allies—as well as Lesbos shortly after the war—marked the end of an important chapter in Greek history and politics. The Athenians were no longer in a position to export their democratic ideas to other poleis. It was only a matter of time before its own democracy was threatened.

Mercenaries. The Athenians were not the only polis to rely heavily on mercenaries in the fourth century B.C.E., which had enormous consequences for Greek political institutions. The basis of polis government had been the phalanx of hoplite citizen soldiers and, in the case of Athens's democracy, the trireme of citizen rowers. When the soldiers and rowers became hired noncitizens—mercenaries—the connection between citizens' political rights and military service was broken. Constant warfare led many Greek citizens to abandon their farms and drift into service as mercenaries, which had agricultural and thus economic consequences, as well as military and political.

Military Technology. The preeminence of the hoplite soldier was also being challenged by changes in military technology and tactics. The citizen farmer had sufficient wealth to be able to purchase his own weapons. Now light-armed tactics, which were pioneered by Pelopidas of Thebes and Iphicrates of Athens, called for more-specialized skills in archery, slinging, siege operations, and the use of the lighter javelin and shield, or *peltê*, of the peltasts. Citizen soldiers rarely had the time or interest to develop these skills. Tyrants such as Jason of Pherae and Dionysius of Syracuse, as well as the Persian king, hired many Greek mercenaries for their armies, an indication that soldiers were now fighting less for their poleis and more for individuals and for money.

The Sacred War. In 355 B.C.E., in response to demands that it stop cultivating sacred land, the federation of Phocis, which lay between Boeotia and Delphi, seized the sanctuary of Apollo at Delphi with the tacit support of Athens. The sanctuary was protected by a group of poleis known as the Amphictyonic Council, which included most of the Greek poleis, but which was dominated by those in Boeotia and Thessaly. Conse-

quently, it fell to Thebes, as the leader of Boeotia, to recover the sanctuary; however, with the sanctuary and its huge treasury in their hands, the Phocians had ample funds with which to hire mercenaries. Led by their generals Philomelus and Onomarchus, the Phocians fought the Thebans in a long war, which was costly for the entire Greek world. Because it was fought over the religious sanctuary at Delphi, it is called the Sacred War. Many of the war's largest battles were fought in Thessaly, where the Phocians entered the sphere of Philip of Macedon. By the end of the war in 347, both Phocis and Thebes were exhausted, and Macedon had become the dominant power over the Greek world.

Sources:

Jack Cargill, *The Second Athenian League* (Berkeley: University of California Press, 1981).

Paul Cartledge, *Agesilaos and the Crisis of Sparta* (London: Duckworth, 1987).

Xenophon, *Hellenica,* translated by Carleton L. Brownson, 2 volumes (Cambridge, Mass.: Harvard University Press, 1985–1986).

POLITICAL ASSEMBLIES OF ATHENS

Limited Democracy. Athens is considered to be the first democracy in the world. Nevertheless, full participation in it was limited to approximately thirty thousand male citizens over the age of eighteen. Women, slaves, *metics* (resident aliens), and children had only limited roles to play.

Voting. Every male citizen over age twenty, after two years of military service, could speak and vote in the *Ekklêsia* (Assembly), which met forty times a year on the Pnyx, a hill overlooking the Athenian marketplace. At least six thousand citizens attended the meetings, which generally lasted only a couple of hours. After debating motions, the Assembly members voted by a show of hands. Its *psêphismata* (votes) dictated foreign policy and major issues concerning the administration of the polis. The Assembly did not by itself institute *nomoi* (laws), but appointed panels to create legislation. It also elected the generals and could initiate political trials, such as *eisaggeliai* (impeachments).

Council. The *Boulê* (Council) consisted of five hundred members, fifty from each of the ten tribes of Athens. Each fifty-man group served as the *prutaneis* (presidents) of the polis for one-tenth of the year, with executive responsibilities and the duty to coordinate the meetings of the Council and Assembly. The Council met every day except holidays in the *bouleutêrion* (Council house) on the edge of the marketplace. It oversaw the activities of approximately six hundred minor and major magistrates who ran everything from the markets to the courts to the religious sanctuaries and festivals. It managed Athens's finances and considered in advance all motions to be put before the Assembly.

Court System. The *dikastêria* (popular courts) were selected by lot on a daily basis from a panel of six thousand who swore a special oath each year. For private disputes, panels of 201 or 401 *dikastai* (judges) were

Voting tokens with the name of the deme, or village, an abbreviation of the office, and the name of the tribe (Agora Museum, Athens)

formed; for disputes that concerned the polis, a court could have from 501 to 1,501 judges. Different disputes were allotted different amounts of time depending on their consequences, but a court could hear and decide several private disputes in a day; public disputes generally each took an entire day. After hearing the prosecution and defense present long, set speeches and then short rebuttals, the judges voted without any direction from a senior magistrate. A majority of votes cast either way decided the dispute.

Protecting the Constitution. The Council of the Areopagus consisted of all those who had served as one of the nine annually elected judicial magistrates, the six *thesmothetai* and the three archons. Before 462 B.C.E. it had wielded considerable power under its mandate "to preserve the constitution," but after this date its powers were limited to the hearing of homicide trials.

Sources:

Mogens H. Hansen, *The Athenian Democracy in the Age of Demosthenes: Structure, Principles, and Ideology,* translated by J. A. Crook (Oxford: Blackwell, 1991).

Charles Hignett, *A History of the Athenian Constitution to the End of the Fifth Century B.C.* (Oxford: Clarendon Press, 1952).

PUNISHMENT

Restitution. The most visible modern form of punishment, imprisonment, was hardly used in the ancient Greek world. The prison at Athens was used only for holding someone accused of a serious crime until his trial, or perhaps until a fine was paid or he suffered execution. Most punishments took the form of restitution, restoring to the injured person what was lost through the injury. Money was the most common form of restitution, and the Athenians decreed that if someone, for instance, stole one hundred drachmas, the restitution should be the original amount doubled. It was up to the injured party to collect the punishment. If the offender refused to pay, the injured party had to bring another suit, the result of which, if he won, would be that the punishment was again doubled. Ultimately the offender could suffer *atimia,* the loss of all civic rights, property, and the protection of the law.

Murder. Homicide and attempted homicide involved religious as well as legal issues. Once accused of murder, that is, intentional killing of a human, a person was excluded from all places of political and religious assembly, including the marketplace. His trial was held in the open air so that no one else was "polluted" through sharing the same space with him. Intentional killing with forethought was punishable by death. Killing without forethought usually resulted in atimia and exile until such time as the killer achieved a reconciliation, perhaps through a financial settlement, with the family of the victim.

Torture. For certain crimes against the state such as treason, besides *atimia* and perhaps execution, a citizen could be tortured in order to extract further information. There was a law forbidding torture of citizens, but once his civic rights were lost, a citizen also lost this protection. Whipping was the preferred method, but, in extreme cases,

A reproduction of a klepsudra (water-clock) used for timing speeches in law courts (Agora Museum, Athens)

Juror's ballots—the solid hubs were for a verdict of not guilty, while the hollow hubs were for a verdict of guilty, circa fourth century B.C.E. (Agora Museum, Athens)

people were also placed on a wheel, which ultimately could dislocate their joints.

Slaves. Since owners were legally responsible for their slaves, they could torture them or put them to death if they misbehaved. Since slaves were present at almost every occasion in Athenian society, they witnessed many things, but since they themselves were not legally responsible, they could not give testimony as witnesses in court. Instead, the two parties to the dispute would agree to methods by which the slave would be tortured. The statements that were achieved in this way were thought by the Athenians to be the most trustworthy possible.

Sources:

Douglas M. MacDowell, *The Law in Classical Athens* (Ithaca, N.Y.: Cornell University Press, 1978).

Stephen Todd, *The Shape of Athenian Law* (Oxford: Clarendon Press, 1993).

THE SECOND PELOPONNESIAN WAR

Showdown. During the Classical Period (480–323 B.C.E.) the Greeks were at war with each other at least one-third of the time. With this fact in mind it might be tempting to consider the great war between Athens with its allies and Sparta with its allies, which is often called "the Peloponnesian War," as just another among many long struggles. No doubt the brilliance of Thucydides' account of the war has contributed somewhat to heightening its profile for historians. For the Athenians, however, it taught important lessons about the nature of their democracy, its ability to conduct war, and the roles to be played by law and popular sovereignty.

An Unsteady Peace. The peace treaty concluded between Athens and Sparta in 445 interrupted hostilities without resolving the causes of the dispute between the two powers. It gave Athens a free hand to dominate its subject allies, one that it exercised quite brutally against the island of Samos in 440. Yet, in general the Athenians did not try to extend their domination over new areas. Pericles, who was both Athens's leading politician and its most authoritative general, was quite happy to let Athenians enjoy the wealth and dominance they already had. In the mid 440s he embarked on a massive building program that gave Athens the physical attributes to match its imperial power, buildings such as the Parthenon and Propylaea on the Acropolis and the *Hēphaistion* near the agora.

There is some evidence that he sent bribes to the Spartans to soften their hostility, but the Spartans themselves had little reason to react. The Athenians were not imposing on their territory. The Spartans' austere lifestyle, which included avoiding the outside world as much as possible, meant that Athens was little direct threat to them.

Political Maneuvering. Nevertheless, Sparta did lead an alliance of states known as the Peloponnesian League, which included Thebes, Corinth, and Megara. Thebes saw itself as the leader of Boeotia, which bordered on Attica, Athens's territory, and the Athenians had strong relations with the Boeotian state of Plataea, which resented Theban ambitions. Corinth also laid groundwork for war. Athens had allied itself in 434 with Corcyra, an island colony of Corinth's that lay on the route between Greece and the rich trading area of Sicily and southern Italy. The Athenians assisted the Corcyraeans in defeating the Corinthian fleet, which allowed the island to sever its ties to its mother city. Meanwhile, Potidaea, one of Athens's allies on the coast of the northern Aegean area known as the Chalcidice, was also a Corinthian colony, and it still received its annual magistrates from the mother city. The Athenians demanded that Potidaea sever these ties with Corinth. The Potidaeans refused, and they and the Corinthians appealed to Sparta for help. The Spartans probably could have been dissuaded from declaring war if Athens had softened its antagonism against Megara, whose markets it was blockading as a result of a border dispute. Nevertheless, the contemporary Athenian historian Thucydides is probably right that war could ultimately not be avoided so long as Athens's ambitions threatened the other Greeks. Modern historians have seen these ambitions in economic terms, citing Athens's needs for grain from the Black Sea, minerals from the northern Aegean, and timber from Thrace and Macedonia.

A New War. Thebes and Plataea caused the actual outbreak of war in 431. The Plataeans, after repulsing a Theban attempt to seize control of their city, massacred 180 Theban prisoners. Anticipating a reprisal, the Plateans sought Athenian help, while the Thebans turned to Sparta. Pericles dictated Athens's strategy at the beginning of the war. The Athenians would counter the Spartans' advantage in hoplite warfare by refusing to meet them on the battlefield. Instead, the Athenians would discipline their impulses to fight, abandon most of the Attic countryside, and withdraw behind the walls that connected Athens and Piraeus. The navy and trading fleets would keep the city fed and supplied. This plan would have been difficult under any circumstances, but the Athenians had not engaged in war on their own territory for over a generation, and many of the men of combat age had never experienced war of any kind. They had grown up in a city that had seen itself as the foremost power of Greece. The first two years of the war proceeded according to Pericles' plans. The Spartans invaded Attica during the campaigning season, laid the country waste, and withdrew, and the Athenian fleet sailed around the Peloponnese on raiding expeditions.

The Plague. In 430 Athens experienced something entirely unexpected: a plague. The crowded conditions of the city and a total lack of knowledge about how to deal with the disease caused the deaths of one-quarter to one-third of Athens's population, including Pericles. Despite this catastrophe, however, Athens's military situation remained much as it had been; what changed was Athens's leadership. Thucydides saw the change in moral terms, and modern historians tend to follow his assessment that Athens's political and military leadership was not up to the standard set by the great general who had given the polis over thirty years of service. The new leadership is described as being led by "demagogues" who pandered to the desires of Athens's demos.

Popular Leaders. Pericles' death in 429 brought a power vacuum in Athens. He had largely eliminated his political opponents from the scene. Capable men of the aristocracy who felt a calling to public service went into the military, where they were often away from Athens for lengthy periods, unable to build popular support with the demos. In Athens what had arisen instead was a new kind of politician, not from the traditional, landholding aristocracy, but of the demos. The new politicians gained their wealth through trade and manufacturing. Their policies were belligerent, and they appealed to the basest motives of the demos, its jealousy and rapacity. Cleon, the son of a wealthy leather tanner, was one of these new politicians.

Cleon. The historical tradition is universally hostile to Cleon. His bravado and aggressiveness were rewarded with his being able to take credit for the capture of several hundred Spartans on the island of Sphacteria in 425, which led the Spartans to sue for peace. Although the proposals were rejected, the prisoners prevented the Spartans from attacking Attica for the next four years. The Athenians responded by increasing the tribute they demanded from their allies. Attempts were even made to make incursions by land into Boeotia.

Discontent. Despite Cleon's successes, he was not able to win over everyone. Some believe that Athens, with its authority invested in an amateur, democratic assembly, had need for people such as Cleon, who devoted themselves to mastering the intricacies of the empire and its administration. As Cleon said in the Mytilenean Debate, which was recorded by the historian Thucydides, "a democracy cannot run an empire." Cleon knew how much money and resources were needed for the empire, especially for his generous doles to the jury courts. When the comic poet Aristophanes criticized him in his early plays, Cleon sued him in court.

Peace of Nicias. The deaths of Cleon and Brasidas at Amphipolis in 422 B.C.E. removed the most belligerent leaders from both Athens and Sparta. Nicias, who had made windfall profits from silver mining, took over the leadership of Athens. Although he catered to the will of the demos as much as anyone, he was sympathetic to the aristocrats and farmers who wanted peace. Since the Spartans wanted peace also, he was able to achieve a peace treaty in 421 B.C.E. without much trouble, and the peace was named for him. Although there are disputes about what was achieved in this first, ten-year part of the Peloponnesian War, it seems pretty clear that despite the losses of the plague the Athenians were the winners. All they had wanted was to continue to hold their empire, and they had achieved this goal.

Alcibiades. Yet, there were restive people in Athens, anxious to put their own mark on Athens's glory. Although Athens and Sparta had achieved a peace treaty, the issues that separated them were still present. A protégé of Pericles, Alcibiades, organized a coalition of poleis in the Peloponnese to check Sparta's dominance over that peninsula. In 418 the armies of Argos, Mantinea, and Elis fought the Spartans at Mantinea and lost. In 416 the Athenians approached the only major Aegean island that was not part of its alliance, Melos and demanded that it join. The Melians were ethnically Dorian; in fact, they were closely tied with the Spartans. They refused an Athenian ultimatum in a debate that was dramatized by the historian Thucydides as the "Melian Dialogue." After a siege the Athenians killed all the Melian men and sold their women and children into slavery.

Sicily. The expedition against Melos was only a preliminary, however, for Alcibiades' greatest ambition: the launching of a fleet to take control of the island of Sicily. Nicias opposed the expedition on the grounds that it would require too many ships, men, and resources. Although he exaggerated the numbers in an attempt to discourage the Athenians, the plan was approved anyway. To make matters worse, he was chosen, against his wishes, as one of the three generals to lead the expedition of 4,500 hoplite soldiers and 94 triremes. Nicias, Alcibiades, and Lamachus made preparations to set off on the largest naval expedition ever by any Greek polis. Shortly before the expedition left, however, accusations were made against Alcibiades that he had profaned the mystery rituals of the cult of Demeter at Eleusis by performing them as part of a drunken party. It was also taken as a bad omen that somebody cut the phalluses off of many of the small statues of the god Hermes, called "herms," that were located throughout the city.

Scandal and Defeat. Alcibiades was temporarily able to face down the accusations against him, but once the expedition was launched and he was away, they resurfaced and Alcibiades was recalled. Because so many of his political supporters were with the fleet, he knew he would have a bad time of it at home, so instead of going to Athens, he went to Argos, and eventually to Sparta. Without him, the expedition to Sicily suffered from indecisiveness. Nicias had to lead it, and he

The site of the Athenian city at Amphipolis in eastern Macedonia, captured by the Spartans in 424 B.C.E.

opposed the whole venture. The Athenians attacked Syracuse, on the eastern coast of Sicily. The Syracusans called on the Spartans for help, and they were quite happy to renew their war against Athens. By 413 B.C.E. the entire expedition to Sicily was wiped out, including further reinforcements sent out from Athens.

Decelea. Meanwhile in Sparta, Alcibiades recommended that in their renewed war the Spartans set up a permanent garrison in Athenian territory at Decelea, and they followed his advice. From Decelea the Spartans were able to continuously harass the Athenians for the next ten years, preventing them from making use of the countryside of Attica.

Oligarchy. The Sicilian disaster led to turmoil both within Athens and among its allies, who now saw the city as weak. With Persian and Spartan help many revolted. At Athens there was anger at the democratic leaders and at the fortune-tellers who had urged on the expedition. Ten men were appointed as *probouloi* (councilors) to preside over measures of economic stringency, a move taken to be a first step toward oligarchy. The reserve of one thousand talents set aside on the Acropolis was used to fund the reforms.

Persian Interference. The reasons for the move to oligarchy are explained by Thucydides. There was a perception that Athens could not survive unless the Persian king stopped financing the Spartans and began helping the Athenians. The Persian king would not act, it was argued, unless Athens adopted an oligarchic government. Alcibiades, who had fled from the Spartans and was now advising the Persian governor Tissaphernes, traveled to the island of Samos and put the plan to aristocratically minded generals such as Pisander. He hoped that the plan might bring about his return to Athens. Initially the democrats at both Samos and Athens were timid. Andro-

cles, a leading democrat who had been responsible for the exile of Alcibiades, was assassinated. The oligarchs were highly organized, employing the connections cultivated in their drinking clubs, the *hetairiai*.

The Four Hundred. A special Assembly was called outside Athens at Colonus, which voted to hand over power to a new Council of Four Hundred. The conservative politician and sophist Antiphon was in charge. The number four hundred was selected because it echoed that of the Solonian Council that predated Cleisthenes'. The new Councilors showed up at the Council House in Athens with a large, armed escort and dismissed the democratically selected Council of Five Hundred. There was a promise given that power would ultimately be in the hands of an Assembly of Five Thousand, a number limited to those who could serve the city either financially or by bearing hoplite weapons. The lower-class *thetes* who manned the fleet were thus to be excluded.

Turmoil. The oligarchs hesitated over recalling Alcibiades, so he made approaches to the democrats at Samos and took his Persian patronage with him. The oligarchs also encouraged those cities that were still subject to them to adopt similarly oligarchic governments, but they tended to revolt instead. Although the oligarchs had claimed that they would pursue the war against Sparta more efficiently than the democrats, once in power they made overtures of peace to the Spartans at Decelea. The navy at Samos elected from its numbers Thrasybulus to lead a democratic reaction. They elected Alcibiades general, who served as a conciliator. Some of the oligarchs were accused of fortifying Eitioneia, near Athens's harbor, to help a Spartan invasion. Soon the Four Hundred were deposed, and Athens was again a democracy.

Loss of Support. Led by Alcibiades, the Athenian navy achieved many successes in the years following 411 B.C.E., and the Spartans were led to offer peace. Yet, the newly restored democracy, which was under the influence of a demagogue named Cleophon, only wanted to pursue war. Alcibiades was welcomed home a hero in 407, but his popularity with Athens's fickle democracy did not last long. A subordinate officer, Antiochus, ignored Alcibiades' orders not to risk battle and was defeated. The loss was relatively insignificant, but Alcibiades was made to take the blame. He was not reelected general the next year and chose to retire.

Arginusae. Despite the loss of this great general, the Athenians enjoyed one last great victory. The Spartan commander Lysander put together a fleet of 140 ships and managed to destroy 30 Athenian ships in a battle near the island of Lesbos. In response, the Athenians took extraordinary steps to assemble the funds necessary to put together a new fleet of their own, 150 ships strong. The two fleets met at Arginusae, near the Turkish coast, and the Athenians won a decisive victory.

Executions. In the aftermath of the battle, however, a storm prevented the Athenian generals from staying to recover the dead from the twenty-five ships that were lost. The democratic Assembly responded by convicting the generals of impiety and executing them. This procedure was completely unconstitutional, as the philosopher Socrates, who happened to be one of those chairing the Assembly meeting that day, tried to point out: Athenians could not be condemned to death by the Assembly but only by a law court. The execution of the generals, one of whom was the son of the great general Pericles, had disastrous consequences for Athens's military prospects, which were already precarious after the retirement of Alcibiades. Athens simply could not afford to lose any more generals.

Aegospotami. The Spartan commander Lysander took advantage of a lapse in Athenian strategy in the Hellespont to surprise the Athenian navy and destroy it in the battle of Aegospotami in 405. Only 20 of 180 Athenian ships managed to escape, and many of them fled to Cyprus. With the loss of its fleet and 3,000–4,000 men, Athens was defenseless. Nevertheless, Lysander did not move immediately to demand Athens's surrender. Instead, he moved through the Aegean, replacing democratic governments loyal to Athens with oligarchic governments loyal to Sparta and forcing the Athenians who lived in and near the various poleis as clerychs to move back to Athens. With its grain supplies cut off by a Spartan embargo, the new arrivals simply exacerbated a famine in Athens.

The Thirty. The Athenians held out for eight months, urged on by the demagogue Cleophon; however, the city finally capitulated in 404, and its Long Walls were torn down. The Spartans were not as severe as some of their allies wanted: they were demanding Athens's total destruction. Instead, Lysander, as he had done with many of the poleis that had been Athens's allies, replaced the city-state's democratic constitution with an oligarchy of thirty select Athenians. Because of their brutal behavior toward their fellow citizens and others living in Athens, this group became despised and known simply as the Thirty or as the Thirty Tyrants.

Political Reforms. The erratic behavior of Athens's democracy in the last years of the war, as well as the fatigue caused by the war itself, must have made the change in Athens's constitution quite appealing to many Athenians. The Thirty were appointed both to run the government and to write new laws according to the *patrios politeia* (ancestral constitution), which would severely limit the franchise, essentially only to the hoplite class, and reform the courts. One of the ways for attacking political opponents in the democracy was malicious prosecution, or *sukophantia*, which the oligarchs promised to end.

Factions. There were differing views among the Thirty, however. Critias led an extremist group that wanted the franchise strictly limited to three thousand citizens and sought to purge not only the most extreme democrats and sycophants, most of whom had at any rate already fled, but also almost anyone who had prospered under the democracy, whether citizen or *metic* (*metoikos*, resident foreigner). Theramenes led a more moderate group, which was willing to broaden the franchise and rejected the wholesale violence of Critias. For his trouble, Theramenes was himself identified as an enemy of the oligarchy and executed, along with approximately 1,500 other victims of the Thirty.

Thrasybulus. A group of democratic exiles had found refuge in Thebes. In 403, led by Thrasybulus, a relatively small group set out for Athens. After defeating a small army at Phyle, on the border of Attica, Thrasybulus's group grew and moved on to Athens. The Thirty responded by stationing a Spartan garrison on Athens's Acropolis, which made the Athenians even more hostile to them. In a battle fought near Athens's port in Piraeus, Critias was killed. Led by their king Pausanias, the Spartans withdrew and, after some negotiations, a reconciliation was achieved among the Athenians. Athens's democracy was restored again.

Sources:

Walter Robert Connor, *New Politicians of Fifth-Century Athens* (Princeton: Princeton University Press, 1971).

Thucydides, *The Peloponnesian War*, translated by Rex Warner (Harmondsworth, U.K.: Penguin, 1954).

WAR ENGINES: LAND AND SEA

Siege Devices. Most Greek cities had elaborate defensive walls and were built on strategically high points. Nevertheless, the Greeks did not develop sophisticated forms of siege craft until well into the historical period. The legendary siege of Troy lasted ten years and was successful only because of the Trojan Horse, a work of deception. From the Persians, the Greeks might have learned about siege ramps and undermining, but their citizen armies did not have the time or resources for these types of activities. The Athenian general Pericles is said to have used siege devices at Samos in 440. They included rams and "tortoises," that is, shells to protect those manning the rams; however, for the most part the Athenians depended on blockades, and they took three years (432–429 B.C.E.) to capture Potidaea in this way.

Dionysius the Elder. Siege craft really developed for the first time in Sicily under Dionysius the Elder, who adopted it from the Carthaginians. In his wars against Carthage (397–396 and 392), he employed arrow-firing catapults, scaling ladders, and most important, towers on wheels. Yet, Macedonians Philip II and Alexander the Great used siege craft most effectively. They developed catapults capable of hurling stones, making it possible to smash fortified walls.

Battering Ram. The trireme was the principal warship of the ancient Greek world. It was a long rowing ship manned by 170 rowers plus 30 marines and archers. Each rower had an oar to himself, and rowers were arranged in three rows from top to bottom. Modern reconstruction and experimentation has shown that the trireme was capable of a speed of nine knots. The main weapon of this vessel was its bronze ram, which was attached to the prow and designed to strike an enemy ship at the waterline. The object was simply to punch a hole that would render the enemy ship waterlogged and unmaneuverable; it was not necessarily sunk. For longer trips sails were used, but they were generally removed and stowed on shore before a trireme went into battle.

Sources:

Lionel Casson, *Ships and Seafaring in Ancient Times* (Austin: University of Texas Press, 1994).

Arnold Walter Lawrence, *Greek Aims in Fortification* (Oxford: Clarendon Press; New York: Oxford University Press, 1979).

John S. Morrison and J. F. Coates, *The Athenian Trireme: The History and Reconstruction of an Ancient Greek Warship* (Cambridge: Cambridge University Press, 1986).

WEAPONRY

Athens v. Sparta. In his speech to the Athenians commemorating the dead who had fallen in the first year of the Second Peloponnesian War (431–404 B.C.E.), Pericles contrasted the Athenians with the Spartans, whose courage, he said, resulted from their "laborious training." Pericles passed over the fact that his own strategy dictated that the Athenians should avoid set battles with the Spartans, whom he considered to be nearly invincible. Nevertheless, the equipment that the two armies brought to the fight was similar, and quite costly, so that only those of comparatively high economic status could fight as hoplite infantry. These soldiers dominated the fighting, and thus also the politics, of the Greek world until the fourth century.

Hoplites. The hoplite wore a helmet, breastplate, greaves, and sometimes arm guards. Each hoplite fought with his shield overlapping that of his neighbor's in the phalanx, a large rectangular formation. The shield, about thirty inches in diameter, was held on the left arm by one strap around the upper forearm and the other, at the rim, held in the left hand. In his right hand the hoplite carried a spear, eight to ten feet long. It was used not for throwing but for thrusting at the enemy phalanx. The hoplite also had a short sword. The hel-

A drawing of an *oxubelês* (sharp-bolt shooter), an antipersonnel weapon of the mid-fourth century B.C.E. (Peter A.B. Smith and Malcolm Swanston)

met, breastplate, greaves, and shield were generally made of bronze, or with leather and wood covered in bronze; the sword and spear points were made of iron.

Transition. In the fourth century, with the shift from citizen to mercenary armies, the more lightly armed *peltasts* became more prevalent. Named for their small, light shield, the *peltê,* they fought with javelins rather than thrusting spears. They could not hope to defeat hoplites in open battle, but they were effective both as an advance guard and at harassing the phalanx from a distance.

Horsemen. Cavalry played only a small role in the fighting forces of the Greek *poleis.* Athens did not create a cavalry force until after the end of the Persian Wars in 479, and the Spartans had none until 424. Horses were extremely costly, and against the hoplite phalanx they were ineffective. Only the Macedonians were able to use them effectively by employing cavalry in greater numbers and arming the riders with lances rather than javelins.

Sources:

Jan G. P. Best, *Thracian Peltasts and Their Influence on Greek Warfare* (Groningen, Netherlands: Wolters-Noordhoff, 1969).

Anthony M. Snodgrass, *Arms and Armour of the Greeks* (Ithaca, N.Y.: Cornell University Press, 1967).

I. G. Spence, *The Cavalry of Classical Greece: A Social and Military History with Particular Reference to Athens* (Oxford: Clarendon Press; New York: Oxford University Press, 1993).

A vase painting of hoplites engaged in battle, circa seventh century B.C.E. (Rome, Villa Giulia. Photo: Max Hirmer)

SIGNIFICANT PEOPLE

ALCIBIADES

CIRCA 450-404 B.C.E.
ATHENIAN STATESMAN AND GENERAL

Controversy. An aristocratic protégé of Pericles and devotee of the philosopher Socrates, Alcibiades was the most flamboyant and controversial man of his times. A man of great charm and ability, he was also self-centered and unscrupulous. He came of age just as Athens appeared to have ended the Second Peloponnesian War with Sparta in 421 B.C.E. Appointed a general the next year, he renounced the Peace of Nicias and encouraged an anti-Spartan alliance between Athens, Argos, Elis, and Mantinea. When the Spartans defeated this alliance at the Battle of Mantinea in 418, Alicibiades avoided ostracism by joining with his political rival Nicias to denounce Hyperbolus, leader of the democratic faction.

Champion and Villain. Alcibiades regained popular support after he won a chariot race at Olympia in 416. The next year he persuaded Athenian leaders to authorize an expedition to Syracuse on the island of Sicily and to appoint him to joint command of the military forces; however, before the expedition set sail, a scandal occurred concerning the Hermae. Someone had mutilated these busts of Hermes, the messenger of Zeus, and in the ensuing investigation, Alicibiades was accused of being the perpetrator.

Defection. Alcibiades sailed to Syracuse while an inquiry was being made into the sacrilege. When he simultaneously received both orders to return home and information that he had been condemned to death in absentia, he made his way to Sparta, where his services were decisive in turning the tide of the war against Athens. He quickly became embroiled in more controversy by seducing the wife of King Aegis II. His attempts in 412 to instigate revolt among the Athenian settlements of Ionia failed, and he soon fled Sparta for Sardis in Asia Minor.

Recall. In 411 Athenian naval authorities requested his services, and Alcibiades redeemed himself by not only defeating the Spartan fleet at Abydos (411) and Cyzicus (410), but also by recovering the vital Black Sea grain route. He returned to Athens a hero in 407 and assumed complete control of the city's war efforts. Nevertheless, within the year Alcibiades lost popular support after a minor naval defeat and fled to Thrace. Still considered by his rivals to be a disturbing influence on Athenian politics, Alcibiades sought refuge with the Persian governor of Phrygia in Asia Minor, where he was murdered at the instigation of the Spartans.

Historical Judgment. Thucydides summed up the Athenians' attitude toward this enigmatic figure: "Although he performed his military responsibilities most favorably for the people, privately everyone objected to his behavior, and having turned their affairs over to others, they quickly destroyed their city."

Sources:

Walter M. Ellis, *Alcibiades* (London & New York: Routledge, 1989).

Plutarch, *Life Stories of Men Who Shaped History, from Plutarch's Lives* (New York: New American Library, 1950).

ALEXANDER THE GREAT

356-323 B.C.E.
KING OF MACEDON

Man and Legend. As the supremacy of the Greek polis gave way to that of Macedon, the center of political power shifted from the *agora* (marketplace) to the royal court of a single man. The accomplishment of Alexander the Great was to transform his father's dominance over Greece into an empire over the entire *oikoumenê*, or "inhabited world." The breathtaking speed with which he used his own courage and tactical brilliance to conquer the

Persian Empire have made his life almost a legend. Later philosophers and essayists like to ascribe to him a visionary ideal of a world united in language and culture. Of these things no one will ever know with great certainty.

A Promising Youth. Alexander III was born in 356 B.C.E., the son of Philip II and Olympias, who was the daughter of King Neoptolemus of Epirus. As a teenager he was tutored by the great Greek philosopher Aristotle. At the age of sixteen he showed enough martial prowess and intellect to be placed in charge of Macedon while his father attacked Byzantium. During Philip's absence he successfully quelled the Maedi, a Thracian people. At the Battle of Chaeronea in 338, he commanded the right wing of the Macedonian army and defeated the Sacred Band of Thebes.

Consolidating Power. Although Alexander the Great is rightly famous for his campaign in Asia, the beginning of his reign was devoted to asserting his right to succeed Philip, eliminating real and potential rivals, and demonstrating once again Macedon's dominance over Greece. As the only fit son of Philip, and one who had demonstrated his skills both on and off the battlefield, Alexander was really the only choice. However, his father had been assassinated, and Alexander took steps to eliminate any potential threats to himself, which was a common device in Macedonian succession. After marching south late in 336 B.C.E. to reassert his hegemony over the Corinthian League, Alexander returned in 335 to crush a revolt by the city of Thebes. He is said to have destroyed every house but that of the famous poet Pindar as a lesson to the rest of the Greeks. Alexander was clearly planning to carry out his father's ambition to attack the Persian Empire, and he did not want to worry about any further uprisings in the Greek world.

The Granicus River. When Alexander set out to cross the Hellespont into Asia Minor in the early spring of 334, it is estimated that he had about 50,000 troops, 43,000 foot soldiers, and more than 6,000 cavalry. He also had about a thirty-day supply of food, which was carried by his fleet. He depended on being resupplied from the lands that he would conquer. The Persian army took up a defensive position on the far side of the Granicus River, where steep riverbanks made it dangerous for the advancing Macedonians. However, Alexander's cavalry met this challenge and drove the Persians back from the riverbank, allowing the foot soldiers to cross the river safely. Alexander took a direct part in the cavalry fighting. He was injured and had to be rescued by his men. Nine out of ten Persians fell in the battle; the remaining two thousand were taken prisoner; and the Persian commander committed suicide. After the battle, Alexander made a point of visiting the ancient site of Troy. He wished to associate himself as much as possible with the legendary hero Achilles, who had been the greatest of the warriors fighting against Troy.

Supplies. Since he was running short of funds, Alexander sent his fleet back to Macedon. From now on his strategy was based largely on taking away the ports that the Persian navy needed, and from which it recruited its ships and men. He established himself at Ephesus, about halfway down the coast in Asia Minor, and began to lay siege to Halicarnassus to the south. The siege was successful, except for a few Persians who held out in the citadel for several months, and here Alexander adopted a method that he would use throughout his conquered territory. He reinstated a woman named Ada, whose rule had recently been usurped, and had himself adopted as her son. As with the Greeks, Alexander was able in this way to employ the form of local government that was familiar to the local people. (The Persians had also used this method on occasion.)

The Gordian Knot. During the winter of 334–333 B.C.E., Alexander dispersed his army, sending the recently married men back to Macedon, another part to Sardis, and taking most of the men south along the coast to Lycia, where it was warmer. In this way, no area was overburdened by the presence of his army. The next spring he assembled his army at Gordium, the ancient capital of Phrygia, which had reached its greatest fame under the famous King Midas in the eighth century B.C.E. In Gordium there was a famous knot of rope with an ancient prophecy: whoever could untie the rope would rule Asia. Tradition has it Alexander "cut the Gordian knot" with his sword, thus giving the source of the expression for solving unsolvable problems.

Issus. From Gordium, Alexander marched south again to the Mediterranean coast in Cilicia. Here he was delayed for several months, and he almost died from a fever. This delay gave the Persian king Darius III time to collect his forces. Like Alexander, Darius had become king in 336, and he was still consolidating his rule. Many in Darius's army were Greek mercenaries. The two armies maneuvered and delayed, each wanting to fight on a field that would give it greater advantage. Since the Persians had a much larger army, they wanted to fight on an open plain. Alexander wanted to fight in a narrow pass. As it turned out, the Persian army circled behind Alexander, and the two armies met at a relatively narrow point on the coast at Issus in late 333 B.C.E. It was a great victory for Alexander. Although they are probably exaggerated, the ancient reports say the Persians lost one hundred thousand men and the Macedonians only five hundred. Alexander's forces even managed to capture Darius's wife and mother, along with his royal camp.

Tyre and Gaza. Darius offered peace, but when Alexander demanded that Darius surrender and recognize Alexander as lord of Asia, the war had to go on. Darius had to retreat in an attempt to reorganize his armies, but Alexander did not pursue him. Instead, he continued his strategy of moving along the Mediterranean coast. Byblos and Sidon quickly surrendered, but the city of Tyre, which was situated on an island just off the coast, withheld a siege for seven months. Alexander had his men build a land bridge out to the island. When ships from Rhodes, Lycia, Byblos, Sidon, and especially from Cyprus, joined his siege, the city was finally captured. Much of the rest of 332 B.C.E. was then devoted to a siege of Gaza, further south along the coast, where Alexander was again wounded.

Alexandria. Egypt was the home of the oldest civilization in the world, and it had long resented Persian domination.

Alexander was welcomed there as Pharaoh, and after a visit to an oracle of Ammon (Zeus) at an oasis in the Libyan desert, he was recognized as a son of the god, and thus a god himself, at least in the eyes of the Egyptians. The Greeks and Macedonians in his army were not happy about Alexander's claiming to be a god, since that conflicted with their traditions, but Alexander seems to have accepted this status in the same way that he adopted the rule and customs of other peoples he had captured. In 332 on an island in the Nile River delta, Alexander also founded the first, and most successful, of many cities that he named for himself. Here he was able to settle many of his retired or disabled veterans. After Alexander's death, Alexandria became the capital of the Ptolemaic Empire, which lasted until the death of Cleopatra in 31 B.C.E.

Peace Overtures. Darius again offered peace terms: Alexander could have all the land he had conquered and a marriage alliance with the Persian king's family; however, Alexander rejected these terms too. He not only wanted revenge for the Persian attacks on Greece, but also wanted to take over the entire Persian Empire. Since the direct path to Persia would have led through an impenetrable desert in modern-day Jordan and Iraq, Alexander retraced his steps up the Mediterranean coast and crossed over modern-day Syria to the upper Tigris River.

Gaugamela. This time, when the armies met in late 331 B.C.E., Darius chose the battlefield. It was at Gaugamela, near the ancient Assyrian capital of Nineveh. The area was wide and level, and Darius even had the land smoothed out to allow for the use of special scythed chariots. They were ineffective, however, since Alexander's light foot soldiers were able to attack their horses with javelins, and the hoplite phalanxes could allow them to pass by harmlessly, kept at a distance by their long sarissas. Alexander's cavalry was able to drive a hole through the middle of the enemy lines and force the Persian king to flee. The Macedonians won another great victory. With the Persian king in flight, the great cities of the Persian Empire, with all their huge wealth, Babylon, Susa, Pasargadae, Persepolis, and Ecbatana, were now Alexander's for the taking. Nevertheless, Alexander took some time seizing these capitals. He had to be careful to keep track of the enormous wealth that now came into his possession. At Persepolis in 330 he finally let his troops help themselves: they looted the city, killed the men, and enslaved the women. As a final act Alexander burned the royal palace, which had been built during the reign of Darius I in the late sixth century B.C.E. This act was certainly a mark of retribution against the Persians.

Decisions. At this point in his campaigns, Alexander had to choose between returning to Macedon or taking the place of the Persian king and continuing his operations to the east. An Old Guard among his Macedonians wanted to return home. They saw contact with Persian culture as a corrupting influence and objected to Alexander's behaving like a Persian king. In 330 this discontent led Alexander to order a series of executions within his army.

Eastern Operations. The Persian king was taken prisoner and subsequently executed by one of his eastern governors, Bessus. Alexander now pursued this pretender to the Persian throne. When he caught him in 329, he had him brutally executed. In the eastern part of what had been the Persian Empire (modern-day Afghanistan and Pakistan), stubborn resistance by local peoples kept Alexander campaigning there for the next three years. Many of his soldiers were not happy about having to fight so far from home, and Alexander's method of settling discharged veterans in conquered cities to counter local resistance caused even more resentment.

The Hydaspes River. Alexander fought his last great pitched battle in 326 B.C.E. on the Hydaspes River against an Indian king, Poros. Here his forces even met elephants, but the result was the same: Alexander's forces won a great victory. King Poros had taken an active part in the fighting, but when he surrendered, Alexander welcomed him as a new ally. The two fought together against Poros's other enemies. Finally this situation was too much for Alexander's men. They had been away from Macedon for eight years. The clothing they had brought from home was worn out, and their equipment was rusting in the monsoon rains. Alexander agreed to turn back.

Homeward Bound. The return trip was not easy, however. As his troops traveled south along the Hydaspes River, they faced a hostile population, and Alexander was wounded by an arrow that pierced his lung. After recovering, he chose a difficult route back, through the Gedrosian Desert on the coast of the Arabian Sea. Many of his soldiers died crossing this region. Back in Persia Alexander found that those he had left in charge were mistreating the local populations, desecrating temples and tombs, and conspiring in treasonous activities. He reasserted control and executed many of the worst offenders.

Persian Influence. His own idea was to achieve a blending of cultures. He saw himself not only as king of Macedon and leader (*hêgemôn*) of Greece, but also as a successor to the kings of Persia. At Pasargadae he therefore took care to restore the plundered tomb of Cyrus the Great, the founder of the Persian Empire. At Susa he held a mass wedding between his own leading men and women of the Persian aristocracy, which was possible because Macedonians allowed polygamy. He himself married two Persian women, daughters of Darius and his predecessor, so that his children might have Persian royal pedigrees. Altogether there were some ten thousand mixed marriages that Alexander had performed, according to Persian customs. He also enlisted thirty thousand Persian youths into his army, dressing them in Macedonian uniforms and giving them Macedonian weapons.

Death. The last two years of Alexander's life were spent in Mesopotamia. There were further rebellions among his Macedonian followers because they resented being pushed aside by Persians, whom they had conquered. Alexander was able to deal with these problems through threats and bluffs. Slowly the accommodation of the two cultures to each other began to take hold. Alexander had many ambitious plans against Arabia, the western Mediterranean, and the Caspian Sea region, but in 323 B.C.E. he fell ill once more with a fever and died.

Influence. The legacy of Alexander has been enormous. The period after 323 B.C.E. is known as the Hellenistic Period because it was a time in which the language, culture, and institutions of Greece, *Hellas*, were spread throughout the Middle East. The time for the polis, however, the independent city-state that was the central political institution of the Greek world, was passed. Alexander's top generals carved up the territory he had conquered and continued to govern until the Romans and Parthians eventually pushed their successors aside centuries later.

Sources:

A.B. Bosworth, *Conquest and Empire: The Reign of Alexander the Great* (Cambridge & New York: Cambridge University Press, 1988).

Donald W. Engels, *Alexander the Great and the Logistics of the Macedonian Army* (Berkeley: University of California Press, 1978).

Peter Green, *Alexander of Macedon, 356–323 B.C.E.: A Historical Biography* (Harmondsworth, U.K.: Penguin, 1974).

John Maxwell O'Brien, *Alexander the Great: The Invisible Enemy* (London & New York: Routledge, 1992).

Plutarch, *The Age of Alexander* (Harmondsworth, U.K.: Penguin, 1973).

DEMOSTHENES

384-322 B.C.E.

ATHENIAN STATESMAN

Reputation. Demosthenes was the most important politician of fourth-century B.C.E. Athens and perhaps the greatest orator of the ancient world. Scribes at the library in Alexandria edited his manuscripts, and Roman, Medieval, and Renaissance scholars reviewed his speeches as part of their oratorical training. A contemporary of Plato and Aristotle, he overcame a speech defect by speaking with pebbles in his mouth and by reciting verse while running.

Legal Savvy. Demosthenes was the son of a sword maker. Since his father died when he was only seven, his first task once achieving legal age was to sue his guardians in order to recover his estate. The skills that he demonstrated in preparing and arguing his case before Athens's popular courts led to his being in high demand as a logographer, or speechwriter, for wealthy clients who were entangled in legal disputes. Demosthenes also began to use his skills in assisting prosecutions against public figures and then in taking on prosecutions himself.

Political Career. At the age of thirty he made his first major speech in the Assembly and soon thereafter became a leader of the popular party and chief spokesman for military preparedness. He strongly opposed the growth of Macedonian power in a series of speeches, the *Philippics* (351–341), which have become classics of political condemnation. Unfortunately, his stance on the issue of Philip II's intentions put him into conflict with the politician Aeschines, whom Demosthenes accused of being a hireling of the Macedonian king.

"On the Crown." After the Macedonians defeated the Athenians and Thebans at the Battle of Chaeronea in 338, Demosthenes came under increasing political attack. Eight years later in the speech "On the Crown," he eloquently replied to Aeschines' charges of cowardice and malfeasance. It is considered by many historians to be the greatest oration ever made in antiquity. (The name of the speech comes from an attempt by Demosthenes' supporters to have him awarded a gold crown for his public service.) As a result of this speech, Aeschines lost popular support and had to go into exile.

Downfall. In 323, Demosthenes was again accused of accepting a bribe. The circumstances of the case are still unclear, but there is some speculation that Demosthenes intended to use the money for civic purposes. This time he was convicted, fined fifty talents, and imprisoned. He escaped from prison and went into exile. The next year he committed suicide in order to avoid capture by Antipater, the successor of Alexander.

Sources:

Werner Jaeger, *Demosthenes: The Origin and Growth of His Policy* (Berkeley: University of California Press, 1938).

James J. Murphy, ed., and John J. Keaney, trans., *Demosthenes On the Crown: A Critical Case Study of a Masterpiece of Ancient Oratory* (New York: Random House, 1967).

PERICLES

CIRCA 495-429 B.C.E.

ATHENIAN STATESMAN

Family Influence. Combining the legislative ability of Solon, the economic understanding of Peisistratus, the political instincts of Cleisthenes, and the military genius of Themistocles, Pericles was the consummate politician of Athens's democracy. He was an Alcmaeonid, a member of one of Athens's most prestigious, and controversial, families. (Some claimed the Alcmaeonids were cursed from their ancestors' involvement in the massacre of the followers of the conspirator Cylon in 632 B.C.E.) His father, Xanthippus, played an important role in Greece's defense against the Persians but was overshadowed by Themistocles, who had once engineered his ostracism.

Man of the People. Pericles began his political career by joining in the prosecution of the statesman and general Cimon, but after Ephialtes' assassination in 462 B.C.E., he assumed the leadership role of the democratic faction in Athens. He championed the rights of the lower class and undertook various legislative measures that gave Athens's citizens more effective control of their government and law courts. Pericles also supported a building program that enhanced the city's beauty and provided a great deal of employment. (Among the edifices erected under his direction were the Acropolis, Parthenon, Propylaea, and Odeon.) He was able to maintain the confidence of the people well enough so that, after having his leading opponent ostracized, he was able to be elected general fifteen years running. He also manipulated Athens's enemies into fighting only when he felt Athens was really ready.

Intellectual. Although Pericles was married to an Athenian woman, his long relationship with Aspasia, a Milesian, is more famous. Together they were the center of an intellectual circle that included the sophist Anaxagoras and the sculptor Pheidias. At times, he had to take steps to defend both of these men in the courts because of some of their revolutionary ideas.

The Plague. During the early stages of the Second Peloponnesian War, Pericles strove to secure Athens's cultural and political leadership in Greece. He expanded Athenian naval forces, reinforced settlements abroad, and improved the defenses of Athens and the port of Piraeus by constructing the third Long Wall. Stricken by the plague in 430, he died the next year. The historian Thucydides, a great admirer of Pericles, summarized his influence this way:

> By his standing, judgement and financial integrity, Pericles was able freely to control the multitude and to lead them instead of being led by them because he never acquired power by improper means. He was never forced to say anything for their pleasure, but, on the contrary, had so high an estimation that he could say something against them that resulted in anger. Whenever he saw them emboldened at the wrong time and through arrogance, he would reduce them to fear with his words; on the other hand, if they were irrationally frightened, he could at once restore them to boldness. It became in name a democracy, but in fact rule by the first man whom the people trusted.

Sources:

Cecil Maurice Bowra, *Periclean Athens* (London: Weidenfeld & Nicolson, 1971).

A. R. Burn, *Pericles and Athens* (London: English Universities Press, 1948).

PHILIP II

382-336 B.C.E.

KING OF MACEDON

Beginnings. Philip II, or Philip of Macedon, was born in 382 B.C.E. As a boy he spent time in Thebes during the height of that city's power. (He was actually a hostage to assure his people's friendliness to the Thebans.) He first came to power in 359 B.C.E. after his brother was killed in battle against the Illyrians, the inhabitants of modern-day Albania.

Rising Power. For several years after his accession and reorganization of his armies, Philip was engaged in securing his northern and western borders. He also took advantage of Athens's difficulties in its Social War (357–355 B.C.E.) to capture Amphipolis, which held a strategically important location on the river Strymon. Since the Macedonians practiced polygamy, he made several marriage alliances, one of which to Olympias, a niece of the king of Epirus, who bore him a son, the future Alexander the Great. One of his most important ventures brought him the region known as the Krenides, which he reorganized under the name Philippi, after himself, and colonized with Macedonians. Philippi was rich in gold mining, and provided Philip with a vital supply of bribe money, which he was able to use effectively.

Peace of Philocrates. Philip entered the Sacred War between Thebes and Phocis in 353. After an initial setback, he won a great victory in 352 in the Battle of the Crocus Field, which gained him control of Thessaly, an area rich in agriculture and in cavalry. From there he besieged Olynthus in 349, the most important city on the northern peninsula known as the Chalcidice. Despite several speeches to the Athenian Assembly, urging the Athenians to come to the aid of Olynthus, the Athenian orator Demosthenes was unsuccessful and Olynthus capitulated. Athens had officially been at war with Philip since his seizure of Amphipolis in 357, but except for patrolling the Aegean coast and checking the Macedonian advance into central Greece at Thermopylae in 352, the Athenians had been unwilling to take decisive action against Philip's increasing power. Demosthenes' political opponent Eubulus had made it illegal even to propose using the state's funds for any military expedition unless Athens itself was directly threatened. Demosthenes finally had to urge support of peace negotiations with Philip, which were concluded in 346 as the Peace of Philocrates.

Political Machinations. Some Athenians, notably the intellectual Isocrates, saw Philip as the true leader of a united Greece and urged him to use persuasive tactics to unify Greece for a renewed campaign against Persia. Demosthenes, however, regarded Philip as a threat both to Athens and to the entire Greek political culture that had endured since the eighth century B.C.E. Philip was an autocrat, and he represented a dictatorial form of politics that was quite foreign to the Greek world. For instance, he arbitrarily moved great portions of his Macedonian population into new settlements in order to achieve his economic and strategic goals. Isocrates seems to have had little trouble accommodating himself to such a culture, but Demosthenes saw no compromise.

Confrontation. In 342 B.C.E. Philip began a campaign to the east of Macedonia, going beyond Amphipolis and Philippi to subdue all of Thrace. While besieging Byzantium, near the entrance to the Black Sea, Philip intercepted 230 grain ships, 180 of which were destined for Athens. Because of this direct attack on Athens's vital food supply, Demosthenes was finally able to rouse the Athenians to decisive action, and the Persians also joined in. They saw which direction Philip's campaigns were heading. Nevertheless, Philip was not greatly worried. He turned his attention first to his northern borders and attacked the Scythians, where he was injured.

Chaeronea. By 338 Philip had recovered and Demosthenes had managed to put together a coalition of almost all the Greek poleis, including Sparta, Corinth, and Thebes, as well as Athens. But at the Battle of Chaeronea, near Thebes, the coalition army was no match for Philip's seasoned troops, and his cavalry, led by his son, Alexander, was able to annihilate the Theban Sacred Band, the Greeks' best fighters. Philip's highly maneuverable phalanxes then defeated the largely defenseless Athenian hoplites. Demosthenes himself was among them, but he escaped to attempt to fortify Athens's defenses.

League of Corinth. As it turned out, Philip did not need to attack Athens; the city surrendered. Philip might have been much more vindictive to the Athenians, but the city still had something he did not—a fleet. He did not want it to fall into the hands of the Persians. He imposed a new political order on the Greeks, however, the League of Corinth, a sort of federated state with Philip himself as its *hêgemôn* (leader). Philip had plans to attack the Persian Empire, so he needed Greek help. He guaranteed the Greek poleis freedom in the running of their own affairs and in commerce so long as they accepted his hegemony. Shortly before the Battle of Chaeronea, the king of Persia had been assassinated, and the instability of the Persian Empire made it a good time for Philip to attack the Persians. A year later, in 337, the *Sunedrion*, or Congress, of the League of Corinth declared war on Persia, and Philip sent an advance force to prepare the way for an invasion; however, internal politics got in the way. In 336 Philip was assassinated by a fellow Macedonian, as a result of court intrigues and jealousies.

Assessment. Within a twenty-three-year period, Philip of Macedon had gained control of Greece and the Balkan peninsula through a skillful use of warfare and diplomacy. He transformed a disunited, semibarbarous Macedon into a rich, powerful kingdom and established the Macedonian army as a professional fighting force. After his death his first son, Alexander III, would make Macedon into the dominant military and political power of the Mediterranean world.

Sources:

Eugene N. Borza, *In the Shadow of Olympus: The Emergence of Macedon* (Princeton: Princeton University Press, 1990).

George Cawkwell, *Philip of Macedon* (London & Boston: Faber & Faber, 1978).

John R. Ellis, *Philip II and Macedonian Imperialism* (London: Thames & Hudson, 1976).

Raphael Sealey, *Demosthenes and His Time: A Study in Defeat* (New York: Oxford University Press, 1993).

SOLON

CIRCA 630–CIRCA 560 B.C.E.
ATHENIAN STATESMAN, POET

Respect. Although Solon was born into a noble family, he was a man of moderate means. He appears to have been a respected merchant whom the people trusted. Around 600 B.C.E. he distinguished himself by publicly reciting a poem that inspired the Athenians to capture Salamis from the Megarians. When competing groups in Athens were about to fall into civil war six years later, they turned to Solon to rule and reconcile them.

Archon. Solon became archon during a period of acute political and economic distress in Athens, and for that reason he was given broad powers to initiate reforms. He ended the practice of Athenians's falling into slavery as a result of their debts and reorganized the government, basing it on wealth rather than birth. He wrote laws that were inscribed for all to see and permitted anyone who wished to seek legal compensation from those who wronged them. In his most important contribution to the development of democracy, he allowed any magistrate's or council's decision to be appealed to a court of law, which was manned by a randomly selected group of Athenians.

Exile. Many of the reforms implemented by Solon were bitterly opposed by certain elements in the city. In order to avoid becoming a tyrant or giving into the temptation of undoing his own reforms, Solon left Athens for a period of ten years. He traveled to Egypt, Cyprus, and Lydia before returning home, where he found the citizenry divided into regional factions. Solon died around 560, at roughly the same time his friend Peisistratus seized power.

Poetry. Solon is known as one of the Seven Wise Men of Greece and is considered to be the first great poet of Athens. In fact, he used poetry a great deal to publicize his efforts, as is seen below:

> I gave to the people as much wealth as sufficient
> Without minimizing or expanding their honor;
> Those having power and respected for their possessions
> To them also I decreed nothing unfair.
> I stood holding a strong shield toward both
> And allowed neither an unjust victory.

Sources:

Emily Katz Anhalt, *Solon the Singer: Politics and Poetics* (Lanham, Md.: Rowman & Littlefield, 1993).

Kathleen Freeman, *The Work and Life of Solon* (Cardiff: University of Wales Press Board; London: H. Milford, 1926).

Ivan M. Linforth, *Solon the Athenian* (Berkeley: University of California Press, 1919).

William John Woodhouse, *Solon the Liberator* (London: Oxford University Press & H. Milford, 1938).

THEMISTOCLES

CIRCA 524-460 B.C.E.
ATHENIAN STATESMAN AND NAVAL COMMANDER

Hero or Villain? The most controversial figure in the Greeks' struggle against the Persians was Themistocles. One historian, Herodotus, accused him of corruption; another, Thucydides, admired him for his far-sightedness and thought him one of the greatest men of his generation. Whatever the historical verdict, Themistocles is one of several Athenian leaders whose great accomplishments only seem to have foreshadowed their downfall at the hands of the people.

Early Life. Historians believe that the family origins of Themistocles made him have strong democratic sympathies. While his father, Neocles, belonged to the aristocratic Lycomid family, his mother was a concubine and possibly not even Greek. As a result, Themistocles did not receive citizenship until 508, when Cleisthenes made it possible for all free men in Athens to become citizens.

Naval Program. In 493 he was elected archon and soon thereafter initiated a series of naval reforms. He ordered the development of the harbor at Piraeus and in 482 requisitioned a large surplus of silver for the enlargement of the fleet to two hundred triremes. In 480 he interpreted a saying of the oracles of Apollo that predicted Greek victory over the Persians so long as the Greeks put faith in Athens' "wooden wall," its fleet of ships. He commanded the combined Greek navy at the Battle of Artemisium, and although it had to retreat, the fleet inflicted heavy losses upon the Persians. Later that same year at Salamis, Themistocles won a stunning victory when he lured the Persians into narrow straits where their superior numbers only caused confusion. He gained tremendous honors around the Greek world for these accomplishments.

Ostracism. Despite this glory, within ten years Themistocles lost favor with the people. His plans to move the capital to Piraeus and to reduce the powers of the Areopagus met with resistance, and he was ostracized from Athens. He lived in Argos for some time, but when evidence appeared that he might be conspiring with the Persians, he was condemned to death by the Spartans. He fled first to the west and then to the east. In a strange twist of events, he finally found refuge with the king of Persia, his former enemy, who made him a provincial governor of several Greek cities in Asia Minor.

Sources:

A. R. Burn, *Persia and the Greeks: The Defence of the West, c. 546–478 B.C.E.* (New York: St. Martin's Press, 1962).

Peter Green, *The Year of Salamis, 480–479 B.C.E.* (London: Weidenfeld & Nicolson, 1970).

Herodotus, *The Histories,* translated by W. Blanco and J. Roberts (New York: Norton, 1992).

Thucydides, *The Peloponnesian War,* translated by Rex Warner (Harmondsworth, U.K.: Penguin, 1954; revised, 1972).

DOCUMENTARY SOURCES

Aristotle, *Constitution of Athens* (circa 335 B.C.E.)—Aristotle was one of the greatest philosophers of all time. He and his students gathered huge amounts of information on everything from plants and animals to poetry and politics. For his research on politics, his team compiled more than 150 *politeiai* (constitutions) of different cities. A *politeia* is really a description of a political system, and the only one of Aristotle's collection that survives is that of Athens. It consists both of a history of Athens down to 403 B.C.E. and a description of the city's government and legal system in the fourth century B.C.E.

Herodotus, *History of the Persian Wars* (circa late fifth century B.C.E.)—written by the "father of history," this account describes Greek and Persian civilizations and the wars fought between them from 490 to 479 B.C.E. Herodotus was a lively writer and storyteller and his work includes a great deal of information that other scientific historians did not consider to cover. He saw history in moral terms: humans must pay for their arrogance. Although a Greek, he was a great admirer of the Persians, and his account is remarkably unbiased.

Homer, *Iliad* and *Odyssey* (circa eighth-seventh centuries B.C.E.)—toward the end of the eighth century B.C.E., poetry that had been composed and transmitted orally for several generations was finally compiled, and scholars credit Homer as its author, although it may have been the work of many poets. *Iliad* tells the story of Achilles, the best of the Greek warriors, assembled in the legendary war against Troy. *Odyssey* describes the voyage home of Odysseus, one of the other Greek warriors at Troy. While these Homeric epics describe legendary events that occurred long before their own time, they also reveal much about the period in which they were composed.

Plutarch, *Parallel Lives*—more than four centuries after the height of Greek civilization, Plutarch (circa 46–circa 120 C.E.) wrote an enormous number of philosophical essays and biographies of famous Greek and Romans. He used a wide range of sources and detailed many events that scholars might not otherwise have known about. His primary contribution as a biographer was in exemplifying various moral behaviors and their significance, rather than historical events.

Thucydides, *History of the Peloponnesian War*—without his skills as an historian, the war between Athens and Sparta (431–404 B.C.E.) that Thucydides describes would never have gained the significance that it has for historians of the ancient world. An Athenian who even served as a general in the war, he describes with insight and complexity the year-by-year progress of the conflict from its beginnings until the year 411. Historians believe that Thucydides wrote his manuscript while he was in exile in Corinth between 423 and 403 but died before completing it.

Xenophon, *Hellenica*—A student of Socrates and a disgruntled Athenian aristocrat who lived most of his adult life among the Spartans, Xenophon took up the narrative of Greek history where Thucydides stopped in 411 and continued it through to 362. Without the charm of Herodotus or the skill of Thucydides, he pursued his own interests in this text, often portraying the Athenians in a negative light while extolling the achievements of the Spartans. As a result, his history is spotty at best, but it is the most important source for the first half of the fourth century B.C.E. (Xenophon is better known as one of the generals who led ten thousand Greek mercenaries out of Asia Minor in 401.)

The speaker's platform on the Pnyx, a hill where legislation was proposed to the Athenian assembly four times a month (Hassia)

First page of the *editio princeps* (1502) of Herodotus's *History of the Persian Wars* (courtesy of the Lilly Library, Indiana University)

CHAPTER SEVEN

LEISURE, RECREATION, AND DAILY LIFE

by JEFFREY S. CARNES

CONTENTS

CHRONOLOGY

208

OVERVIEW

211

TOPICS IN LEISURE, RECREATION, AND DAILY LIFE

Climate and Landscape 212
Clothing and Adornment 213

A Mark of Civilization 218
Food 219
Dangerous Sport. 223
Games 224
Athletes 225
Weaving 228
Housing 229
Female Excellence 231
Leisure and Festivals 233
Symposia 235

DOCUMENTARY SOURCES

238

Sidebars and tables are listed in italics.

800-600* B.C.E.

- Long hair is in fashion for men. This distinctive trait was mentioned in the *Iliad* (circa eighth–seventh centuries B.C.E.), where Homer refers to the Greeks as the "flowing-haired Achaians."

800*

- The Greek diet is based heavily on grains such as wheat and barley, supplemented by such foodstuffs as fish, olives, legumes, onions, garlic, cabbage, artichokes, nuts, and figs. Red meat and dairy products are not popular. The favorite beverage is wine, which is made when grapes are crushed and left to ferment in large jars; the resulting liquid has a 14 percent alcohol content.

- The typical Greek house has a simple design: a series of small rooms situated around a courtyard. The foundation is made of stone while the walls are either stone or brick covered with plaster. Windows are few and the second story is accessible only by a ladder. The *andrôn*, or men's space, is used for dining and entertainment purposes, while women are confined to their own quarters known as the *gunaikeion*.

- Interior decorations include bronze plaques, embroideries, tapestries, and wall paintings. Popular pieces of furniture are the *klismos*, or easy chair, and the *klinê*, a combined bed and couch.

776

- The first Olympic Games are held and include boxing, discus, javelin throwing, the long jump, running, and wrestling . The games were celebrated in honor of Zeus at Olympia and are held in the summer every four years. (The system of dating historical events with reference to the recurring four-year cycle of the Olympics develops much later.)

700*

- Honey becomes a popular sweetener among the Greeks, and they make beehives out of terracotta, wood, and reeds.

- The Eastern practice of lying down while eating is popular among the Greeks.

600*

- The *himation* (similar to a Roman toga) and the short Doric *khitôn* (a thigh-length tunic put on like a shirt) become standard dress for men. Beforehand, men wore the Ionic *khitôn*, which reached to the ankles.

582

- Athletic contests are added to the Pythian Games, which were originally musical competitions. Dedicated to Apollo, the Pythian Games quickly become one of the most prestigious Greek festivals. They are held at Delphi and occur in the summer of the third year of the Olympiad cycle.

* Denotes circa date

- The first Isthmian Games are held in Corinth. They are dedicated to Poseidon and occur every two years in the spring.

573

- The Nemean Games are founded at the city of Nemea at Argos; they are held every two years in honor of Zeus.

566

- Athletic competitions are added to the Panathenaic Festival held every summer to honor the goddess Athena. Other Athenian celebrations include two dedicated to Dionysus, one in the winter (Anthesteria) and the other in early spring (City Dionysia), and a women's autumn festival honoring Demeter (Thesmophoria).

480*

- Popular Greek games include "Odd and Even," played with small objects; dice games; *pessoi,* similar to checkers or chess; and *kottabos,* a drinking game in which a contestant attempts to hit targets with the contents of his wine cup.

430-429

- The Great Plague occurs in Athens. The poor sanitation and crowded housing conditions of the city help spread this and other infectious diseases.

400*

- Urban planning begins in many Greek city-states. Newly founded towns and those undergoing extensive rebuilding lay out streets in a grid pattern. In addition, there is improved treatment of waste, including underground sewage systems and, in some cases, indoor plumbing.

- The himation becomes fashionable for women, replacing the *peplos* (a rectangular garment wrapped around the body). From this point on men and women wear similar outer garments.

- Silk production occurs in Greece with the first garments originating on the Ionian island of Cos.

- Exercise is considered an important aspect of leisure time. The *gumnasion* (exercise area) and *palaistra* (wrestling area) are located near natural springs or brooks to allow men to bathe and share camaraderie.

380-360*

- Plato writes his *Symposium.* This work, in addition to providing information about the sort of activities that went on at all-male symposia, discusses desire, knowledge, and philosophy. Other ancient Greek authors soon adopt the practice of creating fictitious symposium conversations.

- Xenophon's *Symposium* is written around the same time, and although it is less interesting as a literary and philosophical work than Plato's *Symposium*, it shows a more typical dinner party, with drinking and entertainment being as important as serious conversation.

340*

- Clean-shaven faces become fashionable for men. Up until this point, a variety of beard styles (from full to severely trimmed) had been in vogue.

The view southward from the citadel of Mycenae (Nico Mavroyenis for BBC)

OVERVIEW

Climate and Landscape. The physical environment had profound effects on Greek daily life. The type of weather and terrain dictated the needs for clothing and housing and the availability of certain types of food. A mild climate encouraged outdoor social activities and recreation while the mountains caused independent city-states to arise on the plains.

Clothing. The Greeks used a variety of fabrics for clothing, with wool being the most readily available. Outer garments included the *himation* and the *peplos,* while the *khitôn* was the primary undergarment. Sandals were popular footwear and although many people went bareheaded, some hats such as the *pilidion* and *petasos* were used. In the Archaic Period (700–480 B.C.E.) long hair was fashionable for men but became gradually less so by the fifth century. Women's hair was long throughout the period 800–323 B.C.E., and female beauty was considered enhanced by cosmetics of white lead and orchids and assorted pins, brooches, and other jewelry.

Food. The Greek diet was relatively simple. Grains were the most important part of the fare while legumes represented a good source of protein. Olive oil supplied the necessary oils and fats. Except for cheese, dairy products were not a major part of the diet. Meat was a luxury for many people and fish was a favorite treat, although not a significant component of people's diets. The ancient Greeks also ate various vegetables, fruits, nuts, and seasonings. Their favorite beverage was wine.

Games. The Greeks engaged in a variety of leisure activities. Children played with yo-yos while adults had board games such as *pessoi* (which resembled checkers) and various games of chance. Baths, the *gumnasion* (exercise ground), and the *palaistra* (wrestling area) promoted physical training and provided places to socialize. The gumnasion in particular had an erotic role, but eventually its status changed to a place for discussions of philosophy (the schools of both Plato and Aristotle were based in *gumnasia*). Athletic competitions included running, combat sports, throwing and jumping, and equestrian events.

Housing and Furniture. Greek houses were made primarily of stone, clay, and timber. The standard layout of a house was a series of rooms arranged around a courtyard. The Greeks carefully divided their houses into male and female spaces, with special rooms accorded to each sex. The basic types of furniture included chairs and *klinai,* which served as both beds and couches.

Leisure and Festivals. The Greeks had poor timekeeping skills, and the inability to measure precise, consistent divisions of the day affected the rhythm of daily life. Nevertheless, this lack of knowledge did not prohibit the Greeks from holding complex religious and civic festivals. These events served not only to affirm community and religious values, but as festive and often wild occasions, they were a main source of entertainment in the Greek world. Major celebrations included the Panathenaia, Anthesteria, Thesmophoria, and City Dionysia.

Symposia. The word *symposium* comes from the Greek *sumposion,* literally meaning a drinking party. Symposia were perhaps the most complex and interesting of all leisure-time activities. Strictly for men, the symposium had specific guidelines that determined the physical layout of the room (diners reclined on couches), the types of entertainment provided, the amount and type of drinking that went on, and games played by participants.

TOPICS IN LEISURE, RECREATION, AND DAILY LIFE

CLIMATE AND LANDSCAPE

Needs of the People. Perhaps the single biggest factor influencing the daily life of Greece was the climate. Climate determined the sort of vegetation that grew wild, the number and types of trees available, and the sorts of plants and animals that could be cultivated. It affected the needs of the population (demand) and determined as well the ways in which they could meet those needs (supply). Climate influenced demand by determining how much clothing and what kind of shelter would be necessary to protect people from the elements, and also determined how much food would be necessary to sustain life. As for supply, climate determined the sorts of materials available for building, the fibers available for clothing, and the types of foods that were available. Beyond these areas, the effects of climate could be subtle and far-ranging: for example, health is affected by certain types of diet; and the amount of leisure time available in a given society will be influenced by the type of farming that is done and by the amount of surplus food that can be accumulated.

Rainfall and Temperature. The climate of Greece has changed little in the last 2,500 years. (Evidence for this lack of change comes from ancient sources discussing the plants native to the region, which are generally the same ones that flourish there today.) The climate is a type known as "Mediterranean," characterized by cool, wet winters and hot, dry summers, and is similar to the present-day climate of Southern California. More specifically, this term describes a climate in which there is enough rainfall to support dry-farming (i.e., farming without irrigation) in most years; forests are limited in size and density; at least two-thirds of the annual precipitation falls during the winter months of the year; and the summer typically features a prolonged dry spell. For Athens, the average annual precipitation is approximately fifteen inches (thirty-eight centimeters), with 80 percent of that total from October through March. (Los Angeles has a nearly identical amount and seasonal distribution; by way of contrast, temperate-zone U.S. cities such as New York and Houston have rainfall totals averaging forty-eight inches per year, distributed more or less evenly throughout the year.) High temperatures in Athens average eighty-six degrees Fahrenheit (thirty Celsius) from June to September, and fifty-eight (fifteen Celsius)

from October to March; more significantly, the average winter lows are in the mid-forties, and the lowest recorded temperatures are barely below freezing. Thus, frost is not often a problem, allowing the cultivation of frost-sensitive plants such as the olive tree.

Droughts and Famine. More serious in terms of their implications for agriculture are the timing and variability of the rain. Much of the rainfall occurs in short, intense bursts, so that there is a high degree of runoff and the rain is of less help to plants than it might otherwise be. In addition, there is always a high degree of annual variation in the amount of rainfall. While true of any climate, this tendency is aggravated in low-rainfall areas and could be disastrous. Droughts and attendant crop failures were fairly common (although large-scale famine was rare, and usually the result of political causes such as warfare rather than climate), and farming was always a risky enterprise.

Mountains and the Sea. The landscape of Greece is primarily mountainous: there are many small mountain chains, with occasional higher peaks such as Mt. Olympus (9,500 feet). Settlement took place in the plains and sheltered areas between the mountains, a fact which had a profound influence on the development of small, independent *poleis* (city-states). Yet, the landscape had important influences on climate, and thus on daily life as well. For one thing, most rainfall was brought by west winds, which made the eastern parts of Greece (including Attica) somewhat drier than the West and North. For another, the presence of the sea (almost no place on the Greek mainland is more than thirty miles from the sea) acted as a moderating influence on the climate, keeping temperatures within a narrower range than they otherwise would have been.

Greek Character. Greece is a land of stunning natural beauty and a mild climate that encourages life outdoors, so that even leisure time took place outside (at least for men). It was not unusual, then, for Greek thinkers to speculate upon the effects that climate had on the Greek character; and, not surprisingly, to find that their climate somehow made them better than other peoples. Thus, Aristotle found that non-Greek Europeans, due to living in a cold climate, were "full of spirit, but rather lacking in intelligence and skill," while Asians were "better furnished with intelligence and

The sanctuary of Apollo at Delphi (Max Seidal, Mittenwald)

skill, but lack spirit, and for this reason remain slaves." Greeks, however, "living in the middle, have a share of both characteristics, of spirit and intelligence. For this reason they remain free, and have the best political institutions." While scholars would not wish to go so far as Aristotle in saying that climate determined national character, it is hard to overstate the extent to which climate shaped the daily life and routines of most Greeks.

Sources:
Robin Osborne, *Classical Landscape with Figures* (London: G. Philip, 1987).
Robert Sallares, *Ecology of the Ancient World* (Ithaca, N.Y.: Cornell University Press, 1990).
Anthony M. Snodgrass, *An Archaeology of Greece* (Berkeley: University of California Press, 1987).

CLOTHING AND ADORNMENT

Seasons. Keeping warm in most parts of Greece was a problem only in winter, and even then not an especially difficult one, with temperatures rarely approaching freezing. Protection from the sun was more of a problem, but it too was easily accomplished. The absolute need for clothing, then, was relatively small, and its production and use was driven much more by fashion than necessity.

Wool. Most Greek clothing was made of wool, for reasons having to do with economics, technology, and climate.

Wool is warm and water-resistant: to this day it is the best natural fiber for warmth, and its ability to wick away moisture makes it suitable for warm weather as well. The climate of Greece is well-suited not only for humans wearing wool, but also for its original wearers, the sheep. These animals can survive on fairly poor, semiarid pasture land that is incapable of supporting farming (they were, of course, an important source of food as well). For this reason wool was readily available; in addition, it is easy to spin, making it far easier to produce than cotton or silk. Thus, it was far cheaper than other fabrics. Selective breeding took place to improve the quality of wool, and certain regions, such as Miletus, had an especially good reputation for wool production. Goathair was occasionally used as well.

Other Materials. Other fabrics played a minor role. Linen, cultivated in Greece as early as 1200 B.C.E., was fairly common and was used for some tunics and undergarments, since it was less scratchy than wool. It was, however, less durable and more difficult to produce. The stems of the flax plant were dried in the sun, then soaked in water, then dried again, and then beaten with a mallet to separate the husks from the fibers; only then were the fibers ready for weaving. Silk was used as a luxury fiber: the earliest silk known in the Classical world was found in an upper-class grave in Athens, dating to around 400 B.C.E. It was proba-

Marble statues of a woman wearing a *peplos* (a variation of the *khitôn*) and a man wearing a *himation*
(Stadtische Museen, Frankfurt/Main)

bly not imported from China, but instead the product of wild silkmoths on the Greek island of Cos (in the Eastern Aegean). Leather was the usual material for shoes and was used as well for armor, including breastplates and shields. Furs and skins, while readily available, played almost no role in standard Greek dress. They could be used to keep warm in an emergency (the climate did not require their regular use), or by rustics. Wearing fur—especially that of exotic, wild animals—was the mark of the foreign, barbaric, or heroic. Thus, the *maenads*, legendary followers of the god Dionysus, dressed themselves in fawn- and panther-skins; and Heracles wore the skin of the Nemean lion he had slain. Cotton was unknown until Hellenistic times, when its cultivation spread from India into Egypt.

Production. Spinning and weaving were of great economic and symbolic significance for women. Clothing production began with removing the wool from the sheep, which was often accomplished by plucking rather than shearing. The raw wool would then be treated to remove dirt, burrs, and lanolin (an oil, now used as an ointment), combed through and made into balls, dyed, and then spun. To spin, one used a spindle—a tapered rod, made of wood or bone, with a weight at the larger end to increase the momentum of the spindle. The unspun fiber was placed on a shorter rod known as a distaff; the weaver would draw out a few fibers from the wool on the distaff, attach them to the spindle, and let the spindle spin. The weight and rotation of the spindle added twist to the yarn, greatly increasing its strength.

Looms. The spun yarn was then woven on a loom. Until the Roman period, looms varied little in design: they consisted of two upright posts with a transverse beam running across them at the top. Looms typically were leaned up against the wall, rather than being suspended from the ceiling. The individual threads of the warp were attached to the crossbeam, with weights at the bottom to make them hang straight. Horizontal rods were placed through them so that they would alternately be in front of and behind the rods: this allowed the cross-fibers (the weft) to be woven alternately over and under the warp, using a shuttle which was dragged across horizontally. Periodically, a comb would be used to push the weft threads upward to pack them in more tightly.

Dyes. Another advantage to wool is that it takes dyes well, and could be dyed in the fleece before being spun (making it possible to dye large batches conveniently). A variety of sources were used for dyes, including plants, insects, and shellfish. In many cases the wool needed to be treated with special agents (such as iron or alum) for the dyes to hold, and dyeing was normally done by skilled craftspeople. The most famous and expensive dye was the purple derived from whelks (a type of shellfish), known as *porphura*, from which the word *purple* is ultimately derived. Originally developed by Phoenicians from the city of Tyre, this dyeing process was later duplicated in Greek cities, and many cheaper substitute purples were developed. The different shades (ranging from violet to scarlet) remained the most sought-after colors for Greek clothing and other textiles, although the association of purple with social status never became as strong in Greece as it did in Rome.

Patterns. Weaving technique, even in the earliest periods, was quite advanced. It was possible, for example, to produce intricate patterns in a weave by varying the color of the yarn. In Homer's *Iliad* (circa eighth-seventh centuries B.C.E.), Helen "weaves a great web, a red folding robe," and works "into it the numerous struggles of Trojans, breakers of horses, and Achaians, struggles that they endured for her sake at the hands of the war god." Although not much cloth has survived from classical Greece (there is more from the Roman period), depictions of intricately patterned clothing (especially that designed for choruses in drama) reveal the skill of ancient weavers. (Intricate designs could also be embroidered, although this was less common.) Professional weavers, or highly trained slaves, would produce these complex patterns; most clothing, however, was homemade, produced by the women or slaves of the household that wore it. In these cases patterns would be simpler, consisting of geometric shapes or bands of color; many garments, especially those worn by men, were plain and undyed.

Cleaning. Clothing was most often washed in water, but could also be taken to the fuller for cleaning. This process would involve treading it underfoot in a mixture of water, urine, and fuller's earth, then rinsing it in tanks. (A similar process was used to treat wool cloth prior to wearing.) It was normal to patch and repair clothing instead of discarding it: given the scarcity of material goods and the lack of annual changes in fashion, most items of clothing were probably in use for many years.

Types of Clothing. Greek clothing was loose rather than formfitting, and was usually made of large pieces of cloth that were woven into their desired shape rather than tailored. Greek apparel may be divided into two basic types: that which was draped (*periblêma*, literally, "thrown around"), and that which was put on or entered into

(*enduma*). The former category includes all heavier formal or informal outerwear; the latter includes various types of tunics. (Trousers were completely foreign to the Greeks.) Unlike clothing in the modern world, Greek clothing changed little over time: while there might be minor variations in style, the same basic types of garments, cut along the same lines, remained in fashion for centuries. Yet, the Greeks were far from unconcerned with fashion; to them, fashion was tied to small details—ways of draping a mantle, for example, or of tying up a tunic—and to specialized, high-quality production (robes from Corinth and tunics from Amorgos were highly prized). There were not, however, the sort of wholesale changes of garment type or style that characterize the modern fashion system. (Fashions were more changeable, however, for hairstyles, jewelry, and footwear.) In general, clothing was more expensive and difficult to produce than it is in the modern world, and most people owned little of it.

Gender. Another surprise for the modern student of antiquity is the fact that for much of the period men and women wore basically the same clothing: if a woman appeared in public in a man's cloak, it would not cause raised eyebrows. Gender differences, as with fashion, tended to be found in the smaller details and accessories: the decoration of certain garments, the types of fasteners used, hairstyles, and such adornments. Status could also be difficult to determine from clothing: rich people obviously had fancier clothing and kept it in better shape, but there was no separate costume for slaves, and (in contrast with Rome) there was no special garment adopted upon reaching manhood.

Outer Garments. The basic outer garment for men was a mantle known as the *himation*. This garment was a large, rectangular piece of cloth, measuring about nine by six feet, without a hole for the head, which was draped over the body in a variety of ways (sometimes simply or with intricate folds held up by a belt). The himation was similar to the well-known Roman toga (except that the toga consisted of a larger, semicircular piece of cloth). It was put on by being draped over the shoulders and back, then brought around across the front of the body going from right to left. The free, folded end of the himation could then be draped over the crooked left arm, or thrown back over the shoulder for greater freedom of movement. The weight of the cloth would tend to keep it in place, although the garment must have been somewhat prone to slipping, since it was not pinned except in unusual cases (such as emergencies). If greater freedom of movement was required, the himation would be dispensed with altogether. Draping on the wrong side (that is, over the right shoulder) was considered eccentric, ignorant, or rustic. In Plato's *Theaetetus* (circa 360 B.C.E.–355 B.C.E.) Socrates sneers at people who "don't know how to fold the himation over the left shoulder the way freeborn citizens do."

Exposed Flesh. The himation could be draped to cover the right shoulder, although it was common to leave it exposed. This practice was fashionable among many

A Black Figure amphora depicting a customer getting measured for a pair of shoes, circa 520–510 B.C.E. (B.C. Museum of Fine Arts; Francis Bartlett Fund, Boston)

groups, including court speakers and politicians in fifth-century Athens. To have that much exposed flesh on a formal occasion strikes modern readers as odd, but this dress was not at all unusual for the Greeks. Their clothing in general left a lot of uncovered skin, which is due in part to the warm climate, but also to their attitude toward the body, which was viewed with much less modesty than in modern society. This mind-set was particularly true for the male body—athletes competed in the nude—but even to a surprising extent for the female body, considering the culture's desire to keep women under control and out of sight.

Versatility. The himation was a versatile garment, and for some people the only garment. Normally it was worn over a tunic, but Spartan men are said to have worn only the himation after the age of twelve. They were imitated in this style by Socrates and other philosophers who had a taste for simple living, and by those who could not afford any other clothing. For the poor, it could also serve as a blanket.

Cloaks. The other common type of men's outer garment was the *khlamus*, a cloak made of thick, stiff material, pinned up at the shoulder or joined in front of the body. It was worn primarily by soldiers, adolescents, and horseback riders.

Women. For women, the himation came into fashion by the fourth century. Prior to that women had worn the *peplos*, which was a larger rectangle that was wrapped, rather than draped, around the body. Consisting of a rectangular piece of cloth of variable dimensions, the peplos would be wrapped around the body horizontally, then fastened

together over the shoulders with pins. This style would leave one side of the garment open, perhaps exposing the wearer's body. The Spartans—famous for giving women some of the same physical training and freedom as men— were said to wear the peplos in a style that revealed the thighs (earning this style the nickname *phainomêrides*, or "thigh-displayers"). In Athens and elsewhere, less skimpy peploi were more common. A longer garment could be folded over before wrapping, so that the extra material would hang down in the front, giving the appearance of an upper garment over a long skirt. A wider peplos would have extra material on the open side, which would hang down in folds, giving the appearance of a full, elegant garment. If large enough, it could even be pulled up over the head as a veil or hood (women on funeral monuments are sometimes depicted in this manner). The open side could also be sewn or pinned up, giving the whole the appearance of a neat, fairly tight cylinder. In addition, the use of a belt would also allow for a formfitting sort of garment, while creating the opportunity for more folds. Elegant folds were highly valued, to judge from the care which artists of the Classical period took in depicting garment folds in sculpture and vase painting. In addition, the folds in a garment could make a convenient carrying place for objects.

Legend. Herodotus tells a fascinating but fictitious story about the Athenian abandonment of the peplos: Athenian women, outraged at the sole survivor of an expedition against Aigina, stabbed him to death with their brooches. From this point on, Athenian women were forbidden to have brooches; and for this reason they had to give up the peplos and switch to the linen tunic known as the *khitôn*. In fact, wearing of the peplos continued in some areas—it was thought to be Dorian, and therefore a bit rustic and old-fashioned.

Undergarments. The *khitôn* was sometimes an undergarment for a *himation* (not for a *peplos*, which needed none), but it could also be worn alone, in informal contexts or in warm weather. It differed from the other garments in belonging to the class of *enduma*, that is, it was put on like a shirt rather than draped. It was made of two pieces of rectangular cloth (linen or wool) sewn together on the sides and on the shoulders, and was usually sleeveless. There are exceptions, however: women's tunics could be held together by buttonlike discs on the shoulders, around which the cloth could be tied. Sometimes men's tunics were fastened together at the shoulder by pins. Usually a tunic would be drawn in by a belt at the waist; it might also be held in by a wider band (known as the *zôstêr*) higher up. For men the *khitôn* ended at about mid-thigh; for women it was typically somewhat longer. At night, the wearer would remove the belt and use the *khitôn* as a nightshirt.

Work Clothes. A variant on the standard *khitôn* is the *exômis*, which was fastened together on only one shoulder, leaving the other arm free. For this reason, it was a common work costume, for free people and slaves alike. There also existed the full-length Ionic *khitôn* (the shorter one is called Doric), which was a long, cylindrical gown-like garment that reached the ankles. Originally a common garment for men, it fell out of fashion for everyday wear (being replaced by the combination of himation and Doric *khitôn*), but was still used for ceremonial and religious occasions. Among these occasions were chariot races, and the famous Charioteer of Delphi wears an Ionic *khitôn*. Gathered above the waist, it draped in long, parallel folds, with gathered pleats along the side forming a sort of sleeve.

Special Garments. The Doric *khitôn* was usually worn next to the skin, although those who could afford multiple tunics would sometimes wear them in cold weather, or use a softer linen tunic under a woolen one. For the lower body, triangular loincloths were probably common (although underwear is not always depicted in paintings or sculpture) and were regularly worn by menstruating women. Women sometimes wore a *strophion*, a soft cloth band designed to restrain the breasts.

Footwear. Shoes were usually made of leather, although fibrous plant materials could also be used, as could cork or wood for the soles. Evidence from vase paintings suggests that Greeks often went barefoot indoors; regularly going barefoot outdoors, however, was considered a mark of eccentricity, at least by those who could afford shoes (this observation was frequently made in reference to Socrates). Shoes were usually produced by specialized tradespeople and could be bought ready-made or made-to-order: one vase painting shows a cobbler using a customer's foot as an outline for cutting leather.

Sandals and Socks. Sandals were the most common shoe type: easy to construct, cheap, and cool during warm weather. They were tied on rather than slipped into: leather thongs attached to the sole were wound about the ankle and big toe, leaving the upper part of the foot mostly uncovered. Boots were available for travel, military service, and other occasions demanding sturdier footwear. There were also specialized shoes like the *kothurnos*, a high, thick-soled boot worn by tragic actors. Socks (*sokkoi*) were known, but not as common as they are today. They were produced with a knitting technique rather than being woven.

Fashionable Shoes. Women's shoes were more varied in design and often quite elegant and fashionable. A mime by the third-century poet Herodas depicts two urban women shopping for shoes, and the shopowner lists no fewer than sixteen varieties. Unfortunately, scholars have few details on what any of these looked like, and even when there are illustrations on vase paintings, it is often impossible to match these up with the named styles. Designed for formal occasions, many of these shoes were delicate and dyed in various colors. Heels were flat rather than high, and women who wanted to increase their height used cork inserts.

Hats and Accessories. People generally went around bareheaded most of the time. For men, a basic type of hat was the *pilidion*, a plain felt or wool bonnet that could be used as a nightcap, or worn on cold days by slaves and workers, but was not a hat to wear on any occasion when appearance was important. It was worn by the god Hephaestus in his role as patron of workers. A similar design was called the *kunê* (literally, a dogskin cap, although it was usually made of cowhide). The *pilos* was a tall, conical hat that was more fashionable than the pilidion. Perhaps the most familiar Greek hat was the *petasos:* low-crowned and with a broad brim to keep off the sun, it was traditionally worn by travelers (and by Hermes, their patron god). It had a chin strap and when not in use could be pushed back off the head and worn between the shoulders. Felt, being denser than spun and woven wool, was especially good at providing protection from rain. Women wore a version of the petasos known as the *tholia*, and also covered their heads with scarves and cloth headdresses.

Belts and Walking Sticks. Belts were usually thin, simple bands of leather or cloth, although in some cases they could be broader and highly decorated. In addition, a walking stick was a common accessory—useful for balance on uneven roads or rocky areas, and even for holding up the folds of one's himation.

Beauty. Greeks who had sufficient income and leisure devoted much care to their personal appearance, and standards of hygiene were high. For men, there was a tension between the desire to look good (the Greeks were great admirers of youthful male beauty) and the desire to seem naturally beautiful without having to work at it. For women, elaborate attention to beauty was considered perfectly normal. Men were expected to be physically robust and athletic (whether from work, military training, or leisure-time exercise), and sun-darkened skin was considered the norm. Women, by contrast, were supposed to have white, untanned skin, and a man whose complexion was too light might be viewed as somewhat unmanly and suspected of spending too much time indoors with women.

Hair Length. In the Archaic Period (700–480 B.C.E.) it was common for men to wear their hair long: in fact, one of the standard terms for the Greeks in the *Iliad* is "flowing-haired." Like many older fashions, this style fell out of favor in most places by the fifth century, but survived in Sparta, a traditional and conservative society. It was common in Athens for youths to cut off their long hair upon reaching adulthood and to dedicate the hair to a god. Adult men wore their hair at about collar length (a modern term, of course, since the ancient Greeks had no collars) and sometimes paid careful attention to its styling. Barber shops were common, and they seem to have been for the Greeks (as they have been in the present-day United States) popular places to gather and talk. Judging from hairstyles found in sculpture, curled hair must have been common for special occasions, and curling irons are among the personal-care artifacts that have been found in excavations.

Facial Hair. Beards were almost universal for men until after the time of Alexander the Great, although the styles varied a bit. The cheeks were sometimes shaved while the beard was trimmed square or in a point. In the fifth century (when full beards were in fashion), razors were thought of as quintessentially feminine implements, so that a character in a comedy by Aristophanes questions another character's masculinity by accusing him of always carrying a razor.

Hairstyles. Women's hairstyles were, not surprisingly, more elaborate than men's. Women usually wore their hair long (in fact, they rarely cut it) and sometimes kept it curled and piled up on the back of the head or held in place by the *kekruphalos,* a sort of hairnet that gathered it backward off the forehead. Most common was a style in which the hair was braided and drawn into a knot behind the head; hair was worn down over the shoulders on special occasions, such as religious festivals. Slaves, both male and female, had short hair. A variety of hair-care implements have been found by archaeologists: scissors, combs (made of wood, bone, or tortoise shell), and a wide variety of hairpins. It was also possible to dye one's hair, with blond being a popular color, and wigs were available.

Makeup. Cosmetics were widely used by women, especially to achieve the whiteness that was so highly prized. White lead was used, and a type of rouge derived from orchids could be added as a blush. Eyeliner in black or brown was also popular. There were a great variety of perfumes, as well as lotions for skin care. Removal of body hair was the norm (including in many cases pubic hair), which could be accomplished with razors, tweezers, and depilatories. For women, the chief risk in applying makeup was that of appearing too seductive or too much like a *hetaira* (courtesan): a wife was supposed to look appealing to her husband, but somehow not too appealing.

Jewelry. The type of clothing worn in Greece made jewelry a common accessory for both men and women, although women wore quite a bit more. For a peplos and for certain

A MARK OF CIVILIZATION

The cultivation of grapes and production of wine were important parts of the process of civilization. This link was also a commonplace in Greek thought: barbarian peoples were known for liking beer or milk and being ignorant of wine. Thus, in Homer's *Odyssey* (circa eighth-seventh centuries B.C.E.) the Cyclops Polyphemus is tricked by Odysseus, since he is unused to strong Greek wine, and his drunken stupor allows Odysseus and his men to blind him and make their escape from his cave.

Greek attitudes toward drunkenness were less conflicted than in present-day society. While realizing that excessive drinking could be damaging to health and could cause a variety of social ills, the ancient Greeks accepted without question the pleasure that alcohol could provide. In Euripides' play *Bacchae* (circa 406 B.C.E.), the blind prophet Tiresias praises the god Dionysus for his invention of wine:

Mankind, young man, possesses two supreme blessings. First of these is the goddess Demeter, or Earth, whichever name you choose to call her by. It was she who gave to man his nourishment of grain. But after her there came the son of Semele [Dionysus], who matched her present by inventing liquid wine as his gift to man. For filled with that good gift, suffering mankind forgets its grief; from it comes sleep; with it oblivion of the troubles of the day. There is no other medicine for misery. And when we pour libations to the gods, we pour the god of wine himself that through his intercession man may win the favor of heaven.

Although wine was an everyday beverage, and was usually watered down to prevent extreme drunkenness, drinking in the context of the symposium was highly regulated and directed toward achieving a state of pleasurable, but not excessive, inebriation. Wine was mixed in large bowls called *kraters* (Greek *kratêres*), and the number to be consumed at a symposium was a vital decision made by the *symposiarch,* or master of ceremonies. In a fragment of a play by the comic poet Eubulus, Dionysus discusses the proper measure for drinking:

Three kraters only do I propose for sensible men: one for health, the second for love and pleasure, and the third for sleep; when this has been drunk up, wise guests make for home. The fourth krater is mine no longer, but belongs to *hubris;* the fifth to shouting, the sixth to revel; the seventh to black eyes; the eighth to summonses; the ninth to bile; and the tenth to madness and people tossing the furniture about.

types of khitôn pins or brooches were necessary to fasten the garment; and various hairstyles demanded pins and clasps. The historian Thucydides in the late fifth century speaks of upper-class men wearing golden "grasshopper" brooches to hold up their long hair, and this is probably a survival of an Archaic Period practice when men had long hair. In the fifth and fourth centuries, men wore little jewelry except for signet rings, which could be used to place an identifying seal in clay or wax.

Feminine Decorative Items. Women, in addition to functional pieces that held up clothing and hair, wore a variety of purely decorative jewelry: necklaces, bracelets, anklets, and earrings. In the Archaic Period, necklaces were heavy; lighter ones became fashionable later, sometimes with amulets or gems suspended from them. Bracelets and anklets could actually be worn further up the arm or leg and could be plain bands of gold or silver, spiral patterns, or even the form of a snake coiled up on itself. Earrings were designed for pierced ears and, like necklaces, evolved from heavy to light: small circular or patterned studs were the most common type.

Sources:

Robert Flacelière, *Daily Life in Greece at the Time of Pericles*, translated by Peter Green (New York: Macmillan, 1965).

Dorothy M. Johnson, ed., *Ancient Greek Dress* (Chicago: Argonaut, 1964).

Michael L. Ryder, *Sheep and Man* (London: Duckworth, 1983).

FOOD

Plain Fare. By modern standards, the Greek diet was rather plain and lacking in variety, and heavily based on grains (wheat and barley in particular). As one scholar observed: "The typical Greek meal consisted of two courses: the first, a kind of porridge; the second, a kind of porridge"—a humorous exaggeration, but not always that much of one, especially for the poorer classes or in times of scarcity. For the modern student looking at the Greek diet, what is most striking are the absences: foods that were not eaten because they were not known to the Greeks (potatoes, tomatoes, sugar, corn, citrus fruits, coffee, tea, and bananas) or because the Greeks simply did not care for them (butter, beer, and milk). The diet, however, was in many ways similar to that followed in modern Greece, in particular in its dependence on olive oil. Since Greece has the best longevity figures for any country in the European Union (despite lower income levels, which usually depress life expectancy), diet has been cited as a possible explanation. By extension, we may infer that the ancient diet was a healthy one as well, perhaps even more because of limited meat and dairy consumption.

Animal Husbandry. The climate of Greece allowed the cultivation of a wide variety of foods: there was enough water for wheat, barley, and various types of vegetables, and it was warm enough to allow cultivation of olive and fig trees. It was also well suited for grape cultivation, and the presence of the sea made fish a good source of protein. Most parts of Greece were not, however, well suited for large-scale animal husbandry: the soil made raising cattle

and pigs difficult (although sheep filled a useful niche by grazing nonarable pastureland).

Grains. The most significant part of the Greek diet was composed of grains. In fact, the word for grain (*sitos*) was used as a synonym for food, and *opson* (sometimes translated as relish) was a special word for anything other than grain. Cultivated grains included wheat, barley, oats, rye, and millet, with wheat and barley being the most common. Wheat cultivation changed significantly between 800 and 323 B.C.E.: older species of husked wheat (such as spelt and emmer) gave high yields and a laborious process of drying and pounding was necessary in order to extract the grain from the husk. Spelt and emmer were gradually replaced by durum and bread wheats (varieties that still dominate wheat production today), from which the grain could be separated by threshing (breaking up the kernels) and winnowing (using a fan to generate air currents to blow away the lighter husks, leaving the grain behind). Milling technology changed as well, so that flour became finer, with fewer impurities, although it was still coarse by modern standards.

Barley. Since it requires less water when growing than wheat does, barley was a more plentiful and cheaper grain in ancient Greece. Nevertheless, wheat was in greater demand because it has more gluten and produces better bread. For this reason, barley became known as a food for poor people and slaves.

Breads. Grain could be eaten in a variety of ways. The easiest in terms of labor was to cook it with water into a porridge or gruel (similar to modern hot breakfast cereals). Somewhat more appetizing, perhaps, were breads and griddle cakes: barley could be made into a cake known as *maza*, and a variety of breads were known, with the more refined, "whiter" breads being the most valued. Home baking was rare in cities because of a lack of sufficient space to build ovens. Bakeries were plentiful and were usually equipped with brick ovens. To bake bread, a fire was built in the oven and allowed to burn itself out. The embers were swept out, and the bread dough inserted, with the baking accomplished by the heat stored in the bricks.

Ritual Drink. Another common way of consuming grain was in the form of a *kukeôn*, a mixture of barley meal and water that was thin enough to drink. It was the ritual drink served to initiates of the Eleusinian Mysteries and thought to have healthful properties. It was considered a country beverage and could be flavored with local herbs such as thyme and pennyroyal.

Cakes. Equally popular, but much fancier, were cakes—not the sort modern people eat for dessert, but fancy, sweetened breads or pastries. There were a vast array of these, and whole books were written about them. They were considered a delicacy to be eaten as a dessert with fruit after banquets, and many varieties were baked to be used in sacrifices to the gods.

An Attic Black Figure amphora depicting laborers harvesting olives, late sixth century B.C.E. (British Museum, London)

Legumes. Beans, peas, chickpeas, and lentils formed an important part of the ancient Greek diet and were for most people the main source of protein. They could be mashed up and baked into bread, fried, or cooked into soups. An additional advantage was that they could all be easily dried and stored indefinitely.

Oils and Fats. Olive oil was the main source of fat, although other types of vegetable oils such as sesame oil were available, and cheese (which contains butterfat) was also common. Fats are a necessary part of any diet, especially one high in carbohydrates, and in a culture in which most people worked hard, spent much time outdoors, and ate little meat, excessive consumption of fat would rarely have been a problem.

Processing. Olives are inedible when raw and have to be processed for eating (by packing in salt or salt water) or to make oil. For making oil, they had to first be crushed in mills (occasionally large, complicated devices, but most times just a flat stone with a large roller), then pressed to extract the oil. Usually this process was done with green, unripe olives, which were thought to give better oil (this in contrast to modern practice, when black, ripe olives are used). The first pressing produced the "green" oil (what is today called "extra virgin") which was often kept separate and sold at premium prices. Many regions became famous for their oil production, and the high-quality product of these regions could be exported and valued as a luxury item in the same way as vintage wine. Specialty oils were so val-

ued that large amphorae (storage jars) full of oil were given as prizes to victorious athletes in the Panathenaic Games.

Uses. As in the modern world, however, most olive oil was of lower quality and destined for everyday use. In addition to its uses in food, it was an important ingredient in medicines and perfumes, and was the standard fuel for household lamps.

Dairy Products. Milk was primarily the food of foreigners, such as the Scythians, and of shepherds, and the drinking of fresh milk was considered an odd, barbaric practice (for example, in Homer's *Odyssey*, written circa eighth-seventh centuries B.C.E., only the cyclops Polyphemus drinks milk). Given the climate and the extreme perishability of milk, it is hardly surprising that the Greeks rarely drank it. Dairy products had medicinal, cosmetic, and ritual uses, however, and were frequently consumed in the form of cheese. It could be soft and fresh (curds, ricotta, or farmer's cheese are modern analogues), although these were perishable and would have to be eaten quickly. Aged hard cheeses would last much longer and transport better, and the various references to cheese-graters by the comic poet Aristophanes suggest that hard cheese was common. (These types might resemble modern-day Parmesan or Romano.) Sheep's and goat's milk were the most common sources for cheese, not surprisingly given the difficulty of pasturing large flocks of cattle, and modern Greek cheeses like feta and kasseri are probably not too different from their ancient counterparts.

Meat. Consumption of meat varied tremendously from one region to another, although in most places it was quite low for economic reasons. In the *Odyssey* large feasts with consumption of beef are commonplace, which can fool the reader into thinking this practice was standard in ancient Greece. In fact, the *Odyssey* was designed to show a bygone heroic world in which everything was greater and larger than in the present, including the consumption of expensive food; in this way, it actually provides evidence for the rarity of meat consumption. Data from Athens suggests that a sheep might cost about 12 drachmas, a pig about 20, and a cow as much as 80. Given that a semiskilled worker in the fifth century would be paid a drachma per day, meat was usually too expensive for most city-dwellers to buy. Most people, then, ate meat only at public sacrifices, where it was given out for free. For these occasions wealthier citizens would supply sacrificial animals (usually pigs, sheep, goats, and cattle). After the animals were ritually killed and parts of their bodies (usually fat and bones) dedicated to the gods and burned, the remaining meat would be roasted and eaten, being parceled out to the citizens and others who came to participate in the festival. (The Greeks were far too practical to waste a perfectly good animal by giving the gods the better parts. They were also too practical to waste edible flesh, including organ meats and blood—the Spartan national dish, for example, was a thin black stew consisting of pork, blood, salt, and vinegar.) Fair distribution of sacrificial meat was in many instances an act rich with political symbolism, especially in Athens where the official ideology was one of equality. Chickens, ducks, small wild birds, and their eggs also formed a part of the diet and were more affordable. Those who lived in the country could also hunt or trap wild game, including deer, boars, and rabbits.

Fish. The proximity of all parts of Greece to the sea made fish available and a desirable delicacy. It is uncertain, however, how much of a contribution they made to the Greek diet, since they are not especially plentiful in the Mediterranean. In most places they could not have been a significant source of protein, although they provided welcome diversity in an otherwise monotonous diet.

Valuable Catches. Fish were caught mostly along the shoreline, although it was necessary to go out into the open sea for many of the more valuable kinds. Shellfish were also taken from along the shore, as were octopus and squid. The region's few freshwater lakes were a source of fish, especially Lake Copais in Boeotia, famed as a source of eels. Fishing was always a difficult and chancy way to make a living, depending on unseen migrations and shifts in the fish population, although the enduring market for certain highly prized species made some fishermen rich. Much fishing was done with nets, although individuals would also use rods and lines the way modern anglers do.

Preparation. Fish were most often dried or pickled, although in a large city like Athens, which had a harbor only five miles from the city center, fresh fish of many varieties were available. The Athenians, in fact, had a particularly severe case of the general Greek mania for fish, to judge from the many references by Aristophanes and other comic poets. Fish was perhaps the prime example of an *opson*; in fact, the diminutive form of this word, *opsarion*, is the source of the modern Greek word for fish (*psari*). There was nothing Athenians (and many other Greeks) seemed to like so much as fish. Among other things, the ability to consume certain types of fish became a marker of class difference: sardines, sprats, and other small species were affordable by the common people, but eels, tuna, grouper, mullets, and crayfish were reserved for the rich. The fish market was a popular, crowded place, and in Aristophanes' *Frogs* (405 B.C.E.) we hear of a rich man pretending to be poor (to avoid taxation) who gives himself away by buying expensive fish. In his work written in 411 B.C.E., *Thesmophoriazousai* (a fantasy about the redistribution of power), the poor receive greater slices of fish. Plutarch (writing in Roman times but still reflecting older Greek attitudes) tells his readers that if they ever run across a Rhodian dogfish they should buy it, or take it by force if necessary, even at the risk of death. (An exaggeration, not unlike the Japanese proverb about *fugu*, a delicious fish that can be deadly if not properly prepared: "It is madness to eat *fugu*; it is also madness *not* to eat *fugu*.") Fish were popular items at upper-class banquets, and serving a large specimen of a rare type of fish was an excellent way of showing off.

Nutrition. In addition to fish, vegetables provided variety, along with needed vitamins. Onions, garlic, cabbage, lettuce, artichokes, cucumbers, turnips, and radishes were commonly eaten; availability was seasonal and varied from countryside to city. Olives were also eaten, as were some nuts and seeds (sesame, almond, walnut, chestnut, and poppy): these provided fat as well as vitamins, and the seeds were common seasonings for cakes.

Fruits. Apples, pears, grapes, quinces, and pomegranates were readily available and figured not only on the table but also in legend. (Persephone is said to have eaten pomegranate seeds in Hades and thus been doomed to stay there.) The most important fruit, however, was the fig: some scholars claim that no other crop produced more calories per unit of area. Different varieties were cultivated, in part to extend the season of availability. Fresh figs were a treat (although not a particularly rare or expensive one); dried figs were food for slaves or country people, or a sort of emergency food reserve. They were also important as a sweetener, since sugar was unknown to the Greeks.

Honey. The usual sweetener in Greece was honey. Beekeeping had been a carefully practiced art since circa 700 B.C.E. Hives could be made of terracotta, wood, or reeds, and the Greeks were aware of the different flavors that could be produced by altering the bees' diet. The thyme-flower honey of Hymettus (near Athens) was famous, and many other locations had special, sought-after varieties of honey.

Seasonings. Herbs and spices were an important part of Greek cuisine. Most of these were locally grown green plants: basil, bay leaf, chives, fennel, garlic, leeks, mustard, onions, parsley, rosemary, sage, and thyme. There were other, exotic spices that might be imported from distant lands, but the spice trade was still quite undeveloped compared to what it was in Roman times, when trade contact with India and China was more feasible. There was a tendency to flavor food, rather than serve it plain, that survives to this day in the cooking of Mediterranean countries.

Beverages. Water and wine were the only beverages commonly consumed. Milk was unusual and foreign, as was beer. Unfermented fruit juice was too perishable to be practical: rather than make fruit juice that would have to be consumed immediately, Greeks simply ate other fruits and turned grapes into wine.

Alcohol. Wine production was an important factor in the development of civilization and therefore was well advanced and sophisticated by 800 B.C.E. Most modern techniques for training vines (for example, on trellises or trees) were known, and the process of making wine changed little until the advent of modern technology. Grapes were crushed in presses and the juice (known as "must") was placed in large jars to ferment, sometimes with additives such as seawater. Hotter climates produce sweeter wines, with a higher alcohol content, so most Greek wines were in the higher range of possible values for these (perhaps 14 percent alcohol; in the absence of distillation—a medieval invention—there was no hard liquor, and wine was the strongest beverage available). Simple wines would be ready within a few months; others were allowed to ferment longer, although Greek winemakers were unable to stop the fermentation process, and wines would not last for more than four to five years. Since climate and soil determine the essential characteristics of a wine, the development of an export trade from favored wine-producing areas occurred early. Many of the best wines came from Ionian islands (near the coast of Asia Minor) such as Lesbos, Chios, Rhodes, and Thasos.

Popularity. Wine was consumed as an everyday beverage with meals, sometimes mixed with honey or flavored with spices. It was also taken for medicinal purposes as well as to simply get drunk. It was almost always diluted with water: drinking unmixed wine was something done by barbarians or by foolish people who did not care about its effects. The proportion of water mixed in varied according to occasion: heavily diluted wine would be best for children, or for those who needed to maintain sobriety while working; purer wine was suited for banquets and drinking parties. It was the drink of slaves and kings alike (although kings drank better wine), and its use was never seriously questioned. Writers recognized the possibility that excessive drinking could have serious consequences: Pythagoras is said to have claimed that excessive drinking was a training ground for madness, and authors of both fact and fiction tell of alcohol-induced misbehavior ranging from falling off roofs to initiating brawls at weddings. Nevertheless, the Greeks did not have our concept of alcoholism and were quite unselfconscious about enjoying the pleasure and escape from care that drinking could provide. Thus, in the *Bacchae* (circa 406 B.C.E.) of Euripides, the prophet Teiresias praises wine as the gift of the god Dionysus: "Filled with that good gift, suffering mankind forgets its grief; from it comes sleep; with it oblivion of the troubles of the day. There is no other medicine for misery."

Food Preparation. The degree of attention paid to the preparation of food varied according to the amount of income and leisure available. As noted above on housing, most city houses had relatively little space for cooking and lacked ovens, so most urban dwellers bought bread from bakeries. Although a lot of attention was paid to seasoning, methods of preparation must have been simple: boiling, sautéing, or grilling. Prepared foods were available from vendors in the marketplace, inns, and taverns. Between these sources and the number of public festivals at which food was distributed for free, the urban poor may have done little of their own cooking.

Freshness. When cooking was done in the home, it was usually by women or slaves, as were other household tasks. Given the lack of refrigeration, and even of storage space, urban cooks probably bought fresh food on a daily basis (a practice that is still followed in many European cities). In the country, households would aim at self-sufficiency in food and could store large amounts of grain, oil, and wine, and buy whatever opson they needed on occasional trips into town.

Meals. The number of meals taken per day varied: originally three, in fifth-century Athens the usual number was two (although this later reverted to three). Under the older system, breakfast (*ariston*) would be eaten soon after sunrise, with the main meal (*deipnon*) near midday, and a lighter supper (*dorpon*) in the evening. In Athens, the ariston was moved back to later in the day, as was the deipnon, which became an evening meal. (A similar alternation may be found in the United States and parts of Europe, where moving the main meal to the evening is gaining popularity. However, much of the reason for this transition has to do with the demands of urban rather than rural life.)

Etiquette. In houses of sufficient means, meals would be taken in the dining room. Sitting while eating was common, although the fashion for lying down was imported from the East in about 700 B.C.E. and was followed on formal occasions. Utensils would vary according to income and the formality of the occasion: drinking vessels were of pottery, wood, or metal (glass was not commonly used until Roman times). Plates were wood or ceramic. Various examples of highly decorated drinking utensils and plates survive; these items were created by skilled vase painters and were for formal rather than everyday use. Spoons and knives were common; forks were unknown, and most food was eaten with the fingers.

Differences in Diet. Throughout the Greek world each group of inhabitants had different reputations concerning their dietary habits. The Spartans, for example,

Chariot races were difficult and sometimes dangerous. There was much opportunity for skill and cunning, and fair play was ensured by judges and by making competitors swear that they would compete fairly. The following passage comes from Homer's *Iliad* (circa eighth–seventh centuries B.C.E.), with Achilles presiding over a series of competitions to honor his slain comrade Patroclus:

They stood in line for the start, and Achilleus showed them the turn-post far away on the level plain, and beside it he stationed a judge, Phoinix the godlike, the follower of his father, to mark and remember the running and bring back a true story.

Then all held their whips high-lifted above their horses, then struck with the whip thongs and in words urged their horses onward into speed . . . presently after this battle-stubborn Antilochos saw where the hollow way narrowed. There was a break in the ground where winter water had gathered and broken out of the road, and made a sunken place all about. Menelaos shrinking from a collision of chariots steered there, but Antilochos also turned out his single-foot horses from the road, and bore a little way aside, and went after him; and Menelaos was frightened and called out aloud to Antilochos: "Antilochos, this is reckless horsemanship. Hold in your horses. The way is narrow here, it will soon be wider for passing. Be careful not to crash your chariot and wreck both of us." So he spoke, but Antilochos drove on all the harder with a whiplash for greater speed, as if he had never heard him . . . but then the mares of Menelaos gave way and fell back, for he of his

own will slackened his driving for fear that in the road the single-foot horses might crash. . . . But Menelaos of the fair hair called to him in anger: "Antilochos, there is no other man more cursed than you are. Damn you. We Achaians lied when we said you had good sense. Even so, you will not get this prize without having to take an oath."

Eventually Menelaos's claim of foul play is upheld, although he graciously allows Antilochos to keep the prize for first place. The dangers of chariot racing are shown more graphically in Sophocles' *Electra* (circa 497–405 B.C.E.), where the following false report of Orestes' death is given:

Orestes always drove tight at the corners barely grazing the edge of the post with his wheel, loosing his hold of the trace horse on his right while he checked the near horse. In his other laps the poor young man and his horses had come through safe. But this time he let go of the left rein as the horse was turning. Unaware, he struck the edge of the pillar and broke his axle in the center. He was himself thrown from the rails of the chariot and tangled in the reins. As he fell, the horses bolted wildly to the middle of the course. When the crowd saw him fallen from his car, they shuddered. "How young he was," "How gallant his deeds," and "How sadly he has ended," as they saw him thrown earthward now, and then, tossing his legs to the sky— until at last the grooms with difficulty stopped the runaway team and freed him, but so covered with blood that no one of his friends could recognize the unhappy corpse.

were famous for frugality and moderation: they took their meals in communal public messes, drank and ate moderately, and their famous black broth was considered unpalatable by other Greeks. By contrast, the Boeotians were known for high living, overeating, and drinking too much, and were considered to be slow-witted and dull. The citizens of Sybaris in Sicily were considered gourmets, devoted to luxury in all its forms: they were said to have given eel-producers an exemption from taxation. (The word *sybaritic,* meaning devoted to luxury, comes from the name of this town.) Although there is some truth in these assertions (especially those concerning Sparta), they must be taken with a grain of salt, since they reflect not just reality but the prejudices of Athenians and other outsiders, who wished to portray other Greeks as both different and inferior to themselves. Food and its consumption could have a moral dimension largely missing from the present world: "moderation in all things" was a Greek ideal.

Abstention. Some Greeks followed vegetarian diets for religious reasons, although it was not especially common. Followers of the sixth-century philosopher Pythagoras abstained from meat because of their belief in reincarnation: a cow or pig might contain a person's soul. (They also abstained from beans, for reasons that are less clear.) Other philosophers, such as Empedocles, had the same view as did followers of Orphism. Abstention from meat was sometimes also prescribed for medical reasons.

Sources:

James N. Davidson, *Courtesans and Fishcakes: The Consuming Passions of Classical Athens* (London: HarperCollins, 1997).

Robert Flacelière, *Daily Life in Greece at the Time of Pericles,* translated by Peter Green (New York: Macmillan, 1965).

Peter Garnsey, *Famine and Food Supply in the Graeco-Roman World: Responses to Risk and Crisis* (Cambridge: Cambridge University Press, 1988).

Robert Sallares, *Ecology of the Ancient World* (Ithaca, N.Y.: Cornell University Press, 1990).

Charles Seltman, *Wine in the Ancient World* (London: Routledge & Kegan Paul, 1957).

John Wilkins and others, eds., *Food in Antiquity* (Exeter, U.K.: University of Exeter Press, 1995).

William A. Younger, *Gods, Men and Wine* (London: Wine & Food Society, 1966).

A Roman copy of the Discus-thrower sculpted by Myron
in circa 450 B.C.E. (Museo Nationale, Rome)

GAMES

Children's Toys. The Greeks were a competitive peo-ple and loved to play games. Children had more time for play than adults did, and many of their toys were similar to ones used today: for small children, rattles, animal fig-urines, dolls, miniature houses, and pull toys such as char-iots and carts. As they grew older they played with tops, hoops, balls, and knucklebones (the equivalent of dice). Marbles was a popular game, although the marbles would have been made of stone, bone, or some other material instead of glass. (One story claims that the suitors of Penelope played the game as a way of deciding who would have first claim on marrying her.) There were also other small games of skill, such as trying to throw nuts into a circle or bowl (a juvenile version of *kottabos*). Surprising, perhaps, is the fact that the Greeks had yo-yos—double disks made of metal or wood, joined by a short cylindrical bar that a string could be wound around. There are even terracotta versions of these, surviving from shrines where they were dedicated by youths: upon reaching adulthood, children would dedicate their toys to a god. In many cases, however, they offered not the toys themselves, but instead terracotta representations of them—perhaps the original toys were lost, they were being used by a younger sibling, or the young person making the dedication was not quite through playing with them.

Modern Equivalents. Among games involving physical activity were versions of leapfrog and hopscotch; playing with seesaws and swings and giving piggyback rides were also common. There are vase paintings showing balancing games—in particular a game played by adolescents which involved balancing on a greased wineskin. Many of the more physical games shade over into training and athletic competition.

Adult Activities. Adult games were often continuations of childhood games, and if they were competitive in nature, the stakes were raised. Ball games were popular from early on: in Homer's *Odyssey* (circa eighth–seventh centuries B.C.E.) the noise of princess Nausicaa playing catch with her attendants awakens the sleeping Odysseus. Balls were made of strips of leather sewn together and could be stuffed with hair or feathers (a hair-stuffed ball would be hard, like a baseball; feathers would be much softer); some balls may have been inflated with air if made from animal bladders. Team sports were not popular among the Greeks, but ball-playing may have been an exception. One relief from sixth-century Athens shows a man throwing a ball to a group of waiting companions in what looks like a throw-in from out of bounds. Another relief shows two men poised to hit at a ball with curved sticks, similar to a hockey face-off (in this case their companions seem to be standing around waiting their turn, rather than participating). A black-figured vase shows pairs of men, one riding on the other's shoulders, vying for a ball about to be tossed to them by a companion. The Spartans, not surprisingly, found a military use for ball play and invented games in order to improve the physical condition of their youth. As the example from the *Odyssey* shows, ball games were acceptable forms of exercise and play for women, who were excluded from most other forms of athletic competition except in Sparta.

Board Games. Among nonathletic games, board games were popular: one of them, called *pessoi*, resembled check-ers or chess, with players moving oval pieces around a board (divided into thirty-six squares) and into enemy ter-ritory. (In the *Odyssey*, this game was played by Penelope's suitors to amuse themselves after dinner.) Games of chance were ubiquitous, and almost anything could be turned into a competition or the occasion for a bet. A game called "Odd and Even" was played with small objects (knuckle-bones, beans, pebbles, and so forth), and there were many dice games. Dice were made out of knucklebones or terra-cotta and had numbers on each side; the most common game involved throwing three dice, with three sixes being the best result (called "Aphrodite's throw," after the god-dess of love), and three ones being the worst (called "The Dog").

Cockfighting. Animal competitions were also an object for betting. There is evidence for fights among dogs, cats, and weasels, but cockfighting was the most common. Rather than being outlawed (as it is in most modern coun-tries), cockfighting was looked upon with favor: in Athens, an annual competition was organized by the city. Raising and training fighting roosters was an object of much attention, especially for upper-class youths: cockfighting was considered an activity that taught manly courage. Roosters were also appropriate as gifts for a man to give an adolescent lover, as various vase paintings show.

Baths. The more vigorous forms of exercise (running, boxing, wrestling) are best considered not as games, but as part of the daily routine that included spending time at the bath, the *gumnasion* (exercise area), and the *palaistra* (wrestling area). Baths were common in Greek cities by the fourth century and filled an obvious need in a time when there was little indoor plumbing, space was limited, and water difficult to transport. The earliest baths consisted of a series of small tubs arranged around the wall of a room: too small to recline in, they would allow the lower half of the body to be submerged, with heated water available to be poured over the bather. It was an extension of the sort of bath found in private houses, which was basically a large washbasin. Soap was unknown, although a variety of cleaning agents were used: carbonate of soda, potassium lye, and certain types of dirt and chalk.

Daily Routine. Baths became an important part of the daily routine. Admission to private baths in Athens was cheap, and standards of hygiene for all classes were fairly high. Having a bath before dinner was standard practice: even Socrates, famous for his negligence in matters of hygiene and fashion, is depicted in Plato's *Symposium* (circa 380–360 B.C.E.) as having taken a bath before an important dinner party. Baths were well heated at a time when private homes might not be, and Aristophanes jokes about the poor getting burns from standing too close to the fire in the baths. (Spartans, by contrast, rejected hot baths as unmanly, and taking cold baths became fashionable in Athens among those who admired the Spartan way of life.) Eventually, baths large enough to swim in developed, and bathing could be combined with exercise. (Living close to the sea, most Greeks were good swimmers.)

Exercise. Most of all, baths became a place to hang out and pass time, as were the gumnasion and palaistra. The huge bath complexes of the Roman world had not yet developed, so exercise was done elsewhere, perhaps followed by a trip to the bath. Exercise was an important and popular leisure-time activity, but one with significance for the welfare of the state. In a world in which warfare was common, and in which any male citizen was a potential soldier, developing strength and agility was of more than theoretical importance. The main exercise area was the gumnasion, which originated as a place for training *ephebes* (young men) for military service. The name comes from the Greek word *gumnos,* meaning "naked," since exercise in the nude was common (although not universal). Athletes covered their bodies with oil before exercise, and then sprinkled themselves with a layer of dust or sand: this was thought to protect them from chills and changes in temperature. Exercise was often done to musical accompaniment on the *aulos,* a sort of double oboe. Afterward athletes scraped themselves with a curved

ATHLETES

The position of athletes in the Greek world was an honored one, although there were conflicts about what sort of honors were appropriate, and about the value of athletes compared to other members of society. There was often a strong element of class bias: athletes tended to come from well-off families who had enough leisure time to allow for training and competition, and some sources on athletics express clear pro-aristocratic sentiments. The poet Pindar, who was paid by victorious athletes to write odes celebrating their achievements, often praises the aristocratic values of noble birth and inherited excellence, while at the same time exhibiting ambivalence about the process of training. (True excellence had to be inborn, not acquired, although it could be honed with proper instruction.)

One of the main purposes of athletic training was to produce good soldiers; however, athletic performance was a goal in its own right. The Spartan poet Tyrtaeus contrasts pure athletic skill and fighting spirit, and Xenophon reports a conversation in which Socrates argues with a young man who says that he does not need to train because he is a private citizen, not a competitive athlete. Socrates reminds him that as a citizen of the *polis* (city-state), he has an obligation to keep his body in good shape, ready to serve his city at a moment's notice. Attacking the class of specialized, professional athletes from another perspective, Xenophanes in *Poems* (circa 560–circa 478 B.C.E.) complains that athletes get more honor than he does as a poet:

Now, supposing a man were to win the prize for the foot race at Olympia, there where the precinct of Zeus stands beside the river, at Pisa: or if he wins the five-contests, or the wrestling, or if he endures the pain of boxing and wins, or that new and terrible game they call the pankration, contest of all holds: why, such a man will obtain honor, in the citizens' sight, and be given a front seat and be on display at all civic occasions, and he would be given his meals all at the public expense, and be given a gift from the city to take and store for safekeeping. If he won with the chariot, too, all this would be granted to him, and yet he would not deserve it, as I do. Better than brute strength of men, or horses either, is the wisdom that is mine. But custom is careless in all these matters, and there is no justice in putting strength on a level above wisdom which is sound. For if among the people there is one who is a good boxer, or one who excels in wrestling or in the five-contests [pentathlon], or else for speed of his feet, and this is prized beyond other feats of strength that men display in athletic games, the city will not, on account of this man, have better government.

metal tool known as a *strigil* (having slaves or fellow athletes assist in applying and removing oil was common). Provision of oil was a major expense in running a gumnasion, and there are jokes about misers collecting the used oil for use at home (presumably for lighting lamps rather than for cooking).

Special Sites. Originally a gumnasion might be just an open space, usually with a spring or other water supply, next to a shrine of a god or hero. It was often situated next to a grove of trees (most famously in the case of the Academy, the gumnasion made famous by Plato and his followers); permanent buildings were added at a later stage, starting in the fifth century. Athletic training might also take place in the palaistra (literally, "wrestling area"), which was typically smaller than a gumnasion and devoted to wrestling and other combat sports. It was easy to idealize the setting: a character in Aristophanes' *Clouds* (423–418 B.C.E.) reminisces about the old days, when boys spent their time in athletic training rather than learning clever rhetorical tricks: "Ah, I can see you now, as through an idyl moving—you with some companion of your age, modest and manly like you, strolling by the Academy perhaps, or there among the olives, sprinting side by side together, crowned with white reed, breathing with every breath the ecstasy of Spring returning."

A Place to be Noticed. The gumnasion was, because of its setting, a favorite place to pass the time. Those who were not actively engaged in exercise could watch those who were—in fact, the gumnasion was famous as a place for adult males to watch and meet attractive young men. The Aristophanes passage quoted in the last paragraph goes on to describe in graphic detail the beauty of bodies that could be developed by regular exercise. Similarly, in Plato's *Symposium* (circa 380–360 B.C.E.) Alcibiades describes how his attempt to seduce Socrates involved solo wrestling and training in the gumnasion. It was also a place to talk: to gossip, to discuss business or politics, and to devote oneself to intellectual pursuits. By the fourth century, the gumnasion had become a sort of educational center where the leisured classes could enjoy the natural beauty of the setting while discussing philosophy, rhetoric, and science. Plato and his followers frequented the public gumnasion in the Academy district of Athens; similarly, Aristotle established a school in the gumnasion of the Lyceum. The mixed heritage of the gumnasion is illustrated by the subsequent history of the word and other related terms: in English, the *academy* and *academics* are synonyms for education, while the *gymnasium* is a place for exercise. In Germany, a *gymnasium* is a secondary school; while French and Italian words are derived (*lycée* and *liceo*, respectively) from Aristotle's Lyceum.

Gymnastics and Dance. The sorts of exercise practiced for educational purposes by children and youths were continued by adults. These activities included gymnastics and dance, for musical training was an important part of education. Dances in armor, in fact, were an important component of military preparation, and armed dance

competitions were an important part of some festivals. There was also training for the athletic events practiced in the major festivals such as the Olympian Games: running, long jump, boxing, wrestling, discus, and javelin.

Panhellenic Competitions. There were four major Panhellenic athletic competitions: the Olympian, Pythian, Nemean, and Isthmian Games. The Olympian Games took place in the sacred precinct of Zeus at Olympia, and they were held in the late summer of every fourth year, starting in 776 B.C.E. (the four-year pattern has been copied for the modern Olympic Games). The Pythian Games, dedicated to Apollo, took place at Delphi where they started out as a musical competition. After a reorganization athletic contests (and other musical contests) were added, and starting in 582 B.C.E. the Pythian Games were held every four years, in late summer of the third year of the Olympiad cycle. The Nemean Games, sacred to Zeus, were held in the city of Nemea (in Argos) every two years: in July of the second and fourth year of every Olympiad. The Isthmian Games (held in April or May near Corinth) were also biennial and were dedicated to Poseidon. Thus, every year would have a major athletic competition, and these international events were taken seriously enough so that warfare would be suspended by truce to allow the competitions to take place. A certain set of basic events was contested at all festivals, although special musical or athletic ones were added to some of them.

Races. Running races were short by modern standards, consisting of sprints and middle distances. The most important race was the *stadion*, which was the length of one stade (192 meters or 210 yards), the length of the stadium at Olympia and other competition sites. (The English word *stadium* is derived from the Latin word for this distance.) There also existed a *diaulos* (twice the length of a *stadion*) and a *dolikhos* ("long race") consisting of twelve laps (about 1.4 miles). A race in armor was added to the major festivals near the end of the sixth century. Despite the legendary run of Phidippides from Marathon to Athens, there was no marathon competition: few people other than messengers would ever have a reason to run long distances. Other competitions, such as nighttime torch races in festivals, were of uncertain distance.

Training. Runners ran naked and barefoot on a surface of hard-packed sand. Unlike modern track races, which go around an oval, Greek races longer than a stadion involved turning around a post—probably one post for each lane instead of one central post (as in a chariot race). Technique as well as speed were important, and there are vases that show runners practicing starts. Most race training must have taken place outside the gumnasion, but the pleasant suburban locations of most gymnasia provided ample opportunity to practice nearby. Running was also one sport in which there was female competition: women were able to compete in the stadion race at the Heraia, a festival honoring Hera.

Combat Sports. Wrestling was extremely popular, both in practice and in the imagination. Various myths tell of heroes defeating their opponents in wrestling: Heracles kills the giant Antaeus in this way, and also the Nemean lion; Theseus outwrestled the robber Cercyon. Vase paintings show scenes from real and mythological wrestling and reveal the techniques involved. There were two styles of wrestling: upright and ground wrestling. In the former, victory was achieved by throwing your opponent three times, with any full-body fall counting toward a win (contrast modern wrestling, where the shoulders must be pinned). Ground wrestling would continue after a fall, and victory here was achieved by getting one's opponent to admit defeat. Since a fall to the ground was to be avoided at all costs, leg takedowns were extremely risky: neck, arm, and body holds were used instead. The athletes' habit of using oil on their bodies must have increased the difficulty of grabbing an opponent.

Opponents. Wrestling competitions in major festivals involved head-to-head matches, with opponents drawn by lot; weight divisions were unknown, and all competitors were placed in the same pool. (The same procedure was followed for the other combat sports.) An odd number of opponents would lead to one of them having a first-round bye, and it was considered a mark of special distinction to win the competition without having had a bye. Wrestling was practiced as training by men of all ages: in Plato's *Symposium* Alcibiades describes wrestling with Socrates, who would have been in his mid-fifties at the time.

Fisticuffs. Boxing is not quite as widely depicted as wrestling, although it is described in Homer's *Iliad* (circa eighth–seventh centuries B.C.E.). Boxers wore gloves, although these were usually designed to protect the hands rather than to soften the blow. (Softer gloves used for training were an exception to this rule.) Technique was somewhat different from modern-day boxing: it seems that body blows were unknown (either illegal or considered improper), so that all attack and defense concerned the head. Hitting an opponent when he was down, however, was permissible, as vase paintings show. Boxing matches took place in large, open areas rather than a ring, so that cornering an opponent was rarely an option. There were no rounds, and the match ended when one opponent raised his hand to signal submission. Boxing was a slow, cautious affair: the lack of a ring, and the need to defend only the head, must have made most matches games of cat and mouse.

Blood Sport. *Pankration* (Greek *pagkration*) was a mixture of boxing and wrestling: the name implies that every type of force (*pan*, or "all" + *kratos*, or "force") was allowed, and in fact only biting and gouging were forbidden. (Gouging in this case meant putting one's fingers into an opponent's eyes, ears, nose, or mouth.) As with boxing, victory was achieved by getting your opponent to give in, and here the intentional infliction of pain through armlocks, twisting, and strangling were especially effective techniques. A popular technique for getting a stranglehold was called "the ladder," which involved climbing onto an opponent's back. Since there was no penalty for

taking a fall, remaining upright did not always confer an advantage—most matches were decided on the ground, often with one or both opponents covered with blood and seriously injured. Because of the danger of the sport, it was considered especially prestigious.

Throwing. The discus throw developed from the throwing of any sort of weight made of stone or metal. Surviving examples of the discus vary tremendously in weight, from about three to eighteen pounds (the modern discus for men's competitions is two kilograms, or 4.4 pounds). Technique was quite a bit different: rather than spinning in a circle, competitors were able to run forward toward a line before their throw. The sort of body twist used is best illustrated by Myron's famous statue of the Diskobolos (Discus-thrower). At the major festivals the discus was not a stand-alone event, but was contested only as part of the pentathlon.

Javelin. The javelin throw was an event of obvious practical importance for both war and hunting. The chief difference between the ancient and modern javelin competitions is that the Greeks used a throwing strap. This strap was perhaps a foot or a foot-and-a-half in length, and was wound around the shaft of the javelin, with a loop left at the end. The thrower would hook his fingers through the loop while holding the shaft loosely, then throw, using the loop to whip the javelin forward. The unwinding strap would impart a spinning motion to the javelin, thus increasing the distance and the accuracy (a similar principle applies to bullets, which are given a spinning motion by the rifling in gun barrels). At the four major Panhellenic festivals the javelin was a part of the pentathlon, but at the Panathenaic Games there was a separate, highly prestigious competition for throwing the javelin from horseback.

Jumping. The long jump was another event contested only as part of the pentathlon. It was a running jump, with runners landing in soft sand (they would traditionally dig out their own landing pits) and taking off from a board of wood or stone. The evidence from vase paintings shows that technique was similar to that of modern athletes—for example, keeping the legs well in front of the body while in the air. The chief difference between ancient and modern technique is that the Greeks used weights, called *haltêres*, to increase the distance of their jump. The weights (made of stone, with handles on top, or cut into semicircular shapes) would be brought forward on approach, and then swung backward on takeoff. Modern experimentation has shown that this practice can increase the length of the jump considerably, although the famous statistic that Phayllus of Croton jumped fifty-five feet is obviously a fiction. Less formal competitions probably included standing jumps, although there is no good evidence for competition in the high jump.

Other Events. Horse and horse-drawn chariot races were extremely prestigious events at the major festivals. As was the case with the longer running events, the course consisted of a series of out-and-back loops, with a

WEAVING

An extremely important activity for women in ancient Greece was weaving. It was the most visible of women's contributions to the economic health of the *oikos* (household), but in addition acquired tremendous symbolic importance. Weaving became a metaphor for skill, craftiness, and ultimately for storytelling: the English word *text* derives from a Latin word meaning "something woven," and storytelling today is referred to as "spinning a yarn." These associations go all the way back to the earliest days of Greek literature, as the following passages from Homer illustrate. In the first, from Book Three of the *Iliad* (circa eighth–seventh centuries B.C.E.), Iris (messenger of the gods) has come to fetch Helen from her home:

> She came on Helen in the chamber; she was weaving a great web, a red folding robe, and working into it the numerous struggles of Trojans, breakers of horses, and bronze-armored Achaians, struggles that they endured for her sake at the hands of the war god.

Here Helen, the boldest and most self-aware of Greek heroines, is weaving a decorative tapestry, and one which tells a story: in fact, the same story Homer himself is telling, that of the Trojan War being fought for possession of Helen.

The second passage, from the *Odyssey* (circa eighth–seventh centuries B.C.E.), shows the craft of Penelope. Her husband Odysseus has been away from home for twenty years, and various suitors have begun to demand that she leave her house and remarry. She uses weaving as a ruse to evade them, as one of the suitors complains:

> She set up a great loom in her palace, and set to weaving a web of threads long and fine. Then she said to us: "Young men, my suitors now that the great Odysseus has perished, wait, though you are eager to marry me, until I finish this web, so that my weaving will not be useless and wasted. This is a shroud for the hero Laertes [her father-in-law], for when the destructive doom of death which lays men low shall take him, lest any Achaian woman in this neighborhood hold it against me that a man of many conquests lies with no sheet to wind him." So she spoke, and the proud heart in us was persuaded. Thereafter in the daytime she would weave at her great loom, but in the night she would have torches set by, and undo it. So for three years she was secret in her design, convincing the Achaians, but when the fourth year came with the seasons returning, one of her women, who knew the whole of the story, told us, and we found her in the act of undoing her glorious weaving. So, against her will and by force, she had to finish it.

180-degree left-hand turn made around a fixed post. Unlike running courses, however, horse-race courses were longer (about six hundred yards) and were furnished with a single post at each end (rather than a post for each lane); thus, fighting for position and making a tight turn were matters requiring great skill and daring. Racing was a dangerous sport, yet the glory was given not to the rider or charioteer, but to the person who owned (and perhaps trained) the horses. Equestrian events were the province of those who had substantial financial resources, and winning a prize in the major festivals could be a boost to a political career: the Athenian Alcibiades was famous for his chariot victories, as were the tyrants who ruled the wealthy Greek cities of Sicily.

Team Competition. Team sports were absent from the major festivals, although some of the surviving visual evidence suggests that team-based ball games existed outside of the context of formal competition. The Greeks were a highly competitive people, and it is significant that they held competitions not only in athletics, but in drama, music, poetry, and public speaking. However, that competition was almost always on an individual basis, and it has been said that warfare was the only team sport they really enjoyed. Fair play was something given far less emphasis than in present-day society: the idea of being a "good winner" or a "good loser" was foreign to the Greeks. Pindar, writing odes to honor victors in wrestling competitions, takes delight in contrasting their victorious homecoming with the unhappy returns of their defeated opponents, who "slink along back alleyways, shunning enemy eyes and nursing pain, the bite of defeat." Pindar's attitudes were consistent with conventional Greek morality, in which it was considered normal to help one's friends and harm one's enemies: taking delight in the suffering of a foe was nothing to be ashamed of.

Cheating. The lack of sportsmanship is also evident in the prevalence of cheating at the games. Strict rules, oaths to the gods, and careful observation by referees were necessary measures to ensure fair competition. Even so, controversies arose, which was not surprising considering the occasionally high stakes. In addition to glory (which was especially important in the highly competitive male Greek society), there were sometimes substantial financial rewards. Amateurism was unknown in the ancient world: although the four major festivals gave out only crowns of olive, celery, or laurel, victorious athletes often received prizes, either from the festival organizers (at the Panathenaia, the award took the form of large, decorated jars full of olive oil) or from the grateful citizens of their native cities. At Athens, for example, victorious athletes were entitled to receive free meals for life in the public dining room known as the *prutaneion* (where meals were also given to visiting dignitaries). Xenophanes, writing in the sixth century B.C.E., was the first person in the Western tradition to complain that athletes received too much attention while philosophers and intellectuals received too little.

Sources:

Moses I. Finley and H.W. Pleket, *The Olympic Games: The First Thousand Years* (London: Chatto & Windus, 1976).

Robert Flacelière, *Daily Life in Greece at the Time of Pericles*, translated by Peter Green (New York: Macmillan, 1965).

E. Norman Gardiner, *Athletics of the Ancient World* (Oxford: Clarendon Press, 1930).

Michael B. Poliakoff, *Combat Sports in the Ancient World: Competition, Violence, and Culture* (New Haven: Yale University Press, 1987).

David C. Young, *The Olympic Myth of Greek Amateur Athletics* (Chicago: Ares, 1984).

HOUSING

Building Materials. The needs for housing in most of ancient Greece were relatively simple because of the mild climate. Building materials varied somewhat from one region to another, but mostly consisted of stone, clay (used to make bricks and roof tiles), and timber. While marble was used for the facing of fancier buildings, especially in wealthier cities such as Athens, most of the stone used was readily available locally and was often a variety of limestone. Clay was abundant and could be baked (particularly for pottery and other nonarchitectural uses), but unbaked, sun-dried bricks were extremely common in domestic architecture. Timber was widely used in both public and domestic architecture and was available locally or from outside sources, in particular the more temperate regions in Northern Greece and Macedonia.

House Plans. In contrast to the range of architectural styles used for modern housing, the plan and style of most private Greek houses varied little from one city to another, or even from one time period to another. The typical plan consisted of a series of small rooms arranged around a central courtyard, which would be open to the elements. The house would be entered from the street via a door leading into the courtyard itself, often with a small entryway in between. (Since doors opened outward and lacked windows, it was customary in crowded cities for a person leaving home to knock on the door from within, to alert pedestrians to stand clear and avoid being hit.) Unlike most housing in the modern United States, ancient Greek houses in cities were built right next to each other with no intervening space, sharing party walls. Thus, a house would typically have immediate neighbors on three sides, a street on the fourth, and no external lawn or garden area. The courtyard, then, would serve most of the functions of the modern yard—a place to enjoy fresh air, entertain, and work—while providing a degree of privacy not found in most yards. Indeed, the Greek house was typically constructed for maximum privacy: living areas faced away from the street and onto the courtyard, and windows were few and small, in part because the use of glass for windows was unknown in antiquity. In a world in which much of the daily life took place outdoors, face-to-face with others, the *oikos* (house) offered a place of refuge.

Simplicity. Construction and decoration tended to be simple, even for the fairly well-to-do. Walls were built of rubble or sun-dried brick on stone foundations, held together with a mud-based mortar, and usually finished with plaster both inside and out. Often construction was fairly flimsy, so that breaking through the party walls between houses was a favorite technique for burglars (who were sometimes known as *toikhorhukhoi*, or "wall-breakers"). Interior walls were often painted, usually in red or white, to judge from the surviving fragments of painted walls. Floors in most rooms were simply packed earth, although these were probably covered with rugs or mats. In kitchens and dining rooms, however, floors might be made of cement, and in the case of the latter covered with decorative mosaics (which became a common feature in the better houses of the Roman period).

Design Features. Some houses had second stories, but the popularity of this design feature is difficult to determine because surviving archaeological evidence is scant. (Taller, apartment-style buildings became feasible only after stronger building materials were developed by the Romans.) The second floor would be reached by a ladder, by an exterior set of stairs (especially if the second floor was a separate apartment), or, in rare instances, by a fixed staircase. In some cities, second floors were built in such a way as to overhang the street, as a way of gaining additional living space without buying additional land. Roofs were either flat (thus offering additional storage and living space) or sloping, depending on the climate and local traditions (sloping roofs were especially useful in the north to allow the runoff of rain and snow). Sloping roofs were either covered by thatch, terracotta tiles, or some combination of the two.

Men's Room. Many houses had a room specially set aside for receiving and entertaining guests. Called the *andrôn* ("men's area," since most guests were male), it functioned as a dining room as well. The floor was of a hard, durable material (cement or mosaic tile) in order to make cleaning easier. Couches for dining (in formal situations, the Greeks ate lying down) were arranged around the perimeter of the room, and rooms were referred to by the number of couches they could hold. An eleven-couch room was fairly large, perhaps twenty feet across, making it the largest room in the house. The floor near the walls might be raised up, with tables placed in the lower-lying floor in the middle of the room. In order not to isolate the guests on the entry side, the doorway would be off center, near the corner of the room.

Women's Room. Greek men attempted to control female members of their household as much as possible, and this included sheltering them from the outside world. Upper-class women rarely went out without supervision, and there were special areas of the house set aside for them, to which male guests were not admitted. These areas were known as the *gunaikeion* (women's quarters). In some ways, the entire house except for the andrôn was thought of as women's space: men were supposed to spend as much time as possible in public, and a man who chose to spend too much of his leisure time at home with women was viewed with suspicion. The gun-

Terracotta figures of daily life activities: a mother and daughter cooking together; a woman grinding flour for bread; and a woman taking a bath (top: Museum of Fine Arts, Boston; middle and bottom: British Museum, London)

actual space used would have varied with the needs of the individual household.

Hearths. Although the hearth was an important concept for the Greeks (particularly in the form of Hestia, goddess of the hearth, who guaranteed the prosperity of the oikos), few houses actually had permanent hearths or fireplaces; in fact, separate, identifiable kitchen areas were not common before the fourth century. Instead, cooking could be done on small, portable braziers, either in the courtyard or in an interior room, using wood or charcoal (the latter was preferred because it contained more energy in a small volume and burned more controllably). Heating also depended primarily on charcoal, again burned in small vessels. There was no central heating, and ovens were usually found only in larger commercial establishments, such as bakeries and baths. Even so, ventilation was a problem, especially with charcoal, which produces carbon monoxide. It seems that the most common solution was to remove a tile or section of roof after the fire was lit, although some houses had holes designed for the purpose, and there are references in literary sources to terracotta smoke conduits (probably a sort of primitive chimney), which would have been found in fancier houses.

Water Supply. Greek houses lacked running water, so water had to be hauled in from nearby sources such as natural springs, but in many locations they were unavailable or had dried up during the summer. In these cases wells had to be used or cisterns had to be built to collect rainwater (which would generally be allowed to settle and clear before use). By the sixth century engineers had developed the technology for channeling water, so that springs could be tapped and the water led by ground-level terracotta pipes to collect in fountains within the city walls. Gathering water from a nearby fountain would have been a daily task for household members or slaves, who would have to bring enough for drinking, cooking, and personal hygiene. Although Greece has a dry climate, the conservation of rainwater and the diligence and ingenuity of public officials seem to have ensured an adequate water supply for most cities, including Athens, whose population was larger than that of any other Greek city.

Sewage. The disposal of used water and other wastes was a constant problem. Originally, bathing took place inside the house in small, portable tubs; and in cities chamber pots were used for urination and defecation. Yet, public baths developed quickly in the cities, and were common by the fourth century B.C.E., when they had important social as well as hygienic functions. In addition, built-in baths and toilets were in use in Olynthus and presumably elsewhere. In such houses terracotta drainpipes would have led the waste out of the house and into the streets, although in the absence of plumbing it would have been necessary to pour wastewater into the pipes by hand. Even so, provisions for adequate disposal of waste are found starting only in the fourth century. Before that time, there were presumably gutters in the streets, which would accumulate waste that would be washed away by rainwater. This lack of sani-

aikeion might be upstairs, since these areas were more remote and easier to control access to, especially in the absence of fixed staircases. Yet, this situation was not true for all houses: it is in general impossible to identify the function of most rooms from the architectural remains. Similarly, there are no ways of identifying the separate quarters which must have existed for slaves: the

tation certainly must have contributed to the spread of infectious disease such as the great plague of Athens in 430–429 B.C.E., although Greek science and medicine were not advanced enough to recognize the problem (an adequate theory of disease and contagion was developed only in the nineteenth century C.E.). Older cities, such as Athens, never achieved adequate sewage; however, in newer settlements such as Pella in Macedon urban planning allowed for more regular, wider streets with covered sewers that drained the waste from adjacent houses.

Disposal. Nevertheless, there was relatively little garbage to be disposed of in Greece. Much modern trash consists of paper, packaging (including bottles and cans), and other items unknown or rare in Greece. Greek society was far less materially rich than our own: even wealthy people had relatively few possessions, and far fewer of these were disposable than is the case in the United States. In a culture of relative scarcity objects are reused rather than discarded, and the presence of domestic animals (along with the relative scarcity of food) ensured that little food would be thrown out. Even human excrement would often be collected in pits for use as fertilizer. Even so, cities were probably rather unhygienic by modern Western standards, and rodents and insects were common.

Decoration. Throughout the Classical Period (480–323 B.C.E.), decoration and furnishings in private houses were usually modest. This situation was in part because of the relative difficulty of getting luxury goods, but also because of an ideology of equality, in which ostentatious displays of wealth were frowned upon (especially true in Athens and Sparta). In addition to the sort of simple wall paintings mentioned above, there are references to other types of wall decoration: bronze plaques, tapestries, and embroideries. Ceiling decorations are also referred to in wealthy houses, and the Athenian Alcibiades, famous for his extravagant lifestyle, is said to have hired a famous painter to paint frescoes on his walls.

Furniture. As is the case today, furniture and other household objects could be both useful and decorative. A major difference, however, is in the size and portability of ancient furniture, which could be moved easily from room to room and house to house. Tables, chairs, couches, stools, and beds were the primary items of furniture; large cabinets, dressers, and armoires were unknown, with smaller, movable chests and boxes being used for storage (nor were there closets, since clothing was folded and stored flat). Since wood survives only in exceptional conditions, there are few surviving examples of Greek furniture.

Chair Types. Chairs typically had curving backs but no armrests. The most common type was the *klismos,* which might be translated as "easy chair," with a curved, slightly reclined back and plain, curved legs. A fancier variation was the *thronos* (throne), a more solid and upright chair, often highly decorated, and found in palaces and temples rather than in private households. At the low end of the scale was the

The lives of Greek women were lived mostly in private, with little opportunity for participation in public life. Pericles, in his *Funeral Oration* of 431 B.C.E. (as reported by Thucydides), comments on "female excellence," saying that "the best reputation consists of not falling short of their natural character, and that their glory is greatest when they are spoken of least by men—whether they are praised or blamed." In other words, the safest way for a woman to maintain a good reputation is to avoid becoming an object of public scrutiny and to remain in the private world of the *oikos* (household).

A major exception, however, was religious ritual. In Athens, women of the citizen class were priestesses in several public cults and took part in processions at the major festivals. In Aristophanes' *Lysistrata* (411 B.C.E.), an old woman declares her devotion to the city by giving her pedigree, listing the honorific positions she has held:

At the age of seven, I carried the sacred objects; then at ten I ground the barley for Athene; and wearing a saffron robe, I played the Bear-girl in the festival of Brauronian Artemis. After I grew up, and was beautiful, I carried the sacred basket, and wore a necklace of dried figs.

Spartan women had a different way of life, involving much more physical exercise and exposure to the public eye. Plutarch describes the intentions of the Spartan lawgiver Lycurgus in this way:

Lycurgus took particular care about the women as well as the men. He made the young women exercise their bodies by running and wrestling and throwing the discus and the javelin, so that their offspring would have a sound start by taking root in sound bodies and grow stronger, and the women themselves would be able to use their strength to withstand childbearing and wrestle with labour pains. He freed them from softness and sitting in the shade and all female habits, and made it customary for girls no less than boys to go naked in processions and to dance naked at certain festivals and to sing naked while young men were present and looking on. . . . There was nothing shameful in the girls' nakedness, because it was accompanied by modesty and self-control. It produced in them simple habits and an intense desire for good health, and gave the female sex a taste for noble sentiments, since they shared with the males virtue and desire for glory.

diphros (stool), backless and with four straight legs; a common variant—easy to transport and store—was the folding stool, in which the legs crossed, somewhat like a director's chair without arms or back.

Bed and Couch. The *klinê* combined the functions of both bed and couch and was used not only for sleeping and rest, but also for dining, which was often done in a reclining position. It lacked a back and was designed for reclining rather than sitting, typically having one end slanted upward for the purpose. Legs could be slightly curved or straight, and sometimes took the form of animal legs (compare the lions' feet found on sofas and bathtubs in the modern era). The frame of the couch was wooden, but its actual weight-bearing surface consisted of interlaced webbing (of leather or rope) on top of which a thin mattress would be placed. In wealthier homes coverlets, blankets, and pillows might be placed on the klinê. Couches were light enough to allow transport from one room to another, and perhaps outdoors or onto the roof for sleeping during hot weather. Sheets were unknown, and mattresses probably not very soft, so the ancient bed would seem a bit uncomfortable by modern standards.

Table Types. Tables were probably not as popular as in most modern American households, simply because the Greeks had fewer things to put on them—books were rare and lamps were small and stood on separate stands. In wealthier houses there may have been displays of decorative objects, such as the vases, signed by famous artists, which must have been too good for everyday use. But most tables were used during meals, and were light enough to take away when not needed. Tables could have three or four legs and were made of wood, sometimes with metal legs or feet for added durability.

Lighting. Indoor lighting was accomplished with oil-burning lamps. These could be placed on stands, or suspended from chains or cords. Made of metal or clay, they survive in abundance, in a wide variety of sizes. The most common fuel was olive oil, which was stored in a reservoir; a wick was inserted into the lamp nozzle and lit. The technology was far from perfect: such lamps do not produce a lot of light and give off heat as well, unwanted in the summer. They posed a fire hazard, and the use of cheaper grades of olive oil could fill a room with smoke. Even lighting a lamp could prove a problem, since kindling fire was not easy (the usual practice was to keep a flame or embers burning, from which a fire could be rekindled). Outdoors, it was possible to use torches, which would burn with a brighter flame and were necessary to find one's way through the streets on dark nights (there was no street lighting). Insufficient lighting was, however, less of a problem than it might appear, since the Greeks, like most preindustrial peoples, lived according to the rhythm of the day, rising at dawn and spending few of their waking hours in the dark.

Architectural Variations. In addition to the basic plan outlined above, some houses were more elaborate in terms of the courtyards and the rooms that led off them. A common variation in fancier houses was to have a *peristulê*—that is, a series of columns around the courtyard, supporting a small roofed-over area that would provide an outdoor space sheltered from rain and sun. Other houses had a large room off the courtyard that faced south in order to catch as much winter sunlight as possible, with a shallow porch to protect from midday sun. This type is called the *prostas;* a similar design, but with more than one room leading off the porch, is called the *pastas.*

Oikos. The word *oikos* refers to the physical house, but also refers to what is called the "household": the house and its inhabitants. For the Greeks, this was not merely a family unit, but an economic one: occupations and trades tended to be passed from one generation to the next, and all family members were participants. In addition, the *oikos* included nonfamily members: slaves, freedmen or freedwomen, and perhaps guests and lodgers. These social arrangements have important implications for the quality of daily life. First, households tended to be quite a bit larger than the nuclear family: aged parents often lived with their grown children (three- and even four-generation households must have been common given Greek longevity). In addition, there is evidence for various types of extended families, including unmarried female relatives, who would have to be under the care of a *kurios* (head of household). Greek houses were not large: Olynthus, a wealthy fourth century community that took advantage of urban planning, had houses ranging from 1,500 to 3,000 square feet; other, older cities had smaller houses. Therefore, they would have seemed extremely crowded by our standards.

Economics. The *oikos* as economic unit also affected daily life by making the physical house a center of commerce and trade. Artisans did not always have separate premises for their trade: instead, they worked out of the home, so some of the already-precious living area of the house would be given over to work space for shoemaking, metalsmithing, and other crafts. Farmers (including those with houses in town) used their courtyards for activities such as pressing olives or grapes and for storing grain; excavations have revealed wells, cisterns for rainwater, and manure pits in household courtyards.

Lodgers. Not every physical oikos, however, contained a single family. Many households took in lodgers, either renting individual rooms or, sometimes, the entire second floor (more convenient when there was a separate, exterior entrance). This practice was especially common in the larger cities such as Athens, where there was a large transient population, because of the presence of traders and foreign residents (known as *metoikoi*, or metics) and of country residents who had come into town for business or political purposes. Sometimes there were rooms fronting onto the street rather than the courtyard, which could be used as shops and thus rented to outsiders or used by members of the oikos.

Sources:
Robert Flacelière, *Daily Life in Greece at the Time of Pericles,* translated by Peter Green (New York: Macmillan, 1965).

Oswyn Murray and Simon Price, eds., *The Greek City: From Homer to Alexander* (Oxford: Clarendon Press; New York: Oxford University Press, 1990).

G.M.A. Richter, *The Furniture of the Greeks, Etruscans, and Romans* (London: Phaidon Press, 1966).

LEISURE AND FESTIVALS

Rhythms of Life. The amount of leisure time, and the rhythms of daily life, varied tremendously according to location and class. Rich people in Athens and other large cities were not expected to work and would spend their days participating in politics, gossiping, training in the gumnasion (gymnasium), or perhaps engaging in intellectual pursuits. In Sparta, a strict military training regimen reduced the amount of leisure time for all classes. Everywhere and at all times working people and farmers had less leisure time, although this varied seasonally (especially for farmers) and during major civic festivals.

Sundials. Time was structured differently for the ancient Greeks than it is for the modern world. In a society with only poor means of illumination, the daylight hours were too valuable to waste: the habit of getting up at dawn was nearly universal. A further difference is that there were no accurate means of subdividing the day. Two time-telling devices were available: the sundial and the *klepsudra,* a clock that allowed water to drip from one container to another. Yet, these aids were limited since they could not provide accurate and consistent divisions of the entire day. The klepsudra was used to measure small amounts of time—in particular, to limit the amount of time given to speakers in courts. The sundial could measure the whole day, but with rather poor accuracy. Rather than using the location of the shadow on a dial, Greek sundials consisted of an upright pointer (the gnomon) which cast a shadow whose length varied throughout the day. An agreement to meet at a certain time might take the form of "Let's meet when the shadow is ten feet long," but this would only work if both people were using a sundial of the same length and, of course, if the weather was clear. Furthermore, the length of the shadow would vary according to season (longer in winter, when the sun is lower) so that the concept of a fixed division of the day

(a sixty-minute hour or a sixty-second minute) never developed for the Greeks (or the Romans, who used more sophisticated sundials).

Schedules. Many events simply happened early. Since getting out of bed at dawn was standard practice, there was no particular reason not to begin the day's activities then. Moreover, an invitation for dinner at sunset would be easy enough to interpret. Yet, most of the time life was lived with far less precision in regard to time than modern society is accustomed to: nothing could happen on a precise, tight schedule since there was almost no way to make such a schedule.

Calendar. The calendar as well had a significant influence on everyday life. There was no generally agreed upon calendar among the various Greek states: every state had its own, with different names for the months and even different dates for the New Year. Months were named after gods honored in them (Poseidon, for instance), or after festivals that occurred within them (Anthesterion, from the festival Anthesteria). Each month had 29 or 30 days, leaving a year of 354 or 355 days, which meant that an extra month (known as an intercalary month) had to be added about every third year to keep the calendar in line with the seasons. Years were usually reckoned according to the names of civic officials (for example, "in the archonship of Demetrios"), but could also be expressed in terms of Olympiads: that is, four-year periods dating from the first Olympian Games (ancient forerunners of our modern Olympics) in 776 B.C.E. Thus, someone might refer to "the second year of the fifty-first Olympiad" for the year 575 B.C.E., but this method did not become widespread until later.

Weekdays. There was nothing corresponding to the modern notion of the week: that is, no regular, recurring pattern of days, with some set aside for rest. Instead, there were religious festivals, scheduled throughout the year at irregular intervals, that gave working people a

A marble bas-relief depicting animal fights, which provided amusement and an opportunity to gamble in the *gumnasia,* circa 500 B.C.E. (National Archaeological Museum, Athens; David Lees)

break from their daily routine. There were perhaps sixty festival days in the Athenian calendar, and the activities that took place during festivals were some of the most pleasant, and important, of Greek life.

Celebrations. While certain religious occasions such as *thusiai*, or sacrifices, were quite solemn, others were carefree, lighthearted, and even raucous affairs. The large public festivals known as *heortai* were characterized by parades, games, abundant food and wine, music, athletic competitions, and dramatic performances. Modern analogues might include Fourth of July celebrations, St. Patrick's Day parades, church picnics, the Olympic Games, and open-air dramatic festivals such as Shakespeare in the Park. Yet, not one of these contains all the elements of a large Greek festival. Although every Greek city had its own festivals, those of Athens are the best known. The most important Athenian festivals were the Panathenaia, the Anthesteria, the Thesmophoria, and the City Dionysia.

Panathenaia. The Panathenaia was an annual festival, dedicated to the city's patron goddess Athena, and took place in the month of Hekatombaion (late summer, usually equivalent to August). It began with a *pannukhis*, or all-night festival, in which choruses of young men and women would feast, sing, and dance. On the following day the festival's most spectacular event took place: a large procession, which is represented on the Parthenon frieze (now in the British Museum in London). Members of different groups of Athenian society (including resident foreigners) marched or rode on horseback through the city and up to the Acropolis. This procession was followed by sacrifices to Athena, and the roasting and public distribution of the meat. (Distribution was by lot, and the assertion that all citizens were entitled to equal shares was an important part of democratic ideology.) Every fourth year, the festival was expanded into a "Greater Panathenaia," which included competitions in athletics and music, open to citizens of other Greek states. On these occasions, the Panathenaia rivaled the large Panhellenic athletic festivals such as the Olympian Games.

Anthesteria. The Anthesteria was dedicated to Dionysus, especially in his role as god of wine. It took place in the month named after it (Anthesterion), roughly corresponding to February. On the first day of the festival (*Pithoigia*, which literally means "jar-opening"), jars of new wine from the previous autumn's harvest were taken to the sanctuary of Dionysus in the Marshes, opened, and consumed after libations were offered to the god. The second day (*Khoes*) was devoted to a sort of drinking contest: participants, including children and slaves, sat at tables and drank (in silence) khoes filled with wine. The khoes were large vessels, holding about five liters (over one gallon), and participating in one's first Khoes festival was a sort of rite of passage for young people (not unlike a bar mitzvah or first communion). The third day involved offering pots full of seed and vegeta-

ble bran to the dead. The festival as a whole seems to have involved reversals of normal status and practices and was celebrated in most Greek cities that spoke the Ionian dialect.

Thesmophoria. The Thesmophoria was a women's festival honoring Demeter, the goddess of the harvest, and was celebrated in all Greek cities. It took place in the autumn, before the time for the sowing of winter crops. Women set up camps outside the city walls and stayed there for three days. At some time well before the festival, pigs were slaughtered and thrown into pits; during the festival the rotted remains were brought up and placed on altars to Demeter and her daughter Korê, and then mixed with seed in order to ensure a good harvest. Men were excluded from the festival, and participants were supposed to keep the proceedings a secret. In fact, they did so quite well, since modern scholars have little evidence of what actually went on: it seems that the telling of obscene jokes was an element of the festival. Men's curiosity about the proceedings is reflected in the 411 B.C.E. comedy by Aristophanes, *Thesmophoriazousai I* (Women at the Thesmophoria), in which a man tries unsuccessfully to infiltrate the festival.

City Dionysia. The City Dionysia was another festival dedicated to Dionysus, taking place in the month of Elaphebolion (late March). This period was a slack time for agriculture, and the city was full of visitors from the surrounding countryside and from other parts of Greece. The festival began with a procession bringing an image of Dionysus to the theater built in his honor on the south slope of the Acropolis. The following day, a larger procession wound its way through the city, with the participants bearing various symbols of fertility including phalli and loaves of bread. Sacrifices, with public distribution of the meat, followed. The next four days were devoted to dramatic competitions, with each of the city's ten tribes entering one men's chorus and one boys' chorus in the dithyramb (a dramatic choral performance which involved song and dance, but no separate actors). After the dithyramb, competitions in tragedy and comedy performances took place. Three tragedians would compete, each producing three tragedies and one satyr play; and five different comedians would each produce one play. Dramatic performances would be held in the open-air theater dedicated to Dionysus, and would last an entire day.

Sense of Community. What these festivals all have in common, besides their religious elements, is their celebration of community. All members of the community participated—women, slaves, metics, and children—and not just male citizens. Festivals provided the poor with a chance to eat and drink well at public expense. They could also serve as rites of initiation into the community for younger people and allow grown men to show off their power and prestige. For women, they provided a chance to get out of the house and to participate in civic life in ways not normally available to them. Evidence from Aristophanes suggests that the religious rites and festivals were among the most memorable and noteworthy moments in many women's lives: old women in the *Lysistrata* (411 B.C.E.) reminisce about participating in a procession to Artemis and carrying sacred relics to honor Athena. Classicists know relatively little about the daily life of women: much of it must have taken place inside the house and been devoted to housework, weaving, and other crafts. Male sources, with misogyny that is partly serious and partly in jest, suggest that women spent their time in drinking, gossiping, and shopping for clothes and ornaments. The available information about festivals provides a partial corrective to this notion.

Sources:

Richard Hamilton, *Choes and Anthesteria: Athenian Iconography and Ritual* (Ann Arbor: University of Michigan Press, 1991).

Herbert William Parke, *Festivals of the Athenians* (Ithaca, N.Y.: Cornell University Press, 1977).

Arthur Wallace Pickard-Cambridge, *The Dramatic Festivals of Athens* (Oxford: Clarendon Press, 1968).

SYMPOSIA

Significance. One of the most important leisure activities in Greece was the symposium. The symposium was, on the one hand, a drinking party: its name is derived from the words *sun* and *posis* and literally means "drinking together." It was, on the other hand, a complex institution that had important social and political implications. Perhaps no other institution reveals more about the lives of Greek citizen males, and about class and gender ideology.

Exclusive Club. Meals assume a great symbolic importance in all cultures. For the Greeks, eating together had the function of asserting the cohesiveness of the community: all citizens in Athens could get an equal share of sacrificial meat, while Spartan men ate at communal messes to reinforce their sense of being an army, not just a citizen body. The symposium is an application of this principle to smaller, more exclusive groups: not the whole citizen body, but a self-defined, exclusive subset of that group. The symposium was a leisure activity of upper-class males, whose bonding was designed to exclude others: women, noncitizen males, and males who were political or social rivals of the symposiasts.

Evidence. The history of the symposium can be traced back to Homer. In the *Iliad* and *Odyssey* (both written around the eighth and seventh centuries B.C.E.) feasting among the leading warriors is an important social occasion, one by which the harmony of the elite social order is reasserted (in contrast to the breakdowns in the social order caused by war, or by Penelope's unruly suitors). While these are fictitious works, they reflected the ideals of the poet and the audience he composed for, so it may be assumed that formalized aristocratic dining rituals existed well before 700 B.C.E. At about this time, new rituals began to be imported from Lydia, such as the practice of lying down at the table. It

is at this time that the drinking part of the evening (the symposium proper) was separated from the dinner which preceded it, and the complex rituals of the symposium developed.

Proper Etiquette. Sometimes friends, or the members of a club or association, would arrange to share expenses of the meal, each contributing his portion known as an *eranos*. The more exalted form of the symposium, however, involved hosts rich enough to pay the expenses themselves and to provide a suitable atmosphere. Guests upon arrival would remove their shoes and have their feet washed by slaves. Seating was on couches in the *andrôn* (the men's quarters or dining room): five, seven, or eleven couches were the norm, with usually two guests per couch. Larger rooms are not unheard of, but since a primary purpose of the symposium was to create an intimate atmosphere for bonding among the guests, this tended to limit the size of the rooms. Because of the presence of a door in one of the walls, there was a recognizable hierarchy in seating, with a head place for the host, and other places reserved for honored and less-honored guests (the practice of bringing friends along seems to have been common).

Libations. Dinner came first (presumably with wine), then the symposium proper began. First, a slave came around to allow the guests to wash their hands; at this point they were crowned with wreaths of laurel leaves or flowers, and perhaps anointed with perfume. Next, libations were poured to the gods, in particular to Dionysus, the god of wine (here called the *agathos daimôn*, or "good divinity," for giving humans the gift of wine). The libation would involve taking a small sip of unmixed wine (the only time that unmixed wine would be drunk during a well-ordered symposium) and sprinkling a few drops of it on the ground. Hymns to Dionysus were also sung.

Wine Preparation. The next step was to choose a *symposiarch* (leader of the symposium). This person was responsible for fixing the proportions of wine and water, for telling the guests when and how much to drink, and directing the evening's activities (which might consist of speeches, songs, or other contributions from each of the guests). The ritual of mixing and serving wine was a complex one, involving certain shapes of vessels, certain proportions of mixing, and certain ways of drinking. A large open bowl, known as a *kratêr* (the source of the English word *crater*, from its shape), was used for mixing the wine. The water added could be cold or warm (sometimes snow was added, an ostentatious gesture in a country where snow was rare and refrigeration nonexistent). A mixture of half wine and half water was considered dangerously strong; three-to-one and four-to-one seem to be the usual limits. After the wine was mixed, it would be ladled into a jug by a slave, then taken around to serve the individual guests. The cup used by guests might be a goblet or a particular form known as the *kulix*, a shallow, open bowl on a stand and a handle on

A Red Figure drinking cup showing *hetairai*, women companions at the *symposia*, circa 520–510 B.C.E. (Museo Arqueologico, Madrid/Archivo Fotografico)

each side. The shape of the *kulix*, in addition to being useful for playing the game *kottabos*, was desirable since it allowed for decoration on the round, flat interior surface. Cups, bowls, and serving vessels for symposia were usually decorated with scenes appropriate to the symposiastic atmosphere: these could include pictures of Dionysus and scenes of drinking or sexual acts. The effect was to create a symposiastic world that closed in on itself: the symposiasts saw that everything around them reflected the world of the symposium, which would not only increase the intensity and pleasure of the experience, but also help cement the bond among the participants.

Drunkenness. The ideal symposium would involve drinking enough to get drunk, but not enough to make participants lose control. The symposiarch would tell everyone how much to drink: drinking would be in unison, usually involving giving a toast to each guest, or with each guest in turn singing a song. Guests who failed to perform properly would have to pay a forfeit devised by the symposiarch. The symposiarch would also determine the number of kratêrs to be drunk, either beforehand or as he went along. In a play by the comic poet Eubulus, Dionysus announces that three is the appropriate number for sensible people: "one for health, the second for eros and pleasure, and the third for sleep; when the third is finished, wise guests head home." He continues listing the results of additional *kratêres: hubris,* black eyes, shouting, legal proceedings, and finally—after ten of them—"madness and people throwing furniture around." A well-ordered symposium ended with everyone pleasantly drunk, and then heading home in a procession (a *kômos,* from which the word *comedy* may be derived); but as may be expected, things often got out of hand.

Other Activities. The symposium was a place not only for drinking, but for poetry, music, games, talk, and sex—each of these individually, or in various combinations. In the Archaic Period (700–480 B.C.E.), Greek lyric poetry evolved in the context of the symposium: it is often explicitly about how to run a symposium, but it is also concerned with matters such as love. Music was often provided by the guests themselves, who would play the lyre and sing—either the old lyric songs, or patriotic songs (in Athens, a popular song praised Harmodius and Aristogeiton, famed for killing a tyrant), or lyric passages from tragedies. There were also, in the wealthier houses, hired entertainers: in some cases male poets, singers, mimes, dancers, or acrobats, but often flute girls, who provided an exception to the rule that only men attended symposia. Flute girls were not respectable women of the citizen class, and in many cases doubled as prostitutes. The exclusion of women was not merely motivated by a desire to preserve an all-male world, but by a desire to protect women from the sexual attention of men (the same impulse that led to the construction of women's quarters within the house).

Homoeroticism. The symposium also functioned as a place where male homoeroticism could find full expression. Greek adult males were routinely attracted to both women and adolescent males, and the all-male, erotically charged atmosphere of the symposium was a perfect place to forge erotic bonds as well as social and political ones (indeed, the erotic and the political often overlapped, and a youth's choice of lovers could be a way of making alliances for the future). A tomb painting from the Greek colony of Paestum, in southern Italy, has a memorable vignette of symposium culture. Guests are reclining on three couches: on the rightmost couch, a man is courting a youth (depicted as beardless), who responds by touching the man's chest. On the center couch, one of the guests looks back with evident jealousy, while his couch-mate is busily engaged in a game of kottabos.

Popular Game. Although there were other games played at the symposium, kottabos is the best known. The game involved holding one's kulix by the handle (a ring-shaped handle, like that on a coffee mug) and using it to fling the remains of wine toward a target. While doing so, it was customary to shout out the name of one's beloved: winning at kottabos was thought to predict erotic success. Variants included trying to knock a disk off a metal rod, or trying to sink targets floating in a basin of water. The game was also played in public baths and was so much a part of the popular consciousness that the Athenian politician Theramenes parodied it with his dying gesture. Condemned to death by Critias and the Thirty Tyrants, he finished his cup of hemlock, flicked the last drops on the ground, and said "Good health to noble Critias!"

Socrates. There were also conversation and intellectual games of various sorts: charades, riddles, and a variety of word games. In this context can be placed the two surviving literary representations of symposia, those by the fourth-century Athenian authors Plato and Xenophon. In each case, the symposium has Socrates as a guest (both authors were his followers), and the guests take turns making speeches about the nature of desire. In Xenophon's *Symposium* (circa 430–circa 356 B.C.E.) the speeches are frivolous and lighthearted and interspersed with entertainment from mimes, dancers, and acrobats. At the end the eroticism of the dancers inspires the guests to rush home to their wives, and the symposium ends in an orderly (if hasty) way. It is not an entirely typical example (the presence of Socrates reminds us that this is a literary work with philosophical implications), but it is probably accurate in reflecting the mix of entertainment, semiserious conversation, and eroticism that went on at many symposia.

Serious Conversation. Plato's *Symposium* (circa 380–360 B.C.E.) is altogether atypical. A group of guests gather at the house of the tragic playwright Agathon to celebrate the victory he had won in the previous day's dramatic festival. Since they are so hung over from the previous night's celebrations, they decide to dispense with mandatory drinking and allow each guest to drink as much or as little as he

wants. A further break with tradition occurs when the flute girl is sent away, leaving the guests alone to talk about serious matters. Proceeding around the room in turn, each guest makes a speech in praise of Eros, the god of sexual desire. The speeches are complex, philosophical, and entirely devoted to homoerotic desire—women (like the flute girl) are excluded symbolically as well as literally. The climactic speech is that of Socrates, which he claims to have learned from a priestess named Diotima (a complex irony in this all-male world), and which imparts Platonic doctrines on the nature of desire and its relation to the life of philosophy. The symposium reverts to a wilder form, however, when the young political hero Alcibiades crashes the party, and eventually the evening degenerates into wild drinking, with guests falling asleep on their couches and only Socrates left awake at the end. In creating such a fantasy world, Plato showed some of the possibilities inherent in the form of the symposium and also exposed its limitations. After Plato, the fictitious symposium became a popular literary genre, and the word *symposium* today refers not to an occasion for drinking, but for serious conversation.

Women's Equivalent. No formal institution equivalent to the symposium existed for women. Assuredly there were gatherings of women of all classes, especially of those who had leisure time. On many occasions this group activity must have involved sharing meals. Yet, except for public festivals and religious ceremonies, which are well documented, there is relatively little information about women's communal leisure activities. The fact that almost all historical sources were produced by men, combined with the men's reluctance to talk about what women's life in the home was like, leaves modern scholars with little to go on. The standard stereotype about women was that they were overly fond of wine, sex, gossip, and luxury: how much truth, if any, lay behind this is open to debate. In a world in which women were not citizens of the cities they inhabited, and in which they were almost entirely shut off from public life, at-home amusements must have been extremely important.

Sources:

Kenneth J. Dover, *Greek Homosexuality* (Cambridge, Mass.: Harvard University Press, 1977).

François Lissarague, *The Aesthetics of the Greek Banquet: Images of Wine and Ritual* (Princeton: Princeton University Press, 1990).

William J. Slater, ed., *Dining in a Classical Context* (Ann Arbor: University of Michigan Press, 1991).

DOCUMENTARY SOURCES

Aristophanes, *The Comedies* (circa 446–circa 386 B.C.E.)—In many ways the best source for Greek daily life. Aristotle said that tragedy depicted people as being better than they really are, and comedy showed them as being worse than they really are, which is certainly true to the extent that comedy focuses on the basic, the mundane, and the vulgar. Characters in tragedy are concerned with saving their cities from plagues and getting revenge for ancestral wrongs; characters in comedy are concerned with the needs of the body. For this reason Aristophanes' plays provide a wealth of information on housing, sanitation, eating, sex, drinking, clothing, and games. The fragments of the other Athenian comic playwrights, such as Eubulus, also provide insight into ancient Greek daily life, but unfortunately English translations are often difficult to find.

Demosthenes, *The Speeches* (circa 384–322 B.C.E.)—Demosthenes and the other Attic orators such as Lysias and Aeschines reveal much about daily life, although most of it indirectly. Speakers in law courts referred to customs and practices that their audience was familiar with, and for this reason modern readers sometimes have to fill in the blanks themselves.

Homer, *Iliad* and *Odyssey* (circa eighth-seventh centuries B.C.E.)—Like many ancient sources, the work of Homer is not specifically about daily life, but reveals details in passing. The *Iliad* and *Odyssey* are particularly valuable because they are the earliest surviving Greek literature. Because of this reason, they provide evidence for the historical development of certain customs. Of particular value are the descriptions of the household of Odysseus throughout the *Odyssey* (including the layout of the house and the various economic activities, such as weaving, that it supported). For recreation and athletics, the descriptions of games in *Odyssey*, chapter 8, and *Iliad*, chapter 23, are important.

Herodotus, *History of the Persian Wars* (circa late fifth century B.C.E.)—This is the first work of history in the Western tradition. Unlike his successor Thucydides, Herodotus focuses on the personal element in history: on the lives of powerful individuals and the ways in which their moral decisions have political consequences. He is also interested in what is known today as ethnography and anthropology, and thus provides much information about Greek customs and the ways in which the Greeks differed from their non-Greek neighbors.

Hesiod, *Works and Days* (circa eighth century B.C.E.)—This volume provides information about the life of farmers from the earliest years of the period under study.

Pindar, *Epinikia* (circa 518–circa 438 B.C.E.)—These odes were written for athletic victors from the major festivals (Olympic, Pythian, Nemean, and Isthmian Games). The odes reveal fairly little about the contests themselves, but they provide much information on the social context of athletic victories.

Plato, *Symposium* (circa 380–360 B.C.E.)—A description of a fictitious dinner party set in 416 B.C.E., with Socrates, Aristophanes, and other members of the Athenian intelligentsia discussing the nature of Eros. While the dialogue reports a symposium that is in many ways atypical (less drinking than usual, and more philosophy), it nevertheless provides important clues about symposiastic practices.

Sophocles, *Electra* (circa 497–405 B.C.E.)—While tragedy is not as rich as comedy in details of daily life, some individual passages are significant. A good example is the false description of Orestes' death in a chariot-racing accident. Not only does it provide details of how chariot racing was done, but the length of the description (two hundred lines, approximately one-seventh of the length of the play) shows that the audience must have known enough about horse racing to make a speech such as this one appropriate for the genre of the tragic stage.

Xenophanes, *Poems* (circa 560–circa 478 B.C.E.)—The second poem of Xenophanes contrasts the honor paid to athletes with the relative neglect of poets and wise men.

Xenophon, *Symposium* (circa 430–circa 356 B.C.E.)—Not as interesting as Plato's dialogue of the same name, but more typical: this symposium has descriptions of entertainment and games in addition to serious conversation.

CHAPTER EIGHT

THE FAMILY AND SOCIAL TRENDS

by LAURA MCCLURE

CONTENTS

CHRONOLOGY
239

OVERVIEW
244

TOPICS IN THE FAMILY AND SOCIAL TRENDS

Children and
 Education 248

*Military Training and
 Initiation Rites* 250

Conception and
 Childbirth 251

*Sigmund Freud and
 Hysteria* 253

Marriage 254

*A Girl's Experience of
 Marriage* 255

Sexual Misconduct 257

Sexuality 259

A Greek Love Spell 259

Social Roles in the
 Household 264

*Was There Really a
 Trojan War?* 264

Greek Tragedy 265

The Sorrows of Antigone 268

SIGNIFICANT PEOPLE

Aspasia 269

Cleisthenes 269

Draco 269

Lycurgus 270

Pisistratus 270

DOCUMENTARY SOURCES
271

Sidebars and tables are listed in italics.

800* B.C.E.

- The Greek Dark Ages end, and a period begins in which the population expands and city-states emerge. Also, contact is made with Egypt and the Near East.

750*

- The Greek alphabet is developed.
- Greek colonists settle in Ionia, the western coastal region of Asia Minor bordering the Aegean Sea.
- The first oral recitations of Homer's epic tales the *Iliad* and the *Odyssey* occur.

700*

- The poet Hesiod composes *Theogony,* an account both of the origins of the universe and the Greek gods and their interrelation and *Works and Days,* an advice manual mostly concerned with farming.

650*

- The first stone temples are erected by the city-states.
- Ibycus, Sappho, and Anacreon compose their lyric poems.
- The great lawgiver Lycurgus establishes a system of military training that turns Sparta into one of the most powerful city-states in Greece. He also creates a constitution that guarantees political equality for all Spartans.

621*

- Draco prepares the first comprehensive written code of laws for Athens. He proscribes the death penalty for practically all offenses, including adultery.

600*

- The first Greek coins are minted in Lydia.

594*

- The tyrant Solon's reforms promote equality among the citizens of Athens.

560

- Pisistratus and his sons begin a fifty-year rule of Athens and institute state festivals, such as the City Dionysia and Panathenaia, to promote solidarity among citizens.
- Stone statues of youths and maidens begin to appear.

* Denotes circa date

535*
- A transition from Black Figure to Red Figure pottery occurs.
- Eastern influences appear in Athenian art because of the influx of refugees fleeing the Persians.

508*
- Cleisthenes gains support among the Athenian people and overthrows the Pisistradid family. This revolt results in the first democratic government in the history of Western civilization.

490
- The Greeks defeat the Persians at the Battle of Marathon. As a result of this victory, the status of the Athenians increases, and they expand their empire.

479
- The Persians are expelled from Athens but not before destroying the monuments on the Acropolis. The new artistic style exhibited by subsequent art provides a convenient break between the Archaic and Classical Periods.

477
- Athens helps establish the Delian League to protect the city-states from continued threats of Persian invasion. Athens amasses a great amount of wealth by taxing its subject allies.
- Athens begins a period of unparalleled artistic and cultural productivity. Athenian drama increases in popularity.

458
- The first performance of Aeschylus's *Oresteia* trilogy, one of the most important works of literature in Greek history, occurs. Among other things, the play celebrates Athens and its democratic government.

455
- The Sophists, teachers of rhetoric, arrive in Athens.

451
- A law sponsored by the statesman Pericles refuses to recognize as citizens children born of unions between a citizen male and a noncitizen or foreign mother.

440

- The earliest medical writings in the *Hippocratic Corpus* reflect a growing interest in reason and systematic thought.
- Sophocles writes *Antigone,* a play that celebrates human reason and yet, at the same time, reminds people of the importance of family.
- The historian Herodotus composes *History of the Persian Wars.*

431

- The Second Peloponnesian War begins and lasts until 404.
- Euripides writes *Medea,* a play that shows the difficulties of life for ancient Greek women and is one of the poet's most famous works.
- Aristophanes, considered one of the greatest writers of comedies of all time, begins to compose his more than forty politically charged works.

423

- The Athenian general and historian Thucydides is exiled and begins to write his *History of the Peloponnesian War.*

404

- Sparta becomes the most powerful city-state in Greece after winning the Second Peloponnesian War.

399

- The philosopher Socrates is put on trial and condemned to death; the events are later recorded by his pupil Plato in his philosophical dialogues.

390

- Xenophon writes *Economics,* a Socratic dialogue concerned with proper domestic relationships and with managing the household.

384

- Aristotle, one of the greatest philosophers of antiquity and the tutor of Alexander the Great, is born.

380

- Plato writes the *Symposium,* a dialogue in which male poets and philosophers at a drinking party make speeches about love.

359 • Philip II assumes the throne, and Macedon becomes a major power.

356 • Alexander III, or Alexander the Great, son of Philip II, is born.

343 • Demosthenes' oration *Against Neaira* is composed and delivered at a trial.

334 • Alexander the Great begins his military campaigns against Persia. His conquests lead to a massive expansion of Greek power and the spread of Greek language and culture.

323 • Alexander the Great dies of fever in Babylon.

A cup with a painting of Zeus pursuing Ganymede (Ferrara 9351 (T.212 BVP), from Spina. "ARV" 880, 12)

OVERVIEW

The Family. In contrast to more well-documented periods of world history, sources for the family and social trends in ancient Greece are exiguous. Most of the evidence comes from literary texts, and of those, the richest material is the poetry of Homer, composed in the Archaic Period, around 750 B.C.E., and Athenian tragedy, performed between 480 and 404 B.C.E., at the beginning of the Classical era. Literary texts, like modern cinema and novels, may provide insight into some of the underlying ideas the ancient Greeks had about family life and social roles, but they do not always reflect the lives of everyday people. Often they focus on a bygone era filled with kings and queens, aristocrats and warriors, a world in which slaves, children, and commoners figure little. Instead, they tell us more about how the ancient Greeks imagined things should be, rather than how they really were. In the Classical Period, a broader array of sources is available: inscriptions, historical works, and law-court speeches provide more insight into everyday life because they deal with actual people and events.

Homeric Society. Emerging from a dark age in which literacy and other forms of culture were temporarily lost to the Greeks, the Homeric poems combine historical and fictional elements to portray a remote past of mythical kings and their heroic exploits. The *Iliad* and the *Odyssey* (both written circa eighth–seventh centuries B.C.E.) of Homer describe a world divided into small, regional, clan-based chiefdoms, one that harks back to the societies of the late Bronze and the Dark Ages. Homeric society has no written law, only a set of shared customs handed down by word of mouth from generation to generation. Nonetheless, these poems represent the family unit as comprised of a male head of household, a wife, children, and the land, the same social organization found in the Classical Period.

Household. The Greek word *oikos* (household) refers both to the family and its descendants, the clan or tribe, and the physical space they inhabited. Because ancient Greek society was patrilineal, the physical holdings of the household in both the Archaic and Classical Periods passed directly from father to son. This pattern of inheritance closely linked the estate to a particular clan. The Greek household thus became associated with the concept "one's

own," the origins, identity, and material and emotional interests of a given individual.

Guest Friendship. In the Homeric poems, however, the sphere of "one's own" could extend beyond the oikos to other royal households with which heroes and their families had a direct political relationship known as *xenia* (guest friendship). Guest friends formally recognized their connection through the exchange of visits and gifts; after they died, their sons continued these relationships. In the *Iliad*, two heroes on opposite sides of the battle refuse to kill one another once they learn that their grandfathers had been guest friends.

Proving Oneself. Although the Homeric hero closely identified himself with both his clan and significant personal connections outside his immediate oikos, he nonetheless strove to individuate himself, to make a name for himself, to earn immortal glory. He had to show his potential for leadership through both his ability to persuade others and his skill in battle: he had to be a "speaker of words" and a "doer of deeds." At the same time, by earning glory in battle, he increased the prestige not only of himself but also of his family and kingdom. In the *Iliad* the hero Glaucus shows the importance of excelling in battle when he relates his father's advice "to be always among the bravest, and hold my head above others, not shaming the generation of my fathers." The identity of the Homeric hero is thus closely bound with his family and household.

Relationships. Throughout Greek history, the most important family interests were those of the oikos and its members, expressed as the relationship between husband and wife, parent and child, and master and slave. The proper relationship between individuals in the household formed the basis of Greek ethical thought, an idea found in the work of the archaic poet Hesiod. This early concept of justice centered on domestic and private relationships, not on the city or world beyond the house. The just man treated his guests well and did not commit adultery by sleeping with his brother's wife; he showed compassion to vulnerable children and honored his aging parents.

Husband and Wife. One of the most important relationships within the household was between the Homeric hero and his wife. A distinguishing feature of ancient

Greek society, in contrast to many other ancient cultures, was the practice of monogamous marriage: although a man, but not a woman, could have other sexual partners outside of marriage, he had only one legitimate wife. Only her children were fully recognized as heirs to his property, and, after the law of Pericles in 451–450 B.C.E., only her children were considered citizens in classical Athens. In Homeric society the institution of marriage distinguished the concubine, who was literally "spear-won," a prize taken in battle by the hero, and the "wedded wife." A hero could have a strong emotional tie to a concubine, as King Agamemnon had for Chryseis in the *Iliad*. In contrast to later Greek marriage customs, there were few formal markers of marriage in Homeric society. Because there was no city-state, no laws, and no citizenship in the Homeric world, marriages involved a complex system of gift exchange and property negotiations. Women themselves served as objects of exchanges through which alliances between male-governed households were strengthened. Even Helen, the most beautiful woman in Greek myth, exerts no control over her own fate in the *Iliad*, but rather serves as a pawn in a struggle between men.

Wedding Feast. In the absence of a formal ceremony, the relatives and neighbors who participated in the wedding feast witnessed and socially validated the transference of the bride from the house of her father to the house of her husband. In the *Iliad* the shield that the divine blacksmith, Hephaestus, creates for the hero Achilles after his weapons have been lost in battle depicts a wedding celebration and its importance to the community. The brides are shown being escorted from their fathers' houses at night by torchlight to their new homes. The female celebrants sing a special wedding song, the *hymenaeus*, while young men engage in a ritual dance. This scene suggests that Greek marriage in the earliest period involved at least a public recognition of the couple's union.

Means to an End. In the Homeric world, as in later Greece, marriage could serve as a vehicle for achieving political power and authority for a man, especially if he married a woman from a socially significant family. Although a wife technically did not own any of her husband's property, she came to have a vested interest in its prosperity; thus, Penelope protects Odysseus's property from the lawless suitors for almost twenty years, until her husband returns. Women, through their domestic labor and the birth of children, thus played an important role in increasing their husbands' holdings.

The Classical Polis. While the Homeric poems describe a fictional society influenced by earlier social and political ideas, the audience for these poems actually inhabited a new type of political structure, the polis (city-state). City-states emerged in Greece sometime during the eighth century B.C.E., a time roughly coincident with the appearance of the Homeric poems. City-states were relatively small by modern standards and characterized by political autonomy and social homogeneity. Most inhabitants knew each other by name and lived their whole lives

in the same place, often in the same house, if belonging to the landowning class. Many city-states were ruled by a single individual known as a tyrant. This word did not originally have a negative meaning, but referred to a single, aristocratic leader who managed the city, usually beneficently. City-states could also be governed by a small, select group of aristocrats, known as oligarchs. As their wealth and size increased, they erected stone temples that honored individual gods and celebrated their power and glory, beginning around 650 B.C.E.

Colonies. Because opportunities to own land were extremely limited for all but the wealthiest class of citizens, some Greeks of the Archaic Period left their homelands to settle in Greek colonies abroad, in Asia Minor, along the coast of modern-day Turkey, and in Italy. Colonization afforded the average Greek an opportunity to become a landowner. At the same time, colonies increased the public visibility of Greece throughout the ancient Mediterranean world. On the mainland, the scarcity of land created a class system in which rich landowners cultivated an image of themselves as the true aristocrats to whom all others were inferior. They referred to themselves and their families as "the good" and denounced the rest of the population as "the bad," thereby distinguishing aristocrats from commoners.

Protected Interests. One of the main tasks of the city-state was to protect the interests of the individual household. For Hesiod and later writers, the strength of the polis community depended directly upon the preservation of its households and relationships. Indeed, the household was the social precondition that enabled the polis to emerge. Aristotle described the origins of the city as a primitive social and economic unit created to support individual households in their struggle to survive. From these beginnings the city developed into a major ethical force that shaped the characters of its inhabitants.

Athens. Probably the best known of these city-states, along with Sparta and Corinth, is Athens. Because many of the writings come from this period in Greek history, most people employ the term *Greeks* to refer to the Athenians of the Classical Period. Although governed by tyrants in the Archaic Period, the city became the first democracy in the world around 508 B.C.E., when Cleisthenes led a revolution against the rule of the Pisistratid tyranny. The seeds of democracy, however, can be traced all the way back to one of Athens's most famous lawgivers, Solon, who established around 590 B.C.E. a new set of laws that promoted equality among citizens. First, he abolished the practice of debt-bondage, the ability of a creditor to force a man into slavery if he was unable to pay off the debt. Second, he granted citizenship to the foreign artisans living in Athens. Third, he reorganized the citizens into four different property classes, thereby diminishing the power of the aristocratic elite, who previously owned most of the land. Because of these reforms, later Athenians considered Solon the first democrat. Yet, although Athens was a democracy, not everyone could be a citizen. In fact, only about one-sixth of the total Athenian population during the Classical Period could be considered citizens, approximately 50,000 out of 300,000; the rest were slaves, foreigners, or women. While Solon's reforms, and later the democratic government, created more equality between Athenian citizens, it gradually restricted the independent functioning of individual households. Individuals were encouraged to put the city first and to relinquish personal ties in order to serve the city. These changes resulted in an increase of social control over women in particular and the family in general.

Conflict. A central issue during the Classical Period, and one that is critical in understanding the family and social trends, was the increased tension between the household and the state. In the Homeric world, a warrior was required to have loyalty only to his family, friends, and household; there was no concept of a "state" or other political entity. If he committed a crime, he had to make restitution to the victim's family; he was neither prosecuted in a court of law nor sent to jail. In democratic Athens, however, citizens were asked to put the city-state first and personal ties second, a trend that resulted in increased constraints on women. A new kind of dramatic poetry became increasingly important to the Athenians as their city began to grow in power and prestige. This dramatic poetry was a special genre probably invented by Athenians and originally produced only at Athens at a special city festival devoted to the god Dionysus. Almost all of the Greek tragedies explore dynamics within families and their relation to the city-state; many feature striking female characters, powerful matriarchs and dutiful daughters, female rebels, and heroines.

Blood Vengeance. In 458 B.C.E. the playwright Aeschylus dramatized the subordination of family ties to the democratic polis in his *Oresteia* trilogy. In the first play, *Agamemnon*, the poet tells of the return of the great hero, King Agamemnon, to his palace in Argos after fighting for ten years at Troy. His wife, Queen Clytemnestra, entices him into the palace where she murders him in his bath. She kills her husband and his concubine, Cassandra, because he sacrificed their daughter, Iphigeneia, before he left for Troy. By means of her crime, Clytemnestra honors the bond between mother and child. This plot illustrates an ancient principle of blood vendetta in which an injured party may retaliate against an enemy, normally someone outside the family, with impunity. There was no court of law, no codified set of rules, only revenge for a personal crime. In the play that follows, *Libation Bearers*, Agamemnon and Clytemnestra's son, Orestes, after whom the trilogy takes its name, returns to his native Argos to avenge his father's death by killing his mother and her lover. Like his mother, Orestes harms a family member in order to exact justice, but this time the god Apollo sanctions his crime. From a Greek perspective, however, Orestes' revenge was qualitatively different from that of Clytemnestra; his crime was demanded by a god and honored his father and the paternal oikos. In the third play, *Eumenides*, Orestes must stand trial in Athens and defend himself against the Erinyes, primordial creatures who pursue matricides. Orestes is acquitted on the basis of Apollo's argument that the most important tie is not that of mother and child, as Clytemnestra believes, but of husband and wife, because it is sanctioned by the city. At the end of the play, the Erinyes become the Eumenides, the "friendly ones"; cease their hounding of Orestes; occupy the spaces below each household; and ensure the fertility and prosperity of the city. Aeschylus thus departs from the original myth in which Orestes merely visits Athens while fleeing the Erinyes, in order to show the new role played by democracy. The chain of retaliation endorsed by the old system of justice is replaced by a court of law in which the community decides the punishment for individual crimes. What the Greeks formerly considered a private, familial affair now became the business of the democratic city.

Honoring the Dead. Another play, *Antigone* by Sophocles, produced around 440 B.C.E., also dramatized the conflict between the state and the family. In this play a young girl breaks the law established by her uncle, the king, in order to bury her brother's corpse. Her father, Oedipus, ruled Thebes until he discovered that he had killed his father and married his mother. After exiling himself from the city, he bequeaths the throne to his two sons, Eteocles and Polyneices. The brothers quarrel, and Eteocles refuses to relinquish the throne to Polyneices. Polyneices amasses an army in Argos and returns to regain power. A long war ensues, resulting in the deaths of both brothers. Eteocles, as the ruler of Thebes and a political ally, is given a burial with full honors; but his brother, Polyneices, an enemy of the states, is left unburied and dishonored on the battlefield. When the play opens, Creon, the uncle of Antigone and her only remaining sibling, Ismene, has decreed that anyone who attempts to bury Polyneices will be stoned to death. Antigone defies his decree in order to honor her family and the gods of the underworld. When a guard catches Antigone throwing handfuls of dust and singing laments over her brother's body, she is condemned to die in a rocky tomb outside the city. Her fiancé, Haemon, finds that she has hung herself in the cave and straightaway kills himself. Upon hearing this terrible news, Jocasta, the mother of Haemon, also hangs herself. King Creon is left with no surviving family members at the end of the play: he has witnessed the destruction of his own oikos. Like many tragic heroes, he learned his lesson too late; the importance he placed on the city and human law led to the denial of universal and divine law, as well as to a devaluation of women and family. Creon knows that he must pay the price for neglecting this important facet of life. In the end he takes responsibility for his actions: "It was I that killed her," he says. Sophocles' *Antigone* illustrates the importance of the family and women, even in a powerful and wealthy city like Classical Athens.

Political Life. Both the *Oresteia* trilogy and *Antigone* show the extent to which Athenians of the Classical Period were preoccupied with both political issues and the place of the family within the polis. This trend resulted from the premium the polis placed on political life, at the expense of the family. Yet, even in the Athenian democracy, the household and family continued to form the basis of Greek ethical and political thought and therefore played an important role not only in tragic drama but also in the city-state itself.

Ancient Sparta. Known as Lacedaemon, Sparta was another powerful Greek city-state, that, under the leadership of the lawgiver, Lycurgus, adopted a slightly different response to the archaic demand for laws and political order. In this society the city-state functioned almost as an enlarged household that shared wives, children, and property (the latter feature is still found in socialist and communist governments today). Lycurgus created equality among his citizens by redistributing the land and ensuring that each Spartan held the same share. He also established unique marriage and child-rearing practices that reveal a strikingly different attitude toward women from the one found in ancient Athens. Spartan women appear to have had greater social and economic freedom than their Athenian counterparts. They had large *proikes* (dowries), or marriage settlements, that consisted of landed property and movables given by father to daughter upon marriage. Heiresses were free to marry outside their paternal line and still retain a portion of their patrimony, in contrast to Athenian practice. Euripides' play, *Andromache* (circa 425 B.C.E.), seems to have relied on a similar view of Sparta, since it depicts Hermione, the daughter of Helen, as bringing a large dowry into her relatively poor husband's household. The fact that Spartan inheritance laws liberally allowed women to own property—about two-fifths of the land in Sparta was controlled by women—may have contributed to the prominence of women in public and political life.

Gender Roles. Child-rearing and marriage customs also seem to have reinforced the idea of gender role reversal in ancient Sparta. In addition to participating in dances and choruses, Spartan girls received athletic training, an education meant to prepare them for the rigors of childbirth and the production of vigorous male children who would be good warriors. They were also notorious for public nudity, a feature of Spartan life attested in sources as early as the Archaic Period, and a strong contrast to the Athenian practice of female seclusion and physical modesty. Similarly, Spartan marriage customs must have seemed quite barbarian to residents of classical Athens: for example, the laws provided that an older Spartan husband could introduce into his home a younger woman for the purpose of procreation if his marriage had no issue. A man not wishing to marry might "borrow" another man's wife for the production of heirs, as long as he received the husband's

permission. These Spartan practices suggest that a child's legitimacy and citizen status were not as strongly correlated in Sparta as in Athens.

Women in Public. Ancient evidence also indicates that Spartans placed fewer restrictions on the public presence of women, perhaps because they configured public and private spheres in a manner different from the Athenians. Girls' choruses were a regular feature of Spartan life and frequently took place before a mixed audience of both genders. Occasionally, the female choral members would engage in playful teasing of their male audience, rebuking some young men and praising others. At least two female Spartan poets, including Cleitagora, mentioned by Aristophanes, and Megalostrata, existed. Literary sources depict Spartan women as gifted speakers who, according to Plato, received the same education as men, one especially strong in philosophy, rhetoric, and music.

Strong Mothers. Although preserved in a late text, the sayings of Spartan women provide further support for the idea of women's strong public presence. Consisting mostly of mothers exhorting their sons to martial valor or rebuking them for cowardice, the sayings represent Spartan women as fiercely patriotic, indifferent to pain, and yet obedient and deferential to their husbands. In one famous saying, Gorgo, the wife of the Spartan king Leonidas, when asked by an Athenian, "Why do Spartan women alone rule over men?" responded, "Because we alone bear real men."

Communal Living. Spartans were also famous for their practice of communal dining and education. Although the men lived in individual households, they took their daily meals together in a public mess. Spartan fathers did not have final authority over the life or death of their babies, as did fathers in Athens; nor did they introduce their babies to the family hearth and gods within days after their birth. Spartan newborns were brought before a council of elders that determined whether they would live or die. Instead of leaving the education of children to their parents, as was the Athenian custom, the Spartans created a public official responsible for supervising and disciplining the city's children. Similarly, parents were given authority over all children, not just their own, in matters of instruction and punishment. Although their main purpose was to bear sons who would protect the city-state, Spartan girls may have enjoyed more freedom than their Athenian counterparts, appearing more frequently in public and receiving some of the same training as their brothers. These social policies were intended to diminish personal ties, foster loyalty to the state and bravery in battle, and create a superior military force.

TOPICS IN THE FAMILY AND SOCIAL TRENDS

CHILDREN AND EDUCATION

Male Heirs. Because the *oikos* (household) was transmitted from father to son, the birth of male children was critical to the survival of the family. Male children guaranteed that the family line would not die out and that the oikos would remain in the hands of blood relatives. The continued existence of the oikos was so important to men in Classical Athens that the worst curse an enemy could utter was a wish for its destruction. The death of an oikos, in terms of Athenian ideology and religious belief, was a disaster. The commonplace plea in the courts, "that an oikos should not be made empty," indicates the emotional force such a loss evoked in the Athenian jurors. In fact, Athenian law required that children maintain their parents in old age, making offspring vital to the economic and social welfare of parents.

Ritual. The birth of children conferred respect and authority on Athenian women, both in the household and the polis. Women bore sons who would fight for the city, and after 451–450 B.C.E., they imparted citizen status to their offspring. Indeed, female characters in Greek comedy frequently use their standing as mothers to argue for the authority of their proposals. Husbands appeared to have changed their attitudes toward their wives once they had borne offspring, as a passage from a trial speech suggests:

> Members of the jury, when I decided to marry and had brought a wife home, at first my attitude towards her was this: I did not wish to annoy her, but neither was she to have too much of her own way. I watched her as well as I could, and kept an eye on her as was proper. But later, after my child had been born, I came to trust her, and I handed all my possessions over to her, believing that this was the greatest possible proof of affection.

The birth of a child was an important event in the Greek household, marked by religious celebrations. On the fifth day after the birth, a ceremony called *amphidromia* heralded the child's entry into the family. In this ritual the father held the baby while walking around his ancestral hearth, symbolically incorporating the baby into the family. When a male infant was born, he was shown to relatives at a big celebration held on the tenth day, when the father named him. Around this time the child

A Red Figure cup painting of a teacher instructing a child, circa 480 B.C.E. (Staatliche Museen, Berlin. Photo: Bildarchiv Preussischer Kulturbesitz, Berlin)

may have been introduced into his father's hereditary political association, the phratry. This event involved a solemn oath by which the father swore that the child had been born to him from a citizen mother, his wife in marriage. If a child could not prove a legitimate lineage, he was considered a bastard. Such children could only inherit a minimal amount from their fathers' estates; by 403 B.C.E., they were excluded from family religious observances and did not enjoy full citizen rights.

Growth. Babies spent their time in the women's quarters until about age six. In upper-class homes, respected slaves supervised their upbringing; wet nurses breast-fed babies if the mothers were not able to. The nurse functioned as a sort of nanny, while the *Paidagôgos* ("Child Minder") assisted in more formal instruction and later escorted male children to and from school. A child might retain a special affection for his nanny until late in life, as illustrated by Orestes' relationship with his nurse Cilissa in the *Libation Bearers* of Aeschylus (458 B.C.E.). In

A marble grave relief from Salamis of two young warriors, late fifth–early fourth century B.C.E. (Piraeus Museum. Photo: German Institute in Athens)

Sparta, however, boys left home around age six and entered the public educational system that prepared them for military service, while Athenian boys started elementary school at much the same age as they do today. Many kinds of toys were available to children: clappers and rattles for infants; dolls made of clay, wood, or bone, often with moveable limbs and their own miniature furniture and utensils; figurines of horses and chariots; and spinning tops. Greek vases show children rolling hoops or playing ball and even basic playground equipment, such as a swing and a seesaw. Bells served a double purpose of entertaining children and warding off the "evil eye." Small children frequently wore charms or small figurines around their necks. These charms could serve as a form of identification in case they were kidnapped or abandoned. At puberty girls and boys dedicated these playthings to a deity as they prepared for their adult roles.

Elementary and Higher Education. Most ancient Greeks could not read or write until late in the Classical Period, although the extent of public literacy is not known for certain. For the Greeks, education encompassed not only formal schooling, but also upbringing and cultural training in the broadest sense. They regarded poets as their primary teachers, especially in the Archaic Period, but even as late as the end of the fifth century B.C.E., the comic poet Aristophanes repeatedly refers to the dramatist's task as that of educating the citizens. He used the word *didaskalos* (teacher), a cognate of the English word *didactic*, interchangeably with the word *poiêtês* (poet). In the early period, education would have occurred at the male symposium where participants recited poetry and sang traditional songs. Religious festivals in which children recited poetry, like the *Apatouria*, a three-day event honoring new members of the phratry, would have also served an important

After a boy had completed his elementary education, he enrolled in the army, normally between the ages of eighteen and twenty. In fact, a period of military service for men was compulsory in all of the ancient Greek city-states and all Greek males would have fought in a battle in their lifetimes. In the fourth century, the period of military training was referred to as *ephebeia*, meaning "at puberty," after which point one joined either the hoplites (a phalanx formation) or became a sailor in the navy. Youths spent their first year living in barracks near the Athenian harbor, the Piraeus, where they underwent extensive physical conditioning. In the second year, they began active service stationed on the frontiers of Attica. Because military service bridged the critical period between boyhood and adulthood, it resembled a rite of passage, or initiation ritual. Greek myth depicts initiation ritual as involving a boy's separation from and his eventual reintegration into society. Sent on a quest, the boy ventures into the wilderness, endures a contest or struggle, normally with a wild animal, and then returns to his community. Upon his return, he marries and receives political power. The mythic heroes Theseus and Heracles exemplify this process: both confront a series of dangerous creatures that they must kill before they can return home, marry, and become king. Initiation rituals are found in many other cultures, including African, Australian, and Native American stories. Even contemporary religious practices such as confirmation in Catholicism and the bar mitzvah in Judaism represent rites of passage through which the young person becomes an adult member of his or her religious community.

Source: Michael Grant, *A Social History of Greece and Rome* (New York: Scribners, 1992).

educational function. In addition *paiderastia* ("love of boys") may have involved an academic dimension, with the older man serving as a teacher and mentor of the boy. Civic festivals and rituals also inculcated values and beliefs in the young; the dramatic festival at Athens involved various patriotic displays intended to impart lessons of citizenship to spectators. In the Archaic Period, the aristocratic view of education prevailed—that excellence could not be learned, but could only be inherited. With rhetoric becoming increasingly important for advancing political careers in Classical Athens, the Athenians began to view knowledge and excellence as accessible to all through education.

Privileged Few. Little is known about Greek education prior to the fifth century B.C.E. Since the Greek alphabet was not invented until the middle of the eighth century, it is assumed that literacy was not widespread until late in the fourth century. Poets and scribes probably learned their crafts from other practitioners. Individual tutors may have instructed aristocratic children in gymnastics and in music as a broad concept that involved not only instrumentation but also the learning of poems, normally memorized and sung to musical accompaniment. Greek mythology represents the hero Achilles as learning these skills under the tutelage of an imaginary creature, the wise centaur Chiron, who specialized in instructing heroes. Jason, who captured the Golden Fleece, was another one of his pupils. The education of the hero Heracles involves separate instruction in chariot driving, wrestling, archery, and music. Clumsy at lyre playing, the frustrated hero killed his music teacher, Linus, by hitting him over the head with his instrument! In any case, education during the Archaic Period was probably rudimentary, did not involve reading or writing, and was available only to the aristocratic class.

The Basics. In Classical Athens, young boys received at least an elementary education. Pottery shards called *ostraka*, bearing the names of individuals to be exiled from the city, attest to basic literacy among Athenian citizens. Elementary education consisted of three main parts: gymnastics and physical fitness, taught mainly in the *palaistra*, or wrestling school; music, consisting of lyre playing and lyric poetry; and grammar, including reading, writing, arithmetic, and the memorization of important poems, especially the works of Homer. Music included both poetry and dance, with a strong emphasis on performance; indeed, many boys would serve as chorus members in a Greek tragedy before they reached adulthood. Physical education prepared boys for war. Memorization played a large role in ancient education; at a young age, Greek boys could recite from memory vast amounts of poetry, including all of Homer's *Iliad* and *Odyssey* (both written circa eighth–seventh centuries B.C.E.).

Sophists. By the late fifth century B.C.E., a new form of education became available to Athenian boys as they neared adulthood. After a boy finished elementary school, he could further his studies by attending public lectures given by Sophists, receive individual instruction from them, or join one of their schools. The name *Sophist* comes from the Greek adjective *sophos*, meaning "wise." The Sophists were a group of traveling teachers who taught wealthy youths how to speak persuasively in the Assembly and the law courts. All Sophists taught rhetoric, and many believed that all laws, customs, and religious beliefs were the product of social convention and therefore relative. The important thing, in their view, was to make the most persuasive argument, regardless of the moral position. Sophists were normally foreigners, neither Athenian leaders nor citizens, from minor Greek cities. Their public performances often took place both in the private residences of wealthy citizens and at festivals like those of Olympia. With the statesman Pericles as their patron, the Sophists rapidly made inroads into Athenian social and political life.

Subversive Element. The teachings of the Sophists concentrated on political advancement through persuasive speech. By making such skills accessible to the wealthy but nonaristocratic families for a fee, the Sophists aroused the resentment of the upper classes who in the first part of the century had monopolized public discourse simply by virtue of birth. In the Platonic dialogues, Socrates condemns the Sophists for accepting pay on the grounds that the practice compromised the objective pursuit of truth, while his use of trade metaphors in connection with them, most notably in the *Sophist*, identifies them with the merchant and manufacturing classes. Their claim, that *aretê* (aristocratic virtue) could be taught, meant that anyone could advance to a high position in the world of politics. Because the Sophists allowed for a new kind of social mobility, the conservative elite considered them a dangerous source of political subversion.

The Spartan Way. In Sparta education mainly fostered the values necessary for maintaining military prowess. From the age of six or seven, Spartan boys answered to the authority of the state, living in communal quarters separate from their parents. Although their education involved music, reading, and writing, the emphasis was on military training and physical education. In contrast to classical Athens, Spartans allowed their girls to be educated. In order to make them capable of producing strong warriors, the girls received instruction in athletics, as well as in music and dancing.

Sources:

Mark Golden, *Children and Childhood in Classical Athens* (Baltimore: Johns Hopkins University Press, 1990).

William V. Harris, *Ancient Literacy* (Cambridge, Mass.: Harvard University Press, 1989).

Laura McClure, *Spoken Like a Woman: Speech and Gender in Athenian Drama* (Princeton, N.J.: Princeton University Press, 1999).

CONCEPTION AND CHILDBIRTH

Fertility. The true purpose of marriage was procreation; in the Classical Period, it was to produce male offspring who would later fight on behalf of the city-state and participate in its governance. In fact, the birth of offspring was considered a right of Athenian wives; the law made it mandatory for the husband of an heiress to consort with her three times a month. Because of the importance of legitimate heirs to the household and the city, female fertility and childbirth were of great concern to the ancient Greeks. Women turned to female deities such as Hera, Artemis, and Eileithuia, the goddess of childbirth, to assist in conception and childbirth. A couple suffering from infertility might consult Apollo's oracle at Delphi to find a remedy, as did the mythical Athenian king Aegeus, the father of Theseus, or make offerings to the gods. Fertility festivals such as those in honor of the agricultural goddess Demeter ensured women's reproductive power. In labor and delivery women relied on female family members, neighbors, and midwives for help; male doctors were summoned only for the most difficult cases.

Medical Views. By the Classical Period the new science of medicine addressed concerns about female reproduction and attempted to construct theories of the female body.

Many of these theories resulted from speculation rather than scientific observation, partly because dissection of the human body did not occur until the Hellenistic Period. The fact that male doctors normally did not assist women in labor meant that their knowledge of the female body and childbirth was necessarily limited and came mostly from women themselves and their midwives. The writers of the Hippocratic texts therefore put great stock in women's perceptions of their own bodies:

> You cannot disregard what women say about child-bearing. For they are talking about what they know and always inquiring about; they could not be persuaded either by deed or word that they do not know rather more [than you do] about what is happening in their own bodies.

Menstruation. The ancient Greeks viewed the female body as more porous and spongelike in order to explain the process of menstruation. According to Aristotle, a woman's body draws in moisture, converts it to blood, and then expels it during menstruation. If a woman conceives, this blood goes to nourishing the fetus. Male bodies, by contrast, are only porous in the necessary places, such as the glands. The medical writers also represent the female body as soft because of a life of inactivity indoors, and as cold and wet, in contrast to the dry heat of the male body. Indeed, Aristotle makes a biological argument for the superiority of men by developing a theory of heat in the human body. He thought men's bodies generated more heat and therefore were capable of concocting the procreative fluid, semen, while women, because colder, could only produce menstrual fluid. Semen has greater value, in Aristotle's view, because it passes the man's form on to another generation. By this reasoning, Aristotle comes to the conclusion that a woman is inferior to a man:

> A boy actually resembles a woman in physique, and a woman is, as it were, an infertile male; the female, in fact, is female on account of inability of a sort, viz. it lacks the power to concoct the semen out of the final state of the nourishment.

Nonetheless, Aristotle maintains that both men and women produce seeds that mingle to produce a child, with women ejaculating seed into their own wombs. This view represents an improvement over one found earlier in Greek tragedy that says the female contributes nothing to the conception of a child:

> The mother is no parent of that which is called her child, but only nurse of the new-planted seed that grows. The parent is he who mounts. A stranger, she preserves the stranger's seed, if no god interfere. I will show you proof of what I have explained. There can be a father without any mother. There she stands, the living witness, daughter of Olympian Zeus, she who was never fostered in the dark of the womb yet such a child as no goddess could bring to birth.

Here the god Apollo argues that the mother's body serves merely as a vessel or container that nurtures the fetus, while the father provides all of the genetic material. He cites as an example the goddess Athena, who, because

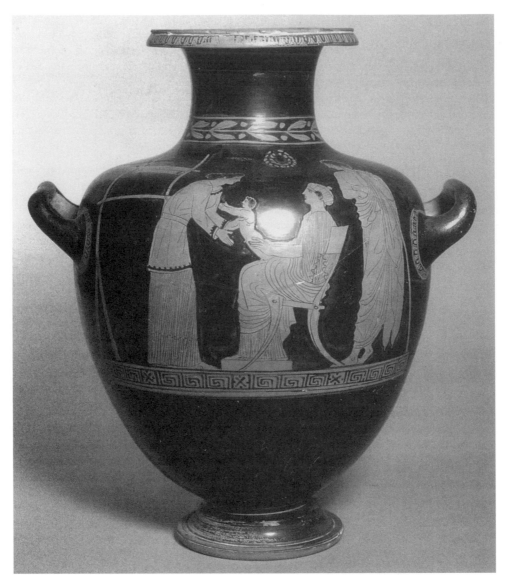

A Red Figure *hudria* painting of a mother, child, and nursemaid (Cambridge, Massachusetts, Harvard University Art Museums, inv. no. 1960.342)

she was born from the head of her father, inherits absolutely no genetic material from her mother. By repeating the word *stranger,* the god further de-emphasizes the blood tie between mother and fetus. Apollo makes this argument because he wishes to defend Orestes against the charge of matricide by showing that his crime is less heinous than that of his mother.

Productive Process. Many ancient medical theories attempt to account for problems in menstruation. In contrast to other ancient cultures, such as the Judaic tradition represented by Leviticus in the Hebrew Bible, the Greeks did not view menstruation as a form of pollution, although they did consider sexual intercourse, childbirth, and contact with the dead to be polluting. The medical writers portray menstruation as productive of health: an absence of menstruation in a nonpregnant woman was thought to produce clots that could travel outside the womb and block other parts of the body, even bringing about hysteria and suicide in teenage girls:

The girls try to choke themselves because of the pressure on their hearts; their will, distraught and anguished because of the bad condition of the blood, forces evil on itself. In some cases the girl says dreadful things: [the visions] order her to jump up and throw herself into wells and drown, as if this were good for her and served some useful purpose.

The corpus also mentions two case studies of older women who apparently rambled and uttered obscenities as a result of amenorrhea.

Wandering Womb. One ancient conception of the female body strikes modern readers as particularly strange. The Greeks considered the uterus to be almost a thinking creature with a mind of its own, "an animal within an animal," as one ancient doctor called it. It could "wander" and easily dislocate itself and respond to smells. One philosophical text from the Classical Period provides another example:

SIGMUND FREUD AND HYSTERIA

Ancient Greek beliefs about the wandering womb and the psychological problems it engendered have parallels in late-nineteenth-century views of hysteria; Sigmund Freud's work with Jean-Martin Charcot in Paris led to his first full-length study of the subject in a book co-authored with Josef Breuer, *Studies in Hysteria* (1895). This book attempted to understand the cause of a set of symptoms found in young women that included various physical pains with no apparent cause, such as a choking sensation (also mentioned in the ancient sources). At first Freud looked for a physiological basis for the illness and performed a famous, almost fatal, operation on Emma Eckstein, under the misguided belief that surgery on her nose would cure her hysteria. He later abandoned this approach and turned instead to exploring the underlying psychological causes of this condition. Freud postulated that hysteria resulted from the repression or blocking of traumatic memories; these repressed memories slipped out or made themselves known through bodily symptoms. Freud's work on hysteria hailed a new era in medicine and inaugurated the new discipline of psychiatry and psychotherapy.

Source: Peter Gay, *Freud: A Life for Our Time* (New York: Norton, 1988).

[Women] have an animal within them eager for conception, which whenever it goes without issue for a long time beyond its proper season, becomes angry and miserable, and wanders everywhere around the body, blocks the outlets for air and prevents respiration, causing extreme helplessness and bringing on all sorts of other diseases.

This image of the uterus as an animal traveling around the body reinforces the stereotype of women as out of control, irrational, and sexually precocious. The medical writers thought that the uterus, because of its tendency to wander, needed to be anchored down by pregnancy or kept moist by sexual intercourse; otherwise, it would become dry and attracted to the moister organs. For this reason, females not regularly having intercourse were considered susceptible to displacement of the womb. Some remedies for drawing the uterus back to its proper place included "odor" therapies in which foul-smelling vapors were applied to nostrils, on the belief that the nostrils and vagina were connected by a long hollow tube.

Labor and Delivery. Medical treatises also discuss labor and delivery, another important aspect of women's reproductive health. Because the ancients did not understand that the uterus is a powerful muscle rather than a simple container, they explained the onset of labor as a result of fetal movements tearing the membranes (not until the first dissection had been performed did this view change). A prolonged or nonprogressing labor was thought to indicate a breech birth, multiple birth, or stillbirth. Remedies

included vigorous shaking (also prescribed for abortion), drugs to facilitate labor, and, as a last resort, embryotomy, a procedure in which instruments extracted the stillborn fetus. Ancient medical practitioners did not perform caesarian sections, a procedure a woman probably would not have survived, given the state of medical knowledge and the lack of sterile conditions.

Midwives. When it came time for delivery, ancient doctors recommended that women deliver their babies on a birthing chair, or on a hard bed if the woman was weak. Midwives advised their patients to use controlled patterns of breathing to alleviate pain, much like the modern-day practice of Lamaze. Sometimes birth attendants passed strong-smelling titems under the woman's nostrils and applied warm cloths to her abdomen to make her more comfortable. After the baby was born, the midwife signaled whether it was male or female, then placed it on the ground to assess whether it was healthy enough to survive. Finally, she judged when to cut and tie the umbilical cord, cleaned and swaddled the baby, and put it to bed. Given the dangers of childbirth in antiquity, it is not surprising to find that maternal mortality was high. Women may have died from exhaustion and hemorrhage during difficult deliveries, especially if they were in poor health or young, as many Greek mothers were, or from diseases induced by pregnancy, such as eclampsia. Because of these dangers, the average life expectancy for adult women was around age thirty-five.

Social Ideology. Many of the Greek medical writings on women simply reinforced social ideology. The importance placed on pregnancy as a healthy and natural state supports the social practice of the early marriage of girls. Indeed, the remedy for most female ailments is to conceive a child. Medical theory also corroborates the idea that women needed the guardianship of men because their physiology predisposes them to irrationality and even insanity. Similarly, theories of the wandering womb represent the female body as lacking regulation, out of control and unpredictable, and in need of guidance.

Birth Control and Infanticide. Both men and women in ancient Greece longed for children in marriage, but economic concerns often forced them to limit the size of their families. Infant mortality was high in ancient Greece, and the precariousness of life for a newborn child naturally reduced family size. However, if an unwanted child was born, a Greek might abandon it in a remote spot. The most likely candidates for exposure were the offspring of illicit unions between slaves or from prostitutes, or those with physical infirmities that might affect their ability to contribute to the family estate. There is some evidence that the Greeks were more likely to expose female babies, for whom the added expense of a dowry might make them particularly burdensome for a poor family.

Economic Considerations. Normally, the first two children of a marriage would not have been exposed, if they were born healthy, whatever their gender. Beyond the first two children, the economic resources of a given family dictated whether or not to rear additional children. The decision whether to raise or abandon a child resided strictly with the father, except in Sparta, where a tribunal of elders had the final say. The law-court speeches from the Classical Period suggest that the average Athenian family might have had five children, although it is unclear how many siblings may have died in childhood, especially since infant mortality was high. Abandoned male children may have been rescued and raised as the adopted heirs of a childless couple, a practice illustrated by the myth of Oedipus. According to the story, a prophecy foretold that Oedipus was destined to kill his father and marry his mother; his father, the King of Thebes, therefore ordered that the child be left to die on a mountainside. A shepherd took pity on him and brought him to Corinth, where another set of parents reared him. Once he had heard the prophecy, Oedipus fled from Corinth, where he thought his birth parents resided, and, through a sequence of complicated events, unwittingly killed his birth father and married his birth mother. The extent to which the Athenians practiced infanticide is still a source of debate, and possibly they turned to this option only as a last resort. No doubt the babies born of slaves or prostitutes and the products of rape or adultery would have been regularly exposed.

Other Techniques. There were also other means of limiting family size. In the days before reliable infertility treatments became available, natural sterility must have played a part in reducing the number of children born to couples. Breastfeeding, the common practice among ancient Greek mothers, also functioned as a natural contraception and ensured that pregnancies would not be spaced too close together, since nursing suppresses menses. Women could also turn to various medical and folk remedies for preventing conception. Measures include holding one's breath during coitus, drinking something cold afterward, or smearing the cervix with olive oil, honey, or cedar resin. One recipe calls for equal measures of pine bark and tanning sumac to be mixed with wine and applied to the cervix a few hours before intercourse. Some of the ingredients in these potions, such as white lead, could be quite dangerous. Once pregnant, a woman could turn to abortifacients. The medical writers recommend injections of oil; baths; potions consisting of linseed, fenugreek, mallow, marshmallow, and wormwood; poultices of meal of lupins, ox bile, and absinthium; or violent physical exercise, such as energetic walking or shaking by oxen. One passage in the *Hippocratic Corpus* advises a woman who wishes to expel the products of conception to jump up and down, kicking her heels to her buttocks! Most of these techniques were probably ineffectual, but some of the herbal therapies indicate an accurate understanding of the science of pharmacology.

Sources:

Lesley Dean-Jones, *Women's Bodies in Classical Greek Science* (Oxford: Clarendon Press; New York: Oxford University Press, 1994).

Sarah B. Pomeroy, *Goddesses, Whores, Wives, and Slaves: Women in Classical Antiquity* (New York: Schocken Books, 1975).

MARRIAGE

Husband and Wife. In Athens marriage practice was normally endogamous, meaning it stayed within the family, although the system did not specify the relatives with whom marriages were to be contracted. The average age of marriage for girls was fourteen, an age thought to ensure that a girl would be a virgin. For males, the age was around thirty, when they were able to serve on the city council and sit as jurors in the law courts, and after they had completed time in the military. The age differential between husband and wife meant that a woman could have remarried several times in her life, and that a dying husband could arrange a future marriage for his young wife. Betrothal was a transaction conducted completely by males, since girls could not perform any legal activity on behalf of themselves. In contrast to men, who often stayed with their fathers' households, especially if firstborn, women upon marriage left the households of their fathers and joined those of their husbands. Marriage thus served as one means of reinforcing ties between unrelated male-governed households. A father frequently sought a husband for his daughter or sister among his male kin, although he might betroth a daughter to a friend as a sign of goodwill, a favor that could be returned. In this way, he drew friends into the kinship group and strengthened ties among their households. The purpose of legitimate marriage was to produce children and heirs, ensuring the continuity of the *oikos* (household) and the ancestral cult. There were added economic benefits: wives provided free labor for farmers and money and property through dowries for the wealthier classes.

Arrangements. In Athens, a marriage was contracted between the girl's father and the groom. First, there was an *egguê* (pledge of marriage) that took the place of our contemporary engagement. In some cases, the bride and groom may never have seen each other, although often marriages were contracted between first cousins and other relatives, a practice particularly popular in classical Athens because it kept the wealth in the family. The main event of the wedding was the procession in a wagon or chariot from the house of the bride to that of the groom (in the courts, this act could be cited as proof of legitimacy of marriage). Since the procession normally took place at night, vases often depict figures carrying torches to light the way. The bride, veiled, mounted a wagon that would take her to her husband's home. On the day of the wedding, the bride's friends and relatives visited her at her new home, bringing gifts, another scene often represented on Attic vases. Well-wishers showered the couple with nuts and dried fruits and then presented them with a basket of bread. The bride ate ritual food: a fruit of many seeds, such as a quince; and sesame cakes, upon entering her husband's house; this was a symbol of his authority over her and of her future fertility. Once a male child had been born to the couple and they had lived together under the same roof, their marriage was considered legally valid.

Natal Family. The mythic prototype for Greek marriage is found in the Homeric *Hymn to Demeter* (circa sixth century B.C.E.), a poem that tells of the abduction of Persephone, the daughter of the agricultural goddess Demeter, by Hades, her uncle and god of the underworld. Like most Greek girls, Persephone marries one of her father's relatives and has no say in the matter. The forcible abduction of the daughter suggests the often violent origins of ancient marriage as reflected in other stories of bride capture, such as the Sabines of Roman myth. Separated from her daughter, the grieving Demeter wanders the world in search of her and even induces famine in the human world in order to force the male gods to return the girl to the light. This part of the story shows how the girl maintained strong ties to her natal family even after marriage. When in the underworld, Persephone eats the seeds of a pomegranate fruit, an act replicated in the actual wedding ceremony, and thus binds herself forever to her husband and his lightless world beneath the ground. In symbolic terms, marriage for the Greek girl enacted a kind of death as she was forced to separate from her natal family and become incorporated into the oikos of her husband's family. In fact, wedding rituals imitated funerary rituals in several important aspects: both involved the cutting of hair, the wearing of garlands, singing, feasting, and the pouring of ritual libations.

Stranger in the House. Because the girl left her natal family to join that of her husband, she was considered a stranger to his hearth and family. Greek literature frequently expresses the suspicion that this status aroused in husbands. For the young wife, on the other hand, inexperience and powerlessness left her vulnerable to harsh treatment from her husband, as the character Medea explains:

And this is the greatest struggle, whether she takes a bad husband or a good one. For divorce does not bring fair repute to a woman, nor may she renounce her husband. But arriving among new customs and laws, she must divine—if she has not learned this lesson at home—how she might best manage her husband. But a man, whenever he grows tired of consorting with those within the house, goes outside and puts an end to his vexation, [turning either to some friend or companion.] But for us it is necessary to look to one soul alone.

Medea's speech raises several relevant points about a girl's experience of marriage. She could not choose her husband, and once married, she was at his mercy. Although able to divorce, she was unlikely to do so, since it might damage her reputation. Finally, a Greek man had access to multiple sex partners, while women had to content themselves with their husbands. Bored or lonely, they were confined to the house, with limited opportunities for social interaction.

Virtues. A funerary epitaph from the Roman period describes the qualities the Greeks valued in married women:

She was fair, good, gentle, and divinely beautiful, faithful to one husband, and to be counted among the heroines of old; therefore for wisdom, discretion and wit she is far above all women.

Above all, the Greek male expected marital fidelity from his wife; the woman in this passage is described as "having only one husband." She is also praised for her beauty and modesty as well as for intellectual attributes such as wisdom and humor.

The Dowry. Upon marriage, a girl brought with her to her husband's house a dowry. It came from her father and remained under the control of the husband during the marriage. The dowry, the female equivalent of the patrimonial inheritance, served as the basis of the woman's maintenance and livelihood in her husband's house. A large dowry enabled fathers to attract the best husbands for their daughters, as well as indicated their social status. It could consist of a considerable fortune; and there is some evidence from the orators that a good one might equal one-tenth of her father's estate. Because a woman had to rely on a *kurios* (guardian) to act for her in the public sphere, she could not dispose of her dowry on her own initiative. A large dowry may have protected a woman and afforded her some power in her husband's house since he would have had to return the money to her father if the marriage broke up. For example, Hipparete, the wife of an Athenian politician, Alcibiades, tried to leave him for bringing home prostitutes. According to an ancient anecdote, he forcibly carried her back home because he could not afford to manage his household without her money. Finally, girls who had no dowry, or only a small one, could still marry; the orators frequently praise the man who marries a penniless girl, especially if an heiress.

Divorce. The anecdote about Hipparete and Alcibiades raises an interesting question: could ancient Greek women divorce their husbands? It is surprising, given the various restrictions placed on women, to find that divorce laws in ancient Athens were fairly liberal. A marriage could be terminated by mutual consent or through the action of either of the spouses. Technically, no ill repute attached to divorce, although Medea's speech quoted above seems to suggest otherwise. When the husband initiated the divorce, he terminated the marriage by sending his wife out of his house. When a wife desired a divorce, she had to rely on her father or other relative to represent her case before the Athenian magistrate who was responsible for handling such actions. Only three such cases of a wife initiating a divorce are recorded from Classical Athens, including that of Hipparete. A father could also take his daughter back from a son-in-law if the two quarreled. Upon divorce, the dowry had to be returned to the woman's guardian, usually her father, while the woman could retain her personal effects and one-half the goods she had produced while in the oikos, as an article of the ancient law code of Gortyn, a city in central Crete, suggests:

> If a husband and wife divorce, she is to keep her property, whatever she brought to the marriage, and half the produce (if there is any) from her property, and half of whatever she has woven within the house; also she is to have 5 staters if her husband is the cause of the divorce. If the husband swears that he is not the cause of the divorce, the judge is to take an oath and decide.

This excerpt reveals the enormous economic contribution women made to their husbands' households and the problems the loss of equity brought about by divorce could cause for men. Further, the Gortyn code indicates that men could be held liable for their conduct toward their wives, with real economic consequences should they fail to comply with behavioral norms. Children, considered to be the property of their father, belonged to his household and thus did not follow the woman when she left.

Inheritance and Property Rights. The Athenians protected the institution of the oikos through a complex system of inheritance laws, particularly in cases where a man might die without a male heir. Every effort was made to keep the estate in the family and to ensure that women could not easily accumulate large estates. Normally, sons inherited their father's property in equal shares unless they had been adopted out of the family, that is, appointed heir to another's oikos, or legally disinherited, a rare occurrence. If the deceased man had direct male descendants (natural or adopted) then they inherited the oikos automatically, by equal division. No daughters or descendants of daughters had any claims in the presence of male heirs. Even their future dowries were not considered an inheritance, but depended upon the generosity of their brothers. Although the oikos was to be divided equally among the sons, there are several instances where the heirs avoided this fragmen-

A cup painting of Persephone and Hades (London E 82, from Vulci. "ARV" 1269, 3)

tation of property. In the absence of sons, there was a strict hierarchy of those who inherited: males related to the deceased came first. Thus, if the deceased had a brother, he would inherit, then a sister; a paternal uncle would win out over an aunt. If a man had no legitimate sons then his oikos would die out, since a daughter in and of herself could not provide the desired continuity of the oikos.

Adoption. Yet, what did happen to a man who had no male heir? Adoption or *eispoiêsis* ("making in") was a fairly common practice in which a man without direct descendants formally declared another man his heir. By law, the adoptee had to be an Athenian citizen. In one comic play, a grumpy old man who has only a daughter adopts his wife's son by another marriage with the formula: "I am formally making you my son, and anything I have, consider it all your own. My daughter here I entrust to your care. Find her a husband . . . ." When this happened, an adopted son had to renounce all rights to his natal oikos because no man could simultaneously become the heir of two households. Individuals in this situation normally adopted a relative because of the implicit moral obligation to keep property within the family. The adopted son, however, was not allowed to make a will, but could only pass the property through his direct descendants. Although married, a woman's natal oikos still retained an active interest in her and her dowry. Even though she could not directly inherit, she could produce sons who could be adopted into the family and inherit the family property; thus a daughter's sons tended to be the preferred heirs adopted into her natal oikos. The keen desire for children and heirs in classical Athens partly explains the practice of suppositious children frequently alluded to in comedy: a childless woman might take a baby from a slave or other woman and pass it off as her own, without her husband's knowledge, just to insure the oikos had an heir.

Heiresses. One exception to this pattern was the heiress, known as the *epiklêros*, a word meaning "with the property" and the technical term for the daughter who could transmit her father's estate in the absence of any sons, natural or adopted, to another man, usually her husband. The epiklêros ensured that a man's oikos did not die out for lack of descendants. A man with an epiklêros could also adopt a son, in which case he could not inherit the property unless he became the girl's husband and kurios. The heiress essentially remained attached to the estate and thereby transmitted the property to her husband upon marriage. For this reason, the father's next of kin could in fact legally claim the heiress as his wife and thus inherit the property:

> The law states that women who have been given in marriage by their fathers and who have been living with their husbands (and who could make better provision for them than a father?), that even a woman thus given in marriage, if her father dies without leaving legitimate sons, becomes subject to the legal power of their next of kin; and many men who have already been living with their wives have been deprived of them.

In fact, marriage to an epiklêros was considered a valid reason for a man to divorce. He could even dissolve the heiress's marriage to another man in order to marry her! However, it was not likely that an epiklêros would have been forced to marry if she already had an adult son, because through her the grandson could inherit the oikos. The institution of the epiklêros therefore may be understood as a kind of safety net for preserving the male-governed oikos in the absence of legitimate sons. The girl in and of herself did not inherit property, but served as a link binding together male relatives and ensuring that the estate remained in the family. Athenian women not only produced legitimate sons and heirs for their husbands but they also provided an alternative supply of heirs for their own natal households. Women were therefore integral to the economic transactions and kinship solidarity of the polis, but their role nevertheless remained mostly passive and always subordinate to the interests of men.

Sources:

Walter K. Lacey, *The Family in Classical Greece* (Ithaca, N.Y.: Cornell University Press, 1968).

Richmond Lattimore, *Themes in Greek and Latin Epitaphs* (Champaign-Urbana: University of Illinois Press, 1962).

Sarah B. Pomeroy, *Goddesses, Whores, Wives, and Slaves: Women in Classical Antiquity* (New York: Shocken Books, 1975).

Cynthia Patterson, *The Family in Greek History* (Cambridge, Mass.: Harvard University Press, 1998).

SEXUAL MISCONDUCT

Adultery. Even though prostitutes and sexual partners other than their wives were available to Athenian men, adultery was not uncommon. The Greek word for adulterer was *moikhos*. From the Homeric poems onward, this type of person is characterized as deceptive, dangerous, and even effeminate. The Trojan prince Paris, for example, is the

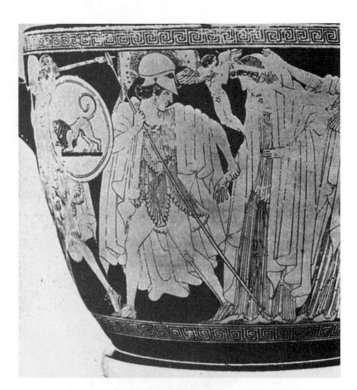

A Red Figure bowl painting of Paris abducting Helen (Boston Museum of Fine Arts, inv. no. 13. 186)

original adulterer in Greek myth, because he abducted the beautiful Helen from her husband's house and brought her to Troy, thereby initiating the Trojan War. In the *Iliad* (circa eighth–seventh centuries B.C.E.), his brother Hector scolds him for his reckless actions: "Evil Paris, beautiful, woman crazy, cajoling, better had you never been born, or killed unwedded." Paris would rather spend his time in the boudoir with the beautiful Helen than on the battlefield.

Preventive Measures. Because Pericles' law of 450–451 B.C.E. decreed that only the legitimate offspring of Athenian parents were entitled to citizenship and full participation in the democratic polis, adultery became more than just a private offence in the Classical polis; it jeopardized the welfare of the city as a whole. Not surprisingly, Greek tragedies from the Classical Period repeatedly show a preoccupation with adultery. A common plot is the trouble wives get into, particularly their involvement with other men, when their husbands are away. For example, Clytemnestra in *Agamemnon* takes on a lover after long years of awaiting her husband's return. The seclusion of women within the house, their segregation from men, and the practice of veiling when in public were all measures geared at protecting them from adultery, and therefore ensuring the legitimacy of a man's children.

Retribution. In the view of the Athenians, the concept of adultery pertained more to women than to men, who were allowed a broad range of sexual partners outside marriage. At the same time, the adulterer, the male participant, received a harsher penalty than the adulteress, even if she initiated the affair. The law allowed a male head of household to kill any man with impunity if he caught them in the

A *kratêr* painting of the murder of Agamemnon, circa 700–480 B.C.E. (Boston Museum of Fine Arts, 63.1246)

act with any of the women under his guardianship, including his mother, wife, sister, or daughter. The speechwriter Lysias describes a situation in which a young wife was seduced by Eratosthenes, a well-known philanderer who caught sight of her at her mother-in-law's funeral, one of the few occasions in which men might come into contact with well-born women not related to them. Her husband, Euphiletus, murdered the lover when he caught them in the act. Eratosthenes' relatives then brought a case against the husband on charges of homicide. Euphiletus won acquittal by arguing that in murdering his wife's seducer, he was actually enforcing the law concerning adulterers, handed down by the lawgiver Draco. It is unclear whether death was always the punishment mandated for adulterers; in Greek comedy, payment, depilation (the practice of removing pubic hair by singeing), and other debasing gestures are some types of compensation demanded of them.

Partner in Crime. The penalty for the woman engaging in adultery was somewhat lighter. The law required a husband to divorce an adulterous wife, although he may not always have followed through with it, especially if it involved repaying a large dowry. It also forbade the adulteress to wear jewelry and to participate in public religious activities. Most husbands, however, refused to initiate a divorce because it meant testifying against their wives in public. Revealing a wife's misconduct would have called into question the parentage and citizenship of a man's children and would have publicly diminished his honor. Why did the Athenians mete out such a harsh punishment to adulterers and not to adulteresses? They considered the woman a passive partner in the crime; in their view women were the easy targets of seducers because they, like children, lacked judgment and self-control. The man, on the other hand, engaged in a premeditated and illegal activity that potentially jeopardized the integrity and stability of another man's household.

Rape. In the Archaic Period, Solon denounced adultery as a crime worse than rape, a view that persisted throughout the Classical Period, and one quite the opposite of our modern thinking on the subject. While an adulterer caught in the act by a husband might be killed, the rapist only had to pay a monetary fine to compensate for his violent crime. Why was the penalty for rape less than seduction or adultery at Athens? Any physical assault, whether sexual or not, against an Athenian citizen man, woman, or child, was considered a serious offense because one of the primary rights of citizenship was physical protection. This central right explains why Athenian laws concerning rape involve a strict social hierarchy of fines, from free man to slave. To the Athenians, adultery potentially undermined both the household and the city. For if an Athenian had an affair with a citizen woman not his wife, his child would have no claim to his property, or familial or religious associations. The woman, on the other hand, would be forced to claim that the child belonged to her husband, thereby upsetting the fragile network of kin and cult connections founded on the legitimacy of offspring. If the woman were caught, all her children would have had difficulty proving their citizen status. In effect, adultery was considered a crime not against an individual, but against the household unit and even against the city itself, since its stability relied, to a great extent, on the welfare of the individual *oikos* (household).

Corrupting Influence. There is yet another reason why the Athenians considered adultery a far worse crime than rape. In their minds, the person who achieves this end by persuasion corrupts the mind as well as the body of the woman, gaining access to her male relative's possessions and jeopardizes the legitimacy of his offspring. For example, Xenophon explains adultery as a more problematic crime than rape because it affects a wife's attitude, her *philia* (love) toward her husband. In the case of rape, her feelings toward her husband would remain unchanged. Similarly, adultery is a habitual activity, occurring more than once, while rape normally involves a single incident.

Sources:

Walter K. Lacey, *The Family in Classical Greece* (Ithaca, N.Y.: Cornell University Press, 1968).

Sarah B. Pomeroy, *Goddesses, Whores, Wives, and Slaves: Women in Classical Antiquity* (New York: Shocken Books, 1975).

Cynthia Patterson, *The Family in Greek History* (Cambridge, Mass.: Harvard University Press, 1998).

SEXUALITY

Double Standard. In sexual matters, the ancient Greeks held to a double standard throughout the Archaic and Classical Periods. Thus we find in the *Iliad* (circa eighth–seventh centuries B.C.E.) that heroes such as Agamemnon may have both a wife at home and concubines won in military conquests. In contrast, a respectable girl was expected to be a virgin upon marriage, and a wife was supposed to have only one sexual partner, her legal

---

A GREEK LOVE SPELL

The ancient Greeks believed that a person could seduce others by using magic potions or uttering special incantations. Below is an example of one such spell, inscribed on a lead tablet from Carthage in North Africa around the first century C.E. The person who commissioned or wrote this text made one critical mistake—he forgot to include the name of his lover, thereby neutralizing the spell!

. . . take away the sleep of that woman until she comes to me and pleases my soul . . . lead [BLANK SPACE] loving, burning on account of her love and desire for me . . . force her to have sex with me [BLANK SPACE]. . . impel, force her to come to me loving, burning with love and desire for me [BLANK SPACE] and drive [BLANK SPACE] from her parents, from her bedroom . . . and force her to love me and give me what I want.

Source: Christopher A. Faraone, *Ancient Greek Love Magic* (Cambridge, Mass.: Harvard University Press, 1999), p. 4.

---

husband. Because contact with wellborn members of the opposite sex was extremely limited in ancient Greek society, particularly in Classical Athens, males turned to other sexual partners—concubines, slaves, prostitutes, flute girls, dancing girls, and boys. Yet, in spite of these social practices, the Greeks believed that women had stronger sexual appetites than men and less control over these impulses, as illustrated by the myth of the seer Teiresias. According to the story, the prophet was turned into a woman for wounding two snakes he encountered copulating on Mount Cyllene; later, he saw them again and was turned back into a man. When Zeus and Hera were arguing over who had the greatest pleasure in sex, men or women, they called in Teiresias to settle the matter. His answer, that women had ten times the sexual enjoyment of men, enraged Hera, who blinded him in revenge.

Love. The Greeks had more than one word to designate love; one they used frequently was *philia*, a term that denoted the affection felt between family members, a husband and wife, or parent and child. Philia also marked the devoted and lasting friendship of two people, but did not have a strong sexual meaning. When the Greeks wanted to describe an intense sexual passion, they used the word *erôs*, from which we derive the English word *erotic*. The Greek poets had much more interest in this type of love than the mutual regard denoted by philia. From Hesiod we learn that the god Erôs loosens the limbs and overwhelms one's reason. Similarly, the lyric poets celebrated erotic love as a powerful, involuntary attraction that enters an individual from without; they frequently used metaphors of illness and pathology, much as we speak of "lovesickness" today.

A poem by the Archaic female poet Sappho describes the physical and emotional disturbances brought about by erôs:

> For whenever I glance at you, it seems that I can say nothing at all, but my tongue is broken in silence, and that instant a light fire rushes beneath my skin, I can no longer see anything; my eyes and my ears are thundering, and cold sweat pours down on me, and shuddering grasps me all over, and I am greener than grass, and I seem to myself to be little short of death.

Lovesickness torments its victims and brings on madness and death in the stricken individual. It induces an unpleasant sensation felt as a goad, sting, or blow. To aid in the pursuit of erotic love, there existed love spells—normally commissioned by men—that might attract a lover and compel him or her to return the feeling. Underlying these depictions is the assumption that erotic love involves a dynamic of mastery and submission, rather than of equality. The lover dominates the passive object of desire but then by turn succumbs to the powerful force of passion, as indicated in the poem by Sappho above.

Standards of Beauty. Greek social custom dictated that respectable women not show themselves to men other than their husbands. They had to cover themselves with veils when going out in public, much like women living under the Taliban regime in contemporary Afghanistan. Otherwise, they were to remain in the dark interiors of the house, where the gaze of men could not penetrate. Nonetheless, literary accounts show women as concerned about their appearance: they used cosmetics, a foundation of white lead to make their skin appear pale, and rouge on their cheeks. They wore special clothing to disguise physical imperfections and to enhance their beauty. Such measures were normally associated with prostitutes, not with reputable women. In one passage, a husband scolds his young wife for using cosmetics and for wearing an ancient version of high heels to make herself more attractive. Greek artistic conventions reflect some of these standards of beauty: vase painters distinguished female figures from male by painting their flesh white, a symbol of their refinement and their life indoors. Artists rarely depict female figures as undressed, unless representing prostitutes or other disreputable women.

The Female Form. For example, statues of girls called Maidens (*Korai*), that served as votive offerings to female goddesses or marked female graves, always wear an ornate costume while their male counterparts always appear naked. These statues show detailed attention to clothing and adornment; there is little sense of the body underneath the drapery. Korai often hold fruit or birds in their hands, symbols of fertility, and stand with the left food forward while the left hand pulls the skirt aside. The right forearm is raised with an offering, a gesture of grace possibly from dance. The Maidens convey daintiness and refinement, not the physical prowess of their male counterparts. They also express the cultural influence of the Ionian East during the late Archaic Period, when Eastern artisans immigrated to Athens to escape the Persians and plied their craft in the

A *Korê* or marble statue of a maiden from the Acropolis, circa sixth century B.C.E. (Athens, Acropolis Museum 679. Photo: Alison Frantz)

city. Indeed, interest in the female form does not appear indigenous to Greece but rather represents an importation from the Near East through the colonies of Asia Minor to the West. In contrast, the only women to appear nude in art during the late Archaic and early Classical Periods are *hetairai* (prostitutes). They appear with frequency on drinking vessels used by men in the symposium.

The Male Form. The male body, on the one hand, was repeatedly glorified in athletic competitions and in art, while on the other hand, it represented a hindrance that had to be overcome by figures such as the Homeric warrior and later, the philosopher. In contrast to the Maidens, male statues of youths (*Kouroi*) wore no clothing. These figures either served as images of deities or as votive offerings to a god set up in a temple or outside it; they also may have functioned as grave markers, as part of the cult of the dead. The Kouros, like its female counterpart, probably originated outside Greece; its pose appears to be borrowed from the Egyptian artistic tradition, although in the Greek version, the weight appears more evenly distributed between the two feet. One Kouros fashioned around 525 B.C.E. and found in a cemetery in Athens called the Kerameikos, bears the inscription: "Stop and grieve at the tomb of the dead Kroisos, slain by wild Ares in the front of battle." These figures embodied the Greek cultural ideal of male strength and physical beauty, normally associated with adolescence. The youths celebrated Hêbê or youthful masculinity, the goddess who embodied the prime of male life, when boys acquired their first beards and were thought to be at the height of their physical powers. A mythic expression of this idea occurs in the story of Herakles, the Greek hero forced to perform fantastic labors to satisfy a hostile king; having completed his labors, he ascends to heaven, to Olympus, the home of the gods, where he marries Hêbê, "Eternal Youth," and lives happily ever after. The Greeks believed that Herakles founded the Olympian games because he combined athletic prowess with the immortality much sought after by athletes and soldiers.

Prostitution. In the world of the Homeric poems, however, prostitution does not exist; there is in fact no reference to prostitution in either the Homeric or Hesiodic poems, although there is concubinage. Prostitution is a phenomenon closely associated with the emergent city-state and the explosion of commercial contacts with the Near East and Egypt during the seventh and sixth centuries B.C.E. Such long-distance trade produced a merchant class and surplus wealth to spend on luxury items. Not surprisingly, one locus for ancient brothels were the harbors and seaports where merchants docked their ships.

Customs and Habits. In the literary sources, accounts of prostitution only begin to appear with any frequency in Herodotus's *Histories* (circa late fifth century B.C.E.). In his chronicles of the strange and wonderful customs and habits of non-Greeks, he speaks of the prostitution of daughters by Lydians as a means of raising dowries, a practice also found among the Egyptian pharaohs. Herodotus also speaks of bride auctions and temple prostitution in Babylon and of the scandals and successes of the courtesan Rhodopis in Egypt. According to stories in circulation at the time, Rhodopis had her own pyramid worth thousands of talents and had the means to dedicate at Apollo's shrine at Delphi. These stories point to the foreign origins of prostitution, or at least to the fact that the Greeks envisioned prostitution as an importation. In fact, many, but not all, prostitutes were foreigners or slaves.

Solon. Although the practice of prostitution may have originated abroad, by the Classical Period it was considered indigenous to Athens. Indeed, one story credits the tyrant Solon with establishing state-run houses of ill repute in order to keep ardent boys away from other men's wives and daughters:

Solon, impelled by the itch which comes in young men's lives, purchased and established female creatures in houses of resort. . . . Solon was the first to found a temple of Aphrodite Pandemos from the profits taken in by the women in charge of the houses.

The story of state-run brothels, whether true or not, points to a widespread association between the city, and later, Athenian democracy (which Solon's reforms facilitated) and those who make their bodies available to others for pay, "a thing democratic," quips another comic fragment.

Types. The Greeks used two main terms for prostitutes. *Porně* referred to a brothel prostitute or streetwalker and was normally a woman from the lowest classes who went with any paying client. The word *hetaira*, on the other hand, designated a woman educated in music and the arts of speaking, who had more control over those with whom she associated. She participated in male drinking parties and often enjoyed the long-term patronage of one man, much like the geishas in Japan. At the drinking party, or *symposium*, a word that means "drinking together," men recited poetry and made speeches, and, as well, were entertained by flute players and prostitutes. There were also male prostitutes and entertainers who performed sexual favors for their clients.

Economic Motivations. These two types of prostitutes may have been distinguished by separate economies: the street women participated in a commodity exchange—theirs was a monetary transaction, sex for pay—while hetaeras relied on a gift economy in which male admirers financed their lifestyle through discrete gifts. Xenophon's portrait of Theodote in his *Memorabilia* exemplifies the latter arrangement: when asked how she manages to support herself, Theodote replies that she has always relied on the favors of friends.

Derision. The *porně*, a name deriving from the verb *pernêmi*, "to sell," appears as an object of derision in Greek poetry from the Archaic Period and later in Attic old comedy in the fifth century B.C.E. In fact, most brothel workers were slaves, the property of their pimps, whose work is repeatedly described as a kind of trade. For both women and men, trade of any sort was considered degrading in Classical Athens. Thus, in comedy and oratory, reference to an individual's parents as engaging in menial trades was the ultimate insult. Equally disgraceful was the suggestion that a rival or his relatives may have prostituted themselves.

Courtesans. Hetairai, in contrast, belonged to the world of luxury and refinement associated with the eastern part of Greece, with Ionia or Asia Minor, now the Turkish coast, especially in the period of the Persian conquests. They wore expensive clothing and had refined manners; as one passage describes them, they did not "stuff their jaws with leeks rolled up into balls" or "greedily bite off pieces of meat in ugly fashion." Their elaborate clothing distinguished courtesans from other women; they wore gold jewelry, garments with purple

A cup painting of two *hetairai* (prostitutes) reclining with male companions at a symposium, circa 470–460 B.C.E. (Basel, Antikenmus. Ka 415. ARV2 868, 45. Photo: Claire Niggli)

borders or drapery so finely woven it was almost transparent and emphasized the contours of their bodies. Well versed in Greek poetry and skilled at speechifying, hetaeras were often associated with famous statesmen, artists, and poets: Pericles had as his hetaira Aspasia, a woman reported to be of great intelligence.

Points of Contact. The slang names attached to prostitutes connote the places they haunted, such as Bridge Woman, Runner, Wanderer, Alley-treader, Ground-beater, or Foot Soldier. Such women endured a nomadic existence, a lifestyle that greatly contrasted the stability of the family estate handed down from generation to generation and the role of wives in preserving it. Street women plied their trade in the harbor district of the Piraeus, or in the Kerameikos, originally a potter's quarters later known for its funerary monuments, near the main entrance to the city and along the central thoroughfare, the Sacred Way. Both the harbor and the Kerameikos were sites of entry into the city, the first point of contact for merchants and travelers from other cities and lands.

Sharing the Wealth. Some prostitutes had an unusual economic independence in a world in which women could not directly own property or control money. Various accounts show prostitutes to have been economic agents, responsible for paying taxes and having the means, in exceptional cases, to finance major works of art and architecture. Celebrated courtesans controlled a great amount of wealth, which they could bestow upon cities and gods, in contrast to the average Athenian woman, who was not allowed to transact business in excess of one *medimnos*, or

a day's ration of grain. There are many late references to companions offering to pay for the rebuilding of city walls and temples. The hetaera Lamia reputedly rebuilt the ruined picture gallery of the Sicyonians, while Cottina dedicated a bronze cow to Aphrodite. Trinkets such as hip belts, breast bands, embroidery, and jewelry were also dedicated to Aphrodite.

Relations Between Men. Ancient Greek society was strongly homosocial, meaning that it privileged friendship between men above most other relationships. In the Homeric world, a man's loyalties were to his family, household, and guest friends. By the Classical Period, social and political ideology encouraged men to understand themselves as citizens first and foremost, with their primary allegiance to the state and to other male citizens, rather than to the personal ties of family and guest friends.

Homoerotic Activity. The social segregation of males and females also contributed to the close bonds formed between men, and probably those of women in the household, although few sources document them. In Classical Athens, males formed strong attachments with each other through military service and participation in public life, two spheres from which women were excluded. Sometimes these attachments were erotic. In contrast to many modern societies, there was widespread acceptance in ancient Greece, at least from the sixth century B.C.E. onward, of homoerotic relationships. Indeed, a famous story about the god Zeus describes his seduction of a beautiful young boy, Ganymede, whom

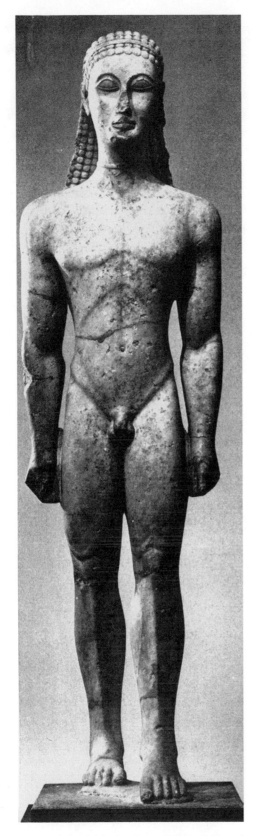

A *Kouros* or a male statue of a youth from Attica, circa late seventh century B.C.E. (Metropolitan Museum of Art, New York)

in love," and had been asked with whom, a boy or a woman, he would not have taken offense at the question. Athenian comedy frequently depicts male characters as captivated by the good looks of a young boy. This pattern of male love may have extended as far back as the Minoan period (2200–1450 B.C.E.) and as late as the end of the Roman Empire in the West (476 C.E.).

Established Norms. The Athenians regarded homoerotic activity as natural and not incompatible with an attraction to women and the prospect of marriage in adult life. Nor did they consider this type of activity to be effeminate or unmanly. Homoerotic relations provided young men with an opportunity for seduction with a partner of equal social and intellectual status, in contrast to the types of liaisons made available by women, prostitutes, and slaves. The Athenians did not classify sexual behavior solely in terms of the gender of the partner, as many contemporary cultures do, but rather evaluated sexual activity according to established norms of behavior appropriate to a person's age, class, and gender. It is therefore difficult to speak of ancient attitudes toward homosexuality because the Greeks simply did not understand that word in the same way that a modern person would. One distinction the Athenians did make, however, was between the sexually active or dominant partner, known as the *erastês* (lover), and the sexually passive or submissive partner, known in male-male relationships as the *erômenos* (beloved), a power dynamic portrayed in literary sources throughout the Archaic and Classical Periods.

Submission. Females were also considered to be submissive and passive by nature; in fact, in comedy, they are directly compared to receptive male partners. The Athenians viewed any sexual relation that involved the submission of a social inferior to someone of higher status as normal, regardless of the gender of the partner. Greek sexual practices therefore embodied social hierarchies of male and female and master and slave. More important, Greek homoerotic love reinforced the idea of a male homosocial culture that depended on the exclusion of women as a means of strengthening its identity.

Platonic Relationship. This amatory relationship, known as *paiderastia* ("love of boys"), represented an Athenian ideal until the end of the Classical Period. In contrast to other types of erotic attachment, paiderastia involved individuals of more or less equal social station: an older male of high birth and an adolescent boy, also from the higher echelon of society. Boys were considered desirable to other males only for a short period of time, from the beginning of puberty, around age sixteen, until they had acquired their first full beard. Although commonplace, paiderastia involved a complex sexual and social interplay: while the older man encountered no criticism for pursuing the boy, the object of his affections fell into disrepute if he yielded to these advances. Athenians may have engaged in such relationships only for a brief period of time before assuming their adult responsibilities such as heading a household and serving in the military.

he abducted and brought to Olympus to serve as his immortal cupbearer. One account of the relationship between the Greek heroes Achilles and Patroclus describes them as lovers. If an Athenian had said, "I am

The close association between adolescence and many homoerotic activities suggests that the practice may have originated in initiation rites that marked the passage from childhood to adulthood. The philosopher Plato, in his *Symposium* (circa 380–360 B.C.E.), cleanses paiderastia of its physical elements and emphasizes the educational dimension. His depiction of male love as the starting point of philosophical inquiry, as intellectual rather than physical, gave rise to the phrase *platonic relationship*. For Plato, the highest ideal is the relationship between men; erotic attachments between a man and a woman, while important for reproduction, have little role to play in his schema.

Disenfranchisement. While a woman in ancient Greece would be harshly criticized for engaging in sexual relations outside marriage, a man could receive public scorn, and even lose his citizen rights, for selling his body to others. Because Solon's legislation protected the body of the citizen male from violation, whether sexual or otherwise, anyone who submitted to degrading sexual behavior from another essentially made himself into a slave. A famous lawsuit, *Against Timarchus,* attempted to prosecute an Athenian politician named Timarchus for just this kind of behavior. Timarchus was thought to have prostituted himself, that is, submitted his body to another and to have taken money for it. Such behavior violated social norms because citizens in ancient Athens were required to be married and to father children. The punishment for this type of sexual misconduct in Athens was disenfranchisement from the city, meaning that the individual could not participate in its democratic institutions, such as the law courts, the Assembly, and the Council (the latter two being the equivalent of our Senate).

Sources:

James N. Davidson, *Courtesans and Fishcakes: The Consuming Passions of Classical Athens* (New York: St. Martin's Press, 1998).

Kenneth James Dover, *Greek Homosexuality* (Cambridge, Mass.: Harvard University Press, 1977).

David M. Halperin, *One Hundred Years of Homosexuality* (New York: Routledge, 1990).

Leslie Kurke, *Coins, Bodies, Games and Gold: The Politics of Meaning in Archaic Greece* (Princeton: Princeton University Press, 1999).

John J. Winkler, *The Constraints of Desire: The Anthropology of Sex and Gender in Ancient Greece* (New York: Routledge, 1990).

SOCIAL ROLES IN THE HOUSEHOLD

Economics. The Greek household was based on a principle of economy: it provided the food, clothing, and shelter necessary to sustain the life of its inhabitants. It was a kind of cottage industry where residents engaged in productive activities such as farming, spinning, weaving, and food preservation that would ensure survival. The household also produced children who would continue to live in it and maintain it for generations. The goal of each oikos was therefore self-sufficiency, the ability to sustain and perpetuate itself for generations.

Women's Work. There was a strict division of labor within the oikos. In Homer's *Iliad* (circa eighth–seventh centuries B.C.E.), the great Trojan hero, Hector, explains to his wife that he must return to the battle to defend his honor

WAS THERE REALLY A TROJAN WAR?

The ancient Greeks believed that their ancestors joined together sometime around 1184 B.C.E. to sail against Troy under the command of several Mycenaean leaders. According to Greek myth, the war began when the Trojan prince Paris (also known as Alexander) kidnapped Helen, the wife of the Spartan king Menelaus, during a visit of *xenia* (guest friendship) and brought her back to Troy. Led by Agamemnon, the brother of Menelaus, armies from several regions in Greece waged a campaign against Troy. With the help of heroes like Achilles, Ajax, and Odysseus, they won the war in the tenth year. A cycle of poems about the outbreak of the Trojan War, the actual battles, and its aftermath, including stories of heroic return, developed in the Dark Age and later influenced Athenian tragedy. Composed before the advent of writing, these stories originally took an oral form, performed by a special class of poets called *aoidoi* to the accompaniment of the lyre. In the nineteenth century C.E., Heinrich Schliemann, a German businessman with an interest in archaeology, set out to discover the lost Troy. What he found was a city, the modern Husarlik in the northwestern part of Turkey, that consisted of several layers, or strata, showing continuous inhabitation from around 3500 B.C.E. to 550 C.E. Subsequent archaeologists have identified the strata known as Troy Six and Seven as the legendary Troy because they coincide with the date traditionally accepted for the Trojan conflict. Although Schliemann and later archaeologists have not been able to substantiate the Trojan War as an historical fact, the myths surrounding this city played a central role in establishing a sense of cultural identity for the Greeks for hundreds of years to come.

Source: Michael Grant, *The Rise of the Greeks* (New York: Scribners, 1988).

and his city and commands her to return to the house: "Go back to our house, and take up your own work, the loom and the distaff, and see to it that your handmaidens ply their work also; but the men must see to the fighting. . . ." As this passage reveals, the Greeks believed that war was the province of men, and the household the realm of women. From the Archaic Period on, women were expected to preserve the things within the house and to produce legitimate male heirs; men, on the other hand, spent their time farming, fighting, and in democratic Athens, governing their city.

Wool Working. Women were responsible for caring for all the members of the household—aging parents, children, and slaves—and for ensuring that they were clothed, fed, and healthy. Their main task was wool working, the process of cleaning and spinning wool into a thread that could be

GREEK TRAGEDY

The greatest contribution of the Athenians may have been dramatic poetry, an invention credited to a man known as Thespis, the first tragic actor, whose name still survives in one of the modern terms for actor, *thespian*. Around 535 B.C.E., the tyrant Pisistratus instituted a new festival in honor of the god Dionysus, called the City Dionysia. Once a year, in early spring, Athenian citizens, probably only men, gathered to watch a trilogy of tragic plays followed by a comic play on each of three successive days. The festival was actually a competition in which leading poets, like Aeschylus, Sophocles, and Euripides, the three best-known tragedians, competed to win first prize. There were also processions, sacrifices and libations, a parade of war orphans, comedy performances, and various types of poetry. The spectators began watching the plays at dawn and stayed all day. They were rude by modern standards; as they sat, they ate food, drank wine, greeted friends, and even threw the occasional bit of food at actors if they thought them particularly bad. The spectacle onstage consisted of three actors and a chorus of about fifteen members, all men, who enacted stories from Greek myth (one play on an historical theme—the Persian War—does exist). Although most of their material was drawn from the heroic past, the tragic poets focused on conflicts between family members and private life, rather than on the glorious deeds of warriors, giving a contemporary meaning to traditional stories.

Sources: Walter K. Lacey, *The Family in Classical Greece* (Ithaca, N.Y.: Cornell University Press, 1968).

Cynthia Patterson, *The Family in Greek History* (Cambridge, Mass.: Harvard University Press, 1998).

woven into a finished piece of cloth. So closely identified was this activity with women that Greek myth represents the Fates as three old women spinning the destinies of mortals. In art, vase painters often indicated female virtue by showing a woman at her loom or engaged in the spinning of wool. In Homer's *Odyssey* (circa eighth–seventh centuries B.C.E.), Penelope uses weaving as a means of keeping her suitors at bay: telling the men she will choose a spouse once she has finished weaving a shroud for her father-in-law, she weaves during the day and unravels the cloth by night, thereby perpetuating a temporal stasis. Women also prepared the dead for burial and assisted in childbirth. A conversation between a husband and his young wife in Xenophon's *Economics* describes this division of labor in the Classical Period:

"It will be your job," I said, "to remain indoors and to send out those members of the household who must work outdoors, and to supervise those who must work indoors, and to receive what is brought in and to allocate what each must

spend, and you must decide what surplus needs to remain, and watch that the expenditure set aside for a year is not used up in a month. When fleeces are brought to you, you must take care that they become cloaks for those who need them. And you must take care that the grain that is stored remains edible. One of your duties, however," I said, "you may find unwelcome, which is, if one of the household slaves is ill, you must see to it that he is looked after."

Women were entrusted with the major responsibility of managing the household and supervising all of its members. If they failed in this task, the oikos ceased to thrive.

Division of Labor. Many Greek writers believed that men's and women's social roles, and the division of labor within the household, resulted from natural differences between men and women. Males, because physically hardier, were considered more suited to outdoor work, while females, because more timid, were thought to have a temperament more appropriate for guarding and caretaking. Individuals who did not conform to these gender roles were looked upon with suspicion and considered socially aberrant. In Xenophon's words, "It is more shameful for a man to stay indoors than to busy himself with outdoor affairs." Men with physical infirmities, such as lameness, made up the lowest strata of society because they were forced to do the menial labor of blacksmiths or other craft indoors, where women normally did their work. The Athenians considered the masculinity of such men to be compromised. Thus, in a comic play cobblers are described as having the white faces characteristic of women because they work indoors. Conversely, women who ventured out of doors ran the risk of losing their good reputations, since only prostitutes, normally foreign women, brazenly showed themselves in public. Of course, women from the poorer families could not avoid venturing forth in public, whether to the marketplace to do their shopping or to draw water from the local fountain, because they had no servants.

The Greek House. Because they were confined to unpleasant indoor quarters, Plato describes Athenian women as "accustomed to a submerged and shadowy existence." The typical Greek house was dark and cramped by modern standards. It was constructed of mud bricks laid on a stone foundation and organized around a rectangular inner courtyard instead of a yard. Most rooms opened on to this inner space, as did a doorway leading to the street. Windows were few, and living quarters were organized away from the street, to maintain privacy. Many houses had a second story that could be reached either by a ladder, or more infrequently, a staircase. Floors consisted of packed dirt. Some sites show sturdier floors where bathing, cooking, and other heavy household chores may have been carried out, although meal preparation could have taken place in the courtyard or on a charcoal brazier.

Special Rooms. Literary sources attest to a special room for men, the *andrôn*, a public room where their drinking parties were held, and to another space reserved especially for women, the *gunaikeion*. The Athenian orator Lysias, in recording the views of a husband who has murdered his

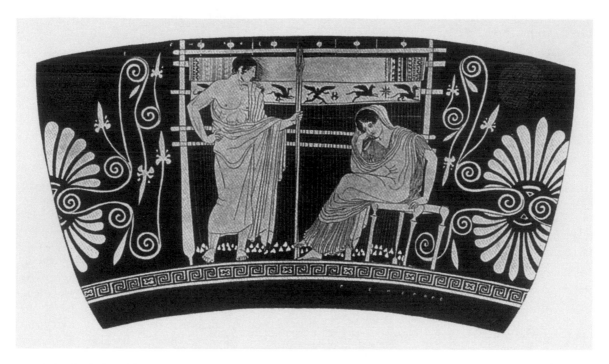

A bowl painting of Penelope at her loom while Telemachus looks on (Marburg University 1016. "ARV" 1233, 19)

wife's lover, provides an example of how the space in a Greek house might have been divided:

> I must explain that I have a small house which is divided into two—the men's quarters and the women's—each having the same space, the women upstairs and the men downstairs. After the birth of my child, his mother nursed him; but I did not want her to run the risk of going downstairs every time she had to give him a bath, so I myself took over the upper story, and let the women have the ground floor. And so it came about that by this time it was quite customary for my wife often to go downstairs and sleep with the child, so that she could give him the breast and stop him from crying.

Separate Quarters. Although archaeologists have not been able to confirm the presence of a separate women's quarters, the traditional arrangement has the women upstairs, as far away from the street, and therefore other men, as possible. They may have been located at the back of the house, or possibly on the second floor, but since the houses would have been constructed of wood, there remains no physical evidence of them. Fancy floors with inlaid mosaic pictures typify the men's quarters, normally a larger room centrally located and abutting the street. Separate living quarters for women were intended to protect their chastity and to keep them away from men as much as possible. Properly secluded females were embarrassed to be seen by men, even their own relatives. It was considered bold and disgraceful for a woman to look directly into a man's eyes, even those of her husband; instead she was to keep their eyes downcast in the presence of men.

Legal Guardianship. Athenian women of the Classical Period could not participate in politics: they could neither vote nor hold public office; they could not own or dispose of property valued at above one *medimnos* (about one day's ration of grain); and they probably could not go to the theater or a trial. Indeed, touching, speaking to, or even looking at a male who was not a family member could incur disgrace, as a passage from a play of Euripides indicates, "it is shameful [for a man] to exchange words with women." Not only were Athenian women not to be spoken to by men, they were also not to be spoken about. In a famous speech commemorating the war dead, the Athenian statesman, Pericles, urged widows to avoid being the subject of gossip: "Your great reputation is not to become worse than your original nature. For your glory is not to be talked about for good or evil among men." In the courtrooms of Classical Athens, orators went to great lengths to avoid mentioning reputable women by name. The mere mention of their names in public, among men, brought disgrace upon women. Instead, the orators referred to upper-class women with indirect phrases, such as "the wife of that man's brother." Although women lived in the city of Athens, they were not citizens: the names of female infants were not inscribed on the lists of citizens, and they were probably not recorded in the phratry, a political association that recognized males born to its members.

Representation. If a woman had public business to conduct, she had to rely on her *kurios* (legal guardian) to represent her. A girl's father was her kyrios until the time she married, when her husband became her legal guardian. His function was primarily economic: he ensured that his ward was properly betrothed and married; he managed her dowry, and acted on her behalf in any financial transaction larger than a day's ration of grain. He was also responsible for any public representation required by his wife or daughter. In an anonymous dramatic fragment, the speech of a young girl suggests how the kyrios might have functioned

Vase painting of female mourners (Copenhagen Natural Museum inv. no. 9195. "ARV" 519, 21)

in a public context: "Father, you should make the speech which I am now making. For it is fitting for you, rather than for me, to think and speak where necessary." The custom of guardianship indicates that the Greeks regarded women as perpetual children who required the guidance and experience of older men. Older women, past the child-bearing years and perhaps widowed, apparently enjoyed a measure of independence and freedom not accorded to younger wives. In addition, although the legal process excluded women, recent scholarship on fourth-century Attic oratory demonstrates that women played an important role behind the scenes, generating disputes between men and encouraging husbands and sons to take legal action; by such means, they contributed to the political status of their households.

Women and Religion. Women also played an important public role in religion. At Athens, they participated in civic festivals like the Panathenaia in honor of Athena, and in other religious festivals reserved for women only, like the Thesmophoria, as well as performed specific ritual duties associated with important stages of life, like weddings and funerals. Indeed, representations of women in Attic drama often involve religious activities.

Mourning Rituals. The Greeks believed that women had an innate affinity for weeping and sorrowful songs, as the character Medea remarks: "Women by nature are given to weeping." Because of their role as caretakers of the body, women had a central part in the mourning of the dead. After washing and dressing the corpse, they sang special songs, called laments. The women of the family stood closest to the body, around the head, with men standing at a distance. This spatial arrangement, in addition to the physical gestures accompanying laments, reinforced the association of women with the body and with physical care. As they lamented, the mourners beat their breasts and heads and tore at their clothing and face with their fingernails. More lamentation accompanied the *ekphora*, the procession in which the corpse was carried out of the house to the cemetery, followed by another round of laments at the tomb. Sometimes a family would hire mourners to honor the dead with a showy display of grief. The rituals surrounding death and burial were perhaps the oldest and least changing art form in ancient Greece. Performed predominantly by women, lamentation represented part of a long tradition that extends even to modern-day Greece. The example of Antigone in classical drama shows how female lamentation affords a means of resisting masculine civic authority. Antigone's desire to bury her brother, while conforming to traditional expectations of female behavior, completely undermines the edicts of Creon and his regime. Her laments give her a public voice in a culture in which women were normally silent.

Female Chorus. Besides performing laments, women in ancient Greece had other religious roles. Girls took part in religious festivals in both the Archaic and Classical Periods as members of choruses that sang in honor of female deities. In Athens, two to four girls, called *arrêphoroi*, from important families were chosen each year to bestow a new garment on a statue of Athena on the Acropolis, the religious center of Athens, as part of the festival of the Panathenaia. At Artemis's sanctuary at Brauron girls, dressed in saffron robes, ran races in honor of the goddess that probably functioned as puberty rites. The female chorus in one of Aristophanes' comedies recounts the ritual activities of their girlhood:

> We are setting out, all you citizens, to say something useful for the city, as we well may, because it reared me in splendid affluence. From the moment I was seven, I served as an arrhephoros; then at ten I was a baker for Athena Arkhêgetis; then I had my saffron robe and was a bear [for Artemis] at the Brauronia; and then I was once a basket-carrier, a lovely girl with a bunch of figs.

This passage shows the rich array of religious experiences afforded young girls as they grew to adulthood, and their importance for the community. By reminding the audience of their religious roles to underscore the validity of their advice, this chorus shows what a fundamental contribution women made to the welfare of the Athenian state.

Fertility Festivals. As mothers and wives, women also participated in state-sponsored fertility festivals such as the Thesmophoria at Athens. At this festival, married women congregated alone for three days near the Acropolis and performed rites in honor of the harvest goddess Demeter. They fasted, sang songs of lament, uttered ritual obscenities, and ended with a feast in honor of birth. During the festival period women set up their own temporary government, and all public business ceased. Husbands were required by law to pay for their wives to attend. Many of the rites performed by women imitated parts of the myth of the abduction of Persephone by Hades and the eventual reunion of the girl with her mother. In the myth, the chasm made by Hades swallowed up the swineherd Euboleus and his pigs; so, too, the participants of the Thesmophoria threw piglets into caves along with pinecones and cakes in the shapes of phalluses and snakes, all objects associated with fertility. Later, women called Bailers, who had abstained from sexual relations for three days, brought up the rotting remains of the objects that had been thrown into the pits. They shouted and clapped as they entered to scare away the snakes thought to inhabit and guard the sacred pits. The women placed the decaying material on altars where individuals wishing for a good harvest could retrieve it and sprinkle it over their fields. These rituals promoted the fertility of Athens, ensuring abundant crops and the birth of children to Athenian couples.

THE SORROWS OF ANTIGONE

The characters and stories of Greek tragedy have had an enduring impact on Western literature and art, and probably none more than *Antigone* (442 or 441 B.C.E.). Sophocles' play influenced many modern writers and thinkers, including Georg Wilhelm Friedrich Hegel, George Eliot, and Virginia Woolf. In the passage below, a guard describes what he saw when he discovered Antigone lamenting over the body of her dead brother, Polyneices:

> . . . then we saw the girl.
> She was crying out with the shrill cry
> of an embittered bird
> that sees its nest robbed of its nestlings
> and the bed empty. So, too, when she saw
> the body stripped of its cover, she burst out in groans
> calling terrible curses on those that had done the deed;
>
> and with her hands immediately
> brought thirsty dust to the body; from a shapely brazen
>
> urn, held high over it, poured a triple stream
> of funerary offerings, and crowned the corpse.

Source: Sophocles, *Antigone,* translated by David Grene (New York: Washington Square Press, 1970), pp. 465–475.

Priestesses. A few exceptional women could serve as priestesses. A fragment from a play by Euripides shows their importance in the Greek city:

> Men's criticism of women is the worthless twanging of a bowstring and evil talk. Women are better than men, as I will show. . . . They manage the household and preserve within the things carried by sea; nor in the absence of the wife is a house tidy or prosperous. Consider their role in religion, for that, in my opinion, comes first. We women play the most important part, because women prophesy the will of Zeus in the oracles of Phoebus. And at the holy site of Dodona near the sacred oak, females convey the will of Zeus to inquirers from Greece. As for the sacred rituals for the Fates and the Nameless Ones [the Erinues], all these would not be holy if performed by men, but prosper in women's hands. In this way women have a rightful share in the service of the gods. Why is it, then, that women must have a bad reputation?

At Dodona, in the north of Greece, female priestesses delivered prophecies to petitioners. Similarly, at Delphi, the Pythia, priestess of Apollo, foretold the future to denizens from all over the ancient world. Priestesses also performed important rites on behalf of other deities, thereby promoting the welfare of the city. Priestesses had an exceptional status in the ancient world: they remained virgins until their service to the god had ended, often when they were past their childbearing years; they did not have children nor did they marry.

In return, they received the esteem and respect of their communities.

Sources:

Elaine Fantha, and others, eds., *Women in the Classical World: Image and Text* (New York: Oxford University Press, 1994).

H. P. Foley, "The 'Female Intruder Reconsidered,'" *Classical Philology*, 77 (1982): 1–22.

Homer, *Iliad*, translated by Richmond Lattimore (Chicago: University of Chicago Press, 1951).

M. Jameson, "Domestic Space in the Greek City-State," in *Domestic Architecture and the Use of Space*, edited by Susan Kent (Cambridge: Cambridge University Press, 1990), pp. 92–113.

Roger Just, *Women in Athenian Law and Life* (London & New York: Routledge, 1989).

Laura McClure, *Spoken Like a Woman: Speech and Gender in Athenian Drama* (Princeton: Princeton University Press, 1999).

"The Politics of Tragic Lamentation," in Alan H. Sommerstein and others, eds., *Tragedy, Comedy and the Polis* (Bari, Italy: Levante editori, 1993), pp. 101–143.

"Private Space and the Greek City," in *The Greek City: From Homer to Alexander*, edited by Oswyn Murray and Simon Price (Oxford: Clarendon Press; New York: Oxford University Press, 1990), pp. 171–195.

SIGNIFICANT PEOPLE

ASPASIA

FLOURISHED MID FIFTH CENTURY B.C.E.
HETAIRA

Companion. Milesian born, Aspasia was a well-known and influential *hetaira* of the Classical Period. She lived with Pericles from 445 B.C.E., after he divorced his wife, until his death in 429 B.C.E. Plato credits her with teaching Pericles the art of rhetoric and records that Socrates enjoyed conversing with her. Her influence over Pericles made her the object of jokes in comedies. After Pericles' death, she became the companion of another politician, Lysicles.

Source:

Simon Hornblower and Antony Spawforth, eds., *The Oxford Classical Dictionary* (Oxford & New York: Oxford University Press, 1996).

CLEISTHENES

CIRCA 570-CIRCA 508 B.C.E.
ATHENIAN STATESMAN

Noble Ideals. Cleisthenes (also spelled Clisthenes) was born into the aristocratic Alcmaeonid family and was the grandson of the tyrant Cleisthenes of Sicyon. In 546 B.C.E. Pisistratus forced his family into exile; little is known of Cleisthenes during his time abroad. Upon returning to Athens he served as *arkhôn* (magistrate) from 525 to 524 and became the people's champion by attempting to implement the democratic reforms of Solon. Isagoras, leader of the city's aristocratic faction, had him expelled in 508, but he was quickly recalled. His political system was based upon locality rather than family and clan. Cleisthenes reorganized the citizens into 139 *demes* (political districts), and this arrangement resulted in a redistribution of power and allowed nonaristocratic citizens an opportunity to participate in government. As a result, Cleisthenes is regarded as the founder of Athenian democracy.

Source:

William George Forrest, *The Emergence of Greek Democracy: The Character of Greek Politics, 800–400 B.C.* (London: Weidenfeld & Nicolson, 1966).

DRACO

FLOURISHED SEVENTH CENTURY B.C.E.
ATHENIAN LAWGIVER

The Code. Draco was responsible for creating a new set of laws in Athens around 621 B.C.E. These statutes were probably the first comprehensive written code of laws in the city. Draco prescribed death for both trivial and serious crimes, hence the word *draconian* is used today to describe repressive legal measures. Around 594 B.C.E. the archon Solon repealed all Draco's statutes except those relating to homicide. These murder laws were publicly inscribed in 409–408 B.C.E. and are partly extant.

Source:

Simon Hornblower and Antony Spawforth, eds., *The Oxford Classical Dictionary* (Oxford & New York: Oxford University Press, 1996).

LYCURGUS

FLOURISHED SEVENTH CENTURY B.C.E.
SPARTAN LAWGIVER

Warrior Society. According to tradition Lycurgus founded Sparta's political system, with its emphasis on military strength, a form of government that survived his rule for generations. Scholars speculate that Lycurgus created the highly militarized communal system following a *Helot* (slave) revolt. He apparently introduced all of Sparta's laws and devised the two organs of government, the *gerousia* (council of elders and the two kings) and the *apella* (assembly). His military and political institutions resembled those of Crete.

Source:

John Boardman and others, eds., *The Oxford History of the Classical World* (Oxford & New York: Oxford University Press, 1986).

PISISTRATUS

DIED 527 B.C.E.
TYRANT OF ATHENS

Descendant of Solon. Pisistratus (also spelled Peisistratus) was born into an aristocratic Athenian family in the sixth century B.C.E.; an ancestor served as an archon in 669–668, and one of his mother's relatives was Solon. He distinguished himself in the war with Megara (570–565) and attempted to seize power in Athens in 560 and 556. At one point he slashed himself and drove his chariot into the *agora* (marketplace) to show the people how his enemies had attacked him. In 546 he finally succeeded in taking control of the city.

Golden Age. Pisistratus ruled Athens by the use of force, but as a *turannos* (tyrant) he was benevolent and law-abiding. Aristotle called his reign the "golden age"; it was noted for the expansion of industry and commerce, domestic tranquility, and neutrality in foreign affairs. A consummate politician, Pisistratus made a point to please the city population as well as the rural majority.

Achievements. During this period Athens grew from a conglomeration of villages into a city, and Pisistratus beautified the marketplace and improved the water supply by building an aqueduct. In rural affairs, he made loans to small farmers for tools and equipment and instituted a system of traveling judges to hear country cases on the spot. Under his reign, religious festivals such as the Panathenaea and the City Dionysia were introduced or expanded. He financed these extensive programs by revenues from the mines at Mount Pangaeum and Laurium in addition to a 5 percent tax on all agricultural products. Pisistratus died in 527 B.C.E. and was succeeded by his sons Hippias and Hipparchus. His encouragement of Athenian prosperity helped to make the city a contending power in Greece.

Source:

Antony Andrewes, *The Greek Tyrants* (London: Hutchinson's University Library, 1956).

DOCUMENTARY SOURCES

Aeschylus, *Oresteia*, 458 B.C.E. The only Greek dramatic trilogy to survive from antiquity (comprised of *Agamemnon, Libation Bearers,* and *Eumenides;* a fourth play called *Proteus* is lost). *Oresteia* sheds light on Athenian conceptions of the family and gender roles and their relevance to a democratic society.

Euripides, *Hippolytus with a Garland,* 428 B.C.E. A play about the quasi-incestuous love between Phaedra and her stepson Hippolytus. (The goddess of love Aphrodite had cursed Hippolytus after he denounced her as the basest of all divinities.)

Euripides, *Medea,* 431 B.C.E. This play relates the tale of Medea, a princess from Colchis, who falls in love with Jason and then kills their sons when Jason weds the daughter of Creon, the king of Corinth. Aside from the relationship between men and women, the text also addresses the issues of moral outrage and the ability of passion to overcome reason.

Homer, *Hymn to Demeter,* circa eighth–seventh centuries B.C.E. Probably written by rhapsodists, this poem provides information on marriage and family roles in ancient Greece.

Homer, *Iliad,* circa eighth–seventh centuries B.C.E. An early epic poem that tells the founding of Hellenic civilization, including the organization of the family, the community, and the relationship of mortals to the gods.

Plato, *Symposium,* circa 380–360 B.C.E. An important text for understanding homoerotic relations in ancient Athens.

Sophocles, *Antigone,* 442 or 441 B.C.E. A play deeply concerned with issues of family and society, produced at the height of the Athenian democracy.

The Pythia (priestess of Apollo) on a Tripod, from the Red Figure Vulci Krater by the Codrus Painter (Antikenmuseum, Staatliche Museen, Berlin)

A Red Figure vase painting of a departure scene (St. Petersburg, The State Hermitage Museum, st. 1428, B809 side A.)

CHAPTER NINE

RELIGION AND PHILOSOPHY

by CAROL POSTER

CONTENTS

CHRONOLOGY
274

OVERVIEW
277

TOPICS IN RELIGION AND PHILOSOPHY

Gods and Goddesses 278
Heros 282
Minor Deities and Monsters . . 283

Hesiod 284
Older Sophists 289
Philosophy: Parameters 290
Philosophy: Tersm, Concepts, and Places 291
Presocratics 293
Fragments of the Presocatics . . . 294
Religion: Parameters 297
Religion: Terms, Concepts, and Places 300
A Spell for Binding a Lover 301

Seven Sages 306
Socratics, Later Sophists, and Cynics 307
Doxographers 308

DOCUMENTARY SOURCES
311

Sidebars and tables are listed in italics.

**800*
B.C.E.**

- A cult dedicated to Apollo, the god of prophecy, purification, healing, music, and archery, begins at Delphi. Apollo is one of the twelve major Olympian gods and the twin brother of Artemis.

- Two major epics from this period are attributed to the poet Homer: the *Iliad,* a tale of the Greek hero Achilles's trials and tribulations during the Trojan War, and the *Odyssey,* the story of Odysseus and his encounters with Athena (goddess of war, wisdom, and the crafts), Poseidon (god of the oceans), and the Underworld. Many later Greek stories of the gods rely heavily on these Homeric poems.

725*

- The first stone temple of Artemis is built at Sparta. One of the twelve Olympian gods, Artemis is the twin sister of Apollo and the patroness of wildlife, women, and childbirth.

700*

- Hesiod composes *Theogony,* a genealogy of the gods that attempts to reconcile conflicting stories and traditions about the deities.

650*

- A school of philosophical thought grows around a group of men later known as the Presocratics. These philosophers include Anaxagoras, Anaximander, Anaximenes, Democritus, Empedocles, Heraclitus, Leucippus, Parmenides of Elea, Pythagoras, Melissus, Thales, Xenophanes, and Zeno. They all attempt to explain the natural world through some sort of divine or rational force.

600

- A temple of Hera (the goddess of marriage) is built at Olympia in the Peloponnese. A major Greek god, she is married to Zeus.

580

- A temple of Artemis is erected at Corcyra.

550*

- The temple of Artemis at Ephesus, in Ionia, one of the Seven Wonders of the World, is finished. Croesus, the king of Lydia, had ordered its erection. The Artemesium becomes famous for its size (over 350 feet by 180 feet) as well as for its ornate artwork. The statue of Artemis is made of gold, ebony, silver, and black stone; the legs and hips are covered with a garment decorated with animals and bees, while the torso has many breasts. (Eastern influences are evident in the statue: it is a mummylike representation, standing straight with the hands extended outward.) The temple is burned in 356 by the madman Herostratus.

* Denotes circa date

500*

- Thinkers later known as the Older Sophists begin to gain recognition in Athens. Renowned for their rhetoric and oratorical abilities, these men include Gorgias of Leontini, Hippias of Elis, Prodicus of Ceos, and Protagoras of Abdera.

458

- Aeschylus writes the *Oresteia,* three plays in which Apollo, Athena, and the Furies (goddesses of vengeance and broken oaths) have prominent roles.

447

- The architects Ictinus and Callicrates begin construction on the Parthenon, the chief temple of Athena on the hill of the Acropolis at Athens.

440

- A temple of Poseidon is finished at Sunium, located along the eastern coast of Greece.

438

- A large gold and ivory statue of Athena, sculpted by Phidias, is dedicated at the Parthenon. Exterior decorations of the building will not be finished for another six years.

430*

- The Temple of Zeus at Olympia (one of the Seven Wonders of the World) is completed. Zeus is the king of the gods and ruler of the heavens. His statue took the sculptor Phidias eight years to finish; it stands almost forty feet tall and is plated with gold and ivory. The god sat on a cedarwood throne decorated with ebony, gold, ivory, and precious stones. He held Nikê (Victory) in his right hand and a sceptre with an eagle in his left.

420

- Construction begins on the temple of Apollo at Bassae, in southern Greece; it is not finished until 400.

406*

- Euripides writes *Bacchae,* a play about Dionysus, the god of ecstasy, intoxication, and wine.

400*

- The Derveni Papyrus, containing a commentary on cosmology, is written. It is the only extant ancient papyrus roll to have been found in Greece itself.

- Antisthenes, the founder of Cynic philosophy, lives a simple and self-sufficient life, shunning personal wealth and comfort. Among his followers are Crates, Diogenes, and Hipparchia.

399

- The philosopher Socrates is tried for corrupting the youth of Athens. He is found guilty and is condemned to death by drinking hemlock. His teachings on beauty, courage, goodness, piety, and virtue (moral excellence) influence many other thinkers. Among the famous Socratic philosophers are Antisthenes, Aristotle, Plato, Speusippus, Theophrastus of Eresos, Xenocrates of Chacedon, and Xenophon.

387

- Plato establishes the Academy in Athens, where he teaches for approximately forty years.

373

- An earthquake destroys parts of Delphi, the seat of the Delphic oracle and temples dedicated to Apollo, Dionysus, and other deities.

335

- Aristotle founds the Lyceum in Athens. Like Plato's Academy, it is organized as a *thiasos,* an association dedicated to the cult of a specific deity, in this case the Muses (goddesses of artistic and intellectual pursuits).

OVERVIEW

Terms. The first difficulty encountered in a discussion of Greek religion and philosophy from 800 to 323 B.C.E. is that there are no direct Greek equivalents for the modern notions of either philosophy or religion. There is no single Greek word for religion; the closest equivalents are phrases meaning "things having to do with the gods." The term *philosophy* was actually invented by the Pythagoreans in the late 6th century B.C.E. Before the invention of the term *philosophy*, someone who was considered wise or knowledgeable about the physical or human worlds was called *sophos* (wise). This category included statesmen, poets, and people who wrote about the natural, human, or divine worlds. Certain groups of thinkers, especially the followers of Pythagoras, Socrates, and Plato, seem to have believed that true wisdom was difficult or impossible to obtain; they thus refused to call themselves wise, but instead called themselves philosophers, which literally means "lovers of wisdom." By the fourth century, the Greeks themselves disagreed about what might properly be called philosophy. Most of what today is termed *science* would have fit under the general rubric of wisdom (*sophia*) around 800 B.C.E., and under philosophy (*philosophia*) by 323 B.C.E.—though then, as now, opinions and definitions always varied from person to person.

Demarcations. What in modern terminology are demarcated by the terms *philosophy* and *religion* could best be described in ancient contexts as attempts to understand the physical, human, and divine worlds, and to influence these by means of language and ritual. For instance, an aspect of the natural world that the ancient Greeks, many of whom were directly involved in agriculture, might have wanted to influence was rainfall. Which sort of attempts to influence or understand rainfall would properly belong to philosophy, which to religion, and which to neither? Building a system of ditches to use existing rainfall most effectively for irrigation affects the physical world by mechanical means, and thus would not be considered a philosophical or religious act. Offering prayers or sacrifices to Zeus or Demeter for rainfall or the prosperity of one's crops would be a religious act. Trying to understand what caused the clouds to rain would be a philosophical inquiry; however, how would modern people categorize an elaborate account of rain as caused by interactions among quasi-divine

forces—religion or philosophy? What about crafting an amulet designed to protect crops against magical attacks—how would this differ from making a scarecrow or lightning rod? At what point do rational explanations of divine forces (which might be called theology) shade over into philosophy? Curing an illness by trying to learn its cause is a standard part of modern scientific medicine. Different ancient medical experts might trace the cause of a disease to an imbalance in cold and hot elements in the body (physics), pollution caused by an offense against the gods (religion), the evil eye (magic), the patient's misunderstanding of the true relationship between soul and body (philosophy), or bad diet (medicine in the modern sense). Is knowledge of diseases (medicine) or ability to persuade the patient to undergo treatment (rhetoric) more important in effecting a cure? Magic, religion, physics, rhetoric, and philosophy all can be used to explain and/or affect the world.

Perspectives. The question of how to divide up various Greek practices and ideas into modern disciplinary categories is not answerable in any precise fashion. The Greeks did not divide up knowledge as present-day scholars do, and, insofar as academics attempt to force Greek thought in modern categories, they necessarily distort it. In antiquity as in the present, people's minds are not divided into neat compartments, in which beliefs about morals, physics, the divine, politics, medicine, astrology, magic, human relationships, and education have no relation to each other. All of the modern ideas are inextricably tangled together. To make matters even more confusing, in antiquity—as now—no two people thought precisely alike. A poor sheep farmer in the Arcadian countryside probably would not have the same beliefs as a wealthy Athenian politician; a Spartan Helot would have a different perspective on justice than a Corinthian oligarch; and a female slave in rural Boeotia probably would not think of love in the same way as a female aristocrat on Lesbos. Disagreements about religion and politics, even within a single family, were probably no rarer in antiquity than today. In other words, any generalizations about Greek thought or religion are at best vague approximations concerning what some Greek people in some places may have thought or believed about certain specific issues, insofar as classicists can reconstruct their ideas.

Late Invention. Philosophy, in a technical sense, was a comparatively late invention. While people, for thousands of years before the invention of writing, may have speculated about matters that would later be considered philosophical, the records of thinkers and ideas the Greeks thought of as philosophical only reach back to the late seventh century B.C.E. and are restricted to those ideas that were transcribed and recopied by later authors; however, this lack of early documentation does not mean that the Greeks suddenly discovered philosophical and scientific thought and abandoned their traditional religious beliefs and practices. Instead, popular religion, especially in the countryside, remained remarkably consistent during the period this book discusses. Poetry (both epic and drama) added an elaborate literary mythos to a substrate of popular religion—one which may not have been believed literally. Official civic cults developed in large cities, in addition to the agricultural festivals of the countryside. In a few cosmopolitan cities such as Miletus, Croton, Elea, and Athens, a small group of educated and relatively wealthy free citizens (overwhelmingly male) read, wrote, and discussed the sort of ideas modern scholars have come to call "philosophical," referring frequently to each others' work and, by the fourth century, sharing a specialized vocabulary.

TOPICS IN RELIGION AND PHILOSOPHY

GODS AND GODDESSES

Major Deities. The Greek pantheon consisted of various gods, heroes, spirits, and cult objects, some of which were worshiped throughout Greece and some of which were purely local. Often multiple deities were worshiped under the name of a single god, or one god would appear under multiple names in different cults. Because of the fluidity of these divinities, often one deity had several unrelated functions or characteristics. The local underground spirits, Theban Amphiaraus and Boeotian Trophonius, for example, were sometimes worshiped as Zeus Amphiaraus and Zeus Trophonius. Were these one, two, three or four gods? At times, it was almost impossible to know which god was which, but, for the Greeks, that was not as important as keeping the gods happy, which was done not by orthodoxy (having the correct beliefs) but by ritual (doing the right things). In fact, on the Athenian Acropolis, there was even an altar of the unknown gods so that one could make sacrifices to all the gods whose names one did not know, thus ensuring that they would not be angry at someone for neglecting them.

Olympian Gods. The Olympian gods were traditionally a group of twelve major gods who appeared in Greek mythology and art. The Olympians were always twelve in number, with eleven appearing in all lists, namely Aphrodite, Apollo, Ares, Artemis, Athena, Demeter, Hephaestus, Hera, Hermes, Poseidon, and Zeus. The twelfth Olympian was at times either Dionysus or Hestia.

Aphrodite (Greek *Aphroditê* or *Kupris*; Latin *Venus*). Aphrodite was the goddess of love, especially sexuality, and fertility. In Homer, she was the daughter of Zeus and Dionë. Hesiod describes her as born out of the *aphros* (seafoam), when the severed genitals of Uranus fell into the sea after he was castrated by his son Cronus. She first came ashore either in Cyprus or Cythera. She was married to Hephaestus, father of her child Erôs (Love), had an affair with Ares, and was mother of Aeneas by the mortal Anchises. She was worshiped as *Aphroditê Ourania* (heavenly love) and *Aphroditê Pandêmos* (popular love), a dichotomy discussed in Plato's *Symposium* (circa 380–360 B.C.E.) and by later philosophical writers. She derived from the older Semitic love deity Ishtar and may have arrived in Greece via Cyprus, where she had a major cult (she was often referred to in poetry as the Cyprian); several Greek authors attest to her Eastern origin.

Apollo (Greek *Apollôn*, Latin *Phoebus* and/or *Apollo*). Apollo was the son of Zeus and Leto and twin brother of Artemis. He was a god of prophecy, music, archery, purification, and healing, and was sometimes associated with the sun. His most famous cults were at Delphi and the island of Delos; his oracles were frequently consulted concerning important civic or personal decisions. Various myths described his love for Coronis (mother of Asclepius), Cassandra, the Cumean Sibyl, Daphne, and Hyacinthus. He had cults, both state and private, throughout Greece. Until recently it was thought that Apollo's origin was entirely non-Greek, but, according to the scholar Walter Burkert, the Apollo of the Classical Period (480–323 B.C.E.) is a composite of at least three prehistoric components: Dorian/Northwest Greek, Cretan/Minoan, and Syro/Hittite. The Dorian component seems to con-

A fifth century B.C.E. relief of Aphrodite being born out of the sea-foam (Museo Delle Terme, Rome, Alinari)

nect him with the Greek word *apella*, the annual gathering of the phratries (local tribal organizations with hereditary membership), of which the admission of new members (by initiation) was an important aspect; this origin would explain his iconic representation as an ephebe. The Cretan/Minoan component accounts for Apollo's identity as a god of healing. He is eventually syncretized with the Cretan god Paiawon; the *paean* is a hymn sung to appease Apollo's wrath. The Syro/Hittite component, which connects him with the Semitic plague god Resep, explains his iconographic representation as an archer and bringer of plague.

Ares (Greek *Arês*, Latin *Mars*). Ares was the son of Zeus and Hera. The Greek *arês* is an abstract noun meaning "war," as well as the name of the war god, associated with violence and strife. Victory itself, however, was characteristic of Athena (she defeated Ares in their battle in Homer's *Iliad* [eighth–seventh centuries B.C.E.]) and was personified and worshiped as the goddess Nikê. Ares was portrayed in art as an armed man driving a chariot to which were harnessed Fear (Phobos) and Terror (Deimos). He had an affair with Aphrodite and played a minor role in the Homeric epics. Although soldiers sacrificed to Ares before battles, he did not have an extensive cult. The Areopagus, a hill where the Areopagus council and court met in Athens, was named after Ares because it was the site of the trial in which Ares was acquitted by the gods of the murder of Poseidon's son, Halirrhothius, who had raped Ares's daughter.

Artemis (Latin *Diana, Lucina*, or *Eileithuia*). Artemis was the daughter of Zeus and Leto and twin sister of Apollo. She was a virgin huntress, patroness of wildlife, women, and childbirth. Myths told of her include her slaying of the hunter Orion and her association with Callisto and Hippolytus. In art she was portrayed as a young woman with bow and arrow, wearing a short chiton, and often accompanied by a deer. She plays a minor role in the *Iliad*. Her best-known sanctuary and festival were at Brauron in Attica. She was called the Mistress of the Wild Animals (Greek *Potnia Thêrôn*), and her cult derived from prehistory when hunters worshiped her by hanging the skins and/or horns of their prey on trees or pillars dedicated to her. In her role as huntress, she was associated with animal sacrifices. Maidens on the verge of marriage performed rituals to avert her anger at their loss of virginity. Women in childbirth invoked the help and protection of *Eileithuia*, who, oddly, was syncretized with the ever-virgin Artemis.

Athena (Greek *Athênê, Athênaiê*, or *Pallas*; Latin *Minerva*). Athena was the daughter of Zeus and Metis. Zeus, on hearing that Metis would bear a son greater than he was, devoured her. Hephaestus used his axe to open Zeus's head, from which Athena emerged in full armor. She was a virgin goddess of war, wisdom, and crafts (especially weaving), and patron deity of Athens. Her most famous temple was the Parthenon, temple of Athena Parthenos (Athena the Virgin) on the Acropolis of Athens, and she had major temples in several other cities as well in her function as the city goddess. She was often referred to as Pallas Athena and

A bronze sculpture of Athena with an owl, circa fifth century B.C.E. (Metropolitan Museum of Art, New York)

world kingdom. Persephonê and Demeter often were worshiped together. In Arcadia, Demeter was worshiped as the consort of Poseidon and associated with horses.

Dionysus (Greek *Dionusos* or *Bakkhos*, Latin *Bacchus* or *Liber*). Dionysus was the son of Zeus and Semelê, the daughter of Cadmus. Semelê, when pregnant by Zeus, was tricked by his jealous wife Hera into requesting that Zeus appear to her in his full godly splendor rather than in mortal form. She was consumed by his lightning, but Zeus saved the unborn Dionysus, whom he placed in his own thigh, from which Dionysus was later born. He, therefore, was referred to as the "twice-born" god. Although the Greeks believed that he was a foreign god who traveled down from Thrace, his worship dates to Mycenaean times. He was the god of wine, intoxication, and ecstasy and patron of the theater. The ecstatic nature of his worship was reflected in various stories concerning his travels. In Euripides's *Bacchae* (circa 406 B.C.E.), Pentheus, king of Thebes, and his family denied Dionysus's divinity. Dionysus caused madness to seize the Theban women. He persuaded Pentheus to attend their ceremonies in disguise; the women discovered Pentheus and dismembered him. The Bacchants (or Maenads), ecstatic followers of Dionysus, were portrayed as wearing animal skins and wreathes, carrying the *thyrsus* (Greek *thursos*, a rod ornamented with ivy and vine leaves and sometimes, a pine cone—in origin probably a phallic symbol), and worshiping their god with music and dance. The maenadic rituals included *sparagmos* (catching a wild animal and rending it limb from limb) and *ômophagia* (eating its raw flesh). The stories about Dionysus were often violent and bizarre, and his cult celebrations featured drunkenness and obscenity.

Hephaestus (Greek *Hêphaistos*, Latin *Vulcanus*). Hephaestus was the son of Zeus and Hera, lamed in early childhood. He was the god of fire and crafts and a skilled smith who forged the shield of Achilles. He married Aphrodite and when his wife was unfaithful to him with Ares, Hephaestus trapped them in a net, thus proving her infidelity. Of the Greek gods, he was the only one portrayed as ugly or physically imperfect. His worship spread from Asia Minor, where he was originally associated with volcanoes, but he had evolved into a smith and craft-god by Mycenaean times. He had major cults in Lemnos and Athens and was worshiped by blacksmiths and other craftspeople.

Hera (Greek *Hêrê*, Latin *Juno*). Hera was the daughter of Cronus and Rhea and both sister and wife to Zeus. Her children included Ares, Hephaestus, and Hêbê. Her cult dated back to the Mycenaean Period, and she was worshiped throughout Greece as a goddess of marriage and patroness of royalty, with major temples at Argos, Mycenae, Samos, and Sparta. She was often portrayed in myth as a jealous wife, wreaking revenge on Zeus and/or his paramours for his many infidelities.

Hermes (Greek *Hermês*, Latin *Mercurius*). Hermes was the son of Maia and Zeus. His cult was celebrated widely from Mycenaean through Classical times. He functioned as a messenger, interpreter, herald, and translator, a god of

was associated with the owl and the olive tree. In her aspect as a war goddess, she was sometimes called *Athena Nikê* (Athena of victory, perhaps a sort of syncretism of Athena and the goddess Nikê); a temple to Athena Nikê was located near the gates of the Athenian Acropolis. Her worship dates back to the Mycenaean Period (1600–1200 B.C.E.), when she may have been called Mistress of Athens. In art she was portrayed as an armed woman, wearing a helmet and bearing an aegis (a goat skin worn as a sort of cloak, or else a skin-covered shield, often with the head of the gorgon Medusa on it).

Demeter (Latin *Ceres*). Demeter was the daughter of Kronos and Rhea, and sister of Zeus. She was the goddess of grain and patroness of agriculture. She sometimes was identified with the Egyptian goddess Isis and the Phrygian Cybelë. She was the mother of Persephonê (by her brother Zeus) and of Plutus (by Iasion). She was worshiped at the Eleusinian mysteries, which included complex initiation ceremonies and the promise of a pleasant afterlife. Another of her important festivals was the Thesmophoria, a festival held before the fields were sown and intended to promote their fertility. An important myth concerning her was that of the rape of Persephonê, a story concerning how the god Hades abducted her daughter Persephonê to his under-

A close-up of a bronze statue of Zeus, circa 460 B.C.E., found off Cape Artemisium (National Archaeological Museum, Athens/Scala)

roads and boundaries (thus of *hermai*, or boundary stones). He escorted souls to the underworld and, in this capacity, was often called upon in curse tablets. His expertise in interpretation (hermeneutics) associated him with oracles and literature. He was the patron of merchants and thieves. As a baby, he stole cattle from Apollo and then placated the angry god by giving him a lyre invented from the shell of a tortoise he had killed. In art he wore winged sandals and a hat, and carried the *caduceus* (herald's staff), around which two ribbons (or snakes) were twined.

Hestia (Latin *Vesta*). Hestia was the daughter of Cronus and Rhea. She was the virgin goddess (or personification) of the hearth which was the center of both Mycenaean palaces and classical private houses. Public buildings called *prutaneia* housed perpetual flames from which individual hearths could be rekindled on ritual occasions. The hearth was considered sacred and could be claimed as a sanctuary. Families would make offerings to Hestia at their own hearths. Although important in daily worship and ritual, Hestia was rarely discussed in mythology and often appeared more as an abstraction of the hearth than as a strongly anthropomorphized deity.

Poseidon (Greek *Poseidaôn*, Latin *Neptunus*). Poseidon was the son of Cronus and Rhea, brother to Hades and Zeus. He was the ruler of the ocean and was associated with earthquakes and horses. He had a son, Triton, by his wife, Amphitrite, and was also father of the Cyclopes. He was widely worshiped in Mycenaean and classical times, especially by sailors. As Poseidon Hippius ("of horses") he was held to have introduced horses and chariots to Greece from Anatolia. In art he appeared as a bearded god, often with a trident (probably originally a fish spear). The Isthmian games at Corinth were held in his honor. He had many major temples, including one on the promontory of Sunium that served as a landmark to sailors.

Zeus (Latin *Iuppiter/Iovis*). Zeus was the son of Cronus and Rhea, brother to Hades and Poseidon. He was the ruler of the heavens, enforcer of justice and guest-friendship, and king of the gods. In epic he was called the "cloud-gatherer," "hurler of thunderbolts," and "the high-thundering." His name is Indo-European, similar to those of other sky gods in Indic, Germanic, and Latin traditions who were also responsible for weather. In art he appeared as a bearded god, sometimes hurling a thunderbolt. The Greek Zeus assimilated features from several other deities; he also was worshiped in a chthonic (underworld) aspect. On Crete where, according to Hesiod he grew to adulthood in concealment from his father, he was a fertility god, and his ritual had an ecstatic character, including celebration of an annual rebirth.

Sources:

Apollodorus of Athens, *The Library of Greek Mythology*, translated by Robin Hard (New York: Oxford University Press, 1997).

Walter Burkert, *Ancient Mystery Cults* (Cambridge, Mass.: Harvard University Press, 1987).

Burkert, *Greek Religion* (Cambridge, Mass.: Harvard University Press, 1985).

Burkert, *Homo Necans: The Anthropology of Ancient Greek Sacrificial Ritual and Myth* (Berkeley: University of California Press, 1983).

Burkert, *Structure and History in Greek Mythology and Ritual* (Berkeley: University of California Press, 1979).

E. R. Dodds, *The Greeks and the Irrational* (Berkeley: University of California Press, 1951).

Lewis R. Farnell, *Greek Hero Cults and Ideas of Immortality* (Oxford: Clarendon Press, 1921).

Farnell, *Outline-History of Greek Religion* (London: Duckworth, 1920).

J. Fontenrose, *The Delphic Oracle: Its Responses and Operations* (Berkeley: University of California Press, 1978).

Timothy Gantz, *Early Greek Myth: A Guide to Literary and Artistic Sources* (Baltimore: Johns Hopkins University Press, 1993).

W. K. C. Guthrie, *The Greeks and Their Gods* (Boston: Beacon, 1951).

Jon Mikalson, *Athenian Popular Religion* (Chapel Hill: University of North Carolina Press, 1983).

H.W. Parke, *Festivals of the Athenians* (Ithaca, N.Y.: Cornell University Press, 1977).

M. L. West, *The East Face of Helicon: West Asiatic Elements in Greek Poetry and Myth* (Oxford: Clarendon Press, 1997).

West, *The Orphic Poems* (Oxford: Clarendon Press, 1983).

HEROES

Cults. The Greeks seem to have been generally believed that there was a "race of heroes," occurring in the period immediately preceding and following the Trojan War (thirteenth-twelfth centuries B.C.E.) Hesiod sets this era in between the Bronze (3000–1100 B.C.E.) and Iron (1100–700 B.C.E.) periods. Most of the heroes were held to have lived in the heroic age or in some mythic period that did not precisely correspond with historical time. Note that these stories were mythical in nature and had little direct correspondence with historical fact, although they may have grown up around historical kernels.

Cadmus (Greek *Kadmos*). The son of Agenor, King of Tyre, Cadmus traveled to Greece in search of his sister, Europa, who had been abducted by Zeus. Cadmus founded the city of Thebes. At the advice of Athena he killed a dragon and planted its teeth in the ground. The buried teeth became armed warriors from whom were descended the aristocracy of Thebes. Cadmus also brought to Greece Phoenician writing, from which the Greek alphabet was derived.

Dioscuri (Greek *Dios kouroi*). The twins Castor and Polydeuces (Greek *Kastôr* and *Poludeukês*, Latin *Castor* and *Pollux*), known as the Dioscuri ("Zeus's Boys"), were sons of Leda. Castor's father was Tyndareus, whereas Polydeuces' was Zeus. When Castor, who was mortal, was badly wounded, his brother, the immortal Polydeuces, agreed to share his immortality with his brother, so both twins spent half the year on Mt. Olympus with the gods and half in the underworld. They were identified with the constellation Gemini (the Twins) and considered protectors of sailors and athletes.

Heracles (Greek *Hêraklês*, Latin *Hercules*). Heracles was the son of Zeus and Alcmena. His twin brother, Iphicles, was mortal, being the son of Alcmena's husband Amphitryon (hence their story involves the same twin motif as the Dioscuri). Heracles was worshiped throughout Greece and known especially for his strength and courage. When he was a baby, he strangled a snake that Hera had sent to kill him. Many stories, often mutually contradictory, were told of his various heroic escapades. In a fit of madness sent by Hera, Heracles had killed his own wife, Megara, and children. He died after putting on a robe poisoned by his jealous second wife, Deianira. He may originally have been an early ruler of Argos or Tiryns, who gradually became a legendary figure, and around whom fabulous stories were woven. His best-known adventures, often portrayed in art, were the twelve labors he performed when serving Eurystheus, King of Tiryns. Many of these involved ridding lands of monsters. His labors performed in the Peloponnese included killing the Nemean lion; killing the Hydra of Lerna, a monster with many heads; capturing alive the Erymanthian Boar; capturing the Hind of Ceryneia; dispersing the Stymphalian Birds; and cleaning the Augean Stables. His labors performed outside the Peloponnese included capturing the Cretan Bull; taming the Horses of Diomedes; securing the Girdle of the Amazon; capturing the Cattle of Geryon; stealing Apples of the Hesperides; and descending to the Underworld and capturing of Cerberus.

Perseus. The son of Zeus and Danaê, Perseus was renowned for killing Medusa. The gods gave him a helmet of invisibility, wings for his feet, and a mirror to enable him to look at Medusa without being turned to stone. After killing Medusa he rescued Andromachë and later either founded Mycenae or immigrated to Persia.

A vase painting of Heracles wrestling with the Nemean lion while Athena watches, circa late sixth century B.C.E. (Museo Civico, Brescia; Hirmer)

Theseus. The son of Aethra and either Aegeus (King of Athens) or Poseidon, Theseus destroyed several monsters and bandits. His most famous exploit was killing, with the help of Ariadne, the Minotaur (half-man, half-bull) of Crete and ending the tribute of seven male and seven female virgins King Minos demanded of Athens as food for the monster. After abandoning Ariadne on Naxos, he became king of Athens. He helped Heracles in an expedition against the Amazons and took their Queen Hippolyta for his wife. A shrine with Theseus's bones was worshiped in Athens, and, though he would have been long dead at the time, he was said to have fought alongside the Athenians at the Battle of Marathon (490 B.C.E.).

Sources:

Apollodorus of Athens, *The Library of Greek Mythology*, translated by Robin Hard (New York: Oxford University Press, 1997).

Walter Burkert, *Ancient Mystery Cults* (Cambridge, Mass.: Harvard University Press, 1987).

Burkert, *Greek Religion* (Cambridge, Mass.: Harvard University Press, 1985).

Burkert, *Homo Necans: The Anthropology of Ancient Greek Sacrificial Ritual and Myth* (Berkeley: University of California Press, 1983).

Burkert, *Structure and History in Greek Mythology and Ritual* (Berkeley: University of California Press, 1979).

E. R. Dodds, *The Greeks and the Irrational* (Berkeley: University of California Press, 1951).

Lewis R. Farnell, *Greek Hero Cults and Ideas of Immortality* (Oxford: Clarendon Press, 1921).

Farnell, *Outline-History of Greek Religion* (London: Duckworth, 1920).

J. Fontenrose, *The Delphic Oracle: Its Responses and Operations* (Berkeley: University of California Press 1978).

Timothy Gantz, *Early Greek Myth: A Guide to Literary and Artistic Sources* (Baltimore: Johns Hopkins University Press, 1993).

W. K. C. Guthrie, *The Greeks and Their Gods* (Boston: Beacon, 1951).

Jon Mikalson, *Athenian Popular Religion* (Chapel Hill: University of North Carolina Press, 1983).

H.W. Parke, *Festivals of the Athenians* (Ithaca, N.Y.: Cornell University Press, 1977)

M. L. West, *The East Face of Helicon: West Asiatic Elements in Greek Poetry and Myth* (Oxford: Clarendon Press, 1997).

West, *The Orphic Poems* (Oxford: Clarendon Press, 1983).

MINOR DEITIES AND MONSTERS

Asclepius (Greek *Asklêpios*; Latin *Aesculapius*). Asclepius was the son of Apollo and a mortal woman, Coronis, daughter of Phlegyas. He was a god (or hero) of healing, who learned his art from the centaur Chiron. His main cult was at Epidauros and included a sacred snake; lesser shrines existed at Athens and Cos. Sick people slept at his shrine, and the god sent them dreams concerning cures for their maladies. (The most detailed extant description of this process is Aristides's *Sacred Tales*). The Asclepiadae, a famous clan or guild of doctors, traced their descent and wisdom from Asclepius.

Atlas. A Titan and the son of Uranus and Gaea, Atlas was punished for rebelling with the other Titans against Zeus. He was condemned to hold up the sky on his shoulders.

Bendis. A Thracian goddess of hunting and fertility (similar to Artemis), Bendis was worshiped in her native land with orgiastic rites. Thracian residents in Piraeus brought her cult with them, and it was established officially in 430–429 B.C.E. In Piraeus, her festival was celebrated by a procession, vigil, and torch race on horseback. This festival is mentioned at the opening of Plato's *Republic* (circa 380–360 B.C.E.).

Centaurs (Greek *Kentauroi*; Latin *Centauri*). Offspring of Ixion and Nephelê, centaurs were beings with the head, torso, and arms of humans and the bodies of horses. They lived on Mt. Pelion, in Thessaly, and were considered wild and uncivilized, with certain exceptions. The centaur Chiron was exceptionally wise and tutored Asclepius, Achilles, and Jason.

Chaos. In Hesiod, Chaos (or the void) was the first phase of the universe, from which were generated Gaea (Earth), Tartarus (the underworld), Eros (Love), Erebus (Darkness), and Nyx (Night).

Cybelë (Greek *Kubêlê*, Latin *Cybele* or *Cybebe*). Cybelë was the Phrygian mother goddess whose consort was Attis. She was a fertility and nature goddess of the type sometimes known as the Agreat Mother" (*Magna Mater*). In the Classical Period (480–323 B.C.E.) she was known to the Greeks and sometimes identified with Demeter, but she did not become important in the Graeco-Roman world until the Hellenistic Period (323–331 B.C.E.).

Cyclopes (Greek *Kuklôpes*). Cyclopes were giants with single eyes in the middles of their heads. In Hesiod's *Theogony* (circa eighth century B.C.E.), they were consid-

ered sons of Uranus (heaven) and Gaea (earth) and helpers of Zeus and Hephaestus. The walls of the ancient cities of Mycenae and Tiryns were called "Cyclopean" because they were believed to have been built by the Cyclopes. In Homer's *Odyssey* (circa eighth–seventh century B.C.E.), the Cyclops Polyphemus, son of Poseidon, lived on an island where he captured and devoured unfortunate humans until he was blinded by Odysseus.

Diônê. Consort of Zeus, Diônê was worshiped primarily at Dodona, and as mother of Aphrodite in Homer. She appeared in Mycenaean tablets. Her name is a feminine version of Zeus; what her relationship was to Hera is unclear.

Dionysus Zagreus. The god Dionysus appears not only in the Olympian Pantheon but also in mystery religions. The aspect of Dionysus, worshiped by the Orphics especially, sometimes can be distinguished from the one found in the Olympian cults and myths by the epithet Zagreus; the stories surrounding him differ in several, but not all, details from the Olympian ones. Dionysus Zagreus, according to the Orphics, was a son of Zeus (in snake form) and Persephonê. Zeus gave the child Dionysus rulership of the world and the Corybantes (guardians of the infant Zeus in Olympian myth) as guardians. The Titans seized Dionysus and tore his body to pieces, devouring all but the heart, which Athena saved. Zeus implanted the heart in Semele, who gave birth to Dionysus. After Zeus punished the Titans by hurling lightning bolts at them, the human race sprang up from the resulting ashes.

Eôs (Latin *Aurora*). Eôs was the daughter of the Titans Hyperion and Thea, and sister of Helius (Sun) and Selenë (Moon). She was the goddess of the dawn and loved, with uniformly unfortunate outcomes, several mortal men, including Cephalus, Orion, and Tithonus.

Eris (Latin *Discordia*). Eris was the goddess or personification of strife or discord who threw the Apple of Discord (inscribed "For The Most Beautiful") among the goddesses Aphrodite, Athena, and Hera during the wedding of Peleus and Thetis—an event that led to the Trojan War (thirteenth-twelfth centuries B.C.E.). In Hesiod there were good and bad strifes, one leading to productive competition and the other to unproductive squabbling.

Erôs (Latin *Cupidus*). The god of love who appears in Hesiod as a quasi-impersonal attractive and generative force, Erôs originally signified intense physical desire, but by the seventh century he acquired a more complex nature. Erôs was personalized as the son of Aphrodite, portrayed in art as a winged child with a bow and arrow. Plato's *Symposium* (circa 380–360 B.C.E.) distinguishes heavenly from common love, the former spiritual and the latter purely physical.

Fates (Greek *Moirai*, Latin *Fata* or *Parcae*). The Fates were daughters of Zeus and Themis, according to Hesiod; generally portrayed as three old women—Clotho (spinner), who held a distaff; Lachesis (apportioner), who pulled the thread; and Atropos (inescapable), who cut the thread.

They determined the fate of each person at birth and thus were often associated with childbearing and found, with Artemis, in cults. Even the gods' powers or honors were apportioned (for example, Poseidon's ruling the sea or Hades, the underworld), and thus the gods could not overturn the decrees of fate. Homer speaks of *Kêres thanatoio*, goddesses of death, who play a role similar to that of the Fates; *kêr* in the abstract means "fate" (in the sense of doom). In later authors the Kêres come to be polluting powers of evil.

Furies (Greek *Erinues, Eumenides, Semnai*, Latin *Dirae, Furiae*). The Furies were goddesses of vengeance, especially concerned with murder, harm done within the family, and broken oaths. They were also known by the positive names of Eumenides (Kindly Ones) and Semnai (Majestic Ones); Aeschylus's play the *Eumenides* (458 B.C.E.) accounted for this dual tradition as an evolution from a harsher to more benevolent type of deity.

Gaea (Greek *Gaia* or *Gê*, Latin *Terra*). Gaea represented the Earth, sometimes quasi-personified as a goddess. Her cult was generally superseded by that of more fully personalized deities. She was the mother and husband of Uranus (Heaven) and mother of the Titans, Cyclopes, Hecatoncheires, Giants, and Furies.

Giants (Greek *Gigantes*). The Giants were a race born from where Uranus's blood fell on and fertilized Gaea (Earth). In epic, Heracles aids the Olympian gods in a battle against the Giants. This battle, the Gigantomachy, was frequently described in literature and portrayed in art.

Gorgons. Winged monsters of quasi-human female shape, the Gorgons had snakes in place of hair. Their glances could turn people to stone. Medusa (Greek *Mêdousa*) was the most commonly portrayed Gorgon, but she also was described as having two sisters, Sthenno and Euryale. Perseus killed Medusa with the help of Athena. Medusa's severed head was often represented in art, and had an apotropaic (warding off evil) function.

Graces (Greek *Kharites*, Latin *Gratiae*). Goddesses personifying beauty and grace, the Graces were daughters of Zeus and associated with joy, blessing, and celebration. Although originally they were not strongly individuated, by the Classical Period they acquired several individual names, including *Thalia* (Flowering), *Auxô* (Grower), *Kalê* (Beautiful), *Euphrosunê* (Joy), and *Aglaia* (Radiant). They traditionally were portrayed as a group of three and appear frequently in minor roles in myth and literature. The Graces had cults in Athens, Orchomenos, and Sparta. They frequently appeared in the company of Aphrodite and Eros.

Hades or Ploutôn (Greek *Aïdôneus*, Latin *Pluto*). Hades was the son of Cronus and Rhea, brother to Zeus and Poseidon. He was the ruler of the Underworld, sometimes confused with Ploutos (Latin *Plutus* or *Dis*), the god of wealth. The two were associated because precious metals were dug up from underground and plants grow from buried seeds. Hades was best known in mythology for his

A bronze statue of a centaur, circa 540 B.C.E.
(Metropolitan Museum, New York)

abduction of Persephonê, daughter of Demeter, to be his queen in the underworld. Mythological descriptions of his kingdom varied, but it usually was described as having three major parts: the Plains of Asphodel where shadowy, and insubstantial shades wandered; Elysium, or the Isles of the Blessed, which was home to dead heroes; and Tartarus, where the enemies of the gods were punished. The river Styx separated Hades from the living world. If the dead had been buried properly (with small coins in their mouths) they could pay Charon to ferry them across the river; the shades of the unburied dead wandered on the banks of the river. The dog Cerberus guarded the gates of Hades and prevented the dead from escaping. In some accounts Minos, Rhadamanthys, and Aeacus judged the dead, sending them to their appropriate fates. Lethë, the river of forgetfulness, was located also in Hades. In Plato's *Republic* (which diverged radically from popular religious belief), souls would drink from Lêthê before being reincarnated, thus forgetting their previous existence.

Hebe (Greek *Hêbê*). Hebe was the daughter of Zeus and Hera, who appeared as a young girl, cupbearer to the gods. She was married to Heracles and sometimes shared a cult with him.

Hecatë (Greek *Hekatê*). Hecatë was the daughter of the Titans Perses and Asterië, or of Coeus and Phoebë, who allied herself with Zeus and the Olympians. She was an ancient chthonian deity whom Hesiod describes as benevolent, but his praise for her may be evidence of a cult and understanding of her, unique to his home in Boeotia. She sometimes overlapped with Artemis (in her role as moon goddess) and was also described as an attendant of Persephonê. She was associated with night, ghosts, and demons; dogs howled at her presence. She was frequently invoked in curse tablets and other magical spells. Her rites were performed at crossroads, where she received dog sacrifices and monthly offerings of food. She rarely appeared in art, but did so occasionally as a triple goddess (much as the Roman Janus, god of doorways, appeared in double form.)

Hecatoncheires. The children of Gaea and Uranus, Hecatoncheires were monsters with one hundred hands, named Cottus, Briareus, and Gyes. They helped Zeus in the war against the Titans.

Helen of Troy. Helen of Troy was the daughter of Zeus and Leda, whose elopement with Paris was described in Homer and mythology as the cause of the Trojan War. She was probably a pre-Hellenic fertility or earth goddess who faded to a demi-goddess and mythological founder of a royal dynasty. She retained a cult at Sparta.

Helius (Latin *Sol*). Helius was the son of the Titans Hyperion and Thea, brother to Selenë (Moon) and Eôs (Dawn), and father of Circë and Phaëthon. He was the Greek personification of the Sun. In art he drives his chariot across the sky from east to west. Helius was a patron deity of Rhodes, but not widely worshiped elsewhere and later identified with Apollo.

Cronus (Greek *Kronos*, Latin *Saturnus*). Cronus was one of the Titans, who were children of Gaea and Uranus. The latter had prevented his older children from being born and confined them inside their mother, Gaea. Because she was in pain from the weight of the sky lying on top of her, Gaea persuaded Cronus, her youngest son, to castrate his father with a sickle. Cronus married his sister, Rhea, and their offspring included many of the Olympian deities (Demeter, Hades, Hera, Hestia, Poseidon, and Zeus). Cronus, knowing one of his sons would supplant him as king of the gods, swallowed all his offspring. Rhea tricked him into swallowing a stone rather than his youngest child, Zeus. When Zeus grew up, he forced his father to regurgitate his siblings. The younger gods fought a war against the Titans and eventually cast them down into Tartarus. The story of Cronus and Gaea has analogues in Phoenician, Babylonian, and Hittite mythology, and may have represented the severing of the heavens from the earth. Cronos appeared in myth and had a festival, the Kronia, in Athens at harvest time, when slaves and masters would feast together.

Leto (Greek *Lêtô*, Latin *Latona*). Leto was a Titan, daughter of Coeus and Phoebë, and mother of Apollo and Artemis. The *Homeric Hymn to Apollo* described how Leto, persecuted by Hera, wandered from island to island, seeking a place where she could give birth to Apollo, until she finally was welcomed by Delos. She shared a cult with her children.

Metis. When Metis (counsel or wisdom) was pregnant, Zeus was advised that her first child would be Athena, and her second, a more powerful god who would overthrow Zeus himself. To prevent this, Zeus swallowed Metis. Thus, wisdom was always inside Zeus.

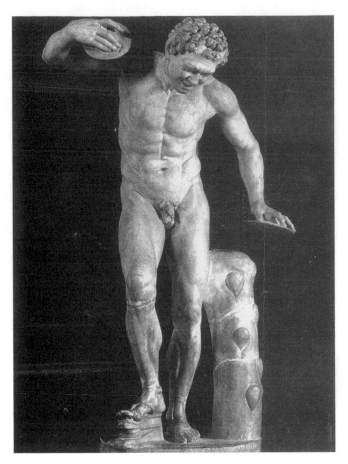

A marble copy of the Dancing Faun satyr made in the third century C.E. from a Greek original (Uffizi Gallery, Florence/Scala 28)

Muses. The daughters of Zeus and Mnemosynë (Memory), the muses were the goddesses of the artistic and intellectual pursuits, often invoked at the beginnings of epics by Hesiod and Homer as the source or inspiration of poetic wisdom, and, of course, of remembering. Different traditions give various numbers of Muses—three, four, or nine; they were always considered as a group, but by Roman times they had also acquired individual identities associated with patronage of specific disciplines: Calliopë (Epic poetry); Clio (History); Euterpë (Flute-playing and elegiac poetry); Melpomenë (Tragedy); Terpsichorë (Choral dance and song); Erato (Lyre and lyric, erotic poetry); Polyhymnia (Hymns to the gods and pantomine); Thalia (Comedy and bucolic poetry); and Urania (Astronomy). They had early cults in Pieria and Mount Helicon and several later minor cults. Several major philosophical schools such as the Pythagorean community, the Platonic Academy, and the Aristotelian Lyceum were actually organized as *thiasoi* (associations for the cult of the Muses). Museums were originally places devoted to the cult of the Muses or, consequently, places where people pursued the cultural activities of which the Muses were the presiding deities.

Nemesis. The goddess or personification of retribution, Nemesis had a wide disparity among her cults that suggests that several distinct goddesses may have been worshiped under her name. One group of stories identified her as a minor goddess pursued by Zeus, who changed into several different forms, especially fish, to avoid him. At her best-known shrine at Rhamnus, she was similar in character to Artemis, but in Boeotia she was worshiped as a goddess of resentment or vengeance. She normally appeared in literature as a goddess of retribution, punishing injustice.

Nereus. The son of Pontus and father of the Nereids, Nereus was an old sea god who was gifted with wisdom and prophecy. In his contest with Heracles he was able to transform himself into many different shapes. He may have had a small cult in Gythium.

Nikê. Hesiod says that Nikê, the Goddess of victory in battle or peacetime contests, was the daughter of the Titan Pallas and of the river Styx, and sister of Zêlos (Rivalry), Kratos (Strength), and Bia (Force). She fought on the side of the Olympians in their war against the Titans and was honored for her loyalty by Zeus. She was often assimilated to, or syncretized with, other gods (such as with Zeus at Olympia, or with Athena at Athens; there is a temple to Athena Nikê on the Athenian Acropolis). She is usually depicted with wings. Soldiers going to war, and even poets competing in dramatic competitions, would pray for her help.

Nymphs (Greek *Numphai*, Latin *Nymphae*). Nymphs were quasi-divine female nature spirits. Each mountain, stream, tree, lake, city, state, or region had its own nymph. They were depicted as young unmarried women, daughters of Zeus. Although long-lived, they were mortal. They had various local cults throughout Greece and were very important in popular religion. There were many small shrines to nymphs in the countryside and caves. They were generally benevolent deities and fond of dancing and music, but appear in folktales as causing difficulties for or seducing unwary or disrespectful travelers. Nymphs were divided into several categories: Dryads (forests and groves); Hamadryads (individual trees); Leimoniads (meadows); Naiads (water); Nereids (ocean); Oceanids (ocean); Oreads (mountains); and Potameids (rivers).

Pan (Latin *Faunus*). Pan was the god of shepherds, portrayed as half-goat, half-human. He was a son of Hermes, native to Arcadia, and associated with wilderness. He was responsible for the fertility of the flocks, and in his rare appearances in mythology he tended to be amorous. Pan supposedly invented the syrinx, a pipe made of seven reeds. When the flocks were unfertile, his statue was flogged to arouse him to fulfill his duties.

Pandora. According to Hesiod, Pandora was the first woman, created by Zeus as revenge on humanity for the tricks of Prometheus. She was made of clay by Hephaestus and endowed with beauty by Aphrodite, craft skill by Athena, and deceit by Hermes. After her marriage to Prometheus's less intelligent brother, Epimetheus, she was prompted by curiosity to open a jar where diseases and other evils were stored, thus bringing evil into the world. Her name means "all gifts" (Greek *pan* + *dôra*), and she

may have been an early earth goddess before being demoted by arrival of a new pantheon.

Persephonê (Greek *Korê*, Latin *Proserpina*). Persephonê was the daughter of Demeter and Zeus. In the *Homeric Hymn to Demeter*, she was described as having been abducted by Hades, who wished to make her his consort and queen of the underworld. Her mother, Demeter, wandered around the world searching for her daughter, eventually stopping at Eleusis, where the Mysteries were founded in her honor. Zeus agreed to restore Persephonê to Demeter if Persephonê had not consumed any food during her sojourn in Hades. On her way back above ground, she consumed several pomegranate seeds. Zeus decreed that Persephonê should thenceforth spend half her life underground with Hades and half above ground with her mother. When Persephonê (the personification of grain) was underground, and Demeter was mourning her absence, no crops grew. Many mystery festivals celebrated Persephonê's return, i.e. the new growth of the crops in early autumn after the end of the summer drought.

Plutus (Greek *Ploutos*). The son of Demeter and Iasion and the god of wealth, Plutus is often identified or confused with Hades because wealth (in the form of precious metals and grain) is underground. He was associated with Demeter and Korë. In popular tales and Aristophanes's play *Ploutos*, he was represented as blind and, thus, visiting the wrong people.

Pontus (Greek *Pontos*). Pontus was the son of Gaea, father of Nereus, and married to Thalassa (a feminine Greek word for sea). He was a personification of the sea.

Prometheus. The son of Iapetus and a nymph (either Thetis or Clymenë), Prometheus was also a Titan. His name means "forethinker." He was portrayed as a wise figure, often a trickster, and sometimes as having created humankind out of clay. He taught humankind arts and crafts and was described in epic as a defender of humanity. He was worshiped among craftspeople in Attica. Hesiod describes his stealing fire from Zeus and giving it to humanity. He also tricked Zeus into choosing for the gods the portion of the sacrifice including the skin, fat, and bones of the sacrificial animals, leaving the meat for mortals. As a punishment (variously for stealing fire from the gods, for the trick concerning the sacrifices, or for not revealing an important secret), Zeus chained Prometheus to a rock, where his liver was gnawed all day by a giant eagle and grew back every night, a punishment from which he was rescued by Heracles.

Rhea (Greek *Rheia*). Rhea was the daughter of Uranus and Gaea and both sister and wife to Cronus. She was the mother of many of the Olympian gods, including Demeter, Hades, Hera, Hestia, Poseidon, and Zeus.

Satyrs and Sileni (Greek *Saturoi* and *Silênoi*). Wood spirits like the god Pan, Satyrs and Sileni were associated with wildlife in remote areas. They had a mixture of human and animal (horse and/or goat) characteristics and were bestial in nature, often drunken and lecherous. They

A relief close-up of the Gorgon Medusa on a pediment of the temple of Artemis at Corcyra, sixth century B.C.E. (Corfu Museum/ Photo German Archaeological Institute, Athens)

formed the choruses of the bawdy comical satyr plays performed after tragedies at the festival of Dionysus and appear with him in art and myth. Sometimes they are portrayed as possessors of important secrets or wisdom.

Tartarus (Greek *Tartaros*). Tartarus was the son of Aether and Gaea and father of Typhon, a monster defeated by Zeus. Tartarus was also the part of the Underworld where those who had rebelled against the gods were sent for punishment.

Themis. A personification of justice, Themis (according to Hesiod) is a Titan, the daughter of Gaea. Zeus and Themis were the parents of the Fates and the Seasons. Themis was sometimes described as the mother of Prometheus. Her cult reflected her origin as an earth goddess, connected in some sources with the Delphic oracle. She was associated with the establishment of religion, sacrifices, divination, and the general harmony of the social order, presiding over the ethical and legal obligations that mortals have to one another and to the gods.

Thetis. A Nereid of surpassing beauty, Thetis excited the lust of the gods. As she was destined to bear a son greater than his father, however, Zeus and Poseidon decided to marry her off to a mortal, Peleus, by whom she bore a son, Achilles. Thetis appeared in the *Iliad* (circa eighth–seventh century B.C.E.), interceding with Zeus on behalf of Achilles.

Titans (Greek *Titanes*, Latin *Titanus*). Children of Gaea and Uranus, the Titans formed the generation of gods before the Olympians and were eventually conquered by them and imprisoned in Tartarus. According to Hesiod, there were twelve Titans, six of each gender. The male Titans were Coeus, Crius, Hyperion, Iapetus, Cronus, and Oceanus; the females were Mnemosynë, Phoebë, Rhea, Tethys, Theia, and Themis. Children of the original twelve Titans, such as Atlas and Prometheus, were also called Titans. Their origins are puzzling. Oceanus, Iapetus, and Cronus are non-Greek names; Mnemosynë (Memory) and Themis (Justice) are personifications of abstract concepts.

Uranus (Greek *Ouranos*). Uranus was the personification of the heavens from whom many of the gods were descended. Uranus impregnated his mother, Gaea, but would not allow the children to be born. With the help of his mother, Cronus castrated his father, and then Gaea brought forth the rest of her children.

Winds. Worship of the Winds was common in Greece. They were portrayed as horses or winged humans who could be beneficial (bringing rain) or destructive. In myth the winds can appear as a poorly differentiated group carried in a sack by Aeolus or as a group of four (Boreas, Zephyrus, Notus, and Eurus) or eight (the aforementioned four plus Kaikias, Apeliotes, Lips, and Skiron). The most commonly named wind gods were: Aeolus (son of Hippotes, given control of the winds, which he kept in a leather bag); Boreas (son of Eos and Astraeus and personification of the North Wind); Zephyrus (West Wind and husband of Iris, the goddess of rainbows); Notus (South Wind); and Eurus (East Wind).

Sources:

Apollodorus of Athens, *The Library of Greek Mythology,* translated by Robin Hard (New York: Oxford University Press, 1997).

Walter Burkert, *Ancient Mystery Cults* (Cambridge, Mass.: Harvard University Press, 1987).

Burkert, *Greek Religion* (Cambridge, Mass.: Harvard University Press, 1985).

Burkert, *Homo Necans: The Anthropology of Ancient Greek Sacrificial Ritual and Myth* (Berkeley: University of California Press, 1983).

Burkert, *Structure and History in Greek Mythology and Ritual* (Berkeley: University of California Press, 1979).

E. R. Dodds, *The Greeks and the Irrational* (Berkeley: University of California Press, 1951).

Lewis R. Farnell, *Greek Hero Cults and Ideas of Immortality* (Oxford: Clarendon Press, 1921).

Farnell, *Outline-History of Greek Religion* (London: Duckworth, 1920).

J. Fontenrose, *The Delphic Oracle: Its Responses and Operations* (Berkeley: University of California Press 1978).

Timothy Gantz, *Early Greek Myth: A Guide to Literary and Artistic Sources* (Baltimore: Johns Hopkins University Press, 1993).

W. K. C. Guthrie, *The Greeks and Their Gods* (Boston: Beacon, 1951).

Jon Mikalson, *Athenian Popular Religion* (Chapel Hill: University of North Carolina Press, 1983).

H. W. Parke, *Festivals of the Athenians* (Ithaca, N.Y.: Cornell University Press, 1977).

M. L. West, *The East Face of Helicon: West Asiatic Elements in Greek Poetry and Myth* (Oxford: Clarendon Press, 1997).

West, *The Orphic Poems* (Oxford: Clarendon Press, 1983).

OLDER SOPHISTS

Distinguished Group. Among the thinkers of fifth century Athens were a group who have come to be called the "Older Sophists." Whether they held any common ideological positions or not is somewhat questionable, as are the criteria by which scholars should decide whether to consider a given thinker a Sophist. The question is further complicated by the shifting meaning of the term. In the fifth century it seemed to be applied mainly to people who were known for their knowledge (for example, Socrates), and those who earned money by teaching advanced pupils (for example, Protagoras), and seemed to be a somewhat neutral term, although often used with pejorative overtones, but by the fourth century the term becomes more specialized, limited to those who taught rhetoric, specifically the ability to speak in assemblies or law-courts. Sophistic skills could promote injustice (such as demagoguery in assemblies or winning unjust lawsuits) or justice (persuading the city-state to act correctly or allowing the underprivileged to win justice for themselves). Conventionally, the term *Older Sophist* is restricted to a small number of figures known from the Platonic dialogues.

Gorgias of Leontini. A leading Sophist, Gorgias of Leontini lived around 485 to 376 B.C.E. and traveled on an embassy from his native Sicily to Athens, where he became famous for the brilliance of his oratorical style. Oratory was notable for importing many poetic features (alliteration, short balanced clauses, elaborate rhythmical devices, ornate language, and such) into prose. The English word *gorgeous* is apparently derived from his name. Two short display orations of his have survived, *Defense of Palamedes* and *Praise of Helen,* and summaries of a philosophical work, *On Non-Being,* which may be considered either a parody or a logical extension of Parmenides's *On Being.* He is the central character in Plato's *Gorgias* (circa 387 B.C.E.) and also discussed in *Meno* (circa 387–380 B.C.E.). In *Gorgias* he defends the notion that rhetoric is the most important and universally applicable of all skills. He argues that orators are more effective doctors than people trained in medicine, giving as an example that he himself would accompany his brother (a doctor) on his rounds and, by convincing people to take their medicines and undergo painful but effective procedures, actually contributed more to their healing than did his brother. In his *Encomium of Helen,* Gorgias offers multiple defenses of Helen's actions, claiming that she could not be blamed for her actions because they can be explained as the result of forcible abduction, the will of the gods, the result of love which is so powerful that not even Zeus is immune to it, or persuasion by means of words which have an almost magical power. Although Gorgias was known for emphasizing the magical power of speech and its deceptive nature, his reputation for immorality is probably not deserved. Even Plato portrayed him as a rather conventionally upright and conservative moralist, despite arguing that the effects of his doctrines and teaching were pernicious.

Hippias of Elis. Known for the breadth of his learning, Hippias, who lived circa 485–415 B.C.E., is portrayed in two Platonic (or possibly pseudo-Platonic) dialogues, *Hippias Major* and *Hippias Minor* (both circa 387 B.C.E.). He claimed expertise in almost every area of wisdom, including mathematics, astronomy, oratory, poetry, grammar, and crafts. According to Plato, he even made his own clothes. He was active in civic life and, like many of the other Sophists, conducted embassies for his city. He is credited with significant original work in geometry as well as poems, orations, and histories (which are not extant).

Prodicus of Ceos. The Sophist Prodicus (mid to late fifth century) appears in Plato's *Protagoras* (circa 387 B.C.E.) and is mentioned in other Platonic dialogues and Old Comedy. He charged substantial fees for instruction and was especially known for his expertise in making fine distinctions among the meanings of words. His most famous composition was *The Choice of Heracles,* in which the hero is offered the choice between a steep, rocky, and difficult route leading up to virtue or a pleasant, smooth, and level road leading down to vice.

Protagoras of Abdera. Probably the first Greek to earn money in higher education was Protagoras (born circa 485). His teaching included such general areas as public speaking, criticism of poetry, citizenship, and grammar. Only fragments quoted by later authors remain of his written works. His prose treatise about the gods began "Concerning the gods, I have no means of knowing whether they exist or not or of what sort they may be. Many things prevent knowledge, including the obscurity of the subject and the brevity of human life." His best-known saying is "Man is the measure of all things; of the things that are, that they are, and of the things that are not that they are not." He is associated with a radical skepticism and relativism about the possibility of knowledge, but, nonetheless, personally appears to have been a fairly traditional moralist. Like Prodicus, he was interested in the meanings and etymologies of words. He taught oratory and interpretation of poetry and claimed to impart virtue by means of these teachings, although, as a teacher of oratory, he also claimed to be able to make the worse (or perhaps weaker) case appear the better (or stronger). When the panhellenic colony of Thurii was founded in 444, Protagoras was appointed to draw up its law code. He is portrayed in Plato's dialogues *Protagoras* and *Theaetetus* (circa 360–355 B.C.E.), and is also mentioned in Attic comedy.

Sources:

Jaqueline de Romilly, *The Great Sophists In Periclean Athens*, translated by Janet Lloyd (Oxford: Clarendon Press, 1992).

G. B. Kerferd, *The Sophistic Movement* (Cambridge: Cambridge University Press, 1981).

PHILOSOPHY: PARAMETERS

Point of Departure. Philosophy, according to Aristotle, begins in wonder. This approach might well describe how not only individuals but also cultures come to philosophize. It is difficult, however, for modern scholars to discover what first impelled the ancient Greeks to engage in abstract speculation; the same problems encountered in trying to understand Greek religion are encountered in examining philosophy, namely those concerning the scope of the term, the variety of differing practices, and the incompleteness of evidence.

Obstacle. Incompleteness of evidence is the single most significant obstacle to understanding early Greek philosophy. The earliest speculative thinkers of Greece existed during a period when literacy was rare. Their work sometimes took the form of poems performed orally and sometimes simply of conversations with their friends and acquaintances for which one must rely on transcriptions or quotations by listeners. Even in the case of authors who themselves wrote their opinions in books, only pieces—quoted or recopied by later authors—survive.

Terminology. The second problem one encounters in studying ancient philosophers is that of which thinkers should be considered under the rubric of "philosophy." The term *philosophia* (love of wisdom) is said to have been invented by Pythagoras and was adopted by Plato and his followers. Many of the thinkers that later Greeks describe as the founders of philosophy, such as Thales, Heraclitus, Parmenides, and Anaxagoras, existed before the term itself was invented. By the time the term came into widespread use in the late fifth and early fourth centuries, its semantic range was itself a subject of contention among those calling themselves philosophers. While the Pythagoreans, and to a lesser degree, Plato and his followers, formed associations dedicated to speculative thought with a quasi-mystical bent, Isocrates claimed that the best form of philosophical knowledge was that of oratory, and that the philosophical life was one of political activism rather than abstract contemplation. A variety of other terms such as *sophist, cynic, physicist, rhetorician, poet, doctor,* and *sage,* was also used to describe many of the people who engaged in activities classicists now include in histories of philosophy; even so, many of these same thinkers engaged in activities that would be considered quite alien to the philosophical, including predicting eclipses, magic, astrology, diplomacy, reciting poems at festivals, and writing speeches for law courts. From an ancient point of view, however, Empedocles, for example, was not a philosopher who dabbled in magic, medicine, and poetry, but simply a wise man (or charlatan, depending on whom you asked) who understood the nature of the cosmos (both the natural and human universe) and used his knowledge to act for the benefit of individuals and communities.

Three Groups. Nineteenth-century scholars, following models established in antiquity—perhaps with an eye more to convenience than accuracy—had tended to divide ancient philosophy into three periods: a confident and scientific one, typified by "Presocratic nature philosophers" or "physicists"; a skeptical one, including the Sophists (and sometimes Socrates), who were concerned with human activities because the external world was unknowable; and a period containing the great synthetic work of Plato, Aristotle, and their schools, followed by a decline into scholastic quibbling and eclecticism. While this scheme of periodization is weak on chronological grounds (many of the so-called Presocratics were contemporary with Socrates and the Older Sophists), it is useful for the student trying to categorize and remember a large selection of unfamiliar thinkers.

Beginnings. Thales, traditionally classed as an Ionian physicist, was often credited with being the first philosopher, but since written records for seventh and sixth century Greece are spotty and unreliable, it is a claim difficult to prove (or disprove). Possibly, though, speculation of the type that was to evolve into philosophy, especially systematic enquiry into the natural world, began in Ionia in the late seventh or sixth century and grew out of two major sources: mythography, which had begun to systematize accounts of the gods and their roles in the creation of the universe and humanity; and Near Eastern and Egyptian science (especially astronomy), medicine, and divination.

Early Ionian thinkers had in common with modern scientists a desire for economical explanations of phenomena. In other words, they tried to bring orderly and simple explanations to bear on the diverse data of daily experiences. Some of them suggested that the variety of physical substances perceived arose out of transformations of a single substance, just as ice, steam, and liquid are forms of water. Others looked for a single ordering principle (usually divine and/or rational, but sometimes mechanical) to account for the regularities which appear in nature (for example, smoke rises but solid objects fall, or that the sun and planets disappear and reappear on fixed schedules).

Natural World. Most of preserved works of the Greek thinkers living in the eastern colonies of Ionia or the western ones of Italy were primarily concerned with the natural world, but their physical speculations were often accompanied by ethical ones. Heraclitus, Xenophanes, and Empedocles all were concerned with what is most valuable in human existence and the nature of the gods and the soul. The atomists, Democritus and Leucippus, derived from their physical conclusions about atoms theories of the best way to cultivate the tranquillity of the soul. Many of the Presocratics had an almost ascetic bent, extending (or perhaps influencing) the traditional Greek value of moderation to a greater level of austerity, condemning, variously, eating of meat, drunkenness, desire for physical pleasure, and loquacity.

Range of Interests. The thinkers who congregated in Athens, whether native or immigrant, included many whose primary interests were in ethics (the proper behavior of individuals), politics (the ordering of cities), and rhetoric (the use of persuasive language). The linguistic focus of early Greek thought began among the Presocratics but expanded considerably with later thinkers. Since people think and communicate by the means of words, to understand things correctly is equivalent to being able to give a correct account of them, and thus understanding things depends to a certain degree on precise use and knowledge of language. Both Socrates and the Sophists, therefore, discussed problems of language and definition, as well as moral and epistemological questions. Meanwhile, Plato and Aristotle had wide-ranging interests, including logic, physics, ethics, theology, biology, politics, rhetoric, and literature. They both founded schools that survived their deaths, and both have continued to influence philosophy to the present day.

Sources:

W. K. C. Guthrie, *A History of Greek Philosophy*, volumes I-VI (Cambridge: Cambridge University Press, 1962–1981).

A. A. Long, ed., *The Cambridge Companion to Early Greek Philosophy* (Cambridge & New York: Cambridge University Press, 1999).

Francis E. Peters, *Greek Philosophical Terms: A Historical Lexicon* (New York: New York University Press, 1967).

H. D. Rankin, *Sophists, Socratics & Cynics* (London: Croom Helm, 1983).

Giovanni Reale, *A History of Ancient Philosophy*, volumes I & II (Albany: State University of New York Press, 1990).

J. O. Urmson, *The Greek Philosophical Vocabulary* (London: Duckworth, 1990).

PHILOSOPHY: TERMS, CONCEPTS, AND PLACES

Academy. Plato's school was located in the Academy, a park outside Athens near a shrine sacred to the hero Academus. The Academy was organized as a *thiasos* (cult dedicated to the Muses) and continued as a philosophical school from its founding by Plato in the fourth century B.C.E. until it was closed by the Emperor Justinian in 529 C.E. Plato's followers, therefore, were referred to as Academics. Plato's Academy has sometimes been called the first university, but there were major differences between its structure and that of modern universities. The Academy did not collect fees from students (they considered demanding fees for knowledge immoral), did not offer degrees, diplomas, or other credentials, and did not have any fixed course of instruction (people would join or leave at any age and might remain members for their entire lives). In certain ways the closest modern institution might be a monastery. Plato himself did not give lectures, although his successors and followers sometimes held formal lectures or discussions. Much of the work of the Academy, which included major discoveries in mathematics, science, and philosophy, seemed to be the outcome of informal discussions. There were, however, regular symposia (drinking parties) at the Academy, during which members celebrated special occasions and engaged in discussions.

Arche (Greek: Arkhê). The First Cause or Origin was called the *arkhê*. Aristotle attributed to the Presocratics the notion that all substances were caused or created from a single substance (water for Thales; air for Anaximenes; fire for Heraclitus; and the Unlimited for Anaximander) which he identified with his own notion of the material cause. Aristotle's account of the Presocratics was probably overly simplistic, but, nonetheless, influential.

Atom. According to the atomic theories of Democritus and Leucippus, the universe is composed of atoms and void. (An atom is the smallest indivisible unit of matter and comes from the Greek term *atomon*, meaning uncut or indivisible.) Atoms consist of uniform and indivisible "being," are of different sizes and shapes, but not substance. The apparent multiplicity of substances perceived with the senses are the result of differing shapes of atoms in different combinations, moving at different speeds.

Cosmos. The cosmos is the ordered universe, as opposed to the chaos from which some poets and philosophers considered it to have evolved.

Divine. Greek thought distinguishes between the divine (*to theion*) and the individual gods (*hoi theoi*). Material or impersonal substances can be considered divine, i.e. greater than the merely human or than other parts of nature, without being considered actual gods. When kings, emperors, or heroes were given divine honors, they were not considered actual gods in the manner of Zeus, but rather they were considered more powerful or capable than ordinary people, much in the way the gods are superior to even the greatest humans.

A mosaic of Plato's Academy, circa 79 C.E., found in the ruins of a villa near Pompeii, Italy (Museo Nazionale, Naples. Photo: Andre Held)

Ethics. The Greeks developed a type of philosophy concerned with individual conduct. Moral philosophy was divided into three parts: ethics (concerned with the individual); oeconomics (modern economics, concerned with the household or extended family); and politics (concerned with the *polis* or city-state).

Form (Platonic). In several of the Platonic dialogues, characters, especially Socrates, discuss the "forms" or "ideas." What these concepts are, precisely, is something that has been debated widely for over two millennia. In Plato's early dialogues (prior to 387 B.C.E.), Socrates and his interlocutors often are presented as arguing over the correct definition of general and abstract terms (beauty, courage, holiness, virtue, justice, etc.). The essence, or Form, of some abstract concept, X, is sometimes presented in a phrase of the pattern "the (form of) X that makes all X things X" (for example,

the Beautiful which makes all beautiful things beautiful) and sometimes as "the X in itself." Whether a Form is an abstract criterion, something with some sort of noncorporeal independent existence, or a divine idea and the relationship of the forms to the particulars, is explored but never definitively answered in the Platonic dialogues.

Fragment. Many early thinker's exact words (*ipsissima verba*) survive today in the works of later authors. For most of the Presocratics and Older Sophists, scholars now possess only fragments (often only one or two clauses) rather than extensive continuous excerpts from their works.

Ipsissima Verba. In discussing Presocratics and Older Sophists, historians distinguish *ipsissima verba*, the thinker's exact words as quoted by later authors, from *testimonia*, summaries or paraphrases of an earlier thinker.

Physics. For the ancient Greeks, physics was the study of the nature (*phusis*) of the sensible world. The Stoics divided philosophy into physics, ethics, and logic.

Recollection. The theory of recollection, advanced in Plato's *Meno* (circa 387–380 B.C.E.), states that since one cannot derive knowledge of the Forms from the particulars, one must have known them before souls descended into bodies. All learning, therefore, is recollection of things we have forgotten, and teaching is a matter of getting rid of false impressions in order to facilitate recollection. Thus Socrates, especially in Plato's *Theaetetus* (circa 360–355 B.C.E.), claims he does not know or teach anything, but merely acts as a midwife to knowledge.

Testimonia. Unlike *ipsissima verba* (verbatim quotations), testimonia consisted of summaries, paraphrases, or discussions of an author's work.

Theology. The term *theologia* was first coined by Plato. It refers to systematic scientific reasoning about the gods, as opposed to popular belief or poetic tradition.

Sources:

W. K. C. Guthrie, *A History of Greek Philosophy*, volumes I-VI (Cambridge: Cambridge University Press, 1962–1981).

A. A. Long, ed., *The Cambridge Companion to Early Greek Philosophy* (Cambridge & New York: Cambridge University Press, 1999).

Francis E. Peters, *Greek Philosophical Terms: A Historical Lexicon* (New York: New York University Press, 1967).

H. D. Rankin, *Sophists, Socratics & Cynics* (London: Croom Helm, 1983).

Giovanni Reale, *A History of Ancient Philosophy*, volumes I &II (Albany: State University of New York Press, 1990).

J. O. Urmson, *The Greek Philosophical Vocabulary* (London: Duckworth, 1990).

PRESOCRATICS

Natural Phenomena. The term *Presocratic philosopher* is used to describe several thinkers who lived in the late seventh through fifth centuries. They shared an interest in trying to explain natural phenomena, though many were also concerned with the nature of the gods, healing, politics, and ethics. The earliest of the Presocratics, including Thales, Anaximenes, Anaximander, and Heraclitus, lived in Ionia, and are sometimes referred to as "Ionian nature philosophers." Two philosophers, Xenophanes and Pythagoras, migrated from Ionia to Italy; these and other philosophers living in Greek colonies in Italy (therefore referred to as an "Italian" school) include Empedocles, Zeno, and Parmenides of Elea. Melissus, though he lived in Samos (native island of Pythagoras), because of his philosophical affiliations with Parmenides and Zeno, is usually grouped with the "Eleatics." Knowledge of these philosophers is rather uncertain and only fragments of most of their work remain, often filtered through a somewhat unreliable doxographical tradition. Many ancient historians of philosophy tended to group thinkers into lines of succession, by constructing lineages of teachers and pupils, and modern accounts often echo these groupings as matters of convenience, even where there are grounds for skepticism concerning the actual historical connections among the various figures so grouped.

Characteristics. There are several striking characteristics shared by many of the Presocratics. The most radical is that it they no longer accepted the world as self-explanatory, but rather sought explanations of the diverse phenomena of ordinary experience in terms of simple underlying causes. Their explanations were often mechanistic, though they could include some sort of divine or rational forces as principles governing the material world. Several Presocratics attempted to achieve unified understandings of the physical, divine, and human worlds. The recent discovery and editing of a partial papyrus text of Empedocles' poem, *Purifications* (fifth century B.C.E.), which almost doubles the number of surviving lines of Empedocles known to modern scholars, demonstrates that even though the Presocratics lived over two thousand years ago, new evidence can radically change perceptions of these distant figures.

Anaxagoras. The son of Hegesibulus of Clazomenae (an Ionian island), Anaxagoras moved to Athens in 480, where he became part of the intellectual and artistic circle surrounding the famous statesman Pericles. He lived in Athens for approximately thirty years, until he was charged with impiety and support of Persia. With the help of Pericles he escaped to Lampsacus, where he founded a school. He wrote a single philosophical work, of which few fragments are extant; ancient accounts of his work are contradictory and unclear. He thought that the physical world was composed of *spermata* (seeds) having fixed qualities. These seeds are infinitely divisible, with each piece containing the qualities of the parent seed. The cosmos began as a mixture of all types of organic and inorganic seeds (blood, bone, gold, or other matter). *Nous* (Mind) alone is separate and unmixed. Nous set the primordial mixture rotating, which separated the types of seed, with the dense, moist, cold, and dark ones tending toward the center and the rarified, dry, hot, and bright ones moving towards the circumference. The sun, stars, and planets are glowing rocks that revolve around a flat earth. He believed eclipses are caused by the moon's passing between the sun and the earth.

Anaximander of Miletus. The author of the first philosophical treatise in prose (circa 546), Anaximander (circa 610–540 B.C.E.) also was known as the author of a complete map of the earth and the inventor of the *gnômôn*, an instrument used in astronomical observation. He thought the first principle of the universe to be the *apeiron* (Indefinite or Unlimited), which he considered divine in nature. Innumerable worlds separate from the Unlimited. The objects of ordinary experience are results of conflicting pairs of opposites that are out of balance. The universe is subject to some sort of natural law, violation of which Anaximander considers "injustice." The earth is suspended in the center of the universe and the sun and planets are fiery substances wrapped in a dark vapor that revolves

HERACLITUS OF EPHESUS
(flourished circa 500 B.C.E.):

Those who step into the same river have different waters flowing ever upon them.

If it were not in honor of Dionysus that they conducted the procession and sang the hymn to the male organ [the phallic hymn], their activity would be completely shameless. But Hades is the same as Dionysus, in whose honor they rave and perform the Bacchic revels.

This ordered universe [*cosmos*], which is the same for all, was not created by any one of the gods or of mankind, but it was ever and is and shall be ever-living Fire, kindled in measure and quenched in measure.

The changes of fire: first sea; and of sea, half is earth and half fiery water-spout. . . . Earth is liquified into sea, and retains its measure according to the same Law as existed before it became earth.

To souls, it is death to become water; to water, it is death to become earth. From earth comes water, and from water, soul.

Much learning does not teach one to have intelligence; for it would have taught Hesiod and Pythagoras, and again, Xenophanes and Hecataeus.

Sea water is the purest and most polluted: for fish, it is drinkable and life-giving; for men, not drinkable and destructive.

Immortals are mortal, mortals are immortal; [each] lives the death of the other, and dies their life.

There is an exchange: all things for Fire and Fire for all things, like goods for gold and gold for goods.

The sun will not transgress his measures; otherwise the Furies, ministers of Justice, will find him out.

PARMENIDES OF ELEA
(flourished circa 475 B.C.E.):

The mares which carry me conveyed me as far as my desire reached, when the goddesses who were driving had set me on the famous highway which bears a man who has knowledge through all the cities. Along this way I was carried; for by this way the exceedingly intelligent mares bore me, drawing the chariot, and the maidens directed the

way. The axle in the naves gave forth a pipe-like sound as it glowed [for it was driven round by the two whirling circles (wheels) at each end] whenever the maidens, daughters of the Sun, having left the Palace of Night, hastened their driving towards the light, having pushed back their veils from their heads with their hands. . . .

And the goddess received me kindly, and took my right hand in hers, and thus she spoke and addressed me: "Young man, companion of immortal charioteers, who comest by the help of the steeds which bring thee to our dwelling: welcome!—since no evil fate has despatched thee on thy journey by this road (for truly it is far from the path trodden by mankind); no, it is divine command and Right. Thou shalt inquire into everything: both the motionless heart of well-rounded Truth, and also the opinions of mortals, in which there is no true reliability. But nevertheless thou shalt learn these things [opinions] also—how one should go through all the things-that-seem, without exception, and test them."

Come, I will tell you—and you must accept my word when you have heard it—the ways of inquiry which alone are to be thought: the one that IT IS, and it is not possible for IT NOT TO BE, is the way of credibility, for it follows Truth; the other, that IT IS NOT, and that IT is bound NOT TO BE: this I tell you is a path that cannot be explored; for you could neither recognize that which is NOT, nor express it.

At this point I cease my reliable theory [Logos] and thought, concerning Truth; from here onwards you must learn the opinions of mortals, listening to the deceptive order of my words.

They have established [the custom of] naming two forms, one of which ought not to be [mentioned]: that is where they have gone astray. They have distinguished them as opposite in form, and have marked them off from another by giving them different signs: on one side the flaming fire in the heavens, mild, very light [in weight], the same as itself in every direction, and not the same as the other. This [other] also is by itself and opposite: dark Night, a dense and heavy body. This world-order I describe to you with all its phenomena, in order that no intellect of mortal men may outstrip you.

Source: Kathleen Freeman, *Ancilla to the Pre-Socratic Philosophers: A Complete Translation of the Fragments in Diels*, Fragmente der Vorsokratiker (Oxford: Basil Blackwell, 1948).

around them. Celestial bodies are seen through holes in the accompanying vapor. Anaximander also was reported to have held that animals and men evolved gradually from earlier entities.

Anaximenes. A follower of Anaximander's, Anaximenes (mid-sixth century) wrote in prose, little of which is extant. He believed that the cosmos (ordered universe) comes to be and perishes in cycles. The universe is surrounded by a divine vapor (*aêr*) which it breathes. This air, when rar-

efied, becomes fire, and, when condensed, wind, cloud, water, earth, and stone. All other substances are variations or combinations of these simpler materials. The earth is a flat disk, floating on air. The sun, moon, and stars are flames exhaled by the earth and circulating around it. The sun at night is concealed behind distant mountains.

Democritus. Born sometime around 470, Democritus was known as the "laughing philosopher" because his ethics emphasized cheerfulness. He is associated with the older thinkers, Protagoras and Leucippus, in the ancient biographies, but the details ancient authors give are contradictory. According to Diogenes Laertius, he wrote many books on such varied topics as ethics, physics, mathematics, music (including philology and literary criticism), and various notes, handbooks, and miscellaneous works. Only a few fragments of his works remain. Both Leucippus and Democritus (whose theories are often confused with each other in ancient accounts) believed that the world consisted of atoms and the void. Atoms were invisibly small, indivisible, undifferentiated matter, differing from each other only in size and shape. The variety observed in the phenomenal world is due to differences in the way atoms are combined with one another (dense or sparse, various shapes) to form larger objects. Atoms themselves do not change, but they do move and suffer random collisions, giving rise to changing phenomena. This world is one of many, and both the natural world and all life evolved gradually from random atoms to more complex structures. The soul is made of small round atoms and perishes with the body. Sensation is the reaction of the soul to *eidôla*, fine particles emanating from all objects and striking sense organs. Democritus recommended that happiness consists of an untroubled soul, the atoms of which are protected from sudden shocks and changes; thus, well-being is a product of moderation, good judgement, and cheerful acceptance of external circumstances. His beliefs strongly influenced Epicurean philosophy.

Eleatic School. The term *Eleatic School* refers to a tradition of philosophy beginning with Parmenides and continued by his pupil Zeno. Melissus, although not personally associated with either of the others, held similar doctrines, and thus is considered an Eleatic. An earlier philosopher, Xenophanes, who was originally from Ionia but traveled widely in Sicily, because of his monotheism, was considered an Eleatic by Aristotle. Empedocles, although influenced by the Eleatics, differed from them on several doctrinal points. Gorgias, who was better known as a rhetorician than as a philosopher, may have been influenced by Empedocles. He wrote an essay *On Non-Being* similar in theme and style to the work of Parmenides.

Empedocles. The son of Meton and grandson of the Empedocles who won the Olympic chariot race in 496, Empedocles (circa 493–433 B.C.E.) was a Sicilian aristocrat and, possibly, follower of Parmenides and/or Pythagoras. He was active in politics in his native city of Acragas. The story that he committed suicide by jumping in the volcano on Mount Aetna is unlikely to be true, but it has inspired many literary works. Empedocles was a polymath, who combined interests in medicine, nature, science, poetry, oratory, mysticism, and politics. He was credited with miraculous healings and claims to divinity, as well as with political and literary influence. Aristotle considered him the founder of rhetoric and, possibly the teacher of Gorgias, and Galen credited him with founding a Sicilian school of medicine. His account of the transmigration of the soul is connected to his notions of the relationships among the elements and the divine. Empedocles denied Parmenides's claim that all reality was permanent and unchanging, but instead suggested that it consisted of permanent elements in changing combinations. These four quasi-divine roots or elements (earth, air, fire, water) mix and separate under the influences of two forces, Love and Strife, giving rise to mortal things (the things we perceive with our senses). The spherical earth is at the center of the universe. A light and a dark hemisphere revolve around it, giving rise to day and night. Matter emits effluences that travel to our eyes, giving rise to vision.

Heraclitus of Ephesus. The son of Bloson, Heraclitus was born into a royal family around 540 B.C.E. He renounced his inherited position, which passed to his brother. His preserved writings are over eighty prose fragments found as quotations in later authors. These may have been parts of a continuous book, or, perhaps, originally composed as a collection of short maxims, or just scattered sayings transmitted in the notes and memories of his followers. (The earliest major sources for Heraclitus are Plato and Aristotle, who wrote more than seventy years after his death.) The most famous of Heraclitus's fragments, and one which is quoted and commented on by several later authors, claimed that one cannot step into the same river twice. He explained this statement by pointing out that if one stepped off a bank twice in the same place, new water would flow over one, the previous waters having flowed downstream. Heraclitus considered the cosmos similar to the river in that even apparently stable objects are always in changing, or in flux, and that the appearance of stability, in rivers or flames (which seem to be his standard cases), is the result of what modern scientists might call dynamic equilibrium. Although the universe always changes, it does not do so at random. The world is composed of opposing elements, of which the most important is fire. The changes of these elements he described as regulated in accordance with *logos*. The role, and even meaning, of *logos* in Heraclitus is unclear. Even ancient Greeks described his sayings as obscure and paradoxical, and the intervening millennia and loss of much of his work have not clarified them. In Greek, logos had an extremely wide semantic range, covering such disparate concepts as reason, logic, ratio, account in the sense of bookkeeping tallies, rational explanation, or word. Perhaps the most that could be claimed with any certainty about the position of logos in Heraclitus is that it functions to maintain order in a constantly changing world. Many of Heraclitus's sayings were polemical, criticizing the claims to wisdom of the masses, the poets, and other philosophers. He argued that true knowledge is universal rather than idiosyncratic, but, nonetheless, known only to the few rather than the many. His work was extremely influential. Cratylus (who claimed that one could not step in the same river even once) and others promulgated his philosophy in classical Athens, Plato and Aristotle discussed him at length, and the Stoics, one of the most important schools of Hellenistic philosophy, followed Heraclitus in several important doctrinal areas.

Leucippus. Little is known of the life of Leucippus (died late fifth century B.C.E.), the teacher of Democritus and the originator of atomic theory. His philosophies are so blended with those of Democritus that it is difficult to distinguish what doctrinal differences, if any, they might have had.

Parmenides of Elea. Born circa 515 B.C.E., Parmenides was an extremely influential thinker who also was involved in civic affairs. He appears in one of Plato's dialogues, *Parmenides* (circa 360–355 B.C.E.), and is mentioned in several others. Socrates, in Plato's *Theaetetus* (circa 360–355 B.C.E.), describes Parmenides as the thinker he admires above all others, and a follower of Parmenides, the anonymous "Eleatic Stranger," is portrayed positively in two other Platonic dialogues, *Sophist* and *Statesman* (both circa 355–347 B.C.E.). Substantial portions remain of his long poem, written in dactylic hexameters. Parmenides's poem consists of three parts, a Proem (introduction), the "Way of Truth," and the "Way of Seeming." The Proem begins with a description of a chariot journey on which Parmenides meets a goddess who instructs him in philosophy, echoing such traditional epic openings as that of the *Theogony* (circa eighth century B.C.E.), in which Hesiod describes the Muses' appearing to him and teaching him about the gods. The goddess tells Parmenides that there are three ways of thinking, namely [it] is, [it] is not, or [it] both is and is not. For an Anglophone reader, the first difficulty encountered in understanding Parmenides is the lack of reference or antecedent to the implied "it," which is the subject of "is." The verb Parmenides uses is *estin*, the third person singular present active indicative of "to be." Because "to be," like all Greek verbs, is inflected (varies its form or ending to indicate tense, voice, mood, and sometimes person and number), subjects are often implied rather than explicitly indicated. Parmenides's "is" has no subject, and so, when he talks about the three paths of "is," "is not," and "is and is not," one can only conjecture about the implied subject. Was he referring to all physical being? Was he formulating a logical theory of noncontradiction or the impossibility of making true negative statements? Was he referring to any given object, or was the ambiguity deliberate? The second section of the poem, the "Way of Truth," begins with the goddess's explaining that since it is impossible to know what is not, and thus also impossible to know what both is and is not (since it partially is not), one can only know what is. Of what is, it is not possible that it is not, and thus it must by its nature be indivisible, unmoved, perfect, complete, permanent, and spherical (descriptions, it is worth noting, that later thinkers, such as Aristotle, would apply to their gods). The world of appearances, in which things are generated and perish and change in attributes and position, is illusory. The goddess also, however, in the third part of the poem, the "Way of Seeming," describes the world of appearances. The connection between these two parts of the poem is obscure, possibly due to the fragmentary condition of the existing text. The "Way of Seeming" presents a cosmology in which things are derived from a pair of opposing forms, Light and Dark, and changing phenomena are accounted for in apparent contradiction to the "Way of Truth."

Pherecydes of Syros. One of the earliest Greek prose writers was Pherecydes, who flourished around 550 B.C.E. He composed a book on cosmology, none of which is extant. From reports of later authors, it appears that his work may have been intermediary in character between systematic mythography and scientific cosmology, thus having affinities with both Hesiod and Thales. His cosmology posits three deities—Zeus, Chronos (time) or Kronos, and Gê or Khthoniê (earth)—as the source of the universe.

Philolaos of Croton or Tarentum. An important Pythagorean, Philolaos was born around 470 and may have written original works on cosmology. It is difficult to establish the contributions of specific Pythagoreans because important works of the school tended to be considered, like physical property, communal (belonging or attributed to either the community as a whole or its founder, Pythagoras).

Pythagoras of Samos. The son of Mnesarchus of Croton and founder of an influential philosophical and religious community, Pythagoras was born in Samos around 580 B.C.E. but immigrated to the Greek colony of Croton in Italy. He was a follower of the god Apollo, and later members of his school considered him a manifestation of the Hyperborean Apollo. He himself did not write, but his sayings were preserved by his followers, although their tendency to attribute all important discoveries, doctrines, or maxims of the school to its founder makes it difficult to distinguish his doctrines from those of his followers. Pythagoras believed in metempsychosis (transmigration of the soul). He thought that the soul was originally divine, descended down to a body, and continued to be incarnated in various plant, animal, and human bodies until it purified itself sufficiently to return to its divine origins. Because Pythagoras and his followers considered the aim of life escape from the cycle of reincarnation, they lived an ascetic life, eschewing meat and meditating in silence. The Pythagoreans probably held all property in common, having philosophical objections to individual ownership. They were active in the government of Croton, but were eventually overthrown and exiled, leading to the destruction of their community in the fifth century. The Pythagoreans were especially interested in mathematics and musical harmony, to which they attributed metaphysical significance. They considered the Limited and Unlimited to be the governing principles of the universe, with the Limited representing order (and goodness) and the Unlimited, disorder. Mathematical understanding of order (especially musical harmony) was seen as a path towards reestablishing divine harmony in the human soul. Their work on mathematics resulted in several advances, including the Pythagorean Theorem for calculating the length of the hypotenuse for right-angled triangles.

For the Pythagoreans the principle of all things was the number and the universe, ordered in harmonic proportions. The sun was at the center of the universe, and the planets, including earth, were spherical and moved around the sun in circular orbits at regularly spaced harmonic intervals (causing a "music of the spheres" or celestial harmony). Pythagorean philosophy was extremely influential in the Classical Period (480–323 B.C.E.) and later. Plato was strongly influenced by the Pythagoreans and discusses Pythagorean cosmology in detail in his dialogue *Timaeus* (circa 355–347 B.C.E.). Several later Platonists, especially Iamblichus, revived Pythagorean philosophy, and it continued to influence philosophy in the late Middle Ages and Renaissance.

Xenophanes of Colophon. A poet and philosopher, Xenophanes (born circa 570 B.C.E.) traveled around Greece, reciting poems. He may have been a major influence on Parmenides. Like many other Presocratic thinkers, he criticized the traditional poetic conception of the gods, arguing that there could only be a single, nonanthropomorphic deity rather than many gods engaged in immoral acts. His deity provides a rational order for the universe. Many of his poems seem concerned with reforming his listeners and advocating some sort of personal seriousness or austerity. He advises, for example, that symposia (parties at which men drank and conversed) be dedicated to serious conversation and not involve excessive consumption of alcohol and asserts that poetry is worth more than athletic contests.

Zeno of Elea. A follower of Parmenides, Zeno appeared in Plato's dialogue *Parmenides* and was credited by Aristotle with the invention of dialectic. He was best known for his paradoxes proving the impossibility of motion, of which two are preserved. In one paradox he argues that an athlete can never cross a stadium, for he first would need to cross half the distance, then half the remaining distance, then half the remaining distance, ad infinitum. The second paradox asserts that if a tortoise is given a head start in a race, Achilles will never be able to catch it, for by the time Achilles reaches the tortoise's previous position, the tortoise will have moved to another position, and when Achilles reaches the tortoise's second position, the tortoise will have moved to yet another position, and so forth.

Sources:

Jonathan Barnes, *The Presocratic Philosophers* (London & Boston: Routledge & Paul, 1979).

Edward Hussey, *The Presocratics* (New York: Scribners, 1972).

John Manley Robinson, *An Introduction to Early Greek Philosophy* (Boston: Houghton Mifflin, 1968).

RELIGION: PARAMETERS

The Divine. The greatest difficulty in discussing Greek religion is that there is no Greek word with a meaning similar to the English term *religion*. The Greeks had gods, considered many things divine or sacred, and performed various actions intended to influence the behavior of the gods, but there was no clear distinction between sacred and secular, clergy and laity, god and hero, or religion and philosophy. Perhaps the best general statement that can be made about Greek religion is that it consists of those things associated with the divine or sacred about which most modern readers disagree with extant ancient authors. Gods, heroes, nymphs, curses, prophecy, divination, astrology, and magic are generally regarded skeptically by modern Western culture, and thus they are categorized as existing within a realm of irrational belief (religion) rather than knowledge (science). For ancient Greeks, especially outside the highly literate and cosmopolitan cities of Asia Minor and Athens, Zeus, the Egyptian gods, or various nymphs were not necessarily part of some distinct realm of the supernatural. They were powerful figures that one worshipped (i.e. to whom one gave offerings) insofar as one needed their help or wanted to avoid their displeasure, in much the same way one paid tribute to the Persian king or heard stories about the kings of distant lands. What was at stake was not the abstract nature of the gods or understanding correct doctrines about them, but rather gaining their favor or avoiding their anger, which was done through some combination of gifts and correct action, such as sacrificing domestic animals to various gods and goddesses, or not violating the laws of hospitality enforced by Zeus. Similarly, the causes of disease, for example, were thought by some Greeks to include the enmity of the gods or pollution inherited from ancestors who had offended the gods and thought by other Greeks to be caused by imbalances in diet or humors. Cures could be obtained by potions (medical or magical), ritual purification, or making offerings to the offended divinities. A prudent person might try all of these different healing modalities.

Explanations. The realm of what is considered "the religious" was much broader in antiquity than it is in modern times. As well as including distinct gods, it also included a variety of nature spirits. Many of the phenomena now understood in terms of science were then explained in divine terms. Thunder, lightning, rain, drought, floods, disease, dreams, earthquakes, tidal waves, sunshine, eclipses, fertility, barrenness, victory or defeat in war, prosperity, or famine—all of these were explained by some Greeks as caused by various deities. Divine help was sought in farming, war, oratory, athletic contests, crafts, healing, childbirth, politics, decision making, and many other aspects of daily life, either by legitimated and officially sanctioned means (sacrifices and oracles) or by more questionable individualistic practices (magic, including curses and necromancy).

Categories. Religion can be divided into two categories, myth and ritual, or story and act. Myths are oral or written accounts of how the divine or supernatural worlds function. Rituals are the acts one performs, including verbal performances such as hymn or prayer, to influence the divine world. Magic is a form of ritual, often performed outside the confines of officially sanctioned practices, to benefit the individual (possibly by harming others) rather than to achieve ends agreed upon by, or useful to, the community. For the ancient Greeks, ritual tended to be more consistent and more primary than myth. In other words, most people performed various traditionally and communally sanctioned ritual acts and had a certain degree of agreement

A painting on an Attic Black Figure *kuathos* of a funeral scene, late sixth century B.C.E. (John R. Freeman)

about how, where, and when those acts should be performed, while the stories about the entities affected by ritual acts displayed a great degree of flexibility. Even in the works of a single author like Hesiod, there are mutually contradictory variants of the same story, as in the case of Pandora and the birth of Aphrodite. Greek religion has sometimes, therefore, been described as a religion of ritual rather than as a "scriptural" religion or a "religion of the book." The difference is that scriptural religions such as Judaism, Christianity, and Islam tend to have written scriptures containing fixed dogma and have developed rituals around their doctrines, whereas the ritually-oriented Greek religion tended to develop myths around ritual; there were, in fact, some rituals for which the associated stories and names of the gods changed over time, while the ritual remained constant. Within each of these categories of stories about the gods and actions directed towards the gods, there are several subdivisions. Stories, or accounts of the gods, can be divided into myths, hymns/sacred performance, epic/tragedy, legend and folktale, mythography, and theology.

Myths. Some stories about the gods were part of a traditional system of belief. These stories appeared in individual poems or art works which are best considered instantiations or representations of the myth. Just as photographs taken from various different angles reveal information about their subjects but are not identical to their subjects, so representations of a myth should not be confused with the underlying belief system. The degree to which Greeks believed their myths varied tremendously; most believed in the tradition as a whole but may have been skeptical concerning many individual stories.

Hymns/Sacred Performance. Poetry about the gods performed at religious festivals often mentioned the gods' deeds. These hymns or sacred performances were often an integral part of ritual. In some cases, a hymn or choral ode could be considered an offering in the same way as a physical votive offering.

Epic/Tragedy. The gods appear in both Homeric epic and tragedy. These artistic portrayals of the divine realm, especially Homer, were certainly influential. The literary accounts often, but not always, agree with the portrayals in classical art. Often, however, the gods as they appear in literature or elite art (expensive pottery, statuary, and so forth) differ from those found in popular ritual. It is difficult to decide whether this variance means different groups had different beliefs, that there was tremendous individual variation in belief, that many Greeks were not concerned about self-contradictions in myth so long as the rituals were efficacious, that artistic license resulted in literary and artistic accounts which no one believed literally, or some combination of these.

Legend and Folktale. Many stories of local heroes or gods do not fit precisely within the tradition of myth, but rather, like the modern stories of Paul Bunyan or George Washington and the cherry tree, form an important corpus of popular stories. Although there is no precise demarcation between the two, generally legends and folktales exist outside both the realm of literature and the integrated system of myth/ritual of official celebrations; they tend to be local rather than Panhellenic, popular rather than elite, and oral rather than written. Often they possess elements of the "tall tale," an exaggerated and humorous story about popular heroes.

Mythography. The tradition of collecting and systematizing myths began quite early in the Archaic Period (700–480 B.C.E.) with such writers as Hesiod and Pherecydes, but flourished most extensively in Alexandria with the later scholars Callimachus and Apollodorus. The collection and resolution of contradictions among myths can be seen as the beginning of the theological impulse.

Theology. The term *theologia*, meaning a rational, philosophical, or systematic approach to the divine, was invented by Plato, but theology, in the sense of attempts to provide complex and coherent accounts of the gods, can certainly be considered an offshoot of mythography, gradually growing more complex, abstract, and divorced from popular and literary tradition.

Ritual. Most Greeks were probably more concerned with ritual, the acts that needed to be done to gain the gods' favor or avert their anger, than with myth, the stories about the gods. Actions related to the gods might include sacrifices, votive offerings, amulets, curse tablets, games and festivals, domestic rituals, and funerary rites.

Sacrifices. When a Greek gave the gods food, it was known as a sacrifice. In blood sacrifices, animals were slaughtered at the altar (or pit, for chthonic deities) and either part or all of the animals burned. Bloodless sacrifices (e.g. cakes, grain, honey, oil, or wine) were placed on altars or poured into the ground.

Offerings and Amulets. Many objects could be given to the gods as payment for favors anticipated or received. Common votives included small terra-cotta figurines, statues, and household items. Amulets were items of jewelry inscribed with apotropaic images or the names of various deities used to ward off evil.

Curse Tablets. One invoked the aid of gods (especially Hermes, Persephonê, and Demeter) in causing misfortune to one's enemies by inscribing lead tablets with curses. The tablets had to be buried in wells, fresh graves, or at the location in which the curse was supposed to take effect. For instance, when cursing an athletic rival, one would leave a tablet at a stadium.

Games and Festivals. Various games and festivals were held throughout Greece in honor of various gods. They ranged from Panhellenic festivals such as the Olympic Games honoring Zeus to civic cults like the Greater Dionysia of Athens, where many of the extant Greek tragedies were first performed in honor of Dionysus. Simpler rural festivals might consist of brief choral performances (singing and dancing by groups of adults or children) and sacrifices to insure the fertility of the soil.

Domestic Rituals. Many Greek ritual observances took place in the household. The hearth, personified as the goddess Hestia, was divine and was a legal sanctuary in the same manner as a public altar or temple. Houses had small outdoor altars at which various rites were performed. Symposia, or drinking parties, began with libations to the gods.

Funerary Rites. Death provided the occasion for a complex series of rituals. Purification of the corpse was followed by elaborate mourning rites, a procession to the graveyard, and sacrifices at the burial. The next steps involved both a period of mourning during which various activities were taboo and regular visits with offerings were paid to the graves of one's dead relatives.

Written Sources. Two major types of evidence exist for Greek religion—written sources and archeological—both of which have limitations. Literary evidence, by its nature, is the expression of the sophisticated ideas of a literate (often urban) elite. Small farmers in rural Arcadia, slaves in Thessaly, itinerant laborers in Boeotia, or Spartan Helots rarely knew how to write, probably. Of materials committed to writing, only a small number were recopied and transmitted so as to survive to the present. Those writings consist of two complete Homeric epics, two epics by Hesiod, thirty-three Homeric hymns, some lyric poetry (Pindar, in substantial quantity, and several other poets), tragedies by three Athenian playwrights, comedies by one early and one relatively late Athenian playwright, ten Attic orators, and limited amounts of historical, philosophical, medical, and miscellaneous writing. These texts are heavily weighted towards Athens and, to a lesser extent, Ionian cities, and many of them date from the fifth and fourth centuries. This list is far from a representative sample even of Greek writing, and many aspects of Greek religion (popular ritual, mystery religions, and folk beliefs) were never committed to writing at all.

Archaeology. Although it provides a much more representative selection of materials, archaeological evidence is frequently difficult to interpret. Terra-cotta figurines unearthed around small rural altars or cave shrines reveals that people in the countryside performed rituals involving altars and figurines. By parallels with literary evidence, one can infer that the figurines were votive (gifts to the gods). Sometimes, by details of the figurines or writing on them, classicists can identify the deity to which they were dedicated. By simply looking at a few figurines and fragments of an altar, however, one cannot learn the details of the rituals performed at the altars, how often or at what times they were performed, the specific purpose of the rituals, or, even more important, what people thought or believed about the deities or the purposes of the rituals. While combining archeological evidence with literary evidence can

A marble relief of Hera and Zeus from the temple of Hera in Selinus, circa 470-450 B.C.E. (Palermo)

yield far better reconstructions of Greek religion than either one alone, that is all they can yield—reconstructions. They will not allow modern readers to get inside the minds of people who died over two thousand years ago and let them observe their thoughts as they marched in the Panathenaic procession or celebrated the Eleusinian mysteries. However, present-day society has to help understand other people, no matter how distant from or close to the modern world they might be, rather than merely represent a radical rupture between a comprehensible present and a mysterious past.

Sources:

Jan N. Bremmer, *The Early Greek Concept of the Soul* (Princeton: Princeton University Press, 1983).

Fritz Graf, *Magic in the Ancient World*, translated by Franklin Philip (Cambridge, Mass.: Harvard University Press, 1997).

Geoffrey Stephen Kirk, *Myth: Its Meaning and Functions in Ancient and Other Cultures* (Cambridge: Cambridge University Press, 1970).

Martin P. Nilsson, *Greek Folk Religion* (New York: Harper & Row, 1961).

Paul Veyne, *Did the Greeks Believe in Their Myths?* translated by Paula Wissing (Chicago: University of Chicago Press, 1988).

RELIGION: TERMS, CONCEPTS, AND PLACES

Afterlife. Greek concepts of the afterlife varied tremendously. Generally, people accepted that some sort of existence continued after death, and thus elaborate funeral rituals existed, including regular family visits to tombs to bring offerings for the dead. People who died prematurely or violently or who were not given adequate burial could become vengeful ghosts. The picture of the afterlife in Homer was gloomy, with the dead portrayed as vague shadowy figures twittering and squeaking in the realm of Hades. Both Hesiod and Homer also described Elysium, or the Isles of the Blessed, as a place inhabited after death by a few favored heroes; it probably was a survival from Minoan beliefs. The mystery religions were unusual in promising some form of pleasant afterlife as a consequence of being initiated and perhaps following some set of ritual and/or ethical practices in life. Certain philosophers, especially the Pythagoreans and others, such as Plato, adopted, with considerable variation, the Egyptian concept of transmigration of the soul.

Altar. Offerings to gods were made at an altar, a raised platform or block of stone. In the case of chthonic deities, a sunken pit performed a similar function. Altars were normally outdoors, though major temples had smaller indoor altars for bloodless sacrifices, in addition to larger outdoor ones. Smaller altars were ubiquitous throughout Greece for both major gods and various minor divinities. Greek houses had hearths sacred to Hestia and small domestic altars.

Amphictyony. Local communities usually formed an amphictyony, or league, to care for a shrine or temple, as well as to enforce various laws connected with the cult, such as enforcing truces during festivals and preventing pollution of the sanctuary. The most important was the one formed around the temples of Apollo at Delphi and Demeter at Thermopylae and which was responsible for the Pythian games. This league fought three major sacred wars over guaranteeing the right of free passage of pilgrims to Delphi, enforcing a vow made to Apollo concerning use of the agricultural lands of Crisa, and maintaining the independence of Delphi. Unlike Christianity and Islam, Greek religion did not have a concept of crusade or jihad; the rather unusual amphictyonic sacred wars were not over conversion or dogma but concerned maintaining a Panhellenic cult and punishing specific acts which interfered with the local activities and autonomy of the cult.

Amulets. Charms, or amulets, were worn for magical, normally apotropaic, purposes, usually as protection against witchcraft, illness, or the evil eye. Various ancient amulets made of a variety of materials have been recovered by archeologists. Many amulets are inscribed with names of deities or magical formulae.

Anthropomorphic. The term *anthropomorphic* means "in the form of a human." Most Greek gods were anthropomorphic, i.e. human in shape and behavior but with certain superhuman characteristics (immortality, ability to transport themselves large distances, invisibility, and so forth).

Apotropaic. The term *apotropaic* means averting or warding off. Various forms of emblems, amulets, statues, and other objects and rituals were used to ward off various inimical powers and influences, including witchcraft, the evil eye, illness, and the anger of the gods. Small charms to ward off the evil eye, made of blue glass with stylized representations of eyes, are still widely sold in Greece.

Archon. In most Greek *poleis,* or city-states, the highest-ranking officials were called archons. In Athens the *arkhôn basileus* (king archon) performed the ceremonial functions which in legendary antiquity were thought to have been performed by kings. These duties included responsibility for the mysteries: the Lenaea, a winter festival in honor of Dionysus; the Anthesteria, a spring festival in honor of Dionysus; and the Areopagus court, which presided over trials concerning murder and certain offenses against the gods.

Astrology. The Greek practice of interpreting signs in the heavens was known as astrology.

Augury. Interpreting the patterns of flights of birds is known as augury.

Blood Offerings. Living animals, usually domestic, were killed during a blood-offerings ceremony. A bull or ox was considered the most impressive sacrifice, but goats, sheep, pigs, and poultry were common. The animal had to be in good health, without defects, and of the right color (light for Olympian gods, black for chthonic gods and the spirits of the dead). Civic ceremonies including blood sacrifices began with a procession. A virgin would carry a sacrificial knife in a basket filled with barley or baked goods, while the other participants followed her, leading the animal, which may have been decorated with ribbons. Water was poured on the hands of the participants, cleansing them, and then sprinkled on the animal's head, so that it would nod, thus consenting to the sacrifice, an important gesture because an unwilling victim was considered a bad omen. After worshipers scattered barley (a preliminary bloodless sacrifice) on the altar and animal, the person performing the sacrifice would kill the animal. The entrails were observed for omens and then roasted on the altar and eaten by the priest and other important individuals. The fat and bones were burnt, rising up in the form of smoke as an offering to the gods; the worshipers cooked and ate the meat. The communal meal was a crucial part of the act of worship.

Bloodless Offerings. Many solid foods, especially fruits, vegetables, cheeses, and cakes, were offered to the gods by being placed on altars or burnt. Liquid bloodless offerings were called libations and usually consisted of oil, honey, or wine.

Burial Customs. Corpses were buried or cremated, with the remains of adults being placed away from populated areas to avoid ritual pollution, although young children might be buried near houses. The bodies of criminals were placed in pits or in the sea. Burial rituals were quite elaborate, including purifications, formal mourning, a procession to the gravesite, and various sacrifices.

Chthonic Deities. The chthonic, or underworld, deities are not an absolute category but rather a way of distinguishing among aspects under which gods were worshiped. Certain functions of the gods, primarily fertility and death, were closely tied to the earth and the realms beneath the earth. Some gods, such as Hades and Hecatë, were exclu-

---

A SPELL FOR BINDING A LOVER

Take wax [or clay] from a potter's wheel and make two figures, a male and a female. Make the male in the form of Ares fully armed, holding a sword / in his left hand and threatening to plunge it into the right side of her neck. And make her with her arms behind her back and down on her knees. And you are to fasten the magical material on her head or neck. . . .

And take thirteen copper needles and stick 1 in the brain while saying, "I am piercing your brain, _____; and stick 2 in the ears and 2 in the eyes and 1 in the mouth and 2 / in the midriff and 1 in the hands and 2 in the pudenda and 2 in the soles, saying each time, "I am piercing such and such a member of her, _____, so that she may remember no one but me, _____, alone."

And take a lead tablet and write the same / spell and recite it. And tie the lead leaf to the figures with thread from the loom after making 365 knots while saying as you have learned, "ABRASAX, hold here fast!" You place it, as the sun is setting, beside the grave of one who has died untimely or violently, placing beside it also the seasonal flowers.

The spell to be written / and recited is: "I entrust this binding spell to you, chthonic gods, . . . to infernal gods and daimons, to men and women who have died untimely deaths, to youths and maidens, from year to year, month to month, day to day, / hour to hour. I adjure all daimons in this place to stand as assistants beside this daimon. And arouse yourself for me, whoever you are, whether male or female, and go to every place and into every quarter and to every house, and attract / and bind her. Attract her, _____, whom _____ bore and whose magical material you possess. Let her be in love with me. . . . Let her not be had in a promiscuous way, . . . nor let her do anything with another man for pleasure, just with me alone. . . .

Source: Hans Dieter Betz, ed., *The Greek Magical Papyri in Translation, Including the Demotic Spells* (Chicago: University of Chicago Press, 1992).

---

sively associated with the underworld. Others, such as Zeus, Demeter, Persephonê, and Hermes, had both earthly and heavenly characteristics and were worshiped in both aspects—one might speak more properly of chthonic worship than chthonic deities. While offerings to heavenly deities were burnt on raised altars, so that the smoke floated up into the sky towards the gods, chthonic offerings were either burnt completely or poured into pits in the ground. Heavenly deities receive white or light-colored animals; chthonic offerings were black or dark. Often the chthonic deities (or deities in their chthonic aspects) were harsher and more vengeful than heavenly ones. The Furies, for example, were primarily chthonic in nature. While scholars used to hold that the chthonic aspects of Greek religion were more primitive than the Olympian ones, archeological evidence does not support that there was a distinct chronological evolution; moreover, *primitive* is a misleading term for early or nonindustrial cultures.

A painting from a sixth century B.C.E. Athenian cup of two men sacrificing a pig (Archives Photographiques, Musée du Louvre, Paris)

Cult. The term cult is taken from the Latin word *cultus*, meaning "care" or "cultivation." For the Greeks one's relationship with the gods was not primarily a question of belief or disbelief, but of performing appropriate ceremonies such as tending and/or caring for the various gods' places and prerogatives. Worship of a god might include giving the god food or drink (bloodless sacrifices), animals (slaughtering the animals at an altar), dedicatory objects (statues, figurines, and so forth), or performances (singing, praying, or dancing in honor of the god). Some of these actions were performed at specific locations (temples or shrines) and some on specific occasions (before drinking, funerals, and festivals). One worshiped, or participated in the cults of, various gods either to obtain benefits or to ward off harm the gods could cause; for example, giving gifts to Asclepius to cure or ward off illness. Cults could be Panhellenic (having participants from all over Greece), regional, or local. Most poleis had official cults and festivals such as the Panathenaea honoring Athena in Athens, the Carnea in honor of Apollo in Sparta, and the Heraea of Hera in Argos.

Curse/Binding Tablets. *Defixiones* were thin lead tablets on which curse or binding spells are inscribed. The person commissioning a curse tablet would usually hire a magician to inscribe a curse on a tablet while performing various magical ceremonies and then bury the tablet. Most of the tablets that have been recovered curse opponents in lawsuits, athletic contests, artistic competitions, or business. Another common category was love charms—the person who commissioned the tablet might ask that the beloved fall out of love with his rival or in love with him. The tablets would request that a deity (usually Demeter, Persephonê, or Hermes of the underworld) inflict damage

on the victim, silencing a tongue in a lawsuit, causing a chariot not to finish a race, or turning customers away from a business rival. The tablets were often buried in wells (which lead down to the underworld), fresh graves (so that the dead could carry the tablet with them to Hades), or the place where the curse was to take effect (for example, an athletic stadium).

Delos. The birthplace of Apollo and Artemis, Delos is a small island (one of the Cyclades) in the Aegean Sea and was a center for worship of Apollo, controlled by Athens during much of the Classical era. Theseus is said to have stopped at Delos on his return from Crete.

Delphi. The most famous oracle of Apollo was located in Delphi on the southern slopes of Mount Parnassus. Delphi was already a holy place in the Mycenaean era (1600–1200 B.C.E.). Archeologists have found many terra-cotta female figures there, possibly associated with the cult of the "holy Pytho," which was mentioned in Homer. The cult of Apollo dates to the eighth century B.C.E. According to myth, an earth goddess and her serpent, Python, were defeated by Apollo, and Apollo took over their sanctuary. Apollo is said to have shared the precinct with Dionysus, each of them taking it in turn for half of the year. The path to the temple was adorned with many statues and treasuries containing offerings to Apollo, some commemorating athletic victories in the Pythian games, and some giving thanks to Apollo for oracles and other favors. Maxims attributed to the Seven Sages were inscribed on the temple. The priestess of the temple, the Pythia, was a woman appointed when she was more than fifty years old; after being selected, she left her family and lived a secluded life. On auspicious days during which people could consult the oracle, she sat on a tripod and was thought (though archeological evidence does not support this theory) to have breathed vapors from a deep chasm. Under the influence of Apollo, she spoke prophecies that were then composed into formal oracles (often in verse) by various priests. Several minor priestesses tended the hearth in the temple. Also in the temple precinct was the *omphalos,* a rock in the shape of a navel, which was said to mark the center of the known world.

Derveni Papyrus. The only substantial ancient papyrus roll to have been found in Greece itself is the Derveni Papyrus. It dates from the fourth century B.C.E. and was partially burned on a funeral pyre. It contains a commentary on Orphic cosmology.

Divination. Greeks had several ways of predicting the future and/or interpreting the wills of the gods. Plant growth, animal behavior, prodigies (unnatural occurrences), the entrails of sacrificial animals, dreams, and celestial phenomena—all were interpreted as significant. Some of the main forms of *mantikê* (divination) practiced in antiquity were augury, haruspicy, dreams, prophecy, astrology, necromancy, and omens.

Dreams. A person's dreams were normally considered prophetic. Artemidorus', *Oneirocritica,* or Dream Book (second century C.E.) describes how to interpret each element of dreams.

Eleusis. A town in Attica near Athens, home to the mystery cult of Demeter and Persephonê, Eleusis shows evidence of continuous habitation and cult activity from Mycenaean through Roman times. There are several successive layers of cult sites, beginning with a Mycenaean megaron that was replaced first by an Archaic temple and then by the *telestêrion*, a large hall with arena-style seats, built by the tyrant Peisistratus and enlarged in the time of Pericles. The Eleusinian Mysteries were both uniquely important to Attica and were also Panhellenic, in the sense that participation was open to anyone who went through the proper initiation rites, including barbarians and slaves.

Epiphany. The actual visible appearances of gods, usually intervening in human affairs, epiphanies were frequent in Homer and common in drama. An actor portraying a god suspended on a crane, known as a *deus ex machina* (god from a machine), often resolved apparently insoluble dilemmas in tragedy. Though the Greeks did not believe that the gods were ordinarily visible in their own times, they did have examples of gods and dead heroes occasionally intervening in momentous events, such as helping the Greeks in their war against Persia. The Athenian tyrant Peisistratus took advantage of this belief when he returned from exile in the sixth century, accompanied by a tall woman dressed like the cult statue of Athena, whom he claimed to be the goddess. The gods were believed to appear often in dreams when people would "incubate" at temples such as those of Asclepius.

Euhemerism. Euhemerus of Messene wrote a novel (circa 311–298 B.C.E.) that advanced the theory that the traditional Greek gods actually had been extraordinarily talented or important people whose deeds were magnified by later generations, until they eventually became considered gods. Modern scholars use the term *euhemerism* to describe theories accounting for mythical stories as distortions of historical narratives.

Festivals. Days officially designated by a community for worship of specific deities, festivals were normally holidays during which no official business (lawsuits, legislative assemblies, instruction in schools, and so forth) could be conducted. Truces were declared for the larger Panhellenic festivals such as the Olympic Games and often local festivals as well. The religious and secular components of festivals were not clearly demarcated. Sacrifices were offered to the gods being honored, but the meat from the sacrifice was shared in a communal feast by the participants. Often games such as chariot and foot races, wrestling, and other athletic contests were held in honor of the gods, but these were opportunities for competition among participants and betting among spectators. Some festivals, especially in the countryside, were simple ceremonies and merry-making celebrating the fertility of the land or the harvest. Choral performances of hymns (singing and dancing in honor of the gods) on simple threshing floors gradually evolved into more elaborate urban artistic forms of the Classical Period

(480–323 B.C.E.). The larger city festivals such as Panathenea and Great Dionysia at Athens, Carnea at Sparta, Heraea at Argos, and Daidala in Boeotia might include theatrical performances, recitations of poetry, and oratorical displays, often staged as competitions with the best performance given an award. Merchants flocked to festivals to hawk their wares to the spectators, and embassies were sent from one city-state to festivals in other poleis, often using the truces negotiated for the festivals and amphictyonic laws allowing the right of safe passage through neighboring areas to festivals as occasions to conduct important negotiations.

Games. Athletic contests were held at various festivals in honor of the gods. Perhaps the most famous were the Olympic Games, held every four years, starting in 776 B.C.E., in honor of the Olympian Zeus. Other famous festivals included the Pythian (at Delphi, in honor of Apollo) and the Nemean (in honor of the Nemean Zeus near Argos) games. The main athletic contests were chariot races, footraces, wrestling, boxing, jumping, and the pankration (combination of wrestling and boxing). Spectators wagered on the outcomes of the games, and vendors sold a variety of foodstuffs and other goods. Orators and poets often entertained the spectators and recited compositions praising the victors.

Haruspicy. The ancient Greeks practiced haruspicy, examining the entrails of sacrificial animals.

Hecatomb. The term *hecatomb* literally means an offering of one hundred oxen, but it was also used to describe any sacrifice of animals.

Herm (Greek *herma*). A stylized sculpture of Hermes (or occasionally another god), the Herm were placed as boundary markers at crossroads, public buildings, and private houses. They consisted of square stone pillars with erect phalluses and a bust of the god, usually with a beard. They were apotropaic (functioned to avert evil). The Herm of the Classical Period probably evolved from early non-anthropomorphic heaps of boundary stones.

Holocausts. A holocaust was a blood offering in which animals were completely burnt rather than the meat's being reserved for a feast. Holocausts were extraordinary forms of sacrifice, specifically reserved for purifications, burials, underworld gods, and for requesting important favors such as victory in an impending battle.

Incubation. An individual could sleep in temple precincts in order that the god may appear to him or her in a dream. The best known example of incubation was at the temples of Asclepius, where sick people would sleep and receive visions of how to cure their illnesses. Often (typically for a fee) priests at the temple would help interpret the visions. Various purificatory rituals and sacrifices were usually conducted by the petitioner before going to sleep. Incubation was also practiced at several other temples, including those of Isis and Sarapis, for purposes of recovering lost objects and seeing the future, as well as curing illness.

Libation (Greek *spondê*). A libation was a liquid offering to the gods, usually wine, milk, honey, or water, either performed alone or in conjunction with sacrifices. Since libations were always part of the ritual performed at the signing of a peace treaty, the Greek word for treaty was *spondai*. At the beginning of symposia (drinking parties), the participants always poured libations of unmixed wine to the Olympian gods and heroes.

Magic. Ancient Greeks used magic (incantations, potions, amulets, curse tablets, necromancy, or other acts or sayings) to influence or understand the world and invoke supernatural beings, whether gods, ghosts, or demons. There was no clear demarcation between magic and religion or gods and demons. The gods and prayers of one nation were often the demons and magic of its enemies; for example, the Christian bishop Augustine believed in the existence of the Greek gods, but he considered them demons rather than entities worth worshiping. Within Greek context, magic can best be described as individual and unsanctioned invocations of the supernatural. While all harmful uses of potions (poisons, love charms, and so forth) and incantations (curses) were considered magical, not all incantations or potions were for harmful purposes. Folk religion and medicine (midwifery) existed on the border between magic and religion, while curses and spells were always magical. Magic, especially when used for harmful purposes, was usually illegal in antiquity, but nonetheless widely practiced. Archeologists have recovered many papyri containing magical spells, as well as curse tablets.

Mystery Cults. The ancient *mysteries* were cults distinguished by the need for initiation and elaborate purification rituals before one could participate in them. They were often concerned with fertility and offered worshipers a promise of a better afterlife if they followed certain rules of conduct and regularly performed certain ceremonies. Certain aspects of the mysteries could only be revealed to initiates and were considered understandable only through experience of the ceremonies rather than explicable in words, an attitude epitomized in the Greek maxim *pathein mathein* ("to experience is to learn"). Few other generalizations can be made with any degree of accuracy about mystery cults in the Classical Period. Some of the better-known mysteries were those of Orpheus, Dionysus, and the Eleusinian.

Necromancy. To engage in necromancy, or calling on the spirits of the dead, was considered an illegal act in ancient Greece.

Olympus. Over 9,500 feet, Olympus is the highest mountain in Greece and, in myth, the home of the Olympian gods. It is located in Northern Greece, on the border between Thessaly and Macedonia, and is part of a range negotiable only by a limited number of passes, thus protecting Greece from invasion from the northeast.

Omens. Many sorts of natural phenomena were interpreted as omens, including the behavior of plants and animals. Tics, itches, and sneezes were also interpreted as omens.

Oracles. The term *oracle* refers either to a god's answer to a worshiper's question, usually predicting future events or giving advice on actions or decisions, or a place or shrine where one could obtain such messages. Among the most important ancient oracles were those of Apollo at Delphi and Zeus at Dodona. Oracular sayings were often cryptic or paradoxical, thus the failure of an oracle was usually attributed to its misinterpretation. A famous example is the one of Croesus, King of Lydia, who was told by the Delphic oracle that if he attacked Persia, a great kingdom would be destroyed. He attacked, and his own kingdom was destroyed.

Orphic. A follower of the cult of Orpheus, Orphic was a legendary musician and was also follower of Dionysus. By the Archaic Period (700–480 B.C.E.), several poems concerning divine mysteries were attributed to Orpheus. These poems included a detailed description of both the cosmos and gods of Orphic belief. The Orphics believed that one's conduct during life affected one's fate in the afterlife. They thought that humans shared with the Titans guilt for the death of Dionysus Zagreus, and that Persephonê demanded some form of atonement from humans before they could progress to a better afterlife. Humans were reincarnated three times, and if they behaved properly in their lives (avoided evil and pollution and were initiated into the Orphic mysteries), they would spend their afterlives on the Isles of the Blessed.

Polis (plural *poleis*). Greece and the various Greek colonies were divided into hundreds of city-states, self-governing administrative entities consisting of a city and the surrounding countryside. There are often distinct names for both the main city of a polis and the polis as a whole; for example, Athens is the main city of Attica, and Sparta, of Lacedaemonia. Often each polis had its own specific official cults.

Pollution (Greek *miasma*). Pollution consisted of defilement, uncleanness, or impurity as a result of violating religious taboos or coming into contact with something unclean, such as a corpse. Acts that clearly violated the laws of the gods (sacrificing with unwashed hands, murder, leaving a corpse unburied, incest, eating human flesh, and so forth) might pollute not only the individual committing the act, but also his family, his descendants for several generations, and even his city, bringing the anger of the gods on everyone with whom the polluted person associated. Significant literary examples include the opening of Sophocles's *Oedipus the King* (circa 497–405 B.C.E.), or the curse of the house of Atreus, described in Aeschylus's *Oresteia* (458 B.C.E.). Certain Greeks believed that illnesses or misfortunes might be the result of some form of pollution associated with their ancestors and would hire wandering purifiers to help them find the cause of the problem and correct it. Acts of purification could be either simple (for example, washing in either fresh or sea water) or quite complex.

Priests. There was no separate clerical caste in ancient Greece, nor was priesthood a profession held by people with special training. Instead, priesthood was an office, in most cases requiring its holder to perform duties only on special occasions. Priests and priestesses were usually appointed by secular officials from a pool of eligible people. Eligibility was determined by gender and age (priestesses at Delphi, for example, were selected from women more than fifty years old). In some cases priests were chosen from specific families (the Eumolpidae and Ceryces for the Eleusinian mysteries); sometimes priestly functions were part of the duties of government officials (for example, the Spartan kings and Athenian archons). While freedom from pollution was necessary (someone who had just killed his mother or violated a sanctuary would be ineligible), priests were not required to be morally or spiritually superior to the general populace, nor, except in the case of mystery religions, did they have any special knowledge about the divinities they served. Priests were responsible for conducting sacrifices and other rituals of the gods they served, in return for which they received part of the sacrifices (the skins of animals, food, and so forth) and sometimes an additional stipend. At smaller shrines priestly duties might require very little time, whereas larger Panhellenic cults (Apollo at Delphi, Zeus at Olympus, and Eleusinian mysteries) might require several temple officials.

Prophecy. Individuals (such as Cassandra in Homer's *Iliad* [circa eighth–seventh centuries B.C.E.] and Aeschylus' *Agamemnon* [458 B.C.E.], or the prophet Tiresias who appeared in Sophocles's *Antigone* [442 or 441 B.C.E.] and *Oedipus Rex*), spoke as the voices, or interpreters, of gods. In the Archaic Period (700–480 B.C.E.), there were individuals who traveled around Greece, practicing various forms of prophecy, purification, and magic as careers.

Sacrifice. A sacrifice was a gift to the gods, an act central to Greek religious practice. Sacrifices were generally offered at places sacred to the gods, either fixed shrines, altars, temples, or hearths, or, in the case of armies, portable altars. Common types of sacrifices included blood offerings, bloodless offerings, and holocausts.

Temple. A temple was a building which housed the image of a deity, and sometimes even the deity, in a manner similar to Near Eastern practice, rather than the Judaeo-Christian one, in which a temple or church is a place for worshippers to congregate. A temple was normally located in a *temenos* (temple precinct), which also might contain various other buildings, including shrines, altars, and treasuries. Temples were similar in structure to, and probably evolved from, Mycenaean *megara*, rectangular halls with entrances through porches (usually with columns) at one of the narrow ends. The main room of a temple, the *naos* or *cella*, contained the cult statue, which usually was placed at the opposite end of the room from the entrance. Temples could be either small and simple or large and ornate, with multiple rows of columns and elaborate friezes. Although there could be a small altar for bloodless sacrifices inside the temple, most sacrifices were performed outdoors at an altar in front of the temple.

Theriomorphic. The term *theriomorphic* means "in the form of an animal." Theriomorphic gods are more typical of the Near East and Egypt than of Greece, although certain Greek household or chthonic deities could appear as snakes. Some divinities, such as Pan and Satyrs, are partially theriomorphic.

Thiasos. A *thiasos* was an association dedicated to the worship or cult of a specific deity. *Thiasoi* functioned as private clubs, with social, as well as cultic, purposes. Many educational institutions were organized as *thiasoi* dedicated to the Muses.

Transmigration. Also known as reincarnation or metempsychosis, transmigration was the belief that after death the soul moved into a new body. Although this notion was common in Egyptian religion, it was not generally believed in Greece during the Classical Period. Pythagoras and his followers were among the limited number of philosophers who believed in transmigration. For this and other reasons, they tended to be vegetarians. One theory held by some of the later Pythagoreans was that in a fixed period (sometimes given as three thousand years) the soul migrated through all the birds of the air, fish of the sea, and beasts of the land, before it finally was reunited with the divine world from which it had descended.

Votive Offerings. Objects given permanently to the gods were called votive offerings. Votives were of two sorts, those given to a god in advance by people desirous of receiving favors from that god or those given in thanks after a favor has been bestowed by a god. Often a person would promise a god some object or action if the god helped him in a certain way (gave victory in battle, healed an illness, or caused success in a financial venture). This manner of dealing with the gods, sometimes referred to by the Latin phrase *do ut des* ("I give that you might give"), is characteristic of Greek religion. Votives are found throughout the Greek world in locations ranging from major temple precincts to small rural shrines. Cities might offer magnificent statues or metal tripods in return for victories, while a farmer might leave a god a small terra-cotta figurine. Common votives included statues resembling the cult image of the god (from full-sized marbles through small terra-cottas), weapons of vanquished enemies, mirrors, tools, or clothing. In the area around Delphi, many cities built treasuries to contain their offerings to the god, which many times overflowed the temple precinct. People could also dedicate themselves to a god, offering either a certain period of service or regular offerings.

Sources:

Apollodorus of Athens, *The Library of Greek Mythology,* translated by Robin Hard (New York: Oxford University Press, 1997).

Walter Burkert, *Ancient Mystery Cults* (Cambridge, Mass.: Harvard University Press, 1987).

Burkert, *Greek Religion* (Cambridge, Mass.: Harvard University Press, 1985).

Burkert, *Homo Necans: The Anthropology of Ancient Greek Sacrificial Ritual and Myth* (Berkeley: University of California Press, 1983).

Burkert, *Structure and History in Greek Mythology and Ritual* (Berkeley: University of California Press, 1979).

E. R. Dodds, *The Greeks and the Irrational* (Berkeley: University of California Press, 1951).

Lewis R. Farnell, *Outline-History of Greek Religion* (London: Duckworth, 1920).

Farnell, *Greek Hero Cults and Ideas of Immortality* (Oxford: Clarendon Press, 1921).

J. Fontenrose, *The Delphic Oracle: Its Responses and Operations* (Berkeley: University of California Press 1978).

Timothy Gantz, *Early Greek Myth: A Guide to Literary and Artistic Sources* (Baltimore: Johns Hopkins University Press, 1993).

W. K. C. Guthrie, *The Greeks and Their Gods* (Boston: Beacon, 1951).

Jon Mikalson, *Athenian Popular Religion* (Chapel Hill: University of North Carolina Press, 1983).

H. W. Parke, *Festivals of the Athenians* (Ithaca, N.Y.: Cornell University Press, 1977).

M. L. West, *The Orphic Poems* (Oxford: Clarendon Press, 1983).

West, *The East Face of Helicon: West Asiatic Elements in Greek Poetry and Myth* (Oxford: Clarendon Press, 1997).

SEVEN SAGES

Wise Men. The Seven Sages were renowned wise men of seventh and sixth century Greece. The earliest list of the Seven Sages, in Plato's *Protagoras* (circa 387 B.C.E.), includes Thales, Pittacus, Bias, Solon, Cleobolus, Myson, and Chilon. Most other writers substitute Periander for Myson. Thales, Bias, Solon, and Pittacus are common to all lists; sometimes Anacharsis, Pherecydes, Epimenides, and Pisistratus appear. Plutarch dramatizes a (mythical) meeting of the Seven at Corinth hosted by Periander. Many of the maxims that appear at Delphi are attributed to the Seven Sages, including *Mêden Agan* ("Nothing In Excess") and *Gnôthi Sauton* ("Know Thyself"). The sages were known for wisdom in its most general sense, encompassing everything from poetry and politics to predicting eclipses. Knowledge of their actual activities, sayings, and ideas is not extensive and it is often difficult to distinguish factual from fictional portraits.

Bias of Priene. Little is known about Bias of Priene, who was born circa 570 B.C.E. He is credited with several poems, songs, and wise sayings and was active in his city, giving speeches concerning legal cases and political decisions. He was praised by Heraclitus, who called him better than the others who claimed wisdom, perhaps for his saying that the majority of men were bad.

Chilon of Sparta. A Spartan ephor in 536 who contributed to increasing his city's power and influence, Chilon had a reputation for wisdom, but few details concerning him have survived.

Cleobolus of Rhodes. The son of Euagoras, Cleobolus of Rhodes flourished circa 600 B.C.E. and wrote many poems and songs. He is also credited with several well-known maxims. His daughter, Cleobolinë, wrote hexameter verses. Little is known of his life.

Periander of Corinth. The son of Cypselus, Periander (died 588 B.C.E.) succeeded his father as tyrant of Corinth. He erected a temple to Apollo and other public buildings. Despite being described as having killed his wife, he was

A bust of Bias of Priene, inscribed with his saying: "Most Men Are Bad" (Vatican Museum)

respected as a diplomat and patron of the arts. During both his reign and that of his father, Corinth founded several important colonies and was a leader in the production of fine pottery.

Pittacus of Mitylene. Living around 650 to 570 B.C.E., Pittacus was a renowned soldier and commander who ruled as elected dictator of Mitylenë for ten years, during which he reformed the laws of the city. Several wise sayings are attributed to him.

Solon of Athens. An Athenian aristocrat, Solon lived circa 630–560 B.C.E. and wrote elegiac and iambic poetry on political and moral subjects. He was first elected archon in Athens around 594 and was responsible for many democratic reforms of the Athenian constitution. He introduced measures to prohibit debtors from being sold into slavery, reformed coinage, and extended citizenship to immigrant craftsmen. Perhaps his most significant reform was to make voting eligibility depend on wealth (with four different property classes having different levels of eligibility for various offices) rather than on birth, thus breaking the political monopoly of the aristocrats.

Thales of Miletus. The actual details of Thales's life and work are so mingled with later accretions that it is difficult to separate truth from fiction. He lived around 600 B.C.E. in Miletus, where he supposedly gave wise advice on political and other matters and predicted a solar eclipse. His primary interests were astronomy and geometry. Aristotle claims that Thales believed that all other substances (including living creatures) somehow derived from transformations of water. Two statements attributed to him are that all things are full of gods and that the magnet had life or soul because it could move iron. According to a rather improbable story, he died by tripping and falling into a well, while gazing at the stars.

Sources:

Francis Macdonald Cornford, *From Religion to Philosophy: A Study in the Origins of Western Speculation* (New York: Harper, 1957).

Hermann F. Fraenkel, *Early Greek Poetry and Philosophy,* translated by Moses Hadas and James Willis (New York: Harcourt Brace Jovanovich, 1975).

Henri Frankfort et al., *Before Philosophy* (Harmondsworth, U.K.: Penguin, 1949).

Werner Jaeger, *The Theology Of The Early Greek Philosophers,* translated by Edward S. Robinson (Oxford: Clarendon Press, 1947).

Bruno Snell, *The Discovery of the Mind,* translated by T. G. Rosenmeyer (Oxford: Blackwell, 1953).

SOCRATICS, LATER SOPHISTS, AND CYNICS

Aristotle. A pupil of Plato, Aristotle (384–322 B.C.E.) founded in 335 B.C.E. his own philosophical school, the Lyceum, slightly to the northeast of Athens. Like Plato's Academy, the Lyceum was legally organized as a *thiasos,* a cult dedicated to the Muses. The buildings of the Lyceum included a *peripatos* (covered court). Because he taught in the peripatos, Aristotle and his followers and called "Peripatetics."

Writings. Aristotle was an extremely prolific writer who also gave many lectures and supervised his students in wide-ranging researches, which resulted in encyclopedic collections of written materials such as the constitutions of all the Greek cities. What has been preserved of Aristotle's work, despite its substantial volume, is a small and rather paradoxically limited selection. Aristotle wrote various exoteric works for publication in the sense of circulation to an audience outside the Academy or Lyceum. These works were mainly philosophical dialogues in the manner of Plato. None of these are extant. Of the encyclopedic collections, a papyrus copy of the *Constitution of Athens* (circa 335 B.C.E.) was discovered in Egypt in 1890, but little else has survived. The extant *Aristotelian Corpus,* which has come to us as a result of repeated recopying in antiquity and the Middle Ages, consists of extensive lecture notes, possibly revised for circulation within his school (and hence known as "esoteric" works, from the Greek *esôteros,* meaning "interior"). This material had disappeared almost completely after the death of Theophrastus, but was rediscovered, brought to Rome, and edited for publication by the grammarians Tyrranion and Andronicus of Rhodes (first century B.C.E.). Because these rediscovered works came to be considered the true teachings of Aristotle ("esoteric" in the sense of secret truth), they became the subject of commentaries; eventually, Aristotle's published works ceased to be read and recopied in the philosophical schools thus, only Aristotle's esoteric corpus has survived intact.

Relation to Plato. Although a devoted student of Plato, Aristotle differed from his teacher in interests and approach—his philosophical differences with Plato were defended with the phrase that he had great love for Plato, but even greater love of the truth. While Plato's work was characterized by literary eloquence, complexity, ambiguity, and a pronounced mystical streak, Aristotle was a more prosaic and scientific thinker, interested in dividing knowledge into precise categories and accumulating vast stores of factual information. Especially the mathematical mysticism that dominated the last period of Plato's life was antithetical to Aristotle, and Aristotle totally rejected the Platonic notion of separated Forms (the existence of universal concepts or templates independent of the particulars in which they were embodied).

Contributions. Aristotle contributed to many areas of knowledge. His prototypical work was in biology, categorizing plants and animals by genus and species, using characteristics that differentiate a member of one species from a member of another as the basis for species membership definition. On a more abstract level, in works including *Prior Analytics, Posterior Analytics,* and *Categories* (all written circa 335 B.C.E.), Aristotle discussed logic, analyzing the relationships of class membership, implication, and truth-value among statements. In physics his most influential contributions again lay in the area of categorization, both of his predecessors' theories and of observable phenomena. He thought that all objects had four "causes" or sources of origin: the material cause (the substance from which they were fashioned), the efficient cause (the tool which did their fashioning), the formal cause (the pattern on which they were based), and the final cause (the purpose for which they were made). Thus, the material cause of a bed would be wood; the efficient, the carpenter who made it; the formal, the blueprint to which it was designed; and the final, its use as an article of furniture for sleeping. Aristotle also made many valuable contributions to the study of metaphysics, rhetoric, poetics, ethics, politics, and many other disciplines, and even to the concept of disciplinarity itself, for example the notion that there are certain subjects and methods proper to each different area of knowledge.

Antisthenes. The son of an Athenian man and a Thracian woman, Antisthenes (circa 443–circa 360 B.C.E.) was a follower of Socrates and originator of Cynic philosophy. He believed that one gained knowledge by investigating the meanings of words, thus following the Socratic interest in definition and the Sophistic focus on correctness of language. Happiness was based on virtue, which was attained through knowledge, rather than material prosperity or physical pleasure. Like Prodicus, he considered Heracles a prototype of virtue. He wrote several philosophical dialogues and orations and a commentary on Homer, which are not extant.

Crates. The son of Ascondas of Thebes, Crates (circa 365–285 B.C.E.) was a Cynic philosopher and followed the teachings of Diogenes, living a self-sufficient and simple life. He renounced a large fortune and lived as a beggar, owning only a walking stick and knapsack. He married Hipparchia, a wealthy woman who abandoned her family to live a Cynic life. They wandered around Greece together, exhorting people to virtue and poverty. Crates's writings included poems, letters, and possibly tragedies, but only a few fragments are extant.

Diogenes the Cynic. A follower of the teachings of Antisthenes, Diogenes the Cynic (circa 400–325 B.C.E.) was renowned for the austerity of his personal life. Although no authentic writings of his have survived, many anecdotes concerning his life remain, many of which are probably later inventions. He was said to have lived in a tub at a temple and owned only his clothes and a bowl. According to one story, when he saw a man scooping up and drinking water with his hands, he cast away the bowl as unnecessary. He believed that happiness could be attained by satisfying physical needs in as simple and uncomplicated a manner as possible, like a dog (Greek *kuôn*, from which Diogenes and his followers took the name *Cynic*). He emphasized the need for independence, such as not depending for one's happiness on external matters, and considered nature (*phusis*) good and conventions unnatural. In literature, both laudatory and satiric, he is portrayed as rejecting conventions of appearance and manners.

Heraclides of Pontus. Born into a wealthy aristocratic family in Heraclea (on the Black Sea), Heraclides traveled to Athens, where he studied and, between 361 and 360, directed Plato's Academy. After having been passed over as Plato's successor, in favor of Speusippus, he returned to his native city, where he opened his own school. His writings, like Plato's, were dialogues, often among famous historical characters (including Empedocles and Pythagoras, who do not appear in Platonic dialogues). His innovations included adding extensive proems to the dialogues and including substantial mythological and anecdotal material; later writers, such as Cicero and Plutarch, emulated Heraclides's literary form. Like many of the Academics, Heraclides probably did significant original work in astronomy and physics, with a somewhat mystical bent. His literary style was widely admired, but so little of his work remains extant that one cannot gauge the originality or quality of his philosophical doctrines.

Hipparchia. The sister of Metrocles of Maronea and wife of Crates, Hipparchia left her wealthy family in order to travel with her husband, exhorting people to the Cynic life. Several anecdotes are told of her, and some letters (probably inauthentic) are attributed to her. In one anecdote, she and Crates were said to have had sexual relations in public, claiming that it was a natural, and thus not shameful, activity.

Isocrates. Originally from a wealthy family, Isocrates (436–388 B.C.E.) later earned his living by writing speeches for law courts and teaching oratory. He argued that Plato and other theoreticians wrongly appropriated the term *philosophia* for themselves and that the word was best applied to those, like himself, whose teaching trained students to know politics and ethics and speak persuasively on

---

DOXOGRAPHERS

The term *doxographer* is used to describe ancient authors who wrote summaries or compilations of the opinions of earlier philosophers. Aristotle was the first to systematically collect opinions of his predecessors, and his work was further extended by his successor, Theophrastus. Several later writers wrote on the lives and opinions of the philosophers and provide extremely valuable resources for understanding the works of those whose writings are no longer extant. One cannot accept the works of the doxographers uncritically, as they often were working from inaccurate sources or were more intent on working out a system (of philosophical successions or of typology of ideas) than in unbiased reporting in the modern sense.

In the first or second century C.E., Aetius wrote an extensive summary of the works of earlier thinkers on natural philosophy. His work is preserved by subsequent writers and provides a crucial source for otherwise unknown materials.

Compendium of the Lives of the Philosophers (circa third century C.E.) by Diogenes Laertius is probably the single most extensive source for many early Greek philosophers' works and biographies. Unfortunately, his work is an almost random compilation of materials from a wide variety of sources; few are reliable, and some are hopelessly garbled in Diogenes's hands.

Flavius Philostratus (born circa 170 C.E.) the son of Verus Philostratus, was a Sophist from Lemnos. He was a member of the court of Julia Domna (wife of the Roman Emperor Septimus Severus), and author of several works, including a *Lives of the Sophists*, which, while focusing on Sophists of his own period, begins with a section on the Older Sophists.

Source: John M. Rist, *The Mind of Aristotle: A Study in Philosophical Growth* (Toronto: University of Toronto Press, 1989).

---

important matters. His view of philosophy is close to what one now might term the liberal arts or humanistic education, and while his work had little effect on technical philosophy, it strongly influenced the history of education.

Plato. As a young man, Plato (circa 428–348/347 B.C.E.) wrote poetry, but was converted to philosophy by Socrates and was among the circle of Socrates's followers. In 387 Plato founded his school, the Academy, where he taught for approximately forty years. His influence on subsequent thinkers could scarcely be overestimated. A modern scholar once described all of philosophy as a series of footnotes to Plato, and philosophers constantly return to him to renew their discipline. While everyone agrees on the importance of Plato, there is almost no agreement on how to interpret his work. Good copies exist of every Platonic work mentioned by ancient authors, and of several works falsely attributed to Plato. There are also several letters attributed to Plato, of which only one, *Epistle VII*, is likely to be authentic. The interpretive problems stem not from missing works but instead from the nature of Platonic writing. All of Plato's extant philosophical works, with the exception of *Epistle VII*, are in the form of dialogues. The characters in the dialogues advance and examine various arguments but rarely come to fixed conclusions. No single character's ideas can be assumed to represent a Platonic doctrine. Plato's writing is even more resistant to interpretation because the dialogues have a complex form, including extravagantly poetic and symbolic myths, irony, humor, and other literary devices. Trying to divorce Plato's ideas from their literary and dramatic context produces conceptual clarity at the expense of faithfulness to Plato. There are also doctrines attributed to Plato by Aristotle and other writers that do not appear in the dialogues.

Early Dialogues. Plato's works have traditionally been divided into three periods, early (circa 387–380 B.C.E.), middle (circa 380–360 B.C.E.), and late (circa 360–347 B.C.E.), although there is no secure basis for establishing an accurate chronology. In the early dialogues *Apology, Euthyphro, Crito, Charmides, Ion, Laches,* and *Hippias Minor,* the main character is Socrates, and he is portrayed as seeking a true definition of some abstract term (piety, virtue, courage, and so forth) by asking questions of interlocutors and demonstrating that their answers are unsatisfactory. The early dialogues normally end in *aporiai* (insoluble problems) and do not reach positive conclusions. Generally, however, characters who consider themselves already wise come off as the most ignorant, and characters who know the limits of their own knowledge and are open to learning, are made to appear the wisest.

Middle Dialogues. In the middle dialogues *Protagoras, Gorgias, Meno, Phaedo, Phaedrus, Parmenides, Republic, Symposium,* and *Theaetetus,* Socrates remains a central character, but he propounds positive doctrines, not all of which are reconcilable with each other. In these dialogues Socrates advances the theory of Forms, that universals (abstract terms such as *beauty, justice, virtue,* or *equality*) exist independently of the *phainomena* (phenomena or "things that appear" [in the physical world]) in which they are instantiated. The phenomena are patterned on or "participate in" the Forms. Since the general Forms cannot be deduced from particular cases, souls must have been acquainted with the Forms before they descended into the body, and thus all learning is really recollection of things known before this lifetime. True knowledge, therefore, is distinct from opinion and comes from reason rather than observation. The goal of philosophy is separation of the soul from the body so that it may return to its divine origin. Moral good for the individual consists in acting in such a way as to improve the condition of the soul; so, for example, one should not indulge in sensual pleasures because, in so, doing the mind is turned from the rational to the physi-

A bust of Socrates (Vatican Museum (314)/photo Scala, Florence)

cal world. This notion of care of the soul leads to the paradoxical conclusion, advanced by Socrates in *Gorgias,* that it is worse to commit than to suffer injustice, because suffering injustice only harms the body, whereas committing injustice harms the soul.

Late Dialogues. *Parmenides* represents a transition to the later dialogues in that the primary speakers are Parmenides and Zeno, and Socrates is represented as a young man, trying to defend the Forms against what becomes a devastating critique. The late dialogues, including *Statesman, Sophist, Philebus,* and *Laws,* emphasize method as much as outcome, focusing on the proper ways of dividing and collecting information in order to produce correct definitions.

Socrates. The Athenian philosopher Socrates (469–399 B.C.E.) devoted much of his life to talking in the gymnasium and marketplace with anyone willing to speak to him about philosophical matters. In personal appearance he was strikingly ugly, his features resembling those of comic masks. He possessed, however, great personal charm or magnetism, which attracted many followers, especially young men from well-to-do families. In 399 he was accused of impiety and corrupting the youth of Athens, and was, by a narrow margin, condemned to death. He refused the offers of several of his friends to help him either pay a fine or escape into exile instead and died by drinking hemlock. His life was marked by a high degree of personal austerity; he seemed indifferent to physical pleasure or even comfort and would occasionally stand still and meditate in silence on some complex problem for many hours before resuming normal activities. He also had what he referred to as a divine sign (*daimonion*, literally "divine thing"), which would appear to him on occasion and forbid him from pursuing certain courses of action.

Different Portraits. Beyond this brief outline of his life, one knows surprisingly little about Socrates, especially given the mass of writings about him. Socrates himself never wrote and did not appear to have any consistent and fixed doctrines. There are substantial portraits of him in Plato, Xenophon, and Aristophanes, and other fragmentary reports, which are not entirely consistent with one another. In Plato, Socrates appears brilliant, arrogant, witty, sarcastic, paradoxical, sceptical, and charismatic by turns, alternately inspiring and infuriating his interlocutors. In Xenophon, Socrates appears rather more conventionally pious, a stern moralist and solid, if not spectacularly brilliant, thinker. Aristophanes shows Socrates as a stereotypical intellectual, clever, unscrupulous, and often devoting his time to speculating about absurd trivialities (measuring how far a flea could jump or determining whether a gnat whistles out of its mouth or its anus). The Platonic portrait is that Socrates has had the greatest influence on the history of philosophy.

Larger Questions. Although in his youth Socrates was interested in natural philosophy, as he grew older he became interested almost exclusively in moral and epistemological questions. He thought that virtue (moral excellence) depended on knowledge, and that if people knew the good then they would do it. Yet, in order to act well, one must know how to define goodness precisely and thus have some methodology that could reliably produce (and judge) definitions. Plato's early dialogues present Socrates conversing with various Athenians over the definition of some general term such as goodness, virtue, courage, piety, or beauty. Generally, Socrates's interlocutors offer up inadequate definitions (frequently examples in place of general definitions), and Socrates disproves a series of increasingly complex accounts until the interlocutors get tired, angry, or have other pressing duties, and the conversations end without resolution. Socrates himself claimed to have no definite knowledge but said that he was like a midwife who, though herself barren, helped bring other people's children to birth and judged them true offspring or stillbirths. He saw ignorance as positive, in the sense that the greatest obstacle to learning is false belief (especially the false belief that one knows things one does not), and thought that by his method of inquiry (*elenchus*), which showed that people held impossible or self-contradictory ideas, he could, like a midwife, help knowledge come to light even if he himself had no positive doctrines to proffer.

Speusippus. On Plato's death in 347, Speusippus succeeded Plato as head of the Academy and was, in turn, upon his own death in 339, followed by Xenocrates. Although only limited fragments and testimonies of Speusippus's work are extant, he appears to have had interests similar to Plato and to have continued in his uncle's tradition, both as leader of the Academy and philosopher. Speusippus was interested in logic, physics (including both biology and cosmology), and ethics and made significant contributions in each field. In logic, Speusippus was interested in the question of definition, and thought that since definitions were based on drawing distinctions, in order to define any given thing, one must have knowledge of everything else in order to see how the thing under consideration differed from other things. His interest in definition involved consideration of both words and things. Among words, it is possible for one word to have multiple meanings, change its meaning when combined with other words, or depend for its meaning on its derivation from other words, and, of course, the same thing can be referred to by multiple words. Definitions, however, are not exclusively verbal. To define the term *dog*, for example, one must investigate how dogs differed from other related species of animal. Speusippus, therefore, wrote ten books collecting observations of similarities and dissimilarities among plants and animals. In theoretical philosophy, Speusippus, like Plato, wrote about Pythagorean mathematics but did not equate the Forms with numbers and denied that the numbers were the source of all things. Little is known of Speusippus's ethics, other than that he considered pleasure morally neutral and goodness a goal, rather than a beginning.

Theophrastus of Eresos. The philosopher Theophrastus (circa 370–286 B.C.E.) was a pupil of Aristotle and his successor as head of the Lyceum. Of his voluminous writings few are extant, namely two treatises on plants, *Characters* (319 B.C.E.), *Metaphysics* (circa 335 B.C.E.), and short works on physics and physiology. He was not so much an original thinker as a cataloguer and systematizer of knowledge and empirical research. He made collections of law codes from various poleis, and, more important for philosophers, collected the opinions of earlier philosophers, on which many later doxographies are based.

Xenocrates of Chacedon. Speusippus's successor as head of the Platonic Academy (339-314), Xenocrates was interested in theology and connected divine to celestial hierarchies in a systematic way that anticipated neoplatonism.

Xenophon. The Athenian aristocrat Xenophon (circa 428–circa 354 B.C.E.) wrote various works concerned with such diverse topics as autobiography, history, politics, the education of a Persian king, hunting, horsemanship, and household management. For the history of philosophy his most important texts are the ones about Socrates, namely *Apology, Memorabilia, Symposium,* and *Oeconomicus* (all four were written circa 430–circa 356 B.C.E.). Xenophon's Socrates is more of a conventional moralist and less of an abstract thinker than the one found in the Platonic dialogues. The question of the relative degree of accuracy of the two Socratic portraits has been widely debated by scholars for several centuries.

Sources:

Jonathan Barnes, *The Cambridge Companion to Aristotle* (Cambridge: Cambridge University Press, 1995).

Harold Cherniss, *The Riddle of the Early Academy* (New York: Russell & Russell, 1962).

Abraham Edel, *Aristotle and his Philosophy* (Chapel Hill: University of North Carolina Press, 1982).

Hans Georg Gadamer, *The Idea of The Good in Platonic-Aristotelian Philosophy*, translated by P. Christopher Smith (New Haven: Yale University Press, 1986).

Richard Kraut, ed. *The Cambridge Companion to Plato* (Cambridge: Cambridge University Press, 1992).

Gerald Press, ed. *Plato's Dialogues: New Studies and Interpretations* (Lanham, Md.: Rowman & Littlefield, 1993).

John M. Rist, *The Mind of Aristotle: A Study in Philosophical Growth* (Toronto: University of Toronto Press, 1989).

W. D. Ross, *Plato's Theory of Ideas* (Oxford: Oxford University Press, 1953).

Kenneth Sayre, *Plato's Literary Garden: How To Read A Platonic Dialogue* (Notre Dame, Ind.: University of Notre Dame Press, 1995).

DOCUMENTARY SOURCES

Aeschylus, *Oresteia* (458 B.C.E.)—a group of three plays (*Agamemnon, Libation Bearers,* and *Eumenides*) which are set just after the end of the Trojan War. Apollo, Athena, and the Furies (the latter transformed at the end of the trilogy into the benevolent Eumenides) all played central roles in the drama, which reveals substantial information about how fifth century Athenians may have conceptualized the gods' role in defining and administering justice.

Euripides, *Bacchae* (circa 406 B.C.E.)—a play that describes how Dionysus traveled to Thebes and established his cult there. In the play, King Pentheus, who refused to recognize the divinity of Dionysus, was torn to pieces by frenzied women. It is one of the main sources for understanding the cult of Dionysus and a type of ecstatic worship unlike the other more orderly civic cults.

Hesiod, *Theogony* (circa 700 B.C.E.)—a literary work concerning the genealogy of the gods. It synthesized various conflicting stories and traditions about the gods into a coherent account.

Homeric, Hymns (eighth–sixth centuries B.C.E.)—like the Homeric epics, the thirty-three *Homeric Hymns* are written in dactylic hexameter and bear evidence of oral or oral-derived composition. Each tells stories about one specific god. They were probably performed at the gods' festivals. Among the longest and most informative of the hymns are those to Aphrodite, Apollo, Demeter, Dionysus, and Hermes.

Homer, *Iliad* (circa eighth–seventh centuries B.C.E.)—a poem, based on a mixture of Mycenaean and later elements, describing the part of the Achaean siege of Troy primarily concerned with the Greek hero Achilles's withdrawal from, and later return to, the fighting. The text of this poem represents a late stage of a tradition originally composed and transmitted orally for many centuries. Many Greek accounts of the gods rely on the Homeric poems.

Homer, *Odyssey* (circa eighth–seventh centuries B.C.E.)—a poem describing the wandering of the hero, Odysseus, on his return from the Trojan War. Athena and Poseidon played important roles in the story, which also contains accounts of the Underworld.

Pindar, *Epinikia* (circa 518–circa 438 B.C.E.)—one of the greatest lyric poets of ancient Greece. Much of his work was lost, except for four *epinikia* or "victory songs," which celebrate the victories of various athlete at the Olympian, Pythian, Isthmian, and Nemean games. These odes are important sources for Greek myths and legends, which Pindar used to illustrate his poetic themes. What is not always known is the extent to which he is relating a variant tradition he has received and when he is innovating a new version.

The Naxian Sphinx from Delphi, circa 560 B.C.E. (Archaeological Museum, Delphi)

SCIENCE, TECHNOLOGY, AND HEALTH

By KEITH M. DICKSON

CONTENTS

CHRONOLOGY
314

OVERVIEW
318

TOPICS IN SCIENCE, TECHNOLOGY, AND HEALTH

Ancient Myths and Legends . . 319

Hephaestus, Wizard of Technology 319

Prometheus the Culture-Giver . .320

Ancient Technology 321

How to Make a Raft. 321

On the Origin of Human Technology and Culture 322

The Early Philosophers 323

The First Manned Flight 324

Early Speculation. 325

The Oath of the Pythagoreans . .325

Heraclitus Speaks 326

Early Speculation: The Cult of Pythagoras . . .327

Sidebars and tables are listed in italics.

Early Speculation: Cycles of Change. 328

Tortoise and Hare 328

Empedocles Speaks 329

Respiration 329

Astronomy or Atheism? 330

Early Speculation:Pluralism . . .330

The Laughing Philosopher 331

Leucippus and Atomism 332

Testimonials from the Temple of Asclepius at Epidaurus 332

Medicine: Social Content . . .333

The Hippocratic Oath. 334

Medicine : The Theory of Healing 334

Hysteria 335

Epilepsy: Divine or Natural? . .336

Medicine: Therapy 338

Plato on the Elements 338

The Science of Plato. 340

Plato's Universe 341

The Science of Plato: Astronomy. 341

Why Snakes Have No Feet 343

The Scientific Research of Aristotle 344

Aristotle on Embryology 346

Teleology of Aristotle 346

The Unmoved Mover and Aristotle : Cosmology 348

SIGNIFICANT PEOPLE
350

Anaxagoras 351

Anaximander 351

Anaximenes. 352

Aristotle. 352

Empedocles. 352

Heraclitus. 353

Plato 353

Pythagoras 354

Thales 354

DOCUMENTARY SOURCES
355

610 B.C.E.

- The astronomer and philosopher Anaximander is born. He becomes known for his theory of the *apeiron* (unlimited)—the eternal substance of the world that contains within itself all contraries such as heat and cold, moist and dry, and so forth. He also claims that all life developed from amphibians.

585

- Thales of Miletus predicts a solar eclipse, which occurs during a battle between the Lydians and Medes. Believing the eclipse is an omen, the two sides conclude a peace treaty.

580*

- The mathematician and philosopher Pythagoras is born at the Ionian colony of Samos. During his lifetime he develops a strong following devoted to political, moral, and social reform. Pythagoras is credited with establishing the functional significance of numbers in the world.

545*

- The philosopher Anaximenes declares that air is the primary substance of the world.

540*

- The philosopher Heraclitus is born. He is known for his cosmology in which fire is the principal element.

530*

- A tunnel is dug through 3,300 feet of solid rock on the island of Samos; its clay pipes carry fresh water to the city.
- A community of Pythagoreans develops at Croton, a small town on the southern Italian peninsula.

520

- The sundial is introduced in Greece.

512

- The Greek engineer Mandrocles constructs a bridge of boats across the Bosphorus, the strait of water separating Europe from Asia Minor.

* Denotes circa date

500*

- Theodorus of Samos is credited with inventing the lock and key, carpenter's square, and turning lathe.

- The Greeks develop iron smelting, using primitive blast furnaces with charcoal stoked by bellows.

- The physician Alcmaeon performs the first recorded dissection of a human body for research purposes. He discovers the difference between veins and arteries and identifies the brain as the center of intelligence.

- The astronomer and philosopher Anaxagoras is born. During his lifetime he asserts that the *nous* (mind, reason, or intelligence) acts upon masses of small particles (the essence of all things) to produce objects.

500

- The newly constructed Samian temple to the goddess Hera is the largest such structure in all of Greece.

490*

- The philosopher, statesman, and poet Empedocles is born. He develops the theory that the physical world is composed of four elements (Fire, Air, Water, and Earth) governed by Love and Strife.

460

- The philosopher Democritus of Abdera is born. He later theorizes that the Milky Way is made up of countless stars.

450*

- The historian Herodotus observes that land is shaped by water that once covered the earth. He is also the first to designate Europe, Africa, and Asia as separate continents.

450

- The logicians Parmenides of Elea, Zeno of Elea, and Melissus of Samos, known as the Eleatics, flourish.

432*

- Meton of Athens discovers the nineteen-year cycle of solar years.

430*
- The optical telegraph is used for the first time in Greece.

430
- A three-year plague devastates the population of Athens. Although its exact nature is unknown, modern scholars speculate that it was either bubonic plague, cholera, or measles.
- Leucippus originates the atomistic theory.

428*
- The philosopher Plato is born in Athens.

420
- Greek scholars begin to compile the *Hippocratic Corpus,* a collection of sixty medical texts. These books describe many common diseases, recommend dry wound dressings, and assert that diseases result from disorders in bodily fluids.

400*
- The mathematician Eudoxus of Cnidus develops the geometric theory of irrational numbers.

399
- Socrates, the teacher of Plato, dies after drinking hemlock in prison.

387*
- Plato begins writing his most famous work, the *Republic;* he does not finish it until around 360 B.C.E.

387
- Plato establishes his school of philosophy known as the Academy in Athens.

384
- The great philosopher and scientist Aristotle is born at Stagira in northern Greece.

380*
- Plato makes a *klepsudra*, or water clock, complete with alarm.

367
- Aristotle joins the Academy.
- Plato visits Syracuse to educate Dionysius II.

350*
- The earliest written description of a human fetus is made.
- Aristotle writes a study on weather and climate called *Meteorologica*.

348*
- Plato dies.

343
- Aristotle becomes the tutor of the thirteen-year-old son of Philip of Macedon, the future Alexander the Great.

335
- Aristotle establishes the Lyceum in Athens. He also begins to write his famous series of texts on logic that later came to be called the *Organon*.

330
- The explorer Pytheas identifies the moon as the cause of tides in the Atlantic.

323
- The mathematician Euclid completes *Stoikheia (Elements),* his landmark work that establishes such basic concepts in geometry as the point and the line.

OVERVIEW

Terms. The word *science* has no exact equivalent in the ancient Greek language. Instead, the Greeks generally used rather broad terms like *philosophia* (love of wisdom) and *epistêmê* (knowledge) to describe the investigation of nature. The sorts of things included in ancient scientific research were equally broad and crossed over into categories that the modern world usually does not consider part of true science at all.

Speculation. Most of the things we now identify as essential for scientific activity are absent from the history of ancient thought. Relatively few examples can be found of Greek thinkers engaging in forming hypotheses, constructing experiments, conducting careful research guided by rigorous methods, keeping detailed records, or proposing and testing and retesting theories. With only occasional exceptions, much of what the Greeks did often seems to a modern reader like pure speculation at best, unsupported by any real scientific methods and procedures. "Which god caused the earthquake?" and "Who put a magic curse on my cow and made it fall sick?" were not the sorts of questions whose answers were likely to result in an objective and scientific understanding of disasters and diseases. In hindsight, it is easy to see how the nature of the questions asked by the ancient Greeks influenced their answers. Only in the work of Aristotle in the middle of the fourth century B.C.E. would Greek scientific activity begin to resemble what we now call science—and even then it would still fall short of our definition.

Contributions. Though they lacked most of the tools, methodologies, and results we consider to be genuinely scientific, the early Greeks nonetheless made lasting contributions to Western science. They were especially influential in their development of the habits of thinking and frames of mind that provide the necessary conditions for scientific research. The Greeks formulated the first genuinely scientific questions and went a long way toward determining what rules should be used to judge the structure and validity of the answers.

Early Thinkers. In the sixth century B.C.E. the Milesians, the earliest group of philosopher-scientists, focused on natural phenomena (earthquakes, storms, and so on) as well as the more cosmological question of what was the ultimate nature of reality. Thales, Anaximander, and Anaximenes were the first to differentiate between what is natural and supernatural. In the quest to uncover universal truths, Pythagoras and his followers determined that reality had a numerical basis.

Turning Point. Change represented a problem to early Greek science, and starting in 500 B.C.E. intellectuals made systematic attempts to explain it. Heraclitus advanced the theory of the *logos* (reason) to explain change, while Parmenides asserted the far more radical idea that reality could never change. Empedocles, Anaxagoras, and Leucippus all supported Parmenides' theory but regarded reality as having more than one element. Leucippus defined the plural elements as *atomon* (indivisible).

Medical Theory. Between 420 and 350 B.C.E. Greek doctors compiled a group of sixty medical texts known as the *Hippocratic Corpus*. A combination of professional textbooks, case studies, and public lectures, the *Hippocratic Corpus* covered a variety of topics, but unfortunately its descriptions of illnesses are nearly impossible to match with modern diagnoses because the ancient Greeks did not understand germ theory. Many Hippocratic writers viewed health as a delicate balance between four "humors" or fluids in the human body: yellow bile, black bile, phlegm, and blood. This theory had a profound impact on Western medicine for centuries to come.

Plato and Aristotle. The philosopher-scientist Plato and his pupil Aristotle contributed immensely to Western scientific thought through their writings and teachings at the schools they established, the Academy (Plato) and the Lyceum (Aristotle). In the *Timaeus* (circa 355 to 347 B.C.E.), Plato offered a discourse on mathematical philosophy that explained the cosmos. Aristotelian research covered a broader range of topics including logic, biology, chemistry, physics, and ethics.

TOPICS IN SCIENCE, TECHNOLOGY, AND HEALTH

ANCIENT MYTHS AND LEGENDS

Narratives. All cultures encode and transmit their values to later generations in the form of narratives. The ancient Greeks are certainly not exceptions to this rule. Before the development of rational thought and expression, they turned to traditional stories or myths for answers. Cosmogonic myths addressed broad questions about the source and nature of the world. How did the universe originate? How is it structured? Who controls its operation? Other myths addressed more specific questions about observable events. What causes storms? Why do crops grow from the earth? How do adult beings create new ones? Where does disease come from? What makes thunder? What exactly are those bright objects that move—some slowly, some rapidly—across the sky by day or night?

Zeus and Poseidon. For the most part, the traditional answers to such questions involved the assumption that

A silver coin from Paestum of Poseidon with a trident (Poseidonia, Kraay 217–222)

HEPHAESTUS, WIZARD OF TECHNOLOGY

In the following passage from Homer's great epic poem, the *Iliad*, a goddess visits Hephaestus at his home and workshop:

She found him sweating as he turned here and there at his bellows busily, since he was working on twenty tripods which were to stand against the wall of his strong-built home.

And he had set golden wheels underneath the base of each one so that, by their own motion, they could wheel into the immortal gathering, and return to his house—a wonder to look at . . .

He set the bellows away from the fire, and gathered and put away all the tools with which he worked in a silver strongbox. Then with a sponge he wiped his forehead clean, and both hands, and his massive neck and hairy chest, and put on a tunic, and took up a heavy stick in his hand, and went to the doorway limping. And in support of their master moved his attendants. These are golden, and in appearance like living young women. There is intelligence in their hearts, and there is speech in them and strength, and they have learned what to do from the immortal gods . . .

Source: Homer, *Iliad*, translated by Richmond Lattimore (Chicago: University of Chicago Press, 1961).

---

powerful, supernatural agents—gods, spirits, demons—were responsible for much of what happened beyond immediate human control. The great god Zeus, lord of the sky, sent rain to irrigate the ground and make plants grow. His bolts of lightning—powerful weapons manufactured by creatures known as Cyclopes—sometimes hit the earth, and wherever they struck, the Greeks erected temples to mark the sacred spot. Earthquakes, on the other hand, were traditionally said to be caused by the god Poseidon, master of horses and the sea. When angered, he would strike his trident against the walls of hollow caves deep below the ground, producing violent tremors at the

PROMETHEUS THE CULTURE-GIVER

This passage, from a play by the great fifth-century tragedian Aeschylus, is a touchstone for what Athenians considered the quintessential signs of human culture. The Titan Prometheus, chained to a rock in the Caucasus Mountains as punishment for stealing fire from Olympus, lists his many contributions to the human race.

Now hear what troubles there were among men, how I found them witless and gave them the use of their wits and made them masters of their minds. . . . For men at first had eyes but saw to no purpose; they had ears but did not hear. Like the shapes of dreams they dragged through their long lives and handled everything in bewilderment and confusion. They did not know of building houses with bricks to face the sun; they did not know how to work in wood. They lived like swarming ants in holes in the ground, in the sunless caves of the earth. For them there was no secure token by which to tell winter nor the flowering spring nor the summer with its crops. All their doings were indeed without intelligent calculation until I showed them the rising of the stars, and the settings, hard to observe. And further I showed them numbering, preeminent among subtle devices, and the combining of letters as a means of remembering all things—the Muses' mother, skilled in craft. It was I who first yoked beasts for them in the yokes and made of those beasts the slaves of trace-chain and pack saddle, so that they might be man's substitute in the hardest tasks. And I harnessed to the carriage, so that they loved the rein, horses, the crowning pride of the rich man's lux-

ury. It was I and none other who discovered ships, the sail-driven wagons that the sea buffets. Such were the contrivances I discovered for man. . . .

Hear the rest, and you will marvel even more at the crafts and resources I contrived. Greatest was this: in former times if a man fell sick he had no defense against the sickness, neither healing food nor drink, nor unguent; but through lack of drugs men wasted away, until I showed them the blending of mild simples with which to drive out all manner of diseases. It was I who arranged all the ways of seercraft, and determined what things come true from dreams, and gave meaning for men to the ominous cries, hard to interpret. It was I who set in order the omens of the highway and the flight of crooked-taloned birds—which of them were propitious or lucky by nature, what kind of life each lead, what their mutual hates, loves, and companionships were. I also taught the smoothness of the vital organs and what color they should be to please the gods, and the dappled beauty of the gall and the lobe. It was I who burned thighs wrapped in fat and the long shank bone, and set mortals on the road to this murky craft. So much for these. Beneath the earth, man's hidden blessing, copper, iron, silver and gold—will anyone claim to have discovered these before I did? No one, I am very sure, who wants to speak truly and to the purpose. One brief word will tell the whole story: all crafts that mortals have came from Prometheus!

Source: Aeschylus, *Prometheus Bound*, edited by Mark Griffith (Cambridge: Cambridge University Press, 1983), pp. 442–471.

---

surface. The development of Western science involved the discovery of different habits of thinking and a different language to express answers that did not involve the existence of gods.

Explanations. Many ancient legends were also aetiological, that is to say, they aimed to explain the origin of familiar objects or practices. The Greeks had an especially rich assortment of stories about three specific technological issues: the wondrous technology enjoyed by the gods; the first inventors of various tools and ways of doing things; and the accomplishments of legendary technicians.

Other Gods and Goddesses. Among gods, it was the lame Hephaestus, god of forge fire and the almost magical craft of metallurgy, who presided over most technology. He was credited with such fantastic creations as automatic doors, robotic servants with the power of speech, and unbreakable nets so fine as to be invisible. The goddess Athena, daughter of Zeus, was also closely involved with technological activity. The bridle and ship were said to be her special inventions. She also controlled the crafts of pottery, weaving, and the manufacture of products from olives and olive wood, both sacred to her. Other legends

attributed the invention of all the basic technologies to the Titan Prometheus, who reportedly gave human beings not only fire, but also the full range of tools and practices essential for their survival.

Daedalus. Finally, several legends surround the famous craftsman Daedalus, along with his son Icarus and his nephew Perdix. The nephew is credited with having invented the first saw, using the backbone of a fish as his model. Daedalus himself constructed the mazelike structure or labyrinth on the island of Crete in which the monstrous Minotaur, half-bull and half-man, was imprisoned. Later, in his attempt to escape from Crete, Daedalus is said to have invented wings for himself and his son by attaching feathers to their arms with molten wax. Daedalus warned Icarus not to fly too close to the sun, but the boy ignored him. The wax melted from his wings, and he plunged to his death in the sea far below. To this day Greeks refer to the area of the Aegean Sea between the islands Patmos and Leros and the coast of Asia Minor as the Icarian Sea to commemorate his tragic flight.

Sources:
William Keith Chambers Guthrie, *The Greeks and Their Gods* (Boston: Beacon, 1951).

Barry B. Powell, *Classical Myth* (Englewood Cliffs, N.J.: Prentice Hall, 1995).

ANCIENT TECHNOLOGY

Trial and Error. The early Greek contributions in technology are few and hard to determine. Most of the basic technological innovations enjoyed by the early Greeks came to them secondhand, from even older cultures in which they had evolved through long, unrecorded ages of trial and error. The fundamental Western methods and tools of agriculture, irrigation, viticulture (wine-making), animal husbandry, metallurgy, mining, transport, navigation, textile manufacture, pottery, and building all have histories that stretch far back into the third and fourth millennia B.C.E. They belong to discoveries and developments made in the far more ancient civilizations of Mesopotamia and ancient Egypt.

Beneficiaries. The Greeks of the Archaic and Classical Periods were the beneficiaries of this development. They took up techniques that had passed anonymously down through other cultures and earlier generations. They used, adapted, extended, and refined them. And in most cases they just as anonymously handed them down to those who came after. The most noteworthy Greek innovations in technology—especially in mechanics and hydraulics—occurred only later, during the Hellenistic Period, from roughly the third through the first centuries B.C.E.

Architecture. At the same time, of course, the ancient Greeks relied on a great variety of skills to make their world habitable. The construction of buildings—especially the temples whose remains still mark the modern Greek landscape—required sophisticated architectural design and a

The ruins of the temple to Hera on Samos, built circa 500 B.C.E. (Photo EM Stresow-Czako)

HOW TO MAKE A RAFT

With a high degree of technological skill—and a little divine help—the hero Odysseus constructed the raft on which he escaped from the island of Ogygia.

He chopped down twenty [trees] in all, and trimmed them well with his bronze ax, planed them expertly, trued them straight to a chalkline.

Kalypso, the shining goddess, at that time came back, bringing him an auger, and he bored through them all and pinned them together with dowels, and then with cords he lashed his raft together . . .

Next, setting up the deck boards and fitting them to close uprights he worked them on, and closed in the ends with broad gunwales.

Then he fashioned the mast, with an upper deck fitted to it, and made in addition a steering oar by which to direct it, and fenced it down the whole length with wattles of osier to keep the water out . . .

Next Kalypso, the shining goddess, brought out the sail cloth to make the sails with, and he carefully worked these also, and attached the straps and halyards and sheets in place aboard it, and then with levers worked it down to the bright salt water.

Source: *The Odyssey of Homer*, translated by Richmond Lattimore (New York: Harper & Row, 1967).

---

mastery of engineering techniques. Blocks of marble and other kinds of stone needed first to be mined and quarried, then cut to shape, transported long distances by both land and sea, and finally erected on-site through the use of ramps, pulleys, cranes, and winches. Several developments, all impossible to credit to a single individual, arose in the slow process of improving ancient techniques. By the mid fifth century B.C.E., for instance, archaeology reveals that iron bars were used (apparently for the first time) to reinforce wood and stone structures.

Herodotus. The ancient Greek historian Herodotus recorded some of the technological marvels of his day. In the year 512 B.C.E., a Greek engineer named Mandrocles reportedly constructed a bridge of boats across the Bosphorus (the strait of water separating Europe from Asia near the modern city of Istanbul, Turkey). The bridge enabled the great Persian emperor, Darius, to cross his army into Europe and wage war against the Greeks.

Three Marvels. Herodotus also mentioned what he considered "three of the greatest engineering feats in the Greek world." The first was a tunnel, eight feet by eight feet and nearly one mile long, cut through a mountain on the island of Samos, in order to conduct water from one side of the island to the other. He credits this construction to the engineer Eupalinus. The second was an artificial harbor on the same island, enclosed by a breakwater running nearly one quarter of a mile into the sea. The third

Plato offers the following myth to explain the origin of human technology, along with its limitations:

Once upon a time, there existed gods but no mortal creatures. When the appointed time came for them to be born, the gods formed them within the earth out of a mixture of earth and fire and the substances compounded of earth and fire. And when they were ready to bring them into the light, they charged Prometheus and Epimetheus with equipping them and allotting suitable powers to each kind. Now Epimetheus begged Prometheus to allow him to do the distribution himself—"and when I have done it," he said, "you can review it." So he persuaded him and got to work. In his allotment he gave to some creatures strength without speed, and equipped the weaker kinds with speed. Some he armed with weapons, while to the unarmed he gave some other faculty and so contrived means for their preservation. . . . He made his whole distribution on a principle of compensation, being careful by these devices that no species should be destroyed.

When he had sufficiently provided means of escape from mutual slaughter, he contrived their comfort against the seasons sent from Zeus, cloaking them with thick hair or hard skins . . . and he planned that when they went to bed the same covering should serve as a proper and natural blanket for each species. He shod them also, some with hooves, others with hard and bloodless skin. Next he appointed different sorts of food for them. . . . Some he allowed to get their nourishment by devouring other animals, and these he made less prolific, while he bestowed fertility on their victims . . .

Now, Epimetheus was not particularly clever, and before he realized it he had used up all the available powers on the brute beasts; the human race was left on his hands unprovided for, and he did not know what to do with them. While he was puzzling over this, Prometheus came to inspect the work, and found the other animals well off for everything, but man naked, unshod, unbedded, and unarmed, and already the appointed day had come when man too was to emerge from within the earth into the daylight. Prometheus, being at a loss to provide any means of salvation for man, stole from Hephaestus and Athena the gift of skill in the arts, along with fire—for without fire it was impossible for anyone to possess or use this skill—and gave it to man. In this was man acquired sufficient resources to keep himself alive, but had no political wisdom. This was in the keeping of Zeus, and Prometheus no longer had right of entry to the citadel where Zeus lived. . . .

By the art they possessed, men soon discovered articulate speech and names, and invented houses and clothes and shoes and bedding and got food from the earth. Thus provided for, they lived in scattered groups; there were no cities. Consequently they were devoured by wild beasts, since they were weaker in every respect, and their technical skill (though a sufficient aid for nurturance) did not extend to making war on the beasts, for they did not have the art of politics, of which the art of war is a part. They tried therefore to save themselves by coming together and founding fortified cities, but when together they injured one another through lack of political skill, and so scattered again and continued to be devoured. Thus Zeus, fearing the total destruction of our race, sent Hermes to impart to men the qualities of respect for others and a sense of justice, so as to bring order into our cities and create a bond of friendship and union.

Source: Plato, *Protagoras and Meno*, translated by W.K.C. Guthrie (London: Penguin, 1956).

was the Samian temple to the goddess Hera, built around 500 B.C.E. and the largest such structure in all of Greece.

Ships. Given how large a role the sea played in ancient Greek life, the construction of ships, both for transport and warfare, was likewise a central activity. The poet Homer's epic poem, the *Odyssey*, takes place in a world in which Greeks and others regularly navigate the Aegean and Mediterranean seas in ships of all different types. During Classical times, the state-of-the-art warship was the trireme. It was developed during the sixth century and set the standard for light, relatively fast attack ships. It was a narrow vessel roughly 120 feet in length and 20 feet wide, and manned by a crew of about two hundred men. In open water it relied on a large, square sail. In battle, the mast was lowered and the ship propelled by banks of rowers at an average speed of around five knots. The name *trireme* means "three-oared" and probably refers to the placement of the rowers in three separate tiers. The prow of the trireme was extended just below the waterline by a long, curved "beak" of wood covered with bronze, making the ship an extremely effective weapon for ramming.

Slave Society. In certain respects, however, the ancient Greek world remained what can be called pretechnological. Practical innovations—the construction of machines, for instance—always lagged far behind abstract and conceptual ones. This situation was due first and in large part to the fact that ancient Greece was a slave society. It has been estimated that, in a representative city on the Greek mainland, as much as one-third to one-half of the total population consisted of slaves. They were mostly captives taken in war or the children bred from them, and their misery is often overlooked or forgotten when we think of the remarkable achievements of the Greeks. For Aristotle, in fact, a slave had the status of a "human tool," whose availability made the need to develop other tools less pressing. Necessity is certainly the mother of invention. The abundant supply of cheap manual labor in the ancient world tended to reduce the need for technological innovations.

Narrow-Mindedness. Another factor that retarded Greek technology was a cultural or ideological one. The minority of Greeks who were educated enough to be concerned with scientific and technological problems were generally less interested in practical issues than in abstract, theoretical ones. Practical solutions, like manual labor, were considered matters for the lower class.

Sources:
Donald Cardwell, *The Norton History of Technology* (New York: Norton, 1994).

John G. Landels, *Engineering in the Ancient World* (Berkeley: University of California Press, 1978).

George Sarton, *A History of Science*, volume 1: *Ancient Science Through the Golden Age of Greece* (Cambridge, Mass.: Harvard University Press, 1952).

THE EARLY PHILOSOPHERS

The Milesians. The philosopher-scientists whom tradition cites as being the earliest were all sixth-century Milesians, residents of the prosperous city of Miletus on the southern coast of what is now modern Turkey. Information about them is thin, and with the exception of a single phrase quoted nearly a millennium after the fact, we have no direct access to their work. Our fragmentary reports of their theories in fact usually come from summaries written much later, and from authors who had their own motives for attributing one idea or another to a particular thinker. Scholars must exercise extreme caution in presenting Milesian ideas and also in interpreting their meaning.

Heaven and Earth. Available evidence indicates two main directions or aims of Milesian research. On the one hand, they were concerned with the investigation of specific natural phenomena, such as earthquakes, lightning, and the behavior of animals. Here they seem to have collected evidence and searched for the simplest and most comprehensive explanations of what those phenomena were and how they operated. On the other hand, they also had much broader, cosmological interest in the ultimate nature of reality: what the universe is made of, where it came from, and what processes seem to govern how it works. Because of their abiding concern with physical reality, later generations of Greek thinkers referred to them as *phusiologoi* (natural scientists).

Thales. One of the Milesians, Thales, is said to have explained earthquakes by claiming that the flat disk of the earth floats on an ocean of water whose waves cause violent tremors on the land above. Although the story that he successfully predicted a solar eclipse in the year 585 B.C.E. probably credits him with greater astronomical skill than he actually had, it does point to an early interest in what later Greeks called *ta meteôra* ("the things above the air"). Some sources in fact mention a book by Thales titled *Nautical Astronomy*—while others claim he wrote two books, *On the*

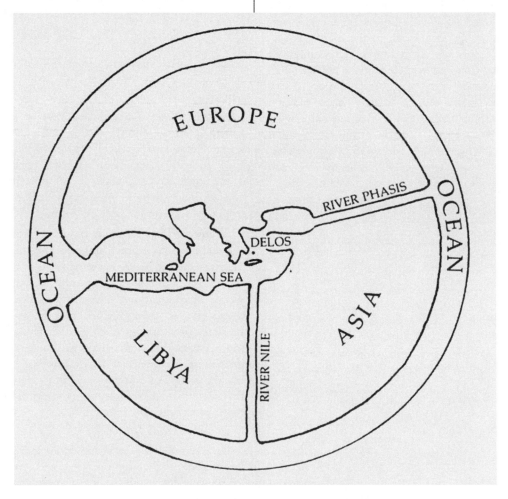

A reconstruction of Anaximander's mid-sixth-century B.C.E. map of the world (J. M. Robinson, *An Introduction to Early Greek Philosophy* [1968], p. 32)

In the following account, the Roman poet Ovid relates the tale of the tragic escape of Daedalus and Icarus from Crete.

[Daedalus] turned his mind toward unknown arts, changing the laws of nature. He laid out feathers in order, first the smallest, a little larger next to it, and so continued, the way that pan-pipes rise in gradual sequence. He fastened them with twine and wax, at middle, at bottom, so, and bent them, gently curving, so that they looked like wings of birds, most surely. And Icarus, his son, stood by and watched him. . . . When it was done at last, his father hovered, poised, in the moving air, and taught his son: "I warn you, Icarus, fly a middle course: Don't go too low, or water will weigh the wings down; don't go too high, or the sun's fire will burn them. Keep to the middle way . . ."

Far off, far down, some fisherman is watching as the rod dips and trembles over the water, some shepherd rests his weight upon his crook, some plowman on the handles of the plowshare, and all look up, in absolute amazement, at those air-borne above. They must be gods!

They were over Samos, Juno's sacred island, Delos and Paros to the right, and another island, Calymne, rich in honey. And the boy thought *This is wonderful!* and left his father, soared higher, higher, drawn to the vast heaven, nearer the sun, and the wax that held the wings melted in that fierce heat, and the bare arms beat up and down in air, and lacking oarage took hold of nothing. "Father!" he cried, and "Father!" until the blue sea hushed him, the dark water men now call the Icarian Sea.

Source: Ovid, *Metamorphoses*, translated by Rolfe Humphries (Bloomington: Indiana University Press, 1955).

Solstice and *On the Equinox*—but since nothing has survived from any of them, it is impossible to determine their content.

Anaximander. Theories about lightning and thunder are attributed to his younger contemporary, Anaximander. This scholar also developed a theoretical model of the solar system: a flat-topped, cylindrical earth in the middle is surrounded by three concentric rings of fire. These rings are hidden by mist that thins out in spots to make holes through which the fire becomes visible to observers on earth. The closest ring has the greatest number of perforations, and thus offers a glimpse of stars; the next, with only one hole, shows the moon; and the most remote is that of the sun. Eclipses are caused when the holes either narrow or else completely (though always temporarily) close. Anaximander also assigned specific widths to each ring, calculated in terms of the diameter of the earth: the ring of stars is nine times its diameter, while those of the moon and sun are eighteen and twenty-seven times as wide, respectively. The geometrical ratio is important, since it indicates an interest in the use of mathematics as a means of uncovering and measuring physical reality. This interest remained a strong one throughout the history of Greek science.

Human Evolution. Anaximander is also said to have claimed that human beings first arose in a watery environment as fishlike creatures, and took on human shape only after a long period of gestation and development. Though this theory is hardly one of evolution, the account nonetheless suggests that Anaximander might have collected fossils and observed different species of marine life. If nothing else, it points to the great variety and breadth of Milesian interests, encompassing what are now the distinct sciences of physics, geology, meteorology, astronomy, and biology.

Aristotelian Influence. It is for cosmology—the theory of the origin and fundamental nature of the world—that the Milesians are best known. Here, however, the greatest caution is needed, since our main source for Milesian cosmology

is the philosopher Aristotle, who lived some two hundred years later. In the course of his research, Aristotle in fact provided what might be called the first history of Greek science and philosophy. Though he is an invaluable source of information that might otherwise have been lost to us, Aristotle also tended to present earlier Greek thinkers as the precursors of his own style of thinking, and this in turn often tended to misrepresent their true ideas and motives.

Material Cause. According to Aristotle, each of the Milesians proposed a different answer to the question of what material things are made of—what he himself called the "material cause" of the world. Thales allegedly said it was water; Anaximander called it the Limitless (*apeiron*); and a third Milesian thinker, Anaximenes, claimed it was air. What exactly each thinker meant may be impossible to recover, but each was probably asking a different question from the one Aristotle later put forth.

Water. If Thales actually thought water was the key, in the sense of the primary substance out of which all things are made, no indication has survived as to how he explained the transformation of water into everything else in the world. Traditional myths of creation, including those told by the Greeks, usually claimed that the world had emerged from the sea, or else from a kind of watery, primordial soup. Thales himself may have had these traditions in mind in making his own claims. In any case, it may be more likely that he saw water as something that was temporally first in the order of creation, as the earliest source rather than the basic ingredient of things.

Cyclical Approach. With Anaximander the situation is more abstract, since he proposed an indeterminate, limitless material as the origin of what is. Rather than a specific substance, like water or air, however, the apeiron is the indefinite and undifferentiated source of everything in the universe. All things naturally come into existence from it through separation, and also dissolve back into it again at regular intervals. The process by which things emerge and return, moreover, seems to have been bound by a kind of moral principle as well, since Anaximander is said to have written (in what may well be our first direct quote from a Greek thinker) that this happens "according to necessity, for they pay penalty and retribution to each other for their injustice according to the arrangement of time." This theory suggests a grand, cyclic process of generation and destruction that ultimately preserves balance and symmetry, as if a law of conservation were at work.

Anaximenes. Evidence provides no clue whether Thales or Anaximander answered the question of just exactly how the universe came into being from water or the Limitless. It is with the third of the Milesians, Anaximenes, that this issue was addressed. His claim that *aêr* ("air" or "mist") is the primary element might at first seem like a step backward from Anaximander's more abstract apeiron. However, this step allowed the youngest Milesian to propose a mechanism for change. Later accounts report that, according to Anaximenes, the condensation and rarefaction of air bring the basic substances of the world into existence. In the words of a late commentator: "Made finer, air becomes fire; made thicker, it becomes wind, then cloud, then (when thickened still more) water, then earth, then stones. Everything else comes into being from these."

Creation. With Anaximenes, then, we have what might be called the first account of the mechanics of creation. The creation of the universe, along with all perceptible changes within it, are here reduced to the operation of two simple, physical processes acting on an equally simple, physical material. It is likely that direct, empirical observation of such natural events as evaporation and freezing offered support for his theory and might even have inspired it.

Sources:

Jonathan Barnes, *Early Greek Philosophy* (Harmondsworth, U.K. & New York: Penguin, 1987).

Charles H. Kahn, *Anaximander and the Origins of Greek Cosmology* (New York: Columbia University Press, 1960).

Geoffrey Stephen Kirk and John Earle Raven, eds., *The Presocratic Philosophers: A Critical History with a Selection of Texts* (Cambridge: Cambridge University Press, 1957).

EARLY SPECULATION

Influence. Though exact details of Milesian speculation are often difficult to capture, its significance is clear and hard to overstate. It is especially important for the degree to which it embodies influential trends that later became more explicit in the history of Greek scientific thought. The Milesians were the first to distinguish consistently between what is natural and what is supernatural, and also to exploit that distinction. These two categories might well be familiar to us now, but for thinkers in the sixth century B.C.E., the difference between them was revolutionary. The theories of Thales, Anaximander, and Anaximenes are as remarkable for what they omit as for what they actually say. Against a background of mythical and religious accounts of the origin and nature of the world, they instead declared that valid explana-

THE OATH OF THE PYTHAGOREANS

According to the Pythagoreans, ten was the essence of all numbers. Moreover, the power of 10 resided in the tetrad, or number 4. If you began at 1 and kept adding each successive number up to four, you arrived at the number 10 (1 + 2 + 3 + 4 = 10). In terms of single units, it was the number 10, but in terms of potentiality, it was the number 4. As a result, the Pythagoreans used to invoke the tetrad as their most sacred oath: "By him who gave the tetrad to our generation, which holds the source and root of eternal reality."

Source: Walter Burkert, *Lore and Science in Ancient Pythagoreanism*, translated by E. L. Minar Jr. (Cambridge, Mass.: Harvard University Press, 1972).

tions of events must be found in regular, rational patterns of natural causes and effects, instead of in the arbitrary will of supernatural forces. Of course, Thales' claim that earthquakes happen because the earth rocks back and forth on choppy water is in reality no more true than the pious belief that they are caused by an angry god named Poseidon, waving his trident at the bottom of the sea. By excluding gods and other supernatural causes from their explanations, however, Thales and the other Milesians created a new way of thinking and talking about the world. Rational claims could now challenge traditional beliefs.

Consistency. Another scientific feature of their work is the fact that the Milesians seem to have focused their attention on studying types rather than particulars. That is to say, they viewed earthquakes, for example, as a class of events instead of as a unique thing that happens now and then, here or there, as Poseidon wills it. For the Milesians, rational accounts should be as comprehensive as possible and, ideally, universally applicable, true for every instance they seek to explain.

Uncovering the Truth. Milesian speculation aimed, as Aristotle later put it, to "save the phenomena" (*sôizein ta phainomena*) by uncovering the universal truths they embody, the rational principles that underlie a multiplicity of singular events. The term *saving* here chiefly means "rescuing" phenomena by building explanatory frameworks in which the events can be understood; without such frameworks, they are simply "lost" and unintelligible. True to this aim, early Greek speculation exhibited a strong tendency to generalize—often (and even absurdly) far beyond the available evidence—in order to include more and more things under a single explanation. The simpler and more inclusive the explanatory framework, after all, the greater its explanatory power and the stronger its claim to being genuine science.

Nature. The fact is that the Milesians might well even be said to have invented nature itself, in the sense that their efforts helped to shape the concept of a naturalistic, rational world. Their work created a new category of events— namely, events whose explanation is not to be found by searching the heavens for signs of divine, supernatural activity. Instead, this new category of nature includes all those

A Moorish astrolabe of the eleventh century C.E.
made from ancient Greek prototypes
(Royal Scottish Museum)

events whose explanations are (or potentially could be) rational. By doing so, the Milesians implicitly defined the object of all later Western science as a collection of regular causes and effects governed by law-like principles. This approach is clearest with Anaximenes, whose identification of condensation and rarefaction as the forces behind all change had the effect of defining the world as an orderly system of simple, physical processes.

Power of Reason. Moreover, if nature is reasonable, it can be understood best by using human powers of reason. This argument may seem obvious, and even a little circular, but it nonetheless marks an important step in the development of scientific thinking. It is a question of which tool is appropriate for which job. If everything that happens in the world results from the behavior of supernatural beings, then events can be understood only in terms of personal decisions made by gods. Since personal decisions are generally influenced by emotions and feelings more than logic, the powers of reason are inadequate to explain and predict them. Nature can be better understood and expressed by rational minds using regular, orderly, law-like principles of reasoning. Hard critical thinking—not blind acceptance of authority, pious emotion, or prayer—opens the way to true knowledge about the world.

Debates. Just as important, this early speculation developed in a context of open debate. The freedom with which the Milesians rejected supernatural explanations already implies a kind of deliberate confrontation, a contest between modern ideas and traditional lore. At the same time, the new thinkers also seem to have been engaged in vigorous, public competition with each other; this approach is indeed a feature of all Greek science, and perhaps of Greek culture as a whole. Anaximander's proposal of the Limitless looks like an abstract challenge to the simple, material stuff claimed by Thales; and in the notion of contracting and expanding air there seems to be an attempt by Anaximenes to solve what was problematic or lacking in both earlier theories. Whether passion for debate reflected Greek political and social conditions—the Milesians lived during a time of political instability, amidst many competing forms of government—or whether it helped create them is a good

HERACLITUS SPEAKS

The *logos* holds always but humans always prove unable to understand it, both before hearing it and when they have first heard it. For though all things happen in accordance with this *logos*, humans are like people with no experience when they experience what I say and do . . .

Although the *logos* is common, most people live as if they had their own private understanding.

Misunderstanding what they have heard, they are like the deaf. This saying describes them: though present, they are absent.

Pigs prefer mud to pure water.

Listening not to me but to the *logos*, it is wise to agree that all things are one.

They do not understand how, though at variance with itself, it agrees with itself. It is a backwards-turning attunement, like that of the bow and the lyre.

An unapparent connection (*harmonia*) is stronger than an apparent one.

On the circumference of a circle, beginning and end are the same.

The name of the bow (*biós*) is life (*bíos*), but its work is death.

Changing, it rests.

God is day night, winter summer, war peace, satiety hunger; he undergoes alteration just as fire, when mixed with spices, gets its name from the scent each gives to it. Different and different waters flow on those who step into the same rivers twice.

Source: Richard D. McKirahan, ed., *Philosophy before Socrates: An Introduction with Texts and Commentary* (Indianapolis: Hackett, 1994).

question. Whatever the answer, the critical climate encouraged these early thinkers to challenge ancient religious beliefs, to analyze claims and counterclaims carefully, to search for compelling evidence to support new theories, and eventually to create a language appropriate for rational, scientific discourse.

Sources:

David C. Lindberg, *The Beginnings of Western Science* (Chicago: University of Chicago Press, 1992).

Geoffrey Ernest Richard Lloyd, *Early Greek Science: Thales to Aristotle* (New York: Norton, 1970).

EARLY SPECULATION: THE CULT OF PYTHAGORAS

Man and Myth. The life and views of Pythagoras are hard to reconstruct, since the man himself inspired a cult and became quickly shrouded in legends spun by his disciples. According to Empedocles, who was strongly influenced by his thinking, Pythagoras "stretched his mind and easily saw each and every thing in ten or twenty generations." His followers were concentrated in the southern Italian town of Croton and remained active as a group from approximately the year 530 through the fourth century B.C.E. In general, they tended to divide themselves into mystics on the one hand and mathematicians on the other. The main concern is with the latter group, though both shared the same premise that the essence of all things could be expressed in numbers.

Structure and Form. The chief proof for this claim that reality is numerical was their observation of the simple ratios that underlie harmony in musical scales—that of the octave (1:2), for instance, in which a string divided in half vibrates twice as fast to produce the same note in a higher register. The fact that some phenomena exhibit a numerical orderliness suggested to the Pythagoreans that the universe as a whole might have a quantitative, mathematical basis. At its best, this theory marked an important shift away from how the Milesians approached nature, since their primary aim seems to have been to isolate the physical material of the world. For this reason, the Milesians are generally identified as materialists. For the Pythagoreans, on the other hand, the search for truth pointed not in the direction of matter but instead of structure and form. Numbers and ratios expressed in numbers were the keys to understanding the essence of reality. The influence of this belief on both the direction and also the language of all later Western science is obvious.

Listeners. At its worst, however, the same insights also tended to promote a kind of mystical speculation among the Pythagoreans. For some of them, especially those who belonged to the mystical group called the *Akousmatikoi* ("Listeners"), numbers had the status of quasidivine objects of worship. The Listeners, that is to say, went far beyond strict, mathematical research and sought to discover numbers beneath all aspects of experience. They assigned numerical values not just to objective relations but also to things and

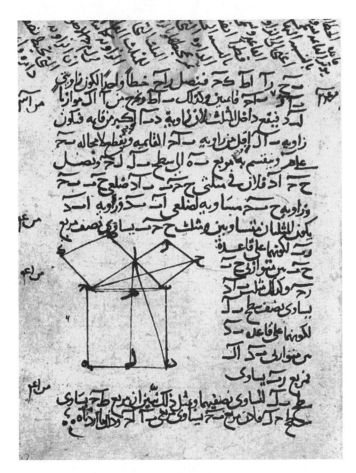

A thirteenth century C.E. Arabic commentary on Euclid with a diagram of the Pythagorean theorem (British Museum)

qualities. The number 3, for instance, was identified as male; 2 as female; and 5 as marriage.

The Universe. The Pythagoreans generalized their discovery of ratios in music into a view of the whole universe itself as "a musical scale and a number." This theory is the source of the famous idea of the "music of the spheres," according to which the moon, sun, planets, and stars were believed to produce different musical notes as they spin through space. To the mind trained to hear them, these notes all blend together into perfect harmony. Here it is easy to see how the same point of departure could produce both pure mathematics and a kind of mysticism. Contemplation of the music of the spheres is simultaneously a scientific and a spiritual act.

Astronomy and Geometry. Empirical investigation and experimentation among the Pythagoreans were more consistent than in the case of the Milesian *phusiologoi*. A great deal of Pythagorean attention was in fact directed to astronomy, in attempts to calculate the relative distances and sizes of the heavenly bodies and to provide accounts of both lunar and solar eclipses. The group was especially noted for its research on acoustics, through the measurement of lengths of vibrating strings and columns of air. They have been credited with classifying numbers into odd and even. Geometry, the science of solid numbers, was also a central part of their work. The proof that bears their name—the Pythagorean theorem (the square of the hypotenuse of a right triangle equals the sum of squares of the other two sides [$a^2 + b^2 = c^2$])—seems to date from the late fourth century B.C.E. Its truth was in fact an old one, known even to the ancient Babylonians as many as five hundred years earlier; what the Greeks did was to provide a conclusive demonstration.

Impact. The major and abiding contribution of the Pythagorean group is what could be called its arithmetization of the world, its view of reality as somehow numerical. Even if it tended to become entangled in mystical beliefs, their basic insight—that the science of numbers is fundamental to every science of nature—had profound influence. Reality is viewed as orderly, regular, mathematical, and easily accessible to rational minds. Nature indeed is number, at least in the sense that mathematics provides the most objective way of talking about natural events. At the same time, Pythagorean work on geometric problems also helped to further hone a scientific language of theorem, evidence, and proof.

Sources:

Walter Burkert, *Lore and Science in Ancient Pythagoreanism* (Cambridge, Mass.: Harvard University Press, 1972).

Cornelia J. de Vogel, *Pythagoras and Early Pythagoreanism: An Interpretation of Neglected Evidence of the Philosopher Pythagoras* (Assen, Netherlands: Van Gorcum, 1966).

EARLY SPECULATION: CYCLES OF CHANGE

Turning Point. The early fifth century is a turning point in the history of Greek science, since it was then that the problem of change first began to be raised in a systematic manner. The Milesians had focused their attention mainly on identifying the basic material of the world; and the Pythagoreans turned away from that material element to look instead at the mathematical structure and form of the world. Neither group directly addressed a simple but crucial fact of everyday observation: things change.

The Cycle of Air. Change is an obvious feature of all things and is directly confirmed by the senses. But what exactly is it? And how does the fact that the world always changes impact on the ability to understand it scientifically? Anaximenes more than any other earlier thinker seems to have speculated on how one thing can turn into another. He claimed that everything is air and proposed condensation and rarefaction as the two processes that account for how air changes into everything else in the world—fire, clouds, rain, rocks, and so forth. This claim is circular. If water, for example, is nothing but condensed air, and fire is air that has been rarefied even more, then air itself is not really a unique element at all, but instead just another phase in an endless cycle. That is, it could just as easily be said that air is nothing but rarefied water or condensed fire. And if this is so, then what sense does it make to claim that air is the primordial reality?

Truth. The problem of change has two main aspects. The first has to do with what passes for an acceptable answer to the question, "What is real?" The ancient Greeks implicitly believed that whatever the true nature of reality is, that true nature must always be true. This truth is what motivated them to "save the phenomena" in the first place, by searching for something fixed and permanent beneath the constantly shifting things and events in the world. Yet, if the answer (as in the case of Anaximenes) is that this fundamental something is sometimes air and sometimes something else, have we really found what we are looking for? Does a changeable reality fit the definition of what reality really should be?

Epistemology. The second aspect of the problem of change has to do with how people can know what is real. What evidence do people have for talking about reality? What basis do people have for judging whether evidence is valid or not? How can people be sure that they know anything at all about reality? These and similar questions mark the beginning of Western epistemology, the study of the relation between the mind and the world. The Greek thinkers of the fifth century B.C.E. put these questions in a more direct form, by contrasting the mind with the senses. The mind insists that reality be permanently true, but the five senses only presents a picture of change; nothing we hear, see, taste, touch, or smell conforms to the idea of a permanent truth. Which is the true path to genuine knowledge of the world, then, reason or sensory experience?

Answers. The first response to these questions was made around 500 B.C.E. by Heraclitus of Ephesus in Asia Minor. The surviving fragments of his book are written in a deliberately obscure and riddling style, making it hard to agree on how exactly to interpret many of his claims. On the one hand, Heraclitus apparently argued that change is indeed the essence of reality itself. He is said to have

---

TORTOISE AND HARE

In this well-known paradox, the Greek warrior Achilleus—whom the poet Homer called "swift-footed Achilles"—must race against the slowest runner imaginable: a tortoise. If only the tortoise is allowed the slightest head start, the Parmenidean logician Zeno is prepared to prove that Achilles can never overtake it. Aristotle reports it as follows:

The so-called "Achilles" paradox claims that the fastest can never overtake the slowest runner in a race, since the runner who comes from behind must first reach the point where the front runner started, and so the slower one always holds a lead.

Another paradox, reported by Aristotle, reads as follows:

If "place" exists, where exactly is it? After all, everything that exists, exists in some "place." As a result, "place" too is in a "place." This goes on to infinity; and so "place" does not exist.

Source: D. J. Allan, *The Philosophy of Aristotle* (Oxford: Clarendon Press, 1970).

Empedocles offered these secrets to prospective disciples: "What drugs there are for ills and what help against old age you will learn, since for you alone I shall accomplish all this. And you will stop the power of the tireless winds which sweep over the earth and destroy the crops with their breath, and again, if you wish, you will bring on compensating breezes. And after black rain you will produce a seasonable drought for men, and after the summer drought you will produce tree-nurturing streams which live in the ether. And you will lead from Hades the power of dead men."

Source: J. Barnes, *The Presocratic Philosophers*, volume 2 (London: Routledge & Kegan Paul, 1979).

In his poem *On Nature* (fifth century B.C.E.), Empedocles draws an analogy to a common implement from daily life in the ancient world—the *klepshudra* or "water-catcher"—to explain how living things breathe:

Everything breathes in and out. All creatures have bloodless vessels in their flesh, extending over the surface of the body, and the skin is perforated with pores at the mouths of those vessels, keeping the blood inside but cutting an easy route for air to pass. When the liquid blood moves away from there, the air bubbles in with a violent surge; and when the blood rushes back, the air is pushed out again. It is just as when a girl plays with a bright brass *klepshudra*. When she puts her beautiful hand over the mouth of the pipe and dips it into shining water, no liquid enters; instead, the air trapped within presses against the many holes and keeps it back, until she uncovers the thick stream. Then, as the air withdraws, an equal amount of water enters. Likewise, when the bronze implement is filled with water and her hand blocks the mouth, the outer air pushes inwards and holds the water back . . . until she removes her hand. Then . . . as air rushes in, an equal amount of water rushes out. So too in the body, when the blood rushing through the limbs moves back and inwards, a stream of air immediately and swiftly rushes in; but when the blood surges up again, an equal quantity of air is breathed back inside.

summed this up in the famous claim that "everything flows" (*panta rhei*): "We step and do not step into the same river," he wrote, "we are and we are not." According to Plutarch, a later commentator:

For it is not possible to step twice into the same river, according to Heraclitus, nor to touch anything twice: due to the velocity of its change, the thing scatters and collects itself again—or rather, it does not come together and depart, approach and withdraw at one time and then at another, but instead does all this simultaneously.

Constant Change. The constantly flowing water of a stream always makes it a different stream from the one into which we just stepped. For that matter, we ourselves also participate in change—our cells, for instance, are constantly dying and being regenerated—so that even the one who steps into the stream is different from the one who stepped there a moment ago. This approach would seem to make any notion of a fixed and permanent reality quite impossible.

Logos. At the same time, however, Heraclitus also insisted on a single unifying principle behind or beneath or within that constant flux. He called this principle the *Logos*—a term that embraces a range of meanings, from "word" or "account" to "reason," "ratio," and "rationality"—and described it as a kind of balance that underlies and also controls all change. Although he identified the Logos with the element fire, it is unlikely that Heraclitus thought of it as a material substance, like the water and air of the Milesians. Fire instead offered a brilliant metaphor for the constantly changing, constantly identical world: "The cosmos . . . was always and is and shall be an ever-living fire kindled in measures and extinguished in measures." The reference to measures once again points to an abiding Greek belief in the ultimate orderliness and measurability of the universe. Beneath or behind or within all change, the Logos remains constant.

The Senses. On the epistemological problem of knowledge—How exactly can one know what is real?—Heraclitus implied that the senses are untrustworthy witnesses that must be brought under the control of the rational mind. After all, how else except by reasoning can one discover the invisible Logos concealed by the world's apparent flux?

Parmenides. Far more radical, however, was the view of the next major thinker, Parmenides, born around 515 B.C.E. in the southern Italian city of Elea. For Parmenides, pure logic alone pointed the way to a truth that completely contradicted every shred of evidence our senses can provide. His main argument, rigorously abstract, is preserved in a poem called *The Way of Truth*. One of its chief aims is to deny that reality could ever be subject to change. The basic argument can be summarized in four points:

(1) Whatever is, *is*—and if it *is*, it is impossible for it not to be;

(2) There was never a time when it was not, because then it would have been nonexistent, and "what is" can never come from what is not, since by definition "what is not" has no reality;

(3) Therefore, "what is" must have *always* been;

(4) If this is true, nothing can ever come into being at all.

A Uniform Whole. The upshot of these dense and knotty claims is that reality always was, is, and will forever be the same. Despite everything our senses report, it is actually static and eternal. There is no coming-to-be or passing-away. Change is an illusion, then: nothing is really born, grows, or dies. Parmenides went even further to claim that reality is perfectly homogeneous—that is, it has no parts, but is instead a single, uniform whole. This approach means that no distinct things exist at all, despite the fact that the evidence of our senses insists on quite the opposite.

Deception. Parmenides' *Way of Truth* is a startling tour de force. It utterly rejects the senses and relies on reason aided only by the new science of logic. This argument marked both a starting point and a challenge for all later fifth-century thought. Logic seemed to demand that his reasoning about the true nature of reality be accepted, or at least that all other claims about reality had to have the same logical structure. Fundamental reality must indeed be permanent and unchanging. Yet, as a result, our five senses are not only untrustworthy but even deceptive, since they present us with a view of the world that, on Parmenides' terms, is totally false. Each of the thinkers who came after him were forced to confront this problem and work out some way of solving it.

Eleatics. On the one hand, philosophers such as Zeno of Elea and Melissus of Samos, both of whom lived around 450 B.C.E. and are collectively known as Eleatics, further refined the tools of logic to support Parmenides. Zeno in particular is

The reverse of a bronze coin from Samos showing Pythagoras holding a scepter and pointing to a globe (Ny Carlsberg Glyptotek, Copenhagen)

famous for a series of logical paradoxes, all of which construct rigorously logical arguments to prove something that completely contradicts intuition and experience. Among the most famous and familiar is the paradox that denies that an arrow can traverse a given space, from A to B, because it would first need to cross an infinite number of fractions of that distance—one-half, one-quarter, one-eighth, one-sixteenth, and so on—in a finite amount of time. Zeno's conclusion, of course, is that motion is logically absurd.

Sources:
Patricia Curd, *The Legacy of Parmenides: Eleatic Monism and Later Presocratic Thought* (Princeton: Princeton University Press, 1998).

Charles H. Kahn, *The Art and Thought of Heraclitus: An Edition of the Fragments with Translation and Commentary* (Cambridge & New York: Cambridge University Press, 1979).

Alexander Mourelatos, *The Route of Parmenides: A Study of Word, Image, and Argument in the Fragments* (New Haven: Yale University Press, 1970).

Wesley Salmon, comp., *Zeno's Paradoxes* (Indianapolis: Bobbs-Merrill, 1970).

EARLY SPECULATION: PLURALISM

Combinations. Attempts were made by the ancient Greeks to save the evidence of the senses and counter the total denial of change. In the 400s, the so-called Pluralists, Empedocles and Anaxagoras, accepted Parmenides' claim that reality is indeed forever changeless, but then went on to assert that it is also fundamentally plural. The universe is a composite of basic, indivisible substances that each enjoy the characteristics of the Eleatic "what is"—namely, each is eternal and unchanging. Since there are many such permanent and timeless entities, however, the world of the senses can be constructed by bringing them together into different combinations.

ASTRONOMY OR ATHEISM?

Tried and convicted of impiety in an Athenian court, Anaxagoras spent the remaining years of his life in exile. The following passage (from the third-century C.E. theologian Hippolytus) records some of the theories that might well have provided the prosecution with ammunition for its case against the philosopher.

The earth (he thinks) is flat in shape, and stays suspended from where it is because of its size, because there is no void and because the air, which is very strong, keeps the earth afloat on it. . . . The sun, the moon, and all the stars are red-hot stones which the rotation of the *aithêr* carries round with it. Beneath the stars are certain bodies, invisible to us, that are carried around with the sun and moon. We do not feel the heat of the stars because they are so far from the earth. Moreover, they are not as hot as the sun and occupy a colder region. The moon is beneath the sun and nearer to us. The sun is larger than the Peloponnese. The moon has no light of its own but derives it from the sun. . . . Eclipses of the moon are due its being screened by the earth or, sometimes, by the bodies beneath the moon; eclipses of the sun, to screening by the moon.

Source: Geoffrey Stephen Kirk and John Earle Raven, *The Presocratic Philosophers: A Critical History with a Selection of Texts* (Cambridge: Cambridge University Press, 1957).

Basic Elements. For Empedocles, the "roots" (*rhizōmata*) of reality are the elements earth, air, fire, and water. They are original substances in the sense that they are uncreated and everlasting, just as Parmenides had demanded reality should be. They are also originative, in that they are the constituents out of which everything that exists is made. He answered the question of how the unlimited number and variety of things in nature could be analyzed back into these four simple elements by claiming that they combine in fixed and definite proportions to create each distinct thing in the world. Bone, for example, is compounded from four parts fire, two parts water, two parts earth; blood is a composite of all four elements in equal proportions. He apparently made no effort to demonstrate these claims experimentally. Despite the brilliant idea of proportion, it would be wrong to see in his work a precursor of modern chemistry.

Love and Strife. Empedocles' system also included two forces that are responsible for the combination and separation of the elements. These are Love and Strife, which work together but in opposite ways to bring everything in the universe into existence. Strife makes each of the elements move apart from the others and gather together. When the power of Strife is supreme, the universe has the shape of four concentric rings of pure earth, water, air, and fire. When Love is dominant, on the contrary, the elements all mingle together to form a homogeneous sphere. The movement from Love to Strife and from Strife back to Love once more is cyclic and eternal, and the world as we experience it comes into being in the periods in between these two extremes of total unity (Love) and total separation (Strife). Over the course of the ages, the world is alternately created, dissolved, and then created all over again.

Anaxagoras. The position taken by Anaxagoras is superficially similar, in that he also regarded reality as plural and composite. Whereas Empedocles analyzed it into the four basic elements, however, Anaxagoras multiplied the number of fundamental entities to include both natural substance—gold, iron, bone, wood, leaf, hair, flesh, and so forth—and such qualities as "hot" and "cold." Each of these substances, according to Anaxagoras, is basic and elementary, and their presence accounts for the great variety of nature. His most famous claim is that "in everything there is a portion of everything." That is to say, any given thing—a piece of bread, for instance—contains a share of every other thing in the world. This peculiar theory might well have been an attempt to explain the transformative process of digestion, through which the food we ingest somehow becomes flesh, hair, blood, and bone. Accordingly, tiny particles of bone, for instance, are present in whatever we might eat; when the food is digested, these particles separate out and go to add themselves to the bone that is already in our body.

Mind. As theories go, this is hardly economical, since it assumes a virtually unlimited number of primary substances. It also, of course, duplicates on the infinitesimal level the variety of visible things whose origin the theory is supposed to explain. In keeping with the rationalism of Greek speculation, Anaxagoras attributed the coming-to-be and dissolution of things to the activity of a cosmic "Mind" (*nous*), which guides all natural processes from within nature itself by making the mixture of infinite primary elements slowly spin and separate out to form all the things of the known world.

Impiety. Anaxagoras is also noteworthy as the first recorded victim of the conflict between science and traditional ideas that had begun with the Milesians some one hundred years earlier. While living in Athens, he is said to have been formally accused of impiety, on the ground that he claimed the sun is a fiery rock somewhat bigger than southern Greece, and not (as a majority of people believed) the great god Helios. Tried and convicted, he was exiled from Athens and spent the years until his death in 428 B.C.E. in a remote corner of the Greek world. While his choice of political associates may have had something to do with the case, his fate also illustrates a genuine tension between subversive new theories and conservative religious belief that was to surface on other occasions in the history of Greek culture.

Sources:

Brad Inwood, *The Poem of Empedocles* (Toronto: University of Toronto Press, 1992).

Malcolm Schofield, *An Essay on Anaxagoras* (Cambridge & New York: Cambridge University Press, 1980).

THE LAUGHING PHILOSOPHER

Democritus of Abdera (circa 460–circa 370 B.C.E.) was known as the "Laughing Philosopher" because of his commentaries on the foibles of man. Only a few fragments of his writings survive.

On sense perception:

Sight takes place by means of a physical impression . . . which does not occur spontaneously in the pupil of the eye. Instead, the air in between the eye and the object is compressed and stamped by both the object and the viewer, since [atoms] are always flowing from everything.

They associated vision with certain images, identical in shape with the object, that constantly streamed from the object and impressed themselves on the eye.

On tastes:

He defines "sweet" as something [made of atoms that are] round and moderately large; "sour," as what is large, round, polygonal, and linear; whatever is "sharp tasting," as the name implies, sharp edges, and is angular, crooked, and linear; whatever is "pungent" is round, small, angular, and crooked; "salty" is angular, moderately large and crooked, with sides of equal length; whatever is "bitter" is round, small, crooked, and smooth; and "oily" is fine, round, and smooth.

On knowledge:

There are two kinds of knowledge: one authentic, one illegitimate. The following belong to illegitimate knowledge: vision, hearing, smell, taste, and touch. The other [sc. rationality] is genuine and distinct from this kind. . . . We must acknowledge that, for this reason, we are separated from reality. . . . In fact, we know nothing about anything . . .

LEUCIPPUS AND ATOMISM

Man of Mystery. Certainly the most original fifth-century contribution to the debate on the nature of change was that of Leucippus (Leukippos) of Miletus. Little is known about his life, except that he lived around 430 B.C.E., wrote two books (*On Mind* and *The Great World System*), and was the teacher of the famous Democritus of Abdera. It is through his pupil that Leucippus's revolutionary insights into the world of nature have mainly been preserved. In turn, the list of works attributed to Democritus runs to more than seventy titles, and includes studies on such diverse subjects as mathematics, farming, medicine, grammar, ethics, and literature. In what remains of his writings on physics or natural science, the atomic theory that Leucippus proposed and Democritus further developed marks a highpoint in ancient speculation.

TESTIMONIALS FROM THE TEMPLE OF ASCLEPIUS AT EPIDAURUS

Heraieus of Mytilene. He had no hair on his head, but an abundant growth on his chin. He was ashamed because he was laughed at by others. He slept in the Temple. The god, by anointing his head with some drug, made hair grow there.

Arata, a woman of Lacedaemon [in southern Greece], suffering from dropsy. While she remained in Lacedaemon, her mother slept in the Temple and saw a dream. It seemed to her that the god cut off her daughter's head and hung up her body in such a way that her throat was turned downwards. Out of it came a large quantity of fluid. Then he took down the body and fitted the head back on the neck. After she had seen this dream the mother went back to Lacedaemon, where she found her daughter in good health. She had seen the same dream.

A man with an abscess in his stomach. When asleep in the Temple he saw a dream. It seemed to him that the god ordered the servants who accompanied him to grip him and hold him tightly so that he could cut open his abdomen. The man tried to get away, but they gripped him and bound him to a door knocker. Then Asclepius cut his belly open, removed the abscess and, having stitched him up again, released him from his bonds. Then he walked out sound, but the floor . . . was covered with blood.

Source: Emma Edelstein and Ludwig Edelstein, *Asclepius: Collection and Interpretation of the Testimonies* (Baltimore & London: Johns Hopkins University Press, 1945).

The Atom. The main features of this theory are direct responses to the demand for an eternally changeless reality offered by Parmenides; and like the answer of the Pluralists, the Atomists too adopted an Eleatic description of their fundamental substance. This material was the atom—from the Greek word *atomon*, meaning "indivisible." Each atom is ungenerated, uniform, unalterable, and incapable of any further division. (Note that this last characteristic distinguishes ancient Greek atoms from the splittable ones of modern physics.)

Three Differences. Infinite in number, the atoms of Democritus differ from each other in three respects only: shape (as the letter 'A' differs from 'N'), arrangement (as 'AN' differs from 'NA'), and relative position (as 'N' is 'Z' turned on its side). Their different shapes are countless, ranging from the smooth, rounded atoms that compose water to the rough, jagged, and uneven ones out of which iron is made. The only other natural reality allowed by Leucippus and Democritus is an infinite void that separates each atom from the others and provides the empty space in which they all continuously move in all directions, often with a whirling motion, and bump into each other. Chance collisions among atoms account for the world of sense experience, since the couplings of hooked atoms or atoms whose shape in some way fit that of others give rise to compound objects. In a fragment from his lost work on Democritus, Aristotle explains the theory as follows:

> The atoms are carried about in the void . . . and as they are carried about, they collide and are bound together in a binding that makes them touch and get close to each other, but which does not actually produce any other single thing. . . . He explains how these entities remain together by reference to how the atoms get entangled with and stuck to each other. For some of them are rough, some hooked, some concave, some convex, and others have countless other different aspects. He thinks they keep hold of one another and stay together until such time as a stronger force from outside touches them, shakes them, and scatters them apart.

Infinity. The apparent coming-to-be and passing-away of things is thus really a rearrangement—joining and separation—of invisible, infinite, and indestructible entities. Moreover, since atoms and void are both infinite, and since motion has always existed, Democritus believed that there must have always been an infinite number of worlds. Each is made of precisely the same unchangeable atoms in different configurations.

Senses. Both the breadth of Democritus's interests and the rational consistency of his atomism are clear from how he applied his theory to explain sense perception, and so also to address the problem of knowledge. First, he believed that our experience of the world is ultimately sensual, the result of physical contact between atoms streaming from objects and entering our organs of perception. Waves of atoms thrown off the surface of a table, for instance, make a kind of impression in the air which then passes as an image into a person's eyes. Different shapes and arrangements of atoms are directly responsible for the variety of possible sensations. For example, the atoms of honey are generally round and smooth in shape, in contrast to the sharp, thin ones of a pungent substance such as vinegar.

Illusion. The data provided by the five senses concern only the shape and arrangement of atoms, however, not the atoms themselves. Everything perceived by the senses is therefore "secondary" and, in a sense, unreal. The chance combinations of atoms do not "actually produce any other single thing," but instead only create the illusion of permanent objects. In actual fact, the atomic arrangements responsible for our sensations of sight, sound, taste, touch, and smell are really impermanent and illusory. The only things that truly exist are atoms per se and the void. Since the senses cannot provide direct access to atoms themselves, only to their shapes and configurations, the rational mind alone has claim to knowledge of reality.

Sources:

David Furley, *Two Studies in the Greek Atomists* (Princeton: Princeton University Press, 1967).

Samuel Sambursky, *The Physical World of the Greeks* (New York: Macmillan, 1956).

MEDICINE: SOCIAL CONTENT

Epidemiology. It is hard to give a precise epidemiology of the ancient Greek world—that is, a clear picture of the kinds of diseases and ailments that were common in the Mediterranean at that time. The preservation of a large body of fifth- and fourth-century Greek medical writings provides less help than might be expected because the categories used by ancient doctors to diagnose their patients were often completely different from modern ones. Many of the symptoms and signs they considered important for identifying diseases are simply irrelevant in modern systems of classification. The same is true of their methods of investigation—the pulse, for instance, was not used as a diagnostic tool until the third century B.C.E.—which often omit what modern doctors consider to be crucial information. Greek physicians neither envisioned nor discussed diseases in the modern language of germ theory, which is only about one hundred and fifty years old. The results are vague descriptions that are impossible to match with contemporary ones.

Palaeopathology. What little can be learned from the texts must be supplemented by the modern science of palaeopathology, which studies skeletal remains for information on diet and health. From these sources, it is likely that dysentery, typhoid and malarial fevers, epilepsy, tuberculosis, diphtheria, rabies, and chicken pox were all common in ancient Greece. Various forms of conjunctivitis (a chronic inflammation of the eyes) seem to have been especially widespread. Evidence also exists for the presence of inheritable conditions such as certain strains of anemia. Beyond that, not much more can be said with any certainty. A devastating plague ravaged the city of Athens (430–427 B.C.E.). Despite the fact that we possess contemporary written accounts of the epidemic, its actual nature is still a matter of debate. Whether it was bubonic plague, cholera, or measles is uncertain.

Hippocratic Corpus. With Greek medicine, scholars are in the unusual position of having direct and rather extensive

A medical record from Epidaurus which records in detail the treatment and recovery of a patient
(AM, Epidaurus)

evidence, instead of the secondhand fragments and quotations in which most other ancient thinkers are preserved. A group of about sixty texts named the *Hippocratic Corpus* and dating from roughly 420 to 350 B.C.E. have survived. The title is deceptive, since these texts represent neither the work of a single author—it is doubtful whether any was actually written by the legendary physician, Hippocrates of Cos—nor even the position of a single medical school.

Authors and Audience. The writings themselves cover a broad range of topics, including anatomy, physiology, pharmacology, embryology, gynecology, epidemiology, surgery, and dietetics. They are obviously the product of a group (or groups) of distinct individuals. Their styles also differ considerably. While some are clearly textbooks for professional physicians, others take the form of detailed, clinical case histories and even public lectures pitched to a nonspecialist audience. These different styles, moreover, imply widely different contexts of use. A book such as the one titled *Airs Waters Places*, for instance, was obviously written as a guide for itinerant doctors, allowing them to

THE HIPPOCRATIC OATH

I swear by Apollo the healer, by Asclepius, by Health and all the powers of healing, and call to witness all the gods and goddesses that I may keep this Oath and Promise to the best of my ability and judgment.

I will pay the same respect to my master in the Science as to my parents and share my life with him and pay all my debts to him. I will regard his sons as my brothers and teach them the Science, if they desire to learn it, without fee or contract. I will hand on precepts, lectures, and all other learning to my sons, to those of my master, and to those pupils duly apprenticed and sworn, and to none other.

I will use my power to help the sick to the best of my ability and judgment; I will abstain from harming or wronging any man by it.

I will not give a fatal dose to anyone if I am asked, nor will I suggest any such thing. Neither will I give a woman means to procure an abortion.

I will be chaste and religious in my life and in my practice.

I will not cut, even for the stone, but I will leave such procedures to the practitioners of that craft.

Whenever I go into a house, I will go to help the sick and never with the intention of doing harm or injury. I will not abuse my position to indulge in sexual contacts with the bodies of women or of men, whether they be freemen or slaves.

Whatever I see or hear, professionally or privately, which ought not to be divulged, I will keep secret and tell no one.

If, therefore, I observe this Oath and do not violate it, may I prosper both in my life and in my profession, earning good repute among all men for all time. If I transgress and forswear this Oath, may my lot be otherwise.

Source: *Hippocratic Writings*, edited by G. E. R. Lloyd (Harmondsworth, U.K. & New York: Penguin, 1978).

---

recognize that doctors in ancient Greece had no formal, institutional status. No standardized course of training and examination authorized them to practice, no special licensing distinguished competent from quack, and no official control guaranteed the overall quality of care. Although some evidence exists of doctors hired at public expense to provide services for a particular community, by far the majority traveled from settlement to settlement like most other artisans, plying their trade alongside healers of all kinds—diviners, exorcists, priests, magicians, herbalists, midwives, athletic trainers, and hawkers of old family recipes and miracle cures. The kind of medicine represented by the *Hippocratic Corpus* was simply one among many therapeutic options. For that matter, in the fifth and fourth centuries, it was definitely considered to be newfangled and strange, and much in need of advertising its benefits in order to attract a clientele. The polemical tones of many of the Hippocratic texts in fact confirm that they were written in direct and often hostile competition with traditional medical practitioners. Just as in the case of Greek natural philosophy, open criticism and public debate accompanied the growth of rational medicine.

Cures. In the middle of the fifth century B.C.E.—and for many hundreds of years afterward, for that matter—an average person's first choice in illness was most probably not to consult a professional Hippocratic doctor at all. Instead, the patient would most likely have turned to a folk remedy. These cures would have brought the person into contact with a variety of individuals and, consequently, different interpretations of disease and means of treatment.

Lore. On the one hand, there existed an ancient tradition of herbal and pharmacological lore, offering treatments for disease based on the medicinal properties of plants and minerals. This lore was the product of centuries of trial and error and undoubtedly offered practical and in some cases effective remedies, as it continues to do today in most parts of the world. On the other hand, popular belief generally explained disease by reference to some kind of supernatural agency. Sickness was caused by offended gods and angry demons, for instance, or else by the sinister workings of magical curses and spells. As a result, people sought remedies tailored to suit what they thought was the true cause of their affliction: prayers, incantations, sacrifices, cleansings, special dietary prescriptions, and ritual behaviors. The author of the Hippocratic text called *On the Sacred Disease* refers with contempt to quasimagical cures for epilepsy that included, among other things, prohibitions against wearing black and touching goats.

Sources:

Lawrence Conrad, and others, *The Western Medical Tradition* (Cambridge & New York: Cambridge University Press, 1995).

G. E. R. Lloyd, ed., *Hippocratic Writings* (Harmondsworth, U.K. & New York: Penguin, 1978).

Guido Majno, *The Healing Hand: Man and Wound in the Ancient World* (Cambridge, Mass.: Harvard University Press, 1975).

MEDICINE: THE THEORY OF HEALING

Asclepius. Throughout the ancient world, belief in the healing powers of the great god Asclepius, son of Apollo, probably drew the most devout support among the general

---

identify and treat diseases specific to particular regions and climates. The *Aphorisms*, on the other hand, which contains practical advice condensed into short, pithy sentences and slogans, was probably meant as a teaching tool.

Doctors. Their diversity offers a rare glimpse of the social context in which early medicine developed. It is important to

public. Hundreds of shrines to Asclepius have been identified across the Mediterranean, and the cult flourished from its official establishment in the fourth century B.C.E. well into Roman and early Christian times. Central to Asclepiadic therapy was the so-called dream cure. After ritual offerings and purifications, the pious patient would sleep in a special dormitory attached to the shrine, and there would be visited in dreams by the god himself. Asclepius would either prescribe a remedy for the patient to purchase later from priests who took care of the temple, or else he might even directly effect the cure.

Man of Torone. The results, advertised on dozens of stone tablets displayed in the precinct of Asclepius's main temple at Epidaurus, were often quite spectacular:

> A man of Torone with leeches. In sleep he saw a dream. It seemed to him that the god cut open his chest with a knife and removed the leeches, which he put into his hands, and then he stitched up his chest again. At daybreak he departed, cured, with the leeches in his hands.

Credibility. Against such a background of tradition, magic, and religion, it was imperative for doctors both as individuals and as a group to distinguish themselves and establish their credibility. Despite ongoing theoretical disputes within the profession, they all consistently rejected supernatural cures as superstitious and firmly endorsed the same rationalist framework that had motivated research since the time of the Milesians in the preceding century. Disease had natural causes, not supernatural ones, and treatment must be rational in order to be scientific and effective.

Health. Earlier thinkers had in fact also concerned themselves with the human body and biological processes. Both Empedocles and Anaxagoras had speculated on the ultimate constituents of flesh and bone, and Alcmaeon of Croton in southern Italy was credited with dissection of an eyeball and discovery of the optic nerve. Even more important was his definition of *health* as the "equal balance" (*isonomia*) within the body of such basic qualities as moist and dry, cold and hot, bitter and sweet. The dominance of any one of them, on the other hand, caused illness.

Four Humors. Alcmaeon's definition was highly influential and productive. While opinions differed widely over which theory of disease to endorse—and even over whether theory was useful at all in a science that was supposed to cure sick individuals, not sickness itself—the *Corpus* still shows a general agreement on basic issues. One of the most common ideas is that of illness as a kind of disequilibrium that needs to be corrected. Specifically, most Hippocratic writers seem to have viewed health as a balance in the relative quantities of certain natural fluids that were present in the human body. This approach is the basis of the well-known theory of the four "humors" (*khumoi*) or "juices": yellow bile, black bile, phlegm, and blood.

Blood. The existence of these fluids seemed to be a matter of simple observation. Blood—all too visible in the case of wounds, hemorrhages, and menstruation—was obvi-

---

HYSTERIA

In a medical diagnosis of hysteria, from the Hippocratic text *Young Girls*, there is a certain degree to which gender biases lurk behind and also implicitly get support from apparently "objective" scientific study:

Many people choke to death as a result of visions, [especially] virgins who do not take a husband at the appropriate time for marriage, [and who thus] experience these visions . . . at the time of their first monthly period. . . . For after their first period the blood collects in the womb in preparation to flow out; but when the mouth of the womb is not opened up, and more blood flows into the womb . . . then [it] rushes up to the heart and to the lungs. When these are filled with blood, the heart becomes sluggish and then, because of the sluggishness, numb and then, because of the numbness, insanity takes hold of the woman: [then] the girl goes crazy because of the violent inflammation, and becomes murderous, because the blood starts to decay. . . . In some cases . . . the visions order her to jump up and throw herself into wells and drown, as if this were good for her and served some useful purpose. . . . When this person returns to her right mind, women give various offerings to [the goddess] Artemis, especially very expensive women's robes. They are deceived, however; the fact is that the disorder is cured when nothing impedes the downward flow of blood. My prescription is that when virgins experience this trouble, they should cohabit with a man as quickly as possible. If they become pregnant, they will be cured.

Source: Mary R. Lefkowitz and Maureen B. Fant, eds., *Women's Life in Greece and Rome: A Source Book in Translation* (Baltimore: Johns Hopkins University Press, 1982).

---

ously crucial for life and also played a central role in religious and magical medicine. It was believed that the quantity of blood in the body regularly reached its height during the spring, when venesection or bloodletting would be used to drain off any harmful excess. A vein would be cut, usually in the wrist or ankle but in other parts of the body too, depending on where the physician felt the most blood had accumulated.

Biles and Phlegm. Forms of dysentery (an intestinal disorder), on the other hand, which were common in the dry, hot summer months, were often accompanied by high fever and vomiting of bile. This reaction was interpreted as the body's spontaneous attempt to purge an abnormal abundance of that fluid. Cold, damp winters, by contrast, seemed to favor overproduction of the white, sticky phlegm that caused colds and respiratory ailments. The fourth humor, black bile (*melaina kholê*), was the most mysterious of the group. It was thought to be observable in excrement and sometimes in the dark fluid of vomit, as well as in blackish, dried blood. Its seasonal peak occurred in the autumn months, dry and cold, when black bile brought on prolonged, chronic ail-

---

ments that were especially difficult to cure, owing to the humor's thick and malignant character.

Regional Differences. This apparent link between humors and seasons was further generalized into an elaborate web of regional, climatic, and meteorological links. The Hippocratic text called *On the Nature of Man* presented the theory in its most systematic form; many other texts assumed it as a basis for their own theorizing. Here the four humors are associated not only with the seasons but also with the four parts of the known world—Europe, Africa, Asia, and Greece—and thus incidentally provided a justification for racial and ethnic stereotyping. The inhabitants of the far north, for instance, dwellers in perpetual winter, tend on the whole to be white, fat, lazy, and mentally slow, because of the abundance of phlegm in their bodies. By contrast, and due to the yellow bile in which their tissues are soaked, Egyptians and Libyans are usually dry and dark, thin and easily agitated southerners. As for the Greeks themselves, they live in by far the best climate and locale in

---

EPILEPSY: DIVINE OR NATURAL?

Below are opening passages from the Hippocratic text *Sacred Disease* in which the anonymous author uses the new scalpel of logic to refute religious and magical claims about the causes of epilepsy and the ways to treat it:

I do not believe that the so-called "sacred disease" is any more divine or sacred than any other disease but, on the contrary, has specific characteristics and a definite cause. Nevertheless, because it is completely different from other diseases, it has been regarded as a divine visitation by those who . . . view it with ignorance and astonishment. The claim of divine origin is kept alive by the difficulty of understanding the malady, but destroyed by the simplistic method of healing they adopt, consisting as it does of purifications and incantations. . . . In my opinion, those who first called this disease "sacred" were the sort of people we now call witch-doctors, faith-healers, charlatans, and quacks. These are exactly the people who pretend to be very pious and to have superior knowledge. Shielding themselves by citing the divine as an excuse for their own perplexity in not knowing what treatment to apply, they held this condition to be sacred so that their ignorance might not be so obvious...

The author gives a list of traditional treatments for epilepsy, both dietary and behavioral, including ritual purifications and a prohibition against touching goats. He is quick to seize on the logical inconsistency of these prescriptions, and to draw them out to their absurd conclusion.

I suppose that none of the inhabitants of inner Libya can possibly be healthy, seeing that they sleep on goat skins and eat goat meat. In fact, they own neither blanket, clothing, nor shoe that is not made of goat skin, because goats are the only animals they have. If contact with or eating of this animal causes and exacerbates the disease while abstinence cures it, then diet alone determines the onset of the disease and its cure. Therefore no god can be blamed and the purifications are useless, and the idea of divine intervention makes no sense . . .

I believe that this disease is not in the least more divine than any other, but has the same nature as other diseases and a similar cause. Moreover, it can be cured no less than other diseases. . . . Like other diseases it is hereditary. If a phlegmatic child is born from a phlegmatic parent, a bilious child from a bilious parent . . . why should the children of a father or mother who is afflicted with this disease not suffer similarly? The seed comes from all parts of the body; it is healthy when it comes from healthy parts, diseased when it comes from diseased parts. Another important proof that this disease is no more divine than any other is the fact that the phlegmatic are constitutionally prone to it while the bilious escape. If its origin were divine, all types would be affected to the same degree.

The true cause of epilepsy, the author states with confidence, is an excess of cold, sticky phlegm in the brain. In the following passage, note first the rather vague anatomy of respiration; and second, the dual purpose ascribed to air:

Should the routes for the passage of phlegm from the brain be blocked, the discharge . . . causes loss of voice, choking, foaming at the mouth, clenching of the teeth and convulsive movements of the hands; the eyes are fixed, the patient becomes unconscious. . . . I will explain the reason for each of these signs. Loss of voice occurs when the phlegm suddenly descends and blocks the vessels so that air can pass neither to the brain nor to the body cavities. For when a man draws in breath through the mouth and nose, the air passes first to the brain, and then the greater part of it goes to the stomach, but some flows into the lungs and blood-vessels. From there it is dispensed throughout the rest of the body by means of the vessels. The air that flows into the stomach cools it, but the air that goes to the lungs and blood-vessels thence enters the body cavities and the brain and has a further purpose. It induces intelligence and is necessary for the movement of the limbs. Therefore, when the vessels are shut off from this supply of air by the accumulation of phlegm . . . the patient loses his voice and his wits. The hands become powerless and move convulsively because the blood can no longer maintain its customary flow. Divergence of the eyes takes place when the smaller blood-vessels supplying them are shut off and no longer provide an air supply; the vessels then pulsate. The froth which appears at the lips comes from the lungs, for when air no longer enters them, they produce froth . . .

Source: *Hippocratic Writings*, edited by G. E. R. Lloyd (Harmondsworth, U.K. & New York: Penguin, 1978).

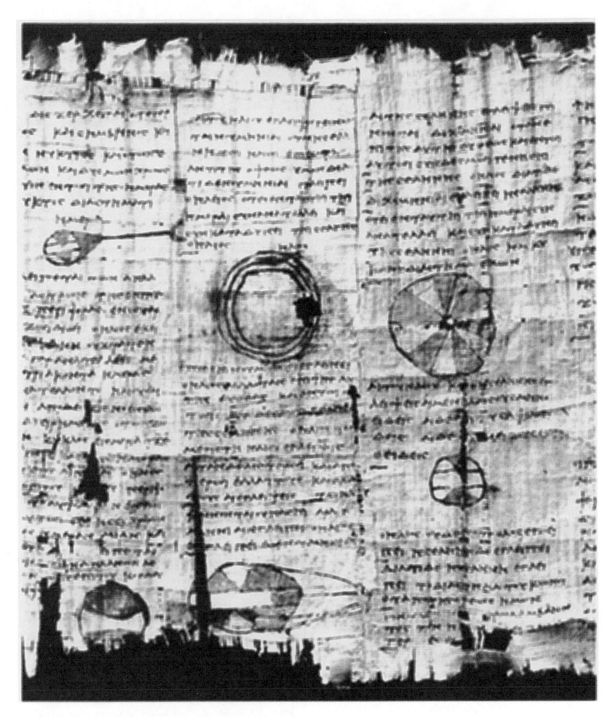

Section of an Alexandrian treatise on astronomy that depicts the movements of planets (Musée du Louvre, Paris)

the whole world, thanks to which their temperament is the most moderate, balanced, and healthiest!

Linkage. These associations provided a structure for still other links. The author of *On the Nature of Man* assigned to each humor a set of qualities—blood (hot and wet), yellow bile (hot and dry), black bile (cold and dry), phlegm (cold and wet)—and in doing so placed them into line with the quartet of elements (fire, air, earth, and water) proposed by Empedocles as the roots of reality. Over the following centuries, this highly influential theory was further expanded to include four stages of life (childhood, adolescence, adulthood, old age), four times of day, four types of fever, four colors, four flavors, four food groups, and even four emotional temperaments or personality types—sanguine, bilious, melancholy, and phlegmatic. In Christian times, the apostles Matthew, Mark, Luke, and John were also included in the linkages.

Sources:

Lawrence Conrad, and others, *The Western Medical Tradition* (Cambridge & New York: Cambridge University Press, 1995).

G. E. R. Lloyd, ed., *Hippocratic Writings* (Harmondsworth, U.K. & New York: Penguin, 1978).

Guido Majno, *The Healing Hand: Man and Wound in the Ancient World* (Cambridge, Mass.: Harvard University Press, 1975).

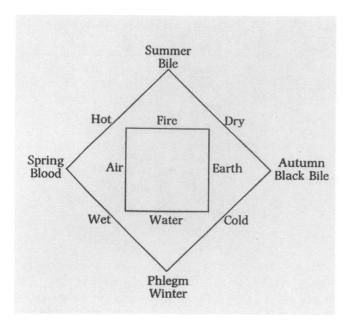

Plan of the Hippocratic humoral system

MEDICINE: THERAPY

Allopathic Remedies. Humoral theory was not just a diagnostic tool, but also provided a framework for therapy. With few exceptions, Hippocratic medicine used diet and regimen as its primary means of cure. Since disease was defined as humoral imbalance, both preventative care and restorative treatment generally took the form of allopathic remedies—that is, a cure by opposites. On the one hand, removal of excess humors was attempted by administering various purgative drugs, some of them unfortunately quite toxic. For instance hellebore, a poisonous herb of the lily family, was frequently used to induce vomiting. On the other, a careful categorization of foods and beverages in terms of what were believed to be their active qualities (hot/cold or wet/dry) offered a way of returning the patient to a balanced condition by prescribing diets to compensate for whichever humoral excess afflicted the body. Imbalances caused by an abnormal amount of black bile (cold and dry), for example, would be treated by a regimen of foods that generate heat and moisture.

Diet. It should be noted that "diet" (*diaita*) in ancient medicine had a far broader meaning than the modern term suggests and meant not simply food and drink but instead an entire style of living. Diet included exercise, bathing, and fixed routines of sleep and waking, as well as the patient's emotional state. The course of therapy, whether after the fact of disease or to prevent its occurrence, was seen as a way the doctor could assist the body's own natural tendency toward equilibrium. Illness was not a supernatural affliction but instead a rational, physiological process that ran a foreseeable course. The expert physician was the one who could accurately predict its phases and prescribe correctly at each stage.

System. The theory of the four humors clearly embodies both the strength and also the weakness of Hippocratic speculation. In this respect it is an emblem of much of ancient science as a whole, for that matter. On the one hand, it is simple, elegant, and rigorously rational. On the basis of a small number of assumptions it generated a complex, highly explanatory, and increasingly comprehensive system that put the human body at the center of a vast network of signs and events in nature. The churning humors, with their alternating cycles of hot and cold and wet and dry, were the microcosm of physical processes in the world at large, driven by the same fundamental laws that govern the production of rain, for instance, or the change from summer to fall. Time, place, climate, season, weather, temperament, age, diet, and habits were all indicators of health or disease, and also suggested the means for diagnosis and treatment. Rather than appealing to divine intervention to account for even the most bizarre and spectacular diseases—such as epilepsy, the subject of *On the Sacred Disease,* which attributes its cause not to God but to phlegm—the system rested on the rationalist foundation of early Greek physics.

PLATO ON THE ELEMENTS

In the *Timaeus* (circa 355–347 B.C.E.), Plato uses the geometrical shape of each element to explain its appearance and behavior:

First, let us ask what we mean when we say that fire is hot. We get a clue from the divisive and cutting effect it has on our bodies. We all feel that fire is sharp, and we should also consider the sharpness of the sides [of the four triangles that compose fire] . . . which make fire cut whatever it touches. We should also remember that the original [pyramidal] shape of fire, more than any other form, has a divisive ability to cut our body into small pieces. This naturally causes the sensation called heat . . .

We give earth the form of a cube, since earth is the most immovable of the four elements and the most malleable of all bodies—and whatever has this nature must necessarily also have the most stable basis. Now, of the two kinds of triangles . . . the one with two equal sides [i.e. the equilateral triangle] naturally has a firmer basis than the kind with two unequal sides [the isosceles triangle]. The cube of earth, then, is made of this former kind of triangle . . .

When earth encounters fire and is dissolved by its sharpness . . . it scatters here and there until its parts meet and blend together again and become earth once more. However, when water forms again after having first been divided by fire or air, may become one part fire and two parts air; and a single volume of air can be divided into two parts of fire . . .

Source: *The Dialogues of Plato,* fourth edition, 4 volumes, translated by Benjamin Jowett (Oxford: Clarendon Press, 1953).

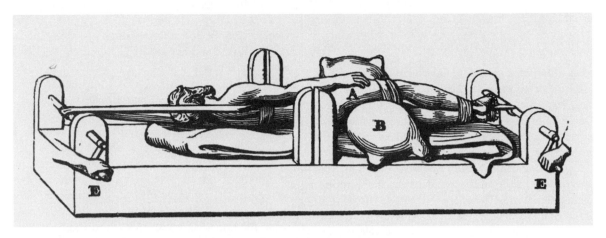

A drawing of the Hippocratic Bench which provided traction to reset fractures and heal broken bones

Speculation. At the same time, the humoral theory was obviously also sheer speculation with hardly any basis in empirical methods and real physiology. What is conspicuously lacking from a modern point of view are any signs of experimental rigor to match the rigor of theorizing. It is true that Hippocratic writers sometimes point to observable events to support their claims, as when one author refers to evidence gained from the autopsy of a goat as proof that phlegm in the brain causes epileptic seizures. For the most part, however, humoral theory developed and existed in a highly rarefied atmosphere, as a closed system that was true on its own terms and so incapable of ever being disproved. Moreover, as a framework for understanding disease and a guide for its treatment, it continued in effect for at least two millennia, well into the seventeenth century C.E., with results that often did far more harm than good to the patient. For instance, in reference to the practice of venesection to purge blood, which was still in use up until 1900, the historian Guido Majno in *The Healing Hand* (1975) remarked that "medicine has never produced a greater absurdity"—nor a more dangerous one, it might be added.

Limits. Not to minimize genuine Hippocratic contributions, however, the limits in which early Greek doctors worked must be kept in mind. Their fanciful understanding of physiology resulted from poor anatomical knowledge. This problem in turn was in large part due to strong religious prohibitions against opening the human body. The famous Hippocratic *Oath,* in fact, expressly forbids the practice of surgery. For the most part—and wisely, given the lack of sanitary conditions for treatment—invasive medical procedures were avoided.

Observation. Moreover, the *Hippocratic Corpus* does in fact also contain evidence of conscientious and detailed observation of facts. The importance of observation was especially emphasized because it provided material for the fine art of prognosis. Here the physician, after examining a patient, would try to describe the prior course of the disease and also predict its outcome. The prognosis also acted as a public display to showcase the physician's expertise—and so too the legitimacy of his profession—since "he will improve his reputation as a doctor and people will feel confident about putting themselves in his hands."

Hippocratic Faces. Therefore the authors of the books that go under the name of *Epidemics* provided careful, day-by-day descriptions of individual case histories and the climatic conditions in which they arose, sometimes covering as much as four months of continuous medical history. The text named *Prognosis* is devoted to painstaking descriptions of the patient's face, eyes, complexion, hands, feet, movements, and overall behavior—including sleep patterns, upright and recumbent posture ("how he lies in bed"), and types of breathing. These disciplined, rigorous empirical records gave rise to the so called "Hippocratic Faces," a collection of diagnostic signs to guide the physician in identifying diseases and anticipating what course they would run. The following is representative:

Nose sharp, eyes sunken, temples hollow, the ears cold and drawn back with their lobes twisted, the skin of the face hard, stretched, and dry, and its color pale or dusky. If this is the appearance of the face at the onset of the disease, and it is impossible to base a diagnosis on other signs, the patient should be asked if he has insomnia, severe diarrhea, or ravenous hunger. If he affirms any of these, the case should be considered less severe . . . since its crisis will be reached in a day and a night. But if he affirms none of them. . . .

For sheer accuracy of observation, such case histories went unrivaled for at least two thousand years. Equally valuable insights and, on the whole, more successful styles of therapy—if often painful ones—are also found in a group of texts devoted to the diagnosis and treatment of fractures, dislocations, and head wounds.

Women's Health. Several texts in the *Corpus* deal with gynecological issues. These studies of female anatomy and physiology suggest communication between the exclusively male Hippocratics and the anonymous women who treated conditions specific to women and acted as midwives. Little is known about female patients and female caregivers at this time, however, for ancient Greek culture was vigorously misogynist, denying women both a place and a voice in society.

Hysteria. The writings on female-related health issues tend to exhibit a mixture of keen observation and pure mythology, legitimate research and blind sexism. Accordingly, a male fetus grows on the right (stronger) side of the womb, a female on the left. Male sperm contributes the essential substance of the future child; the mother merely provides a place for incubation. The uterus itself, for that matter, was believed to be an independent and highly mobile organ, which sometimes "wandered" through the body in search of the vital moisture it craved. By squeezing or knocking against other organs in the course of its travels, it drove young women to fits of nervous anxiety, giddiness, delirium, spells of choking and fainting—in short, to what was called "hysteria," from the Greek word *hustera,* meaning "womb." In such cases most doctors prescribed marriage as a cure.

Embryology. Medical theory intersected philosophical ideas in the case of embryology. The treatise *On the Nature of the Child* is remarkable as the first systematic observation on record of the development of an embryo, using hen's eggs incubated over a period of twenty days. For the most part, however, such empirical work took second place to debate over the much broader issues of generation and growth. Here the main question was that of the nature of the plant or animal seed, and how a fully formed and differentiated being could grow from it. The answer proposed and generally accepted by physicians and philosophers alike was that the seed is composed of elements drawn and distilled from every part of the body, and therefore essentially contains each of its substances—tissue, bone, hair, blood, and so on.

Interdependence. The resemblance between this theory—known as *pangenesis* (Greek *paggenesis*)—and theories put forward by some of the pluralists and atomists is obvious. It emphasizes how interdependent all branches of what are now distinguished as separate disciplines—philosophy, physics, chemistry, biology, medicine—originally were. Many physicians were at the same time practicing philosophers, in fact, and quite a few physicists dabbled in medicine. It also points to the ongoing, open, and interdisciplinary nature of research in fifth- and fourth-century Greece.

Sources:
Lawrence Conrad, and others, *The Western Medical Tradition* (Cambridge & New York: Cambridge University Press, 1995).

G. E. R. Lloyd, ed., *Hippocratic Writings* (Harmondsworth, U.K. & New York: Penguin, 1978).

Guido Majno, *The Healing Hand: Man and Wound in the Ancient World* (Cambridge, Mass.: Harvard University Press, 1975).

THE SCIENCE OF PLATO

Impact. Plato is now best known as the main representative of idealist philosophy in the West and the founder of the Academy, the first Western university. He is far less often recognized, however, as a mathematical philosopher (or philosophical mathematician), even though that is how he might have preferred to describe himself.

Forms. His purely philosophical activity also influenced Greek scientific research, although that influence was certainly a mixed and not always encouraging one. Plato's idealism on the whole tended to devalue the world of the senses as an unstable realm of continual "coming-to-be" and "passing-away." It is but a pale shadow of the real world of the Forms. If the world we perceive is unreal, however, then research into natural phenomena is correspondingly of less value and importance than efforts to comprehend the ideal Forms on which things in our world are modeled. Truth is to be found not in the visible but instead in the intelligible world and must be accessed by reason and not by sensory experience. Why waste time using the imperfect senses to learn more about a world that is ultimately an illusion?

Parmenides. In his epistemological position, Plato clearly owed much to Parmenides, who likewise rejected the senses in favor of pure, abstract logic. On these terms, Plato judged the value of a particular line of scientific research by how much it uncovered patterns in the natural world that pointed the mind toward the eternal, ideal realm of changeless Being. For the most part, only geometry and astronomy, both highly mathematical, seemed to live up to this high standard. The emphasis here on mathematics also reveals a Pythagorean influence on Plato.

Cosmology. Central to an understanding of Platonic science is the late dialogue known as the *Timaeus* (circa 355 to 347 B.C.E.). There, Plato gives what he calls a "plausible story"—the best that can be offered, given the fact that it aims to explain the dim world of the senses. Specifically, he provides an account of the arrangement of all things in the world by a divine artisan or Demiurge (*dêmiourgos*). Unlike the God of the Judeo-Christian and Islamic traditions, the Demiurge is not a creator in the strict sense of the word, since he works with preexistent matter. Further, he is not even all-powerful, since matter itself can stubbornly resist his efforts to form it in one way or another. He is instead a god who shapes, and who does so by keeping one eye fixed on the eternal Forms, which provide him with patterns for the things in this world. From this starting point, and in the form of a mythic tale that perhaps should not be not taken too literally, Plato goes on to construct an entire cosmology. It intends it to be as comprehensive as possible, combining mathematics, physics, biology, and physiology into a unique and complex system.

Geometrical Shapes. His debts to earlier Greek thinkers are fairly easy to identify. From Empedocles he borrowed the notion that all substances are compounded from the four basic "roots," earth, water, air, and fire. In a much more radical move, however, and certainly with Pythagorean inspiration, he identified each of these four with a solid geometrical form. Fire is a four-sided figure, or tetrahedron, and resembles a pyramid. Earth is a cube and thus has six sides. Air is an octahedron, or eight-sided polygon. The last and most complex element, finally, is the twenty-sided icosahedron of water. Greek geometry, whose exact details in the century before Plato are hazy at best,

For before the heavens came into being, there were no days or nights, no months or years. But now, at the same time as [the Demiurge] framed the heavens, he devised their coming into being. . . . Time, then, came into being together with the universe so that just as they were begotten together, they might also be undone together, should there ever be an undoing of them. . . . He brought into being the Sun, the Moon, and five other stars, in order to create time. These are called 'wanderers' [*planêtai*], and they came into being to set limts to and stand guard over the counting of time. When the god had finished making a body for each of them, he placed them into [seven] orbits. He set the Moon in the first circle, around the earth, and the Sun in the second, above it. The Dawnbringer [the Morning Star, or Venus] and the star said to be sacred to Hermes [Mercury] he set to run in circles that equal the Sun's in speed . . .

Source: *The Dialogues of Plato,* fourth edition, 4 volumes, translated by Benjamin Jowett (Oxford: Clarendon Press, 1953).

had already determined that these four shapes—plus a fifth, the dodecahedron (twelve sides)—are the only regular geometrical solids.

Triangles. Plato then went on to analyze each of these shapes even further, namely into a combination of one or the other of two basic types of triangles: the right and the equilateral. Two right isosceles triangles, for instance, or else four equilateral ones, can be joined to form one face of a cube; the whole solid itself, then, would equal 6 x 4 or 24 triangles. The element air, identified with an octahedron, can be broken down into eight such triangles; water, the icosahedron, is made up of twenty.

Problem of Change. Bizarre as this theory might seem to modern eyes, it makes sense and even has some recognizable strengths within its own. To begin with, it marks an advance over Empedocles and the other Pluralists, since it reduces their four elements to a single, fundamental reality. Moreover, by analyzing fire, air, water, and earth into four, eight, twenty, and twenty-four triangles, respectively, it takes care of a major problem that the Empedoclean system leaves unresolved. According to Empedocles, each of the four roots is fundamental and basic, in the sense that it is incapable of any further analysis. Air, for instance, cannot be broken down into smaller, constituent parts, nor can it ever change into anything else—despite the fact that direct observation offers plenty of evidence that air indeed condenses into water, and water evaporates into air. How can these simple changes be explained if each of the four roots permanently keeps its own form?

Transformation. Plato's composite elements, by contrast, can be easily transformed into one another by the simple addition or subtraction of the triangles out of which they are

made. Remove two triangles from earth, for instance, and the result will be fire. This results in a kind of chemistry of combinations and proportions that is similar to the one that Empedocles proposed, but which operates on a much more fundamental level. Further, Empedocles' vague talk of "four parts fire, two parts water, two parts earth" as a recipe for the production of "bone," for example, could now be replaced by seemingly more precise mathematical formulas, such as the one Plato offers to account for how (one icosahedron of) water changes in the process of boiling into (two octahedra of) air and (one tetrahedron of) fire: $20 = \{2 \times 8\} + 4$.

Math and Nature. What is perhaps most important of all about the cosmological account in the *Timaeus* is the fact that it completes the project begun by the Pythagoreans. In their belief that numbers are the basic reality, the Pythagoreans had sought (both mystically and mathematically) to uncover the hidden numerical structure of the world. In this respect, they mathematized nature. Plato's own work in the *Timaeus* carries this process to its logical conclusion by identifying ultimate reality with geometrical forms. The earlier Greek thinkers were materialists: the fundamental "stuff" of the world was always seen by them as precisely that— "stuff"—that is, as a physical entity. Although Plato's four elements (earth, air, fire, and water) are material, however, his system reduced them to the far more abstract, nonmaterial shapes of the triangles. The physical world could now be constructed, broken down, and remade again by combining geometrical parts. Once this had been accomplished, the old questions of what reality is made of and how it undergoes all its innumerable changes seemed that much closer to being resolved. Moreover, the preferred language in which acceptable answers to these questions were to be cast was from then on decidedly the language of mathematics.

Sources:

D. R. Dicks, *Early Greek Astronomy to Aristotle* (Ithaca, N.Y.: Cornell University Press, 1970).

David C. Lindberg, *The Beginnings of Western Science: The European Scientific Tradition in Philosophical, Religious, and Institutional Context, 600 B.C.E. to C.E. 1450* (Chicago: University of Chicago Press, 1992).

Samuel Sambursky, *The Physical World of the Greeks* (New York: Macmillan, 1956).

THE SCIENCE OF PLATO: ASTRONOMY

Planes. The *Timaeus* is not limited to mathematical cosmology. It also covers issues of astronomy, biology, and human physiology. In Plato's astronomical scheme, for instance, a spherical earth lies at the center of a greater sphere of the heavens, on whose inner surface the stars are embedded like bright nails. As the outer sphere turns, the stars are carried around the earth in a daily rotation. The sun, moon, and the other planets revolve at different speeds around what is known as the ecliptic. If the earth's equator is extended outward to the sphere of the fixed stars, it forms a plane called the celestial equator. The ecliptic is an imaginary circular plane tilted about twenty-three degrees to the celestial equator. The path of the sun along the ecliptic intersects the celestial equator at the fall and spring equinoxes, the two days each year when day and night have equal lengths.

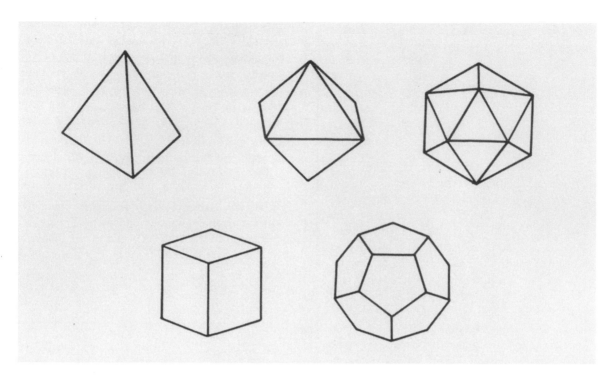

The five geometrical solids of Plato: tetrahedron, octahedron, icosahedron (l.-r., top row); cube and dodecahedron (l.-r., bottom row) (Courtesy of J.V. Field)

Planetary Motion. It was well known in the ancient world that the planets sometimes move erratically. At times they seem to change speed—to speed up or slow down—in their revolution "around the earth," and sometimes they even appear to move backward. One of Plato's most significant contributions to astronomy was his claim that these apparently irrational movements could be explained by supposing that each planet moved on not one but several circular tracks. He proposed that planetary motion should be thought of as a combination of orbits within orbits, in which the clockwise turns of one track, for instance, would cause the adjacent track to move counterclockwise, and so on. This view, he felt, might result in the creation of a regular, geometrical model of what looked like highly irregular behavior. If successful, what better example could there be of discovering order behind disorder, and so of "saving the phenomena"? The impact of this notion on Greek and much of later western astronomy was to be profound.

Astronomy. It is indeed in the science of astronomy that the ancient Greeks made their greatest and most influential advances. Here more than in any other field of research, mathematical and mechanical models were constructed, applied, analyzed, challenged, then further refined and applied again in an effort to "save the phenomena."

Turning Point. The fourth century B.C.E. marks a turning point in early astronomical work. Prior to this period, there was Anaximander's sixth-century model. He had proposed a system in which sun, moon, and stars orbit a cylindrical earth on tracks whose diameters are respectively twenty-seven, eighteen, and nine times earth's diameter. His theory clearly owes more to love of symmetry than any empirical observation Anaximander ever could have made.

Philolaos. The Pythagoreans, too, had speculated about the nature and shape of the heavens. Philolaos, a member of the group who lived in the last half of the fifth century, surprisingly theorized that the earth is not located at the center of the universe, but instead orbits around a "central fire." He further theorized that another or "counter-earth" orbited the fire at a point always precisely opposite the position of the earth and was therefore never actually visible to us. He is said to have used its existence to explain why lunar eclipses happen more often than eclipses of the sun.

Practical Applications. The observation of the heavens also had practical value in the ancient world. To begin with, it was regularly carried out as part of such nontheoretical business as farming and navigation. For Greeks no less than for the Babylonians long before them, constellations marked off cardinal points, provided means of keeping time, and also predicted seasonal change. A considerable body of oral, anonymous lore had developed on this basis and was used both for reckoning at sea and also to determine cycles of planting and harvest.

Calendars. The need for accurate civic and religious calendars likewise encouraged astronomical observation, since here precise counting was required to measure the terms of public offices and to establish the all-important dates of festivals in honor of the gods. This need was especially great given the fact that the ancient Greek world traditionally measured time on the basis of the phases of the moon. Such lunar calendars had months of roughly twenty-nine or thirty days, resulting in a twelve-month year about 348 days long. This lunar year had to be reconciled somehow with the somewhat greater number of days (365) that resulted when a year was measured by the course of the sun.

Intercalation. Around 432 B.C.E. Meton of Athens accurately calculated how many additional or intercalary days should be added to the lunar calendar over the course of a nineteen-year cycle in order to bring it into alignment with the solar calendar. One of his contemporaries, Euctemon, also measured the exact lengths of each of the four seasons, based on careful observations of the equinoxes and solstices. (The solstices, in June and December, are the two days on which the sun reaches its farthest northern and southern positions along the ecliptic.)

Irregularities. The primary aim of fourth-century Greek astronomy was the task set for it by Plato. In the *Timaeus* he had proposed that it should be possible to construct a rational, geometric account of the motion of the stars, sun, moon, and the five known planets (Mercury, Venus, Mars, Jupiter, and Saturn). From the viewpoint of an observer on earth, their movements exhibit both orderliness and also strange, puzzling irregularities. Plato's challenge was to design a model that would save those irregularities by making them regular and rational.

Celestial Movement. In order to construct a geometric model that would precisely reproduce these movements, several different motions had to be taken into consideration:

(1) On the one hand, there is the steady, daily revolution of all the celestial bodies around the earth from east to west—or so it seemed, assuming a geocentric universe, namely one in which the earth rests unmoving at the center while all the other heavenly bodies turn around it;

(2) Over the course of many weeks and months of nights, the constellations also seem to follow a longer, slower orbital path from east to west. Some disappear from view at certain seasons, but then always reappear in roughly the same place in the sky at roughly the same time each year. Their imaginary track through the heavens forms the circle or belt called the zodiac;

(3) Further, the sun, moon, and planets themselves move in the opposite direction, from west to east, against the background of constellations. They all follow the same path—the tilted orbit known as the ecliptic—but they do so at varying speeds, ranging from a single month for the moon to nearly thirty years for the planet Saturn to make one zodiacal orbit;

(4) Most problematic of all were the "stations" and "retrograde" movements of the planets. The name *planet* in fact derives from the Greek verb *planasthai*, which means "to wander." Unlike the sun, moon, and "fixed" stars, the planets moved irregularly and therefore required a special explanation. When observed over the length of a year, planets such as Mars seem to stop in the course of their normal, easterly movement through the zodiac and to hold still for several nights. They then appear to move backward (retrograde), east to west, sometimes for as long as a month, before continuing on an easterly course again.

Apparent Anomalies. Plato's challenge to the students in his Academy, to the astronomers of his own and later generations, was to produce a systematic account of this peculiar and seemingly unsystematic motion. Here it is important to

WHY SNAKES HAVE NO FEET

In the following passage from his work *Parts of Animals* (circa 335 B.C.E.), Aristotle applies his classification of animals into blooded and bloodless, along with his notion of immanent teleology—the fact that every single thing in nature has an innate purpose—to explain why snakes have no feet:

The reason for the footlessness of snakes is that nature does nothing in vain but in every case looks out for the best possible arrangement for each thing, saving its special entity and essence. Besides, as we have said before, no blooded animal can move at more than four points [that is, they can have no more than four feet]. Clearly, those blooded animals that are disproportionately long in relation to the rest of their body, as are snakes, cannot have feet. For they are not the sort to have more than four—then they would be bloodless [such as insects, for instance]—but with two or four feet they would be practically immobile, so slow and useless the movement would have to be.

Source: Anthony Preus, *Science and Philosophy in Aristotle's Biological Works* (Hildesheim, Germany & New York: G. Olms, 1975).

note Plato's underlying assumption—characteristically Greek, and at the same time also characteristically scientific—that these anomalies are not real but instead only apparent. Behind those visible oddities, Plato believed, are movements that are actually uniform, orderly, and mathematically expressible. This assumption still motivates modern astronomy, along with all the other sciences of the West. The actual search for a solution to the problem of planetary motion as Plato had posed it in fact occupied Western astronomers for the next two thousand years.

Eudoxus of Cnidus. The challenge was taken up first by Plato's own associate, the astronomer Eudoxus of Cnidus (circa 408–355 B.C.E.). He was indeed a gifted polymath with a rather broad range of interests. The tradition credits him with research on mathematics, geography, medicine, and music along with astronomy. Precious little of his work survives, however, and his writings are on the whole patched together from quotations found in the works of Aristotle and Simplicius, a scholar of the sixth century C.E.

Eudoxan Model. Eudoxus's solution to the problem of how celestial bodies move was to propose not one but a whole series of four simple, circular movements for each of the planets, and three each for the sun and moon. The result is a highly ingenious geometrical model. Spheres within spheres within spheres move in complex, contrary rotations, like cogs in a machine, all perfectly regular and orderly. The combined movements all together produce the illusion of irregular, wandering planets.

Rotating Spheres. In his solution, each of the four spheres assigned to a planet produces one element of its total movement. To understand how it works, imagine the earth surrounded by four concentric, turning spheres; these constitute the system of a single planet—Mars, for instance. The planet itself rides along the equator of the smallest or innermost sphere (D), but its overall movement is also a result of the motions of each of the three increasingly larger ones (C, B, and A). Their motions are as follows: the largest and outermost sphere (A) turns from east to west once every twenty-four hours on an axis that runs north to south. This motion accounts for how, to a terrestrial observer, Mars seems to orbit the earth at just that speed. Modern astronomy, of course, now correctly attributes this to Earth's own rotation. The next sphere (B) rotates far more slowly and in the opposite direction, west to east, against the backdrop of the constellations. It turns once every twenty-two months, since this period is the actual time it takes Mars to complete one circuit through the zodiac. Rather than being perfectly north-south, the axis of this second sphere is tilted a little, at right angles to the ecliptic. This detail helps account for apparent changes in the speed and position of Mars at various times over the course of two years. As for the motions of the two innermost spheres (C and D), these are the most important. Eudoxus designed them to account for the bizarre stations and retrograde movements that drew so much scientific attention to the planets in the ancient world. After all, this is what had motivated Plato's demand for a rational solution in the first place. By tilting the axes of these two spheres at certain specific angles to each other, and by making them rotate in opposite directions at equal speeds, Eudoxus produced the appearance of a curving movement called a *hippopede*, or "horse-fetter."

Planetary Paths. The hippopede is a path shaped like a figure eight. As Mars moves back and forth along it, the planet makes a looping motion. This configuration combines with its slow, easterly movement along the zodiacal track and the fast east-west spin of its daily rotation to create the illusion of a planet that periodically stops, stands still, goes back, and then moves again. From the fixed point of an astronomer on earth, the model Eudoxus proposed seemed to answer Plato's challenge successfully.

Mathematical Theory. The Eudoxan solution is a remarkably imaginative leap. It moves from erratic, irregular sensory data to a vision of the uniform and orderly events that can explain them. Moreover, it is a leap of the mind more than the eye, an astonishing stretch of the imagination, guided by rules of geometry. It is a feat of sheer mathematical theorizing, for in the absence of telescopes and other tools for measurement it completely lacked empirical support.

Revisions. The model has many weaknesses. In particular, it could not account for changes in planetary brightness. From observation, any given planet regularly gets dimmer at certain times of year, then brighter again—a fact which modern astronomy explains in terms of its varying distance from earth. Nonetheless, the model designed by Eudoxus established the standard pattern for addressing the question of how planets move. Later astronomers tinkered with his geometry, adding or subtracting orbital paths in ever more ingenious and intricate combinations to pro-

duce the observed effect. Eudoxus had proposed a total of twenty-seven spheres as the minimum number necessary to replicate the apparent movements of the planets. They were increased to thirty-four by Callippus of Cyzicus, an astronomer who lived around 330 B.C.E. Aristotle added an additional twenty-two spheres, to bring the total number up to fifty-six. Heraclides of Pontus (fl. 350 B.C.E.) complicated the model even further by proposing a theory of "epicycles." According to this approach, the planets Venus and Mercury actually orbit the sun while the sun itself orbits the earth. He is also credited with the striking minority view that the earth itself rotates on an axis while the surrounding heavens stay at rest!

Elliptical Model. The strange movements of the planets remained a central problem for astronomy for nearly two millennia after Plato had first made it a scientific challenge. In fact, not until the seventeenth century were models in which the planets move around inside perfectly circular spheres finally abandoned. They were then replaced by a model in which their orbits are instead elliptical. The one who proposed this new shape was none other than the great German scientist Johannes Kepler (1571–1630), one of the founders of modern astronomy. The various solutions to Plato's problem indeed changed over time, and new tools—such as the telescope, first used after 1609—brought the heavens ever closer to the eye. What never changed, however, was the demand that had first been expressed by the ancient Greeks. The observable phenomena far in the sky, above and around the earth, had to be "saved" by constructing models of the universe that conformed to laws of geometry. The orderliness of those far distant worlds was first dreamed of in the mathematical imagination of ancient Greeks.

Sources:

D. R. Dicks, *Early Greek Astronomy to Aristotle* (Ithaca, N.Y.: Cornell University Press, 1970).

David C. Lindberg, *The Beginnings of Western Science: The European Scientific Tradition in Philosophical, Religious, and Institutional Context, 600 B.C.E. to C.E. 1450* (Chicago: University of Chicago Press, 1992).

Samuel Sambursky, *The Physical World of the Greeks* (New York: Macmillan, 1956).

THE SCIENTIFIC RESEARCH OF ARISTOTLE

Breadth and Scope. In Aristotle there is a consistent pattern of deliberate, conscientious research on as broad a range of scientific fields as were recognized in antiquity, along with the creation of entirely new fields that had previously been unknown: logic, epistemology, cosmology, medicine, physiology, psychology, biology, zoology, botany, optics, acoustics, physics, dynamics, mathematics, astronomy, rhetoric, political science, ethics, and literary theory. Roughly 30 of his more than 150 books have survived. It should also be remembered that Aristotle was as deeply committed to teaching and cooperative work as he was to independent research. Just as important as his own writings, therefore, is the long tradition of scientific research that he set in motion and that continued to operate through many later generations of researchers, teachers, and students at the Lyceum.

Rules of Logic. Aristotle gave a remarkable degree of attention to the language of science and the structure of scientific claims. This approach was partly his response to the epistemological problems Greek philosophers and scientists had faced for at least one hundred years. It will be remembered that in the early fifth century, Parmenides profoundly influenced the direction of Greek science and philosophy by using the new tool of logic to construct an argument that made rational sense but at the same time seemed to contradict everything the five senses suggested about the world. Whether one supported or rejected Parmenides' argument, all subsequent thinkers nonetheless at least had to conform to the same rules of logic he had used.

Apodeixis. Aristotle's concern with scientific language was partly also his own recognition that claims must meet rigorous criteria and standards in order to be true. If *epistêmê* (scientific knowledge) is genuine, after all, it must be based on *apodeixis* (valid proof). How, then, is it possible to recognize when a proof is valid or not? Are there rules that govern how valid proofs are put together? Are there logical steps that can be taken to test an argument for fallacies and inconsistencies? Are there clear, objective measures that can be applied to any given claim in order to refute it if it is false and confirm it if it is true?

The Tool. In a group of books known collectively as the *Organon* (circa 335 B.C.E.), Aristotle carefully analyzed these and similar questions. The result of his efforts is a finely detailed and rigorously argued exposition of the nature of reasoning. Here, and for the first time in any consistent and comprehensive way, he established the structure of valid, logical demonstrations and mapped out the shape of different kinds of premises—axioms, definitions, hypotheses—that provide the starting points for scientific claims about the world. He categorized types of arguments, investigated their forms, distinguished between abstract and empirical claims, and spelled out the basic rules an argument must follow in order to be logical. He then went on to determine what degrees of certainty each different branch of science was capable of giving, based on the kinds of proofs it was able to offer for its claims. The Greek word *organon* means "utensil" or "implement," and in this painstaking work on the grammar of proofs, Aristotle indeed fashioned a tool that has shaped and continues to shape all later scientific discourse.

Criteria. For Aristotle, scientific knowledge is knowledge of the essential *aitiai* (causes) of any given thing. These causes are four in number, and in the case of any given thing it is necessary for all of them to be investigated and identified before true knowledge of that thing is possible. A valid, scientific account of something—whether it is inanimate (stone, water, spoon) or living (tree, animal, person), artificial (statue, table, machine) or natural (catfish, flower, embryo)—must fully explain: what it is made of; what shape or form it has; what made it what it is; and what purpose or function it serves.

Four Causes. These four criteria correspond to what are usually termed the *material cause, formal cause, efficient (moving) cause,* and *final (telic) cause.* They form the basis not only of Aristotelian physics, but also of his understanding of each and every thing and event in the world as a whole. They provide the basic answers to every question that can possibly be asked, from why a rock falls when dropped to what kind of life a human being ought to live. For example, a chair mostly has wood as its material cause; this is what it is made of. Its formal cause is what makes this mass of wood a chair and not, say, a bookshelf or a coatrack or a desk. In a word, the formal cause accounts for its shape, which clearly does much to define what any given lump of matter is. This chair was made in a factory by a worker, who thus provided its motive or efficient cause, namely, the series of acts by which the wood took on its shape. Finally, this chair was made for a specific purpose—its final or telic cause—which is to support persons comfortably as they sit.

Nature. Of course, the same truths hold for natural no less than artificial things. For instance, an acorn's material cause is the woody stuff it is made of. Its formal cause is identical with the shape it has, which distinguishes it as an acorn and not, for example, a pine cone. Its efficient cause is the oak tree that produced it. (Notice here that the efficient cause is not necessarily the same as a human agent; it does not matter that the tree was not conscious of producing the acorn.) Last, its final cause is the goal toward which the acorn naturally tends, namely to grow into an adult oak itself.

Interpretations. Obviously, the idea of "cause" is somewhat narrower for many people than it was for Aristotle. People generally mean by it the individual or thing that directly produces a certain effect. That is to say, people tend to identify cause with what Aristotle calls the efficient cause. His idea of material and formal causes was meant as a direct response to Plato, whose philosophy of idealism made the ideal Form alone real and entirely detached from matter. For Aristotle, on the contrary, form and matter are inseparable. Although the word *dog* can be defined in a universal way, so as to include all real dogs in its description, there is still no ideal Dog apart from actual, living ones.

Final Cause. By far the most important of the causes for Aristotle, however, is the final or telic one—from the Greek word *telos,* meaning "end" or "goal." Its sense is clear in the case of an artificial thing like a chair, since here the final cause is identical to the purpose or function for which the craftsman made it. Final causes also operate in the world of natural things, as in the case of the mature oak that is the ultimate goal of the acorn's development. There is a major difference between the final cause of artificial and natural things, however. As far as the natural world goes, Aristotle firmly insists

ARISTOTLE ON EMBRYOLOGY

Aristotle's description of the "navel-string" links embryo to placenta in a species of dog-fish called the "smooth shark." Disbelieved for nearly two millennia, its existence was finally confirmed by researchers in the middle of the nineteenth century.

The so-called smooth shark has its eggs in between the wombs, like the dog-fish; these eggs shift into each of the two horns of the womb and descend, and the young develop with the navel-string attached to the womb. . . . The navel-string is long and adheres to the underside of the womb—each string being attached as it were by a sucker—and also the center of the embryo in the place where the liver is situated. . . . When young, the embryo has its head pointing upwards, but downwards when it becomes strong and has completed its growth. Males are generated on the left-hand side of the womb, and females on the right-hand side, and males and females on the same side together. If the embryo is cut open, then its internal organs (such as the liver) are found to be large and supplied with blood, just as in quadrupeds.

A passage from Aristotle's description of the development of a chicken embryo, another classic example of meticulous empirical observation:

When the egg is now ten days old the chick and all the parts are distinctly visible. The head is still larger than the rest of the body, and the eyes larger than the head, but still sightless. The eyes, if removed about this time, are found to be larger than beans, and black; if the outer membrane is peeled off, there is a white and cold liquid inside, which glitters quite a bit in the sunlight, but there is no hard substance at all. Such is the condition of the head and eyes. At this time also the larger internal organs are visible, along with the stomach and the arrangement of the viscera; and the veins that stretch from the heart are now close to the navel. A pair of veins extends from the navel, one toward the membrane that envelops the yoke—which, by the way, is now liquid—and the other towards the membrane that contains both of the others: namely, the membrane within which the chick lies and the membrane of the yolk, along with the intervening liquid. On the tenth day the white is at the extreme outer surface, reduced in quantity, glutinous, firm, and with a pale color.

Source: *The Complete Works of Aristotle, The Revised Oxford Translation*, edited by Jonathan Barnes (Princeton: Princeton University Press, 1984).

---

guins, not mice. Democritus and the Atomists had claimed that all things in the world are the temporary result of purely random atomic collisions. Atoms bump into each other by chance and stick together to form certain objects, which break up when a stronger outside force splits them apart again. On the contrary, Aristotle claims that each and every natural thing exhibits a genuine purposiveness. Propelled by an inner drive—an immanent teleology—each moves steadily toward realizing its own specific kind of perfection. Each strives to actualize its innate potential.

Actual v. Potential. The distinction between what is *energeia* (actual) and what is *dunamis* (potential), in fact, was the key to Aristotle's approach to the old Parmenidean dilemma of change. The puzzle had already been occupying Greek thinkers for more than a century: How can something come into being? Not from nothing ("what is not"), since nothing does not exist. Not from something, for whatever already exists is already in existence, and therefore has no need to come into being at all. Aristotle's concept of dunamis neatly cuts through that logical knot. An acorn, for example, indeed is an oak, at least in the sense that it has the potential to grow into one; while in another sense, it is not actually an oak at all. It has the dunamis to be something else, even if this other something has not yet been actualized in the world. The concept of potential thus lets something come into being from nothing, namely from what does not really exist yet. Change—the movement from being potential to being actual—is logically possible after all. The evidence of the senses, which show us a world of constant change, is finally vindicated!

Sources:

J. L. Ackrill, *Aristotle the Philosopher* (Oxford & New York: Oxford University Press, 1981).

Jonathan Barnes, *Aristotle* (Oxford & New York: Oxford University Press, 1982).

D. R. Dicks, *Early Greek Astronomy to Aristotle* (Ithaca, N.Y.: Cornell University Press, 1970).

Pierre Pellegrin, *Aristotle's Classification of Animals*, translated by Anthony Preus (Berkeley: University of California Press, 1986).

Samuel Sambursky, *The Physical World of the Greeks* (London: Routledge & Kegan Paul, 1956).

TELEOLOGY OF ARISTOTLE

Biology and Physiology. Aristotle applied his ideas of dunamis and immanent teleology most successfully in his works on biology and physiology. These subjects account for the largest share of his extant writings, in fact, and include such important texts as *History of Animals, Parts of Animals, Movement of Animals, Generation of Animals,* and the group of essays known as the *Short Natural Histories* or *Parua Naturalia.* These volumes, all of which were written sometime around 335 B.C.E., exhibit Aristotle's best balance between theory and observation.

Specimens. His research on plants and animals is indeed remarkable for its depth of detail and empirical rigor. These

---

that no god exercises providential control over things and that nature itself also has no deliberate, conscious aim. That is to say, there is no equivalent in nature to the craftsman in the realm of art and manufacturing.

Immanent Teleology. The different ends toward which natural things grow—seeds into plants, for instance, or children into adults—are instead internal or immanent in the things themselves. Acorns naturally become oaks, not pine trees; penguins give birth to pen-

qualities were generally lacking among the earlier Greek scientists, who tended to devote themselves more to theoretical speculation than to observation and experiment. Relying on specimens gathered widely throughout the known world, however, Aristotle himself distinguished more than five hundred different species of animals, performed frequent dissections, and made precise records of anatomical descriptions. His discussion of unusual features of the placenta of a species of dogfish, for example, was finally verified in the middle of the nineteenth century. All of this highly detailed work was accomplished without the aid of any modern instruments such as the magnifying glass and microscope. The overall system of zoological classification (taxonomy) he constructed remained in effect until the great Swedish biologist Linnaeus in the eighteenth century.

Reproduction. Aristotle's investigations in this field were not limited to anatomy and classification, however, but also ranged widely and deeply over physiology, nutrition and growth, locomotion, sensation, and reproduction. With reference to this last topic, Aristotle used rigorous logic to reject the idea of pangenesis. Most of the Hippocratic medical writers had believed that in both plants and animals, the seed draws its material from the parent's whole body. Aristotle proposed instead the idea that the male parent supplies the formal and the efficient cause of the offspring, whereas the female contributes only the matter. This approach was consistent both with his theory of four causes and with his sexism as well.

Nutritive Soul. Aristotle was also deeply interested in the variety of living creatures in nature and what accounted for the differences among them. In *History of Animals* and especially in *On the Soul* (circa 335 B.C.E.), he identified the soul of a living creature with its formal cause, in the belief that form is what provides each thing with its true definition and essential characteristics. For Aristotle, the entire natural world is a vast hierarchy of different types of souls. Plants have what he termed a nutritive soul, which is the cause of their growth, nourishment, and reproduction.

Sensitive Soul. According to Aristotle, animals are superior to plants because, in addition to a nutritive soul, they also have a sensitive soul, which gives animals the ability to experience their surroundings. Among animals as a class, moreover, there is a hierarchy that runs from those that possess only one of the senses—clams, for instance—right up to the higher animals, which have all five. Aristotle also felt that the sensitive soul in animals that have all or at least most of the five senses gives them the power of locomotion. Since they can fully sense the world, they can also move toward what is good and away from what harms them.

Rational Soul. At the top of the hierarchy of earthly creatures come human beings. Along with the capacities of growth, nourishment, reproduction, sensation, and locomotion, people also have the higher capacity of reason. According to Aristotle, the rational soul makes reason possible.

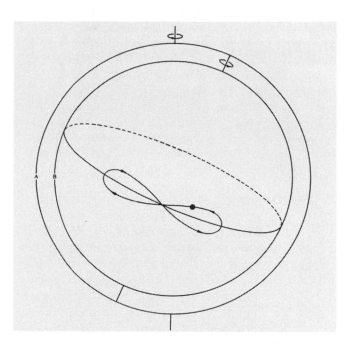

A diagram of the Eudoxan spheres and hippopede

Chain of Being. This graduated scale is indeed just one series of links in a much larger Chain of Being, which stretches from the lowest to the highest order of things, both inanimate and living. Here Aristotle used his theory of causes and his idea of immanent teleology as explanatory tools to connect all things in the universe into a single, systematic, comprehensive, and rational whole. At the same time, the hierarchical order of things in the world is reflected in a similar ordering of all the branches of science that study them.

Matter and Elements. At the lowest link in the chain is pure matter; it is the material out of which everything is made, but it lacks form and purpose. Next come the four elements (earth, air, fire, water), which Aristotle borrowed from Empedocles. Plato did the same thing, but whereas he went on to analyze the elements into abstract geometric entities, Aristotle reduced them to combinations of sensible qualities (hot/cold and wet/dry). Their character and behavior are completely determined by what Aristotle identified as their formal and final causes. It should come as no surprise that, even though they are inanimate, each of the four elements nonetheless still exhibits immanent teleology. Fire naturally moves up, for instance, away from the center of the world, while rocks move in the opposite direction. For Aristotle, this movement does not happen because of the force of gravity. In fact, the true nature of gravity was not fully appreciated for more than two thousand years after Aristotle, until Sir Isaac Newton formulated his famous law of gravitation in the seventeenth century. Instead, Aristotle believed the behavior of a falling rock must be explained in terms of its natural tendency to move downward. Because it is made of earth, it naturally moves toward the place where the greatest mass of earth is located.

Sources:

J. L. Ackrill, *Aristotle the Philosopher* (Oxford & New York: Oxford University Press, 1981).

Jonathan Barnes, *Aristotle* (Oxford & New York: Oxford University Press, 1982).

D. R. Dicks, *Early Greek Astronomy to Aristotle* (Ithaca, N.Y.: Cornell University Press, 1970).

Pierre Pellegrin, *Aristotle's Classification of Animals,* translated by Anthony Preus (Berkeley: University of California Press, 1986).

Samuel Sambursky, *The Physical World of the Greeks* (London: Routledge & Kegan Paul, 1956).

THE UNMOVED MOVER AND ARISTOTLE: COSMOLOGY

Dynamics. In his *Physics* (circa 335 B.C.E.), Aristotle was the first to formulate and then explore such common Western scientific concepts as force, movement, speed, place, weight, mass, distance, and resistance. He used them to develop a theory to account for what he called "forced" or "unnatural motion" here on earth. Natural motion occurs when an object obeys its immanent tendency to move, as when a rock falls down. Unnatural motion, on the other hand, is motion that is imparted to a body from the outside, as when a rock is thrown up in the air, against its nature. Aristotle's *Physics* is the beginning of the science of dynamics.

Celestial Bodies. The laws that govern the motion of celestial bodies are the subject of three books also written around 335 B.C.E. In *Meteorology, On the Heavens,* and the *Metaphysics,* science and philosophy together reach their highest point of speculation. Aristotle's observation of the movements of the planets and stars led him to postulate the existence of an entirely new, fifth element. His reasoning was influenced greatly by his discoveries in the study of dynamics. The four terrestrial elements, inherited from Empedocles, naturally move either up or down. Moreover, they tend to move along linear vectors—that is, in straight lines—and they always stop once they have reached their natural destinations. The stars and planets, however, behave quite differently. On the one hand, they all move in regular and circular patterns, as the mathematician and astronomer Eudoxus had so elegantly shown. On the other, and even more remarkable, the stars and planets never stop. Their movement is perpetual and ceaseless, unlike anything that can be observed here in the earthly world. Aristotle reasoned that they must therefore be made of something nonterrestrial, something much more refined and perhaps even divine. This "something" is *aithêr*—an eternal material in constant circular motion, unaffected by the impermanence that touches everything on earth.

The Universe. On the basis of these five elements, then, and in keeping with his new laws of dynamics, Aristotle proceeded to construct a comprehensive picture of the entire universe. (The theory would remain virtually the same for more than 1,500 years.) At the center of the cosmos is our dense planet. It is made of elemental earth (cold and dry) that has naturally collected here. The earth's spherical shape is confirmed, among other things, by the shadow it casts on the moon during lunar eclipses. Ideally, if the four lower elements existed in an unmixed state, the earth would be surrounded by perfectly concentric rings of water, air, and fire. This configuration is how the elements naturally tend to collect, with the heaviest at the center and the lightest at the outermost ring. However, most things in the world are in reality mixtures of earth, water, air, fire, and water, and each element is rarely found in an unadulterated condition.

Rotational Tracks. In Aristotle's cosmology, the orbit of the moon begins precisely where fire, the lightest terrestrial element, achieves its farthest reach. Everything above this point is made of *aithêr,* the fifth and purest element of all. Beginning with the moon, a system of aitherial bodies extends out to the largest sphere of the universe. Next after the moon comes the sun, then the five known planets, and finally the fixed stars. The stars are fixed because they were believed to be embedded in the inner wall of the outermost sphere and to turn along with its slow movement. Aristotle further refined the geometrical model that Eudoxus had designed, and his celestial bodies move along a total of fifty-six rotational tracks within tracks within tracks within tracks. In his system, moreover, each orbiting sphere touches both the sphere above and the sphere below it. In this way, celestial motion is communicated from heaven's outermost circle down into the dense, sublunary region. The spheres turn in a complex pattern of rotations and counterrotations, producing what appears in the night sky to an observer on earth.

Mechanical Model. They were meant to do much more than just produce an illusion. Aristotle connected all fifty-six spheres together, made each touch the next sphere in line, and made motion pass all the way down the line of spheres from beginning to end. This changed the Eudoxan model of the universe in a radical way. Eudoxus, after all, had proposed a geometrical model. It was an abstract, theoretical answer to an intriguing puzzle that Plato had said was in need of some solution. His concern was principally with calculating the minimum number of circular tracks that were necessary to imitate the observed movement of the sun, planets, and stars. As a result, his answer was more like a design hypothesis than a blueprint for a model that could actually work. By physically linking each sphere to the next, Aristotle transformed this geometrical model into a dynamic and mechanical one. The fifty-six spheres in his system are like the cogs in a divine machine, and their turns and counterturns are really meant to show how the heavenly bodies actually behave as they move through celestial space. Rather than being merely hypothetical, the spheres in his model obey the laws of both physics and dynamics, at least as Aristotle conceived them. The result is a working model, not simply an abstract sketch. This set the precedent for over two millennia of astronomical models built to reflect the real shape of the universe.

Natural Movement. Aristotle's theory of causes required that the eternal, perfectly circular movement of all the celestial bodies starting with the moon be natural, not forced. Forced motion, after all, is contrary to nature, and in the end it is always defeated by the tendency every object has to move in the way that is proper to it. That is the reason why rocks always fall to earth, despite how much effort we might put into throwing them up in the air. The moon, sun, planets, and

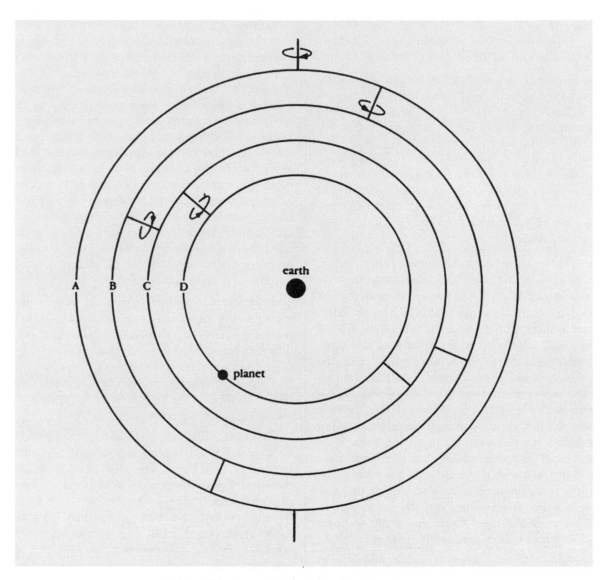

Eudoxan spheres for a single planet in orbit around the earth

stars continue to move around and around forever because this is in keeping with their immanent teleology.

Displacement. However, where does this motion come from? What causes it? A rock, for instance, falls because it is made of the element earth, because earth is the heaviest element, and because the heaviest always moves toward the center. Once a rock reaches the center, however, it stops moving. If we ask why a certain specific rock actually moves, then, the only answer can be that someone or something at some time removed it from its natural place at the center. The rock falls because it has been displaced, and it is attempting to return to its proper "home."

Infinite Regress. What about the celestial bodies, then, the ones that are all made of *aithêr,* the pure fifth element? They eternally move in a circle because this is their natural way; it expresses their immanent teleology. Yet, where does their motion come from? What could have started it? Aristotle reasoned that the source of celestial motion must logically be something that does

not itself move. Otherwise, any attempt to understand it gets stuck on an endless treadmill of what is called infinite regress, where each answer only raises the same question all over again. If the source of celestial movement is something that also moves, then it must get its own motion from some other source, and then that source must itself be either moving or unmoved. If it is moved, then the question is thrown back yet another step. To avoid spinning the logical wheels forever, then, reason demands that the ultimate source of motion is something that is unmoved.

Prime Mover. At the source of all movement, celestial and earthly, Aristotle theorized the existence of what he called a Prime or Unmoved Mover. He identified it with God, and this God is the most complete being imaginable. Unlike everything else in the universe, which naturally strives to fulfill its inner goal or immanent teleology, God is already fully actualized. In God there is nothing potential—no dunamis at all—but only *energeia* (pure reality). Since God is complete, God has no need of anything else; this means that God is perfectly autonomous and self-sufficient. God is entirely separate from all other things.

Function. What does God, the Unmoved Mover, do for all eternity? The only thing such a being could do, in keeping with its perfect reality, is to spend all of eternity contemplating itself. God cannot act, after all, since action would imply that God does not already have what it needs, or that God wants something else. It is impossible, however, for God to want anything because He is by definition perfect and complete. If God cannot act, then, God must think, and the universe offers no other object of thought worthy enough of God except for God himself.

Desire. How, then, does this most perfect being, entirely absorbed in thinking about itself, make the stars and planets move? It cannot do so in the way that an efficient or moving cause makes things happen. After all, it is not as if the Unmoved Mover turns some kind of heavenly crank, which turns the sphere of the stars, which turns the spheres of Saturn, which turn the spheres of Jupiter, and so on. Instead, God makes things move in the way that a final or telic cause works. God is a totally perfect being, fully actualized—in fact, the only such being in the entire universe. As a result, God embodies the desire that every natural thing has to realize its potential and thus achieve its own perfection. Since God represents what is ultimately real, God is the ultimate aim of immanent teleology. God is the goal that every existing thing—from rock to fire to seed to human soul to wandering planet—naturally seeks to become. The whole universe turns out of desire for God.

Connections. At this stage, Aristotle passes from science to theology and religion, and thus well beyond the limits of this chapter. For Aristotle, however, these boundaries are not as definite as they are for modern people, since his world was far more interconnected than ours. No clear line separates physics from theology. The fact is that theology is simply what every rational person should study after completing the study of physics. In turn, physics leads naturally to the study of God as the Unmoved Mover of the cosmos. Everything is bound together—biology, zoology, physics, astronomy, dynamics, theology—because the theory of the four causes offers a complete and comprehensive theory of every thing and action in the universe.

Influence. The range of his theories has much to do with Aristotle's profound influence on subsequent generations of philosophers and scientists, especially throughout the ancient world and from the thirteenth century up through the Renaissance. First, his work addressed and offered answers to questions that had occupied Greek thought for upward of three centuries: What is reality made of? How does it change into the variety of things that we experience through our senses? What causes this change? How is the universe structured? How can phenomena be saved? How can reality be apprehended? How do we know that we know? How can we prove it? How can our knowledge be communicated? Here Aristotle did not just propose grand, unified solutions to specific problems. He also analyzed the language itself in which scientific claims should be cast in order to be genuinely objective.

Scientific Disciplines. Aristotle also contributed greatly to the content and in some cases even the definition of a variety of scientific disciplines. Many of the different branches of research that make up the various departments in a modern university were either created by Aristotle or else given their first, clear definition by him. The sheer range and scope of Aristotle's scientific attention have seldom ever been matched.

Research. Moreover, in founding the Lyceum, Aristotle created the first genuinely scientific research community in the West. He also gave it a genuinely scientific research agenda—into physics, mechanics, dynamics, medicine, geometry, astronomy, zoology, biology, botany, chemistry, and mineralogy, to name the most important fields. That agenda has driven western scientific investigation ever since. Along with the agenda, finally, Aristotle bequeathed a set of methodological procedures—especially those of logical argument and detailed, empirical observation—by which all science still continues to be guided.

Sources:

J. L. Ackrill, *Aristotle the Philosopher* (Oxford & New York: Oxford University Press, 1981).

Jonathan Barnes, *Aristotle* (Oxford & New York: Oxford University Press, 1982).

D. R. Dicks, *Early Greek Astronomy to Aristotle* (Ithaca, N.Y.: Cornell University Press, 1970).

Pierre Pellegrin, *Aristotle's Classification of Animals,* translated by Anthony Preus (Berkeley: University of California Press, 1986).

Samuel Sambursky, *The Physical World of the Greeks* (London: Routledge & Kegan Paul, 1956).

SIGNIFICANT PEOPLE

ANAXAGORAS

CIRCA 500-CIRCA 428 B.C.E.

ASTRONOMER AND PHILOSOPHER

Modern Ideas. Anaxagoras was born in Clazomenae, Anatolia (in present-day Turkey). Around 480 B.C.E. he moved to Athens, where he lived for thirty years and taught a variety of students, including Pericles and possibly Socrates. Unfortunately, few of the writings of Anaxagoras have survived. When he declared that the Sun was an incandescent stone, he was prosecuted for impiety, although the charge was more a political attack on Pericles. He then went into exile and spent his last years at Lampsacus.

Cosmology. Aside from discovering the true cause of eclipses, Anaxagoras made some interesting assertions concerning the physical universe. He declared that natural objects are composed of infinitesimally small particles containing mixtures of all qualities. Accordingly, the *nous* (mind, reason, or intelligence) acts upon masses of these particles to produce objects. It seemed to him quite impossible that anything should come into being from what does not exist. For example, when ingested, simple and homogeneous nourishment such as bread or water helps produce hair, veins, arteries, sinews, bones, skin, and all the other parts of the human body.

Sources:

Felix M. Cleve, *The Philosophy of Anaxagoras: An Attempt at Reconstruction* (New York: King's Cross Press, 1949).

Geoffrey Stephen Kirk and John Earle Raven, eds., *The Presocratic Philosophers: A Critical History with a Selection of Texts* (Cambridge: Cambridge University Press, 1957).

ANAXIMANDER

610-CIRCA 545 B.C.E.

ASTRONOMER AND PHILOSOPHER

Historical Record. Thought to have been a pupil of Thales, Anaximander of Miletus wrote treatises on geography, astronomy, and cosmology. However, only one sentence of his writings survives, so the writings of later scholars form the primary source of information about his discoveries. Anaximander is credited with having drawn the first map of the world. One hundred years later, the historian Herodotus found it simplistic and amusing:

> It makes me smile to see how many people have made circular pictures of the earth, and how not a single one has done it sensibly! They all make the river Okeanos run around the earth as neatly as if were drawn with a compass, and make Asia and Europe equal in size!

If Anaximander's map fit this description, its shape owed less to exploration and actual measurement than to a scientific desire for order and symmetry.

Evolution. Anaximander believed the world derived from a source called the *apeiron* (unlimited). His notions about the origin of animal and human life, though fanciful, bear an uncanny resemblance to modern evolutionary theories. Later writers report his claim that people must have originally been born from nonhuman creatures, on the ground that human (unlike animal) offspring require a long period of nursing and care in order to survive. If they had originally been born into the world from (and as) human beings, he reasoned, the species would have perished in the first generation. On this assumption, he argued that in the beginning, fishlike creatures arose from warm water and earth. Human beings grew inside them, enclosed like embryos, and remained within their protective envelopes until they reached the age of puberty. Then "the fishlike creatures burst apart and men and women who were now able to feed and take care of themselves stepped forth" onto dry land.

Sources:

Charles H. Kahn, *Anaximander and the Origins of Greek Cosmology* (New York: Columbia University Press, 1960).

Paul Seligman, *The Apeiron of Anaximander: A Study in the Origin and Function of Metaphysical Ideas* (Westport, Conn.: Greenwood Press, 1962).

ANAXIMENES

FLOURISHED CIRCA 545 B.C.E.
PHILOSOPHER

Universal Building Block. No information survives about the life of Anaximenes, the last of the Milesians, except that he is said to have been the pupil of Anaxagoras. His theory that *aêr* (air, mist, or vapor) is the fundamental element of the universe marks a genuine advance over earlier theories because it provides a dynamic mechanism to account for physical changes in the world. According to Anaximenes, cycles of condensation and rarefaction and contraction and expansion determine the transformation of "thin" air into increasingly denser air: "Clouds occur when air gets thickened; when compressed further, rain is squeezed out; and hail occurs when the falling water condenses." In the case of snow, a lower temperature and some wind would cause the water to get frothy and white.

Source:

G. E. R. Lloyd, *Early Greek Science: Thales to Aristotle* (New York: Norton, 1970).

ARISTOTLE

384-322 B.C.E.
PHILOSOPHER AND SCIENTIST

Significance. Aristotle is one of the greatest intellectual figures in history. More than any other ancient Greek thinker, he helped define Western rationalism and scientific methodology. In fact, until the end of the seventeenth century, Western intellectual culture was labeled Aristotelian. His greatest achievements were in the study of formal logic and pioneering the field of zoology, in which his theories were not replaced until the 1800s.

Student and Teacher. Born in 384 B.C.E. at Stagira, a small coastal town in northern Greece, Aristotle grew up in an environment that offered him many rich opportunities to observe and think about the natural world. His father, Nicomachus, was court physician to Amyntas II, king of Macedonia. His later interest in biology has often been attributed to his father's influence upon him. At the age of seventeen, Aristotle went to Athens to study under the famous Plato, with whom he stayed for the next twenty years. After Plato's death in 348 or 347, Aristotle spent some years in the islands of the eastern Aegean, apparently studying and collecting specimens of plant and animal life. He was then invited back to the royal court of Macedon to serve as tutor to the young prince Alexander, known to later ages as Alexander the Great. In 335, Aristotle returned to Athens and there established an institute called the Lyceum, where he worked and taught until his death in 322.

Works. The interests of Aristotle were vast, and he wrote on many subjects, including biology, botany, chemistry, ethics, history, literary theory, logic, physics, political theory, psychology, metaphysics, rhetoric, and zoology. Most of his extant works are edited compilations of lectures he delivered at the Lyceum. Among his major works written before 335 B.C.E. are *On the Heavens, History of Animals, Parts of Animals, Physics, Progression of Animals,* and *On Sophistical Refutations.* His major works written after 335 B.C.E. include *Categories, Metaphysics, Nicomachean Ethics, On the Soul, Poetics, Politics, Prior Analytics, Posterior Analytics,* and *Rhetoric.*

Sources:

D. J. Allan, *The Philosophy of Aristotle* (Oxford: Clarendon Press, 1970).

Jonathan Barnes, *Aristotle* (Oxford & New York: Oxford University Press, 1982).

Malcolm Schofield Barnes and Richard Sorabji, eds., *Articles on Aristotle,* 3 volumes (New York: St. Martin's Press, 1977).

Harold Cherniss, *Aristotle's Criticism of Plato and the Academy* (New York: Russell & Russell, 1944).

John Ferguson, *Aristotle* (New York: Twayne, 1972).

Felix Grayeff, *Aristotle and His School* (London: Duckworth, 1974).

Werner Jaeger, *Aristotle: Fundamentals of the History of His Development,* second edition, translated by Richard Robinson (Oxford: Clarendon Press, 1948).

EMPEDOCLES

CIRCA 490-430 B.C.E.
PHILOSOPHER, STATESMAN, POET

Beginnings. Like Pythagoras, the charismatic Empedocles was a magnet for legends; unlike Pythagoras, though, he might well himself have actively done all he could to encourage them. Born into an aristocratic family in Acragas, Sicily, around 490 B.C.E., he seems to have vigorously supported the democratic faction in the politics of his home city. The proximity of Acragas to Croton and Elea in southern Italy brought him into contact with both Parmenides and the Pythagoreans, and strong traces of their influence are evident in his own work.

Showman. A flashy and flamboyant showman, Empedocles is said to have traveled extensively through the western Mediterranean, dressed in expensive purple robes, bronze boots, and a golden crown. He professed extraordinary power over the natural world, as well as the means to perform miraculous cures. While Aristotle hailed him as the inventor of rhetoric, Galen regarded him as the founder of Italian medicine. Nothing remains of his writings except for brief sections from two poems, *On Nature* and *Purifications*.

Four Elements. Empedocles maintained that all matter is composed of Fire, Air, Water, and Earth, and these four ingredients, in turn, are governed by Love and Strife. In addition, Empedocles believed in the transmigration of souls, declaring that those who have sinned must wander the earth in various mortal bodies for thirty thousand seasons and perform purifying acts such as abstaining from eating animal flesh. According to legend, Empedocles died after jumping into the volcanic crater atop Mount Etna in an attempt to convince others of his divinity.

Sources:
Jonathan Barnes, *The Presocratic Philosophers*, volume 2 (London: Routledge & Kegan Paul, 1979).

Helle Lambridis, *Empedocles: A Philosophical Investigation* (Tuscaloosa: University of Alabama Press, 1976).

HERACLITUS

CIRCA 540–CIRCA 480 B.C.E.

PHILOSOPHER

An Enigma. For the ancient world, Heraclitus (also spelled Heracleitus or Hêrakleitos) was always *skoteinos*, "dark" and "obscure." This reputation was due as much to his riddling, prophetic style as to the exact nature of the mysterious logos or reason he saw hidden beneath the flow and flux of appearances. Tradition has it that, despite the political privileges that came from his birth into one of the aristocratic families of Ephesus, he rejected leadership in favor of the life of a misanthropic hermit, living alone in the mountains, eating plants and grass. Haughty and aloof, rude and enigmatic, he was famous for his caustic wit and his rejection of most other thinkers as learned but far from intelligent or wise.

Fire. The one book that Heraclitus apparently wrote, *On Nature*, or *Muses* (circa 500 B.C.E.), is lost, and later scholars have summarized his teachings. Heraclitus believed that fire is the basis of the universe, writing that the world order is an "ever-living fire kindling in measures and being extinguished in measures." The contest between opposite forces (Good and Evil, Hot and Cold, Love and Strife) is a major theme of his teachings. Heraclitus supposedly died at the age of sixty after burying himself up to the neck in hot cow dung in an attempt to cure himself of dropsy.

Source:
David Sider, "Heraclitus," in *Ancient Greek Authors, Dictionary of Literary Biography*, volume 176, edited by Ward W. Briggs (Columbia, S.C.: Bruccoli Clark Layman/Detroit: Gale Research, 1997), pp. 176–181.

PLATO

CIRCA 428–348 OR 347 B.C.E.

PHILOSOPHER

Influence. Plato is a member of the great trio of ancient Greek intellectuals—the other two being Socrates and Aristotle—who established the philosophical foundations of Western culture. Almost every ancient philosopher who came after him wrote in response to Plato's theories. In fact, scholars studied his logical, epistemological, and metaphysical writings throughout the Middle Ages and the Renaissance.

Aristocles. Plato was born in Athens, the son of Ariston and Perictione. He was originally called Aristocles, after his grandfather, but was given the nickname "Plato" (after the Greek word *platus*, meaning broad, apparently in reference to either his physique, broad forehead, or intellect). He studied under Socrates until the philosopher's death in 399 B.C.E. and then began a series of travels that led him to Megara, Egypt, Cyrene, Sicily, and Magna Graecia (the Greek seaport colonies of southern Italy). Returning to Athens in 387, Plato founded his school of philosophy known as the Academy, where one of his most famous students was Aristotle.

Works. The extant works of Plato are in the form of dialogues in which his mentor, Socrates, takes a leading role. His greatest dialogue, *Republic*, the first book of which was written sometime before 387 B.C.E., describes the construction of an ideal state. *Apology* was also written prior to 387 B.C.E. and purports to be Socrates' speech at his trial. Three other important works were composed sometime between 380 and 360 B.C.E.: *Symposium* (a study on ideal love); *Phaedrus* (a critique of the prevailing conception of rhetoric); and *Phaedo* (a discourse on immortality of the soul and Socrates' last conversation before death). One of Plato's famous late dialogues is *Timaeus* (circa 355–347 B.C.E.), which contains his theory of the universe and the story of Atlantis.

Sources:
John Glucker, *Antiochus and the Late Academy* (Göttingen: Vandenhoeck und Ruprecht, 1978).

John Earle Raven, *Plato's Thought in the Making: A Study of the Development of His Metaphysics* (Cambridge: Cambridge University Press, 1965).

Alice Swift Riginos, *Platonica: The Anecdotes Concerning the Life and Writings of Plato* (Leiden: Brill, 1976).

C. J. Rowe, *Plato* (New York: St. Martin's Press, 1984).

A. E. Taylor, *Plato, the Man and His Work,* fifth edition (London: Methuen, 1948).

PYTHAGORAS

CIRCA 580–CIRCA 500 B.C.E.
PHILOSOPHER AND MATHEMATICIAN

Croton. The details of Pythagoras's life are lost in a blur of legends invented by his disciples. Pythagoras was born sometime around 580 B.C.E. in the eastern Aegean, and after travels in Egypt and Babylonia reportedly settled in the Greek city of Croton in southern Italy. There he lived as the head of a religious and philosophical community rumored to be nearly three hundred in number. It eventually gained wide political influence in Croton, but after twenty years of virtual rule the group devolved into factions. In the ensuing violence many members were killed while others fled into exile. Pythagoras sought refuge in a temple in the neighboring city of Metapontum, and there he starved to death.

Contributions. Although none of his writings have survived, Pythagoras is credited with the theory of the functional significance of numbers. Nonetheless other discoveries attributed to him such as the incommensurability of the side and diagonal of a square and the theorem for right triangles were probably developed by some of his later followers. Overall, his contribution to Greek intellectual tradition has more to do with mystical wisdom than it does with scientific scholarship.

Listeners and Learners. Upon his death, the cult split into two groups: the *Akousmatikoi* (Listeners), who cultivated his religious, mystical, and ethical teachings, and the *Mathêmatikoi* (Learners), who continued his work in mathematics, astronomy, and music. The former were all sworn to observe strict rules of purity and abstinence, along with rigid dietary prohibitions that seem to have included vegetarianism, based on a belief in the reincarnation of the soul after death (the meat a person eats might once have been a man). According to a roughly contemporary anecdote, Pythagoras once stopped someone from beating a small dog because he recognized in its barking the voice of a dead friend, who had obviously been reborn as the puppy.

Beliefs. Some of the rules of behavior of the Akousmatikoi cult reportedly included never stir a fire with something made of iron and always put your right shoe on first, but always wash your left foot before you wash the right one. Meanwhile, the Mathêmatikoi believed that the fundamental principles of the universe were arranged in ten contrary pairs: limit and unlimited; odd and even; one and many; right and left; male and female; rest and motion; straight and curved; light and dark; good and bad; and square and oblong.

Sources:
Walter Burkert, *Lore and Science in Ancient Pythagoreanism* (Cambridge, Mass.: Harvard University Press, 1972).

Peter Kingsley, *Ancient Philosophy, Mystery, and Magic: Empedocles and Pythagorean Tradition* (Oxford: Clarendon Press; New York: Oxford University Press, 1995).

THALES

CIRCA 625–CIRCA 547 B.C.E.
PHILOSOPHER

Mystery. Thales of Miletus lived and worked in the prosperous port city of Miletus on the coast of Asia Minor. Tradition credits him with a variety of ingenious solutions to practical problems, but Thales left no writings to posterity. Much of what is known about him comes from Aristotle, who regarded him as the first real *phusiologos* or natural scientist. Thales held that water was the basic building block of all matter.

Achievements. Thales allegedly visited Egypt, where he is supposed to have learned geometry, studied the rise and fall of the Nile, and determined the height of pyramids by measuring their shadows. He is said to have designed a canal that split the deep Lydian river Halys in two, diverting some of its flow into another channel so that the army of Croesus could safely cross it. His prediction of a solar eclipse in the year 585 B.C.E. was well known in the ancient world. When mocked on account of his poverty, he is said to have noted by observing the stars that there would be a large crop of olives at the next harvest. Thales then borrowed money from friends and used it to buy up all the olive presses in Miletus. When harvest arrived and the demand for presses was high, he rented them out at many times their original purchase price and thus made a large profit. Aristotle, who tells this story, states that it proves that philosophers could be rich if they wanted to, but they are not really interested in money.

Source:
G. E. R. Lloyd, *Early Greek Science: Thales to Aristotle* (New York: Norton, 1970).

DOCUMENTARY SOURCES

Note: With the exception of the Hippocratic medical writings, the works of the sixth- and fifth-century Greek scientists are preserved entirely in fragments quoted by later writers, in some cases as much as one thousand years after the fact. This situation applies to the following scientists covered in the preceding chapter: Alcmaeon, Anaxagoras, Anaximander, Anaximenes, Democritus, Empedocles, Euctemon, Heraclitus, Leucippus, Melissus, Meton, Parmenides, Philolaos, Pythagoras, Thales, and Zeno. Their fragments, along with whatever ancient biographical information and commentary survives, have been compiled and edited by Hermann Diels in the multivolume work, *Die Fragmente der Vorsokratiker* (1903). The works of the fourth-century astronomers Callipus, Eudoxus, and Heraclides have suffered the same fate, and are known today only through summaries by other Greek writers.

Aristotle produced his various works circa 335 B.C.E. The *Organon*, a later collective title for six separate works (*Categories, On Interpretation, Prior Analytics, Posterior Analytics, Topics,* and *On Sophistical Refutations*), is devoted to the principles of logical reasoning. It is essential for establishing the methodology used by Aristotle in his scientific writings.

The group of works on the physical world includes the *Physics, On the Heavens, On Generation and Corruption,* and *Meteorology.* For the most part, these titles clearly indicate their respective contents. *On Generation and Corruption* deals with the concepts of change, motion, growth, action, and passivity as they apply to physical things in the world.

Aristotle's biological research is contained in the works *History of Animals, Parts of Animals, Movement of Animals, Generation of Animals,* and also in a collection of writings called *Parua Naturalia* (Short Natural Histories). As a group of works, they represent the most systematic and comprehensive set of investigations into taxonomy, zoology, and biology prior to the nineteenth century. To this same group should be added his work *On the Soul,* in which Aristotle deals with issues that cross the boundary between modern biology and psychology: growth, nutrition, sensation, imagination, movement, thought, and rationality.

Herodotus wrote the *History of the Persian Wars* sometime in the late fifth century B.C.E. This volume deals with events leading up to the unsuccessful Persian invasion of Greece in 480 B.C.E., and it is also a rich source of anecdotal information about fifth-century cultural (and occasionally technological) history.

Hippocrates of Cos lived around 425 B.C.E., and the works that have survived under his name constitute a relatively large body of short essays. For convenience they can be divided into two main groups, one general and largely theoretical, the other more practical.

The general group includes such theoretical works as *Aphorisms, Ancient Medicine, Precepts, Sacred Disease, Humors, Nature of Man, The Art,* and *Places in Man,* along with the work titled *Airs Waters Places,* which offers a survey of the different sorts of disease to be encountered in different parts of the world and during the four seasons. The *Oath* also belongs to this group, as it states the basic moral rules by which physicians who belong to the Hippocratic school must abide.

More specific and practical texts include *Nutriment, Prognostic, Regimen in Acute Diseases, Regimen in Health I-IV, Epidemics I-VII, Breaths, Dentition, Wounds in the Head, In the Surgery, Fractures, Diseases I-III, Glands, Fleshes, Ulcers,* and *Hemorrhoids.*

Hippocratic embryological and gynecological theories are found in the essays *Seven Months' Child, Diseases of Women I-III, Generation, Nature of the Child, Superfetation,* and *Young Girls.*

Plato's mathematics, cosmology, and astronomy can be found in his dialogue called *Timaeus* (circa 355–347 B.C.E.). Here, in the form of "a plausible myth," Plato offers an account of the creation and organization of the universe.

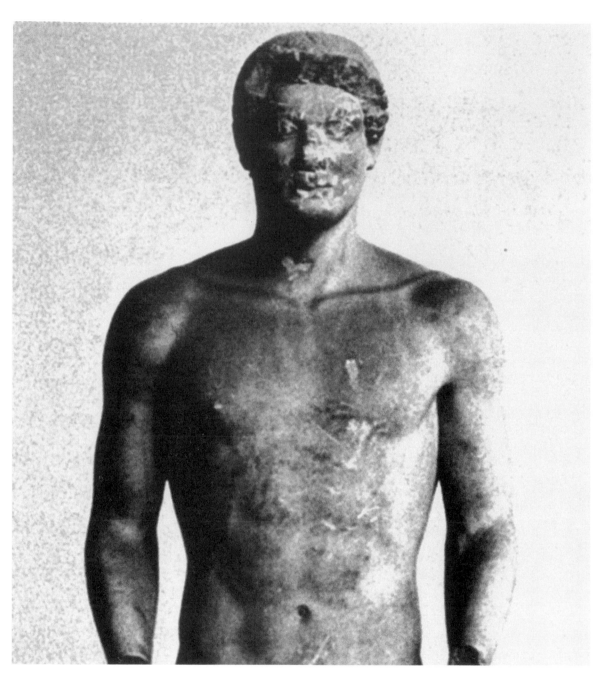

Kouros of Aristodidos, circa 510–500 B.C.E. (Athens NM 3938. Photo: Jeffrey M Hurwit.)

GLOSSARY

Abacus: Block-shaped part of column capital immediately beneath the epistyle.

Aêr: Air or mist. According to Anaximenes, the world is composed of *aêr* transformed by expansion and contraction into water, earth, and all other natural things. Cf. English *air*.

Aetiological Myths: Stories that provide accounts of the origin of familiar objects or practices.

Agathos Daimôn: Literally, the "good divinity." A name given to Dionysus, under which he was toasted at the beginning of a symposium.

Agôgê: The term used for the Spartan training or upbringing that emphasized strict military discipline.

Agora: The gathering place or market; the commercial and political center of the polis.

Aithêr: The lightest and purest element imaginable. Aristotle believed that the moon, sun, stars, and other heavenly bodies were made of aither, and he considered it a fifth element, along with earth, air, fire, and water. Cf. English *ether*.

Aitiai: The Four Causes of Aristotle. In order to have scientific knowledge about something, it is necessary to know (1) what material it is made of; (2) what form it has; (3) who (or what) made it; and (4) what is its function.

Akousmatikoi: The "Listeners," a mystical sect of Pythagoreans who worshipped numbers and numerical ratios. Cf. English *acoustic*.

Akropolis or Acropolis: A citadel located on elevated ground, usually containing the major temples and shrines.

Akrôtêrion (Plural = Akrôtêria): Sculpted figure placed on top of the apex and corners of a pediment.

Alabastron: A slim oil container with rounded end, narrow neck, and flaring mouth.

Allopathic Remedy: An attempt to cure a disease by treating it with something whose characteristics are opposite to those of the disease. Hippocratic doctors believed that an excess of phlegm (cold and wet), for instance, should be cured by giving the patient foods that are hot and dry.

Amphictyony: From the Greek *amphiktiones* meaning "dwellers-around"; a league of devotees connected to a religious sanctuary and the maintenance of its cult. As the word implies, they were mostly regional, but the most important, such as the Delphic amphictyony, had representatives from many parts of Greece.

Amphidromia: Literally, "a running around." A religious ceremony that marked the birth of a child and in which the father of the house carried the five-day-old infant around the ancestral hearth.

Amphora: A slender, two-handled clay vessel used for the transport of various commodities.

Andrôn: Literally, "belonging to men." A space in the Greek house reserved for men and demarcated from the rest of the house by its location near the street and sometimes by its mosaic floors. This area was used as a dining room for dinner parties and symposia.

Angareion or Aggareion: A Persian system of mounted relay messengers.

Anthestêria: Athenian festival honoring Dionysus, and involving the tasting of wine from that year's vintage.

Aoidos: Singer. A preliterate poet depicted in the Homeric poems who sings of the legendary deeds of heroes accompanied by the lyre.

Apeiron: Limitless. According to Anaximander, the universe began as a vast, boundless material in which everything was completely mixed together—a cosmic soup out of which the world as it is known today slowly separated.

Apodeixis: Proof. One of the greatest contributions of ancient Greek science is rules for proving claims in a rational and logical manner.

Apotropaic: From the Greek *apotrepein* meaning "avert"; designed to turn away evil. Modern Italians wear a small gold horn to avert the *malocchio* or "evil eye"; modern Greeks and Turks hang a decorative blue glass eye as a wall ornament for similar reasons.

Arkhôn or Archon: Ruler. The highest public office in archaic Athens to which nine individuals were originally appointed and later chosen by direct election. After the reforms of Cleisthenes, the nine archons were replaced by ten generalships, one of which was held by Pericles.

Areios Pagos or Areopagus: The Hill of Ares in Athens where the aristocratic council of former archons met.

Aristocracy: Rule by "the best," whether morally, economically, or militarily.

Ariston: Breakfast. Typically eaten just after sunrise, although in Athens it tended to be a mid-morning meal (one of two daily meals rather than three).

Arrêphoroi: "Those who carry the garment." The girls who carried the new garment and other sacred things for the goddess Athena at the Panathenaea.

Aruballos or Aryballos: A round, narrow-necked, usually miniature-sized bottle for oil or perfume.

Atomon: Unsplittable. Scientists such as Democritus believed that everything is made of invisible, indivisible bits of matter. Each "atom" has a different shape and can stick to other atoms to form larger objects. Cf. English *atom*.

Aulos: A musical instrument with reeds and two pipes.

Basileus: "King"; initially a local ruler; by the Classical Period the term referred to a local magistrate or a foreign king.

Bilingual Vase: A vase that has black-figure style on one side and red-figure style on the other.

Black Figure Technique: Type of pottery painting in which black silhouette figures are incised and have color added to them.

Caryatid: Sculpted female figure supporting an entablature.

Celestial Equator: An imaginary plane extending from the earth's equator out into space. The sun and planets appear to move through the sky along a line that is tilted about twenty-three degrees in relation to the celestial equator.

Cella: Central room of a Greek temple that housed the cult statue.

Centauromachy: Battle between the heroes known as Lapiths and centaurs, who gate-crashed the wedding of the king of the Lapiths and tried to rape the women, but were repelled.

Chryselephantine: Constructed of gold and ivory; such statues usually had a wooden core.

Chthonian or Chthonic: From the Greek *khthôn* meaning "ground" or "earth"; of or pertaining to the underworld. Chthonic gods are broadly distinguished

from sky gods (the latter, in Greece, are situated on Mount Olympus).

City Dionysia: The dramatic festival at Athens in honor of the god Dionysus where the Athenians watched plays produced by the tragic and comic poets.

Clerychs: Athenian "stakeholders" who received a parcel of land near a potentially hostile ally as part of a colony; a council of ten local rulers who formed an oligarchic government loyal to Sparta.

Comedy: "Revel-singing"; humorous dramatic performance, formally organized in Athens from the early fifth century B.C.E.

Contrapposto: A stance in which the body's weight is supported on one leg, so that a contrast is formed between the tension of one side with the relaxation of the other.

Cosmogonic Myths: Stories that provide accounts of the origin and nature of the world.

Dactylic Hexameter: The poetic meter of Greek epic and didactic. Greek poetry was based on recurring patterns of long and short syllables, and this meter was made up of six dactyls (one long and two short syllables) or their equivalent per line.

Deipnon: A midday meal, typically the biggest meal of the day. In Athens, it was moved forward to become an evening meal.

Deltos: A pair of wooden tablets hinged together, with the inside surfaces coated with beeswax, for writing.

Dêmiourgos: The god who makes the world out of pre-existing matter in Plato's book *Timaeus* (355–347 B.C.E.).

Dentil: Toothlike projection on an Ionic epistyle.

Diaulos: A footrace twice the length of a *stadion*.

Didactic: Instructional; used especially of poetry containing technical information, such as Hesiod's *Works and Days*.

Didaskalos: The word for teacher, used of poets in their capacity as educators of citizens.

Diaita: Special foods, drinks, baths, and exercises prescribed by ancient Greek doctors. Cf. English *diet*.

Dikastai: Judges in the Athenian courts, who served as both judge and jury.

Dinos: Large, round-bottomed bowl, requiring a separate stand, sometimes used for mixing wine.

Diolkos: A stone-paved pathway across the Isthmus of Corinth, used for transporting ships and their cargos across the Isthmus.

Dionysus: A complex and multifaceted god, best known as the god of wine.

Diphros: A stool, either having four straight legs, or four curved, crisscrossing legs that would allow it to be folded up for storage or transport.

Dithyramb: A type of narrative choral song, originally associated with Dionysus, and thought to have been the origin of tragedy.

Dokimasia: The scrutiny of new citizens and magistrates performed by the Athenian council.

Dolikhos: A longer footrace, covering usually twelve *stadia*.

Dorpon: An evening meal, lighter than the *deipnon*.

Drakhma or Drachma: "A handful"; the most common Athenian currency in circulation; roughly equivalent to two dollars in modern U.S. currency.

Dunamis: An inner potential to act in a certain way that is special to every single thing in the world; for example, seeds grow into plants, fire moves upward, and so forth; the theory was developed by Aristotle. Cf. English *dynamic, dynamo.*

Ecliptic: An imaginary circle drawn in space, about twenty-three degrees above the celestial equator. It marks the apparent paths of the sun and planets around the earth.

Eileithuia or Eileithyia: "The Coming." The Greek goddess of childbirth.

Eispoiesis: "Making in." The legal process of adoption an Athenian citizen without issue could undertake to ensure his *oikos* (household) had an heir.

Ekkuklêma: "Thing wheeled out"; a low trolley used to display the result of off-stage action in tragedy (often a corpse).

Ekphora: "Carrying out." The funeral procession in which the corpse was carried from the deceased's house to his tomb; often depicted on late Geometric pottery.

Ekphrasis: Literary description of a work of visual art.

Eleusinian Mysteries: A popular religious cult based in Eleusis, a town near Athens.

Emporion: A trading post or settlement.

Encaustic: Painting technique involving application of pigments mixed with hot wax.

Enduma: Clothing (such as the *khitôn*) designed to be entered into or pulled onto the body.

Energeia: Reality; the opposite of dynamis. For instance, when a thing fulfills its dynamis—when a seed grows into a mature plant, it achieves its true energeia. Cf. English *energy.*

Egguê or Engyê: "In pledge." The process of betrothal in which a father pledged his daughter to another man.

Entablature: All parts of an architectural order above the columns.

Entasis: The vertical, convex curve of a column.

Epeisodion: "Addition"; that part of a tragedy between two choral odes.

Ephebe: From the Greek *ephêbos* meaning "on the brink of youth." This term originally meant a boy (eighteen-twenty years old) who had reached the age of puberty, but in Classical Athens it came to refer to a youth on the threshold of manhood. As a liminal figure, the ephebe embodies both the excitement of imminent adulthood and the poignant freshness of adolescence. The ephebe, in Athens, underwent *dokimasia* (a rite of passage involving an official public scrutiny) and was registered as a full-fledged citizen. He then presented himself for two years of military training.

Ephors: The "overseers" who served with the Spartan kings.

Epic: A long narrative poem in Greek, composed in dactylic hexameters.

Epidemiology: A study of the types and patterns of diseases that regularly occur in a particular region.

Epiklêros: "With the property." A girl who transmitted her father's property to another man through marriage if he had died with no direct male heirs.

Epistêmê: Accurate, rational, logical, scientific knowledge.

Epistemology: The branch of philosophy that studies the relation between the mind and the world and that attempts to answer such questions as: What is true? and How is knowledge possible? During the fifth century B.C.E., epistemology became a central concern of Greek thinkers.

Epistyle: Line of blocks extending above columns to support upper part of building.

Eranos: A banquet to which all guests contributed.

Erastês: "Lover." The active, older male partner in a homoerotic relationship.

Erinues: Snaky, winged creatures born from the earth. They pursue mortals guilty of matricide or fratricide and drive them mad.

Erômenos: "Beloved." The passive or submissive partner in an erotic relationship.

Erôs: Love that always has a sexual component.

Eupatrids: "Sons of good fathers"; the term used to describe early Athenian aristocrats.

Euthuna: The audit performed on all magistrates in Athens as they gave up their duties.

Exodos: "Exit"; the last part of a tragedy, including everything after the last stasimon.

Exômis: A type of *khitôn* which left one shoulder exposed; a common work garment.

Flute: Vertical concave channels or grooves on columns.

Fresco: Wall painting produced by application of pigments to wet or damp plaster.

Frieze: Zone above the epistyle; decorated with metopes and triglyphs in Doric order and sculpture or dentils in Ionic.

Fullers: Tradespeople responsible for cleaning and processing raw wool or finished garments.

Gerousia: The council of twenty-eight elders, plus the two kings, at Sparta.

Gigantomachy: Mythic battle in which the Olympian gods, helped by Heracles, assert their supremacy by defeating a race of giants who attempt to overthrow them.

Gnômôn: An upright pointer in a sundial or similar time-telling device.

Gumnasion: A place for exercising. Like the Roman baths or the modern health club, it acquired social functions and even became a place for learning and philosophy. Cf. English *gymnasium*.

Gunaikeion: "Belonging to women." The space in the Greek house occupied by women, located either on the second story or at the back of the house. While women might enter the *andrôn*, men from outside the family would not normally enter the *gunaikeion*.

Haltêres: A set of weights used in the long jump to increase the distance jumped.

Harmosts: "Arrangers"; the term for the Spartan governors of subject cities.

Hebe: "Youth." The age at which a young man gets his first beard when he is at his prime; also a goddess who symbolized this period in life.

Hektêmoroi: "sixth-parters"; the indentured poor in Athens, before the reforms of Solon.

Hêgemôn: A leader or ruler.

Helots: The local slave population in and around Sparta.

Hêmerodromoi: "Day-runners"; long-distance runners used to carry messages over land.

Heortê (Plural = Heortai): Festivals. These celebrations were both religious and civic at the same time and involved a large variety of leisure activities.

Hestia: Goddess of the hearth and protector of the household.

Hetaira: "Female companion." An upper-class prostitute, usually educated and skilled in music, who participated in the male symposium.

Hetairia: An aristocratic club.

Himation: A garment consisting of a large rectangular piece of cloth that was draped over the body. The standard outer garment for men (by the sixth century) and for women (by the fourth century).

Hippopede: Horse fetter. The astronomer Eudoxus claimed that each of the planets travels along a special track shaped like a figure-8, resembling a kind of bridle used in the ancient world.

Homoioi: "Equals."

Hoplite: A soldier armed with a full set of weapons (*hopla*).

Hupokritês: "answerer" or "interpreter"; an actor.

Hustera: Uterus. Some ancient Greek doctors thought that hysteria—a condition whose symptoms included uncontrollable weeping, shortness of breath, irrational behavior, and fainting—was a strictly female ailment that happened whenever the uterus "wandered" around inside the body, bumping into other organs. Cf. English *hysteria* and *hysterical*.

Hydria: Three-handled vase used for carrying water.

Immanent Teleology: The Aristotelian theory that every natural thing has as part of its makeup an inner goal toward which it tends. Aristotle identified this with the fourth or "final" cause.

Isonomia: "Equality in the law"; an early term used to describe Athenian democracy.

Isonomia: The equal balance of certain qualities (hot/cold, wet/dry) in the human body. This notion advanced by the philosopher Alcmaeon strongly influenced the Hippocratic idea of the four "humors."

Kantharos: Drinking cup with high handles, frequently used by Dionysus on Greek painted pottery.

Kekruphalos: A hairnet worn by women to gather the hair backward and off the forehead.

Kêrux (Plural = Kêrukes): A herald or official messenger.

Kêrukeion: A staff carried by a herald to identify him as a messenger and protect him from harassment.

Khitôn: A tunic, for men or women, that was put on over the head rather than draped. The Doric *khitôn* was thigh- or knee-length; the older Ionic *khitôn* reached the ankles.

Khlamus or Chlamys: A cloak made of thick, stiff material, joined at the shoulder or in front of the body.

Khoes (Singular = Khous): A liquid measure. Drinking khoes of wine was part of the celebration at the Anthesteria.

Khumoi: Fluids. Ancient Greek doctors believed that the relative amounts of four bodily fluids determined sickness and health: blood, yellow bile, phlegm, and black bile. Cf. English *humor*.

Klepsudra: A water clock, in which water dripping from one vessel to another would mark off a fixed amount of time. It was used for timing specific events, such as speeches in law courts.

Klinê (Plural = Klinai): A couch or bed. This piece of furniture lacked a back and was designed for reclining rather than sitting. Usually one end was slightly elevated, which would allow the user to be propped up while dining, or maintain slight head elevation while sleeping.

Klismos: A type of chair having a curved, slightly reclined back and plain, curved legs.

Kommos: "Dirge"; used more generally of any singing shared between the chorus and actor(s).

Kômos: A procession following a symposium, in which the participants make their way home.

Korê (Plural = Korai): "Maiden." A traditional statue of a young girl from the Archaic Period that marked female graves or served as votive offerings to female deities.

Koruphaios: "Head man"; the leader of a chorus.

Kothurnos: A high-soled shoe worn by actors in tragedies.

Kottabos: A game played at symposia and sometimes elsewhere in which the participants flick the dregs of their wine at a target.

Kouros (Plural = Kouroi): "Youth." A traditional statue of a warrior from the Archaic Period that marked male graves or was dedicated to a god.

Kratêr: A large bowl for mixing wine and water.

Kukeôn: A mixture of barley meal and water, often flavored with herbs or honey.

Kulix: A shallow, two-handled cup for drinking at a symposium. Often decorated with scenes of drinking or sex.

Kunê: A plain cap, made of leather.

Kurios: "Guardian." A legal term that refers to the man, usually a father or husband, entrusted with the welfare of a daughter or wife.

Lekuthos: Tall, one-handled oil bottle.

Lênaia: "Wine-pressing"; an Athenian dramatic festival held every year in January/February of the modern calendar.

Linear B: A syllabic form of writing used by Mycenaean Greeks.

Logographos: "Writer of words"; a ghostwriter for speeches, but also used of early writers of other sorts of prose.

Logos: In general a rational, logical account or explanation of something. For Heraclitus, the logos has the broader sense of a rational, ordering principle that remains the same despite all the apparent changes in the world. Cf. English *logic* and *-logy*.

Loutrophoros: Vase shaped for holding water in a marriage ritual.

Lyric: "Suited to the lyre"; sung poetry, usually more emotional than spoken verse.

Maenads: In myth, female followers of Dionysus. They are often depicted wearing the skins of wild animals, such as fawns and leopards.

Mathêmatikoi: The "Learners," or scientific followers of Pythagoras, who devoted their attention to research on acoustics, geometry, and astronomy. Cf. English *mathematics*.

Maza: A griddle cake made from barley meal.

Medimnos: A measure of grain employed by the Athenians, about twelve gallons.

Megaron: From the Greek *megas* meaning "great"; the great hall of a Mycenaean palace, typically with a central hearth.

Mêkhanê: "Machine"; a crane used for introducing deities onto the Greek stage.

Melaina Kholê: Black bile, one of the four bodily "humors" that were thought to be responsible for health and sickness. Greek doctors believed an excess of black bile caused serious, chronic illnesses. Cf. English *melancholy*.

Metic: Literally, "one dwelling with"; a resident foreigner.

Metope: Slab, usually blank, but sometimes decorated, between two triglyphs of a Doric frieze.

Moikhos: An adulterer. A man who seduces other men's wives and who may be punished by death if caught.

Monôidia: "Solo song."

Mousikê: "(The art) belonging to the Muse"; includes the semantic field of its descendant "music," but is actually much wider for the Greeks, including what modern scholars call "literature."

Nous: The divine mind that controls all events and processes in the world; the theory of Anaxagoras.

Obol: One of the smallest units of Athenian currency; made of bronze or iron, it resembled *obeliskoi* (nails), hence its name; six obols equaled one drachma.

Ode: A song, often choral.

Oikos: The household, a concept that included all family members: the husband, wife, and children, as well as slaves, animals, and property.

Oinokhoê: Vase used for pouring liquids, usually wine.

Oligarchy: Rule by a few.

Olpê: Jug with round mouth and sagging belly.

Opisthodomos: Back porch of a Greek temple.

Opson: A "treat" or a "delicacy." Used for any food other than grain.

Orkhêstra: "Dancing place"; usually a round area in a Greek theater, used by the chorus.

Ostracism: The Athenian process of banishing a citizen for ten years in order to preserve political stability.

Ostrakon (Plural = Ostraka): A pottery shard on which Athenians inscribed the names of those citizens whom they wished to drive out of the city for political misconduct.

Paggenesis or Pangenesis: The ancient theory that a plant or animal seed is drawn from every part of its parent's body, and therefore contains all the parts into which the seed will grow as it matures.

Pagkration or Pankration: A combat sport in which almost all fighting techniques were allowed.

Paiderastia: "Love of boys." The erotic relationship between males of equal status, normally an older aristocratic man and a wellborn youth (not a *boy* as the term is used today).

Palaeopathology: The modern science that studies human and animal remains in order to learn about nutrition and disease in ancient societies.

Palaistra: Similar to the *gumnasion*, but devoted to wrestling and other combat sports.

Panathênaia: In Athens, the large annual festival honoring Athena. Every four years in August it was expanded into a major panhellenic event.

Panhellenism: The idea of a united Greece.

Pannukhis: An all-night festival or portion of a festival.

Panta Rhei: "Everything flows." According to Heraclitus, the world is in a constant state of change and flux, like a river.

Parabasis: "Coming forward"; part of Old Comedy when the chorus addressed the audience on behalf of the poet.

Parodos: "Entry"; the entry and first song of the chorus in a drama.

Pastas: A house design in which there was more than one south-facing room off the courtyard, allowing for maximum exposure to the winter sun.

Pediment: Triangular space formed by slanting roof at the ends of a Greek building, usually a temple.

Pelikê: Two-handled vase used for storage.

Peltast: A lightly armed soldier.

Pentecontor: The chief type of warship used in the Archaic Period; the name means "fifty-oars," but not all pentecontors had that many. Anywhere from forty to sixty oarsmen were arrayed in two ranks on either side provided the propulsion.

Peplos: A women's garment consisting of a large piece of cloth draped around the body and fastened at the shoulders.

Periblêma: Clothing (such as the *himation*) designed to be wrapped around the body.

Perioikoi: "Those dwelling around"; people ethnically akin to the Spartans but not enjoying Spartan citizenship.

Peristyle: Covered colonnade surrounding a building or court.

Pessoi: A game resembling checkers.

Petasos: A man's hat with a crown and a broad brim, which provided protection from the sun. For this reason, it was the standard hat for travelers.

Phainomêrides: Literally, "thigh-revealers." A style of *peplos*, loosely fastened on one side.

Phalanx: A closely packed formation of hoplite soldiers.

Philia: "Affection." The feeling of love between members of a household, husband and a wife, parents and children, or between friends.

Phratry: From the Greek *phratria*, meaning a localized organization with hereditary membership. Members of a phratry were known as *phrateres* (Latin *fratres*, "brothers"). To join a phratry one had to be initiated. In some locales, phratries were subgroups of the *phulê* ("tribe," "clan," extended kinship group) and themselves might be subdivided into groups known as *genê* (extended family).

Phusiologoi: Literally, meaning "those who give a rational logos (account) of physis (nature)." The name given to ancient Greek thinkers—such as Thales, Anaximander, and Anaximenes—who devoted their attention to studying natural phenomena.

Pilidion: A plain bonnet made of wool or felt. A practical but unfashionable garment.

Pillars of Herakles: The ancient name for the Strait of Gibraltar, a point which marked for the ancients the beginning of the vast unknown.

Pilos: A tall, conical hat.

Pithos: A large, round-bodied clay vessel used for the storage and transport of various commodities.

Poiêtês: "Poet." The word used to designate a person who composed poems, particularly plays.

Polis (Plural = Poleis): "City-state." The basic political unit of ancient Greece, characterized by ethnic homogeneity and governmental autonomy.

Politeia: The constitution of a *polis*.

Pornê: "Prostitute." A woman who worked in a brothel or sold her body on the streets for money.

Porphura: A highly prized, expensive purple dye derived from the shellfish *porphura*.

Presbeutês: An ambassador or envoy.

Probouloi: Councilors given extraordinary powers.

Proïx (Plural = Proïkes): "Dowry." A gift of property or money given from the bride's father to the groom to support his daughter and her future children.

Prologos: "Prologue"; the part of a play before the entry of the chorus.

Pronaos: Front porch of Greek temple.

Prostas: A house design in which there was a south-facing room off the courtyard, allowing for maximum exposure to the winter sun.

Prothesis: Lying in state and ritual mourning of a deceased person, commonly depicted on Late Geometric pottery.

Prutaneion: A public building serving as the symbolic center of the *polis* (city-state). It could be used for the entertainment of important guests; in Athens, victorious athletes were given free meals for life at the prutaneion.

Prutanis: A sort of presidency, elected by lot to head the Athenian state.

Psuktêr: Bulbous vase used as wine cooler.

Red Figure Technique: Type of vase painting in which the background is painted (usually black), leaving the figures the colour of the clay which are then decorated with washes, glazes, and color.

Relief Sculpture: A type of sculpture in which figures emerge partly from a sunken background.

Retrograde Movement: The apparently backward movement of planets at certain times of the year. Much of fourth-century B.C.E. Greek astronomy was devoted to designing a model of the solar system that could account for this kind of movement.

Rhizômata: The four basic elements or "roots"— earth, air, fire, and water—that Empedocles claimed made everything in the universe.

Satrap: A Persian governor.

Satyr: A mythical follower of Dionysus, with a horse's or goat's legs and tail; satyr plays had a chorus of men dressed up as these creatures.

Sitos: Literally, "grain," but in practice the word came to mean food of any sort.

Skyphos: A two-handled drinking cup.

Skutalê: A special staff used by Spartan magistrates to decode messages sent to them on leather strips by the Spartan government.

Sokkoi: Socks, typically produced by a sort of knitting technique rather than weaving.

Sophist: From *sophos,* meaning "wise." A teacher of rhetoric who instructed young men how to make the best argument.

Sôizein Ta Phainomena: According to Aristotle, an attempt by early Greek scientists to "save the phenomena"—that is, to provide a rational account (logos) of things and processes in the world. Without such an account, natural phenomena are unintelligible and thus "lost."

Sphyrelaton Technique: Construction of figures by hammering thin metal sheets over a form, then nailing them to a wooden core.

Stadion (Plural = Stadia): A distance equivalent to 192 meters (210 yards). Also a footrace covering this distance.

Stamnos: Two-handled vase used for storage.

Stasimon: "Standing (song)"; an ode sung by the chorus after the parodos.

Stasis: Political strife.

Stele: Upright stone slab, often used as a grave-marker, sometimes with inscriptions and relief sculpture.

Stereobate: The stepped foundation of a stone temple.

Stoa: Long, rectangular construction with a roof extending from the back wall to a row of supports in front.

Strophion: A band worn by women to restrain the breasts.

Stylobate: Portion of the floor of a building on which the columns rest.

Sukophantia: Troublesome litigation, brought for the sake of politics or intimidation rather than to right wrongs.

Sumposion or Symposium: Literally, "drinking together." An all-male drinking party in which participants sang songs, recited poems, and were entertained by musicians and *hetairai.*

Sunoikein: "To live together." The term used to recognize the validity of a marriage in ancient Greece.

Sussitia: The common dining centers of Sparta.

Symposiarch: Literally, "leader of the symposium." A symposiarch would be chosen from among the guests at a symposium and would be a sort of master of ceremonies, in charge of entertainment, conversation, and drinking.

Syncretism: Identification of one god with another (as of Apollo and the Sun).

Synoicism or Sunoikismos: The unification of a large area into a single polis.

Talent: A weight used in commercial trade, the equivalent of about 26 kilograms.

Ta Meteôra: Literally, these are "the things above the air," namely everything that modern science includes in the categories of meteorology and astronomy. As early as the Milesians, the Greeks showed a keen interest in explaining the movements of the stars and planets. Cf. English *meteor* and *meteorology.*

Telos: Goal. The final or "telic" cause of the four Aristotelian aitiai. For Aristotle, everything in the universe—inanimate things no less than living creatures—has an inner purpose or function that defines its true nature.

Temenos: From the Greek *temnein,* meaning "cut off"; a piece of land such as a grove dedicated to a god as a sacred precinct. Often a temenos had a temple built on it.

Tempera Technique: Use of medium such as egg yolk to bind colors in painting.

Terracotta: Baked clay.

Tesserae: Small pieces of stone used in composing mosaics.

Thesmophoria: A state-sponsored fertility festival in honor of Demeter and Persephone attended only by women.

Thesmothetai: Senior magistrates in Athens with judicial responsibilities.

Tholia: A broad-brimmed hat for women (equivalent to the *petasos*).

Thronos: a fancy type of chair, from which the English word *throne* is derived. Solid and upright (as opposed to the reclining *klismos*), it was typically found in palaces and public buildings rather than in private houses.

Thulê: An "island" glimpsed by the explorer Pytheas in the North Sea in the late fourth century B.C.E.; it came to represent the furthest reach of the earth in ancient thought.

Thusia: A public sacrifice.

Toikhorukhoi: Literally, "wall-breakers." A common Greek word for burglars, derived from their practice of breaking through walls (which were often thin) instead of through doors or windows.

Tragedy: "Goat-song"; a serious play (not necessarily with an unhappy ending).

Trapezite: Literally, "the man at the table": a money-changer.

Trierês: A trireme, the standard warship of the late Archaic and Classical Periods. Approximately 170 oarsmen were arrayed in three banks on each side to provide propulsion.

Triglyph: Slab in the frieze area of Doric temple that has grooves carved in it.

Tripod: Tall, three-footed cauldron, usually bronze, sometimes functioned as a dedication in sanctuaries, a prize in athletic competitions, or to conduct sacrifices.

Tyranny: A form of government formed outside the existing constitution.

Wanax: An early Greek term for a lord.

White Ground Technique: Type of painting common on mid- to late-fifth-century Attic funerary vases which had a white clay slip covering them, sometimes with added colors as decoration.

Xenia: "Guest-friendship." A relationship between adult males from unrelated households, recognized by the mutual exchange of gifts and visits.

Xoanon (Plural = Xoana): Primitive statue made of wood, usually as cult statue.

Zôstêr: A cloth band used to hold up a *khitôn*.

GENERAL REFERENCES

GENERAL

Antony Andrewes, *The Greeks* (New York: Knopf, 1967).

Peter D. Arnott, *An Introduction to the Greek World* (London: Macmillan; New York: St. Martin's Press, 1967).

John Boardman, Jasper Griffin, and Oswyn Murray, eds., *The Oxford History of the Classical World* (Oxford & New York: Oxford University Press, 1986).

Nancy Demand, *A History of Ancient Greece* (New York: McGraw-Hill, 1996).

William E. Dunstan, *Ancient Greece* (Fort Worth, Tex.: Harcourt College Publishers, 2000).

Michael Grant, *The Ancient Mediterranean* (London: Weidenfeld & Nicolson, 1969).

Grant, *The Rise of the Greeks* (New York: Scribners, 1988).

Grant, *A Social History of Greece and Rome* (New York: Scribners, 1992).

Simon Hornblower, *The Greek World 479–323 B.C.* (London & New York: Methuen, 1983).

Hornblower and Antony Spawforth, eds., *The Oxford Classical Dictionary,* third edition (Oxford: Oxford University Press, 1999).

Nicholas F. Jones, *Ancient Greece: State and Society* (Upper Saddle River, N.J.: Prentice Hall, 1997).

D. Brendan Nagle, *The Ancient World: A Social and Cultural History* (Upper Saddle River, N.J.: Prentice Hall, 1999).

Anton Powell, ed., *The Greek World* (London & New York: Routledge, 1995).

Anthony M. Snodgrass, *Archaic Greece: The Age of Experiment* (London: Dent , 1980).

Chester G. Starr, *The Ancient Greeks* (New York: Oxford University Press, 1971).

THE ARTS

David Bain, *Actors and Audience: A Study of Asides and Related Conventions in Greek Drama* (Oxford: Oxford University Press, 1977).

H. C. Baldry, *Ancient Greek Literature in Its Living Context* (New York: McGraw-Hill, 1974).

William R. Biers, *The Archaeology of Greece: An Introduction* (Ithaca, N.Y. & London: Cornell University Press, 1996).

John Boardman, *Athenian Black Figure Vases: A Handbook* (London: Thames & Hudson, 1974).

Boardman, *Athenian Red Figure Vases, The Archaic Period: A Handbook* (London: Thames & Hudson, 1975).

Boardman, *Athenian Red Figure Vases, The Classical Period: A Handbook* (London: Thames & Hudson, 1989).

Boardman, *Greek Art* (London: Thames & Hudson, 1996).

Boardman, *Greek Sculpture: The Classical Period. A Handbook* (London: Thames & Hudson, 1978).

Cecil Maurice Bowra, *Early Greek Elegists* (Cambridge, Mass.: Harvard University Press, 1938).

David A. Campbell, *The Golden Lyre: The Themes of the Greek Lyric Poets* (London: Duckworth, 1983).

David Castriota, *Myth, Ethos, Actuality: Official Art in Fifth-Century B.C. Athens* (Madison: University of Wisconsin Press, 1992).

J. N. Coldstream, *Geometric Greece* (London: Benn, 1977).

J. J. Coulton, *Ancient Greek Architects at Work: Problems of Structure and Design* (London: Elek, 1977).

Kenneth J. Dover, *Aristophanic Comedy* (London: Batsford, 1972).

P. E. Easterling and B. M. W. Knox, eds., *The Cambridge History of Classical Literature,* volume 1, *Greek Literature* (Cambridge & New York: Cambridge University Press, 1985).

John Ferguson, *A Companion to Greek Tragedy* (Austin: University of Texas Press, 1972).

E. D. Francis, *Image and Idea in Fifth-Century Athens: Art and Literature After the Persian Wars,* edited by

Michael Vickers (London & New York: Routledge, 1990).

Hermann Fränkel, *Early Greek Poetry and Philosophy: A History of Greek Epic, Lyric, and Prose to the Middle of the Fifth Century,* translated by Moses Hadas and James Willis (Oxford: Blackwell, 1975).

Michael Grant, *Greek and Roman Historians: Information and Misinformation* (London & New York: Routledge, 1995).

W. K. C. Guthrie, *A History of Greek Philosophy,* 6 volumes (Cambridge: Cambridge University Press, 1962–1981).

Richard Hamilton, *The Architecture of Hesiodic Poetry* (Baltimore: Johns Hopkins University Press, 1989).

Jeffrey M. Hurwit, *The Art and Culture of Early Greece, 1100–480 B.C.E.* (Ithaca, N.Y. & London: Cornell University Press, 1985).

Franciscus Junius, *The Literature of Classical Art,* 2 volumes, edited and translated by Keith Aldrich, Philipp Fehl, and Raina Fehl (Berkeley: University of California Press, 1991).

George A. Kennedy, *The Art of Persuasion in Greece* (Princeton: Princeton University Press, 1963).

Geoffrey Stephen Kirk, *The Songs of Homer* (Cambridge: Cambridge University Press, 1962).

Mary R. Lefkowitz, *The Lives of the Greek Poets* (Baltimore: Johns Hopkins University Press, 1981).

Albin Lesky, *A History of Greek Literature,* translated by James Willis and Cornelis de Heer (London: Methuen, 1966).

Peter Levi, *A History of Greek Literature* (New York: Viking, 1985).

Warren G. Moon, ed., *Polykleitos, the Doryphoros and Tradition* (Madison: University of Wisconsin Press, 1995).

Ian Morris and Barry Powell, eds., *A New Companion to Homer* (Leiden, Netherlands & New York: Brill, 1997).

Sarah P. Morris, *Daidalos and the Origins of Greek Art* (Princeton: Princeton University Press, 1992).

Robin Osborne, *Archaic and Classical Greek Art* (Oxford & New York: Oxford University Press, 1998).

Arthur Wallace Pickard-Cambridge, *The Dramatic Festivals of Athens* (London: Oxford University Press, 1968).

J. J. Pollitt, *The Art of Ancient Greece: Sources and Documents* (Cambridge & New York: Cambridge University Press, 1990).

Tom Rasmussen and Nigel Spivey, eds., *Looking at Greek Vases* (Cambridge & New York: Cambridge University Press, 1991).

Edward Schiappa, ed., *Landmark Essays in Classical Greek Rhetoric* (Davis, Cal.: Hermagoras, 1994).

Nigel Spivey, *Greek Art* (London: Phaidon, 1997).

Andrew Stewart, *Art, Desire and the Body in Ancient Greece* (Cambridge & New York: Cambridge University Press, 1997).

Stewart, *Faces of Power: Alexander's Image and Hellenistic Politics* (Berkeley: University of California Press, 1993).

Stewart, *Greek Sculpture: An Exploration,* 2 volumes (New Haven: Yale University Press, 1990).

David F. Sutton, *The Greek Satyr Play* (Meisenheim am Glan: Hain, 1980).

Peter Toohey, *Epic Lessons: An Introduction to Ancient Didactic Poetry* (London & New York: Routledge, 1996).

A. J. B. Wace and Frank H. Stubbings, eds., *A Companion to Homer* (London: Macmillan; New York: St. Martin's Press, 1962).

COMMUNICATION, TRANSPORTATION, AND EXPLORATION

L. Sprague de Camp, *The Ancient Engineers* (Garden City, N.Y.: Doubleday, 1963).

Lionel Casson, *Ships and Seafaring in Ancient Times* (Austin: University of Texas Press, 1994).

Casson, *Travel in the Ancient World* (London: Allen & Unwin, 1974).

B. F. Cook, *Greek Inscriptions* (Berkeley: University of California Press; London: British Museum, 1987).

Donald W. Engels, *Alexander the Great and the Logistics of the Macedonian Army* (Berkeley: University of California Press, 1978).

Robert Garland, *The Piraeus: From the Fifth to the First Century B.C.* (Ithaca, N.Y.: Cornell University Press, 1987).

Peter Garnsey, *Famine and Food Supply in the Graeco-Roman World: Responses to Risk and Crisis* (Cambridge & New York: Cambridge University Press, 1988).

Henry Hodges, *Technology in the Ancient World* (London: Allen Lane, 1970; New York: Knopf, 1970).

Gillian Hutchinson, *Medieval Ships and Shipping* (London: Leicester University Press, 1994).

Manoles Korres, *From Pentelicon to the Parthenon: The Ancient Quarries and the Story of a Half-worked Column Capital of the First Marble Parthenon* (Athens: Melissa, 1995).

J. G. Landels, *Engineering in the Ancient World* (Berkeley: University of California Press, 1978; London: Chatto & Windus, 1978).

Sian Lewis, *News and Society in the Greek Polis* (Chapel Hill: University of North Carolina Press, 1996; London: Duckworth, 1996).

J. S. Morrison and J. F. Coates, *The Athenian Trireme: The History and Reconstruction of an Ancient Greek Warship* (Cambridge & New York: Cambridge University Press, 1986).

Colin Renfrew, *Archaeology and Language: The Puzzle of Indo-European Origins* (London: Cape, 1987).

H. T. Wallinga, *Ships and Sea-power before the Great Persian War: The Ancestry of the Ancient Trireme* (Leiden, Netherlands & New York: Brill, 1993).

LEISURE, RECREATION, AND DAILY LIFE

James N. Davidson, *Courtesans and Fishcakes: The Consuming Passions of Classical Athens* (London: HarperCollins, 1997).

Kenneth J. Dover, *Greek Homosexuality* (Cambridge, Mass.: Harvard University Press, 1977).

Moses I. Finley and H. W. Pleket, *The Olympic Games: The First Thousand Years* (London: Chatto & Windus, 1976).

Robert Flacelière, *Daily Life in Greece at the Time of Pericles,* translated by Peter Green (New York: Macmillan, 1965).

E. Norman Gardiner, *Athletics of the Ancient World* (Oxford: Clarendon Press, 1930).

Peter Garnsey, *Famine and Food Supply in the Graeco-Roman World: Responses to Risk and Crisis* (Cambridge: Cambridge University Press, 1988).

Richard Hamilton, *Choes and Anthesteria: Athenian Iconography and Ritual* (Ann Arbor: University of Michigan Press, 1991).

Dorothy M. Johnson, ed., *Ancient Greek Dress* (Chicago: Argonaut, 1964).

François Lissarague, *The Aesthetics of the Greek Banquet: Images of Wine and Ritual* (Princeton: Princeton University Press, 1990).

Oswyn Murray and Simon Price, eds., *The Greek City: From Homer to Alexander* (Oxford: Clarendon Press; New York: Oxford University Press, 1990).

Robin Osborne, *Classical Landscape with Figures* (London: G. Philip, 1987).

Herbert William Parke, *Festivals of the Athenians* (Ithaca, N.Y.: Cornell University Press, 1977).

Arthur Wallace Pickard-Cambridge, *The Dramatic Festivals of Athens* (Oxford: Clarendon Press, 1968).

Michael B. Poliakoff, *Combat Sports in the Ancient World: Competition, Violence, and Culture* (New Haven: Yale University Press, 1987).

G. M. A. Richter, *The Furniture of the Greeks, Etruscans, and Romans* (London: Phaidon, 1966).

Charles Seltman, *Wine in the Ancient World* (London: Routledge & Kegan Paul, 1957).

William J. Slater, ed., *Dining in a Classical Context* (Ann Arbor: University of Michigan Press, 1991).

Anthony M. Snodgrass, *An Archaeology of Greece* (Berkeley: University of California Press, 1987).

John Wilkins, and others, eds., *Food in Antiquity* (Exeter, U.K.: University of Exeter Press, 1995).

David C. Young, *The Olympic Myth of Greek Amateur Athletics* (Chicago: Ares, 1984).

William A. Younger, *Gods, Men and Wine* (London: Wine and Food Society, 1966).

THE FAMILY AND SOCIAL TRENDS

Margaret Alexiou, *The Ritual Lament in the Greek Tradition* (Cambridge: Cambridge University Press, 1974).

Averil Cameron and Amélie Kuhrt, eds., *Images of Women in Antiquity* (Detroit: Wayne State University Press, 1983).

Elaine Fantham, and others, eds., *Women in the Classical World: Image and Text* (New York: Oxford University Press, 1994).

Helene P. Foley, comp., *Reflections of Women in Antiquity* (New York: Gordon & Breech Science Publishers, 1981).

David M. Halperin, *One Hundred Years of Homosexuality: And Other Essays on Greek Love* (New York: Routledge, 1990).

Halperin, John J. Winkler, and Froma I. Zeitlin, eds., *Before Sexuality: The Construction of Erotic Experience in the Ancient Greek World* (Princeton: Princeton University Press, 1990).

Madeleine M. Henry, *Prisoner of History: Aspasia of Miletus and Her Biographical Tradition* (New York: Oxford University Press, 1995).

S. C. Humphreys, *The Family, Women, and Death: Comparative Studies* (London & Boston: Routledge & Kegan Paul, 1983).

Virginia J. Hunter, *Policing Athens: Social Control in the Attic Lawsuits, 420–320 B.C.* (Princeton: Princeton University Press, 1994).

Roger Just, *Women in Athenian Law and Life* (London & New York: Routledge, 1989).

Mary R. Lefkowitz and Maureen B. Fant, comps., *Women's Life in Greece and Rome* (Baltimore: Johns Hopkins University Press, 1982).

Zeitlin, *Playing the Other: Gender and Society in Classical Greek Literature* (Chicago: University of Chicago Press, 1996).

POLITICS, LAW, AND THE MILITARY

Antony Andrewes, *The Greek Tyrants* (London: Hutchinson's University Library, 1956).

Aristotle, *The Athenian Constitution,* translated by P. J. Rhodes (Harmondsworth, U.K. & New York: Penguin, 1984).

Paul Cartledge, *Sparta and Lakonia: A Regional History, 1300–362 B.C.* (London & Boston: Routledge & Kegan Paul, 1979).

J. K. Davies, *Democracy and Classical Greece* (Hassocks, U.K.: Harvester, 1978; Atlantic Highlands, N.J.: Humanities, 1978).

Victor Ehrenberg, *From Solon to Socrates: Greek History and Civilization During the Sixth and Fifth Centuries B.C.* (London: Methuen, 1968).

Debra Hamel, *Athenian Generals: Military Authority in the Classical Period* (Leiden, Netherlands & Boston: Brill, 1998).

Mogens Herman Hansen, *The Athenian Democracy in the Age of Demosthenes: Structure, Principles, and Ideology,* translated by J. A. Crook (Oxford & Cambridge, Mass.: Blackwell, 1991).

Victor Davis Hanson, *The Wars of the Ancient Greeks: And Their Invention of Western Military Culture* (London: Cassell, 1999).

Douglas M. McDowell, *The Law in Classical Athens* (London: Thames & Hudson, 1978).

J. S. Morrison and J. F. Coates, *The Athenian Trireme: The History and Reconstruction of an Ancient Greek Warship* (Cambridge & New York: Cambridge University Press, 1986).

William Kendrick Pritchett, *Ancient Greek Military Practices, Part I* (Berkeley: University of California Press, 1971).

Michael M. Sage, *Warfare in Ancient Greece: A Sourcebook* (London & New York: Routledge, 1996).

Raphael Sealey, *A History of the Greek City-States, ca. 700–338 B.C.* (Berkeley: University of California Press, 1976).

I. G. Spence, *The Cavalry of Classical Greece: A Social and Military History with Particular Reference to Athens* (Oxford: Clarendon Press, 1993; New York: Oxford University Press, 1993).

RELIGION AND PHILOSOPHY

Apollodorus of Athens, *The Library of Greek Mythology,* translated by Robin Hard (New York: Oxford University Press, 1997).

Jonathan Barnes, *The Cambridge Companion to Aristotle* (Cambridge: Cambridge University Press, 1995).

Barnes, *The Presocratic Philosophers* (London & Boston: Routledge & Kegan Paul, 1979).

Hans Dieter Betz, ed., *The Greek Magical Papyri in Translation, Including the Demotic Spells* (Chicago: University of Chicago Press, 1992).

Jan N. Bremmer, *The Early Greek Concept of the Soul* (Princeton: Princeton University Press, 1983).

Walter Burkert, *Ancient Mystery Cults* (Cambridge, Mass.: Harvard University Press, 1987).

Burkert, *Greek Religion* (Cambridge, Mass.: Harvard University Press, 1985).

Burkert, *Homo Necans: The Anthropology of Ancient Greek Sacrificial Ritual and Myth* (Berkeley: University of California Press, 1983).

Burkert, *Structure and History in Greek Mythology and Ritual* (Berkeley: University of California Press, 1979).

Harold Cherniss, *The Riddle of the Early Academy* (New York: Russell & Russell, 1962).

E. R. Dodds, *The Greeks and the Irrational* (Berkeley: University of California Press, 1951).

Abraham Edel, *Aristotle and his Philosophy* (Chapel Hill: University of North Carolina Press, 1982).

Lewis R. Farnell, *Greek Hero Cults and Ideas of Immortality* (Oxford: Clarendon Press, 1921).

Farnell, *Outline-History of Greek Religion* (London: Duckworth, 1920).

J. Fontenrose, *The Delphic Oracle: Its Responses and Operations* (Berkeley: University of California Press, 1978).

Kathleen Freeman, ed., *Ancilla to The Pre-Socratic Philosophers: A Complete Translation of the Fragments in Diels, Fragmente der Vorsokratiker* (Cambridge, Mass.: Harvard University Press, 1948).

Hans Georg Gadamer, *The Idea of The Good in Platonic-Aristotelian Philosophy,* translated by P. Christopher Smith (New Haven: Yale University Press, 1986).

Timothy Gantz, *Early Greek Myth: A Guide to Literary and Artistic Sources* (Baltimore: Johns Hopkins University Press, 1993).

Fritz Graf, *Magic in the Ancient World,* translated by Franklin Philip (Cambridge, Mass.: Harvard University Press, 1997).

W. K. C. Guthrie, *The Greeks and Their Gods* (Boston: Beacon, 1951).

Guthrie, *A History of Greek Philosophy,* Volumes I-VI (Cambridge: Cambridge University Press, 1962-1981).

Edward Hussey, *The Presocratics* (New York: Scribners, 1972).

G. B. Kerferd, *The Sophistic Movement* (Cambridge: Cambridge University Press, 1981).

Geoffrey Stephen Kirk, *Myth: Its Meaning and Functions in Ancient and Other Cultures* (Cambridge: Cambridge University Press, 1970).

Richard Kraut, ed., *The Cambridge Companion to Plato* (Cambridge: Cambridge University Press, 1992).

A. A. Long, ed., *The Cambridge Companion to Early Greek Philosophy* (Cambridge & New York: Cambridge University Press, 1999).

Georg Luck, ed., *Arcana Mundi: Magic and the Occult in the Greek and Roman Worlds: A Collection of Ancient Texts* (Baltimore: Johns Hopkins University Press, 1985).

Jon Mikalson, *Athenian Popular Religion* (Chapel Hill: University of North Carolina Press, 1983).

Martin P. Nilsson, *Greek Folk Religion* (New York: Harper, 1961).

H. W. Parke, *Festivals of the Athenians* (Ithaca, N.Y.: Cornell University Press, 1977).

Francis E. Peters, *Greek Philosophical Terms: A Historical Lexicon* (New York: New York University Press, 1967).

Barry B. Powell, *Classical Myth* (Englewood Cliffs, N.J.: Prentice Hall, 1995).

Gerald Press, ed., *Plato's Dialogues: New Studies and Interpretations* (Lanham, Md.: Rowman & Littlefield, 1993).

H. D. Rankin, *Sophists, Socratics & Cynics* (London: Croom Helm, 1983).

Giovanni Reale, *A History of Ancient Philosophy*, Volumes I & II (Albany: State University of New York Press, 1990).

John M. Rist, *The Mind of Aristotle: A Study in Philosophical Growth* (Toronto: University of Toronto Press, 1989).

John Manley Robinson, *An Introduction to Early Greek Philosophy* (Boston: Houghton Mifflin, 1968).

Jaqueline de Romilly, *The Great Sophists In Periclean Athens,* translated by Janet Lloyd (Oxford: Clarendon Press, 1992).

W. D. Ross, *Plato's Theory of Ideas* (Oxford: Oxford University Press, 1953).

Kenneth Sayre, *Plato's Literary Garden: How To Read A Platonic Dialogue* (Notre Dame, Ind.: University of Notre Dame Press, 1995).

Rosamund Kent Sprague, ed., *The Older Sophists: A Complete Translation by Several Hands of the Fragments in Die Fragmente der Vorsokratiker,* edited by Hermann Diels (Columbia: University of South Carolina Press, 1972).

J. O. Urmson, *The Greek Philosophical Vocabulary* (London: Duckworth, 1990).

Paul Veyne, *Did the Greeks Believe in Their Myths?,* translated by Paula Wissing (Chicago: University of Chicago Press, 1988).

M. L. West, *The East Face of Helicon: West Asiatic Elements in Greek Poetry and Myth* (Oxford: Clarendon Press, 1997).

West, *The Orphic Poems* (Oxford: Clarendon Press, 1983).

SCIENCE, TECHNOLOGY, AND HEALTH

J. L. Ackrill, *Aristotle the Philosopher* (Oxford & New York: Oxford University Press, 1981).

Aristotle, *The Complete Works of Aristotle: The Revised Oxford Translation*, edited by Jonathan Barnes, 2 volumes (Princeton: Princeton University Press, 1984).

Jonathan Barnes, *Aristotle* (Oxford & New York: Oxford University Press, 1982).

Barnes, *Early Greek Philosophy* (Harmondsworth, U.K. & New York: Penguin, 1987).

Robert S. Brumbaugh, *Plato's Mathematical Imagination: The Mathematical Passages in the Dialogues and Their Interpretation* (Bloomington: Indiana University Press, 1954).

Walter Burkert, *Lore and Science in Ancient Pythagoreanism,* translated by Edwin L. Minar Jr. (Cambridge, Mass.: Harvard University Press, 1972).

D. S. L. Cardwell, *Turning Points in Western Technology: A Study of Technology, Science and History* (New York: Science History Publications, 1972).

Marshall Clagett, *Greek Science in Antiquity* (New York: Abelard-Schuman, 1955).

S. Marc Cohen, and others, eds., *Readings in Ancient Greek Philosophy: From Thales to Aristotle* (Indianapolis: Hackett, 1995).

Lawrence I. Conrad, and others, *The Western Medical Tradition, 800 B.C. to A.D. 1800* (Cambridge: Cambridge University Press, 1995).

Patricia Curd, *The Legacy of Parmenides: Eleatic Monism and Later Presocratic Thought* (Princeton: Princeton University Press, 1998).

William Cecil Dampier Dampier-Whetham, *A History of Science and Its Relations with Philosophy & Religion* (Cambridge: Cambridge University Press, 1929).

D. R. Dicks, *Early Greek Astronomy to Aristotle* (Ithaca, N.Y.: Cornell University Press, 1970).

J. Dreyer, *A History of Astronomy from Thales to Kepler* (New York: Dover, 1953).

Emma J. Edelstein and Ludwig Edelstein, *Asclepius: A Collection and Interpretation of the Testimonies* (Baltimore: Johns Hopkins University Press, 1945).

Ludwig Edelstein, *Ancient Medicine: Selected Papers of Ludwig Edelstein,* edited by Owsei Temkin and C. Lilian Temkin, translated by C. Lilian Temkin (Baltimore: Johns Hopkins University Press, 1967).

Empedocles, *The Poem of Empedocles: A Text and Translation With an Introduction,* by Brad Inwood (Toronto: University of Toronto Press, 1992).

Benjamin Farrington, *Greek Science, Its Meaning For Us,* 2 volumes (Harmondsworth, U.K.: Penguin, 1944–1949).

Roger French, *Ancient Natural History: Histories of Nature* (London & New York: Routledge, 1994).

David Furley, *Cosmic Problems: Essays on Greek and Roman Philosophy of Nature* (Cambridge & New York: Cambridge University Press, 1989).

Furley, *The Greek Cosmologists,* volume 1, *The Formation of the Atomic Theory and Its Earliest Critics* (Cambridge & New York: Cambridge University Press, 1987).

Furley, *Two Studies in the Greek Atomists: Study I, Indivisible Magnitudes; Study II, Aristotle and Epicurus on Voluntary Action* (Princeton: Princeton University Press, 1967).

W. K. C. Guthrie, *The Greeks and Their Gods* (London: Methuen, 1950).

J. Donald Hughes, *Pan's Travail: Environmental Problems of the Ancient Greeks and Romans* (Baltimore: Johns Hopkins University Press, 1994).

John Humphrey, John P. Oleson, and Andrew Sherwood, eds., *Greek and Roman Technology: A Sourcebook* (London & New York: Routledge, 1998).

Charles H. Kahn, *Anaximander and the Origins of Greek Cosmology* (New York: Columbia University Press, 1960).

Kahn, *The Art and Thought of Heraclitus: An Edition of the Fragments With Translation and Commentary* (Cambridge & New York: Cambridge University Press, 1979).

G. S. Kirk and J. E. Raven, *The Presocratic Philosophers: A Critical History with a Selection of Texts* (Cambridge: Cambridge University Press, 1957).

Morris Kline, *Mathematics in Western Culture* (New York: Oxford University Press, 1953).

J. G. Landels, *Engineering in the Ancient World* (Berkeley: University of California Press, 1978).

David C. Lindberg, *The Beginnings of Western Science: The European Scientific Tradition in Philosophical, Religious, and Institutional Context, 600 B.C. to A.D. 1450* (Chicago: University of Chicago Press, 1992).

G. E. R. Lloyd, *Early Greek Science: Thales to Aristotle* (New York: Norton, 1970).

Lloyd, ed., *Hippocratic Writings,* translated by J. Chadwick and W. N. Mann (Harmondsworth, U.K. & New York: Penguin, 1978).

Lloyd, *Magic, Reason, and Experience: Studies in the Origin and Development of Greek Science* (Cambridge & New York: Cambridge University Press, 1979).

Lloyd, *The Revolutions of Wisdom: Studies in the Claims and Practice of Ancient Greek Science* (Berkeley: University of California Press, 1987).

Lois N. Magner, *A History of Medicine* (New York: M. Dekker, 1992).

Guido Majno, *The Healing Hand: Man and Wound in the Ancient World* (Cambridge, Mass.: Harvard University Press, 1975).

Richard D. Mohr, *The Platonic Cosmology* (Leiden, Netherlands: Brill, 1985).

Alexander P. D. Mourelatos, *The Route of Parmenides: A Study of Word, Image, and Argument in the Fragments* (New Haven: Yale University Press, 1970).

O. Neugebauer, *The Exact Sciences in Antiquity* (Copenhagen: Munksgaard, 1951).

Neugebauer, *A History of Ancient Mathematical Astronomy,* 3 volumes (Berlin & New York: Springer-Verlag, 1975).

Pierre Pellegrin, *Aristotle's Classification of Animals: Biology and the Conceptual Unity of the Aristotelian Corpus,* translated by Anthony Preus, revised edition (Berkeley: University of California Press, 1986).

Anthony Preus, *Science and Philosophy in Aristotle's Biological Works* (Hildesheim, Germany & New York: Olms, 1975).

Wesley C. Salmon, ed., *Zeno's Paradoxes* (Indianapolis: Bobbs-Merrill, 1970).

Giorgio de Santillana, *The Origins of Scientific Thought: From Anaximander to Proclus, 600 B.C. to 300 A.D.* (Chicago: University of Chicago Press, 1961).

George Sarton, *A History of Science,* volume 1: *Ancient Science Through the Golden Age of Greece* (Cambridge, Mass.: Harvard University Press, 1952).

Malcolm Schofield, *An Essay on Anaxagoras* (Cambridge & New York: Cambridge University Press, 1980).

Gregory Vlastos, *Plato's Universe* (Seattle: University of Washington Press, 1975).

C. J. de Vogel, *Pythagoras and Early Pythagoreanism: An Interpretation of Neglected Evidence on the Philosopher* (Assen, Netherlands: Van Gorcum, 1966).

SOCIAL CLASS SYSTEM AND THE ECONOMY

M. M. Austin and P. Vidal-Naquet, *Economic and Social History of Ancient Greece: An Introduction,* translated by Austin (Berkeley: University of California Press, 1977).

John Boardman, *The Greeks Overseas* (Baltimore: Penguin, 1964).

Thomas James Dunbabin, *The Western Greeks: The History of Sicily and South Italy from the Foundation of the Greek Colonies to 480 B.C.* (Oxford: Clarendon Press, 1948).

Moses I. Finley, *The Ancient Economy* (Berkeley: University of California Press, 1973).

George Leonard Huxley, *Early Sparta* (Cambridge, Mass.: Harvard University Press, 1962).

A. H. M. Jones, *Sparta* (Cambridge, Mass.: Harvard University Press, 1967).

Nicholas F. Jones, *Ancient Greece: State and Society* (Upper Saddle River, N.J.: Prentice Hall, 1997).

Russell Meiggs, *Trees and Timber in the Ancient Mediterranean World* (Oxford: Clarendon Press, 1982).

Humfrey Michell, *Sparta* (Cambridge: Cambridge University Press, 1952).

Anton Powell and Stephen Hodkinson, eds., *The Shadow of Sparta* (London & New York: Routledge for the Classical Press of Wales, 1994).

GEOGRAPHY

John Boardman, *The Greeks Overseas* (London: Penguin, 1964).

Charles W. Fornara, *The Nature of History in Ancient Greece and Rome* (Berkeley: University of California Press, 1983).

James S. Romm, *The Edges of the Earth in Ancient Thought* (Princeton: Princeton University Press, 1992).

Robert Sallares, *Ecology of the Ancient World* (Ithaca, N.Y.: Cornell University Press, 1990).

Samuel Sambursky, *The Physical World of the Greeks*, translated by Merton Dagut (London: Routledge & Kegan Paul, 1956; New York: Macmillan, 1956).

Richard J. A. Talbert, ed., *Atlas of Classical History* (London: Croom Helm, 1985; New York: Macmillan, 1985).

J. O. Thomson, *Everyman's Classical Atlas* (New York: Dutton, 1961).

The World of Athens: An Introduction to Classical Athenian Culture, Joint Association of Classical Teachers (Cambridge: Cambridge University Press, 1984).

CONTRIBUTORS

Michael S. Allen is studying religion in the Honors College at the University of South Carolina. He plans to pursue advanced study at Oxford University.

Jeffrey S. Carnes is Associate Professor of Classics at Syracuse University, New York. He received his Ph.D. in Classics from the University of North Carolina at Chapel Hill, where he was a Morehead Fellow. His research interests include Greek lyric poetry, mythology, literary theory, and gender studies. He is the author of *The Uses of Aiakos: Pindar and the Aiginetan Imaginary* (forthcoming) and many essays and book chapters. During the 2000–2001 academic year he is teaching at the Intercollegiate Center for Classical Studies in Rome.

Keith M. Dickson has taught at Wheaton College, Massachusetts, the University of California, Berkeley; the University of California, Davis; Beijing Normal University Foreign Language Institute; and Beijing Language and Culture University; he is currently Associate Professor of Classics at Purdue University, Indiana. He has published articles on palaeography, Greek epic and choral poetry, ancient magic, and ancient medicine. He is the author of three books: *Agnellus of Ravenna: Lectures on Galen's De Sectis* (1981), *Nestor: Poetic Memory in Greek Epic* (1995), and *Stephanus the Philosopher and Physician: Commentary on Galen's Therapeutics to Glaucon* (1998).

William E. Hutton received his Ph.D. in Classics from the University of Texas at Austin in 1995 and has taught at the Universities of Wisconsin and Calgary and at Truman State University, Missouri. Since 1997, he has been Visiting Assistant Professor of Classical Studies at the College of William and Mary, Virginia. He is a founder and managing editor of the Suda On-Line project (www.stoa.org/sol), and is currently in the process of completing a book on the Greek travel writer Pausanias.

Borimir Jordan is Professor of Classics at the University of California, Santa Barbara. He has been Visiting Professor at the University of California, Berkeley; University of California, Los Angeles; and Dartmouth College, New Hampshire. He received his graduate education at the University of California, Berkeley, and the American School of Classical Studies at Athens. He completed his postgraduate education in Roman law at the University of California, Berkeley, Law School. His fields of study include Greek history, religion, epigraphy, and archaeology. His major publications include books on naval history and religion and articles on Herodotus, Thucydides, Greek religion, Spartan social history, Athenian constitutional history, and the use and sources of energy in antiquity.

John T. Kirby is Professor of Classics and Comparative Literature and Chair of the Program in Comparative Literature at Purdue University, where he also founded the interdisciplinary Program in Classical Studies. His books include *Secret of the Muses Retold: Classical Influences on Italian Authors of the Twentieth Century* (2000), *The Comparative Reader: A Handlist of Basic Reading in Comparative Literature* (1998), *The Rhetoric of Cicero's Pro Cluentio* (1990), and *World Eras: The Roman Republic and Empire, 264 B.C.E.–476 C.E.* (forthcoming).

Laura McClure is Associate Professor of Classics at the University of Wisconsin, Madison. Her primary areas of research are Athenian drama and the Classical tradition and women in the ancient world. She is the author of *Spoken Like a Woman: Speech and Gender in Athenian Drama* (1999) and co-editor of a forthcoming volume on women's voices in ancient Greece. She has also published articles on Greek tragedy, pedagogy, and the classical tradition.

David C. Mirhady teaches at Simon Fraser University, British Columbia, Canada. He has published several articles and book chapters on ancient political theory, philosophy, and rhetoric and law. He has co-edited a collection of papers on *Peripatetic Rhetoric After Aristotle* (1994) and published translations of several works of the Athenian intellectual Isocrates. He is currently at work on a commentary on the political and legal works of Theophrastus of Eresus and on various aspects of Greek law and legal procedure.

Kelly Olson is Assistant Professor in the Department of Classical Studies at the University of Western Ontario, London, Ontario, Canada. Her research interests include Greek and Roman art, social history, women, and the family. She has co-edited *The Classical Collection at the David and Alfred Smart Museum of Art* (1998) and authored entries on Roman glass and coins. In addition she has published reviews and articles on ancient costume and gender in antiquity. She is currently working on a book about female clothing and adornment in ancient Rome.

Neil O'Sullivan is a Senior Lecturer in the Department of Classics and Ancient History at the University of Western Australia, Nedlands. He is a graduate of the Universities of Melbourne and Cambridge, and his chief research interests are ancient literary criticism, the first Sophistic, and Old Comedy. He is the author of *Alcidamas, Aristophanes and the Beginnings of Greek Stylistic Theory* (1992) and was co-editor of the journal *Antichthon* from 1993 to 1998.

Patrick O'Sullivan is a Lecturer in Greek literature, language, art, and philosophy at the University of Canterbury, Christchurch, New Zealand. Among his chief research interests is the intellectual history of the Archaic and Classical Greek world, with a focus on the reception of poetry, ancient psychological and cognitive theories, and visual aesthetics. He has written on aspects of Greek art and drama, especially Aeschylus, and is working on a project on Greek concepts of visual imagery from Homer to Plato.

Carol Poster is Associate Professor of English at Montana State University. Her publications include verse translations of Aristophanes' *Clouds* and Plautus's *Stichus*, and essays on ancient philosophy and rhetoric in *American Journal of Philology*, *Phoenix*, *Philosophy and Rhetoric*, *Rhetoric Society Quarterly*, and other journals and essay collections. Her book, *Writing the Ineffable: The Rhetoric of Ontology in Early Greek Thought*, is forthcoming. She has been a visiting fellow at the Tanner Humanities Center (University of Utah) and the Project on Rhetoric of Inquiry (University of Iowa).

INDEX OF PHOTOGRAPHS

Acharnians: Fragment of a third-century C.E. papyrus commentary on Aristophanes' poem (Brussells Mus. Roy. Inv. E. 5972) 59

Achilles painter: An Athenian white-ground *lekuthos* (late fifth century B.C.E.) showing a warrior departing from home (National Museum, Athens [1818]/ photo TAP) 66

Achilles slaying Penthesileia, the Amazon queen: An Athenian amphora from the late sixth century B.C.E. (British Museum, London [B210]) 69

Acropolis: *Korê*, or marble statue of a maiden, circa sixth century B.C.E. (Athens, Acropolis Museum 679, Photo: Alison Frantz) 260

The Acropolis in Athens: the Parthenon is the large structure to the right, while the Propylaia, the grandiose entrance, is on the left. The temple of Athena Nikê is in front of the Propylaia (Archivo Iconografico SA). 80

Aeschylus 85

Aeschylus' tragic play the *Eumenides:* Play scene detail on a fourth-century B.C.E. vase (British Museum, London) 82

Agamemnon: A *kratêr* painting of his murder, circa 700–480 B.C.E. (Boston Museum of Fine Arts, 63.1246) 258

Agora of ancient Athens (Photo: Ekdotike Athenon SA, Athens) 136

Al Mina with Mount Kasius in the background 154

Alcibiades 198

Alexander the Great 198

Alexander the Great at the Battle of Issus in 333 B.C.E.: Mosaic detail (circa 300 B.C.E.) found in Pompeii (Naples, National Museum; Photo: Andre Held) 183

Alexandrian treatise section on astronomy that depicts the movements of planets (Musée du Louvre, Paris) 337

Alphabets of the various Greek city-states and regions (from Anthony Snodgrass, *Archaic Greece* [1980], p. 80) 100

Amasis Painter: An Athenian amphora with a painting of dancers performing for Dionysus, mid-sixth century B.C.E. (Cabinet des Médailles, Bibliothèque Nationale, Paris [222] / photo Hirmer Verlag GmbH, Munich) 72

Amphipolis: The site of the Athenian city in eastern Macedonia, captured by the Spartans in 424 B.C.E. 194

Anaxagoras 351

Anaximander's mid-sixth-century B.C.E. map of the world: Modern reconstruction (J. M. Robinson, *An Introduction to Early Greek Philosophy* [1968], p. 32) 323

Aphrodite being born out of the seafoam: A fifth century B.C.E. relief (Museo Delle Terme, Rome, Alinari) 279

Apollo, Artemis, and Leto: Beaten bronze figures from the temple of Apollo at Dreros on Crete, circa 700 B.C.E. (National Archaeological Museum, Athens (1) / photo TAP) 74

Aristophanes 86

Aristophanes: Fragment of a third-century C.E. papyrus commentary on *Acharnians* (Brussells Mus. Roy. Inv. E. 5972) 59

Aristotle 352

Artemis, Apollo, and Leto: Beaten bronze figures from the temple of Apollo at Dreros on Crete, circa 700 B.C.E. (National Archaeological Museum, Athens (1)/photo TAP) 74

Aspasia 269

Athena watches Heracles wrestling the Nemean lion: A vase painting, circa late sixth century B.C.E. (Museo Civico, Brescia; Hirmer). 283

Athena with an owl, bronze sculpture, circa fifth century B.C.E. (Metropolitan Museum of Art, New York) 280

Athena Parthenos by Pheidias, orginially made in circa 440 B.C.E.: A modern reconstruction (Royal Ontario Museum, Toronto) 55

An Athenian amphora from the late sixth century B.C.E. showing Achilles slaying Penthesileia, the Amazon queen (British Museum, London [B210]) 69

An Athenian amphora with a painting of dancers performing for Dionysus; attributed to the Amasis Painter, mid-sixth century B.C.E. (Cabinet des Médailles, Bibliothèque Nationale, Paris [222]/ photo Hirmer Verlag GmbH, Munich) 72

An Athenian cup (circa late sixth century B.C.E.) with a painting of a pirate ship chasing a Greek merchantman (photo British Museum) 125

Athenian cup painting of two men sacrificing a pig, sixth century B.C.E. (Archives Photographiques, Musée du Louvre, Paris) 302

Athenian grave stele of an unknown man, circa fourth century B.C.E. (National Archaeological Museum, Athens (869) / photo TAP) 160

An Athenian Red Figure kalyx *kratêr* (wine mixing bowl) by the Niobid Painter, mid-fifth century B.C.E. (Musée du Lourve, Paris [G341]/ photo Réunion des Musées Nationaux) 71

The Athenian treasury on Delphi, built with the booty taken from the Persians after the Battle of Marathon in 490 B.C.E. (Courtesy of Ecole Française d'Archéologie, Athens) 24

An Athenian white-ground *lekuthos* attributed to the Achilles painter (late fifth century B.C.E.) and showing a warrior departing from home (National Museum, Athens [1818] / photo TAP) 66

Attic Black Figure amphora depicting laborers harvesting olives, late sixth century B.C.E. (British Museum, London) 220

Attic Black Figure *kuathos* painting of a funeral scene, late sixth century B.C.E. (John R. Freeman) 298

Attica: *Kouros,* or a male statue of a youth, circa late seventh century B.C.E. (Metropolitan Museum of Art, New York) 263

The Avenue of Lions on the island of Delos (Photo: Robert Tobler, Lucerne) 145

Bias of Priene: A bust inscribed with his saying "Most Men Are Bad" (Vatican Museum) 306

A Black Figure amphora depicting a customer getting measured for a pair of shoes, circa 520–510 B.C.E. (B.C. Museum of Fine Arts; Francis Bartlett Fund, Boston) 216

A Black Figure amphora painting of merchants weighing grain, circa 550-530 B.C.E. (Metropolitan

Museum of Art, New York) 141

A Boeotian terracotta of a plowman with his horses (Musée du Louvre, Paris, France) 134

A bowl painting of agricultural laborers on the road to market (Musée du Louvre, Paris, France) 139

A bowl painting of Penelope at her loom, while Telemachos looks on (Marburg University 1016. "ARV" 1233, 19) 266

A bronze sculpture of Athena with an owl, circa fifth century B.C.E. (Metropolitan Museum of Art, New York) 280

A bronze statue of a centaur, circa 540 B.C.E. (Metropolitan Museum, New York) 285

A bronze statue of Zeus, circa 460 B.C.E., found off Cape Artemisium (National Archaeological Museum, Athens/Scala) 281

A bronze statuette of a hoplite, circa late sixth century B.C.E. (Peter Newark Military Pictures) 174

A centaur, bronze statue, circa 540 B.C.E. (Metropolitan Museum, New York) 285

A chariot tablet found at Knossos on Crete (drawing from John Chadwick, *The Decipher of Linear B* [Cambridge: Cambridge University Press, 1976], p. 108. Reprinted by permission of the publisher) 104

Chora, Mykonos: Storage jar, mid-seventh century B.C.E. (Archaeological Museum, Mykonos) 159

Codrus Painter: The Pythia (priestess of Apollo) on a Tripod, from the Red Figure Vulci Krater (Antikenmuseum, Staatliche Museen, Berlin) 271

Corinth: The site of the ancient city with the remains of the sixth century B.C.E. temple of Apollo in the foreground (National Tourist Organization of Greece, photo V. and N. Tombazi) 142

A Corinthian pyxis, circa 600-575 B.C.E. (Ashmolean Museum, Oxford) 67

A cup painting of Persephone and Hades (London E 82, from Vulci. "ARV" 1269, 3) 256

A cup painting of two *hetairas* (prostitutes) reclining with male companions at a symposium, circa 470–460 B.C.E. (Basel, Antikenmus. Ka 415. ARV2 868, 45. Photo Claire Niggli) 262

A cup with a painting of Zeus pursuing Ganymede (Ferrara 9351 (T.212 BVP), from Spina. "ARV" 880, 12) 243

Dancing Faun satyr: A marble copy made in the third century C.E. from a Greek original (Uffizi Gallery, Florence/Scala 28) 286

Jacques Louis David's 1814 painting "Leonidas at Thermopylae," (Louvre, Cliché de Musees Nationaux, Paris) 48

Delos: The Avenue of Lions (Photo: Robert Tobler, Lucerne) 145

Delphi: The sanctuary of Apollo (Max Seidal, Mittenwald) 213

Delphi: The stadium for the Pythian Games (Melia) 144

Delphi's theater (A.G.E. Fototstock) 65

Demosthenes 201

Dionysus: An Athenian amphora with a painting of dancers performing for him; attributed to the Amasis Painter, mid-sixth century B.C.E. (Cabinet des Médailles, Bibliothèque Nationale, Paris [222] / photo Hirmer Verlag GmbH, Munich) 72

Discus-thrower, sculpted by Myron in circa 450 B.C.E.: A Roman duplicate (Museo Nationale, Rome) 224

Epidaurus: A medical record which records in detail the treatment and recovery of a patient (AM, Epidaurus) 333

Ergotimos's François Vase, an Athenian Black Figure *kratêr* painted by Kleitias, circa 570 B.C.E. (Museo Archiologico, Florence) 70

Etruscan merchant vessel: Tomb painting, Tarquinia, Italy, circa early fifth century B.C.E. (photo courtesy of Mario Moretti) 120

Euclid: A thirteenth century C.E. Arabic commentary with a diagram of the Pythagorean theorem (British Museum) 327

Eudoxan spheres and hippopede diagram 347

Eudoxan spheres for a single planet in orbit around the earth 349

Eumenides, the tragic play composed by Aeschylus: Play scene detail on a fourth-century B.C.E. vase (British Museum, London) 82

Eupalinus: A view of the tunnel built by the engineer on Samos, circa 530 B.C.E. (Deutsches Archäologisches Institut, Athens) 157

Euripides 86

Female mourners: Vase painting (Copenhagen Natural Museum Inv. 9195. "ARV" 519, 21) 267

The figure of a seer from the east pediment of the temple of Zeus at Olympia, circa 460 B.C.E. (Photo: Hirmer Verlag GmbH, Munich) 77

The François Vase, an Athenian Black Figure *kratêr* made by Ergotimos and painted by Kleitias, circa 570 B.C.E. (Museo Archiologico, Florence) 70

Funeral scene: Attic Black Figure *kuathos* painting, late sixth century B.C.E. (John R. Freeman) 298

Ganymede being pursued by Zeus: Cup painting (Ferrara 9351 (T.212 BVP), from Spina. "ARV" 880, 12) 243

Gorgon Medusa: A relief on a pediment of the temple of Artemis at Corcyra, sixth century B.C.E. (Corfu Museum/Photo German Archaeological Institute, Athens) 288

Greek coins (British Museum, London) 153

A Greek road in southern Italy that later became the Roman Via Appia (A. F. Kersting) 126

Hades and Persephone: Cup painting (London E 82, from Vulci. "ARV" 1269, 3) 256

Hecataeus of Miletus's map of the world, circa 500 B.C.E.: A modern reconstruction 30

Helen being abducted by Paris: A Red Figure bowl painting (Boston Museum of Fine Arts, inv. no. 13. 186) 257

Hera and Zeus: A marble relief from the temple of Hera in Selinus, circa 470-450 B.C.E. (Palermo) 300

Heracles wrestling with the Nemean lion while Athena watches: A vase painting, circa late sixth century B.C.E. (Museo Civico, Brescia; Hirmer) 283

Heraclitus 353

Hermes and one of the Kharites: A relief detail (Louvre, Paris) 117

"Hermes and Infant Dionysus," a sculpture attributed to Praxiteles, but possibly a fourth-century B.C.E. copy (Archaeological Museum, Olympia) 79

Herodotus 87

Herodotus's *History of the Persian Wars:* First page of the *editio princeps* [1502] (courtesy of the Lilly Library, Indiana University) 206

Herodotus's map of the world, originally made circa 430 B.C.E. (Thames & Hudson Ltd, London, from O. A. W. Dilke: "Greek and Roman Maps," (1985); used by permission of the publisher and Cornell University Press) 34

Hetairai (prostitutes) reclining with male companions at a symposium, circa 470–460 B.C.E. cup painting (Basel, Antikenmus. Ka 415. ARV2 868, 45. Photo Claire Niggli) 262

Hetairai, women companions at the *symposia*: Red Figure drinking cup painting, circa 520–510 B.C.E. (Museo Arqueologico, Madrid / Archivo Fotografico) 236

Hippocratic Bench, which provided traction to reset fractures and heal broken bones 339

A hoplite, bronze statuette, circa late sixth century B.C.E. (Peter Newark Military Pictures) 174

Hoplites engaged in battle: A vase painting, circa seventh century B.C.E. (Rome, Villa Giulia. Photo: Max Hirmer) 197

Juror's ballots: the solid hubs were for a verdict of not guilty, while the hollow hubs were for a verdict of guilty, circa fourth century B.C.E. (Agora Museum, Athens). 192

The Kharites and Hermes: A relief detail (Louvre, Paris) 117

A klepsudra (water clock) used for timing speeches in law courts: A modern reconstruction (Agora Museum, Athens) 191

Korê from the Acropolis, circa 490 B.C.E. (Akropolis Museum, Athens) 78

A *Korê,* or marble statue of a maiden, from the Acropolis, circa sixth century B.C.E. (Athens, Acropolis Museum 679. Photo: Alison Frantz) 260

Kouros of Aristodidos, circa 510–500 B.C.E. (Athens NM 3938. Photo-Jeffrey M Hurwit) 356

A *Kouros,* or a male statue of a youth, from Attica, circa late seventh century B.C.E. (Metropolitan Museum of Art, New York) 263

A *kratêr* painting of the murder of Agamemnon, circa 700–480 B.C.E. (Boston Museum of Fine Arts, 63.1246) 258

Lapiths battling a centaur: A metope from the south side of the Parthenon, 440s B.C.E. (British Museum, London) 81

Leonidas: A modern statue of the Spartan king and general near the battlefield at Thermopylae (Sonia Halliday Photographs) 185

"Leonidas at Thermopylae," painted by Jacques Louis David in 1814 (Louvre, Cliché de Musees Nationaux, Paris) 48

Leto, Artemis, and Apollo: Beaten bronze figures from the temple of Apollo at Dreros on Crete, circa 700 B.C.E. (National Archaeological Museum, Athens (1)/photo TAP) 74

Leuctra: A battlefield monument commemorating the defeat of the Spartans by Epaminodas in 371 B.C.E. 188

Linear B tablet from the Mycenaean Period (1600–1200 B.C.E.) discovered at Knossos on Crete (from John Chadwick, *The Mycenaean World* [Cambridge: Cambridge University Press, 1976], p. 16. Reprinted by permission of the publisher) 103

A loan made by the Sanctuary of Zeus to the polis of Locri; inscribed on a bronze tablet, circa 350-250 B.C.E. (Reggio Calabria, Museo Nazionale Cat. 346/I/ photo credit Andrea Baguzzi, Milano5) 97

A map of Alexander the Great's military campaigns 36

A map of Greece 40

A map of Greece and the Mediterranean during the time period 800–323 B.C.E. 32

A map of Greek colonies founded between 750 B.C.E. and 500 B.C.E. (Sarah B. Pomeroy, and others, *Ancient Greece: Political, Social, and Cultural History* [1999]; used by permission of Oxford University Press) 108

A map of the principal sea routes used by Greek mariners during the period 800 to 323 B.C.E. 38

A marble bas-relief depicting animal fights, which provided amusement and an opportunity to gamble in the *gumnasia*, circa 500 B.C.E. (National Archaeological Museum, Athens; David Lees) 233

A marble grave relief from Salamis of two young warriors, circa late fifth–early fourth century B.C.E. (Piraeus Museum. Photo German Institute in Athens) 249

Marble statues of a woman wearing a *peplos* (a variation of the *khitôn*) and a man wearing a *himation* (Stadtische Museen, Frankfurt/ Main) 214

A medical record from Epidaurus, which records in detail the treatment and recovery of a patient (AM, Epidaurus) 333

A metope from the south side of the Parthenon showing Lapiths battling a centaur, 440s B.C.E. (British Museum, London) 81

A Moorish astrolabe of the eleventh century C.E. made from ancient Greek prototypes (Royal Scottish Museum) 326

Mosaic detail (circa 300 B.C.E.) found in Pompeii and showing Alexander the Great at the Battle of Issus in 333 B.C.E. (Naples, National Museum; Photo: Andre Held) 183

Mycenae: The view southward from the citadel (Nico Mavroyenis for BBC) 210

Myron's Discus-thrower, sculpted in circa 450 B.C.E.: A Roman duplicate (Museo Nationale, Rome) 224

The Naxian Sphinx from Delphi, circa 560 B.C.E. (Archaeological Museum, Delphi) 312

Nemean lion being wrestled by Heracles while Athena watches: A vase painting, circa late sixth century B.C.E. (Museo Civico, Brescia; Hirmer) 283

The Nereid Monunment, circa 400 B.C.E. (British Museum, London) 57

Niobid Painter: An Athenian Red Figure kalyx *kratêr* (wine mixing bowl), mid-fifth century B.C.E. (Musée du Lourve, Paris [G341]/ photo Réunion des Musées Nationaux) 71

Paestum: A silver coin of Poseidon with a trident (Poseidonia, Kraay 217-222) 319

A painting of a two-banked warship found on a Theban bowl, circa late eighth century B.C.E. (from John Sinclair Morrison, *Greek Oared Ships, 900-322 B.C.* [1968], plate 19) 121

The Panathenaic Way, the main thoroughfare by the agora of Athens (David Hurn/Magnum, Paris) 116

Paris abducting Helen: A Red Figure bowl painting (Boston Museum of Fine Arts, inv. no. 13. 186) 257

Parthenon: A metope showing Lapiths battling a centaur, 440s B.C.E. (British Museum, London) 81

Penelope at her loom while Telemachos looks on: Bowl painting (Marburg University 1016. "ARV" 1233, 19) 266

Penthesileia, the Amazon queen, being slayed by Achilles: An Athenian amphora from the late sixth century B.C.E. (British Museum, London [B210]) 69

Periander 158

Pericles 201

Persephone and Hades: Cup paint-

ing (London E 82, from Vulci. "ARV" 1269, 3) 256

Pheidias's Athena Parthenos, orginially made in circa 440 B.C.E.: A modern reconstruction (Royal Ontario Museum, Toronto) 55

Philip II 202

Pindar 89

Plan of the Hippocratic humoral system 338

Plato 353

Plato's academy: A mosaic detail, circa 79 C.E., found in the ruins of a villa near Pompeii, Italy (Museo Nazionale, Naples. Photo: Andre Held) 292

Plato's five geometrical solids: tetrahedron, octahedron, icosahedron (l.-r., top row); cube and dodecahedron (l.-r., bottom row) (Courtesy of J. V. Field) 342

The Pnyx: A hill with a speaker's platform where legislation was proposed to the Athenian assembly four times a month (Hassia) 205

Poseidon: The temple to the god on Cape Sunium in Attica (M. Nicholson/*Ancient Civilizations*) 28

Poseidon with a trident: An image on a silver coin from Paestum (Poseidonia, Kraay 217-222) 319

Praxiteles' sculpture "Hermes and Infant Dionysus"; possibly a fourth-century B.C.E. copy (Archaeological Museum, Olympia) 79

Priene: A model of the Ionian city (formerly Staatliche Museen, Berlin) 111

Pythagoras 354

Pythagoras holding a scepter and pointing to a globe: An image on the reverse of a bronze coin from Samos (Ny Carlsberg Glyptotok, Copenhagen) 330

Pythagorean theorem: A thirteenth century C.E. Arabic commentary on Euclid (British Museum) 327

The Pythia (priestess of Apollo) on a Tripod, from the Red Figure Vulci Krater by the Codrus Painter (Antikenmuseum, Staatliche Museen, Berlin) 271

Pythian Games: The stadium for the

events at Delphi (Melia) 144

Ostraka of Themistocles, circa 480 B.C.E. (Agora Museum, Athens) 177

Oxubelês (sharp-bolt shooter), an antipersonnel weapon of the mid-fourth century B.C.E. (Peter A.B. Smith and Malcolm Swanston) 196

The Rampin Horseman, circa 540 B.C.E. (Acropolis 590, head in Louvre, 3104. Photo: Jeffrey M Hurwit) 76

A reconstruction of Anaximander's mid-sixth-century B.C.E. map of the world (J. M. Robinson, *An Introduction to Early Greek Philosophy* [1968], p. 32) 323

A Red Figure bowl painting of Paris abducting Helen (Boston Museum of Fine Arts, inv. no. 13. 186) 257

A Red Figure cup painting of teachers instructing children, circa 480 B.C.E. (Staatliche Museen, Berlin. Photo Bildarchiv Preussischer Kulturbesitz, Berlin) 248

A Red Figure drinking cup showing *hetairai*, women companions at the *symposia*, circa 520–510 B.C.E. (Museo Arqueologico, Madrid/ Archivo Fotografico) 236

A Red Figure *hudria* painting of a mother, child and nursemaid (Cambridge, Massachusetts, Harvard University Art Museums, inv.no. 1960.342) 252

A Red Figure vase painting of a departure scene (St. Petersburg, The State Hermitage Museum, st. 1428, B809 side A.) 272

Salamis: A marble grave relief of two young warriors, circa late fifth–early fourth century B.C.E. (Piraeus Museum. Photo German Institute in Athens) 249

Sanctuary of Asclepius in Epidaurus: The theater dates from the fourth century B.C.E. (Scala) 61

The sanctuary of Apollo at Delphi (Max Seidal, Mittenwald) 213

Sanctuary of Zeus: A loan made to the polis of Locri; inscribed on a bronze tablet, circa 350-250 B.C.E. (Reggio Calabria, Museo Nazionale Cat. 346/I/photo credit

Andrea Baguzzi, Milano5) 97

Sappho 91

Sappho: Fragment of a second-century-C.E. papyrus text of her poems (Bodleian Library, Oxford) 64

Siphnian Treasury: Detail of the North frieze, late sixth century B.C.E. (Photo courtesy of Ecole Française d'Archéologie, Athens) 54

Socrates: A bust (Vatican Museum (314)/photo Scala, Florence) 309

Solon 203

Sophocles 92

Spartan ruins 150

The speaker's platform on the Pnyx, a hill where legislation was proposed to the Athenian assembly four times a month (Hassia) 205

A stone quarry used by the ancient Greeks in Italy (National Archaeological Museum, Athens. Photo: Jean Mazenod) 155

A storage jar from Chora, Mykonos, mid-seventh century B.C.E. (Archaeological Museum, Mykonos) 159

A surviving fragment of the decree for the Athenian expedition to Sicily in 415 B.C.E. (Epigraphical Museum, Athens) 39

Symposia: A Red Figure drinking cup showing *hetairai* (women companions), circa 520–510 B.C.E. (Museo Arqueologico, Madrid/ Archivo Fotografico) 236

Symposium: Two hetairas (prostitutes) reclining with male companions, circa 470–460 B.C.E. cup painting (Basel, Antikenmus. Ka 415. ARV2 868, 45. Photo Claire Niggli) 262

Tarquinia, Italy, tomb painting of an Etruscan merchant vessel, circa early fifth century B.C.E. (photo courtesy of Mario Moretti) 120

Telemachos watching Penelope at her loom: Bowl painting (Marburg University 1016. "ARV" 1233, 19) 266

The temple at Segesta, in the northwestern part of Sicily (Photo: Leonard von Matt. Buochs) 146

Temple of Apollo at Corinth: The

remains of the sixth century B.C.E. structure in the foreground (National Tourist Organization of Greece, photo V. and N. Tombazi) 142

Temple of Artemis at Corcyra: A relief of the Gorgon Medusa, sixth century B.C.E. (Corfu Museum/ Photo German Archaeological Institute, Athens) 288

Temple of Hera in Selinus: A marble relief of Hera and Zeus, circa 470-450 B.C.E. (Palermo) 300

Temple of Zeus at Olympia: The figure of a seer from the east pediment, circa 460 B.C.E. (Photo: Hirmer Verlag GmbH, Munich) 77

Temple to Hera on Samos: Ruins of the structure built in circa 500 B.C.E. (Photo EM Stresow-Czako) 321

Terracotta figures of daily life activities: a mother and daughter cooking together; a woman grinding flour for bread; and a woman taking a bath (top: Museum of Fine Arts, Boston; middle and bottom: British Museum, London) 230

A terracotta figurine of a reveller and his young slave (British Museum, London) 148

Thales 354

The theater at the sanctuary of Asclepius in Epidaurus, dating from the fourth century B.C.E. It is one of the best surviving examples of a Classical Greek theater (Scala). 61

Theban bowl: A painting of a two-banked warship, circa late eighth century B.C.E. (from John Sinclair Morrison, *Greek Oared Ships, 900-322 B.C.* [1968], plate 19) 121

Themistocles 204

Themistocles: Two ostraka, circa 480 B.C.E. (Agora Museum, Athens) 177

Thucydides 92

Thucydides: Fragment of a third-century-B.C.E. papyrus with the text of book 1 of his history (Hamburger Staats- und Universitatsbibliothek) 63

A trireme from the Classical Era: A modern reconstruction (Paul Lipke/Trirene Trust, Montague, Mass.) 123

The Tyrannicides: A Roman copy of the monument which stood in the agora at Athens (Naples, Museo Nazionale) 156

A vase painting of a messenger reporting news of Persian defeat to King Darius I (NAM, Naples; Photo: Soprintendenza alle Antichità di Napoli) 182

Voting tokens with the name of the deme, or village, an abbreviation of the office, and the name of the tribe (Agora Museum, Athens) 191

Vulci Krater (Red Figure) by the Codrus Painter: The Pythia (priestess of Apollo) on a Tripod (Antikenmuseum, Staatliche Museen, Berlin) 271

Zeus and Hera: A marble relief from the temple of Hera in Selinus, circa 470-450 B.C.E. (Palermo) 300

Zeus, bronze statue, circa 460 B.C.E., found off Cape Artemisium (National Archaeological Museum, Athens/Scala) 281

Zeus pursuing Ganymede: Cup painting (Ferrara 9351 (T.212 BVP), from Spina. "ARV" 880, 12) 243

INDEX

A

Academy (Plato), 211, 226, 291, 307, 308, 318, 340, 353
  depicted in mosaic, *292*
  heads of, 310
Acharnians (Aristophanes), 86, 93, 125
Achilles
  depicted on Athenian amphora, *69*
  depicted on Nereid Monument, *57*
Achilles painter, 73
Achilochus of Paros, 60
Acropolis, 51, 52, 54, 89, 136, 180, 185
  built under Pericles's direction, 202
  kore from, *78*
  marble statue of maiden, *260*
Actors
  face masks, 83–84
  tragedies, 81, 82, 83, 84
Actual *vs.* potential concept, 346
Adoption, 256
Adornment, 213, 216, 217–219
Adultery, 257–259, 259
Aegean Islands, 145
Aegean Sea, 98, 99
Aegospotami, Battle of, 195
Aeolians, 131
Aeolic language groups, 101
Aeschines, 65, 94
Aeschylus, 50, 75, 82, 85, 94, 106
  Agamemnon, 85, 105, 106, 271, 305, 311
  Eumedines, 85, 246, 271, 311
  Libation Bearers, 85, 246, 248, 271, 311
  Oresteia, 85, 92, 246, 271, 304, 311
  Persians, 82, 85, 186
  Prometheus Bound, 85, 320
  Seven Against Thebes, 85, 94
  Suppliant Women, 85
Aetius, 308
Afterlife concepts, 300
Against Timarchus, 264
Agamemnon, 62
  kratêr painting depicting murder of, *258*
Agamemnon (Aeschylus), 85, 105, 106, 271, 305, 311
Agathon, 93
Agesilaus (king of Sparta), 187, 188
Agesilaus (Xenophon), 159
Aggareion, 104–105
Agiad family (Sparta), 178
Agias portrait, 88
Aglaophon, 90
Agogê, 178, 187
Agora, 104, 176, 180
Agriculture, 132, 133, 140, 141, 143, 212
  Athens, 135
  Corinth, 142

laborers depicted on bowl painting, *139*
  Sparta, 148, 149
  Thessaly, 153
Airs Waters Places (Hippocrates), 333, 355
Aithiopis, 63
Ajax (Sophocles), 82
Al Mina, 110–111, 153–154
  view of, *154*
Alcaeus, 64, 69, 91
Alcestis (Euripides), 75, 83, 87
Alcibiades, 147, 178, 184, 193, 198, 226
  chariot victories, 228
  Second Peloponnesian War, 194, 195
Alcmaeon of Croton, 335, 355
Alcmaeonid family, 147, 155, 178, 180, 201, 270
Alcman, 64
Alcohol, 222
Alexander the Great (Alexander III), 56, 81, 152, 173, 198–201
  Alexandria, 199–200
  ascendance of, 183
  death, 50, 200–201
  depicted by Lysippus, 88
  depicted on mosaic, at Battle of Issus, *183*
  eastern operations, 200
  Gaugamela, 200
  Gordian knot, 199
  Granicus River victory, 199
  Hellenization, 29
  homeward trip, 200
  Hydaspes River, 200
  influence, 201
  Issus, 199
  man and legend, 198–199
  map of military campaigns, *36*
  military campaigns, 35–36
  patron of arts, 85
  Persian influence, 200
  power consolidation, 199
  siege craft usage, 196
  student of Aristotle's, 352
  supplies, 199
  Tyre and Gaza, 199
  youth, 199
Alexandria, 35, 199–200
Allopathic remedies, 338
Alphabet(s), 102, 174–175, 250
  epic poetry, 61
  facilitation of trade, 154
  Greek, 103, 107, 154
  various Greek city-states and regions, *100*
  See also Language
Altars, 300
Amasis Painter, 69–70
  Athenian amphora attributed to, *72*
Amassis (pharaoh of Egypt), 157
Ambassadors, 105

Amphictyony, 300
Amphicytonic Council, 185, 190
Amphipolis, *194*
Amphorae, 71
  Achilles depicted, slaying Penthesileia, *69*
  dancers performing for Dionysos, *72*
  Kyrenia shipwreck, 122
  merchants weighing grain, *141*
  olive harvesting depicted, *220*
  shoe measurement depicted, *216*
Amulets, 299, 300, 304
Anabasis (Xenophon), 64, 125, 159
Anacreon of Teos, 64, 112
Analatos painter, 68
Anavysos Kouros, 77
Anaxagoras, 202, 318, 335, 351, 355
  exile, 330, 331
  Presocratic philosopher, 290, 293
Anaximander of Miletus, 29, 31, 318, 324, 342, 351, 355
  astronomer and philosopher, 351–352
  Periodas Gês, 32
  Presocratic philosopher, 293–294
  reconstruction of mid-sixth-century B.C.E. world map, *323*
Anaximenes, 293, 318, 324, 328, 352, 355
Ancient Medicine (Hippocrates), 355
Andocides, 65
Andromache (Euripides), 247
Andromachus, 156
Animal husbandry, 219
Animals
  Aristotle's research on, 346–347
  in art, 67, 75, *233*
  competitions, 224–225
  domesticated, 117–118
  in mosaics, 73
  sacrifice, *302*, 303
Antenor, 155
Anthesteria, 211, 234
Anthropomorphic, 300
Antigone (Sophocles), 92, 246, 268, 271, 305
Antigonos, 86
Antipater, 201
Antiphon, 64, 65, 94
Antisthenes, 307
Apelles of Colophon, 73, 85–86
Aphaia, temple to, 54
Aphorisms (Hippocrates), 334, 355
Aphrodite, 278, *279*
Aphroditê Anaduomenê (Aphrodite Rising from the Sea), 86
Aphroditê of Cnidos (Cnidia) (Praxiteles), 79, 81, 91
Apollo, 278–279
  bronze figure, from temple of Apollo at Dreros, Crete, *80*
  oracle of, Delphi, 176, 302, 304

sanctuary of, at Delphi, *213*
    temple at Bassai, 56
"Apollo the Lizard Slayer," 79
Apollodorus, 72, 93, 299
Apology (Plato), 309, 353
Apology (Xenophon), 310
Apotropaic, 300
Apoxuomenos (Lysippus), 81, 88
Aratus, 59
Arcadian Confederacy, 189
Arcado-Cypriot language group, 101
Archaeology
    Homeric poems, 60, 63
    religion, 299–300
    source for economic/social history, 159
Archaic Period
    archaeological evidence, 159
    Athens, 134
    coinage introduced, 151
    documentary sources, 125
    epic poems, 60
    fashion for men and women, 211
    financial centers, 143–144
    Greece during, 174–176
    hairstyles, 218
    jewelry, 219
    literature, 49, 50
    polis, 131, 172
    political tensions, 108
    politics of Homer, 174
    population movements, 140
    social and agricultural crisis, 133–134
    symposia, 236
    trade, 153, 155
    travelers, 112
    tyranny, 156
Archaic smile, 54, 77
Arche (First Cause or Origin), 291
Archelaus of Macedonia, 87
Archilochus of Paros, 112
Architects, 155
Architecture, 51, 53–57
    Early and High Classical Periods, 54, 56
    Early Archaic Period, 53, 76
    Grecian and Roman revival, 52
    influence from abroad, 53
    Later Classical Period, 56
    Later Geometric Period, 53
    Middle and Later Archaic Periods, 53–54
    Parthenon, 56
    technology, 321
    temples, 56
    treasuries, 54
    variations in fourth century, 56–57
    See also Houses/housing; Temples
Archon, 301
Areopagus Council (Athens), 178, 179, 181, 186, 191
Ares, 278, 279
Arginusae, 195
Argos, 172
Argument, 73
Arion, 112, 121
Aristides, 184, 185, 186
    Sacred Tales, 283
Aristocrats, 147
Aristophanes, 50, 57, 58, 66, 86, 125, 225, 249
    Acharnians, 96, 93, 125

Assembly women, 86
Banqueters, 86
Clouds, 58, 86, 93, 226
Cleon's lawsuit, 193
Comedies, The, 238
fragment of third century papyrus
    commentary on *Acharnians*, *59*
Frogs, 86, 93, 125
Knights, 58, 86
Lysistrata, 99, 235
poet and playwright, 86, 93
portraits of Socrates, 310
Thesmophoriazousai, 86, 234
Wasps, 58, 86, 93
Aristotelian Corpus, 307
Aristotle, 33, 50, 73, 84, 133, 290, 352
    atomism, 332
    biological research, 355
    Categories, 307, 352
    on climate and national character, *212*
    Constitution of Athens, *204, 307*
    cosmology, 324, 348–350
    on embryology, 346
    four causes and scientific knowledge, 345
    Generation of Animals, 346, 355
    History of Animals, 346, 347, 352, 355
    logic, 345
    Lyceum, 226, 318, 350, 352
    Metaphysics, 348, 352
    Meteorology, 348, 355
    Movement of Animals, 346, 355
    Milesian speculation, 325
    Nichomachean Ethics, 352
    opinion on polis, 172
    Organon, 345, 355
    origins of tragedy, 81
    paradoxes, 328
    Parts of Animals, 343, 346, 352, 355
    Physics, 348, 352, 355
    Poetics, 50, 57, 73, 94, 352
    Politics, 94, 159, 173, 352
    on Polygnotus, 90
    portion of papyrus text of *Constitution of Athens*, *74*
    Posterior Analytics, 307, 352
    Prior Analytics, 307, 352
    Prime Mover theory, 349–350
    range of interests, 291
    relation to Plato, 307, 353
    Rhetoric, 352
    rhetoric, 184
    on Satyrs, 75
    scientific research, 31, 344–346
    source for Heraclitus of Ephesus, 295
    teleology, 346–347
    theories on conception, 251
    tutor of Alexander the Great, 199
    on war booty, 145
    writings, 66, 307, 352, 355
Armies, 152
    citizen, 176, 190, 197
    Macedonian, 182–183
Arrian, 35, 39
Art
    documentary sources, 94
    female form in, *260*
    forms of, 53–84
    legacy of Greek, 51–52
    male form in, *263*

    pottery, painting, and mosaics, 51, 66–73
    sculpture, 51, 75–81.
    significant people in, 85–93
    See also Architecture; Literature
Art, The (Hippocrates), 355
Artaxerxes II, 187
Artemidorus
    Dream Book *(Oneirocritica)*, 302
Artemis, *80*, 278, 279
Artemis at Ephesus, 53
Asclepius, 283, 332, 334–335
Aspasia, 269
Assembly (Athens), 180, 190–191
Assemblywomen (Aristophanes), 86
Assyria, 75
Assyrians, 152
Astrolabe
    Moorish, made from ancient Greek
        prototypes, *326*
Astrology, 301, 302
Astronomy, 327
    early, 323, 324
    science of Plato, 341–344
    section of Alexandrian treatise, *337*
Athena, 278, 279–280
    bronze sculpture, *280*
    depicted in temple to Aphaia, 54
    Parthenon, 54
    temples to, 54, 56
Athena Nike, temple of, 56
Athena Parthenos, model of Pheidias's, *55*
Athena Parthenos (Pheidias), 89
Athena Promakhos (Pheidias), 89
Athenian Empire, 173, 187
Athenian expedition to Sicily
    surviving fragment of decree for, *39*
Athenian treasury (Delphi), *24*
Athenians
    class divisions, 179
    tribal divisions, 180
Athens, 33, 50, 107, 118, 131, 132, 134–138, 172, 176–181
    adultery in, 259
    agriculture, 135
    Archaic Period, 134
    Areopagus Council, 178, 179, 181, 186, 191
    Assembly, 180, 190
    art during Early and High Classical
        Periods, 54
    Boulê, 180
    Classical Period, 134
    Cleisthenes, father of democracy, 180, 269
    coins, 152, 180
    Constitution of Draco, 178
    court system, 180–181, 190–191
    Delian League, 185
    democratic practices, 173
    disenfranchisement, 264
    divorce laws, 256
    education, 249, 250
    equality, 181
    governing bodies, 180
    government of Pisistratids, 157
    grave stele of unknown man, *160*
    Greek tragedy and, 49
    imperialism, 137, 185
    imports, 137
    Ionia as subject state, 145
    land ownership, 134–135

Marathon, Battle of, 181, 184
marriage, 254
metics, 135
military service, 180
occupations, 135
oratory and rhetoric, 183–184
outdoor theaters, 83
peace treaty with Sparta (445), 192
Persian Menace, 184–187
plague (430–427 B.C.E.), 333
political assemblies, 190–191
political rights, 135
publication of speeches, 73
punishment, 191–192
reforms, 186
rivalry with Sparta, 173, 178
roads, 113
Second Peloponnesian War, 73, 138, 173, 192–195
slaves, 135–137
social trends, 245–246
Social War, 190
Sparta contrasted with, 176
taxes, 135
tourism, 140
tyrants, 179
view of northwestern side of agora, *136*
voting, 190
wealth, 135
weapons, 196
See also Sparta
Athletes, 225
Athletic competitions, 224, 226–228
documentary sources, 238
lyric poetry, 89
male form, 260–261
religion, 303
Atlas, 283
Atomism, 291, 332–333
Atomists, 346
Attalids, 51
Attica
kouroi and korai, 77
"New York kouros," 77
pottery, 66, 68, 76
"red figure" vases, 70–72
Attic-Ionic language group, 101
Atticism, 64–65
Augury, 301, 302
Auxerre goddess, 76
Avenue of Lions (Delos), *145*

B

Bacchae (Euripides), 83, 87, 218, 311
wine, 222
Bacchylides of Ceos, 64, 94
Bakeries, 219, 222
Balkan Peninsula, 98
Ball games, 224
Banking, 135
Banqueters (Aristophanes), 86
Barbarians, 33
Barbaroi, 29, 33
Barley, 219
Baroque period, Greek legacy in art during, 52
Bassai, temple to Apollo, 79

Baths, 211, 225, 230
Battering ram, 196
Battle of Leuctra, 189
commemorative monument, *188*
Battle of Mantinea, 189, 198
Battle of Marathon, 181, 184
Beacons, 106
Beauty standards, 260
Beds and couches, 231
Beekeeping, 221
Belts, 217
Bendis, 283
Berlin Korê, 77
Berlin painter, 71
Bernini, Giovanni, 52
Beverages, 219, 222
Bias of Priene, *306*
Biles and phlegm, 335–336
"Bilingual vases," 71
Binding tablet, 302
Biology, Aristotle's works on, 346
Birds (Aristophanes), 86
Birth control, 253
Black-figure style painting, 157
amphora depicting shoe measurement, *216*
amphora showing merchants weighing grain, *141*
pottery, 51, 68
Blood, 335
Blood offerings, 301
Blood sport, 227
Blood vengeance, 246
Bloodless offerings, 301
Bloodletting, 335, 339
Board games, 224
Boeotia, 138, 187
Boeotian Confederacy, 189
Boeotian League, 138
Botticelli, Sandro, 86
Boulê (Athens council), 180
Boxing, 227, 303
Brasidas, 92
Bread and breadmaking, 219
depicted in terra cotta figure, *230*
Breuer, Josef, 253
Bride auctions, 261
Bronze, 155
artwork, 111
sculpture, 75, 76, 90
tablet recording loan made by Sanctuary of Zeus, *97*
tripods, 75
Bronze Age, 107, 149, 154, 155, 172
"Bronze Town," 154
Brothels, 261
Burials, 267, 301, 303
Byron, Lord George Gordon, 52
Byzantium, 109

C

Cadmus, 282
Cakes, 219
Calendars, 233, 342–343
Callicrates, 56
Callimachus, 299
Callippus of Cyzicus, 344, 355

Calumny (Apelles of Colophon), 73, 85–86
Canon (Polyclitus), 78, 90
Carthage, 108, 147
Cartography, 29
Caryatids, 56
Castor, 282
Categories (Aristotle), 307, 352
Celebrations, 234
Celestial bodies, 348, 349
Census classes, 133–134
Centauromachy, 56, 79
Centaurs, 75, 78, 79, 284
Cephisodotus, 79
Ceramic ware, 153
Chaeronea, Battle of, 203
Chain of Being, 347
Chairs, 231
Change
Aristotle's approach to, 346
early speculation on, 328–330
Plato's explanation of, 341
Chaos, 284
Character, Greek, influence of climate on, 212–213
Characters (Theophrastus of Eresos), 310
Charcot, Jean-Martin, 253
Chares, 88
Chariots
monuments, 91
racing, 223, 227–228, 303
tablet, *104*
Charmides (Plato), 309
Charms, 300
Charondas of Catana, 156, 173
Cheeses, 220
Cheilon, 149
Chigi Vase, 54, 68
Childbirth, 248, 253
Children, 248–249
birth ritual, 248
education, 249–251
growth, 248–249
male heirs, 248
slaves, 136
Sparta, 247, 248
teacher depicted, with child on cup painting, *248*
toys, 224, 249
Chilon of Sparta, 306
Chionides, 57
Choice of Heracles, The (Prodicus of Ceos), 289–290
Choral odes
Doric dialect, 101
Greek tragedies, 82
Chorus
actors and, in Greek tragedies, 82
face masks, 83–84
female, 268
in Old Comedy, 58–59
role of, in Greek tragedy, 83
Satyr plays, 75
Chthonic deities, 301
Cicero, 308
Cimon, 90, 186, 201
City Dionysia, 234, 265, 270
City states, 107, 245
architecture, 51
archons, 301

borders, 107–108
drama, 49–50
emergence of, 66, 131
growth and development, 131
protected interests, 245
social hierarchy, 147
temple architecture, 53–54
typology, 131–132
Civic buildings, 51
Civic cults, 278
Classical Period
artists, 51
Athens, 134
economic crisis, 138–140
education, 249
Greek tragedy, 84
hetaira, 269
house decoration/furnishings, 231
instability, 147
literature, 49, 50
Peloponnesian War, 192
polis, 172
political life, 246
Pythagorean philosophy, 297
ship design, 118, 119
ship size, 121
Sparta, 148, 151
Cleisthenes, 134, 147, 178, 204, 245, 269
as founder of Athenian democracy, 180, 269
ostracism introduced, 181
Cleitagora, 247
Cleobolus of Rhodes, 306
Cleomenes I, 158
Cleon, 58, 86, 184, 193
Cleophon, 195
Climate, 212–213
effects on Greek daily life, 211
Cloaks, 216
Clothing, 211, 213–217
cleaning, 215
color and patterns, 215
exposed flesh, 215–216
production, 214
travelers, 117
types of, 215
undergarments, 217
versatility, 216
work, 217
Clouds (Aristophanes), 58, 86, 93, 226
Coasting, 120–121
Cockfighting, 224–225
Codes, 106
Coins, 73, 112, 140, 153
Athenian, 152, 180
introduction, 151
Colonies, 37–38, 108, 245
Colonization, 31, 33, 98, 108–110, 132, 140–142
expeditions, 140
modern model, 140–141
settlements, 140
sharers of land, 141
Sicily, 146
social and economic causes, 140
Colossus of Rhodes, 88
Combat sports, 226–227
Comedies, The (Aristophanes), 238
Comedy, 49, 50, 57–59
divisions, 57
documentary sources, 93

fantasy, 58
limitations, 57
obscenity, 58
playwrights, 86
political commentary, 58
qualities, 57–58
role in the Lênaia, 59
See also Tragedy
Commerce, 132, 135, 140, 153
seaborne, 37
ships, 119
Sicily and Southern Italy, 146
See also Trade
Communication
documentary sources, 125
Linear A and Linear B, 102, 103, 174, 175
movement of information, 104–107
Community, 234–235
Compendium of the Lives of the Philosophers
(Diogenes Laertius), 308
Conception, 251
Constitution of Athens (Aristotle), 204, 307
portion of first-century-C.E. papyrus text,
74
Constitution of the Lacedaemonians (Xenophon), 159
Constitution of the Spartans (Xenophon), 64
Construction
roads, 113–114
shipbuilding, 119
temples, 152
Contraception, 254
Contrapposto pose, 73, 78
Cooking, 230
Corax of Syracuse, 73
Corinth, 107, 118, 131, 137, 142–143
emporium, 153
pottery, 67, 76
roads, 113, 115
site of ancient, 142
tyrants, 156
Corinthian columns, 51, 56
Corinthian League, 199
Corinthian War, 188
Cosmetics, 218, 260
Cosmogonic myths, 319
Cosmology
Aristotelian, 324, 348–350
Platonic, 340, 341
Cosmos, 291
Council of Athens, 190
Council of Four Hundred, 194
Council of the Areopagus, 191
Courtesans, 261–262
Courts
Athens, 180–181, 190–191
water-clock for timing speeches, 191
Craftsmen, 136, 143
Crates, 307–308
Cremation, 301
Crete, 100, 148, 172
Critias, 64, 195
Crito (Plato), 309
Croesus (king of Lydia), 143
Cronus, 286
Crop failures, 212
Ctesias of Cnidus, 29, 32
Cult of Pythagoras, 327–328
Cults, 132, 302
Asclepius, 335

heroic, 282
"holy Pytho," 302
mystery, 304
Cuneiform writing system, 102
Cures, 334
diet, 338
dream, 335
Curse tablets, 299, 302, 304
Cybelë, 284
Cycles of Change, 328–330
Cyclopes, 284, 319
Cyclops (Euripides), 75, 87, 94
Cylon, 156, 178, 180
Cynegeticus (Xenophon), 64
Cynics, 307, 308
Cypria, 63
Cypselus, 176
Cyrene, 110
Cyrillic alphabet, 103
Cyrus the Great, 37, 173, 200
Cyrus the Younger, 187

D

Daedalic style, 54, 76
Daedalus, 320, 324
Daily life, 211
clothing and adornment, 213–219
documentary sources, 238
food, 219–223
games, 224–228
housing, 229–232
leisure and festivals, 233–235
symposia, 235–237
Dances, 83, 226
Dancing Faun satyr, 286
Darius I (king of Persia), 31, 158, 181, 200
messenger depicted on vase painting,
reporting news of Persian defeat, 182
Darius III (king of Persia), 199, 200
Dark Ages, 107, 131, 140, 172
David, Jacques Louis, 52
"Leonidas at Thermopylae," 48
De Chirico, Giorgio, 52
Death rituals, 267
Debt, 133, 140, 179, 203, 245
Declea, 194
Defense of Palamedes (Gorgias of Leontini), 289
Deities
chthonic, 301
major, 278–282
minor, 283–289
Delian League, 33, 54, 146, 185, 186, 187
Delos, 302
Avenue of Lions, 145
Delphi, 155, 300
Athenian treasury, 24
Naxian Sphynx, 312
oracle of, 38, 185, 302, 304
Panhellenic sanctuaries at, 75
priestesses, 305
Pythian Games, 226
roadways, 113
sanctuary of Apollo, 143, 213
stadium at, for Pythian Games, 144
treasuries, 54
Deltos, 104

Demeter, 278, 280
Democracy
    Cleisthenes as founder of, 180, 269
    influence of, on literature, 49, 50
    limits to, in Athens, 190
    Solon's reforms, 245–246
    See also City-states; Phalanx
Democritus, 291, 294–295, 331, 346, 355
    atomic theories, 291, 332
Demosthenes, 50, 65, 94, 159, 184, 201
    death, 201
    "On the Crown", 201
    and Philip II of Macedon, 202, 203
    Philippics, 201
    Speeches, The, 238
Departure scene, Red Figure vase painting, *272*
Derveni Papyrus, 302
Deus ex machina, 303
Diadoumenos (Polyclitus), 90
Dialects, 101
Didactic poetry, 49, 59–60, 93
Die Fragmente der Vorsokratiker (Diels), 355
Diels, Hermann, 355
Diet, 211, 219–223
Dinarchus, 65, 94
Dio Chrysostom, 56
Diogenes Laertius
    Compendium of the Lives of the Philosophers,
        308
Diogenes the Cynic, 308
Diolkos, 116
Dionë, 284
Dionysius I, 147
Dionysus (son of Zeus), 280
Dionysus Zagreus, 284
Dioscuri, 282
Diplomacy, 187
Dipylon Vase, 66
Discus-thrower (Myron), 78
    Roman copy of sculpture by Myron, *224*
Disease, 333, 335
    diagnosing, 339
    epilepsy, 336
    therapy, 338
Disenfranchisement, 264
Displacement, 349
Dithyramb, 64, 81
Divination, 302
Divine, the, 291, 297
Division of labor, 265
Divorce, 255, 256, 257
Doctors, 334, 335, 339
Dodona, oracle of, 38, 304
Dorian Greeks, 131
Dorian Spartans, 149
Doric language group, 101
Doric order columns, 51, 53, 56
Doruphoros (Polyclitus), 78, 90
Douris, 71
Dowries, 255–256
    divorce and return of, 256
    prostitution, 261
Doxographers, 308
Draco, 152, 156, 269–270
    Constitution, 178
    law code, 179
    laws against adultery, 258
Drama, 49–50, 51
    Doric dialect, 101

playwrights, 85
Satyr play, 75, 83
See also Comedy; Tragedy
Dreams, 302–303, 332
    cures and, 335
    incubation, 303
Droughts, 212
Drunkenness, 218, 236
Dyes, clothing, 215
Dynamics, Aristotelian, 348

E

Early and High Classical Periods
    pottery, 72–73
    sculpture, 78
Early Archaic Period
    pottery, 67–68
    sculpture, 75–76
Early Geometric Period
    pottery, 66
Ecclesiazusae, 58
Eckstein, Emma, 253
Economic activities, 132, 143–145
    dedications to gods, 143
    farming, 143
    financial centers, 143–144
    "first fruits," 144
    religious cults, 143
    transport and exchange of goods and
        services, 155
    war, 144–145
Economic conditions
    birth control and infanticide, 253
    Classical Period, 138–140
    colonization, 141
    households, 264
    prostitution, 261, 262
    Sparta, 148, 149, 150–151
    technological advances, 152–153
Economics, 292
Economics (Xenophon), 265
Education, 250–251
    elementary, 250
    privileged few, 250
    Sparta, 149–150, 251
    See also Academy; Lyceum
Egypt
    influences on Greek art, 53, 75, 77
    papyrus, 104
Egyptians
    construction techniques, 152
    shipbuilding, 99
Ekphrasis, 94
Eleatic School, 295, 330
Electra (Euripides), 87, 94
Electra (Sophocles), 92, 223, 238
Elegy, 60–63, 93
Elements, 347
Eleusinian Mysteries, 219, 280, 303, 304
Elgin, Lord, 52
Eliot, George, 268
Embryology, 340, 346
Emergency messages, 105–106
Empedocles, 223, 290, 291, 295, 308, 318, 335,
    341, 352–353
    influence on Aristotle, 347, 348

On Nature, 329, 353
philosopher, statesman, poet, 293, 352–353
Purification, 293, 353
on Pythagoras, 327
quoted, 329
Empedocles (Olympic chariot racer), 295
Empirical observation, 350
Emporion (Emporium), 110, 153
Encomium of Helen (Gorgias of Leontini), 289
Engineering, 321–322
England, 52
Envoys, 105
Eôs, 284
Epaminodas
    Battle of Mantinea, 189, 198
    monument commemorating defeat of
        Spartans by, *188*
Ephesus, temple of Artemis at, 53
Ephialtes, 186, 201
Ephorus, 85
Epic Cycle, 63
Epics, 60–63
    documentary sources, 94
    Homeric, 299
    poetry, 49, 59, 174
    See also Homer: *Iliad*; *Odyssey*
Epidemics, 339
Epidemiology, 333
Epigonoi, 63
Epilepsy, 336
Epinicians (Pindar), 89
Epinikia (Pindar), 238, 311
Epiphanies, 303
Epistemology, 328
Epistle VII (Plato), 309
Epitrapezios (Lysippus), 88
Equality, 173, 181, 245
Erechtheum, 136
Ergotimos, 69
    François Vase, *70*
Erôs, 284
Erotic love, 259–260
Ethics, 291, 292
Ethnographers, 29, 32, 33
Etiquette, 222
    household, 222
    symposia, 235
Euclid
    Arabic commentary (thirteenth century
        C.E.), with diagram of
        Pythagorean theorem, *327*
Euctemon, 343, 355
Eudoxan spheres and hippopede, *347*
Eudoxus of Cnidus, 343–344, 348, 355
Euhemerism, 303
Euhemerus of Messene, 303
Eumenides (Aeschylus), 85, 246, 271, 311
Eupalinus, *157*, 321
Eupatrids, 178
Euphronius, 71
Euripides, 50, 58, 75, 85, 86–87, 265
    Andromache, 247
    Bacchae, 83, 87, 218, 311
    chorus in plays, 82–83
    Cyclops, 75, 87, 94
    Electra, 87, 94
    fragment, papyrus anthology of lyric
        passages from tragedies of, *82*
    Helen, 87

Hippolytus with a Garland, 271
Medea, 271
Orestes, 87
Phoenician Women, 92
Trojan Women, 58
Eurypontid family (Sparta), 178
Euthycrates, 88
Euthydikos Korê, 77
Euthymenes, 31
Euthymides, 71
Euthyphro (Plato), 309
Eutychides, 88
Evolution, 324
Exekias, 70
Exercise, 211, 224, 225–226
Exile
      Anaxagoras, 330, 331
      law code of Draco, 179
      political leaders, 103
      punishment for murder, 191
      Themistocles, 186
Explorers and exploration, 29, 31–32, 98, 99
Exports, 139

F

Face masks, 83–84
Family, 244
      conception and childbirth, 251–254
      documentary sources, 271
      limiting size of, 253–254
      marriage, 254–256
      social roles in household, 264–267
Famine, 212
Fantasy, 58
Farms and farming, 143, 157
      Athens, 135
      Corinth, 142
      dry, 212
      population control, 141
      Sparta, 149
      See also Agriculture
Farnese Heracles (Lysippus), 88
Fashion, 215
Fates, The, 284–285
Feigned Madness of Odysseus (Parrhasius), 88
Female chorus, 268
Female excellence, 231
Fertility, 251
Festivals, 211, 234, 299, 301, 303
      calendar, 233
      fertility, 268
      religious, 268
      See also Games
Financial centers, 143–144
First Peloponnesian War, 173, 187
Fish, 219, 221
Flame codes, 106
Flavius Philostratus, 308
Folktales, 299
Food, 211, 219–223
      breads, 219
      cakes, 219
      dairy products, 220
      fish, 221
      fruits, 221
      grains, 219

honey, 221
legumes, 220
meal times, 222
meat, 221
oils and fats, 220
preparation, 222
ritual drink, 219
seasonings, 221–222
Sparta, 151
Foot travel, 116–117
Footwear, 211, 217
      measuring for shoes depicted on amphora, *216*
Forests, 153
Form (Platonic), 292, 309, 340
Four Hundred, Council of, 194
François Vase, 68–69, *70*
French Neoclassical style, 52
Frescoes, 68, 72, 73, 92
Freud, Sigmund, 253
Frogs (Aristophanes), 86, 93, 125
Fruits, 221
Fuel, 154–155
Funeral Oration (Pericles), 231
Funerals, 267
      monuments and markers, 77, 79
      rituals, 300
      scene depicted on Black-figure kyathos, *298*
Funerary vases, 66, 68
Furies, The, 285
Furniture, 211, 231

G

Gaea, 285
Galen, 353
Games, 211, 224–228, 299
      cheating, 228
      Panhellenic competitions, 226
      religion, 303
      symposia, 237
Garbage disposal, 231
Gender roles, 247, 265
Genealogies, 63
Generation of Animals (Aristotle), 346, 355
Geographers, 29–32
Geography, 33, 98, 172
Geometric design, 66, 67
Geometric Period, 53
Geometric Renaissance, 103
Geometry, 327–328
      Plato's analysis, 340–341
      Plato's solids, *342*
Gerousia, The (Spartan senate), 178
Giants, The, 285
Gift-exchanges, 156
Gigantomachy, 54, 56, 285
Gods and goddesses, 278–282, 283–289, 320
Gold, 155
Gordian knot, 199
Gorgias of Leontini, 73, 81, 94, 184, 289
      Defense of Palamides, 289
      Encomium of Helen, 289
      On Praise of Helen, 81, 94, 289
Gorgias (Plato), 94, 289, 309
Gorgons, 285

Graces, 285
Grain, 143, 219
Grapes, 218, 219, 222
Grave monuments, 81
Gravity, 347
Great Dionysia, 59, 83, 303
Great World System, The (Leucippus), 332
"Greater Greece," 109
Greece
      map of (800–323 B.C.E.), *32*
      map of, during Second Peloponnesian War, *40*
Greek civilization
      assessment, 99
      documentary sources, 39
      expansion, 98
      geography, 98
      technologies, 99
Greek War of Independence, 52
Griffins, 76
Ground wrestling, 227
Guest-friendship, 156, 244
Gumnasion, 225, 226
Gyges (king of Lydia), 143
Gymnastics, 226
Gynecological health, 339–340

H

Hades, 285
Hadrian (emperor of Rome), 54, 113
Hairstyles, 211, 217, 218
Hanno, 31, 32
Haruspicy, 303
Hats, 217
Healing
      diet, 338
      incubations, 303
      theory, 334–337
Healing Hand, The (Majno), 339
Health, 335
      documentary sources, 355
      women's, 339–340
      See also Medicine
Hebe, 285
Hebrew language, 103
Hecataeus, 63
      Periodos Gês, 39
Hecataeus of Miletus, 30
      map of world by, *30*
      Periodos Gês, 30, 32, 39
Hecatë, 285–286
Hecatomb, 303
Hecatoncheires, 286
Hegel, Georg Wilhelm Friedich, 268
Hegemony, 187
Heiresses, 256, 257
Helen (Euripides), 87
Helen of Troy, *257*, 286
Helius, 286
Hellen, 33
Hellenic League, 184, 185
Hellenica (Xenophon), 64, 125, 159, 189, 205
Hellenistic Period, 50, 173, 201
Hellenization, 29
Helots, 148, 149, 151, 177, 186, 187
Hephaestus, 278, 280

in passage in *Iliad*, 319
temple to, in Athens, 56
Hera, 278, 280
marble relief depicting, from temple of
Hera in Selinus, *300*
temples to, 53, 54
Heracles, 51, 172, 282
depicted in architectural sculptures, 54
depicted wrestling with Nemean lion, *283*
Heraclides of Pontus, 308, 344, 355
Heraclitus of Ephesus, 290, 291, 295, 318, 353,
355
on change, 328–329
fragment, 294
quoted, 326
Heralds, 105
Herbs, 221
Hercules. *See* Heracles
Herm, 303
Hermes, 105, *117*, 278, 280–281
"Hermes and Infant Dionysos," *79*
Hermes Carrying the Infant Dionysus (Praxiteles),
91
Hero cults, 61
Herodotus, 29, 50, 63, 87, 94, 101, 102, 204
on early maps, 32, 351
History of the Persian Wars (Histories, The),
33, 34, 39, 63, 87, 102, 106,
107, 109, 112, 115, 125, 159, 204, *206*, 238,
261, 355
legend about peplos, 216–217
map of world by, *34*
on Sostratus of Aegina, 124
technological advances recorded by, 321
travels of, 33
Heroes, 244, 282–283
Heroic Age, 63
Hesiod, 87–88, 259, 282, 298, 299
afterlife portrayal, 300
Aprodite references, 278
epics, 299
poet, 87–88
Theogony, 49, 88, 93, 174, 284, 296, 311
Works and Days, 49, 59, 88, 93, 125, 159,
174, 238
Hestia, 278, 281
Hetairas, 261, 262
Hieroglyphics, Egyptian, 102
Hieron of Syracuse, 89
Highwaymen, 38
Himation, *214*, 215, 216
Himilco, 31
Hipparchia, 308
Hipparchus, 157, 158, 179, 180, 270
Hippias, 147, 157, 158, 179, 180, 181, 184, 270,
289
Hippias Major (Plato), 289
Hippias Minor (Plato), 289, 309
Hippocrates of Cos, 333, 355
Aphorisms, 334, 355
Humors, 355
Nature of Man, 355
Sacred Diseases, 334, 336, 338, 355
Hippocratic Bench, *339*
Hippocratic Corpus, 254, 318, 333, 334, 339
"Hippocratic Faces," 339
Hippocratic Oath, 334, 339, 355
Hippolytus, 330
Hippolytus (Euripides), 87, 271

Hipponax, 60
Histiaios, 157
History, 49, 50, 63–64, 87
documentary sources, 94
Homeric poems, 62
History of Animals (Aristotle), 346, 347, 352, 355
History of the Peloponnesian War (Thucydides),
50, 92, 125, 159, 173, 192, 205
History of the Persian Wars (Histories, The)
(Herodotus), 33, 34, 39, 63
87, 102, 125, 159, 204, *206*, 238, 261, 355
quote from, 106, 107, 109, 112, 115
first page of editio princeps, *206*
Holocausts, 303
Homer, 87, 88, 101, 147
afterlife portrayal, 300
Aprodite references, 278
cult of "holy Pytho," 302
epics, 60–63
epiphanies, 303
family and social trends in poetry, 244
gift exchanges in poems of, 156
Greek alphabet, 175
Hymn to Demeter, 254, 271, 287
Iliad, 39, 49, 60, 63, 88, 94, 125, 204, 205,
271, 305, 311
Odyssey, 36, 39, 49, 60, 75, 94, 122, 125,
204, 205, 311
personal background, 60
physical world of, 36–37
politics, 174
Homeric Hymns, 311
Homicide
Draco's laws, 178
Homeric world, 175
Homoeroticism, 236–237, 262–263
Homosexuality, 141, 263
Honey, 221
Hoplite, 172, 177, 181, 182, 200, 250
bronze statuette, *174*
challenges to, 190
vase painting of, *197*
weaponry, 196
Horace, 50
Horsemanship (Xenophon), 64
Horses, *117*–118
Hospitality theme
Homeric poems, 62
Satyr plays, 75
Household, 244
ritual observances, 299
social roles, 264–269
Housing/houses, 211, 229–232, 265
architectural variations, 232
building materials, 229
decoration, 231
design, 229
disposal, 231
furniture, 231–232
hearths, 230
lighting, 232
lodgers, 232
men's room, 229
sewage, 230–231
simplicity, 229
special rooms, 265–266
water supply, 230
women's room, 229–230, 266

Human figures
central to Greek art, 51
korê, 77, 101, 260
kouros, 77, 78, 260, 263
in late Geometric Period sculpture, 75
in mosaics, 73
Parthenon frieze, 79
on vases, 66, 67
Humor, 57, 58
Humors, 335–337
Hippocratic speculation, 338–339
Hippocratic system, *338*
linkages, 336–337
Humors (Hippocrates), 355
Husbands and wives, 244–245, 254
Hygiene, 217
Hymn to Demeter (Homer), 254, 271, 287
Hymns, 49, 298
Hyperbolus, 198
Hyperides, 65, 94
Hysteria, 253, 335, 340

I

Iambics, 60–63
Ibycus, 64, 112
Icarus, 320, 324
Ictinus, 56
Identity, Greek, 176
Iliad (Homer), 39, 49, 60, 63, 88, 94, 125, 204,
205, 271, 305, 311
chariot racing, 223
family and social trends, 244
feasting, 235
fragment of second century B.C.E. papyrus
text of, *61*
geographical reality, 36
influence, 49, 238, 271, 311
justice, 175
passage on Hephaestus, 319
politics, 174
prophecy, 305
quotes from, 53, 62, 115
weaving described, 215, 228
women's household work, 264
Iliou Persis, 63
Ilisos relief, 81
Illnesses, 333
cures, 334
Imperialism, 137, 185
Imports
Athens, 137–138
Corinth, 143
Incision, pottery, 67–68
Incubation, 303
Indo-European language family, 99
Infant mortality, 253
Infanticide, 141, 253
Infertility, 251
Infinite regress, 349
Infinity, 332
Ingres, Jean-Auguste-Dominique, 52
Inheritance, 255, 257
male heirs, 248
property rights, 256
Sparta, 247
Initiation rites, 250

Ion (Plato), 309
Ionia, 53, 145–146
Ionian Greeks, 131, 145, 178, 181, 184
Ionian nature philosophers, 293
Ionic order columns, 51, 53, 56, 57
Iphicrates of Athens, 190
Ipsissima verba, 292
Iron, 108, 109, 155
Iron Age, 172
Isaeus, 65, 94, 159, 184
Isagoras, 270
Isocrates, 65, 94, 159, 184, 202, 308
Isthmia, 143
Isthmian Games, 38, 143, 226, 311
Isthmus of Corinth, 143
Italian Renaissance, Greek legacy in art during, 52
Italy
    Southern, 146–147
    stone quarry used by ancient Greeks, *155*
Ivory sculptures, 75

J

Javelin throwing, 227
Jewelry, 75, 218–219
Juror's ballots, *192*
Justice, 175
    Constitution of Draco, 178
    social relationships, 244

K

Kairos (*Opportunity*) (Lysippus), 79, 88
Keats, John, 52
Kepler, Johannes, 344
King's Peace, 188, 189
Kleitias, 69
    François Vase, *70*
Kleiton, 94
Kleophrades painter, 71
Klepsudra, 233
Knights (Aristophanes), 58, 86
Knossos on Crete
    chariot tablet drawing, *104*
    Mycenaean Period Linear B tablet, *103*
Koinê, 101
Korê, 77, *78*, *260*
Kottabos, 237
Kouros, 77, 78, 260, 263
    Kroisos (Anavysos Kouros), 77
    Kouros of Aristodidos, 77, *356*
    New York Kouros, 77
Kratêr
    Athenian Red-figure kalyx, by Niobid
        Painter, *71*
    François Vase, *70*
    funeral, 66, 67
Kritian Boy, 78
Kroisos (Anavysos Kouros), 77
Kurbeis, 104
Kyrenia shipwreck, 121–122

L

Labor
    household division of, 265

slave, 136, 143, 147
Lacedaemonians (Spartans), 149
Lacedaemon (Sparta), 247
Laches (Plato), 309
Laconians (Spartans), 178
Land ownership, 134–135
Land transport, 139
Landscape, 211, 212–213
Language, 99–102
    dialects, 100–101
    expansion, 100
    foreigners, 101
    four groupings, 101
    Indo-European family, 99
    interpreters, 101–102
    origins, 99–100
    social indicators, 101
    written, 174–175
Lapiths, 78, 79
Late Geometric Period
    pottery, 66
    sculpture, 75
Later Classical Period
    painting, 73
    sculpture, 79, 81
Later Sophists, 307–311
Latin language, 51
Law
    adultery, 257–258
    codes, 156, 173
    documentary sources, 196–197
    Draconian code, 269–270
    inheritance, 256, 257
Laws (Plato), 159, 309
League of Corinth, 203
Leather, 214
Legends, 172, 174, 299, 319–320
Leisure, 211, 212, 233–234
    documentary sources, 238
    games, 224–228
    symposia, 235–237
Lekuthos, white-ground, *66*, 73
Lemnian Athena (Pheidias), 89
Lênaia, 59, 86
"Leonidas at Thermopylae" (David), *48*
Leonidas (king of Sparta), 184, *185*
Leto, *80*, 286
Leucippus, 291, 296, 318, 332–333, 355
Leuctra, Battle of, 189
Levant, the, 75
Libation, 301, 304
Libation Bearers (Aeschylus), 85, 246, 248, 271,
    311
Life expectancy, 219
Life of Lycurgus (Plutarch), 177
Lighting, 232
Lincoln Memorial (Washington, D.C.), Grecian
    influence on, 52
Linear A, 102, 103
Linear B, 102, *103*, 174, 175
Linen, 213
Linnaeus, Carolus, 347
Literacy, 103, 154, 250
Literature, 49–51
    comedy, 57–59
    didactic poetry, 59–60
    documentary sources, 93–94
    elegy and iambics, 60
    epics, 60–63

family and social trends in, 244
    history, 63–64
    lyric poetry, 64
    oratory, 64–65
    philosophical writings, 65–66
    rhetoric, 73, 75
    Satyr plays, 75
    tragedy, 81–84, 85, 265
Little Iliad, 63
Lives of the Sophists (Flavius Philostratus), 308
Loans, 133, 140, 157, 180
Logic, 345, 350
Logographic writing system, 102
Logos, 329
Long Walls, Athens, 187
Looms, 214–215
Love, 259–260
Lucretius, 59
Lyceum, 307, 318, 352
    heads of, 310
    scientific research, 344, 350
Lycomid family, 204
Lycurgan social order in Sparta, 149
Lycurgus of Sparta, 65, 94, 148, 149, 156, 173,
    231, 247, 270
Lyric, 64
    documentary sources, 94
    poetry, 49, 64, 89, 299
Lysander, 187, 195
Lysias, 65, 94, 159, 184
Lysippus, 52, 79, 81, 86, 88
Lysistrata (Aristophanes), 86, 99, 125, 231, 235
Lysistratus, 88

M

Macedon, 182
    warfare in, 182–183
Magic, 297, 304
Maidens, in sculpture, 77
Majno, Guido, 339
Mantinea, Battle of, 189
Manufacturing, 132, 135, 176
Maps, 29, 32, 36, 38, 351
    Alexander the Great's military campaigns,
        36
    Greece (800–323 B.C.E.), *32*
    Greece during Second Peloponnesian War,
        40
    Greek colonies between 750 B.C.E. and 500
        B.C.E.,
        108
    by Hecataeus of Miletus, *30*
    Herodotus's, *34*
    reconstruction of Anaximander's, *323*
    sea navigation, 120
    sea routes used by Greek mariners, *38*
Marathon, Battle of, 106, 173, 181, 184
Marathon Boy, 81, 91
Marble, 91, 119, 155
Mariners, 119
Maritime culture, 98–99
Marriage, 244–245, 254–257
    adoption, 256
    arrangements, 254
    bride as stranger in husband's house, 255
    divorce and, 256

dowries, 255–256
girls' experience of, 253, 255
heiresses, 257
husbands and wives, 244–245, 254
inheritance and property rights, 256
natal family, 254–255
postponement, 141
procreative purpose, 251
Sparta, 247
Mathematics, 327–328, 341
Matter, 347
Mauslous, 51, 57
Mausoleum, 51, 57, 81, 91
Meat, 221
Medea (Euripides), 87, 271
Medical record from Epidaurus, *333*
Medicine, 318
documentary sources, 355
female reproduction, 251
social content, 333–334
theory of healing, 334–337
therapy, 338–340
Mediterranean world, 37
Medusa, 285, *288*
Meidias painter, 73
"Melian Dialogue," 193
Melissus of Samos, 293, 330, 355
Memorabilia (Xenophon), 63, 94, 310
Men
cloaks, 216
hairstyles, 211, 217–218
hats, 217
marriage, 244–245
outer garments, 215
relations between, 262
room for, in household, 229
statue showing *himation*, *214*
tunics, 217
Meno (Plato), 289, 293, 309
Menstruation, 251, 252
Mercenaries, 112, 190, 197
Merchants, 98, 107, 111, 112, 124, 140, *141*
Mesopotamians, 99
Messengers
vase painting, reporting news of Persian defeat to Darius I, *182*
Messenia, 148, 151, 177
Metalwork, 111
Metamorphoses (Ovid), 324
Metaphysics (Aristotle), 348, 352
Metaphysics (Theophrastus of Eresos), 310
Metempsychosis, 296, 305
Meteorology (Aristotle), 348, 355
Metics, 134, 135, 136
Metis, 286
Meton of Athens, 343, 355
Metopes, 78, 79, *81*
Michelangelo, 52
Middle and Later Archaic Periods
pottery, *69*
sculpture, 77
Middle Comedy, 57
Midwives, 251, 253, 339
Milesians, 323
debates, 326–327
early speculation, 325–327
Miletus, 145, 157
Military
campaigns of Alexander the Great, 35–36

documentary sources, 196–197
innovations, 152
leaders, 175
technology, 190
Military service, 250
Athens, 180
citizens' political rights connected to, 173, 190
Sparta, 151
See also Warfare
Milk, 220
Miltiades, 185
Mines and mining, 135, 136, 138, 139
Minoan civilization, 100, 102, 172
Minos (king of Crete), 172
Minotaur, 75, 172
Mnesicles, 56
Money, 152
Monsters, 283–289
Moral philosophy, 292
Mosaics, 73
Alexander the Great depicted at Battle of Issus, *183*
Plato's academy depicted, *292*
Mothers, 247, 248
Mount Olympus, 212
Mount Parthenius, 114
Mountains, 29, 98, 113, 172, 212
Mourning, 267, 299
Movement of Animals (Aristotle), 346, 355
Murder, 191
Muses, 286
Music
education, 250
Greek poetry and, 49
symposia, 236
training, 226
"Music of the spheres," 327–328
Mycenae, 50, 107, 172
southward view from citadel, *210*
Mycenaean Era (1600–1200 B.C.E.), 51, 149
Mycenaean Period
architecture and sculpture, 53
linear B, 102, 174, 175
Linear B tablet, *103*
Myron, 78
Discus-thrower statue, *224*, 227
Mystery cults/religions, 300, 304
Mythography, 299
Myths and mythology, 63, 297, 298, 319–320
in art, 51, 52
didactic poetry, 60
Geometric Period figurines, 75
paintings in tombs, 73
pottery, 69, 70
Satyr plays, 75
Mytilenean Debate, 193

N

Napoleon, 52
Narratives and vase painting, 68
Natural History (Pliny the Elder), 68
Nature and natural world
mathematics, 341
Milesian speculation, 325–326
philosophy, 291, 323–325

religious context, 277
Nature of Man (Hippocrates), 355
Naucratis, 111, 153, 154
Navies, 37, 146, 204
Navigation, 120
Naxian Sphinx (Delphi), *312*
Near East influences on Greek art, 53
Necromancy, 302, 304
Nemea, 143
Nemean Games, 38, 226, 303, 311
Nemesis, 286–287
Neolithic Period, 100
Neoptolemos, 86
Nereid Monument, *57*
Nereus, 287
New Comedy, 50, 57
New York Kouros, 77
Newton, Sir Isaac, 347
Nichomachean Ethics (Aristotle), 352
Nicias, 184
Peace of, 193, 198
Nicomedes, 91
Nikandre statue, 76
Nikê, 287
Nile River (Egypt), 35
Niobid Painter, 72, 73, 90
Athenian Red Figure kalyx kratêr by, *71*
Nostoi, 63
Nude Hero (Apelles of Colophon), 86
Number theories, Pythagorean, 327–328
Nutrition, 219–222
Nutritive soul, 347
Nymphs, 287

O

Oar-driven warships, 99, 118, 119, 122–124
Oarsmen, 137
Obscenity, 58
Ode on a Grecian Urn (Keats), 52
Odeon, 202
Odysseus After Slaying the Suitors (Polygnotus), 90
Odyssey (Homer), 36, 39, 49, 60, 75, 94, 122, 125, 174, 204–205, 311
ball games, 224
Cyclops Polyphemus reference, 68, 75, 218, 284
details from daily life, 238
family and social trends, 244
feasting, 235
home to Ithaca, 122
justice, 175
meat, 220
milk, 220
Odysseus builds a raft, 119
quotation from, 62, 76
raft-making described, 321
relationship with writing, 61
weaving described, 228
Oeconomica, *159*
Oedipus and the Sphinx (Ingres), 52
Oedipus at Colonus (Sophocles), 92
Oedipus of Thebes, 172
Oedipus Rex (Sophocles), 82, 84, 304, 305
Offerings, 299
Oidipodeia, 63
Oikistês, 37–38

Oikonomikos (Xenophon), 159, 310
Oikos, 232, 244, 264, 265
    male heirs, 248
    marriage, 254
Old Comedy, 50, 57, 58, 86
"Older Sophists," 289–290, 292, 308
Oligarchy, 194
Olive harvesting depicted on Black Figure
    amphora, 220
Olive oil, 111, 139, 211, 219, 220
Olympia
    sanctuaries, 51, 75, 143
    seer figure from pediment of temple of
        Zeus, 77
    temple to Zeus, 54, 56
Olympia (trireme model), 124
Olympian gods, 278
Olympian Oration (Dio Chrysostom), 56
Olympias, 199
Olympic Games, 38, 176, 226, 234, 299, 303,
    311
Olympus, 304
Omens, 302, 304
Omphalos, 30
On Being (Parmenides), 289
On Generation and Corruption (Aristotle), 355
On Mind (Leucippus), 332
On Nature (Empedocles), 329, 353
On Non-Being (Gorgias of Leontini), 289
On Praise of Helen (Gorgias of Leontini), 81, 94,
    289
On Sophistical Refutations (Aristotle), 352
"On the Crown" (Demosthenes), 201
On the Heavens (Aristotle), 348, 352, 355
On the Nature of Man, 336, 337
On the Nature of the Child, 340
On the Navy Boards (Demosthenes), 125
On the Soul (Aristotle), 347, 352, 355
Oneirocritica (Dream Book) (Artemidorus), 302
Opportunity (Kairos) (Lysippus), 79, 88
Oracles, 185, 302, 304
Oral forms of communication, 102
Oral poetry, 61, 174
Oratory, 64–65, 73, 75, 94, 183–184, 201
Oresteia (Aeschylus), 85, 92, 246, 271, 304, 311
Orestes (Euripides), 87
Organon (Aristotle), 345, 355
Orientalizing influence, 68, 75–76
Orphic mysteries, 304
Orphism, 223
Ostracism, 103, 181
    Themistocles, 204
Ostraka, 103, 107, 181, 250
Outdoor theaters, 83
Ovid, Metamorphoses quotation, 324
Oxybeles (antipersonnel weapon), 196

P

Paiderastia, 263
Painters, 85
Painting, 93
    black-figure technique, 51, 68, 69, 71, 157
    documentary sources, 94
    fresco, 68
    large-scale, 72
    Later Classical Period, 73

Platonic criticism of, 68
    red-figure technique, 51, 70–72
    vase, 52, 67, 68, 111
Palaistra, 225
Paleopathology, 333
Palinode, 64
Pamphilus of Sicyon, 85
Pan, 287
Panaenus, 53, 56
Panathenaia, 180, 211, 228, 234, 267, 270, 303
Panathenaic Way, 116
Pandora, 60, 287
Pangenesis, 340, 347
Panhellenic competitions, 226
Panhellenism, 184–185
Pantheon, deities within, 278, 284
Papyrus, 104, 107
Parabasis, 58–59
Parallel Lives (Plutarch), 205
Parchment, 104
Paris adducting Helen, depiction of, 257
Parmenides of Elea, 289, 290, 293, 295, 318, 331,
    345, 355
    fragment, 294
    influence on Plato, 340
    in Plato's dialogues, 309
    On Being, 289
    Way of Truth, 329, 330
Parmenides (Plato), 296, 297, 309
Parrhasius, 72, 88–89, 93, 94
Parry, Milman, 61
Partheneia, 64
Parthenon, 51, 52, 54, 56, 116, 185
    built under Pericles's direction, 202
    description of, 56
    metope from south side, Lapiths battling
        centaur, 81
    sculpture, 79
Parts of Animals (Aristotle), 343, 346, 352, 355
Parva Naturalia (Aristotle), 355
Pasion, 136
Pastoral literary genre, 50
Pausanias, 51, 72, 91, 113, 114, 117, 185, 195
Pax Romana, 50
Peace (Cephisodotus), 79
Peace of Antalcidas, 188
Peace of Callias, 187
Peace of Nicias, 193, 198
Peace of Philocrates, 202
Peisistratus, 54, 132, 147, 179, 180, 203
Pelopidas of Thebes, 189, 190
Peloponnesian League, 137, 148, 192
Peloponnesian Wars
    First Peloponnesian War, 173, 187
    emergency messages, 105–106
    grain imports, 143
    map of Greece during the Second
        Peloponnesian War, 40
    plague, 193, 202
    political maneuvering, 192
    Second Peloponnesian War, 58, 73, 92, 134,
        138, 173, 192–196
    Sparta's manpower shortages, 151
    Thucydides's history of, 50
Peltasts, 197
Peplos, 77, 216
    marble statue of woman wearing, 214
Perfumes, 218
Periander of Corinth, 132, 156, 157, 158, 306

Pericles, 184, 201–202, 293
    Acropolis, 51, 54, 56, 89, 192
    Aspasia and, 262, 269
    death, 193
    family lineage, 147, 178
    Funeral Oration, 231
    reforms, 186
    Sophists and patronage of, 250
    statesman, 201–202
Periodos Gēs (Anaximander of Miletus), 32
Periodos Gēs (Hecataeus of Miletus), 30, 32, 39
Periokoi, 148–149
Persephonë, 287
Perseus, 172, 282
Persian Menace, The, 184–187
Persian Wars, 137, 197
Persians, 145, 173, 179
    Alexander the Great's victories over, 200
    battles with Greeks, 184
    King's Peace, 188
    relay messengers, 104
Persians (Aeschylus), 82, 85, 186
Phaedo (Plato), 31, 39, 309, 353
    fragment of papyrus text, 65
Phaedrus (Plato), 309, 353
Phalanx, 181, 196, 200
    basis of political organization, 173, 176,
        177, 190
    Macedonian, 182
Pharmacological lore, 334
Pheidias, 53, 54, 56, 78, 89, 94, 202
    Athena Parthenos, 89
    Athena Promakhos, 89
    Athena statue in Parthenon, 56
    model of Athena Parthenos, 55
    praise for Zeus figure by, 56
    Zeus at Olympia, 89
Pheidippides, 106
Pheidon of Argos, 157
Pherecydes of Syros, 296, 299
Phidippides, 226
Philebus (Plato), 309
Philip II (king of Macedon), 33, 56, 73, 85, 173,
    182, 190, 202–203
    assassination, 183, 199
    assessment, 203
    Battle of Chaeronea, 203
    father of Alexander the Great, 202
    League of Corinth, 203
    peace of Philocrates, 202
    political machinations, 202
    rising power, 202
    siege craft usage, 196
    See also Alexander the Great (Alexander III)
Philippics (Demosthenes), 201
Philoctetes (Sophocles), 92
Philolaus of Croton or Tarentum, 90, 296, 342,
    355
Philosophers, early, 323–325. See also Aristotle;
    Plato; Socrates
Philosophy, 49, 50, 65–66, 277–278
    Academy, 291
    beginnings, 290–291
    documentary sources, 94, 311
    natural world, 291
    origin of term, 277
    parameters of, 290–291
    range of interests, 291
    terms, concepts, places, 290, 291–293

Philoxenus, 149
Phoenician Women (Euripides), 94
Phoenicians, 49, 103, 107
    colonization, 108
    dyeing processes, 215
    influence on Greek civilization, 99, 154
    shipbuilding, 99
    trade, 108, 109, 110, 121
Phryne, 91
Physics, 293, 345
Physics (Aristotle), 348, 352, 355
Physiology, 346
Picasso, Pablo, 52
Pillars of Herakles, 36
Pindar, 36, 64, 89–90, 94, 199, 225, 228, 299
    Epinicians, 89
    Epinikia, 238, 311
Pirates, 38, 136
Pisistratid tyranny, 245
Pisistratus, 157, 158, 270
Pittacus of Mitylene, 306
Places in Man (Hippocrates), 355
Plague, 333
Planetary motion
    Eudoxus of Cnidus on, 343–344
    Plato's proposal on, 342, 343
Planets, Eudoxan spheres for, *349*
Plants, 346–347
Plataea, 192
Plato, 50, 247, 277, 290, 300
    Academy, 211, 226, 291, 307, 308, 318,
      340, 353
    Apology, 309, 353
    Aristotle's relation to, 307
    astronomy, 341–344
    Charmides, 309
    contributions, 307
    critique of painting, 68
    Crito, 309
    dialogues, 66, 309
    elements, 338, 347
    Epistle VII, 309
    Euthyphro, 309
    Forms, 340
    fragment of papyrus text of *Phaedo, 65*
    geometrical solids of, *342*
    Gorgias, 94, 289, 309
    Hippias Major, 389
    Hippias Minor, 289, 309
    Ion, 309
    Laches, 309
    Laws, 159, 309
    Meno, 289, 293, 309
    on origin of technology and culture, 322
    Parmenides, 296, 297, 309
    Phaedo, 31, 39, 309, 353
    portraits of Socrates, 310
    Protagoras, 94, 289, 306, 309
    range of interests, 291
    relation to Aristotle, 353
    Republic, 94, 173, 284, 309, 353
    rhetoric, 184
    science of, 340–341
    Sophist, 296, 309
    source for Heraclitus of Ephesus, 295
    Statesman, 296, 309
    Symposium, 225, 226, 237, 238, 271, 309,
      353
    Theaetetus, 215, 293, 296, 309

theologia, 299
Timaeus, 297, 318, 338, 340, 341, 353, 355
    works, 94
Platonic relationships, 263–264
Pliny, 51, 68, 85, 88, 93
Ploutôn, 285
Pluralism, 330–331
Pluralists, 330, 341
Plutarch, 177, 231, 308
    Life of Lycurgus, 177
    Parallel Lives, 205
Plutus, 287
Poems (Xenophanes), 225, 238
Poetics (Aristotle), 50, 57, 73, 94, 352
Poetry, 49, 73
    Archaic Age, 112
    didactic, 59–60
    elegy and iambics, 60
    epic, 174, 299
    lyric, 64, 89, 299
    philosophical, 65
    popular religion, 278
    Solon of Athens, 179, 203
    tragedies, 83
Poets, 112, 249
Poleis, 29, 33
Polis, 172, 173, 176, 180, 186, 245, 304
    cults, 304
    decline, 187–190
    emergence, 131
    equality, 173
    family ties subordinated to, 246, 247
    warfare, 176
Political life, 246–247
Political organization, 107
    Cleisthenes's reforms, 180
    phalanx, 173, 176, 177, 190
Political rights, 135
Politics, 37, 291, 292
    documentary sources, 204–205
    political assemblies of Athens, 190–191
Politics (Aristotle), 94, 159, 173, 352
Pollution, 304
Polychromy, 69
    pottery, 68
Polyclitus of Argos, 52, 78, 81, 88, 90
    Canon, 78, 90
    Diadoumenos, 90
    Doruphoros, 78, 90
Polycrates of Samos, 64, 132, 145, 157, 158
Polydeuces, 282
Polyglotism, 102
Polygnotus, 56, 72, 73, 90, 93, 94
Pontus, 287
Population control, 141, 253–254
Poros (king of India), 200
Poseidon, 278, 281–282, 319
    cult, 143
    depicted on silver coin, with trident, *319*
Posterior Analytics (Aristotle), 307, 352
Pottery, 37, 140–141, 153, 157
    Athens, 139
    "black figure" style, 68
    Boeotian terra cotta of plowman with
      horses, *134*
    Corinthian, 142–143, 156
    daily life activities depicted through terra
      cotta figures, *230*
    Early Archaic Period, 67–68

Eastern influence and new styles, 68
human figures, 66, 67
Late Geometric Period, 66
Middle and Later Archaic Periods, 68–69
mourning scenes, 66–67
painted, 51
"red figure" vases, 70–72
regional variations, 69–70
terra cotta figurine of reveler and slave, *148*
trade, 111
wealth and fame, 66–67
Zeus pursuing Ganymede depicted on cup,
    243
    See also Amphorae
Pratinas of Phleius, 75
Praxitelean "S" curve, 79
Praxiteles, 57, 79, 80, 81, 90–91
Precepts (Hippocrates), 355
Pregnancy, 253
Presocratic philosophers, 65, 94, 290, 291, 292,
    293–297
Presocratics, 293–297
Priene, *111*
Priestesses, 231, 268–269, 302, 305
Priests, 305
Prime Mover, 349
Prior Analytics (Aristotle), 307, 352
Prisons, 191
Private messages, 107
Prodicus of Ceos, 289–290
Prognosis, 339
Progression of Animals (Aristotle), 352
Prometheus, 287, 320
Prometheus Bound (Aeschylus), 85, 320
Pronomos Vase, 75
Property rights, 149, 256. *See also* Inheritance
Prophecy, 302, 305
Propylaea, 202
Prose, 50
Prostitution, 141, 261
Protagoras of Abdera, 65, 184, 290
Protagoras (Plato), 94, 289, 306, 309
Proto-Attic style, 68
Protogenes, 73, 85
Protogeometric style, 66
Psammetichus (king of Egypt), 53, 157
Ptolemaic Empire, 200
Ptolemy I, 85
Public speaking, 183–184
Punishment, 191–192
Purifications (Empedocles), 293, 353
Pynx
    speaker's platform, for proposing
      legislation, *205*
Pythagoras of Samos, 290, 293, 296–297, 354
    cult of, 327–328
    depicted on bronze coin from Samos, *330*
    philosophy as term, 277
    transmigration of the soul, 305
    vegetarianism, 223
Pythagorean theorem, 328
    Arabic commentary on Euclid with
      diagram of, *327*
Pythagoreans, 90, 277, 290, 296, 297, 305
    cosmology, 342
    impact, 328
    influence on Plato, 340, 341
    tetrad as sacred oath, 325
    transmigration of the soul, 300

Pytheas, 31–32
Pythia on a tripod, *271*
Pythian Games, 38, 226, 300, 302, 303, 311
Pyxis, Corinthian, *67*

Q

Quarries, *155*

R

Rainfall, 212
Ramp technology, 152
Rampin Horseman, *76, 77*
Rape, 259
Rape of the Daughters of Leucippus, The
    (Polygnotus), 90
Raphael, 52
Rational soul, 347
Reason, power of, 326
Recollection theory, 293
Record keeping, 103
Recreation
    documentary sources, 238
    games, 224–228
Red-figure style painted pottery/vases, 51, 70–72
Reincarnation, 296, 305
Relativism, 65
Relay messengers, 104
Religion, 132, 277
    archaeology, 299–300
    Aristotle's theories, 349–350
    categories, 297–298
    curse tablets, 299
    the divine, 297
    documentary sources, 311
    epic/tragedy, 298–299
    explanations, 297
    funerary rites, 299
    games and festivals, 299
    hymns/sacred performance, 298
    legend and folktale, 299
    myths, 298, 299
    offerings and amulets, 299
    parameters of, 297–300
    ritual, 299
    sacrifices, 299
    terms, concepts, and places, 300–305
    theology, 299
    women's roles, 267
    written sources, 299
Religious cults
    economic activity, 144
    economic life, 143
    helots, 149
Religious festivals, 211, 233
    educational function, 249–250
    female choruses, 268
    Greek tragedies and, 83
Renaissance, 52
Renfrew, Colin, 100
Reproduction, 251–254
    Aristotle's investigations, 347
    labor and delivery, 253
    menstruation, 251
    "wandering womb" conception, 252–253

Republic (Plato), 94, 173, 284, 309, 353
Restitution, 191
Rhea, 287
Rhetoric, 49, 50, 65, 183–184, 291
    impact, 73, 75
    speech and argument, 73
Rhetoric (Aristotle), 352
Riace Bronzes, 78–79, 89
Rituals, 219, 297, 299
Roads, 99, 106, 113, 157
    construction techniques, 113–114
    heavy-freight, 115–116
    precursor to Roman Via Appia, *126*
    route between Argos and Tegea, 114–115
    wheel ruts, 114
Rodin, Auguste, 52
Roman alphabet, 103
Roman Empire, 50
Roman Period, 51
Romans, 50, 113
Rome, 50
Rule of law, 173
Running races, 226

S

Sack of Troy (Polygnotus), 90
Sacred Band of Thebes, 189, 199, 203
Sacred Disease (Hippocrates), 334, 336, 338, 355
Sacred Tales (Aristides), 283
Sacred War (355–346 B.C.E), 173, 190, 202
Sacrifices, 299, 305
Sail-driven ships, 118, 119
Sailors, 119, 120, 250
Salamis, 184, 204
Samos
    Polycrates's rule of, 158
    temple to Hera on, 53, *321*
    view of tunnel built by Eupalinus, *157*
Sanctuaries, 53, 143, *213*, 300
Sanctuary of Zeus
    inscribed bronze tablet recording loan made
        by, *97*
Sandals, 217
Sappho, 49, 91, 94, 112, 260
    fragment of second-century-C.E. papyrus
        text of poems, *64*
Sataspes, 31
Satyr plays, 75, 83
Satyrs, 287
    Dancing Faun, *286*
Schliemann, Heinrich, 63, 264
Science, 277, 318
    Aristotle's contributions to, 350
    documentary sources, 355
    of Plato, 340–341
    See also Astronomy; Medicine; Nature and
        natural world; Technology
Scopas, 56, 57, 73, 81, 91–92
Sculptors, 155
Sculpture, 51, 52, 91–92, 157
    bronze, 76, 90
    Early and High Classical Periods, 78
    Early Archaic Period, 75–76
    influence from abroad, 53
    Late Geometric Period, 75
    Later Classical Period, 79, 81

legacy of Classical Greek, 51–52
    maidens, 77
    Middle and Later Archaic Periods, 77
    Parthenon, 79
Scylax of Caryanda, 31
Sea
    influence on Greek climate, 212
    map of routes, *38*
    transport, 113, 118–124
Seasons
    clothing, 213
    humors linked to, 336–337
Second Athenian League, 189, 190
Second Messenian War, 177
Second Peloponnesian War, 58, 73, 92, 134, 138,
    173, 192–195
    emergency messages, 105–106
    grain imports, 143
    map of Greece during, *40*
    plague, 193, 202
    political maneuvering, 192
    Sparta's manpower shortages, 151
    Thucydides's history of, 50
Semitic languages, 103
Senses, the
    atomism, 332–333
    cycles of change, 328, 329
    pluralism, 330
Sensitive soul, 347
Settlements, 176, 212
Seven Against Thebes (Aeschylus), 85, 94
Seven Sages (Wise Men of Greece), 203, 302,
    306–307
Seven Wonders of the Ancient World
    Colossus of Rhodes, 88
    Mausoleum at Halicarnassus, 51, 57, 91
    temple of Artemis at Ephesus, 53
    Temple to Zeus at Olympia, 54, 56
Severe Style, 78, 79
Sewage, 230–231
Sexuality, 259–264
    courtesans, 261–262
    disenfranchisement, 264
    double standards, 259
    female form, 260
    Greek love spell, 259
    homoerotic activity, 262–263
    love, 259–260
    male form, 260–261
    misconduct, 257–259
    prostitution, 261
    relations between men, 262
    standards of beauty, 260
Shakespeare, William, 57
Ships and shipbuilding, 99, 119, 152, 153
    Athenian cup with painting of pirate ship
        chasing Greek merchant ship, *125*
    coasting, 120–121
    design, 118, 122
    Etruscan merchant vessel, *120*
    Ionia, 145
    Kyrenia shipwreck, 121–122
    military use, 123–124
    oared, 122
    propulsion, 122–123
    size, 121
    specialization, 119
    technology, 322
    trade routes, 121

trireme, 123
winds and rigging, 119–120
Shipwrecks
Kyrenia, 121–122
Ulu Burun, 118, 119
Shoes, 217
Short Natural Histories or *Parva Naturalia*
(Aristotle), 346
Shrines, 300
Sicily, 50, 146–147, 193
Second Peloponnesian War, 193, 194
slaves, 148
Siege devices, 195
Sileni, 287
Silk, 213
Silver, 155, 157
Siphian Treasury, *54*
Sixth-sharers, 133
Skiagraphia, 72
Skytale, 105
Slave revolts, 137
Slave society
pretechnological, 322
Slaves and slavery, 133, 134, 143, 146, 147
Athens, 135–137, 178
Boeotia, 138
depicted in terra cotta figurine, *148*
hairstyles, 218
native, 148
pretechnological, 322
prostitutes, 261
punishment, 192
Solon's reforms of, 179, 203
Sparta, 173
types of, 147–148
Social class system, overview, 131–132
documentary sources, 159
Social organization, 147–148
Social trends, 244–247
documentary sources, 271
Social War, 190, 202
Socks, 217
Socrates, 64, 94, 195, 225, 226, 277
bust of, *309*
clothing, 216
death sentence, 173
forms and ideas, 292
Platonic critique of painting, 68
in Plato's dialogues, 309, 310, 353
Plato's relation to, 308, 310
range of interests, 291
Socratics, 307
contributions in, 307–311
Solon of Athens, 141, 152, 156, 203
brothels, 261
law codes, 173, 179
poetry, 60, 159, 203
reforms, 133–135, 245–246, 270
Seven Sages, 306
statesman, 203
Songs, 83. *See also* Chorus
Sophist (Plato), 296, 309
Sophists, 64–66, 73, 81, 184, 250–251, 290
influence of, on Euripides, 87
Later, 307–311
Older, 289–290, 308
Sophocles, 50, 70, 83, 92, 185, 255, 265, 268
Ajax, 82
Antigone, 92, 246, 268, 271, 305

Electra, 92, 223, 238
Oedipus at Colonus, 92
Oedipus Rex, 82, 84, 304, 305
Philoctetes, +3
playwright, 92, 94
satyr plays, 75
Trackers, 75
Sostratus of Aegina, 124, 155
Soul, Aristotle's types of, 347
Southern Italy, 146–147
Sparta, 33, 50, 107, 118, 131, 148–151, 176–181,
184, 186
Agiad family, 178
Athens contrasted with, 176
austerity, 149
Battle of Leuctra, 189
characteristics, 148
Classical Period, 151
constitution, 177, 178
discipline, 150
dress code, 149, 150
education, 149–150, 249, 251
empire, 151
farming, 149
food consumption, 151
gender roles, 247
Gerousia, The, 178
good government, 178
hegemony, 187, 189
imperialism, 137
infanticide, 254
Lycurgan social order, 149
military service, 151
military state, 177
peace treaty with Athens (445), 192
property, 149
rivalry with Athens, 173, 178
ruins, *150*
Second Peloponnesian War, 138, 192–195
slaves, 148
social structure, 148–149
social trends, 247
weapons, 196
women, 231
See also Athens
Spartans, 173
ball games, 224
diet, 222–223
monument commemorating defeat of, by
Epaminodas, *188*
site of Athenian city at Amphipolis,
captured by, *194*
skytale, 105
Spartiates, 148, 149, 151
Spears, 182
Speculation, 325–327
Cult of Pythagoras, 327–328
Cycles of Change, 328–330
Pluralism, 330–331
Speeches, 64–65, 73, 184
Speeches, The (Demosthenes), 238
Spells, 301
Speusippus, 310
Sphyrelaton method, 76
Spices, 221
Spinning, 214, 265
Sports
blood, 227
combat, 226–227

discus throwing, 227
javelin throwing, 227
jumping, 227
races, 226
religion, 303
team, 228
Stadiums, 143
at Delphi, for Pythian Games, *144*
Stage machinery, Greek tragedy, 84
Statesman (Plato), 296, 309
Sterility, 254
Stesichorus, 64, 69
Stoa Poikilê, Athens, 72, 90
Storage jar, Mykonos, *159*
Stories of Heroes, 63
Storytelling
Homeric poems, 61
weaving related to, 228
Strabo, 35, 39
Streetwalkers, 261
Studies in Hysteria (Freud and Breuer), 253
"Succession myths," 88
Sundials, 233
Sung poetry, 64
Suppliant Women (Aeschylus), 85
Sybaris, 146
Syllabic writing, 102–103
Symbolism, legends, 172
Symposia, 211, 235–237
Academy, 291
Symposium (Plato), 225, 226, 237, 238, 271, 309,
353
Aprodite references, 278
paiderastia, 264
wrestling, 227
Symposium (Xenophon), 63, 237, 238, 310

T

Ta Indika (Ctesias of Cnidus), 32
Tarentum, 146
Tartarus, 288
Taxes, 135, 138, 140, 179
Teachers, 112, 249
Team sports, 228
Technology, 151–153, 318
ancient, 321–323
architecture, 321
beneficiaries, 321
documentary sources, 355
Herodotus, 321
narrow-mindedness, 322–323
ships, 322
slave society, 322
"three marvels," 321–322
trial and error, 321
Telegoneia, 63
Teleology, 345, 346–347
Telescope, 344
Temperature, 212
Temple of Apollo, Delphi, 155, 300
bronze statuettes at, 76
remains of sixth century B.C.E., *142*
Temple of Apollo, Dreros, Crete
beaten bronze figures of Apollo, Artemis,
Leto, *80*
Temple of Artemis, Corcyra

relief close-up of Gorgon Medusa on pediment of, *288*

Temple of Artemis, Ephesus, 86

Temple of Athena Alea, Tegea, 81, 91

Temple of Hera (Selinus)
marble relief of Hera and Zeus from, *300*

Temple of Poseidon, *28*

Temple of Zeus, Olympia, 157
pedimental sculptures, 78
seer figure from east pediment, *77*

Temples, 51, 53, 91, 143, 146, 157, 300, 305
to Aphaia, 54
healing, 332
healing through sleeping, 335
incubations, 303
Ionia, 145
prostitution, 261
ruins of temple to Hera on Samos, *321*
sculptures, 76, 78, 79, 81
transportation, 116

Testimonia, 293

Tetralogies, 64

Thales of Miletus, 290, 306–307, 318, 323–324, 325, 354

Theaetetus (Plato), 215, 293, 296, 309

Theater, 83, 143. *See also* Comedy; Drama; Tragedy

Thebais, 63

Thebes, 33, 50, 172, 173, 192

Themis, 288

Themistocles, 139, 146, 184, 201, 204
ostraka, *177*

Theognis, 49

Theogony (Hesiod), 49, 88, 93, 174, 284, 296, 311

Theology, 293, 299, 349–350

Theophrastus of Eresos, 308, 310
Characters, 310
Metaphysics, 310

Theramenes, 195

Theriomorphic, 305

Thermopylae, 202
battle, 184
temple of Demeter, 300

Theseus of Athens, 172, 283

Thesmophoria, 211, 234, 267, 268, 280

Thesmophoriazousai (Aristophanes), 86, 234

Thespis, 57, 81, 82, 265

Thessaly, 153
slaves, 148

Thetis, 288

Thiasos, 305

Thirty Tyrants, 195

Thirty Years' Peace, 173

Thrasybulus, 157, 158, 195

Thucydides, 92–93, 137, 194, 204, 219
on Alcibiades, 198
fragment of third-century-B.C.E. papyrus with text of book 1
historian and general, 92–93, 94
history of, *63*
History of the Peloponnesian War, 50, 92, 125, 159, 173, 192, 205
"Melian Dialogue," 193
on Pericles, 202

Tiberius (emperor of Rome), 88

Timaeus (Plato), 297, 318, 338, 340, 341, 353, 355

Timber, 137, 146, 153, 157

Timekeeping, 233

Timoleon, 147

Timotheus, 93

Tiryns, 172

Tisias, 73

Tisicrates, 88

Titanomakhia, 63

Titans, 288

Titian, 52

Tomb cult, 61

Tombs, 73

Topography, 131

Tortoise and hare paradox, 328

Torture, 191–192

Tourism, 140

Toys, 224, 249

Trackers (Sophocles), 75

Trade, 37, 109, 110, 111, 132, 155, 172
carrying, 111–112
facilitation of, 154
households, 175
items, 111
networks/routes, 29, 108, 121
posts, 153–155
routes, 29, 121

Traders, 31

Traffic, roads and land, 113–118

Tragedy, 49, 73, 81–84, 85, 265, 299
comedy contrasted with, 57–59
deus ex machina, 303
documentary sources, 94
essential features, 82
face masks, 83–84
family dynamics, 246
and humor, 57, 58
interaction between actors, 83
origins, 81–82
outdoor theaters, 83
playwrights, 85, 86–87, 92
production and finance, 83
relationship between chorus and actor, 82–83
role of chorus, 83
Satyr plays and origins of, 75
stage machinery, 84
structure, 82
See also Comedy

Transmigration of the soul, 296, 300, 305

Transportation
documentary sources, 125
domestic animals, 117–118
exchange of goods and services, 155–156
land, 139
patterns and practices of, 107–112
roads and land traffic, 113–118
sea, 118–124
technologies, 99
wagon rides, 115

Travelers, 98
ancient Greek, 38
Archaic Age, 112
clothing, 117

Treasuries, 54

Trireme, *123*, 152, 196, 322

Trojan Horse, 195

Trojan War, 36, 62–63, 101, 172
attempts at substantiation of, 264
cause of, 286
race of heroes preceding/following, 282
scenes from, in art, 51

Trojan Women (Euripides), 58, 87

Troy, 63, 174
Schliemann's search for, 264

Truth, 328

Tyrants, 132, 140, 145, 147, 156–157, 176, 178
city-states, 245
Roman copy of monument to tyrannicides, *156*
the Thirty, 195

Tyrtaeus, 60, 225

U

Ulu Burun wreck, 118, 119

Underworld deities, 301

Universe
Aristotle's theories, 348
early philosophers, 325
Plato's, 341
Pythagorean viewpoint, 327–328

Upright wrestling, 227

Uranus, 288

V

Vase paintings, 68, 80, 111
departure scene, *272*
female mourners, *267*

Vases, 52, 140
funerary, 66
"red figure," 70–72
See also Amphorae; Pottery

Vassals, 140

Vegetables, 221

Vegetarians, 223, 305

Vehicles, 99, 118

Venesection, 335, 339

Via Appia, Greek precursor to, *126*

Via Egnatia, 113

Virgil, 59

Visual art. *See* Architecture; Art; Painting; Pottery; Sculpture

Vitruvius, 91

Voting
Athens, 190
tokens, *191*

Votive offerings, 305

Vowels, 103

W

Wagons, 115, 118

Walking sticks, 217

Warfare, 132, 144–145, 173, 176
Alexander the Great, 199–200
booty, 140, 143, 144
documentary sources, 204–205
Homeric poems, 62
Macedonian art of, 182–183
Philip II, 203–203
polis in decline, 187–190
war engines, 195–196

Warriors
bronze sculptures, 78

depicted on amphorae, 73
depicted on grave relief from Salamis, *249*
depicted on pottery, 66, 67
Warships, 152, 196
    slaves, 137
    two-banked, *121*
Wasps (Aristophanes), 58, 86, 93
Water, 230, 324
Water-clock
    reproduction of, for timing speeches in law
        courts, *191*
Way of Truth, The (Parmenides), 329, 330
Ways and Means (Xenophon), 159
Wealth (Aristophanes), 86
Weapons, 173, 176, 190, 196–197
    Athens *vs.* Sparta, 196
    Macedonian, 182–183
    oxybeles, *196*
Weather, 211, 212
Weaving, 214, 228, 264–265
    bowl painting of Penelope at loom, with
        Telemachos looking on, *266*
    looms, 214
    patterns, 215
Weddings, 245, 267
Wheat cultivation, 219
Widows, 266, 267
Wigs, 218
Winckelmann, J. J., 52
Winds, worship of, 289
Wine, 111, 211, 218, 222–223
Wise men, 306–307
Wives and husbands, 244–245, 254
Women
    ball games, 224
    beauty, 217, 260
    companions of symposia, depicted on
        drinking cup, *236*
    "female excellence," 231
    hairstyles, 211, 218
    hats, 217
    health, 339–340
    heiresses, 257
    household work, 264

lack of information about leisure by, 237
legal guardianship, 266
marriage, 244–245
mourners depicted on vase, *267*
offspring and status of, 248
peplos, *214*, 216
priestesses, 268–269, 302, 305
prostitutes, 261–262
in public, 247
religion, 235, 267
representation, 266–267
room for, in household, 229–230
running, 226
shoes, 217
slaves, 136
Sparta, 247
Spartan, 149, 150, 151, 247
spinning and weaving, 214
symposia, 236
weaving, 228, 264–265
Wool, 264
    clothing, 211, 213
    dyes, 215
Woolf, Virginia, 268
Works and Days (Hesiod), 49, 59, 88, 93, 125,
    159, 174, 238
Worship
    blood offerings, 301
    wind, 289. *See also* Religion
Wrestling, 226–227, 303
Writing, 49, 107, 174–175
    deltos, 104
    Homeric poems, 61
    ostraka, 103
    papyrus and parchment, 104
    stone inscriptions, 104
    syllabic, 102–103
    types of writing systems, 102
    See also Alphabet; Language; Literature

X

Xanthipppus, 201

Xenocrates of Chacedon, 310
Xenodamus, 149
Xenophanes, 228, 291, 293, 297
    Poems, 238
Xenophon, 63–64, 66, 94, 125, 159, 189, 225,
    310–311
    Apology, 310
    Constitution of the Lacedaemonians, 159
    Constitution of the Spartans, 64
    Cynegeticus, 64
    Economics, 265
    Hellenica, 64, 125, 159, 189, 205
    Horsemanship, 64
    Memorabilia, 63, 94, 310
    Oikonomikos, 159, 310
    Poems, 225, 238
    portraits of Socrates, 310
    Symposium, 63, 237, 238, 310
Xerxes (king of Persia), 31, 63, 82
Xoana, 76

Y

Young Girls, 335

Z

Zaleucus of Locri, 156, 173
Zeno of Elea, 293, 295, 297, 309, 330, 355
Zeus, 278, 282, 319
    altar in Pergamon dedicated to, 51
    bronze statue, *281*
    marble relief depicting, from temple of
        Hera in Selinus, *300*
    oracle at Dodona, 304
    temple at Olympia, 54, 56
Zeus at Olympia (Pheidias), 89
Zeuxis, 72, 89, 93, 94
Zoology, Aristotle's construction of, 347